Windows XP Pro

THE MISSING MANUAL

*The book that
should have been
in the box*

What the Reviewers Said*

Pogue is a clear and gifted writer who is able to cut through the technobabble and show the reader how to solve problems and get stuff done. The Missing Manual is an ideal companion for both first-time XP users and more experienced users who find themselves flummoxed by the software.

—Larry Blasko, Associated Press

A visit to *www.missingmanuals.com* can offer instant relief to headaches generated by mounting XP glitches. David Pogue, a columnist for *The New York Times* and the genius behind the Missing Manual series of books, has adapted his easy-to-follow, humorous style of writing to help us survive our often-exasperating bouts with computer mania. This is an extremely easy-to-follow guide to everything you need to know about Windows XP without insulting our intelligence, as we sometimes find in the 'Idiots' or 'Dummies' series of books, giving us step-by-step solutions to our problems.

—Mike Berman, Scripps Howard News Service

A masterful treatment of Windows XP, written in a direct and lively style.

—Ed Laskowski, The Vista PC Journal

I enjoyed following the pages in this sensibly written guide. It is the way to go for first-time and intermediate PC fans. The author's warm, witty, and jargon-free writing style is applied to every nook of Windows XP.

—Sam Gardner, PC News

[This book is] outstanding in the way it presents its subject matter and in the amount of material it covers, yet manages to present it all in an easily understood manner. If you are looking for a good book on Windows XP, this is it. I highly recommend it for beginners as well as for more advanced users, for the learning of Windows XP as well as for troubleshooting. It is truly 'the book that should have been in the box' and will help you get the most out of your Windows XP computer.

—Gerhard R. Fischer, Charlotte Bytes

This book will help first-time and intermediate PC fans greatly, and it has enough depth to aid experienced Windows users, too…Since it stays clear of jargon, and does an excellent job of explaining any technical terms it has to use, a beginner should have no problem understanding the material.

—Bob Esch, The Databus

If you've ever struggled with XP (and if that's the OS on your notebook or desktop, you're lying if you say you haven't), this book offers rock-solid advice as well as terrific tips on every crumb XP has to offer.

— Michael Cahlin, Emerging Tip World

* *From reviews of* Windows XP Home Edition: The Missing Manual, *this book's predecessor.*

Windows XP Pro

THE MISSING MANUAL

David Pogue, Craig Zacker, and L.J. Zacker

POGUE PRESS™
O'REILLY®

Beijing • Cambridge • Farnham • Köln • Paris • Sebastopol • Taipei • Tokyo

Windows XP Pro: The Missing Manual

by David Pogue, Craig Zacker, and L.J. Zacker

Published by Pogue Press/O'Reilly & Associates, Inc.,
1005 Gravenstein Highway North, Sebastopol, CA 95472.

January 2003:	First Edition.
May 2003:	Second Printing.
August 2003:	Third Printing.
January 2004:	Fourth Printing.
February 2004:	Fifth Printing.

ISBN: 0-596-00348-X

Table of Contents

Part Three: Windows Online

Part Four: Plugging into Windows XP

Part Five: Life on the Network

Part Six: Appendixes

The Missing Credits

About the Authors

David Pogue is the weekly computer columnist for the *New York Times* and the creator of the Missing Manual series. He's the author or co-author of 25 books, including six in this series and six in the "For Dummies" line (including *Magic, Opera, Classical Music,* and *The Flat-Screen iMac*). In his other life, David is a former Broadway show conductor, a magician, and a pianist (*www.davidpogue.com*).

He welcomes feedback about Missing Manual titles by email: *david@pogueman.com*. (If you need technical help, however, please refer to the sources in Chapter 5.)

Craig Zacker is a writer, editor, and networker whose computing experience began in the days of teletypes and paper tape. After earning a Masters Degree in English and American Literature from New York University, Craig worked extensively on the integration of Windows NT into existing internetworks, supported fleets of Windows workstations, and was employed as a technical writer, content provider, and Webmaster for the online services group of a large software company. Since devoting himself to writing and editing full-time, Craig has authored or contributed to many books on networking topics, operating systems, and PC hardware. He has also developed online training courses for the Web and published articles with top industry publications. For more information, see *http://www.zacker.com*.

L.J. Zacker began working with mainframe and personal computers in the mid 1980s, and has since worked as a network administrator, programmer, and security consultant for mainframe systems and PC LANs. Now a full-time author and editor, L.J. has contributed to numerous books and articles for various publishers including Microsoft Press, SAMS Publishing, and *Windows 2000* magazine.

About the Creative Team

Nan Barber (copy editor) co-authored *Office X for the Macintosh: The Missing Manual* and *Office 2001 for Macintosh: The Missing Manual*. As the principal copy editor for this series, she has edited the titles on iPhoto, Mac OS 9, AppleWorks 6, iMovie, Dreamweaver 4, and Windows XP Home Edition. Email: *nanbarber@mac.com*.

Rose Cassano (cover illustration) has worked as an independent designer and illustrator for 20 years. Assignments have spanned everything from the nonprofit sector to corporate clientele. She lives in beautiful Southern Oregon, grateful for the miracles of modern technology that make living and working there a reality. Email: *cassano@cdsnet.net*. Web: *www.rosecassano.com*.

Phil Simpson (design and layout) works out of his office in Stamford, Connecticut, where he has had his graphic design business since 1982. He is experienced in many facets of graphic design, including corporate identity, publication design, and corporate and medical communications. Email: *pmsimpson@earthlink.net*.

Acknowledgments

The Missing Manual series is a joint venture between the dream team introduced on these pages and O'Reilly & Associates: Tim O'Reilly, Mark Brokering, and company.

I'm grateful to all of them, and to and Chuck Brandstater, John Cacciatore, Danny Marcus, and Sada Preisch for their proofreading smarts. Thanks to David Rogelberg for believing in the idea, and above all, to Jennifer, Kelly, and Tia, who make these books—and everything else—possible.

The Missing Manual Series

Missing Manual books are designed to be superbly written guides to computer products that don't come with printed manuals (which is just about all of them). Each book features a handcrafted index; cross-references to specific page numbers (not just "See Chapter 14"); and a promise never to use an apostrophe in the possessive word *its*. Current and upcoming titles include:

- *Dreamweaver MX: The Missing Manual* by David Sawyer McFarland

- *Windows XP Home Edition: The Missing Manual* by David Pogue

- *Photoshop Elements 2: The Missing Manual* by Donnie O'Quinn

- *Switching to the Mac: The Missing Manual* by David Pogue

- *Mac OS X: The Missing Manual, Second Edition,* by David Pogue

- *Office X for Macintosh: The Missing Manual* by Nan Barber, Tonya Engst, & David Reynolds

- *iPhoto: The Missing Manual* by David Pogue, Joseph Schorr, & Derrick Story

- *AppleWorks 6: The Missing Manual* by Jim Elferdink & David Reynolds

- *iMovie 2: The Missing Manual* by David Pogue

- *Mac OS 9: The Missing Manual* by David Pogue

Introduction

For years, the evolution of Microsoft Windows ran along two different tracks. First, there were the home versions: Windows 95, Windows 98, and Windows Me. These were the Windows for everyday individuals. They were compatible with just about everything on earth, including games of every description—but where stability was concerned, they weren't what you'd call Rocks of Gibraltar.

Second, there were the corporate versions of Windows: Windows NT and Windows 2000. These versions of Windows rarely froze or crashed, and they featured industrial-strength security. However, they weren't anywhere near as compatible as the home versions of Windows. If you tried to run the Barney the Dinosaur CD-ROM at work, for example, you were out of luck (if not out of a job).

This schizophrenic approach to the evolution of Windows entailed its share of drawbacks. It meant twice as much engineering effort for Microsoft, twice as much tech-support knowledge by computer companies, and twice as much work for software companies, which had to ensure compatibility with both systems. It wasn't even so great for you, the PC fan, because you had to worry about compatibility with each piece of software you bought. And it was entirely possible to get confused when sitting down in front of a PC running a different version of Windows.

The goal of Windows XP was simple: Combine the two versions of Windows into a single new operating system that offers the best features of both.

For the most part, Microsoft succeeded. Ending the era of dual operating systems offers both you and Microsoft huge simplicity benefits—now there's only one operating system to learn, discuss, and troubleshoot. It also offers a big payoff to hardware and software manufacturers, who now have to ensure compatibility with only one operating system.

If you're used to one of the home versions, you may be surprised by some of the resulting changes; under the colorful, three-dimensional new skin of Windows XP Home Edition lurks Windows 2000, which includes some of its beefy security features. This book will help you get through them.

If you're accustomed to Windows 2000 or Windows NT, you'll probably be happy to hear that XP Professional is built on the same bulletproof frame. All you have to get used to are XP's greater compatibility with a wide range of hardware and software, and Windows' new look (and even that can be turned off, if you like).

Either way, you've entered a new age: the unified Windows era. Now you, Microsoft, and software companies can get used to the notion that everybody is using the same Windows. (There are still two different *editions* of Windows XP —Professional and Home Edition—but they're not really two different operating systems, as noted on page 17.)

About This Book

Despite the many improvements in Windows over the years, one feature hasn't improved a bit: Microsoft's documentation. In fact, with Windows XP, you get no printed user guide at all. To learn about the thousands of pieces of software that make up this operating system, you're expected to read the online help screens.

Unfortunately, as you'll quickly discover, these help screens are tersely written, offer very little technical depth, and lack examples and illustrations. You can't even mark your place, underline, or read them in the bathroom. In Windows XP, many of the help screens are actually on Microsoft's Web site; you can't see them without an Internet connection. Too bad if you're on a plane somewhere with your laptop.

The purpose of this book, then, is to serve as the manual that should have accompanied Windows XP Pro. In these pages, you'll find step-by-step instructions for using almost every Windows feature, including those you may not even have quite understood, let alone mastered.

Windows XP Pro: The Missing Manual is designed to accommodate readers at every technical level. The primary discussions are written for advanced-beginner or intermediate PC users. But if you're a first-time Windows user, special sidebar articles called Up To Speed provide the introductory information you need to understand the topic at hand. If you're an advanced PC user, on the other hand, keep your eye out for similar shaded boxes called Power Users' Clinic. They offer more technical tips, tricks, and shortcuts for the veteran PC fan.

About the Outline

This book is divided into six parts, each containing several chapters:

- Part 1, **The Windows XP Desktop,** covers everything you see on the screen when you turn on a Windows XP computer: icons, windows, menus, scroll bars, the Recycle Bin, shortcuts, the Start menu, shortcut menus, and so on.

- Part 2, **The Components of Windows XP,** is dedicated to the proposition that an operating system is little more than a launch pad for *programs.* Chapter 6 describes how to work with applications in Windows—launch them, switch among them, swap data between them, use them to create and open files, and so on.

  This part also offers an item-by-item discussion of the individual software nuggets that make up this operating system. These include not just the items in your Control Panel folder, but also the long list of free programs that Microsoft threw in: Windows Media Player, Movie Maker 2, WordPad, and so on.

- Part 3, **Windows Online,** covers all the special Internet-related features of Windows, including the wizards that set up your Internet account, Outlook Express (for email), Internet Explorer 6 (for Web browsing), chatting or videoconferencing with MSN Messenger, and so on.

- Part 4, **Plugging into Windows XP,** describes the operating system's relationship with equipment you can attach to your PC—scanners, cameras, disks, printers, and so on. Special chapters describe faxing, fonts, troubleshooting your PC, and preventing problems from even arising.

- Part 5, **Life on the Network,** honors the millions of households and offices that now contain more than one PC. If you work at home or in a small office, these chapters show you how to build your own network; if you work in a corporation

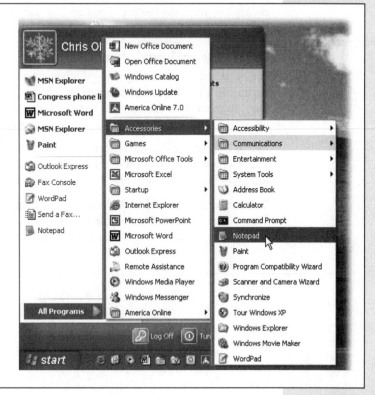

Figure I-1:
In this book, arrow notations help to simplify folder and menu instructions. For example, "Choose Start→All Programs→Accessories→Notepad" is a more compact way of saying, "Click the Start button. When the Start menu opens, click All Programs; without clicking, now slide to the right onto the Accessories submenu; in that submenu, click Notepad," as shown here.

where some highly paid professional network geek is on hand to do the trouble-shooting, these chapters show you how to exploit XP Pro's considerable networking prowess.

At the end of the book, two appendixes provide guidance in installing this operating system and a menu-by-menu explanation of the Windows XP Pro desktop commands.

About→These→Arrows

Throughout this book, and throughout the Missing Manual series, you'll find sentences like this: "Open the Start→My Computer→Local Disk (C:)→Windows folder." That's shorthand for a much longer instruction that directs you to open three nested icons in sequence, like this: "Click the Start menu to open it. Click My Computer in the Start menu. Inside the My Computer window is a disk icon labeled Local Disk (C:); double-click it to open it. Inside *that* window is yet another icon called Windows. Double-click to open it, too."

Similarly, this kind of arrow shorthand helps to simplify the business of choosing commands in menus, as shown in Figure I-1.

About Shift-Clicking

Here's another bit of shorthand you'll find in this book (and others): instructions to *Shift-click* something. That means you should hold down the Shift key, and then click before releasing the key. If you understand that much, the meaning of instructions like "Ctrl-click" and "Alt-click" should be clear.

About MissingManuals.com

You're invited and encouraged to submit corrections and updates to this book's Web page at *www.missingmanuals.com*. (Click the book's name, and then click the Errata link.) In an effort to keep the book as up-to-date and accurate as possible, each time we print more copies of this book, we'll make any corrections you've suggested.

Even if you have nothing to report, you should check that Errata page now and then. That's where we'll post a list of the corrections and updates we've made, so that you can mark important corrections into your own copy of the book, if you like.

In the meantime, we'd love to hear your suggestions for new books in the Missing Manual line. There's a place for that on the Web site, too, as well as a place to sign up for free email notification of new titles in the series.

Part One:
The Windows XP Desktop

1

A Welcome to Windows XP

Microsoft Windows XP is the latest and, technically speaking, the best version of the most-used software in the world. If you recently bought a new PC, Windows XP probably came preinstalled. If you already own a computer (running Windows 98, Me, or 2000, for example), you can buy Windows XP separately to upgrade your machine (see Appendix A).

No matter how you get it on your PC, however, you'll be spending a lot of time with Windows XP. It's your computer's face; it's the first thing that greets you when you turn on your machine, and the last thing you see before it blinks off.

What It's For

Windows is an *operating system,* the software that controls your computer. It's designed to serve you in several ways:

- **It's a launching bay.** At its heart, Windows is a home base, a remote-control clicker that lets you call up the various software programs (applications) you use to do work or kill time. When you get right down to it, applications are the real reason you bought a PC.

   Windows XP is a well-stocked software pantry unto itself; for example, it comes with such basic programs as a Web browser, email program, simple word processor, and calculator. Windows XP comes with eleven games, too, several of which you can play live against other people on the Internet. (Chapter 7 covers all of these freebie programs.)

   If you were stranded on a desert island, the built-in Windows XP programs could suffice for everyday operations. But if you're like most people, sooner or later, you'll buy and install more software. That's one of the luxuries of using Windows: You can choose from a staggering number of add-on programs. Whether you're a left-handed beekeeper or a German-speaking nun, some company somewhere is selling Windows software designed just for you, its target audience.

- **It's a file cabinet.** Every application on your machine, as well as every document you create, is represented on the screen by an *icon* (see Figure 1-1). You can organize these icons into little onscreen file folders. You can make backups (safety copies) by dragging file icons onto a floppy disk or blank CD, or send them to people by email. You can also trash icons you no longer need by dragging them onto the Recycle Bin icon.

My Computer   Congress   Sunset.jpg
phone list.doc

Microsoft Word   Backup CD

Figure 1-1:
Your Windows world revolves around icons, the tiny pictures that represent your programs, documents, and various Windows components. From left to right: the icons for your computer itself, a word processing document, a digital photo (a JPEG document), a word processor program (Word), and a CD-ROM inserted into your computer.

- **It's your equipment headquarters.** What you can actually *see* of Windows is only the tip of the iceberg. An enormous chunk of Windows is behind-the-scenes plumbing that controls the various functions of your computer—its modem, screen, keyboard, printer, and so on.

Getting Ready for Windows

To get the most out of Windows with the least frustration, it helps to become familiar with the following concepts and terms. You'll encounter these words and phrases over and over again—in the built-in Windows help, in computer magazines, and in this book.

The right mouse button is king

One of the most important features of Windows isn't on the screen—it's under your hand. The standard mouse has two mouse buttons. You use the left one to click buttons, highlight text, and drag things around on the screen.

When you click the right button, however, a *shortcut menu* appears onscreen, like the ones shown in Figure 1-2. Get into the habit of *right-clicking* things—icons, folders, disks, text in your word processor, buttons on your menu bar, pictures on a Web page, and so on. The commands that appear on the shortcut menu will make you much more productive and lead you to discover handy functions you never knew existed.

This is a big deal: Microsoft's research suggests that nearly 75 percent of Windows users don't use the right mouse button, and therefore miss hundreds of timesaving shortcuts. Part of the rationale behind Windows XP's redesign is putting these functions out in the open. Even so, many more shortcuts remain hidden under your right mouse button.

Tip: Microsoft doesn't discriminate against left-handers…much. You can swap the functions of the right and left mouse buttons easily enough.

In the Control Panel window (page 253), open the Mouse icon. When the Mouse Properties dialog box opens, click the Buttons tab, and turn on the "Switch primary and secondary buttons" checkbox. Then click OK. Windows now assumes that you want to use the *left* mouse button as the one that produces shortcut menus.

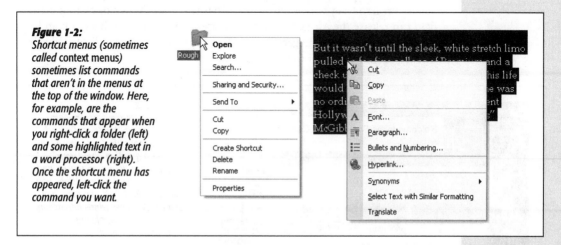

Figure 1-2:
Shortcut menus (sometimes called context menus) *sometimes list commands that aren't in the menus at the top of the window. Here, for example, are the commands that appear when you right-click a folder (left) and some highlighted text in a word processor (right). Once the shortcut menu has appeared, left-click the command you want.*

Windows wizards conduct a lot of interviews

A *wizard* is a series of screens that walks you through the task you're trying to complete. Wizards make configuration and installation tasks easier by breaking them down into smaller, more easily digested steps. Figure 1-3 offers an example.

There's more than one way to do everything

No matter what setting you want to adjust, no matter what program you want to open, Microsoft has provided five or six different ways to do it. For example, here are the various ways to delete a file: press the Delete key, choose Delete from the File menu at the top of a window, drag the file icon onto the Recycle Bin, or right-click the file name and choose Delete from the shortcut menu.

Pessimists grumble that there are too many paths to every destination, making it much more difficult to learn Windows. Optimists point out that this abundance of approaches means that almost everyone will find, and settle on, a satisfying method for each task. Whenever you find a task irksome, remember you have other options.

You can use the keyboard for everything

In earlier versions of Windows, underlined letters appeared in the names of menus
and dialog boxes. These underlines were clues for people who found it faster to do
something by pressing keys than by using the mouse.

The underlines are hidden in Windows XP, at least in disk and folder windows (they
still appear in your individual software programs). If you miss them, you have two
options:

- Make them come back full-time, using the control panel's Display program (see
  page 263).

- Make them reappear only when you summon them—by pressing the Alt key, Tab
  key, or an arrow key whenever the menu bar is visible. (When operating menus,
  you can release the Alt key immediately after pressing it.) In this book, in help
  screens, and computer magazines, you'll see key combinations indicated like this:
  Alt+S (or Alt+ whatever the letter key is).

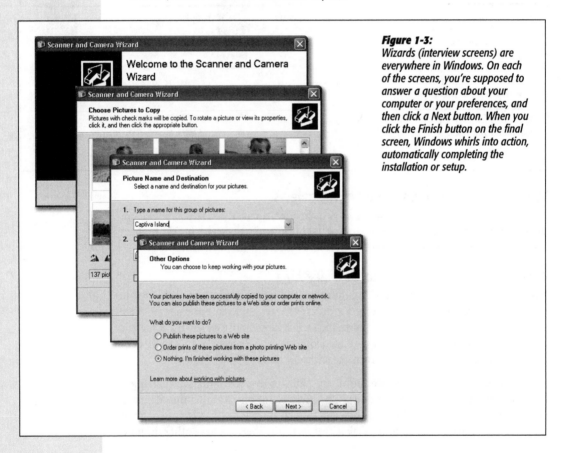

Figure 1-3:
*Wizards (interview screens) are
everywhere in Windows. On each
of the screens, you're supposed to
answer a question about your
computer or your preferences, and
then click a Next button. When you
click the Finish button on the final
screen, Windows whirls into action,
automatically completing the
installation or setup.*

Tip: Pressing the Windows logo key (next to the Alt key on recent keyboards) opens the Start menu *and* turns on its little underlines. Microsoft assumed, logically enough, that if you're enough of a keyboard lover to have opened the Start menu from the keyboard, you're probably going to want to use the keyboard to trigger the commands *in* the Start menu, too.

Once the underlines are visible, you can open a menu by pressing the underlined letter (F for the File menu, for example). Once the menu is open, press the underlined letter key that corresponds to the menu command you want. Or press Esc to close the menu without doing anything. (In Windows, the Esc key always means *cancel* or *stop*.)

If choosing a menu command opens a dialog box (see Figure 1-4), you can trigger its options, too, by pressing Alt along with the underlined letters. (Within dialog boxes, you can't press and release Alt; you have to hold it down while typing the underlined letter.)

As shown in Figure 1-4, it's a rare task indeed that you can't perform entirely from the keyboard.

Figure 1-4:
Here's how you might print two copies of a document without using the mouse at all. First, press Alt+F, which opens the File menu (left). Then type the letter P, which represents the Print command. Now the Print dialog box appears (right). Press Alt+C to highlight the Copies box, type the number of copies you want, and then press Enter to "click" the Print button. (The Enter key always means, "Click the default button in the dialog box—the one with a shadowed border.")

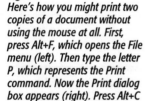
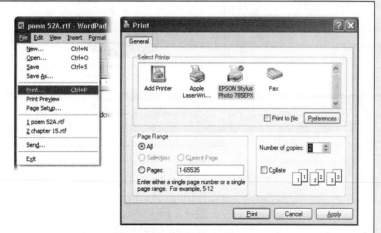

You could spend a lifetime changing properties

You can't write an operating system that's all things to all people, but Microsoft has sure tried. You can change almost every aspect of the way Windows looks and works. You can replace the gray backdrop of the screen (the *wallpaper*) with your favorite photograph, change the typeface used for the names of your icons, or set up a particular program to launch automatically every time you turn on the PC.

When you want to change some *general* behavior of your computer, such as how it connects to the Internet, how soon the screen goes black to save power, and how quickly a letter repeats on the screen when you hold down a key, you use the Control Panel window (see Chapter 9).

Many other times, however, you may want to adjust the settings of only one *particular* element of the machine, such as the hard drive, the Recycle Bin, or a particular application. In those cases, simply right-click the corresponding icon. In the resulting shortcut menu, you'll often find a command called Properties. When you click it, a dialog box appears containing settings or information about that object, as shown in Figure 1-5.

Tip: As a shortcut to the Properties command, just highlight an icon and then press Alt+Enter.

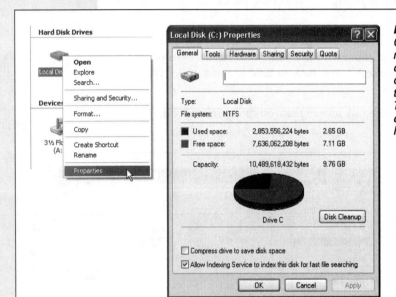

Figure 1-5:
One quick way to find out how much space is left on your hard drive is to right-click the corresponding icon and choose the Properties command (left). The Properties dialog box appears (right), featuring a handy disk-space graph.

It's also worth getting to know how to operate *tabbed dialog boxes,* like the one shown in Figure 1-5. These are windows that contain so many options, Microsoft has had to split them up into separate panels, or *tabs.* To reveal a new set of options, just click a different tab (called General, Tools, Hardware, Sharing, Security, and Quota in Figure 1-5). These tabs are designed to resemble the tabs at the top of file folders.

Tip: You can switch tabs without using the mouse by pressing Ctrl+Tab (to "click" the next tab to the right) or Ctrl+Shift+Tab (for the previous tab).

Every piece of hardware requires software

You can't walk six feet into the room at a computer user group meeting without hearing people talk about their *drivers*. They're not talking about their chauffeurs (unless they're Bill Gates); they're talking about the controlling software required by every hardware component of a PC.

The *driver* is the translator between your PC's brain and the equipment attached to it. Windows requires a driver for anything you might attach to, or install inside, your computer—mouse, keyboard, screen, CD-ROM drive, scanner, digital camera, palmtop, and so on. Without the correct driver software, the corresponding piece of equipment doesn't work at all.

When you buy one of these gadgets, you receive a CD containing the driver software. If the included driver software works fine, then great. If your gadget acts up, however, remember that equipment manufacturers regularly release improved (read: less buggy) versions of these software chunks. (You generally find such updates on the manufacturers' Web sites.)

Fortunately, Windows XP comes with drivers for over 12,000 components, saving you the trouble of scavenging for them on a disk or on the Internet. (That's one of XP's big advantages over Windows 2000, which was driver-poor by comparison.) This gigantic library is the heart of Microsoft's heavily advertised *Plug and Play* feature (Chapter 14), which lets you connect a new gadget to your PC without even thinking about the driver software.

It's not meant to be overwhelming

Windows has an absolutely staggering array of features. You can burrow six levels down, dialog box through dialog box, and never come to the end of it. There are enough programs, commands, and help screens to keep you studying the rest of your life.

It's crucial to remember that Microsoft's programmers created Windows in modules—the digital-photography team here, the networking team there—with different audiences in mind. The idea, of course, was to make sure that no subset of potential customers would find a feature lacking.

But if *you* don't have a digital camera, a network, or whatever, there's absolutely nothing wrong with ignoring everything you encounter on the screen that isn't relevant to your setup and work routine. Even Bill Gates doesn't use every single feature of Windows XP.

What's New in Windows XP

Windows XP is the most dramatic Windows overhaul since the introduction of Windows 95. As noted in the Introduction, Microsoft's goal in creating XP was gigantic: It wanted to merge its home line (the friendly but cranky Windows 95, 98, and Me) with its corporate line (the unattractive but rock-solid Windows NT and 2000) into a single, unified operating system that offers the best of both.

But this flowing of two streams into a single mighty river is only the beginning. Some of the following features will seem new only if you're used to Windows 2000, and others only if you're coming from, say, Windows Me. The rest of this section is an overview of the other goodies Windows XP offers.

Stability

The biggest news in Windows XP is that it's based on Windows 2000. Its features, including *protected memory* (if one program crashes, it isn't allowed to poison the well of memory that other programs use) and strong network security features, give you vastly improved stability. In fact, it's possible to go for weeks without having to restart a crashed PC (as opposed to days or, well, minutes with Windows Me). That's not to say that individual programs don't still bomb now and then—they do—but they no longer take down your whole computer.

Here's what else Microsoft has done to make your PC more stable:

- **System File Protection.** Before Windows XP (and Me), the installer for some new piece of software might have replaced some important Windows file with an older version, resulting in instability or crashes. When an installer tries to do that in Windows XP, it gets the door slammed in its face.

  Of course, if its installer is unable to replace the component it wants to replace, your new software might not run. However, thanks to System File Protection, you'll at least be no worse off than before you performed the installation.

- **System Restore.** Windows XP memorizes the condition of its own system files before you perform any kind of installation. If you find your PC doesn't work properly after installing some new piece of software, you can "roll back" your computer to its earlier, healthy condition. Once again, you've just undone the installation, so you can't use that new piece of software or equipment, but you've also saved lots of time troubleshooting. System Restore is a quick alternative to trying to return your machine, step by step, to the way it was before things went wrong. Bear in mind, though, that System Restore can't recover or monitor any changes to your own files (documents, email, and so on)—only system files and programs.

- **More careful driver management.** As noted above, you need driver software for every component of your PC. Windows XP interrupts you with a warning message whenever some installer tries to put an incompatible driver onto your system. And if that roadblock fails, you can use the Driver Rollback feature (page 435) to restore any driver that got replaced by a flakier one.

- **AutoUpdate.** Like any software company, Microsoft regularly releases small fixes, patches, and updates to Windows. In the old days, it was your job to read the magazines or scan the Web sites for news about these updates. Windows XP takes over that task for you; whenever you're connected to the Internet, Windows invisibly sneaks over to the Microsoft Web site, checks for updates to your software components, downloads any that it thinks you need, and pops up a window offering to install the patch for you. (You can turn off this feature if it feels too much like Big Brother.) See Chapter 16 for details.

A Cosmetic Overhaul

As you've probably discovered already, Windows XP looks much more modern and colorful than its cosmetically challenged predecessors. The taskbar and window borders are now a shimmering, backlit blue; the redesigned icons have a 3-D shadowed look; tiny animations liven up the desktop; and the Recycle Bin is now in the lower-right corner, as though it's the period at the end of a screen-size paragraph.

Other functional and cosmetic enhancements:

- When the taskbar gets crowded, it now automatically consolidates the window buttons of each program. If you're working on six Word documents, you might see just a single Microsoft Word button on the taskbar, which you can use as a pop-up menu to switch to a specific document.

- The Start menu is now a better-organized, two-column affair—recently used programs are listed in the left column, and everything else (My Documents, My Computer, Control Panel, Search, and so on) is in the right.

- The Control Panel can open in two different views: either as a window full of icons, as before (Classic View), or in tidy function-related categories (Category View). The beginning of Chapter 9 makes this new setup clear.

- There must be a neat freak on the XP design team, because Windows XP is practically obsessive about keeping your desktop and taskbar clear of clutter. A new installation of Windows XP presents you with an immaculate desktop graced by only a single icon, the Recycle Bin. (Of course, computer companies may still install desktop icons on new PCs.) The software even interrupts you every few weeks, offering to sweep away rarely used desktop icons into a special folder. Similarly, the *notification area* (once called the taskbar *tray*) hides little buttons that you rarely use (page 98). If it could, Windows XP would reach out to pluck bits of spinach from your teeth.

By the way, if you don't care for the XP cosmetic changes, you can turn them off selectively, which makes your desktop look and work just as it did in previous versions of Windows (you'll find instructions throughout this book in special sidebar boxes labeled "Nostalgia Corner"). You can also turn off the various animations, drop shadows, and other special effects for a measurable speed boost on slower PCs (see page 122).

Pictures, Music, and Movies

Windows XP gets a gold star for its new picture, music, and movie features. For example, the simple act of plugging a digital camera into your PC opens a dialog box that offers to transfer your photos from camera to hard drive.

Windows XP comes with version 8 or 9 of Media Player, which lets you play movies, listen to distant radio stations over the Internet, burn music CDs, and transfer music files to your portable MP3 player. Chapter 8 tells all.

Miscellaneous Touch-Ups

Nips and tucks are everywhere in Windows XP. For example:

- XP machines start up and wake up faster than in previous Windows versions.

- Desktop windows now offer a left-side *task pane* (Figure 1-6) that offers one-click access to jobs you might need to do.

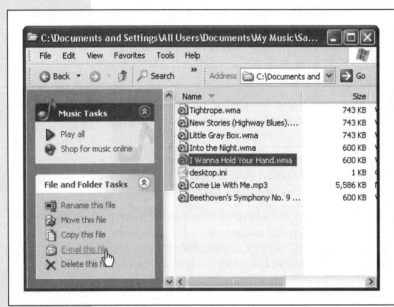

Figure 1-6:
The new task pane commands are sometimes extremely useful ("Set as desktop background" when you click a picture file). Other times, they're invitations to send money to Microsoft and its partners ("Shop for music online," "Order prints online"). In any folder containing photo or music files, like the MP3 files shown here, controls appear that let you conduct a slide show, or a concert of your MP3 files, right there on the desktop.

- Windows XP comes with Internet Explorer 6, an upgraded Web browser that offers better security features and a couple of nifty picture-viewing options (Chapter 11).

- XP offers a few useful technologies expressly for laptop owners, including ClearType (for easier-to-read text on flat-panel screens) and improved battery management.

- Frightened Web users can take some comfort in XP's new, built-in *firewall* software, which blocks hacker invasions from the Internet (page 312).

- Windows Messenger lets you exchange instant messages with people on your MSN, Hotmail, or Windows Messenger "buddy list" over the Internet. If your PC has a microphone and speakers, you can also talk to your pals toll-free. Windows Messenger even turns your PC into a videophone, if it has a video camera.

- *Remote Assistance* means that, in times of troubleshooting, you can extend an invitation to someone geekier than yourself to see, and even take control of, your

PC from across the Internet. For anyone who's ever lived through the exasperating experience of trying to troubleshoot a friend's computer over the phone ("Now do you see a message on the screen? What does it say? No, no, that's the Recycle Bin…"), this is a big deal.

Professional Edition vs. Home Edition

It's *mostly* true that there's really just one Windows XP. The Professional and Home editions look alike, generally work alike, and are based on the same multigigabyte glob of software code.

But as with a pizza, insurance policy, or Toyota Camry, you can pay a little more to get a few extras tacked on. Buying the Professional Edition equips you with these goodies. Many of them are interesting primarily only to professional corporate network nerds, to be sure, but all are described in this book:

• **Remote Desktop.** If your XP Pro machine has a permanent Internet connection (like a cable modem or DSL), you can connect to it from any other Windows machine via the Internet (or office network). You can see what's on its screen and manipulate what you find there—a great feature when you're traveling with a laptop.

• **Corporate domain membership.** XP Pro computers can be part of a *domain*—a group of networked computers, usually in big corporations (Chapter 19), that system administrators can maintain as a unit. Computers running the Home Edition can't join a domain and aren't affected by the changes the administrator makes to the domain settings.

• **Administrative shares.** Windows XP Pro creates several *shared folders* for use by administrators and operating system services that manage the computer environment on the network. For security reasons, and to limit problems like somebody deleting essential files, XP Pro doesn't give everyday employees access to these folders.

• **Remote Installation Service (RIS).** RIS is a technical process that helps administrators install operating systems and software via the network without having to physically visit the computer.

• **Acknowledgment of high-horsepower chips.** If your computer has multiple processors inside, or the Intel Itanium processor, only XP Pro exploits them.

• **Offline files.** This feature lets you "sign out" certain files and folders when you're about to leave the office with your laptop. When you return, the documents you've edited are automatically copied back to their starting places on the network.

• **Roaming profiles.** This feature lets you sit down at any PC on the office network, log on, and see your own personal desktop, even though you're not at your own personal PC.

• **Group and local policy settings.** *Group policies* let administrators set up various groups on the network domain (one for Marketing, one for Accounting, as so on). That way, the administrator can apply the same security and management settings to all employees in that group, in one fell swoop.

Local group policies let administrators customize and fine-tune the underlings' PCs. For example, the admin can prevent you from using certain programs (like chat programs) and specify what your Start menu and taskbar look like. (If a local group policy conflicts with a network domain group policy, the group policy usually wins.)

• **Polyglot heaven.** You can make Windows XP change the language it uses for dialog boxes, menus, help files, dictionaries, spelling checkers, and so on. Microsoft refers to this feature as the Multilingual User Interface. Over 60 languages are included in both versions of Windows XP, but only XP Pro includes a toolbar (the Language bar) that lets you change the language on your computer at any time.

• **File protection.** In XP Pro, you can protect individual files or folders by encrypting them, so that not even the most diligent spy or hacker can open them.

• **NTFS Permissions.** XP Pro gives you much greater control over who (in your home, school, or office) can access which files, folders, or programs—whether over the network or when logging in directly. Details in Chapter 17.

• **Internet Information Services (IIS).** XP Pro can turn your PC into a Web, mail, and FTP server using this software. (This feature may be familiar to Windows 2000 fans.)

• **Dynamic disks.** If you have more than one hard drive, you can set up XP Pro to treat them all as single massive disk. (Details in Chapter 15.)

The Dark Side of Windows XP

Despite all of the improvements, Windows XP doesn't come without its share of controversy. Let us count the ways in which the new operating system has raised eyebrows and hackles.

Activation (Copy Protection)

Windows XP marks the first time Microsoft has ever copy-protected Windows, meaning you can't install Windows XP on more than one PC from the same CD. (Technically, the CDs are all identical. What you really can't use more than once is your serial number.) If you have a desktop PC as well as a laptop, you have to buy Windows XP twice, and Microsoft will give you only a 10 percent discount on the second copy. If you make the attempt, the second PC refuses to operate after 30 days.

How does it know that you're being naughty? When you first install Windows XP, the operating system inspects ten crucial components inside your PC: the hard drive, motherboard, video card, memory, and so on. All this information is transmitted, along with the 25-character serial number on the back of your Windows XP CD (the Product Key), to Microsoft's database via your Internet account. The process takes about two seconds, and involves little more than clicking an OK button. You have just *activated* Windows XP.

Note: If you don't have an Internet connection, activation is a much more grueling procedure. You have to call a toll-free number, read a 50-digit identification number to the Microsoft agent, and then type a 42-digit confirmation number into your software. Do whatever it takes to avoid having to endure this fingertip-numbing ritual.

Later, if you try to install the same copy of Windows XP onto a different computer, Windows XP will check in with Microsoft and discover that the new machine's components aren't the same. It will conclude that you have tried to install the same copy of the operating system onto a different machine—and it will lock you out.

This aspect of Windows XP has frightened or enraged many a computer fan. In truth, though, it isn't quite as bad as it seems. Here's why:

- If you buy a new PC with Windows XP already installed, you don't have to activate anything; it's already been done.

- Copies of Windows XP that are distributed within corporations don't require this activation business, either.

- No information about *you* is transferred to Microsoft during this activation process—only a list of the components in your PC make the trip. (Later in the installation process, you're also asked to *register* your copy of Windows—a completely different affair. This time, personal information *is* transmitted to Microsoft—but this part is optional.)

- Don't believe the Internet Chicken Littles who claim that activation will shut down your PC if you try to upgrade the memory or another component. In fact, you would have to replace four of the ten key components within a period of four months—your basic hardware-upgrade frenzy—before Windows XP stopped recognizing your computer. And even then, you could just call Microsoft to obtain a new activation number.

Tip: Your PC's note to itself that Windows has been properly activated is stored in two little files called Wpa.dbl and Wpa.bak. (They're in your My Computer→Local Disk (C:)→Windows→System32 folder.) If you ever decide to replace your hard drive, back up these little files before you remove your original drive. (Copy them onto a floppy, for example.)

Then, after installing the new hard drive and installing Windows XP onto it, copy the Wpa.dbl and Wpa.bak files into exactly the same folder. Windows XP will be perfectly content that it's running on a legitimate, properly activated computer.

Privacy Concerns

Microsoft is making more of an effort than ever to compile a massive database of its customers. There's nothing particularly sneaky about it, though, because Microsoft collects this information only with your permission.

Here are three times when you'll be asked to send information back to Microsoft:

- **During registration.** As noted earlier, registration means "sending your name and address to Microsoft just after starting up Windows XP for the first time." Registering ensures that you'll be on Microsoft's mailing lists, so you won't miss a single exciting Microsoft marketing message. Fortunately, it's optional.

- **After a crash or freeze.** When things go really wrong with your software, Windows XP, like Office XP before it, seeks your permission to send a bug report back to the mother ship. No information about you is supposed to go along for the ride—only a description of your PC and some technical specs that describe what was going on at the time of the crash. However, it's technically possible for some scraps of your document to show up in the report.

Microsoft collects these bug reports by the thousands. Its hope, of course, is that it will be able to spot patterns that help pinpoint the causes of these crashes.

UP TO SPEED

Windows XP: The Buzzword-Compliant Operating System

You can't read an article about Windows XP without hearing certain technical buzzwords that were once exclusively the domain of computer engineers. Here's what they mean:

Preemptive multitasking. Most people know that multitasking means "doing more than one thing at once." Windows has always been capable of making a printout, downloading a file, and letting you type away in a word processor, all at the same time.

Unfortunately, the Windows 95/98/Me version of multitasking works by the rule of the playground: The bully gets what he wants. If one of your programs insists on hogging the attention of your PC's processor (because it's crashing, for example), it leaves the other programs gasping for breath. This arrangement is called *cooperative* multitasking. Clearly, it works only if your programs are in fact cooperating with one another.

Windows XP's *preemptive* multitasking system brings a teacher to the playground to make sure that each program receives a fair amount of time from the PC's processor.

The result is that the programs get along much better, and a poorly written or crashing program isn't permitted to send the other ones home crying.

Multithreading. Multithreading means "doing more than one thing at once," too, but in this case it's referring to a single program. Even while your video editing program is exporting your movie, for example, you may be able to continue editing at the same time.

Memory protection. In Windows XP, every program runs in its own indestructible memory bubble—another reason XP is so much more stable than its predecessors. If one program crashes, it isn't allowed to poison the well of RAM that other programs might want to use, as it would in Windows Me.

That doesn't mean paradise—programs may still freeze or quit unexpectedly. The world will never be entirely free of sloppy programmers. But your PC itself will soldier on with its other programs unaffected.

- **When you try to use one of the Internet features.** Some of Windows XP's most attractive features, including MSN Messenger and Web page publishing, require you to have a *Passport*—Microsoft's form of Internet identification. All you have to reveal in this case is your email address. You can refuse, of course, but then Microsoft won't let you use those features.

Microsoft swears up and down that it has no ulterior motives in compiling this data. But if it makes you nervous, just decline in each case.

Microsoft Data Formats

Microsoft makes no secret of the fact that it wants its own software technologies to predominate, especially when it comes to the Internet and multimedia. For example, the Java software required by many online banking and investment Web sites is no longer part of the standard Internet Explorer Web browser installation (because of legal squabbles with Sun, Java's creator). Windows Media Player can't understand QuickTime movie files or RealAudio files, either—and, in fact, can't even turn your CDs into standard MP3 files.

Fortunately, you'll find workarounds for all of these limitations (see Chapter 8 and Chapter 11).

The Desktop and Start Menu

When you turn on a Windows XP Pro computer for the first time, you may think that you're simply seeing the traditional Windows startup process as redesigned by a West Coast graphic designer. If it's a new computer, you may also receive a big hello from the company that sold it to you.

If you've just performed a *clean installation* of Windows XP (page 625), or if it's a brand-new PC, you may now be treated to a series of blue "Welcome to Microsoft Windows" setup screens. This Setup Wizard guides you through setting up an Internet account, *activating* your copy of Windows (page 18), setting up *accounts* for different people who will be sharing this computer (page 497), and so on. Appendix A has a complete description of this process.

Logging In

What happens next in the startup process depends on which of XP Pro's two "personalities" you're seeing, which is determined by what kind of network you're connected to.

Eager though you may be to dive in, taking a minute to learn the difference is essential if you hope to understand what appears on screen when you log in and why it may not match the examples you see online and in magazines and books.

Domains vs. Workgroups

Unlike Windows XP Home Edition, which was designed primarily for individuals to use, well, at home, Windows XP Pro serves two masters. Although it works very well for home PCs, it's also designed to thrive in massively networked corporations.

As a result, Windows XP Pro has two distinct personalities, each of which presents different features, a different logon sequence, and different levels of security. What you get when you log in depends on what kind of network your PC is connected to:

- A **domain network** is a group of computers and other network gear that's centrally maintained by an administrator, thanks to a special, master computer called a *domain controller*. That highly paid professional can set up and troubleshoot all files and security settings on all domain PCs without having to visit each one in person.

    You, the employee, can generally sit down at any computer in the domain and log on with your user name and password. At that point, you find the same files, folders, and disks available to you as you did at your own computer. For more information on domains, see Chapter 19.

- A **workgroup** is the kind of network in most homes and small offices: a small cluster of machines connected via network cables or wireless cards, as described in Chapter 18. Instead of enjoying central administration, as in a domain, you have to configure all settings for accounts and shared folders independently on each computer. If you have five PCs, and you'd like to be able to access all of their

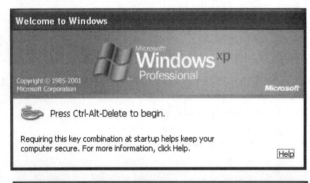

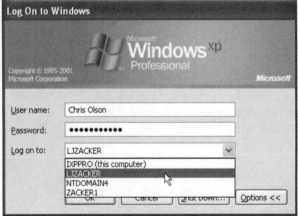

Figure 2-1:
Top: When your computer is a member of a network domain, you're probably greeted by this message when you start up the PC. To proceed, press Ctrl+Alt+Del (a ritual that may be familiar if you've used Windows 2000).

Bottom: This is the Classic Logon dialog box, which appears next. Type your name and password and then click OK or press Enter.

files from across the network, you must set up an account for yourself (a name and password) five times. (Clearly, workgroups get to be a real hassle as they grow larger than about ten machines.)

As you read this book, this is the category you're interested in if your PC is at home, sits in a small office, or isn't part of any network at all.

Tip: If you're not sure whether your computer is a member of a workgroup or a domain, choose Start→Control Panel→System, and then click the Computer Name tab. This dialog box shows the name of your computer and the name of its domain or workgroup.

Logging In, Continued

Now that you know which XP Pro personality your computer has adopted, you can see why the login process isn't the same for everybody.

- **If your PC connects to a corporate domain,** you encounter the startup box shown in Figure 2-1. Press Ctrl+Alt+Del to proceed to the "Classic" Logon dialog box. Type your name in the User Name text box, type your password in the Password text box, and then click OK (or press Enter). You arrive at the desktop.

- **If your PC is part of a workgroup (or no network at all),** you may encounter the Welcome dialog box shown in Figure 2-2. Click your name in the list, type your password if you're asked for it, and click the little right-pointing arrow button (or press Enter). You arrive at the desktop.

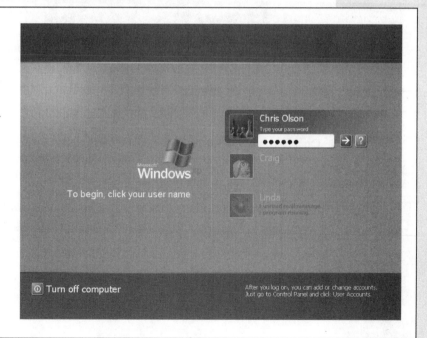

Figure 2-2:
If there are several accounts on a standalone or workgroup PC—that is, if more than one person uses it, each with his own account—the machine presents this screen each time you turn it on. See Chapter 17 for much more on this business of user accounts and logging in.

• **If it's a standalone PC that nobody else uses,** no big deal. You arrive at the Windows XP desktop.

The Elements of the XP Desktop

Once you're past the heart-pounding excitement of the new startup logo and the Setup Wizard, you reach the digital vista shown in Figure 2-3. It's the Windows desktop, now graced by a pastoral sunny hillside that should look familiar to anyone who has ever watched "Teletubbies."

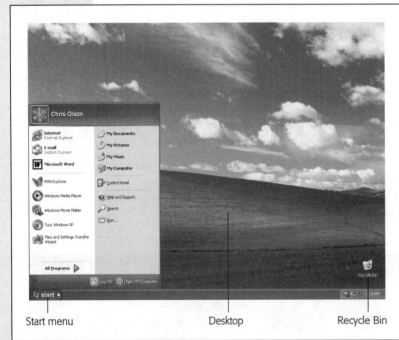

Start menu   *Desktop*   *Recycle Bin*

Figure 2-3:
Everything you'll ever do on the computer begins with a click on one of these three elements: a desktop icon, the Start button (which opens the Start menu), or the taskbar, which is described in Chapter 3. (The Start menu, now in a new, improved two-column format, lists every significant command and software component on your PC.) Some people enjoy the newly streamlined Windows XP desktop. Others deliberately place additional icons on the desktop—things like favorite programs and documents—for quicker access. Let your personality be your guide.

On a fresh installation of Windows XP, you may be surprised to discover that Microsoft has gone cleanliness-crazy. A new installation of Windows XP on a new computer presents an absolutely spotless desktop, utterly icon-free except for the Recycle Bin. Even the familiar My Computer, My Documents, and My Network Places icons seem to be missing. (If you've upgraded from an older version of Windows, you'll still see your old icons on the desktop. Furthermore, the company who sold you your PC may have stocked the desktop with a few of its own icons—but you get the point.)

Those former desktop icons are now in your Start menu, which appear when you click the Start button in the lower-left corner of your screen (Figure 2-3). The following pages cover the Start menu in detail.

The Start Menu

Windows XP is composed of 40 million lines of computer code, scattered across your hard drive in thousands of files. The vast majority of them are support files, there for behind-the-scenes use by Windows and your applications. They're not for you. They may as well bear a sticker saying, "No user serviceable parts inside."

That's why the Start menu is so important. It lists every *useful* piece of software on your computer, including commands, programs, and files. You can use the Start menu to open your applications, install new software, configure hardware, get help, find files, and much more.

When you click the Start button at the lower-left corner of your screen, the Start menu pops open, shooting upward. Its contents depend on which options you (or your computer's manufacturer) have put there; Figure 2-4 illustrates an example. The new, multi-column structure of the Start menu is one of the most radical developments in Windows XP.

The new Start menu is divided into four chunks. One area, the *pinned items list,* lists programs you use every day and is yours to modify. Another, the *most frequently used programs list,* lists programs you use often and is computed automatically by Windows. The final two sections list Windows features and standard Windows programs. Figure 2-4 describes the function of each section.

NOSTALGIA CORNER

Restoring the Desktop Icons

The desktop icons that once provided quick access to important locations on your PC—My Computer, My Documents, My Network Places, and Internet Explorer—have been swept away by the digital broom of Microsoft's clean-freak XP designers.

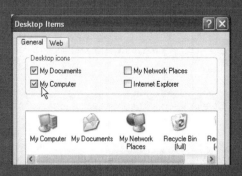

You can still get to these locations; they're listed in your Start menu now. On one hand, you can now open these folders and programs without having to hide whatever windows are covering up your desktop. On the other hand, opening them now requires two mouse clicks (including one to open the Start menu)—an egregious expenditure of caloric effort.

If you miss the old arrangement, it's easy enough to put these icons back on the desktop. To do so, right-click the desktop and then choose Properties from the shortcut menu.

Now the Display Properties dialog box appears. Click the Desktop tab. Below the list of backgrounds, click the Customize Desktop button. As shown here, awaiting your summons are checkboxes for the usual desktop icons: My Documents, My Computer, My Network Places, and Internet Explorer. Turn on the ones you'd like to install onto the desktop, putting check marks in the appropriate boxes, and then click OK twice. Your old favorite icons are now back where they once belonged.

Tip: If you're a keyboard-shortcut lover, you can open the Start menu by pressing the Windows logo key on the bottom row of your keyboard. (If you're using one of those antique, kerosene-operated keyboards that lacks a Windows key, press Ctrl+Esc instead.)

Once it's open, you can use the arrow keys to "walk" up and down the menu (or type the first letters of the command you want), and then press Enter to "click" the highlighted command.

Start menu items graced by a right-pointing triangle arrow (such as Accessories in Figure 2-4) have *submenus*, also known as *cascading menus*. As you move your mouse pointer over an item that has such an arrow, the submenu, listing additional options, pops out to the right (you don't have to click). It's not unusual for submenu items to have arrows of their own, indicating—what else?—additional submenus.

This discussion describes the items in the Start menu from the bottom up, left to right, the way your mouse encounters them as it moves up from the Start button.

Tip: To change your name and icon as it appears at the top of the new Start menu, use the User Accounts program in the Control Panel, as described on page 503.

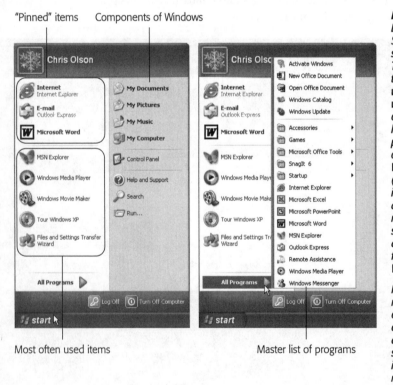

"Pinned" items   Components of Windows

Most often used items   Master list of programs

Figure 2-4:
Left: In Windows XP, the Start menu is divided into several distinct sections. The top left section is yours to play with. You can "pin" whatever programs you want here, in whatever order you like. The lower-left section lists the programs you use most often, according to Windows XP's calculations. (You can delete individual items here but you can't add items manually or rearrange them.) The right-side column provides direct access to certain Windows features and standard Windows programs.

Right: The All Programs menu superimposes itself on the standard two-column Start menu, listing almost every piece of software you've ever installed. You can rearrange, add to, or delete items from this list.

Start→Log Off

This command is at the heart of Windows XP's *accounts* feature, in which each person who uses this PC gets to see his own desktop picture, email account, files, and so on (see Chapter 17). When you're logged into a network domain this is one of the most important features of all. You should log off your computer any time you walk away from it, especially if your computer stores confidential information. If this is a home computer and it doesn't store confidential information you can safely ignore this option forever.

Choosing this command may present either of two dialog boxes, depending on whether your computer is logged into a network domain, or whether or not you log on to a standalone or workgroup computer that has the Windows XP feature called *Fast User Switching* turned on.

Note: You cannot use Fast User Switching on a computer that logs on to a network domain.

- **Immediate log off.** If you see the dialog box shown at bottom in Figure 2-5, two possibilities exist. The first is that you're logged into a network domain. When

NOSTALGIA CORNER

Return to the Old Start Menu

The newly designed XP Start menu has its charms, not the least of which is its three-dimensional glowing effect. But it's also confusing to old-time Windows users, and slower to open, particularly on PCs that aren't quite state of the art.

Fortunately, it's easy enough to switch back to the organization and design of the old, single-column Start menu. Just right-click the Start button. Now, from the shortcut menu, choose Properties.

In the Taskbar and Start Menu Properties dialog box that appears, you'll see the option to return to the old Start menu design—what Microsoft calls Classic Start menu—staring you in the face, complete with an illustration. Click that button, click OK, and enjoy going back to the future.

When you use the Classic Start menu, you'll notice a few differences in the behavior of the Start menu commands. For example, the Log Off command bears your actual account name ("Log Off Chris"), and of course the Programs command isn't a second, separate menu superimposed on the Start menu. (But you knew that, of course, because you're already accustomed to the older Start menu.)

Incidentally, on the assumption that you *really* liked Windows better the old way, turning on the Classic Start menu also restores several icons to your immaculate desktop: My Documents, My Computer, Internet Explorer, and My Network Places. (They disappear when you switch back to the modern Start menu.)

To restore the new Start menu, repeat the procedure—but this time, in the dialog box shown here, turn on Start Menu instead.

---

you click Log Off (or press Enter), Windows closes all open programs and then presents the classic Welcome to Windows dialog box so that the next person can log on.

The second possibility is that, on your standalone or workgroup computer, you or someone with local Administrator privileges on your computer has turned off Fast User Switching. If you click Log Off (or press Enter), Windows closes all open programs and presents a new Welcome screen (Figure 2-2) so that the next person can sign in. If you haven't saved your work, each application gives you an opportunity to do so before closing.

If you click Cancel in either case, you're sent right back to whatever you were doing.

- **Switch User/Log Off.** If you see the dialog box shown at the top of Figure 2-5, then Fast User Switching is turned on (as it is on any fresh Windows XP Pro installation for a standalone or workgroup computer). It's among the most use-

Figure 2-5:
Top: On workgroup computers, if Fast User Switching is turned on, this is what you see when you choose Start→Log Off. No matter which button you click, you return to the Welcome screen. The only difference is that clicking the Switch User button leaves all of your programs open and in memory, and the Log Off button takes a few moments to close them.

Bottom: On domain-network computers (or any computer where Fast User Switching is turned off), a dialog box like this appears when you choose Start→Log Off. If you click the Log Off button, Windows quits your programs and then takes you to the Classic Logon dialog box.

ful new features in Windows XP, since it lets somebody else log into the computer, opening up his own world of documents, email, desktop picture, and so on. Meanwhile, whatever *you* had up and running remains open behind the scenes. After the interloper is finished, you can log on again to find all of your open programs and documents exactly as you left them on the screen.

Although this is a handy Windows XP feature, it can also be the least secure. When user accounts aren't assigned passwords, anyone can access anyone else's information as easily as clicking the person's name.

Tip: On your Windows XP Professional standalone or workgroup computer, you turn Fast User Switching off in Start→Control Panel→User Accounts. Click the link called "Change the way users log on or off."

Figure 2-6:
Just how down is off? Top: Here's what you probably see if you work in a company with a domain network. Click the command in the drop-down menu that corresponds to the degree of down-ness you want—Log Off, Shut Down, Restart, Standby, Hibernate, or Disconnect. Or type the first letter of the command you want. (For Standby, press S twice.)

Bottom: On a workgroup PC, your Shut Down dialog box may look like this instead. As you see here, the secret Hibernate button appears only when you press the Shift key.

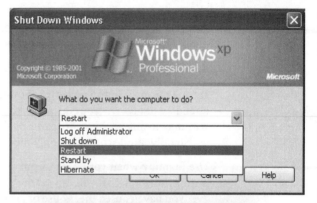

Start→Shut Down (Turn Off Computer)

In Windows XP Pro, this menu item is more powerful than its name implies. Choosing it opens a dialog box that offers several variations on "shut down" (see Figure 2-6).

- **Standby** puts your computer to "sleep." This special state of PC consciousness reduces the amount of electricity the computer uses. It remains in suspended animation until you use the mouse or keyboard to begin working again. (This feature is available only if your computer offers it *and* you've turned it on in the Power Options program in the Control Panel.)

  How the PC sleeps depends on its power-saving features. Usually, the hard drive stops spinning and the screen goes dark. Whatever programs or documents you were working on remain in memory.

Warning: This information is stored only in memory, not on your hard drive. If your computer loses power, you lose all of the information that was stored in memory. To be absolutely safe, save your open documents before putting the PC in Standby.

  If you're using a laptop on battery power, Standby is a real boon. When the flight attendant hands over your microwaved chicken teriyaki, you can take a food break without closing all your programs or shutting down the computer. And best of all, Standby mode consumes only the barest trickle of battery power.

  Use Standby when you want to put your computer to sleep on cue. It's worth noting, however, that you can set the computer to stand by automatically whenever you haven't used the mouse or keyboard for a while. You can even make it so that the computer won't wake up again unless you type in a certain password. Page 286 has the details on these extra features.

- **Shut down** quits all open programs (or, in some cases, prompts you to do so), offers you the opportunity to save any unsaved documents, and then exits Windows. Most modern PCs then turn off automatically.

Note: If you're logged on to a workgroup network, this command may be called Turn Off.

  If your older model requires you to manually press the Power button, you must wait until a message appears on the screen telling you that it's safe to turn off the computer (which may take more than a few seconds).

Tip: You don't have to open the Start menu to turn off the computer. Just press the power button. (If that makes the PC sleep or *hibernate* instead, see page 286.)

- **Restart** quits all open programs, then quits and restarts Windows again automatically. The computer doesn't turn off. (You might do this to "refresh" your computer when you notice that it's responding sluggishly, for example.)

- **Log off** quits all programs, disconnects from the network, and then displays the Welcome screen so that the next person can log in. (The PC doesn't restart.)

- **Disconnect** appears as an option only if your computer is connected to a Windows 2000 Server machine that's running Terminal Services. (If you use this feature, you know who you are.) When you choose it, your terminal session disconnects, but the server remembers what you were doing. When you reconnect to Terminal Services, you return to your previous session. Everything looks as it did before you disconnected.

- **Hibernate** shuts down the machine after it *memorizes* the state of your software, including all open operating system files, applications, and documents. Behind the scenes, it saves all this memorized information into a file on your hard disk. As a result, the Hibernate command doesn't work unless you have a lot of free disk space. The more RAM your computer has, the more disk space you'll need. (As with Standby, this feature is only available if your computer offers it and you've turned it on in the Power Options Control Panel program.)

Note: On a workgroup computer, you may not see the Hibernate command. It doesn't appear in the Turn Off Computer dialog box unless you hold down the Shift key. When you do, the Standby option changes to say Hibernate (see Figure 2-6).

The beauty of this feature is that when you start the computer again, everything returns to the way it was when you shut down—*fast*. The same documents appear, the same programs are running, and so on. Hibernate, in other words, offers the speed and convenience of Standby, with the safety of Turn Off.

GEM IN THE ROUGH

Hibernation as a Shutdown Technique

When you shut down the computer in Hibernation mode, the next startup is lightning-fast. As soon as the startup procedure begins, Windows notices the hibernation file on the hard drive, says, "Hey, everything's in place," and loads the file into memory. After you push the power button, everything reappears on the screen faster than you can say, "Redmond, Washington." After you've enjoyed the speed of a power up from Hibernation mode, the normal startup seems unbearably slow.

This instant-on characteristic makes it tempting to use the hibernation feature *every* time you shut down your computer. But when your PC hibernates, Windows doesn't have a chance to quit and then restart, as it would if you use the Restart command or shut the computer down. As a result,

Windows never gets the opportunity to flush your computer's memory or perform the other domestic chores of a modern operating system. Consequently, Windows may seem to slow down over time.

Furthermore, the Plug and Play feature described in Chapter 14 might not work when you plug in some new piece of equipment. That's because Windows ordinarily recognizes such new arrivals during the startup process—and when your computer hibernates, there *is* no startup process.

The solution is to compromise. Use the Hibernate mode *most* of the time, but shut the computer down or restart it every now and then. (If you bought your PC with Windows XP Pro preinstalled, you may have noticed that it starts up faster than before, anyway.)

As with the Standby feature, you can configure your computer to hibernate auto-matically after a period of inactivity, or require a password to bring it out of hibernation. See page 283 for details.

Note: Some older computers don't come with the necessary circuitry (technically, *BIOS support*) for the Hibernate command. In that case, the Hibernate choice doesn't appear, even when you press Shift.

Start→All Programs

For most people, the Start→All Programs command is the most important func-tion of the Start menu. It's the master list of every program on your computer. (The installer for any new program generally installs its own name in this menu; see Fig-ure 2-7.) You can jump directly to your word processor, calendar, or favorite game, for example, just by choosing its name from the Start→All Programs menu.

Tip: When the Start menu is open, you can open the All Programs menu in a number of ways: by clicking the All Programs menu, by pointing to it and keeping the mouse still for a moment, or by pressing the P and then the right-arrow keys on your keyboard.

Speaking of keyboard fanaticism: Once the programs list is open, you can also choose anything in it without involving the mouse. Just type the first letter of a program's name—or press the up and down arrow keys—to highlight the name of the program you want. Then press Enter to seal the deal.

Clearly, the graphic designers were on vacation the day Microsoft came up with this one. The All Programs menu appears *superimposed* on the regular Start menu, add-ing a third column in a second layer—not the most elegant visual solution, to be sure, but at least easy to find.

The Startup folder

The Start→All Programs menu also lists the *Startup folder*, which contains programs that load automatically every time you start Windows XP. This can be a very useful

---

NOSTALGIA CORNER

Restoring the Single-Column Programs List

If you have a lot of programs, the All Programs menu may itself consume multiple columns on your screen. If this columns-on-columns effect makes you a bit dizzy, just re-place it with the simple, one-column, scrolling Programs menu of Windows gone by.

To do so, right-click the Start button, then choose Proper-ties from the submenu. Next, click the Customize button, click the Advanced tab, and scroll down the list of options

until you see Scroll Programs. Turn on the checkbox and then click OK twice.

Now your programs list may still be too tall for the screen. But you can scroll the list by pointing to the tiny black tri-angle arrow (at the top or bottom of the menu) without clicking. And of course, you can always select items in the list from the keyboard.

---

feature; if you check your email every morning, you may as well save yourself a few mouse clicks by putting your email program into the Startup folder. If you spend all day long word processing, you may as well put Microsoft Word or WordPerfect in there.

In fact, although few PC users suspect it, what you put into the Startup folder doesn't have to be an application. It can just as well be a certain document you consult every day. It can even be a folder or disk icon whose window you'd like to find open and waiting each time you turn on the PC. (The My Documents folder is a natural example.)

Figure 2-7:
The Start→All Programs menu may list the actual application (such as Microsoft Word) that you can click to launch the program. But it may also list a program group, a submenu that lists everything in a particular application folder. Some software programs install a folder on the All Programs menu, like the Office Tools folder shown here, that contains commands for launching the software, uninstalling the software, running specific utilities, opening the help files, and so on.

Of course, you may be interested in the Startup folder for a different reason: to *stop* some program from launching itself. This is a particularly common syndrome if somebody else set up your PC. Some program seems to launch itself, unbidden, every time you turn the machine on.

Tip: All kinds of programs dump components into this folder. Over time, they can begin to slow down your computer. If you're having trouble determining the purpose of one startup program or another, visit this Web page, which provides a comprehensive list of every startup software nugget known, with instructions for turning off each one: *www.pacs-portal.co.uk/startup_index.htm*.

Fortunately, it's easy to either add or remove items from the Startup folder:

1. **Click the Start button. Point to All Programs. Right-click Startup and choose Open from the shortcut menu.**

   The Startup window opens, revealing whatever is inside.

   To delete an icon from this folder, just right-click it, choose Delete from the short-cut menu, and answer Yes to send the icon to the Recycle Bin. Close all the windows you've opened and enjoy your newfound freedom from self-launching software. The deed is done.

   To add a new icon to the Startup folder, on the other hand, read on.

2. **Navigate to the disk, folder, application, or document icon you want to add to the Startup folder.**

   Doing so requires familiarity with one of two folder-navigation schemes: My Computer or Windows Explorer. Both are described in the next chapter.

3. **Using the right mouse button, drag the icon directly into the Startup window, as shown in Figure 2-8.**

   When you release the button, a shortcut menu appears.

4. **Choose Create Shortcuts Here from the shortcut menu.**

   Close all the windows you've opened. From now on, each time you turn on or restart your computer, the program, file, disk, or folder you dragged will open by itself.

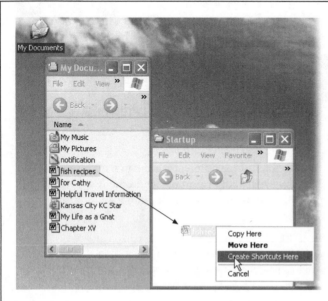

Figure 2-8:
It's easy to add a program or document icon to your Startup folder so that it launches automatically every time you turn on the computer. Here, a document from the My Documents folder is being added. You may also want to add a shortcut for the My Documents folder itself, which ensures that its window will be ready and open each time the computer starts up.

Tip: To find out what something is—something in your Start menu, All Programs menu, or indeed anywhere on your desktop—point to it with your cursor without clicking. A small yellow tooltip appears, containing a text description. (If the tooltip doesn't appear, it might be that the window you're pointing to isn't the *active* window on your desktop. Click the window and then try again.)

Start→Run

Use the Run menu item to get to a *command line*, as shown in Figure 2-9. A command line is a text-based method of performing a task. You type a command, click OK, and something happens as a result.

Working at the command line is becoming a lost art in the world of Windows, because most people prefer to issue commands by choosing from menus using the mouse. However, some old-timers still love the command line, and even mouse-lovers encounter situations where a typed command is the *only* way to do something.

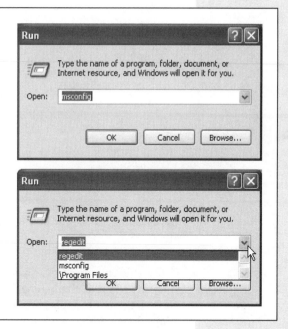

Figure 2-9:
Top: The last Run command you entered appears automatically in the Open text box. You can use the drop-down list to see a list of commands you've previously entered.

Bottom: The Run command knows the names of all of your folders and also remembers the last few commands you typed here. As you go, you're shown the best match for the characters you're typing. When the name of the folder you're trying to open appears in the list, click it to save having to type the rest of the entry.

If you're an old-time PC veteran, your head probably teems with neat Run commands you've picked up over the years. If you're new to this idea, however, the following are a few of the useful and timesaving functions you can perform with the Run dialog box.

Launch a Program

As noted later in this discussion, one of the most important Start menu commands is the All Programs menu, where you'll find the name of almost every application on your computer. You can open any of these programs one at a time by typing its *program file name* in the Open text box and then pressing Enter. That's an extremely useful shortcut for both pros and novices alike, because it's frequently faster to launch a program this way than to use the Start→All Programs menu.

Unfortunately, the program file name isn't the same as its plain-English name; it's a cryptic, abbreviated version. For example, if you want to open Microsoft Word, you must type *winword*. That's the actual name of the Word program icon as it sits in your My Computer→Local Disk (C:)→Program Files→Microsoft Office→Office folder. Some other common program-file names are shown here:

Program's real name	Program's familiar name
iexplore	Internet Explorer
explorer	Windows Explorer
write	WordPad
msworks	Microsoft Works
msimn	Outlook Express
wmplayer	Windows Media Player
palm	Palm Desktop
sol	Solitaire
winmine	Minesweep
control	classic Control Panel
regedit	The Registry Editor
cleanmgr	Disk Cleanup
defrag	Disk Defragmenter
calc	Calculator

Tip: To discover the program file name of a favorite program, see "Which One's the Program?" on page 67.

If, like efficiency freaks worldwide, you believe that it's generally faster and more efficient to do something using the keyboard than using the mouse, get this: You can perform this entire application-launching stunt without using the mouse at all. Just follow these steps in rapid succession:

1. **Press the Windows logo key on the bottom row of your keyboard.**

   Doing so makes the Start menu pop open.

2. **Press the letter R key.**

   That's the underlined letter for the Run command, whose dialog box now opens.

3. **Type the program file's name in the Open box.**

If you've typed the name before, just type a couple of letters; Windows XP fills in the rest of the name automatically.

4. **Press Enter.**

Windows opens the requested program instantly. Keystrokes: 4, Mouse: 0.

Launch Any Program or Document

Using the Run dialog box is handy for launching favorite applications, because it requires so few keystrokes. But you can also use the Run dialog box to open *any* file on the computer—if you're willing to do some additional typing.

The trick here is to type in the entire *path* of the program or document you want. (See the box below if you're new to the idea of file paths.) For example, to open the family budget spreadsheet that's in Harold's My Documents folder, you might type *C:\Documents and Settings\Harold\My Documents\familybudget.xls.*

(Of course, you probably wouldn't *actually* have to type all that, since the auto-complete feature attempts to complete each folder name as you start to type it.)

Tip: Typing the path in this way is also useful for launching applications that don't appear in the Start→All Programs menu. (If a program doesn't appear there, you must type its entire pathname—or click Browse to hunt for its icon yourself.)

For example, some advanced Windows XP utilities (including the *Registry Editor,* an advanced diagnostic program) are accessible only through the command line. You also need to use the Run command to open some older DOS programs that don't come with a listing in the All Programs menu.

Open a Drive Window

When you click My Computer on your Start menu, you'll discover that Windows assigns a letter of the alphabet to each disk drive attached to your machine—the hard drive, CD-ROM drive, floppy drive, and so on. The floppy drive is A:, the hard drive is usually C:, and so on. (There hasn't been a B: drive since the demise of the two-floppy computer.)

UP TO SPEED

The Path to Enlightenment about Paths

Windows is too busy to think of a particular file as "that family album program in the Program Files folder, which is in the My Programs folder on the C: drive." Instead, it uses shorthand to specify each icon's location on your hard drive—a series of disk and folder names separated by backslashes, like this: *C:\program files\pbsoftware\ beekeeperpro.exe.* This kind of location code is that icon's *path.* (Capitalization doesn't matter, even though you may see capital letters in Microsoft's examples.)

You'll encounter file paths when using several important Windows features. The Run dialog box described in this section is one; the Search command is another. As you'll see in the next chapter, when you choose the Search command, Windows identifies the location of each file it finds for you by displaying its path.

By typing a drive letter followed by a colon (for example, *C:*) into the Run box and pressing Enter, you make a window pop open, displaying the contents of that drive.

Open a Folder Window

You can also use the Run dialog box to open the window for any folder on your machine. To do so, type a backslash followed by the name of a folder (see Figure 2-9, bottom). You might type, for example, *\Program Files* to see your complete software collection.

Note: The Run command assumes that you're opening a folder on Drive C. If you want to open a folder on a different drive, add the drive letter and a colon before the name of the folder (for example, *D:\data*).

If you're on a network, you can even open a folder that's sitting on another computer on the network. To do so, type two backslashes, the computer's name, and then the shared folder's name. For instance, to access a shared folder called Budgets on a computer named Admin, enter *\\admin\budgets*. (See Chapter 20 for more on sharing folders over the network.)

It might make you feel extra proficient to know that you've just used the *Universal Naming Convention,* or UNC, for the shared folder. The UNC is simply the two-backslash, computer name\folder name format (for example: *\\ComputerName\foldername*).

Tip: In any of these cases, if you don't remember the precise name of a file or folder you want to open in the Run dialog box, click the Browse button to display the Browse dialog box, as shown in Figure 2-10.

Figure 2-10:
The Browse dialog box, which makes frequent appearances in Windows XP, lets you navigate the folders on your computer to find a file. The five icons at the left side make it easy to jump to the places where you're most likely to find the document you want. If you enter a drive letter and a colon in the Run dialog box before clicking the Browse button (like C:), the Browse dialog box opens with a display of that drive's contents.

Connect to a Web Page

You can jump directly to a specific Web page by typing its Web address (URL)—such as *www.realbigcompany.com*—into the Run dialog box, and then pressing Enter. You don't even have to open your Web browser first.

Once again, you may not have to type very much; the drop-down list in the Run dialog box lists every URL you've previously entered. Simply click one (or press the down arrow to highlight the one you want, and then press Enter) to go to that site.

Start→Search

The humble Search command looks no more special than anything else on the Start menu. In Windows XP, however, it's a newly revised powerhouse that's far more complex to navigate. Microsoft has even given it a new name—Search Companion. You'll probably use it often.

The Search function can quickly find all kinds of computer-ish things: file and folder icons, computers on your network, Web sites, email addresses, and phone numbers.

Finding Files and Folders

If you save your files exclusively into the My Documents folder (page 60), you'll have little need to use the Search function to locate your files. You'll always know where they are: right there in that folder.

Every now and then, however, you won't remember where you filed something, or you'll download something from the Internet and not be able to find it again, or

---

NOSTALGIA CORNER

Who Let the Dog Out?

Microsoft is at it again, adding cutesy cartoon characters to its software. Fortunately, the Search program works just as well without the dog as with it.

If you'd just as soon not have little Rover eyeing you with his little anthropomorphic 3-D eyes while you do your searching, it's easy enough to get rid of him. Either click "Turn off animated character" on the current menu, or click directly on the animated character to open up the panel illustrated here.

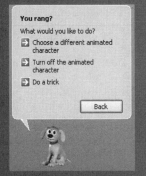

Click "Turn off the animated character" to get rid of the dog. (You must still sit through one final animation while it saunters away.)

On the other hand, if this kind of thing seems to make computers less intimidating for you, click "Choose a different animated character" instead. You'll find that Microsoft has provided not just one, but several provocative little characters that can occupy the bottom of your Search panel—a wizard, some yuppie woman in a flying car, and a surfboard kid whose face appears to be made of a banana. Click Next until you see the one you want, and then click OK.

Finally, if you do decide to tolerate Microsoft's animation attempts, don't miss the "Do a trick" link that appears when you click the animated character.

---

you'll install something and not know where to look for it. In those situations, the Search command is just what you need (Figure 2-11). It lets you look for a particular file or folder based on its description—by its name, size, date stamp, and so on.

The Search command can also look for the words *inside* your files. That's a powerful feature if you remember having typed or read something, but can't remember what you named the file.

Starting a search

Microsoft wanted to make absolutely sure you'd be able to find the Search command. It has provided at least seven different ways to begin a search:

- Choose Start→Search.

- Press F3 or Windows key+F (that's the Windows logo key on the bottom row of most keyboards).

- If a disk or folder window is already open, press Ctrl+E, click the Search toolbar button, or choose View→Explorer Bar→Search.

In each case, the Search window appears, as shown in Figure 2-11.

Figure 2-11:
Left: The basic Search panel. You might expect that Microsoft had learned its lesson about cute anthropomorphic cartoon characters. Microsoft Bob and Clippy the paper clip, for example, have both gone to the great CompUSA in the sky. But Microsoft is at it again, now with Rover, the search-companion dog. He wags and sometimes even barks as you perform your search.

Right: If you click the desktop itself and then press F3, or if you click the "More advanced search options" checkbox that occasionally appears, the Search panel may look slightly different, as shown here.

Windows XP comes with a set of canned searches (listed at left in Figure 2-11) designed to help you find what you're looking for faster. Click the green arrow next to the one you want (or click the *words* next to the arrow).

Pictures, music, or video

When you click this link, the Search panel changes (Figure 2-12, left). Turn on the checkboxes you want, and type in part of the file name.

Tip: As a bonus, this kind of search can also find text inside the *metadata* stored with each multimedia file—the behind-the-scenes descriptive information like pixel dimensions (for photos), and rock group name or music genre (for music files). You can type, for example, *Beatles* into the "All or part of the file name" text box to turn up MP3 files recorded by that band, or *800 x 600* into the text box to find JPEG files of precisely that size.

Figure 2-12:
Left: This panel appears to help you search for multimedia files. Middle: You're all set to search for documents that you've created or downloaded.

Right: This kind of search is slower, but more complete—it searches for everything, including program files and Windows system files. (It doesn't, however, search for metadata in picture, movie, and music files, as does the first kind of search.)

Documents (word processing, spreadsheet, and so on.)

This link produces the panel shown second from left in Figure 2-12. It comes set to search only for documents—files that *you* can create or download. In other words, it doesn't bother looking through hidden files, system files, application files, and so on. And it doesn't find the names of folders at all—just files.

All files and folders

Clicking this link produces the panel shown at right in Figure 2-12. This is the slowest kind of search, because it searches the thousands of hidden in-system files as well as the ones that you've created yourself.

This kind of search offers a number of useful power features:

- **A word or phrase in the file.** Sooner or later, it happens to everyone: A file's name doesn't match what's inside it. Maybe a marauding toddler pressed the keys, inadvertently renaming your doctoral thesis "xggrjpO#$5%////." Maybe, in a Saturday afternoon organizing binge, your spouse helpfully changed the name of your "ATM Instructions" document to "Cash Machine Info," without realizing that it was a help file for Adobe Type Manager. Or maybe you just can't remember what you called something.

The "A word or phrase in the file" option searches for words *inside* your files, regardless of their names. It's extremely slow, since Windows has to read every single file, which it does only slightly faster than you could. (But there's a workaround—see page 54.) Furthermore, this kind of search works only if you can remember an *exact* word or phrase in the missing document. Even punctuation has to match exactly.

Finally, the text you enter should be unique enough to assume it only exists in the file you're looking for; if you search for, say, *Microsoft*, Windows will find so many files that the search will be pointless.

- **Look in.** Use this drop-down menu if you want to limit your search to a single folder or disk. Every disk attached to your PC at the moment—your hard drive, Zip disk, CD-ROM, and so on—shows up in this list. (To search your whole computer, choose My Computer and then proceed.)

- **When was it modified? What size is it?** When you click one of the double-down-arrow circle buttons, like this one, you expand the Search panel for additional options. For example, the "When was it modified?" feature lets you find only files or folders you created or changed in a certain date range (see Figure 2-13), and the "What size is it?" feature lets you screen out files larger or smaller than a number of KB you specify.

- **More advanced options.** These controls offer even more choices (again, see Figure 2-13). For example, you get a "Type of file" drop-down menu that lets you confine your search to only compressed files or Word documents. **Search system folders** makes Windows look inside all of the folders that contain the operating

---

UP TO SPEED

Typing in the File Name

No matter which kind of search you undertake, Windows XP offers you the chance to look for a file whose name you know by typing its name into the "All or part of the file name" text box on the Search panel.

You don't have to type the entire file name—only enough of it to distinguish it from the other files on your computer. Capitals don't matter, and neither does the position of the letters you type—if you type *John,* Windows will find files with names like Johnson, Peterjohn, and DiJohnson.

You can also search for all files of a specific type, such as all Word files, by typing **.doc*—that is, an asterisk, a pe-

riod, and then the three-letter filename extension of the kind of file you want. (See page 172 for more on filename extensions.) The asterisk is a wild card meaning, "any text at all."

To narrow the search, you can enter both a partial name *and* an extension, such as *mom*.doc.* This will turn up Word files named Mom's Finances.doc, Moment of Truth.doc, and so on.

Finally, note that Search can find these files even if the filename extensions themselves are *hidden* (page 189).

---

system itself—not something you'll generally find useful. Likewise, **Search hidden files and folders** makes the Search program find matching files among the thousands that Windows generally hides from you (see page 89).

Search subfolders is much more practical. It looks for files within folders *inside* the disk or folder you've specified. Turn this option off only when you know for sure that the file you need is in the disk or folder you're starting with, but *not* within any subfolders there. Skipping the subfolders makes the search process much faster. **Case sensitive** instructs the Search program to match the capitalization of the characters you enter; searching for files containing "dentist" won't find files containing "Dentist." And **Search tape backup,** of course, searches for the specified files on your tape-backup system, if you have one.

Windows uses the checkboxes you turn on *in addition* to any data you entered into the basic search fields.

Figure 2-13:
By clicking the double-down-arrow circle buttons, you can expand the Search panel considerably (shown here scrolled down so far that you can't even see the file names you're searching for). The search shown here will find Word documents created during June 2002 in the My Documents folder.

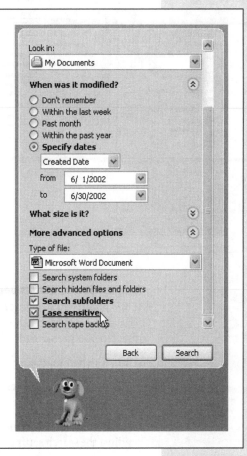

Managing the Found Files and Folders

Once you've set up the search, click the Search button (or press Enter). As the search proceeds, the screen changes. On the right side of the window, you now see a list of files and folders whose names contain what you typed in the blank. (Figure 2-14 shows this list.)

Note: Anything that Windows XP finds in your My Documents folder shows up twice in the list. Repeat to yourself each morning: "It's not my fault."

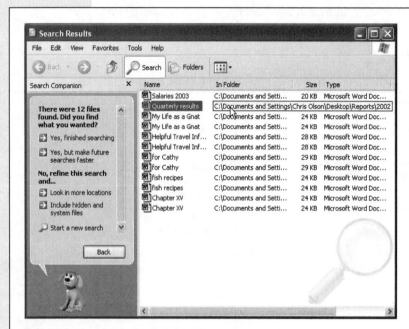

Figure 2-14:
You can manipulate the list of found files much the way you'd approach a list of files in a standard folder window. For example, you can highlight something in the list by typing the first couple of letters of its name, or move up or down the list by pressing the arrow keys. You can also highlight multiple icons simultaneously. Highlight all of them by choosing Edit→Select All, highlight individual items by Ctrl-clicking them, drag vertically over the list to enclose a cluster of them, and so on.

Using the Search Results panel

At this point, you can proceed in many different ways. A few of these ways are listed in the panel at the left side of the window (the exact assortment depends on the kind of search you performed).

- **Yes, finished searching.** Click to close the whole left panel (and lose the dog).

- **Yes, but make future searches faster.** Click this link to turn on Indexing Service, described on page 54.

- **Refine this search.** Windows XP often offers you a number of links that let you adjust the search settings you just used. For example, you may opt to perform the search again, this time including hidden and system files, or restrict the search to a different folder or disk, and so on.

- **Sort results by category.** Click the double-down-arrow circle button to open controls that let you sort the list—by name, date, and so on.

- **View results differently.** Click this double-down-arrow circle button to change the view of the results window—to Details, Tiles, or Thumbnails view, for example (see page 82).

- **Start a new search.** Click this option to start all over with new search parameters.

Using the results list

You can also manage the list of found files by treating the right side of the window just as you would any desktop window. For example:

- **Read all about it.** If you point to the name of a found icon, a pop-up rectangular balloon displays a little paragraph identifying the file's path, full name, modification date, size, and other information.

- **Find out where something is.** The In Folder column just to the right of an icon's name shows you exactly where it is on your machine, using the standard Windows path notation described on page 39.

Tip: You may have to widen the column to see the complete pathname; to do so, drag the dividing line at the top of the column, to the right of the In Folder column heading. Alternatively, point to the location information without clicking. As shown in Figure 2-14, a pop-up *tooltip* appears, revealing the complete folder path.

- **Open the file.** If one of the found files is the one you were looking for, double-click it to open it. This, in fact, is what most people do most of the time when using the Search program. In many cases, you'll never even know or care *where* the file was—you just want to get into it.

- **Jump to an icon in its home folder.** If you want to view the found file in its native habitat, sitting somewhere on your hard drive, right-click the icon in the Search window and choose Open Containing Folder from the shortcut menu. The Search window instantly retreats to the background, as Windows opens the folder and then highlights the icon in question, sitting wherever it is on your hard drive.

- **Move or delete the file.** You can drag an item directly out of the found-files list onto the desktop, directly onto the Recycle Bin icon, or into a different folder, window, or disk. (For more on moving icons, and all related hazards, see Chapter 4.)

- **Send To, rename, or create a shortcut.** After highlighting an icon (or icons) in the list of found files, you can use any of the commands in the File menu: Send To (which lets you move the icon to one of several standard folders), Rename, and so on. See page 134 for more on shortcuts.

Tip: You can also right-click a found icon to copy, move, rename, or create a shortcut to it. Just choose from the resulting shortcut menu.

- **Adjust the list.** By clicking the column headings of the results window, you can sort the list of found files in a variety of ways: by name, size, date modified, and so on. (You can reverse the order by clicking the column heading a second time.) You can also adjust the relative widths of the columns just by dragging the column-name dividers. And, as with almost any Windows window, you can drag the lower-right corner of the window to make it bigger or smaller.

- **Save the search setup.** By choosing File→Save Search, you can immortalize the search you've just set up. You might use this feature if you perform the same search each day—if, for example, you like to round up all the documents you created yesterday for backing up.

Windows XP automatically names the search file with a description it derives from the criteria you entered into the search fields, and adds the extension *.fnd* (for example, *Files Named Budget.fnd*). You can save the resulting search icon anywhere you like.

To use the search criteria again, double-click the saved *.fnd* file. The Search window opens, with your data already entered. Click the Search button to get the canned search underway.

Searching for Printers

When you're logged on to your Windows network domain, you search for Active Directory printers by clicking "Printers, computers or people" on the first Search screen. (Chapter 19 explains all about Active Directory.)

Note: The Find Printers dialog box isn't available to workgroup computers. If your PC is on such a network, use the Printers and Faxes option instead to locate, view, or add printers.

If you're part of a network domain, on the other hand, you can use *either* the "Printers, computers or people" to search for Active Directory printers or using the "Printers and Faxes" feature to add, locate, or view printers that are used by your PC. (Chapter 13 discusses the Printers and Faxes feature in detail.)

GEM IN THE ROUGH

Using Search to Clean Up Your Drive

You don't have to restrict your use of the Search feature to finding files you can't locate on your own. You can use its power to gather files for general hard-drive housekeeping.

If you have files about the same subject scattered in a variety of folders, you can use the Search command to gather them together. For example, search for all files with the word "budget" in the file name. Create a new folder, select all the found files in the Search Results pane (documents, spreadsheets, accounting reports, and so on), and drag

any *one* of them into the new folder to move them en masse.

You can also search for the backup files your software creates, such as files with the extensions *.xlk* (Microsoft Excel) or *.wbk* (Microsoft Word). They take up disk space, and you'll probably never use them. You can round them up using the Search command, and then delete them as a group from the Search Results pane.

On the next screen, click "A printer on the network" to open the Find Printers dialog box, as shown in Figure 2-15. On the Printers tab, click the In box's down arrow to select the entire directory or specific domain that you want to search, or click Browse to locate the domain. It isn't necessary to enter any further search criteria, but if you do want to get more specific, you have a few search options available:

Figure 2-15:
The Find Printers dialog box lets you refine your search criteria using the Printer, Features, and Advanced tabs. Left: The Printer tab lets you enter basic search information. Middle: On the Features tab, you can get more specific in your search for the perfect printer: whether it prints in color or on both sides of the paper, for example. Right: The Advanced tab affords you the most specific search of all. You can use formulas to specify search criteria like the language the printer "speaks" or the minimum print resolution you need.

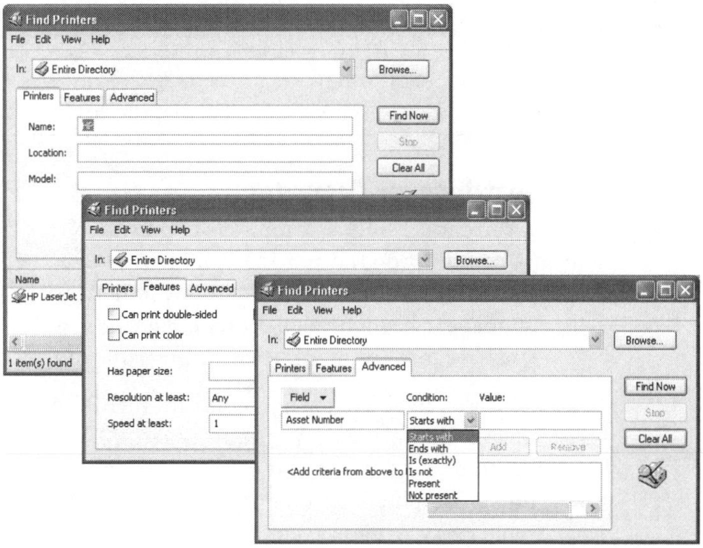

- On the Printers tab, if you know the name (or part of the name) of the printer you're searching for, type it in the Name text box.

  If you want a list of all printers (or only the printers that fulfill the criteria you entered) in a particular location, enter the location's name in the Location text box.

Tip: If the Location text box is already filled in, it's because your network administrator has set up the Windows network to display the printers nearest to you. If the Location text box isn't filled in and you don't enter a location to search, Windows will search the entire Windows domain for printers, using whatever criteria you've entered.

  If you're trying to locate a specific printer model (you have a certain affinity for HP printers, say), enter the model name in the Model text box.

- On the Features tab, you can get even more specific with your search criteria, such as whether the printer can print double-sided pages or in color. You can even specify page size and resolution.

- The Advanced tab gives you additional fields to specify search criteria, like the number of pages the printer can churn out per minute. (This is a good option if you're in a big hurry.) See Figure 2-15 for details.

After you've entered your search criteria, click Find Now. When the PC finishes the search, a list of printers that fulfill your criteria appears. Connect to one of them by right-clicking its name and then choosing Connect from the shortcut menu.

Tip: As with the "All files and folders" search, you can save the search you've just set up by Choosing File→Save Search. To use the search criteria again, double-click the saved .*fnd* file. When the Find Printers dialog box opens, click the Find Now button to commence the canned search.

Searching for Computers

If you click "Printers, computers or people" on the first Search screen, and then click "A computer on the network" on the next one, the Search program lets you type in the name of another computer on your network (if you're on one). If you search for *ac,* the search will turn up *accounts, packages,* and so on. There's no browse function; you have to know at least part of the name of the computer you want to find.

Of course, if you're trying to find another PC on the network, you can simply open the My Network Places window (page 57), which shows you icons representing all the computers on your network. So why would you ever use the Search function to find a computer? Because it sometimes finds computers that My Network Places can't. Every Windows veteran has lost count of the number of times computers have been missing from My Network Places. In such cases, the Search function is the reliable way to locate the computer and thus access its contents.

Searching for People

If you click "Printers, computers or people" on the first Search screen, you'll find, on the second screen, an option called "People in your address book." This tantalizing option lets you type in somebody's name; the Search program can consult any of several "White Pages" Web sites online in an attempt to track down that person's email address and telephone number. It can also search your own Windows address book when you want to check someone's phone number or other information.

Note: This option has additional power when used on a corporate domain network. See Chapter 19 for more on domains, and page 50 for more on searching for people (or their phone numbers) on yours.

Searching your address book

As one of the bonus freebie programs that come with Windows XP, you get a program called Address Book. (It's an address book.) You can look at yours by choosing Start→All Programs→Accessories→Address Book, although the place you're likely to use it the most is when you're in an email program like Outlook Express, which is described in Chapter 12.

In any case, clicking "People in your address book" brings up the dialog box shown in Figure 2-16.

Searching phone books on the Internet

No matter how social a person you are, it's theoretically possible somebody out there has managed to elude your address book. There may be times that you want to look up the phone number or email address of someone who's not only not in your address book, but not even in your *physical* phone book. Fortunately, you live in the Internet age, where a number of Web sites serve as worldwide "White Pages."

Use the Look In drop-down list (see Figure 2-16) to display a list of these people-finding Web sites (Bigfoot, WhoWhere, and so on). Now choose a search service; as a little experimentation will quickly demonstrate, some of these sites work better than others.

Figure 2-16:
Windows assumes that you want to search your address book for a certain name or email address. Enter information in one or more fields—you can use partial words—and then click the Find Now button. All matching entries appear at the bottom of the window.

You must be connected to the Internet to use this feature (or your browser must be configured to start your Internet connection automatically when it opens; see page 316). The dialog box that appears has two tabs:

• The **People** tab provides a place to enter a name, email address, or both. Use this tab if you know that information, and need a street address or a telephone number.

• The **Advanced** tab lets you narrow your search. As you can see in Figure 2-17, you can make some very fine distinctions when describing the person you're trying to find.

Figure 2-17:
A straightforward name search by no means turns up every one of the 200 million Internet citizens, but it's occasionally successful in turning up a few matches for the name you specify.

When you're finished setting up your search, click the Find Now button. The Search program uses your existing Internet connection to send the query off to the chosen Web site. After a few minutes, you'll get a response, even if it's "No response."

Unfortunately, the technology gods don't smile on this feature. Sometimes you get outdated email addresses. And sometimes you get no results at all—the search Web sites do one quick pass of their databases and then return an error message. That message might say simply that the person couldn't be found, or it might say, "The search could not be completed within the time specified for this directory service." (In other words, the search engine took a quick look, didn't find an exact match, and doesn't want to keep looking.)

Tip: Instead of using the Find People dialog box, it's frequently more productive to work directly on the directory Web page. After choosing the search engine you want to use from the drop-down list, click the Web Site button. In a flash (or in a few minutes, depending on the speed of your Internet connection), you're on the Internet and the browser window displays the search engine you selected. Working from the search engine directly on the Web instead of using the Search feature as an intermediary offers more powerful choices for searching.

Searching the Internet

Any old computer can search for the files on its own hard drive. The Search Companion's special twist, however, is that it lets you use exactly the same program to search for information on the World Wide Web.

To put the program into search-the-Internet mode, click Search the Internet on the main Search panel (shown at left in Figure 2-11). The "What are you looking for?" panel appears, complete with a place to type a search phrase.

When you click the Search button, your PC goes online and submits that request to MSN Search, which is Microsoft's version of a search page like Google or Yahoo.

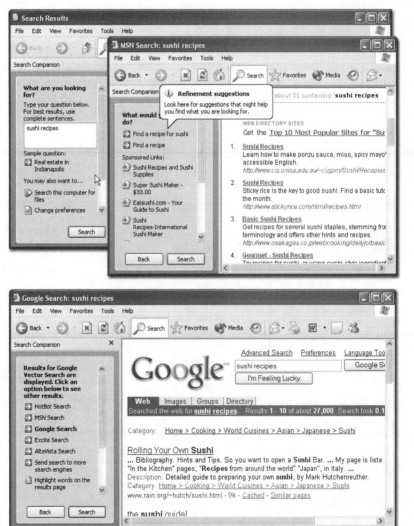

Figure 2-18:
Top left: When you search the Internet, don't mind the "Sample question" that appears beneath the search blank; it's simply designed to give you some ideas of the ways you can phrase your search requests.

Top right: You get a list of Web pages that contain the text you seek, along with some suggestions on ways to "refine your search" (such as visiting Microsoft's commercial partners to buy books, music, and so on). The best part is the "Automatically send your search to other search engines" link (not shown). If you click it, Windows puts each of the major search pages only one click away.

Bottom: From here, you can generally read the first paragraph of text that appears on the Web page, go to the page by clicking its link, and so on.

Windows now goes online, sends your search request to the selected Web site and, after a moment, shows you the results of its search: a list of Web pages containing the text you typed (see Figure 2-18).

The Indexing Service

The regular Windows XP Search command can locate words inside your files—a handy feature when you're trying to turn up a document whose contents you know, but whose name you can't remember. Just don't try it on a deadline; it's painfully slow.

To eliminate that delay, Microsoft has programmed Windows XP with an optional feature that does something ingenious. Like a kid cramming for an exam, it can read, take notes on, and memorize the contents of all of your text-based files: text files, HTML documents, Microsoft Office files, email, and so on. (You can make it understand other kinds of documents, too, if you buy additional filters made by third-party software companies.)

After *indexing* your hard drive in this way, XP can pinpoint text or file properties in seconds. The only downside is that you sacrifice a few megabytes of disk space to the hidden "card catalog."

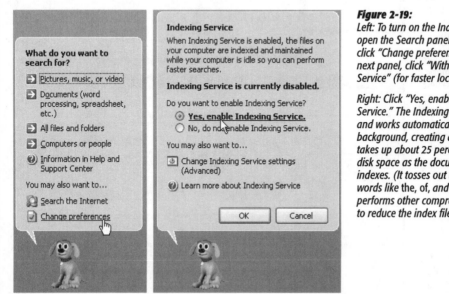

Figure 2-19:
Left: To turn on the Indexing Service, open the Search panel and then click "Change preferences." On the next panel, click "With Indexing Service" (for faster local searches)."

Right: Click "Yes, enable Indexing Service." The Indexing Service starts and works automatically in the background, creating a file that takes up about 25 percent as much disk space as the documents it indexes. (It tosses out unhelpful words like the, of, and a, and performs other compression tricks to reduce the index file size.)

If that's a tradeoff you're willing to make, you'll definitely enjoy the Windows XP *Indexing Service*, as it's called (just as it was in Windows 2000).

To index your files, proceed as shown in Figure 2-19.

Once the Indexing Service has completed its analysis of the files on your machine—which can take many hours—you don't need to do anything special when searching for words inside your files. Just enjoy the amazing speed with which your Search program now rounds up files according to their contents or properties—and enjoy

---

POWER USERS' CLINIC

Indexing Service to the Max

There's more to Indexing Service than just using the regular Search Companion program. You can actually use a specialized query-submission *language* to perform extremely targeted searches.

It turns out, for example, that Indexing Service logs much more than just the words inside your files. It also notes and records their *properties*, or file attributes. They go by the names of *Access* (the last time somebody opened the file), *DocAppName* (the name of the program that created the file), *DocAuthor* (whoever created the document, in programs that offer this feature), *DocLastPrinted* (when the document was last printed), *DocSlideCount* (number of slides in a PowerPoint file), *DocWordCount* (number of words in a text file), *Size* (size of the document, in bytes), *Write* (date last modified), and so on.

(Want to see the complete list of the searchable attributes? Cancel your appointments for the afternoon, and then follow the steps indicated in Figure 2-20. Click Query the Catalog, the Tips for Searching link, and then the Query Syntax button.)

To perform a property search using the Search program, click the "A word or phrase in the file" text box shown in Figure 2-11. Then type the @ symbol, followed by the property type you want, an = sign (or < or >), and the value in question. In other words, here's how you would look for a Word document with at least 1500 words in it:

@DocWordCount >1500

Similarly, if you want to round up documents you've printed within the last 50 hours, you could type this into the "A word or phrase in the file" text box—

@DocLastPrinted >-2d2h

—because you express times and dates relative to the current time by using a minus sign and then *h* for hours, *d* for days, *w* for weeks, *m* for months, *y* for years, and so on.

It's worth noting that that @ business is shorthand for a much more complex and flexible system, which Microsoft will be phasing in during the coming years. The more complex syntax uses *property tags* that look something like the HTML tags that form Web-page code, like this:

{prop name=write} >2002/6/5 12:00:00 {/prop}

(This particular phrase would find documents modified after noon on June 5, 2002.)

These tags are useful in another case, too: Everyday searches for words inside your files tell Windows to round up files containing those words in *any* order. If you search for *Long John Silver,* you'll get documents containing a sentence like, "It took John a long time to find the silver."

But if you enclose the search phrase with the *phrase* tags, you'll get only files that contain *exactly* the phrase you typed: *{phrase} Long John Silver {/phrase}.* In other words, you can use the {phrase} tags the way you use quotation marks on a Web search engine.

Clearly, you can get very deep into the Indexing Service querying language, combining the various search phrases by joining them with a & symbol, using wild card characters (*), even using UNIX-style regular expressions. (*Indexing Service: The Missing Manual,* anyone?)

---

the fact that the Indexing Service will *continue* to keep itself up to date, automatically indexing any files you create or edit.

Note: When Indexing Service is turned on, capitalization doesn't matter, and Windows ignores short words like *of, it, is,* and so on. Note, too, that Indexing Service refuses to search folders that belong to other people with accounts on your PC (unless, of course, they marked those folders as Shared). Chapter 20 has full details.

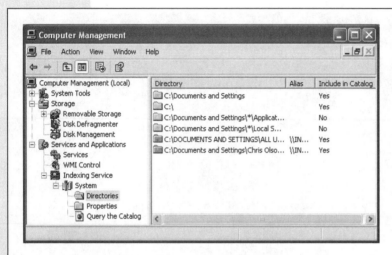

Figure 2-20:
Power users have vast amounts of control over what gets cataloged when Indexing Service is set loose. This display, for example, offers Yes and No indicators regarding which folders have been indexed. To get here, choose Start→Control Panel→Administrative Tools→Computer Management. In the list, click the + buttons to expand Services and Applications, then Indexing Service, then System.

Start→Help and Support

Choosing Start→Help and Support opens the new, improved Windows Help and Support Center window, which is described in Chapter 5.

FREQUENTLY ASKED QUESTION

The View from a Window

The My Computer window at home and the My Computer window on my PC at work don't look alike. What's up with that?

The difference is that your PC at work is probably on a network domain, and the one at home belongs to a smaller, less formal workgroup network (see page 23 for details on these differences). As you'll discover over and over again, the Windows XP Pro experience is slightly different depending on which kind of network you're on.

On a computer that's part of a domain, you see only two

sections: "Hard Disk Drives" and "Devices with Removable Storage" (as shown at top in Figure 2-21).

On a workgroup PC, you get a third section, called "Files Stored on This Computer" (Figure 2-21, bottom). It lists the My Documents folders for each person who has an account on—and who has logged on to—this computer.

Why? Because in a corporation, your files probably aren't even *on* your PC. They probably sit on some centralized server machine elsewhere on the network. So there probably *aren't* many "files stored on this computer."

Tip: Once again, speed fans have an alternative to using the mouse—just press the F1 key to open the Help window.

Start→Control Panel

This extremely important command opens an extremely important window: the Control Panel, which houses two dozen programs you'll use to change almost every important setting on your PC. It's so important, in fact, that it gets a chapter of its own (Chapter 9).

Start→My Network Places

In previous versions of Windows, a My Network Places icon used to appear on everybody's desktop. Of course, for the millions of non-networked PC users in their home offices and bedrooms, it never made much sense. In Windows XP Professional, in fact, My Network Places appears only when your PC joins a network—and then only in the Start menu. (You can also put its icon on the desktop yourself, as described on page 266.)

In any case, once it's there, choosing this command opens the My Network Places window, which displays icons for the computer, disks and folders other people on the office network have made available for rummaging. (Much more on this topic in Chapter 20.)

Start→My Computer

The My Computer command is the trunk lid, the doorway to every single shred of software on your machine. When you choose this command, a window opens to reveal icons that represent each disk drive in your machine, as shown in Figure 2-21. (Note to power users: Technically, My Computer displays a different icon for each hard drive *partition.*)

For example, by double-clicking your hard-drive icon and then the various folders on it, you can eventually see the icons for every single file and folder on your computer. (The My Computer icon no longer appears on the desktop—unless you put it there, as described on page 266.)

Tip: You don't have to live with "My This, My That" as the names of the important Windows folders. You can easily rename them, as described on page 57.

Start→My Music, My Pictures

Clearly, Microsoft imagined that most of its Windows XP customers would be multimedia mavens, decked out with digital cameras and MP3 music players. To hammer home the point, it has stocked your My Documents folder with My Pictures and My Music folders to store digital photos and music files, respectively.

If you do indeed have a digital camera or MP3 player (and it's Windows XP–compatible), you'll probably find that whatever software came with it automatically dumps your photos into, and sucks your music files out of, these folders. You'll find much more on this topic in Chapter 8.

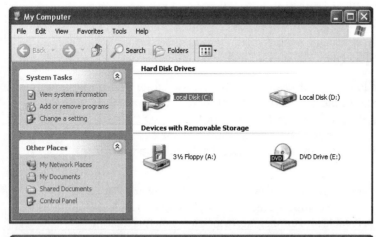

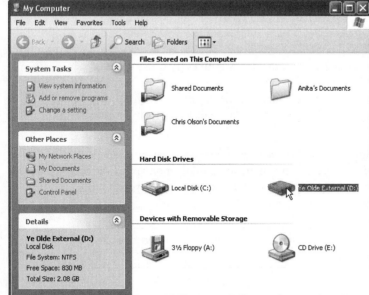

Figure 2-21:
The My Computer window is divided into two sections on a computer that's a member of a network domain, and three sections on a computer that's a member of a workgroup. Top: The screen you see when your computer joins a network domain. At the top of the screen comes a list of hard drives, followed by a list of removable-disk drives. This computer has one floppy drive, two hard drives (or one partitioned hard drive, as described in Appendix A), and one CD-ROM drive. (If there's a disk in the CD-ROM drive, you get to see its name, not just its drive letter.)

Bottom: If your computer is a member of a workgroup, you see an additional section at the very top of the screen, which has an icon for the My Documents folder of each person who has an account on this computer. When you select a disk icon (on either type of computer) by clicking it, the Details pane on the left side of the window displays its file system, capacity, and amount of free space.

Tip: If you don't feel the need to stare at these folder names in your Start menu day after day, it's easy enough to get rid of them. Right-click the Start menu; from the shortcut menu, choose Properties. In that dialog box, click the Start Menu tab, click Customize, and then click the Advanced tab. Now scroll down in the Start menu items list until you see My Music or My Pictures. Click "Don't display this item," and then click OK.

Start→My Recent Documents

You should see the My Recent Documents menu command in your Start menu by default. If you don't, you can turn it on using the techniques described in the box below.

There's one good reason for turning on this menu: It adds to your Start menu a submenu listing the last 15 documents you've opened. Using a list of recent documents can save you time when you want to reopen something you've worked on recently, but you're not in the mood to burrow through folders to find its icon.

Note, however, that:

- Documents appear on the "recently used" list only if your applications are smart enough to update it. Most modern programs (including all Microsoft programs) perform this administrative task, but not all do.

- The Documents list doesn't know when you've deleted a document or moved it to another folder or disk; it continues to list the file even after it's gone. In that event, clicking the document's listing produces only an error message.

NOSTALGIA CORNER

Restoring the Traditional Folder Listings

Some of the commands that populated the Start menus of previous Windows versions no longer appear in the home version of Windows XP. That's by design, of course: Microsoft is trying to make its new operating system look less overwhelming to the newcomer.

But if you miss some of the old folders—My Network Places and My Recent Documents, for example—it's easy enough to put them back.

Right-click the Start menu. From the shortcut menu, choose Properties. Now the Taskbar and Start Menu Properties dialog box appears; on the Start Menu tab, click the Customize button, and then the Advanced tab.

In the scrolling list, you'll find a checkbox that makes My Network Places appear in the Start menu. Windows 2000 veterans may also want to turn on "Display as Connect to menu" under Network Connections, so that you have a handy submenu of network connections in your Start menu. If you scroll all the way to the bottom of the list, you'll also see an option that adds System Administrative Tools to your All Programs menu and even to your Start menu. (You can read about these technical utilities in Chapter 16.)

At the bottom of the dialog box, turn on "List my most recently opened documents" to add the My Recent Documents command to your Start menu. Click OK twice to return to the desktop and try out your changes.

Tip: Of course, there's another easy way to open a document you've recently worked on. To start, simply launch the program you used to create it. Many programs maintain a list of recent documents at the bottom of the File menu; choose one of these names to open the corresponding file.

Start→My Documents

This command opens up your My Documents folder, which, until Windows XP, appeared as an icon on your desktop. It's designed to hold the data files you and your programs create.

Of course, you're welcome to file your documents *anywhere* on the hard drive, but most programs propose the My Documents folder as the target location for newly created documents.

Sticking with that principle makes a lot of sense for three reasons. First, it makes navigation easy. You never have to wonder where you filed some document, since all your stuff is sitting right there in the My Documents folder. Second, this arrangement makes backing up easy, in that you can drag the entire My Documents folder right onto a Zip disk or blank CD.

Third, remember that Windows XP has been designed from the ground up for *computer sharing.* It's ideal for any situation where different family members, students, or workers share the same PC. Each person who uses the computer will turn on the machine to find her own separate, secure set of files, folders, desktop pictures, Web bookmarks, preference settings—and My Documents folder. (Much more about this feature in Chapter 20.)

Customizing the Start Menu

As millions of Windows users have demonstrated, it's perfectly possible to live a long and happy life without ever tampering with the Start menu. For many people, the idea of making it look or work differently comes dangerously close to nerd terri-

---

UP TO SPEED

The Not-My-Documents Folder

Whenever you log on, Windows XP provides a My Documents folder just for you. (It actually sits in the My Computer→Local Disk (C:)→Documents and Settings→ [Your Name] folder.)

This feature can be confusing if you're not expecting it. For example, if you stop by the computer after somebody else has logged in, none of your stuff is where you expect to

find it—specifically, in the My Documents folder. That's because the computer no longer opens *your* documents folder when you choose Start→My Documents.

If this happens to you, check the name that appears at the top of the Start menu. It identifies who's currently logged on—and whose documents are showing up in the My Documents window.

---

tory. (It's true that listing your favorite files there gives you quicker access to them—but it's even easier to use the Quick Launch toolbar, as described on page 103.)

Still, knowing how to manipulate the Start menu listings may come in handy someday, and provides an interesting glimpse into the way Windows works.

Note: Thanks to the User Accounts feature described in Chapter 17, any changes you make to the Start menu apply only to *you.* Each person with an account on this PC has an independent, customized Start menu. When you sign on to the machine using your name and password, Windows XP loads *your* customized Start menu.

Figure 2-22:
Top: The only task you can perform on this first screen is to turn off the new, Windows XP double-column Start menu design to return to the older, single-column Classic Start menu design of Windows versions gone by. The good stuff awaits when you click the Customize button.

Bottom: Here's the General tab of the Customize Start Menu dialog box. (The Clear List button refers to the lower-left section of the Start menu, which lists the programs you use most often. Click Clear List if you don't want to risk your supervisor coming by while you're up for coffee, and noticing that your most recently used programs are Tetris Max, Myst III, Tomb Raider, and Quake.)

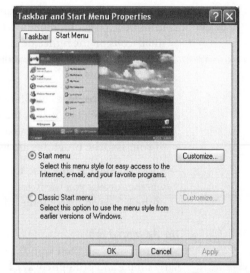

Basic Start Menu Settings

Microsoft offers a fascinating set of customization options for the Start menu. It's hard to tell whether these options were selected by a scientific usability study or by a dartboard, but you're likely to find something that suits you.

To view and change the basic options, right-click the Start menu; choose Properties from the shortcut menu. Now the Taskbar and Start Menu Properties dialog box opens, as seen in Figure 2-22.

The General tab

When you click the Customize button, you see the dialog box shown at right in Figure 2-22. Here you're offered a random assortment of Start menu tweaks:

- **Select an icon size for programs.** Turning on "Small icons" gives you smaller icons next to the commands in the left column of the Start menu. (You *always* get small icons on the right side and in the All Programs menu.) As a result, the Start menu is more compact. Consider converting to small icons as your All Programs menu gets crowded.

- **Number of programs on Start menu.** The number here refers to the lower-left column of the Start menu, the one that lists programs used most often. By increasing this number, you make the Start menu taller—but you ensure that more of your favorite programs are listed and ready to launch.

- **Show on Start menu.** Use these checkboxes and drop-down menus to specify whether or not you want your Web browser and email program listed at the top of the left-hand Start menu column—and if so, which ones.

The Advanced tab

Microsoft may call these options Advanced, but they affect the Start menu in some fairly simple and profound ways. Here, in fact, is where you'll find the on/off switches for every single command on the *right side* of the Start menu, among other things.

- **Open submenus when I pause on them with my mouse.** When this checkbox is turned on, you don't actually have to click a submenu to view its options.

FREQUENTLY ASKED QUESTION

Opening the Control Panel Window When You Can't

OK, I'm with you—I turned on "Display as a menu" for the Control Panel, so now I can open any Control Panel program directly from my Start menu. Trouble is, now I can't open the Control Panel window itself! Nothing happens when I click the Start→Control Panel command. How do I open the Control Panel window?

Ah, there's a troublemaker in every class.

Click the Start button to open the menu, slide up to Control Panel, and then *right-click* Control Panel. Choose Open from the shortcut menu. You're back in business.

- **Highlight newly installed programs.** Whenever you (or some techie in the building) install a new program into the Start menu, it shows up with orange highlighting for a few days. The idea, of course, is to grab your attention and make you aware of your expanded software suite. If you could do without this kind of reminder, then just turn off this checkbox.

- **Control Panel, My Computer, My Documents, My Music, My Pictures, Network Connections.** Beneath each of these headings, you'll find three options. The middle one, "Display as a menu," is extremely useful. It means that instead of simply listing the name of a folder (which is what "Display as a link" means), your Start menu sprouts a submenu listing the *contents* of that folder, as shown at bottom in Figure 2-23.

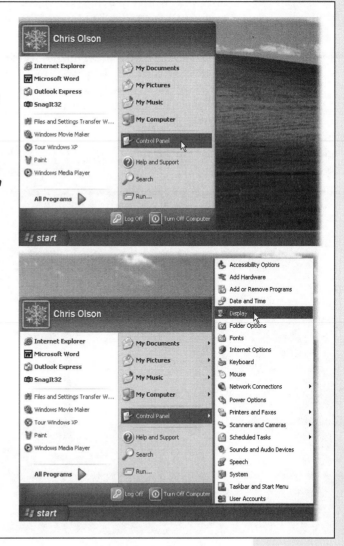

Figure 2-23:
Top: When "Display as a link" is selected for Control Panel, you, like generations of Windows users before you, can't open a particular Control Panel program directly from the Start menu. Instead, you must choose Start→Control Panel, which opens the Control Panel window; now it's up to you to open the program you want.

Bottom: Turning on "Display as a menu" saves you a step. You now get a submenu that lists each program in the Control Panel folder. By clicking one, you can open it directly. This feature saves you the trouble of opening a folder window (such as Control Panel or My Documents), double-clicking an icon inside it, and then closing the window again.

("Don't display this item," of course, removes the folder in question from your Start menu altogether. That's a good point to remember if you ever set down your PC and discover that, for example, the Control Panel appears to have disappeared.)

- **Enable dragging and dropping.** Turning on this checkbox has two benefits. First, it lets you customize your Start menu just by dragging icons onto it, as described in the next section. Second, it lets you right-click Start menu items, which produces a useful shortcut menu containing commands like Rename, Properties, and Remove from This List. (If this checkbox is turned off, right-clicking Start menu items has no effect.)

- **Favorites menu.** This option adds a Favorites command to the Start menu that lists your favorite Web sites (see page 334) and icons (files, folders, and so on; see page 642). Thereafter, you can use the Start menu to launch Internet Explorer and travel directly to the selected site.

- **Help and Support, Run command, Search.** These checkboxes govern the appearance of the corresponding commands in the Start menu. For example, if you've absorbed the fact that pressing the F1 key always opens the Windows help program, you may as well reclaim the screen space occupied by this command in the Start menu by turning it off here.

NOSTALGIA CORNER

Options for the Classic Start Menu

If you've turned on the Classic (single-column) Start menu as described on page 64, clicking the corresponding Customize button shown in Figure 2-22 offers its own dialog box full of options.

Some are the same options described on these pages. The rest either control which commands are listed in the menu (checkboxes beginning with the word Display) or turn certain commands into submenus (checkboxes beginning with the word Expand). This is a very handy feature when applied to the Control Panel, for example.

Finally, note the option called Use Personalized Menus. When this checkbox is turned on, Windows watches you and studies your behavior (that is, even more than usual).

If it notices that you haven't been using certain Start menu commands, Windows hides them, making the menu listing shorter, as shown here at left.

The double-arrow button at the bottom of the All Programs menu indicates that there's more to the list than you're

seeing; click it to see the full menu, as shown here at right.

Some people find it disconcerting that Personalized Menus *changes* the Start menu frequently, making it difficult to get used to the positions of familiar items. Other people find that this feature makes the All Programs menu and its submenus easier to use, because it frees them from hunting through commands that they don't use much.

- **Network Connections.** If you find yourself switching between different methods of getting online (or onto a network)—for example, switching your laptop between the cable modem when you're at home and its dial-up modem when you're on the road—turn on "Display as Connect to menu." From now on, you'll be able to switch network connections just by choosing from the submenu in your Start menu.

- **Printers and Faxes.** Turn on this checkbox if you'd like your Start menu to provide direct access to the Printers and Faxes folder, or the icons that appear for each printer and virtual fax machine you've installed (see Chapter 13).

- **Scroll Programs.** This option changes how the Start→All Programs menu looks when there are too many programs listed to fit on the screen. Ordinarily when this situation arises, a second All Programs menu appears to the right of the first one, continuing the list. But if you turn on this checkbox, all your programs appear instead on one massive, scrolling programs list. As you scroll down past the last visible name, the top of the All Programs menu scrolls off the screen.

Adding Icons to the Start Menu

Usually, when you install a new program, its installer automatically inserts the program's name and icon in your Start→All Programs menu. There may be times, however, when you want to add something to the Start menu yourself, such as a folder, document, or even a disk.

The "free" sections of the Start menu

In the following pages, you'll read several references to the "free" portions of the Start menu. These are the two areas that you, the lowly human, are allowed to modify freely—adding, removing, renaming, or sorting as you see fit:

- **The top-left section of the Start menu.** This little area lists what Microsoft calls *pinned* programs and files—things you use often enough that you want a fairly permanent list of them at your fingertips.

- **The All Programs menu.** This, of course, is the master list of programs (and anything else—documents, folders, disks—you want to see listed).

These two legal areas are highlighted back in Figure 2-4.

In other words, most of the following techniques don't work when applied to the listings in the *right* column, nor the lower-*left* quadrant of the Start menu, where Windows XP lists the programs you use most frequently.

Method 1: Drag an icon directly

Microsoft wouldn't be Microsoft if it didn't provide at least 437 different ways to do this job. Here are three of the world's favorites:

1. **Locate the icon you want to add to your Start menu.**

   It can be an application (see the box on page 67), a document you've created, a folder you frequently access, one of the programs in your Control Panel's folder, or even your hard drive or floppy-drive icon. (Adding disks and folders to the Start menu is especially handy, because it lets you dive directly into their contents without having to drill down through the My Computer window.)

Tip: Adding an application name to your All Programs menu requires that you find the program *file*, as described on page 67. To do so, either use the Search command described earlier in this chapter, or use the Windows Explorer window described in Chapter 3. You'll find your program files in the My Computer→Local Disk (C:)→Program Files folder.

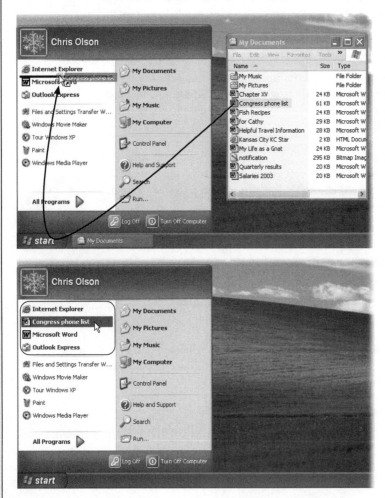

Figure 2-24:
Top: You can add something to the top of your Start menu by dragging it (from whatever folder it's in) onto the Start button to open the Start menu, and then dragging it directly into position. (Once the Start menu is open, you can also drag it onto the All Programs button—and once that menu is open, drag it anywhere in that list.)

Bottom: When you release the mouse, you'll find that it's been happily ensconced where you dropped it. Remember, too, that you're always free to drag anything up or down in the "free" areas of the menu: the circled area shown here, and the All Programs list.

2. Drag it directly onto the Start button.

If you release the mouse now, Windows adds the name of the icon you've just dragged to the bottom of the list at the top-left section of the menu (Figure 2-24, right).

But if "Enable dragging and dropping" is turned on, as described in the previous section, you're free to drop it wherever you want among the items listed in the top-left section of the menu (Figure 2-24, left).

Similarly, if you drag to the Start button and then onto the All Programs command without releasing the mouse, you can place it exactly where you want in the Start→All Programs menu.

Tip: After making a mess of your Start→All Programs menu by dragging icons onto it, you may want to restore some order—specifically, alphabetical. That's easy: Just right-click anywhere on the open All Programs menu and choose Sort By Name from the shortcut menu.

Method 2: Use the Add Listing Wizard

If you've placed your Start menu into the single-column Classic mode, the same drag-and-drop routine works for adding new programs. But you can also use one of Microsoft's wizards for the same purpose. Right-click the Start button; choose Properties from the shortcut menu; and click Customize to view the Add, Remove, and Sort buttons available to you there.

Method 3: Use the Start Menu folders

Windows XP builds the All Programs menu by consulting the contents of two critical folders:

- **Documents and Settings→All Users→Start Menu→Programs folder.** This folder contains shortcuts for programs that are available to everybody who has an account on your machine (Chapter 17).

FREQUENTLY ASKED QUESTION

Which One's the Program?

I want to add a program to my Start menu like you said. But where is the program's icon?

To discover the program file name of a favorite program, open your My Computer→Local Disk (C:)→Program Files folder. Inside you'll find folders containing all of your applications—and inside each of *these* folders, you'll find icons for each application's components. Right-click the window, choose View→Details from the shortcut menu, and look for an icon whose Type column says "application."

OK, I did that. But in the program's folder, there are 15 million little files that all say they're applications. How do I know which is the actual application file?

First, you can usually recognize which application is the primary one both by its short-form name and by its icon. *WinWord* is probably a good hint that you've found Word for Windows, for example. Second, the instructions from the software company may tell you which file to click.

• **Documents and Settings→[Your Name]→Start Menu→Programs folder.** In this folder, you'll find shortcuts for the programs that *you* have added to the Start menu—and they appear only when *you* have logged into the machine.

Figure 2-25 shows you these two locations in Windows Explorer.

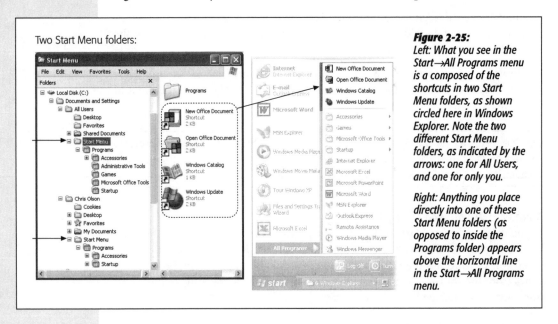

Two Start Menu folders:

Figure 2-25:
Left: What you see in the Start→All Programs menu is a composed of the shortcuts in two Start Menu folders, as shown circled here in Windows Explorer. Note the two different Start Menu folders, as indicated by the arrows: one for All Users, and one for only you.

Right: Anything you place directly into one of these Start Menu folders (as opposed to inside the Programs folder) appears above the horizontal line in the Start→All Programs menu.

In other words, instead of the fancy icon-adding wizards and drag-and-drop schemes described earlier, you may prefer to fine-tune your Start menu the low-tech way. Just open the relevant Start Menu folder. (Right-click the Start button; from the shortcut menu, choose either Open All Users [to view the list of programs for the masses] or Open [to see the list of your personal programs.]) You can add shortcut icons to, remove them from, or rename them in your Start→All Programs menu just by manipulating the shortcuts in this folder.

Removing Icons from the Start Menu

When it comes time to prune an overgrown Start menu, there are three different sets of instructions, depending on which section of the Start menu needs purging.

• **The lower-left section.** Right-click the item you've targeted for extinction, and then choose "Remove from This List" from the shortcut menu.

• **The right-hand column.** Right-click the Start button; choose Properties from the shortcut menu; click Customize; click the Advanced tab, scroll down, and turn off the checkboxes for the items you want expunged.

Note: If you're using the Classic Start menu view, right-click the Start button; choose Properties; click Customize; and then turn off the checkboxes in the "Advanced Start menu options" list box.

- **The "free" areas.** (This means the upper-left section and the All Programs list.) You can ditch items from these areas just by *dragging* them off the menu—onto the desktop, for example, or even directly onto the Recycle Bin icon.

Or, if you prefer, just right-click the file, folder, program, or disk name in the All Programs menu, and then choose Delete from the shortcut menu. It disappears instantly. To remove items from the upper-left section, right-click on the item, and then choose "Remove from This List" from the shortcut menu.

In both cases, you're only deleting the *shortcut* that appears on the menu. Deleting items from the Start menu doesn't actually uninstall any software.

Renaming Start Menu Items

Not many people are aware that they can change the Fisher-Price naming conventions of Windows (My Documents, My Pictures, My First Operating System…).

In fact, you can rename anything you choose in the Start menu—and not just in the free areas. Click the Start menu to open it, right-click the command you want to rename, and choose Rename from the shortcut menu. The name of the command—even My Documents or My Computer—sprouts a little editing box. Type the new name and then press Enter.

Reorganizing the Start Menu

To change the order of listings in the "free" portions of the Start menu, just drag the commands up and down the lists as you see fit. As you drag an item, a black line appears to show you the resulting location of your dragging action. Release the mouse when the black line is where you want the relocated icon to appear.

Tip: If you change your mind while you're dragging, press the Esc key to leave everything as it was.

You can drag program names from the lower-left section of the Start menu, too—but only into one of the "free" areas.

Add folders to hold submenus

Start menu listings accompanied by a right-facing triangle arrow represent folders. For example, clicking Start→All Programs→Games reveals a submenu that lists all the games that come with Windows (see Figure 2-26).

Without these folders consolidating the All Programs menu, you'd need one of those very expensive 95-inch monitors to see the entire list of applications. Fortunately, you can create Programs menu folders of your own and stock them with whatever icons you like. For instance, you may want to create a folder for CD-ROM-based games, eliminating those long lists from the All Programs menu.

To add a folder to the All Programs menu, follow these steps:

1. **Open the Start menu. Right-click All Programs. From the shortcut menu, choose Explore.**

The subfolders you are about to create in the All Programs menu will show up only when *you* are logged on. (If you want to make a change that affects *everybody* with an account on this computer, choose Explore All Users from the shortcut menu instead.)

In any case, the Start Menu Explorer window appears.

Figure 2-26:
Some Programs menu items have submenu folders and sub-submenu folders. As you move through the layers, you're performing an action known as "drilling down." You'll see this phrase often in manuals and computer books—for example, "Drill down to the Calculator to crunch a few quick numbers."

2. **Click the Programs folder.**

   Its contents are listed in the right pane, as shown in Figure 2-27.

3. **Choose File→New→Folder.**

   Or, if your right mouse button hasn't been getting enough exercise, right-click a blank spot in the right pane, and then choose New→Folder from the shortcut menu.

4. **When the new folder item appears, type a folder name and then press Enter.**

   Close the Start Menu window, if you like.

Your new folder appears at the bottom of the Start→All Programs menu. Feel free to drag your new folder up or down on the menu.

Now you can put your favorite file, folder, disk, or application icons *into* this new folder. To do so, drag an icon onto the Start→All Programs menu, and then, without releasing the mouse, onto the new folder/submenu you created. Of course, the first time you do this, your newly created folder submenu just says "Empty"; drag the icon onto that "Empty" notation to install it into your submenu. Then drag as many other icons as you like into this new folder.

You can even create folders *within* folders in your Start→All Programs menu. Just repeat the instructions given earlier—but following step 2, click the + sign next to the first folder you added. Then continue with step 3.

Figure 2-27:
The listings on the All Programs menu appear in the right pane. Notice that some of the items have folder icons; these are the folders that hold submenus. If you click Programs (in the left pane) before creating the new folder, you'll create a folder within the body of the All Programs list. To add a folder whose name will appear above *the line in the All Programs menu, click Start Menu (in the left pane) before creating a new folder.*

Windows, Folders, and the Taskbar

Windows got its name from the rectangles on the screen—the windows— where every computer activity takes place. You look at a Web page in a window, type into a window, read email in a window, and look at the contents of a folder in a window—sometimes all at once. But as you create more files, stash them in more folders, and launch more programs, it's easy to wind up paralyzed before a screen awash with cluttered, overlapping rectangles.

Fortunately, Windows is crawling with icons, buttons, and other inventions to help you keep these windows under control.

Windows in Windows

There are two categories of windows in Windows:

- **Desktop windows.** These windows, sometimes called Windows Explorer windows, include the windows that open when you double-click a disk or folder icon. This is where you organize your files and programs.

- **Application windows.** These are the windows where you do your work—in Word or Internet Explorer, for example.

Nonetheless, all windows have certain components in common (see Figure 3-1).

- **Title bar.** This top strip displays the name of the window. Drag it like a handle when you want to *move* the window on the screen.

- **Minimize button.** Click this box to temporarily hide a window, shrinking it down into the form of a button on your taskbar (page 96). You can open it again by clicking that button. *Keyboard shortcut:* Press Alt+Space bar, then N.

- **Maximize button.** Click this button to enlarge the window so that it fills the screen, gluing its edges to the screen borders. At this point, the maximize button turns into a *restore down* button (whose icon shows two overlapping rectangles), which you can click to return the window to its previous size. *Keyboard shortcut:* Press Alt+Space bar, then X.

Tip: You can also maximize or restore a window by double-clicking its title bar.

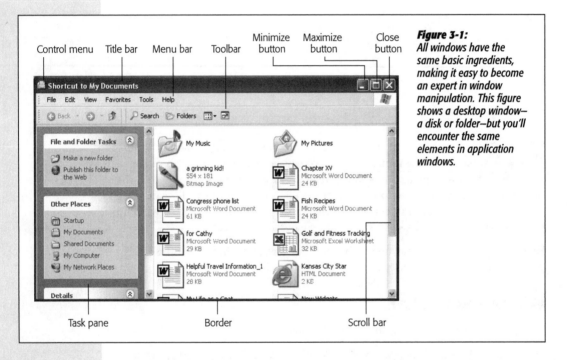

Figure 3-1:
All windows have the same basic ingredients, making it easy to become an expert in window manipulation. This figure shows a desktop window— a disk or folder—but you'll encounter the same elements in application windows.

- **Close button.** Click the X button to close the window. *Keyboard shortcut:* Press Alt+F4.

- **Menu bar.** Click a menu title (such as File or Edit) to open a menu, revealing a list of commands available for that menu in this window. *Keyboard shortcuts:* Press Alt+[underlined letter in menu], or press F10 to activate the menu bar in the active window and *then* press the underlined letter.

- **Toolbar.** Some windows offer rows of one-click shortcut buttons as equivalents for the menu commands that Microsoft thinks you'll use frequently. (More on toolbars at the end of this chapter.)

- **Scroll bar.** A scroll bar appears on the right side or bottom of the window if the window isn't large enough to show all its contents (as described in the box at the bottom of this page).

- **Address bar.** This bar lets you type in a Web address or the address of a folder on your PC (page 39); when you press Enter or click Go, that Web page (or a list of the contents of that folder) appears.

- **Control icon.** The icon next to the title is actually a menu that offers commands for sizing, moving, and closing the window. You can double-click it to close a window. Otherwise, it's not very useful, because its commands duplicate the other doodads described here.

- **Borders.** You can change the size of a window by dragging these edges. Position your pointer over any border until the pointer turns into a double-headed arrow. Then drag inward or outward to reshape the window. (To resize a full-screen window, click the restore down button first.)

Tip: You can resize a window in both dimensions at once just by dragging one of its corners. The diagonally striped ribs at the lower-right corner may suggest that it's the *only* corner you can drag, but it's not; all four corners work the same way.

The Task Pane

At the left side of every desktop window is a special, independent blue panel. For novices in particular, it's one of the most useful new features in Windows XP.

The programmers at Microsoft were clearly frustrated at having built so many interesting features into Windows that nobody knew existed. Most of these features appeared only when you right-clicked something—a folder, file, or whatever. But by

---

UP TO SPEED

Scroll Bar Crash Course

Scroll bars are the strips that may appear at the right side or bottom of a window. The scroll bar signals you that the window isn't big enough to reveal all of its contents.

Click the arrows at each end of a scroll bar to move slowly through the window, or drag the square handle (the *thumb*) to move faster. (The position of the thumb relative to the entire scroll bar reflects your relative position in the entire window or document.) You can quickly move to a specific part of the window by holding the mouse button down on the scroll bar where you want the thumb to be. The scroll bar rapidly scrolls to the desired location and then stops.

If your mouse has a little wheel on the top, you can scroll (in most programs) just by turning the wheel with your finger, even if your cursor is nowhere near the scroll bar. You can turbo-scroll by dragging the mouse upward or downward while keeping the wheel pressed down inside the window.

Finally, keyboard addicts should note that you can scroll without using the mouse at all. Press the Page Up or Page Down keys to scroll the window by one "windowful," or use the up and down arrow keys to scroll one line at a time.

Microsoft's research, as many as 75 percent of Windows users never right-click *any-thing*. They've been missing out on all of these features.

The idea behind the *task pane,* therefore, is to unearth the list of features that once lurked (and still lurk) inside shortcut menus. The contents of this blue panel change depending on the kind of window you're viewing (Figure 3-2), but the idea is always the same: to wave a frantic little software flag in front of your eyes, so that you'll notice some of the possibilities that are only a click away.

In a standard desktop window, for example, the task pane lists frequently sought commands like "Make a new folder," "Publish this folder to the Web," and "Share

Figure 3-2:
The task pane is divided into functional blocks: tasks at top, places below that, file and folder info below that. If the pane becomes too long, you can either use the scroll bar or collapse sections of the pane by clicking the round buttons.

Middle: When you click a file, you get its specs or a preview of its contents.

Right: Depending on the folder template you've chosen, you may get picture- or music-specific tasks.

NOSTALGIA CORNER

Hiding and Shrinking the Task Pane

The task pane is plenty useful for plenty of people, but it's a glutton for screen space. It adds a two-inch sidecar onto every window, which you can't hide or show on a folder-by-folder basis—and can't make narrower.

When window space is tight, you can eliminate the task pane in either of two ways. First, note that Windows po-litely removes the pane altogether when the window be-comes so narrow that half of it would be the task pane. Try dragging the right edge of a window slowly to the left; even-

tually, you'll see the task pane blink out of sight. (Widen the window again to make it reappear.)

Second, you can get rid of the task pane on a computer-wide basis. In any folder window, choose Tools→Folder Options. In the resulting dialog box, click "Use Windows Classic folders" and then click OK.

Now the task panes are gone—at least until you return to the same Folder Options dialog box and click "Show com-mon tasks and folders" to make them return.

this folder" (with other people on your office network). Below that list of File and Folder Tasks is a box (Other Places) that offers one-click links to frequently accessed locations on your PC: My Computer, My Network Places, and so on.

Finally, at the bottom of every desktop task pane is a Details area. If you click a file icon, this panel displays its size, name, type, modification date, and (if it's a picture) dimensions. If you click a disk icon, you're able to see how full it is and how much it holds. If you select several icons at once, this panel shows you the sum of their file sizes—a great feature when you're burning a CD, for example, and don't want to exceed the 650 MB limit.

Depending on the *template* that's been applied to a folder (page 82), you may also see special multimedia task links: "View as a slideshow" and "Print this picture" for graphics files, "Play All" and "Shop for music online" for music folders, and so on. (Chapter 8 details these topics.)

The Explorer Bar

The new task pane occupies the space at the left side of a window, exactly where the Explorer bar appeared in previous versions of Windows.

But the Explorer bar is still available. By using the View→Explorer Bar command, you can make the task pane disappear, to be replaced by your choice of the following kinds of information:

- **Search.** By choosing View→Explorer Bar→Search, you bring up the Windows XP Search program described in Chapter 2. *Keyboard shortcut:* Ctrl+E, or F3.

- **Favorites.** As you might guess, this list offers quick access to your "bookmarked" Web sites from Internet Explorer. But it can also list folder windows, documents, and other icons to which you'd like easy access. (As noted on page 64, you can also access your Favorites from the Start menu.) *Keyboard shortcut:* Ctrl+I.

   To add a certain window to this list—My Documents, for example—open it on the screen and then choose Favorites→Add to Favorites (or press Alt+A, A). Name the window, if you like, and then click OK.

   Or, to add an icon (file, folder, disk) to the list of Favorites, just drag it directly into the Favorites bar. Now it's listed in your Favorites menu and in your Favorites bar.

- **Media.** This panel, new in Windows XP, offers a set of controls for playing music CDs, music files, and movie files, right there in your folder window. Of course, Windows Media Player (Chapter 8) is the galactic headquarters for this kind of task. But if you just want to play an MP3 file as background music for your work, this is a great shortcut (see Figure 3-3).

- **History.** This panel works exactly like the one in a Web browser, in that it shows you a list of Web sites you've recently visited, sorted by the date of the visit ("2 Weeks Ago," for example). *Keyboard shortcut:* Ctrl+H.

Tip: Many people miss the fact that the History panel also contains a handy recent-*documents* tracker, one that's even more complete and permanent than the My Recent Documents folder described on page 59. To see the list of documents you've recently opened—including your own files, Help files, and so on—just click the My Computer icon in the history list. (If you opened a document on another machine across the network, click its name instead.)

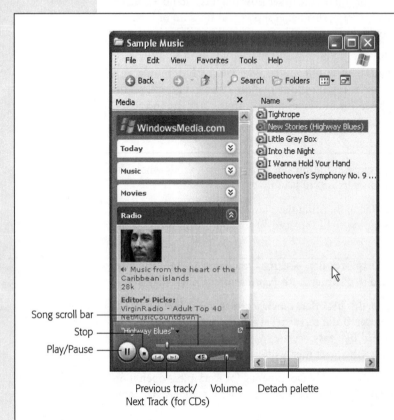

Song scroll bar

Stop

Play/Pause

Previous track/   Volume   Detach palette
Next Track (for CDs)

Figure 3-3:
The controls here represent the "front end" for playing video clips, audio CDs, and sound files. Don't miss the double-down-arrow circle buttons, which take you directly to the Web sites where you can find music, video, or even radio stations to play. The little "Detach palette" button in the upper-right corner turns this panel into a floating palette that you can park anywhere on the screen.

- **Folders.** Choosing View→Explorer Bar→Folders (or simply clicking the Folders button on the standard window toolbar) opens the Windows Explorer–like folder tree that's described on page 116.

- **Tip of the Day.** This option actually has nothing to do with the left-side panel of a window. Instead, it opens a new strip at the *bottom* of the window, displaying a useful tip or trick for using Windows. (Any other Explorer bar panel you've opened at the left side of the window stays right where it is.)

- **Discuss.** This option is worthless unless an administrator has set up a SharePoint Portal Server (a corporate software kit that permits chat sessions among employees). If so, you can use this panel to control which discussion group you sign up for, or to insert fragments of your chat into a document you're working on.

Sizing, Moving, and Closing Windows

Any Windows window can cycle among three altered states:

- **Maximized** means that the window fills the screen. Its edges are glued to the boundaries of your monitor, and you can't see anything behind it. It expands to this size when you click its maximize button (see Figure 3-1)—an ideal arrangement when you're surfing the Web or working on a document for hours at a stretch, since the largest possible window means the least possible scrolling.

Tip: When a window is maximized, you can *restore* it (as described below) by pressing Alt+Space bar, then R.

- When you click a window's **minimize** button (Figure 3-1), the window disappears. It hasn't actually closed, however; it's simply reincarnated as a button on the taskbar at the bottom of the screen. You can bring the window back by clicking this taskbar button, which bears the window's name. Minimizing a window is a great tactic when you want to see what's in the window behind it.

- A **restored** window is neither maximized nor minimized. It's a loose cannon, floating around on your screen as an independent rectangle. Because its edges aren't attached to the walls of your monitor, you can make it any size you like by dragging its borders.

Tip: Double-clicking the title bar alternates a window between its maximized (full-screen) and restored conditions.

Moving a window

Moving a window is easy—just drag the title bar.

Most of the time, you move a window to get it out of the way when you're trying to see what's *behind* it. However, moving windows around is also handy if you're moving or copying data between programs, or moving or copying files between drives or folders, as shown in Figure 3-4.

Closing a window

You can close a window in any of the following ways:

- Click the close button (the X in the upper-right corner).

- Press Alt+F4.

- Double-click the Control icon in the upper-left corner.

- Single-click the Control icon in the upper-left corner, and then choose Close from the menu.

- Right-click the window's taskbar button, and then choose Close from the shortcut menu.

- In desktop windows, choose File→Close.

- Quit the program you're using, log off, or shut down the PC.

Be careful: In many programs, including Internet Explorer, closing the window also quits the program entirely.

Tip: If you see *two* X buttons in the upper-right corner of your screen, then you're probably using a program like Microsoft Word. It's what Microsoft calls an MDI, or *multiple document interface* program (see page 157). It gives you a window within a window. The outer window represents the application itself; the inner one represents the particular *document* you're working on.

If you want to close one document before working on another, be careful to click the *inner* Close button. Clicking the outer one exits the application entirely. If you have multiple documents open within one application, you can close the active document by pressing Ctrl+F4. The program *may* ask if you want to save the document before closing it, but nothing is certain, so get in the habit of pressing Ctrl+S before you press Ctrl+F4.

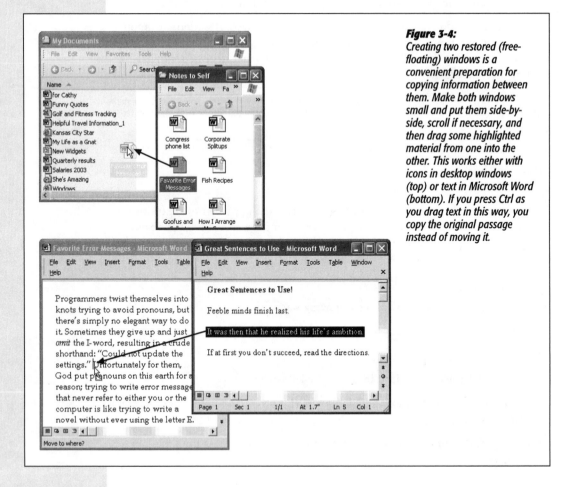

Figure 3-4:
Creating two restored (free-floating) windows is a convenient preparation for copying information between them. Make both windows small and put them side-by-side, scroll if necessary, and then drag some highlighted material from one into the other. This works either with icons in desktop windows (top) or text in Microsoft Word (bottom). If you press Ctrl as you drag text in this way, you copy the original passage instead of moving it.

Working with Multiple Windows

Many people routinely keep four or five programs open at once, like a calendar, word processor, Web browser, and email program. Others (computer book authors, for example) regularly work in just one program, but have several document windows open at once, representing several chapters. Clearly, learning how to manage and navigate a flurry of overlapping windows is an essential Windows survival skill.

Active and inactive windows

When you have multiple windows open on your screen, only one window is *active*, which means the following:

- It's in the foreground, *in front* of all other windows.

- It's the window that "hears" your keystrokes and mouse clicks.

- The title bar is vivid blue and the background (inactive) window title bars are a lighter, more faded blue. (You can change this color scheme, as described on page 271.)

Of course, just because a window is in the background doesn't mean that it can't continue with whatever assignment you gave it—printing, downloading email, and so on. If a background program needs to pass a message to you (such as an error message), it automatically pops to the foreground, becoming the active program. When you respond to the message (usually by clicking OK), Windows XP sends the program *back* to the background.

Tip: To activate a background window, click anywhere on it. If other windows are covering up the background window, click its name on the taskbar (described in the next section).

You can also rotate through all the open windows and programs by pressing Alt+Tab. A little panel appears in the center of your screen, filled with the icons of open folders and programs; each press of Alt+Tab highlights the next in sequence. (Alt+*Shift*+Tab moves you one *backward* through the sequence.) Upon releasing the keys, you jump to the highlighted window, as though it's a high-tech game of Duck Duck Goose.

Of course, you won't become a true Zen master of window juggling until you've explored the multiple-window command center itself—the taskbar (see page 96).

The Desktop Window Overhaul

Windows' windows look just fine straight from the factory: all the edges are straight, and the text is perfectly legible. Still, if you're going to stare at this computer screen for half of your waking hours, you may as well investigate some of the ways these windows can be enhanced for better looks and greater efficiency. As it turns out, there's no end to the tweaks Microsoft lets you perform.

Icon and List Views

You can view the files and folders in a desktop window in any of several ways: as small icons, jumbo icons, a tidy list, and so on. Each window remembers its own view settings.

To change the view of a particular open window, choose one of these commands from its View menu (or from the little ▦▾ icon on the toolbar): Filmstrip, Thumbnails, Tiles, Icons, List, or Details. Figure 3-5 illustrates each of these options.

Some of these views are new in Windows XP. Filmstrip view, for example, is a home run for anyone with a digital camera or scanner. It turns the folder window into a slide show machine, complete with Next and Previous buttons beneath an enlarged picture, as well as buttons that rotate the image on the screen. (You get this view automatically when you open your My Pictures folder.)

Figure 3-5:
The new **Filmstrip** view (upper left) creates a slide show right in the folder window. **Thumbnails** view (upper right) is also good for photos—or anyone who would like a larger target for clicking each icon. (Tip: If you press Shift as you switch to Thumbnails view, you hide the file names. Do it again to bring the names back.)

In the new **Tiles** view (middle left), your icons appear at standard size, sorted alphabetically into vertical columns—with name and file details just to the right. **Icons** view (middle right) sorts the icons horizontally in rows, displaying only their names. The **List** view (lower left) packs, by far, the most files into the space of a window. **Details** view (lower right) is the same as List view, except for the additional columns of information that reveal the size, the icon type, and the date and time the item was last modified.

Tip: In Filmstrip view, try right-clicking inside the large image of your photo. The resulting shortcut menu offers a number of very useful options, including Rotate commands, "Set as Desktop Background," and "Send To" (which lets you fire the picture off to somebody by email).

As a message may tell you, rotating certain pictures may force Windows to recompress them, sometimes reducing the quality by a fractional amount. In general, the quality loss isn't visible to the eye, but if you're concerned, duplicate the file to preserve the original before rotating.

Changing the sorting order

Windows XP starts out arranging the icons alphabetically in two different groups. Folders come first, followed by the list of loose files in a second group.

But you don't have to be content with an alphabetical list. Windows XP is wildly flexible in this regard, letting you sort a window's contents in any of 32 ways.

To change the sorting criterion, choose View→Arrange Icons By, and then choose from the drop-down menu. The sorting possibilities listed here depend on which *columns* you've made visible in Details view (described in the next section). Generally, though, you'll find these options:

GEM IN THE ROUGH

Folder Templates

In previous Windows versions, people with too much time on their hands could choose their own HTML templates to dress up the backgrounds of their open folder windows. In XP, if you want the blank area behind your icons to be solid mauve, for example, or decked out with a replica of your home page, you're out of luck.

There is still a Customize This Folder command in the View menu, though. (It's available in the View menu of any folder you've created yourself—just not built-in folders like My Documents.) It produces the dialog box shown here. Using the drop-down menu at the top, you can choose to apply any of seven canned folder templates to the currently open folder.

In the Windows XP sense, *template* here means *predefined*

view setting (thumbnail, filmstrip, or whatever) and set of task pane options. Ever wonder why your My Pictures folder always opens up in Filmstrip view, with useful tasks like "View as a slide show" on the task pane? Now you know: It's been given the Pictures template in this dialog box.

Three of the templates listed here are designed for folders that contain music files (MP3 files and such), one is for documents of any file type, two are for picture folders, and one is for videos. Clearly, Microsoft designed this feature for its own benefit (for the My Pictures and My Music folders, specifically). However, if you create other multimedia folders of your own, you now know how to make them resemble Windows XP's ready-made folders.

- **Name** arranges the files alphabetically.

- **Type** arranges the files in the window alphabetically by file *type,* such as Word documents, applications, JPEG files, and so on. (Technically, you're sorting files by their *filename extensions* [see page 172].)

- **Size** arranges files by size, smallest first. (Folders are unaffected; Windows never shows you the sizes of folders in its list views.) In the My Computer window, this option says Total Size and lists your disks by their capacity.

- **Free Space** is an option only in the My Computer window. Needless to say, it shows you how much space is left on each of your disks.

- **Show in Groups** is a fascinating enhancement in Windows XP. In any view except Filmstrip and List, it superimposes *headings* on your sorted list of icons, making the window look like an index (see Figure 3-6). When sorting the list by size, for example, the headings say Tiny, Small, Medium, and Folders. When sorting by modified date, you see headings called Yesterday, Last week, Earlier this month, and so on. It's an inspired idea that makes it much easier to hunt down specific icons in crowded folders.

- **Auto Arrange,** available only in Icon and Tile views, isn't actually a sorting method, it's a straightening-up method. It rearranges the icons so they're equally spaced and neat. (You can use this command on the desktop, too, which is one way to avoid CWDS [Cluttered Windows Desktop Syndrome].)

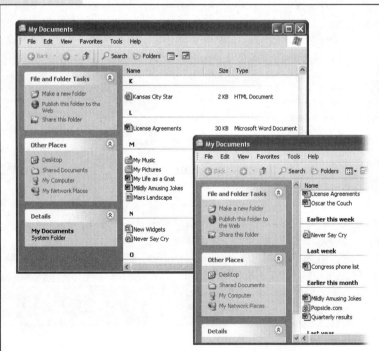

Figure 3-6:
Show in Groups is a useful new view option (available in all views except Filmstrip and List) that superimposes a set of "filing tabs" on any window, with headings that reflect the date, size, name, type, and so on. It's perfect for scanning a crowded list. These examples show sorting by name (left) and by modified date (right). In the My Computer window, the effect is slightly different: Your folders and disks are listed in headings called, for example, Files Stored on This Computer, Hard Disk Drives, and Devices with Removable Storage.

- **Align to Grid** is slightly different. Whereas Auto Arrange always keeps icons or tiles in a tight, equally spaced clump, Align to Grid snaps dragged icons into position against an invisible underlying grid, even if they're scattered across the broad space of an open window (instead of clustered together in the upper-left corner). In other words, this feature is generally useful only when Auto Arrange is turned off.

Note: You can't reverse the sort *order* of your icons (from Z to A, for example), except in Details view, described next.

Manipulating the Details view

You gotta love Details view. Clearly, Microsoft does: it's endowed Details view with much more flexibility and power than the other views.

First, there's the obvious advantage of being able to see the size and date of the objects in neat columns, as shown in Figure 3-5. Second, you can sort the contents by file size, type, or date simply by clicking the appropriate column heading.

Tip: If you click the same column heading again, the sorting order is reversed. For instance, clicking the Date Modified column once places your files into oldest-files-first sequence; a second click puts the *newest* file first. A small arrow on the column heading points up or down to indicate the order of the sort. (This doesn't work if "Arrange in Groups" is turned on.)

Third, you can rearrange the column sequence just by dragging their headings horizontally.

Finally, you can manipulate the columns in a number of ways:

- To add more columns to the window, providing even more information about each icon, right-click any column heading and choose column names from the resulting drop-down menu. As you'll quickly discover, many of these column headings are useful only in folders that contain certain kinds of files—Date Picture Taken is for digital photos, Album Title is for music files, and so on.

- For even more control over the columns, choose View→Choose Details to open the dialog box shown in Figure 3-7. Turn on the checkboxes beside the columns you want. You can even determine their sequence just by clicking a column name, and then clicking Move Up or Move Down (although, as noted above, it's much easier to drag the column headings in the window yourself).

- Once you've opened the Choose Details window, you *could* change the width of a column by editing the number at the bottom in the "Width of selected column (in pixels)" text box—but that's for geeks. It's much more natural to adjust column widths just by dragging the vertical divider bar (between column headings) from side to side.

Tip: When adjusting the width of a column, here's a technique that's even better than dragging: *Double-click* the divider between one column name and the next. Doing so automatically expands the column to a width that's precisely wide enough to reveal the widest item in that column (exactly as in Microsoft Excel).

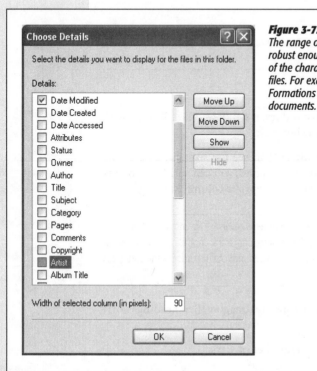

Figure 3-7:
The range of information you can display in the window is robust enough to satisfy even the terminally curious. Some of the characteristics listed here are for specific types of files. For example, you won't need a column for Audio Formations in a folder that holds word processing documents.

Standard Folder Views

Now that you've twiddled and tweaked your system windows into a perfectly efficient configuration, you needn't go through the same exercises for each folder. Windows XP can immortalize your changes as the standard setting for *all* your windows.

Choose Tools→Folder Options→View tab. Click the Apply to All Folders button. When Windows XP asks whether you're sure you know what you're doing, click Yes.

At this point, all of your disk and folder windows open up with the same view, sorting method, and so on. You're still free to override those standard settings on a window-by-window basis, however. And if you change your mind *again,* seeking to make all of your maverick folder windows snap back into line with the standard settings, choose Tools→Folder Options→View tab and click the Reset All Folders button.

Uni-Window vs. Multi-Window

When you double-click a folder, Windows can react in one of two ways:

- **It can open a new window.** Now you've got two windows on the screen, one over-lapping the other. Moving or copying an icon from one into the other is a piece of cake. Trouble is, if your double-clicking craze continues much longer, your screen will eventually be overrun with windows that you must now painstakingly close again.

- **It can replace the original window with a new one.** This only-one-window-at-all-times behavior keeps your desktop from becoming crowded with windows. If you need to return to the previous window, the Back button takes you there. Of course, you'll have a harder time dragging icons from one window to another using this method.

Whatever you decide, you switch windows between these two behaviors like this: Choose Tools→Folder Options→General tab in any desktop window. In the result-ing dialog box, click "Open each folder in the same window" or "Open each folder in its own window," as you like. Then click OK.

The "Folder Options" Options

If you choose Tools→Folder Options from any folder window and then click the View tab (see Figure 3-8), you see an array of options that affect all of the folder windows on your PC. When assessing the impact of these controls, "earth-shatter-ing" isn't the adjective that springs to mind. Still, you may find a few of them useful.

Here are the functions of the various checkboxes:

- **Automatically search for network folders and printers.** When you turn on this checkbox, Windows explores your network every few seconds in hopes of detect-

---

POWER USERS' CLINIC

Eliminating Double-Clicks

In many ways, each desktop folder window is just like In-ternet Explorer. It has a Back button at the top, an Address bar strip just below that, a Favorites menu, and so on.

If you enjoy this computer-as-browser effect, you can ac-tually take it one step further. You can set up your PC so that *one* click, not two, opens an icon. It's a strange effect that some people adore, and others turn off again as fast as their little fingers will let them. Either way, you should try it out.

Choose Tools→Folder Options→General tab. Select "Single-click to open an item (point to select)." When you turn on this option, you can even turn the icon names into

underlined links by selecting "Underline icon titles consis-tent with my browser" or "Underline icon titles only when I point at them." Click OK.

If a single click opens an icon, you're entitled to wonder: How does one *select* an icon (which you'd normally do with a single click)? Answer: Just point to it for about a half-second, letting the mouse hover over the listing with-out clicking. To make multiple selections, press the Ctrl key as you point to additional icons.

Of course, the PC-as-Web analogy isn't quite complete—you still won't see advertising banners across the top of your desktop windows. Maybe next year.

---

ing shared folders and network printers that recently have been turned on or off. That way, your Network Places and Printers windows will be up to date when you open them.

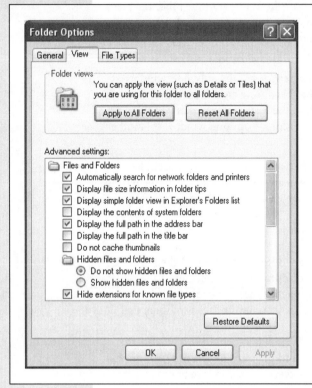

Figure 3-8:
Some of the options in this list are contained within tiny folder icons. Double-click one of these icons to expand the list and reveal the options within it. For example, you won't see the "Do not show hidden files and folders" option until you have expanded the "Hidden files and folders" folder icon.

- **Display file size information in folder tips.** A *folder tip* is a rectangular balloon that appears when you point to a folder—a little yellow box that tells you what's in that folder and how big it is on the disk. (It appears only if you've turned on the "Show pop-up description" checkbox described below.) Talk about tweaky: you turn off *this* checkbox if you want to see the description but not the size.

- **Display simple folder view in Explorer's Folders list.** When you've turned on this option, clicking a folder in Windows Explorer (page 116) expands its listing, showing you its contents. It also simultaneously *closes* any other folder you've previously expanded.

- **Display the contents of system folders.** When you open certain windows that "belong" to Windows XP itself—the Windows folder or Program Files folder, for example—you see nothing but an enormous, full-window message that says, "These files are hidden." Microsoft grew weary of answering tech-support calls from clueless or mischievous customers who had moved or deleted critical system files from these folders, rendering their PCs crippled or useless. The company concluded that the simplest preventive measure would be to make them invisible (the files, not the PCs).

This checkbox is responsible for that safety feature. If you consider yourself a cool customer when it comes to power-user techniques like fooling around with important Windows folders, you can turn this box on. You won't see that "These files are hidden" message any more. (Of course, even if this checkbox is turned off, you can still view the hidden files by clicking the "Show the contents of this folder" link in the task pane of any such window.)

- **Display the full path in the address bar.** When this option is on, Windows reveals the exact location of the current window in the Address bar (if it's showing)—for example, *C:\Documents and Settings\Chris\My Documents.* See page 39 for more on folder paths.

- **Display the full path in the title bar.** Same idea, but this time the path of the open folder or file shows up in the *title bar* of the window. Seeing the path can be useful when you're not sure which disk a folder is on, for example. Unfortunately, you also get the full path in the window's taskbar button—or more specifically, the first couple words of the path, which aren't usually helpful. In that case, just point to the taskbar button to see the rest of the pathname appear in a tooltip (if "Show pop-up description" is turned on, as described on page 91).

- **Do not cache thumbnails.** This option refers to the new Thumbnails view, a window view that's primarily useful for looking at folders full of pictures. When Windows *caches* such images, it memorizes the little pictures that constitute your thumbnails, so that they'll appear faster the next time you open the window. You save a tiny bit of memory by turning on this checkbox, but you'll wait a lot longer every time you open a folder whose contents are in Thumbnails view.

- **Hidden files and folders; Hide protected operating system files (Recommended).** As noted above, Windows XP hides certain files and information that, if deleted or changed by mistake, could cause you hours of troubleshooting grief by damaging the operating system or your programs. (Certain files and folders remain hidden *even* if you have turned on "Display the contents of System folders.") Yes, Big Brother is watching you, but he means well.

By changing these settings, you, the confident power user, can make the hidden files and folders appear (they'll show up with dimmed icons, as though to reinforce their delicate nature). But you'll have the smoothest possible computing career if you leave these options untouched.

- **Hide extensions for known file types.** Windows XP normally hides the three-letter *filename extension* on standard files and documents (Word files, graphics files, and so on), in an effort to make Windows seem less technical and intimidating. Your files wind up named Groceries and Frank instead of Groceries.doc and Frank.jpg.

Power users often make these extensions reappear by turning off this option; see page 173 for more on this topic.

- **Launch folder windows in a separate process.** This geekily worded setting opens each folder into a different chunk of memory (RAM). In certain rare situations, this largely obsolete arrangement is more stable—but it slightly slows down your machine and unnecessarily uses memory.

- **Managing pairs of Web pages and folders.** For some reason, this new Windows XP option shows up only if you've also installed Microsoft Office. This feature affects Web pages that you save to your hard drive (by choosing, in Internet Explorer, File→Save As, and then choosing the "Web Page, Complete" option in the "Save as type" drop-down list). For such a tiny feature, quite a bit of explanation is required.

   When saving a Web page in this way, you generally wind up with two separate icons on your desktop: an HTML document that contains the Web page's code (and the words on the page), plus a similarly named folder full of the graphics (and scripts) that appeared on that page.

   The "Show and manage the pair as a single file" option here is a strange but useful one. It means that whenever you move or delete *one* of these two icons (the HTML document and the graphics folder), the other one automatically accompanies it. The idea, of course, is to help you avoid breaking the connection between these items—for example, leaving the graphics behind when you copy the text file to another disk.

   If you turn on "Show both parts and manage them individually," of course, Windows doesn't preserve any such link. If you drag or delete the text file, you leave behind the graphics folder.

   (The strangest option in all of Windows XP is the final one, "Show both parts but manage as a single file." It produces exactly the same effect as "Show and manage the pair as a single file." Go figure.)

- **Remember each folder's view settings.** Ordinarily, every folder and disk window memorizes its own view setting (List, Details, Thumbnails, or whatever) independently.

   But if you turn *off* this checkbox, each folder inherits the view setting of the window it's *in*. If you open My Documents, for example, and switch it to Tiles view, all the folders inside it will open into Tiles view windows, too. Furthermore, if you change one of those inner folders to Details view, for example, it won't stick. Instead, it will switch right back to Tiles the next time you open it.

   If you're clever, then, here's how you could set your PC to employ the same view setting all the time (Details view, for example): turn on this option *and* use the Apply to All Folders button described on page 86.

- **Restore previous folder windows at logon.** Every time you log off the computer, Windows forgets which windows were open. That's a distinct bummer, especially if you tend to work out of your My Documents window, which you must therefore manually reopen every time you fire up the old PC.

  If you turn on this useful checkbox, then each time you log on, Windows XP will automatically present you with whichever windows were open when you last logged off.

- **Show Control Panel in My Computer.** Turn on this checkbox if you'd like to see a Control Panel icon in the My Computer window, as in previous versions of Windows.

- **Show encrypted or compressed NTFS files in color.** This feature won't make much sense until you've read page 454, which explains how Windows XP Professional can encode your files for security, and page 449, which explains how Windows XP (any version) can compact your files to use less disk space.

  This option turns the names of affected icons green and blue, respectively, so that you can spot them at a glance. On the other hand, encrypted or compressed files and folders operate quite normally, immediately converting back to human form when double-clicked. In other words, knowing which ones have been affected isn't particularly valuable. Turn off this box to make them look just like any other files and folders.

- **Show pop-up description for folder and desktop items.** If you point to (but don't click) an icon, a taskbar button, a found item in the Search program, or whatever, you get a pop-up tooltip—a floating yellow label that helps identify what you're pointing to. If you find these tooltips distracting, turn off this checkbox.

- **Use simple file sharing.** See page 574 for details on this simplified, but not especially secure, file-sharing system.

Note: The changes you make in the Folder Options settings are global; they affect *all* desktop windows.

Window Toolbars

On the day it's born, every Windows XP desktop window has a standard *toolbar* across the top (see Figure 3-9). A toolbar is simply a strip of one-click buttons like Back, Forward, Search, and so on.

But by choosing View→Toolbars, or right-clicking a blank spot on a toolbar and pointing to Toolbars on the shortcut menu, you can add or hide whichever toolbars you like, on a window-by-window basis. Three different toolbars are available from the View menu: Standard Buttons, Address Bar, and Links.

Tip: As anyone in the U.S. Justice Department could probably tell you, the Internet Explorer Web browser is deeply embedded in Windows itself. These window toolbars are perfect examples: They appear not only in desktop windows but also in Internet Explorer when you're browsing the Web. In fact, you'll probably find them even more useful when you're browsing the Web than when browsing your desktop folders.

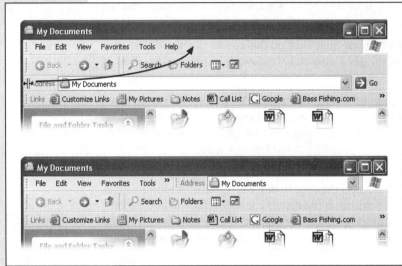

Figure 3-9:
Top: The three basic toolbars that you can summon independently for any desktop window—and also in Internet Explorer.

Bottom: By dragging the vertical left-side handle of a toolbar, you can make the displays more compact by placing two or more bars on the same row. You can even drag one right up into the menu bar, as shown here, to save additional vertical space.

The Standard Buttons Toolbar

This toolbar helps you navigate your desktop (or the Web). The desktop version contains buttons like these:

- **Back, Forward.** On the Web, these buttons let you return to Web pages you've just seen. At the desktop, they display the contents of a disk or folder you've just seen. If you're using one-window-at-a-time mode (see "Uni-Window vs. Multi-Window" on page 87), these buttons are your sole means of getting around as you burrow through your folders.

Tip: In both Internet Explorer and at the desktop, you can click the tiny down-pointing black triangle on the Back or Forward button to see a drop-down menu of every Web page (or desktop window) you visited on your way to your current position. Similarly, if you point to one of these buttons without clicking, a tooltip indicates which Web site or folder you'll go to if you click.

- **Up.** This button, short for "up a level," displays the contents of the folder that *contains* the one you're examining. If you're looking at the contents of, say, the Idaho folder, clicking this button would open the USA folder that contains it.

- **Search.** Opens the Search panel described on page 41. *Keyboard shortcut:* F3.

- **Folders.** Hides or shows the master map of disks and folders at the left side of the window, re-creating the two-panel Windows Explorer navigational display described in the next chapter.

- **Views.** Opens a short menu listing the different window views: Tiles, Thumbnails, Details, and so on. (In other words, it duplicates the View menu on the menu bar.) For details on these views, see page 82.

These are just the buttons that Microsoft proposes. You're free to add any of several other buttons to the toolbar or delete ones you never use. You can also change the size of these buttons—a useful feature, considering that the factory settings provide fairly porky icons with both pictures and text labels.

To begin the customizing process, right-click a blank spot on the toolbar. Choose Customize from the shortcut menu to open the Customize Toolbar dialog box (Figure 3-10).

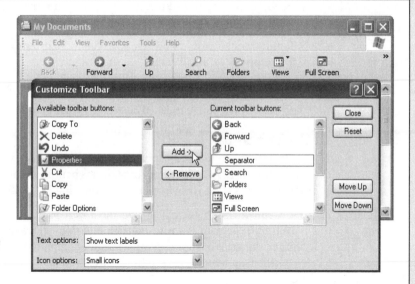

Figure 3-10:
The Customize Toolbar dialog box opens in front of the window you were viewing, so you can see the relationship between the window and the dialog box settings. For instance, notice that the right pane of the dialog box lists the current toolbar buttons; the top-to-bottom listing matches the left-to-right arrangement of the toolbar on the window. The Separator is the thin vertical line on the toolbar.

- To remove a button from the toolbar, click its name in the right pane and then click Remove.

- To move a button left or right on the toolbar, just drag its name up or down the right-side list. (Ignore the Move Up and Move Down buttons; they're for suckers who don't know about the dragging trick.)

- To add a button to the toolbar, click it in the left pane and then click Add.

Here are some of the most useful buttons in the left-side list, for your toolbar-adding consideration. **Properties** saves you a right-click whenever you want to examine an icon's Properties dialog box. **Full Screen** expands the window to fill the entire monitor, in the process replacing all of the toolbars with a single, tiny-iconned control strip at the very top of the screen). To recover from Full Screen view, click the (shrunken) Full Screen icon a second time.

Finally, **Folder Options** opens the dialog box illustrated in Figure 3-8, saving you a couple of menu clicks. This is a great button to have available if you find yourself wanting to make the task pane (page 75) appear and disappear often.

- To add a separator (a vertical divider line) between buttons, click Separator in the left pane and then click Add. Use the Move Up and Move Down buttons at the right of the dialog box to position it.

  Each button's text label generally appears to the right of its button instead of underneath, thanks to the Text Options→"Selective text on right" setting. (As is implied by the name, Windows doesn't put a label next to *every* icon—just the ones it likes.) If you prefer, you can choose "Show text labels" (which displays the labels *underneath* the icon buttons), or for the maximum space savings, "No text labels," from this drop-down menu. (There's no way to display *only* labels without the pictures.)

- To put the standard jumbo Windows XP toolbar buttons on a little diet, choose Icon Options→"Small icons."

- To return everything to its Windows XP factory settings, click Reset.

Click Close when you're finished customizing the Standard toolbar.

The Address Bar

In a Web browser, the Address bar is where you type the addresses of the Web sites you want to visit. At the desktop, the Address bar obeys your commands in all kinds of ways. Here's what you can type there (pressing Enter afterward):

- **A Web address.** You can leave off the *http://* portion. Just type the body of the Web address, such as *www.sony.com,* into this strip. When you click Go or press Enter, the icons in your desktop window are replaced by the actual Web page you specified. Suddenly you're in Internet Explorer.

Tip: By pressing Ctrl+Enter, you can surround whatever you've just typed into the Address bar with *http://www.* and *.com.* See Chapter 11 for even more typing shortcuts along these lines.

- **A search phrase.** If you type some text into this strip that isn't obviously a Web address, Windows assumes that you're telling it, "Go online and search for this phrase." From here, it works exactly as though you've used the Internet search feature described on page 53.

- **A folder name.** You can also type one of several important folder names into this strip, such as *My Computer, My Documents, My Music,* and so on. When you click Go or press Enter, that particular folder window opens.

Tip: The little down-arrow button at the right end of the Address bar is very useful, too. It offers a list of the primary locations on your PC (My Computer, My Documents, your hard drives, and so on) for instant location-jumping.

- **A program or path name.** In these regards, the Address bar works just like the Run command described on page 37.

In each case, as soon as you begin to type, a drop-down list of recently visited Web sites, files, or folders appears below the Address bar. Windows XP is trying to save you some typing. If you see what you're looking for, click it with the mouse, or press the down arrow key to highlight the one you want and then press Enter.

Tip: You don't really need the little Go button; pressing Enter is much faster. If you agree, right-click the Go button and then choose Go Button from the shortcut menu (so that the checkmark disappears), thus removing it altogether.

The Links Toolbar

At first glance, you might assume that the purpose of this toolbar is to provide links to your favorite Web sites. And sure enough, that's what it's for—when you're using Internet Explorer.

Although few realize it, you can drag *any icon at all* onto the toolbar—files, folders, disks, programs, or whatever—to turn them into one-click buttons. In short, think of the Links toolbar as a miniature Start menu for places and things you use most often. You can see desktop folders and documents installed there, for example, in Figure 3-9.

To add your own icons, just drag them from the desktop or any folder window directly onto the toolbar, at any time. Here are a few possibilities, just to get your juices flowing:

- Install toolbar icons of the three or four programs you use the most (or a few documents you work on every day). Sure, the Start menu can also serve this purpose, but only the Links toolbar keeps their names in view.

- Install toolbar icons for shared folders on the network. This arrangement saves several steps when you want to connect to them.

- Install toolbar icons of Web sites you visit often, so that you can jump directly to them when you sit down in front of your PC each morning.

You can drag these links around on the toolbar to put them into a different order, or remove a link by dragging it away—directly into the Recycle Bin, if you like. (They're only shortcuts; you're not actually deleting anything important.) To rename something here—a good idea, since horizontal space in this location is so precious—right-click it and choose Rename from the shortcut menu.

Tip: When you're viewing a Web page, dragging a Web link from this toolbar directly into the Address bar takes you to that particular Web page. But when you're viewing a folder window, dragging one of these Web links to the Address bar creates–in whatever desktop window is open–an *Internet shortcut file.* When double-clicked, this special document connects to the Internet and opens the specified Web page.

The Taskbar

The permanent blue stripe across the bottom of your screen is the taskbar, one of the most prominent and important elements of the Windows interface (see Figure 3-11).

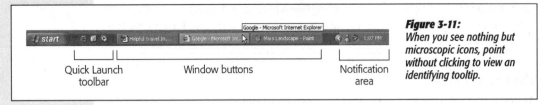

Figure 3-11:
When you see nothing but microscopic icons, point without clicking to view an identifying tooltip.

The taskbar has several segments, each dedicated to an important function. Its right end, the *notification area,* contains little status icons that display the time, whether or not you're online, whether or not your laptop's plugged in, and so on. The main portion of the taskbar, of course, helps you keep your open windows and programs under control. You can even dress up your taskbar with additional little segments called toolbars, as described in the following pages.

This section covers each of these features in turn.

The Notification Area

In Windows XP, Microsoft has chosen a new name for the area formerly known as the tray (the group of tiny icons at the right end of the taskbar): the notification area. (Why use one syllable when eight will do?)

The purpose is much the same: to give you quick access to little status indicators and pop-up menus that control various functions of your PC. Many a software installer inserts its own little icon into this area: fax software, virus software, palmtop synchronization software, and so on.

INFREQUENTLY ASKED QUESTION

The Radio Toolbar

Didn't there used to be another toolbar–the radio toolbar? How am I supposed to tune in my favorite Internet radio stations?

It's gone from Windows XP. When you're in the mood for a little classical music as you crunch numbers, use the new Media Explorer bar panel instead (page 77).

Tip: To figure out what an icon represents, point to it without clicking so that a tooltip appears. To access the controls that accompany it, try both left-clicking and right-clicking the tiny icon. Often, each click produces a different pop-up menu filled with useful controls.

Despite the expansion of its name, you'll probably discover that this area is much smaller than it used to be. On a new PC, for example, you may find little more than the current time.

Tip: By double-clicking the time display, you open the Date and Time Control Panel program. And if you point to the time without clicking, a tooltip appears to tell you the day of the week and today's date.

That's because Microsoft's XP anti-clutter campaign reached a fever pitch when it came to this component of the operating system. The designers of Windows had noticed that software companies large and small had been indiscriminately dumping little icons into this area, sometimes for prestige more than utility.

Therefore, Microsoft laid down two policies concerning this critical piece of screen real estate:

- Even Microsoft's own usual junk—the speaker icon for volume control, the display icon for changing screen resolution, the battery icon for laptops, and so on—is absent on a fresh XP installation. If you want to add these controls to the notification area, you must do it yourself, using the corresponding Control Panel programs as described in Chapter 9.

- Notification area icons that you don't use often will be summarily hidden after a couple of weeks. See Figure 3-12 for details.

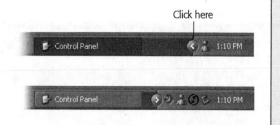

Figure 3-12:
If you see a < button, Windows is telling you that it has hidden some of your notification-area icons. Click this button to expand the notification area, bringing all of the hidden icons into view (bottom).

Click here

Window Buttons

Every time you open a window, whether at the desktop or in one of your programs, the taskbar sprouts a button bearing that window's name and icon. Buttons make it easy to switch between open programs and windows: Just click one to bring its associated window into the foreground, even if it has been minimized.

The taskbar is the antidote for COWS (Cluttered Overlapping Window Syndrome). In fact, if you work with a lot of windows, you'll run smack into one of the biggest and most visible changes in Windows XP: taskbar button *groups*.

In the old days, opening a lot of windows might produce the relatively useless display of truncated buttons, as illustrated in Figure 3-13. Not only are the buttons too narrow to read the names of the windows, but the buttons appear in chronological order, not software-program order.

The new Windows taskbar does two things that no Windows taskbar has done before. First, when conditions become crowded, it automatically groups the names of open windows into a single menu that sprouts from the corresponding program button, as shown at bottom in Figure 3-13. Click the taskbar button bearing the program's name to produce a pop-up menu of the window names. Now you can jump directly to the one you want.

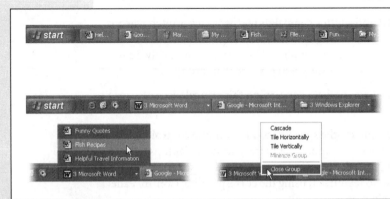

Figure 3-13:
Top: The old taskbar wasn't much help in managing a bunch of windows.

Middle: Nowadays, a crowded taskbar combines its buttons.

Bottom left: Click one of these button groups to see the list of windows it's concealing.
Bottom right: Right-click to operate on all windows at once.

Second, even when there is plenty of room, Windows XP aligns the buttons into horizontal groups *by program*. So you'll see all the Word-document buttons appear, followed by all the Excel-document buttons, and so on.

NOSTALGIA CORNER

Turning Off Notification Area Auto-Hiding

In general, the temporary removal of notification area icons you haven't used in a while is a noble ambition. Most of the time, you truly won't miss any invisible icons, and their absence will make the icons you *do* use stand out all the more.

Still, you can tell Windows to leave your tray alone—to leave every notification area icon in full view all the time. To do so, right-click a blank area of the taskbar; from the drop-down menu, choose Properties. At the bottom of the resulting dialog box, turn off the "Hide inactive icons" checkbox, and click OK.

If that seems a little drastic, don't miss the Customize button just to the right of that checkbox. It opens a list of every tray icon that would normally appear, if it weren't for Windows XP's efforts. Click in the Behavior column to produce a pop-up menu for each item. Choose the status you want for each individual tray icon: "Hide when inactive," "Always hide," and "Always show." Finally, click OK.

Despite these dramatic changes, most of the following time-honored basics still apply:

- To bring a window to the foreground, making it the active window, click its button on the taskbar. (If clicking a button doesn't bring a window forward, it's because Windows has combined several open windows into a single button. Just click the corresponding program's button as though it's a menu, and then choose the specific window you want from the resulting list, as shown in Figure 3-13.)

- To *hide* an active window that's before you on the screen, click its taskbar button—a great feature that a lot of PC fans miss. (To hide a background window, click its taskbar button *twice:* once to bring the window forward, again to hide it.)

- To minimize, maximize, restore, or close a window, even if you can't see it on the screen, right-click its button on the taskbar and choose the appropriate command from the shortcut menu (Figure 3-13, bottom). It's a real timesaver to close a window without first bringing it into the foreground. (You can still right-click a window's name when it appears in one of the consolidated taskbar menus described earlier.)

- To arrange all visible windows in an overlapping pattern as shown in Figure 3-14, right-click a blank spot on the taskbar and choose Cascade Windows from the shortcut menu.

- To arrange all non-minimized windows in neat little boxes, each getting an equal rectangular chunk of your screen, right-click a blank spot on the taskbar and choose Tile Windows Vertically or Tile Windows Horizontally from the shortcut menu.

Figure 3-14:
When you've cascaded your windows, click any title bar to bring its window to the foreground. After you've clicked a few title bars and worked in several windows, you'll need to choose Cascade Windows again to rearrange all your open windows. (By right-clicking a consolidated taskbar button, you can cascade only the windows of one program. If you want to cascade all windows of all programs, right-click a blank part of the taskbar.)

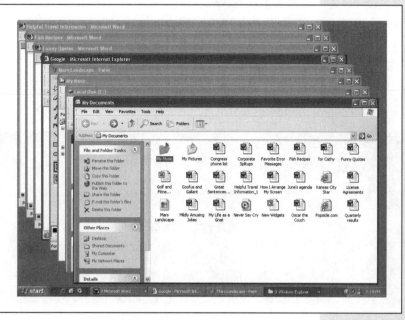

• To minimize all the windows in one fell swoop, right-click a blank spot on the taskbar and choose Show the Desktop from the shortcut menu—or just press the Windows logo key+D.

Tip: When the taskbar is crowded with buttons, it may not be easy to find a blank spot to click. Usually there's a little gap near the right end. You can make it easier to find some blank space by *enlarging* the taskbar, as described on the facing page.

• If you change your mind, the taskbar shortcut menu always includes an Undo command for the last taskbar command you invoked. (Its wording changes to reflect your most recent action—"Undo Minimize All," for example.)

• To close the windows from different programs all at once, Ctrl-click their taskbar buttons to select them. Then right-click the last one you clicked, and choose Close Group from the shortcut menu.

The Quick Launch Toolbar

At the left end of the taskbar—just to the right of the Start button—is a handful of tiny, unlabeled icons. This is the Quick Launch toolbar, one of the most useful features in Windows. See page 103 for details on this and other toolbars.

Customizing the Taskbar

You're not stuck with the taskbar exactly as it came from Microsoft. You can resize it, move it, or hide it completely. Most people don't bother, but it's always good to know what options you have.

Moving the taskbar

You can move the taskbar to the top of your monitor, or, if you're a true rebel, to either side.

To do so, first ensure that the toolbar isn't *locked* (which means that you can't move or resize the taskbar—or any of its toolbars, for that matter). Right-click a blank spot on the taskbar to produce the taskbar shortcut menu. If "Lock the taskbar" is checked, select it to make the checkmark disappear.

NOSTALGIA CORNER

Bringing Back the Old Taskbar

The new taskbar's tendency to consolidate the names of document windows into a single program button saves space, for sure.

Even so, it's not inconceivable that you might prefer the old system. For example, once Windows stacks the names of your documents, you no longer can bring a certain applica-

tion to the front just by clicking its taskbar button. (You must actually choose from its menu, which is a lot more effort.)

To make Windows XP display the taskbar the way it used to, right-click an empty area of the taskbar and choose Properties from the shortcut menu. Turn off the "Group similar taskbar buttons" checkbox and then click OK.

Now you can drag the taskbar to any edge of the screen, using any blank spot in the central section as a handle. Release the mouse when the taskbar leaps to the edge you've indicated with the cursor.

When the taskbar is on the left or right edge of the screen, Windows XP widens it automatically so that you can read the button names, which remain horizontal. (Ergonomic studies have indicated that keeping your neck bent at a 90 degree angle to read vertical buttons isn't so hot for your spine.)

Tip: No matter which edge of the screen holds your taskbar, your programs are generally smart enough to adjust their own windows as necessary. In other words, your Word document will shift sideways so that it doesn't overlap the taskbar that you've dragged to the side of the screen.

Resizing the taskbar

Even with the new button-grouping feature, the taskbar can still accumulate a lot of buttons and icons. As a result, you may want to enlarge the taskbar to see what's what.

Begin by making sure that the taskbar isn't locked, as described earlier. Then position your pointer on the inside edge of the taskbar (the edge closest to the desktop). When the pointer turns into a double-headed arrow, drag toward the desktop (to enlarge the taskbar) or toward the edge of your monitor (to minimize it).

Note: If you're resizing a taskbar that's on the top or bottom of the screen, the taskbar automatically changes its size in full taskbar-height increments. You can't fine-tune the height; you can only double or triple it, for example.

If it's on the left or right edge of your screen, however, you can resize the taskbar freely.

Hiding the taskbar

If you're working on a smallish monitor, you may wish that the taskbar would make itself scarce now and then—like when you're working on a word processing or Web page document that needs every pixel of space you can get.

Fortunately, it's easy to make the taskbar hide itself until you need it. Start by right-clicking a blank spot on the taskbar, and then choose Properties from the shortcut menu. The Taskbar and Start Menu Properties dialog box appears, offering these options:

- **Keep the taskbar on top of other windows.** This option—the factory setting—permits no other window to cover up the taskbar. Your program windows automatically shrink as necessary to accommodate the taskbar's screen bulk. (If you turn off this option, full-screen application windows overlap the taskbar.)

Tip: To open the taskbar when it's not visible, just press Ctrl+Esc, or press the Windows logo key on your keyboard.

• **Auto-hide the taskbar.** This feature makes the taskbar disappear whenever you're not using it—a clever way to devote your entire screen to application windows, and yet have the taskbar at your cursor tip when needed.

When this feature is turned on, the taskbar disappears whenever you click elsewhere, or whenever your cursor moves away from it. Only a thin blue line at the edge of the screen indicates that you have a taskbar at all. As soon as your pointer moves close to that line, the taskbar joyfully springs back into view.

Hiding the taskbar manually

When, on some random Tuesday, you decide to get the taskbar out of your hair *temporarily*—when reading a vast spreadsheet, for example—don't bother with the checkboxes described in the previous paragraphs. There's a quicker way to hide the taskbar: just drag it forcibly off the screen. Point to the inside edge of the taskbar, so that your cursor becomes a double-headed arrow, before dragging down.

Once again, a thin blue line represents the hidden edge. You can grab that line like a handle to pull the taskbar back onto the screen when you want it.

Taskbar Toolbars

Taskbar *toolbars* are separate, recessed-looking areas on the taskbar that offer special-function features. You can build your own toolbar, for example, stocked with documents related to a single project. (Somewhere in America, there's a self-help group for people who spend entirely too much time fiddling with this kind of thing.)

To make a toolbar appear or disappear, right-click a blank spot on the taskbar and choose from the Toolbars shortcut menu (Figure 3-15). The ones with checkmarks are visible now; select one to make the toolbar (and checkmark) disappear.

TROUBLESHOOTING MOMENT

Retrieving a Lost Hidden Taskbar

Sometimes, after manually hiding the taskbar (or going too far when you're trying to make it smaller), you can't get it back. The thin blue line disappears, or your mouse pointer won't turn into a double-headed arrow when you position it on the thin line. Here's how to fix the problem:

1. Press Ctrl+Esc. This keystroke selects the taskbar, even though you can't see it (although you can now see the Start menu).

2. Press Esc to make the Start menu disappear. (The taskbar is *still* selected, even though you can't see it.)

3. Press Alt+Space bar to bring up a shortcut menu.

4. Choose Size from the shortcut menu; this changes your mouse pointer into a four-sided shape. Don't click anything.

5. Press the arrow key that points toward the center of the screen (from the taskbar's perspective). As you do, the taskbar reappears.

6. Resize the taskbar very carefully to avoid repeating all of these steps.

Quick Launch Toolbar

The Quick Launch toolbar, once you've made it appear, is fantastically useful. In fact, in sheer convenience, it puts the Start menu to shame. It contains icons for functions that Microsoft assumes you'll use most often. They include:

- **Show Desktop**, a one-click way to minimize (hide) *all* the windows on your screen to make your desktop visible. Don't forget about this button the next time you need to burrow through some folders, put something in the Recycle Bin, or perform some other activity in your desktop folders. *Keyboard shortcut:* Windows key+D.

- **Launch Internet Explorer Browser**, for one-click access to the Web browser included with Windows XP.

- **Windows Media Player**, for one-click access to the music and movie player included with Windows XP (see Chapter 8).

The buttons detailed above are only hints of this toolbar's power, however. What makes it great is how easy it is to add your *own* icons—particularly those you use frequently. There's no faster or easier way to open them (no matter what mass of cluttered windows is on your screen), since the taskbar displays your favorite icons at all times.

To add an icon to this toolbar, simply drag it there, as shown in Figure 3-16. To remove an icon, just drag it off the toolbar—directly onto the Recycle Bin, if you

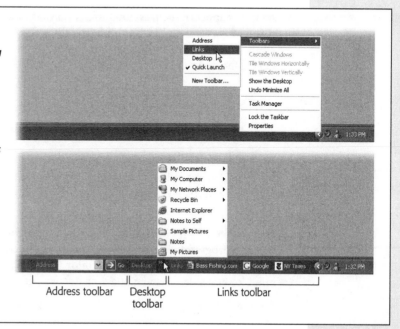

Figure 3-15:

Top: Make toolbars appear by right-clicking a blank area on the taskbar, if you can find one.

Bottom: Toolbars eat into your taskbar space, so use them sparingly. If you've added too many icons to the toolbar, a >> button appears at its right end. Click it to expose a list of the commands or icons that didn't fit.

Address toolbar   Desktop toolbar   Links toolbar

like. (You're not actually removing any software from your computer.) If you think you'll somehow survive without using Windows Media Player each day, for example, remove it from the Quick Launch toolbar.

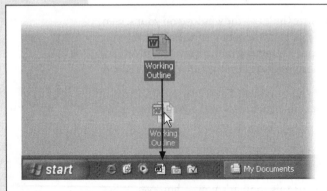

Figure 3-16:
You can add almost any kind of icon (an application, document file, disk, folder, Control Panel, or whatever) to the Quick Launch toolbar just by dragging it there (top); a thick vertical bar shows you where it'll appear. The only challenge is to find the folder that houses the icon you want to add. If it's an application, see page 67 for hints on finding the actual icon of the program in question.

Desktop Toolbar

The Desktop toolbar offers quick access to whichever icons are sitting on your desktop—Windows Media Player, Word, and so on. This toolbar also provides quick access to icons that used to appear automatically on previous versions of Windows: My computer, My Network Places, My Documents, Recycle Bin, and Internet Explorer.

When it first appears, the Desktop toolbar may take the form of a >> button at the right end of the taskbar. The button is actually a pop-up menu that lists your desktop stuff. This could be useful if your screen becomes filled with windows, thus obscuring the desktop.

Address Toolbar, Links Toolbar

These toolbars are exactly the same as the window toolbars described on page 91— except that they appear in the taskbar at all times, instead of in desktop windows.

Language Bar Toolbar

The floating Language bar, shown in Figure 3-17, automatically appears on your computer's desktop and in the Toolbars menu when you install either of two components:

- **Text services.** That's Microsoft's catch-all phrase for certain text-related add-on software programs: a second keyboard layout, handwriting recognition, speech recognition, or an Input Method Editor (IME), which is a system that lets you input for example, Asian language characters with a standard 101-key keyboard.

- **Another language.** As described in Appendix A, you can install multiple input languages on your computer and, using the Language bar, switch between them when the mood strikes. The language for the operating system doesn't change— only what characters appear onscreen when you type.

The buttons and options available on the Language bar depend on which text services you've installed and what application you're using. Microsoft Excel 2002 accepts speech recognition, for example, but Notepad doesn't.

Right-clicking the Language bar displays a shortcut menu where you can change its settings (see Figure 3-17). The shortcut menu lets you minimize the Language bar (Figure 3-17), make it transparent, shorten the bar by hiding its text labels, and so on. Only two of these options aren't self-explanatory:

- **Additional icons in taskbar.** When you minimize the Language bar, the taskbar shows only the icon for the language you're currently using (like EN for English, as shown in Figure 3-17.) If you'd like to run the Language bar minimized with all of the installed text-service icons at your disposal, turn on this option and then minimize. Now you can click the text-service icons on the taskbar.

- **Settings.** This option opens the Text Services and Input Languages dialog box, shown in Figure 3-17. In this dialog box, you select the installed input language you want to use when you boot up your computer, the text services that you prefer for each installed input language, and the Advanced keystroke settings for switching between input languages. For example, you can assign Left Alt+Shift+E to change to English (United States).

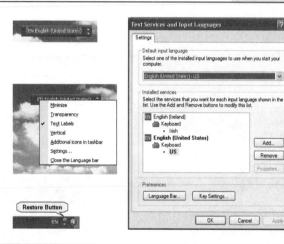

Figure 3-17:
Top left: The floating Language bar. Right-clicking this toolbar displays its shortcut menu.

Middle left: The shortcut menu for the Language bar lets you change Language bar settings, such as transparency, vertical (orientation), and minimize.

Bottom Left: When you minimize the Language bar, it shrinks down to the taskbar for easier access.

Right: The Text Services and Input Languages dialog box appears when you select Settings from the shortcut menu. Here you can change the current input language, set hot keys for language switching, and so on.

Redesigning Your Toolbars

To change the look of a toolbar, unlock the taskbar (using its shortcut menu), and then right-click any blank spot within the toolbar. (If the taskbar isn't unlocked, you won't see the toolbar's shortcut menu. When you're finished making changes to the toolbar, lock the taskbar again if you wish.)

Tip: How much horizontal taskbar space a toolbar consumes is up to you. Drag the perforated border at the left edge of a toolbar to make it wider or narrower. That's a good point to remember if, in fact, you can't *find* a blank spot to right-click.

The resulting shortcut menu offers these choices:

- **View** lets you change the size of the icons on the toolbar.

- **Open Folder** works only with the Quick Launch and Links toolbars (or toolbars you've created yourself). It opens a window that lists what's in the toolbar, so that you can delete or rename the icons. (Of course, you can also delete or rename any icon on these toolbars by right-clicking it and choosing Delete or Rename from the shortcut menu. But the Open Folder command is a better bet when you're

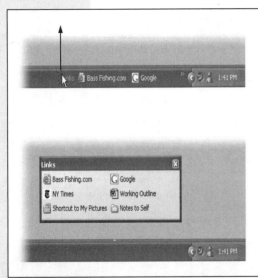

Figure 3-18:

To park a toolbar in a different location, drag upward on the "perforated" handle at the left edge (top). The result is a strange sort of floating toolbar (bottom); it's now an onscreen, perpetually available launcher. (Use tooltips, or choose Show Text from its shortcut menu, to identify the icons.) If you drag the toolbar to an edge of the screen, it glues itself there like a second taskbar.

FREQUENTLY ASKED QUESTION

The Not-So-Amazing Disappearing Toolbar

Hey, what's going on? I made a custom toolbar, and actually spent quite a lot of time on it. And then, when I needed more space on my taskbar, I right-clicked it and chose Close from the shortcut menu.

Now I want it back, but when I right-click a blank area on the taskbar and choose Toolbars, my custom toolbar isn't listed there! How do I get it back?

You've discovered an unfortunate little quirk of custom

toolbars: they don't really exist. All you've done is add a folder listing to your taskbar, as fleeting as the morning dew. If you close a custom toolbar, it no longer appears on that shortcut menu; it's gone forever.

The folder from which you created it, however, is still hanging around. To get the toolbar back, you need to create it all over again (as described in this section)—but at least you don't have to create its folder from scratch.

---

performing more extensive surgery on the toolbar, since you're able to work in a window that isn't nearly as claustrophobic as the toolbar itself.)

• **Show Text** identifies each toolbar icon with a text label.

• **Show Title** makes the toolbar's name (such as "Quick Launch" or "Desktop") appear on the toolbar.

• **Close Toolbar** makes the toolbar disappear.

• **Always on Top** and **Auto-Hide** appear on a toolbar's shortcut menu *only* when you've detached the toolbar, turning it into a floating palette as described in the next section. They make any toolbar as flexible as the taskbar, at least when it comes to hiding itself on cue.

If you turn on Always on Top, then document windows can't cover up your tool-bar. And if you turn on Auto-Hide, a toolbar that you've attached to one edge of your screen hides almost completely, until you point to it with your cursor.

Figure 3-19:
The major folders of your computer are displayed in the New Toolbar dialog box. Click the + sign to expand a disk or folder—and continue to expand disks and folders—until you find the folder you're seeking. Or you can create a new folder for your toolbar anywhere on the hard drive.

Moving toolbars

You don't need to keep toolbars on the taskbar; you can move them to any spot on the screen that you find handy, as shown in Figure 3-18. (The taskbar must first be unlocked, as described on page 100.) To return the toolbar to its original location, drag its title bar back onto the taskbar.

Creating toolbars

The Quick Launch area of the taskbar is such a delight that you may actually de-velop a syndrome called Quick Launch Envy—you'll find that having only one isn't enough. You might wish to create several different Quick Launch toolbars, each stocked with the icons for a different project or person. One could contain icons for all the chapters of a book you're writing; another could list only your games.

Fortunately, it's easy to create as many different custom toolbars as you like, each of which behaves exactly like the Quick Launch toolbar.

The short way

Windows XP creates toolbars from *folders;* so before creating a toolbar of your own, you must create a folder (unless you already have a folder that's filled with the stuff you want to toolbarize).

Here's the easiest way to turn a folder into a toolbar: Just drag the folder icon until your cursor strikes the edge of your monitor (any edge except the one where the taskbar is). When you let go, you'll see a brand-new toolbar whose buttons list the contents of the folder you just dragged. From here, it behaves just like any other toolbar. You can right-click it to make the icons smaller, you can drag it into the center of the screen to make it a floating palette, and so on.

The long way

The drag-and-drop method is new to Windows XP. The old way is still around, however, for people who bill by the hour.

To begin, right-click a blank spot on the taskbar. From the shortcut menu, choose Toolbars→New Toolbar to open the New Toolbar dialog box, as shown in Figure 3-19. Find and click the folder you want, and then click OK.

Your new toolbar is on the taskbar. Feel free to tailor it as described in the previous discussions—by changing its icon sizes, hiding or showing the icon labels, or adding new icons to it by dragging them from other desktop windows.

TROUBLESHOOTING MOMENT

The Disappearing Language Toolbar

Did you turn the Language bar off, and now can't get it back?

You've probably changed an important option ("Turn off advanced text services") at the Control Panel level.

To check this option, choose Start→Control Panel, and then (in Classic view) opening the Regional and Language Options icon. Click the Languages tab, and then click Details. The Text Services and Input Languages dialog box appears.

On the Settings tab, you'll probably see that the Language Bar button is dimmed, preventing you from turning on the Language bar and making changes to it.

To make the Language bar available, click the Advanced tab. In the System Configuration section, turn off "Turn off advanced text services" and then click Apply. You've just undone the damage.

Click the Settings tab and then the Language Bar button to ensure that the "Show the Language bar on the desktop" checkbox is selected, and then click OK. The Language bar should once again appear on your desktop and in the Toolbars shortcut menu.

Organizing Your Stuff

Every disk, folder, file, application, printer, and networked computer is represented on your screen by an icon. To avoid spraying your screen with thousands of overlapping icons seething like snakes in a pit, Windows organizes icons into folders, puts those folders into *other* folders, and so on.

This folder-in-a-folder-in-a-folder scheme works beautifully at reducing screen clutter, but it means that you've got some hunting to do whenever you want to open a particular icon.

Helping you navigate and manage your files, folders, and disks with less stress and greater speed was one of the primary design goals of Windows—and of this chapter.

Tip: To create a new folder to hold your icons, right-click where you want the folder to appear (on the desktop, or in any desktop window except My Computer), and choose New→Folder from the shortcut menu. The new folder appears with its temporary "New Folder" name highlighted. Type a new name for the folder and then press Enter.

UP TO SPEED

Directories vs. Folders

Before Windows took over the universe, folders were called *directories*, and folders inside them were called *subdirectories*. Keep that in mind the next time you're reading an old user guide, magazine article, or computer book.

The Folders of Windows XP

The top-level, all-encompassing, mother-ship window of your PC is the My Computer window. From within this window, you have access to every disk, folder, and file on your computer. Its slogan might well be: "If it's not in here, it's not on your PC."

To see it, choose Start→My Computer, or double-click its icon on the desktop, if you've put it there (page 27). (And if it is on your desktop, remember that you can rename it something that's a little more, well, dignified, by clicking it and then pressing the F2 key.)

No matter how you open the My Computer window (Figure 4-1), you generally see several categories of icons:

Figure 4-1:
Top: The My Computer window, shown here on a corporate-network PC, is the starting point for any folder-digging you want to do. It shows the disk drives of your PC. If you double-click the icon of a removable-disk drive (like your CD-ROM drive, Zip drive, or Jaz drive), you receive only an error message unless there's actually a disk in the drive.

Bottom: The My Computer window on a workgroup computer (that is, not part of a corporate domain network) includes all the perks included on a network computer with the added advantage of the "Files on This Computer" category.

- **Hard Disk Drives.** These icons, of course, represent your PC's hard drive (or drives, if you've installed or attached additional ones). Most people, most of the time, are most concerned with the Local Disk (C:), which represents the internal hard drive preinstalled in your computer. (You're welcome to rename this icon, by the way, just as you would any icon.)

- **Files on This Computer.** This category appears only if your computer is a member of a *workgroup*, not if it's part of a domain network (see page 23). These folders, which bear the names of people with accounts on that PC (page 497), store links to all files and preferences for each person.

- **Devices with Removable Storage.** Here, Windows is talking about your floppy drive, CD or DVD drive, Zip drive, and so on.

Tip: Ordinarily, if your name is, say, Chris, you're not allowed to open the Frank's Documents folder; if you've been given a *Limited* XP account (page 501), then double-clicking it produces only an error message. That's the Windows XP security system at work.

But My Computer also contains a folder called Shared Documents. This folder is like the community bulletin board, in that everybody who uses this PC is free to deposit things, take things out, and read whatever resides there. See Chapter 20 for details.

- **Scanners and Cameras.** This is where you see the icons for any digital cameras or scanners you've installed.

- **Other.** You may also see a Control Panel icon here—if, for example, you added it as directed on page 91.

What's in the Local Disk (C:) Window

You might be surprised to learn that your main hard drive window doesn't actually contain anything much that's useful to you, the PC's human companion. It's organized primarily for Windows' own benefit.

If you double-click the Local Disk C: icon in My Computer—that is, your primary hard drive's icon—a direly worded message lets you know that these files are hidden. "This folder contains files that keep your system working properly," it says. "You should not modify its contents." (Figure 4-2 shows a similar message.)

All of this important-sounding prose is aimed at the kind of person who, before the invention of this warning message, fearlessly or naïvely cruised through the important system files of their PCs, deleting and moving files until the computer was inoperable (and then calling Microsoft for tech support).

Truth is, the C: drive also contains a lot of stuff that *doesn't* belong to Windows—including your files. So when you're just looking (but not touching) the Windows system files, or when you want to burrow around in your own folders, it's perfectly OK to click the "Show the contents of this folder" link. Suddenly the C: drive's formerly invisible contents appear. They include these standard folders:

Documents and Settings

Windows XP has been designed from the ground up for *computer sharing*. It's ideal for any situation where different family members, students, or workers share the same machine.

In fact, in Windows XP, each person who uses the computer will turn on the machine to find his own secure set of files, folders, desktop pictures, Web bookmarks, font collections, and preference settings. (Secure, at least, from other people who don't have *administrative* accounts. Much more about this feature in Chapter 17.)

Like it or not, Windows considers you one of these people. If you're the only one who uses this PC, fine—you can simply ignore the sharing features. But in its little software head, Windows XP still considers you an account holder, and stands ready to accommodate any others who should come along.

In any case, now you should see the importance of the Documents and Settings folder. Inside are folders named for the different people who use this PC. In general, Limited account holders (page 509) aren't allowed to open anybody else's folder.

If you're the sole proprietor of the machine, there's only one account folder here—and it's named for you, of course. If not, there's a folder here for each person who has an account on this PC. (As noted above, if your PC isn't part of a corporate domain network, icons for these folders also appear in the My Computer window. Those are only pointers to the *real* folders, which are here in Documents and Settings.)

This is only the first of many examples in which Windows imposes a fairly rigid folder structure, but this approach has its advantages. By keeping such tight control over which files go where, Windows XP keeps itself pure—and very stable. Furthermore, keeping all of your stuff in a single folder will make it very easy to back up your work.

Program Files

This folder contains all of your applications—Word, Excel, Internet Explorer, your games, and so on. But that isn't the impression you get when you first open the folder (Figure 4-2).

Fortunately, making them appear on your screen is easy enough: Simply click the words "Show the contents of this folder." They appear just below the "These files are hidden" message, and also in the task pane. (The Local Disk (C:) drive window works the same way.)

This peculiar behavior requires some explanation. A Windows program isn't a single, self-contained icon. Instead, each is accompanied by a phalanx of support files and folders like the ones shown in Figure 4-2. Nestled among all of these auxiliary files is the actual application icon, which can't even run if it's separated from its support group.

As mentioned previously, Microsoft and other software companies grew weary of taking tech-support calls from people whose programs stopped working after being moved around. Finally, as a preemptive strike, Microsoft simply made them invisible. The "These files are hidden" message is meant to say: "Nothing to see here, folks. Move along."

So how are you supposed to launch your programs if you can't see them in the Program Files folder? Just take your pick of a half-dozen ways, all of which are described in the beginning of Chapter 6.

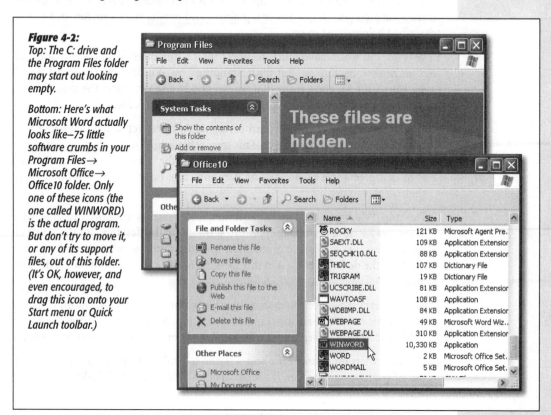

Figure 4-2:
Top: The C: drive and the Program Files folder may start out looking empty.

Bottom: Here's what Microsoft Word actually looks like—75 little software crumbs in your Program Files→ Microsoft Office→ Office10 folder. Only one of these icons (the one called WINWORD) is the actual program. But don't try to move it, or any of its support files, out of this folder. (It's OK, however, and even encouraged, to drag this icon onto your Start menu or Quick Launch toolbar.)

Windows or WINNT

Here's another folder that Microsoft wishes its customers would simply ignore. This most hallowed folder contains Windows itself, the thousands of little files that make Windows, well, Windows. Most of these folders and files have cryptic names that appeal to cryptic people.

Note: This folder is usually called Windows; however, it's called WINNT if you upgraded your operating system from Windows 2000. In the remaining pages of this book, let the term "Windows folder" refer to "the folder called Windows or WINNT, depending on whether or not you upgraded your machine from Windows 2000."

In general, the healthiest PC is one whose Windows folder has been left alone. (One exception: The Fonts folder contains the icons that represent the various typefaces installed on your machine. You're free to add or remove icons from this folder.)

Your Account Folder

Everything that makes your Windows XP experience your own sits inside the Local Disk (C:)→Documents and Settings→[Your Name] folder. This is where Windows stores your preferences, documents, pictures and music, Web favorites and *cookies* (described below), and so on.

In general, you won't have much business interacting directly with this folder, except perhaps to back it up. But understanding how Windows works—and how it keeps your stuff separate from that of everybody else who uses the machine—is much easier once you've had a tour of your own account folder.

- **Cookies.** A cookie is a small (and controversial) preference file that some Web sites deposit on your hard drive. This special file is how sites recognize you when you visit them again. A cookie is responsible for the "Hello, [Your Name]!" message that greets you when visiting Amazon.com, for example. Windows keeps them in this folder.

- **Desktop.** When you drag an icon out of a folder or disk window and onto your Windows XP desktop, it may *appear* to show up on the desktop. But that's just an optical illusion—a visual convenience. In truth, nothing in Windows XP is ever *really* on the desktop; it's just in this Desktop *folder,* and mirrored on the desktop area.

  Remember that everyone who shares your machine will, upon logging on (Chapter 17), see his own stuff sitting out on the desktop. Now you know how Windows XP does it: There's a separate Desktop folder in every person's account folder.

  You can entertain yourself for hours trying to prove this. If you drag something out of your Desktop folder, it also disappears from the actual desktop. And vice versa.

- **Favorites.** See page 642 for a definition of favorites. For now, it's enough to note that this folder stores shortcuts of the files, folders, and other items you designated as favorites. This information can be handy if you want to delete a bunch of your favorites all at once, rename them, and so on.

Tip: This folder may also contain a Links folder. It's the folder representation of the Links toolbar described on page 95.

- **My Documents.** Windows XP makes it look like you're setting up your nest (your documents, photos, music files, and so on) in the My Documents folder—the one that opens when you choose Start→My Documents. And whenever you save a new document (when you're working in Word, for example), the Save dialog box proposes storing the new file in this folder.

Behind the scenes, however, My Documents is actually just one of several folders in your own account folder. It's a good idea to back this one up periodically.

- **Start menu.** This folder is the true home for the icons whose names appear in your Start menu. By renaming, deleting, or adding to the contents of this folder, you can quickly and easily reorganize your Start menu.

Your account folder actually holds much more than this, but the rest of the folders are hidden, reserved for use by Windows itself. The hidden folders include: Application Data (which your programs may use to store user-specific settings and files), Local Settings (Internet Explorer's history list and cache file, for example), NetHood (shortcuts for the icons in your My Network Places window), My Recent Documents (document shortcuts, the ones that show up in the optional My Recent Documents submenu of the Start menu), and SendTo, which is described later in this chapter.

Navigating My Computer

Most of the time, you can get where you're going on your computer using the commands, programs, and folders listed in the Start menu. But when you need to find something that isn't listed there—when you need to burrow manually through the labyrinth of folders on the machine—Windows offers two key methods of undertaking a folder quest.

First, you can open the My Computer window, as described at the beginning of this chapter. From there, you double-click one folder after another, burrowing ever deeper into the folders-within-folders.

NOSTALGIA CORNER

Turning Off Simple Folder View

When it set about creating Windows XP, Microsoft left no stone unturned in its reevaluation of every existing Windows feature—and Windows Explorer is no exception.

You may have noticed, for example, that vertical dotted lines no longer indicate how deeply you've burrowed in your "tree" of folders within folders, as shown at left in Figure 4-3.

There's an even more important change, too. When you click a *folder icon* (not its + button) on the left side of an Explorer window, Windows expands that folder's listing *and* instantly closes whichever folder you previously expanded. In other words, it's much harder to get lost in the navigation of your folder tree by expanding the listings of too many folders within folders.

But if you really want to open two different "branches" (subfolders) of your folder tree simultaneously—to compare the contents of two folders simultaneously, for example—the process is easy enough: Just click the little + symbols beside folder names instead of clicking the folder names themselves. When you click the + buttons, Explorer works exactly as it did in previous versions, leaving open the listings for the subfolders you've already opened.

That still doesn't bring back the dotted lines, however. If you really prefer the old Explorer in all regards, choose Tools→Folder Options→View Tab in any open folder window. Turn off "Display simple folder view in Explorer's Folders list," and click OK. Now Explorer looks exactly as it did in previous Windows versions.

Tip: As you navigate your folders, keep in mind the power of the Backspace key. Each time you press it, you jump to the *parent* window of the one you're now looking at–the one that contains the previous folder. For example, if you're perusing the My Pictures folder inside My Documents, pressing Backspace opens the My Documents window.

Likewise, the Alt key, pressed with the right and left arrow keys, serves as a Back and Forward button. Use this powerful shortcut (instead of clicking the corresponding buttons on the Standard toolbar) to "walk" backward or forward through the list of windows most recently opened.

Navigating with Windows Explorer

The second method of navigating the folders on your PC is called Windows Explorer—for long-time Windows veterans, a familiar sight. (Note that some people use the term "Windows Explorer" to refer to everyday folder windows. In this book, the term refers exclusively to the split-window view shown in Figure 4-3.)

Using this method, you work in a single window that shows every folder on the machine at once. As a result, you're less likely to lose your bearings using Windows Explorer than burrowing through folder after folder, as described above.

You can jump into Explorer view using any of these methods:

- Shift–double-click any disk or folder icon.

- Right-click a disk or folder icon (even if it's in the Start menu) and choose Explore from the shortcut menu.

- Click Folders on the Standard toolbar.

- Choose View→Explorer Bar→Folders.

- Choose Start→All Programs→Accessories→Windows Explorer.

- Choose Start→Run, type *explorer,* and then press Enter.

No matter which method you use, the result is a window like the one shown in Figure 4-3.

As you can see, this hierarchical display splits the window into two panes. The left pane displays *only* disks and folders. The right pane displays the contents (folders *and* files) of any disk or folder you click. You can manipulate the icons on either side much as you would any other icons. For example, double-click one to open it, drag it to the Recycle Bin to delete it, or drag it into another folder in the folder list to move it elsewhere on your machine.

This arrangement makes it very easy to move files and folders around on your hard drive. First, make the right pane display the icon you want to move. Then, set up the left pane so that you can see the destination folder or disk—and drag the right-side icon from one side to the other.

When the panel is too narrow

As shown in Figure 4-3, expanding a folder provides a new indented list of folders inside it. If you expand folders within folders to a sufficient level, the indentation may push the folder names so far to the right that you can't read them. You can remedy this problem with any of the following actions:

• Adjust the relative sizes of the window halves by dragging the vertical bar between them.

• Position your mouse pointer over a folder whose name is being chopped off. A tooltip balloon appears to display the full name of the folder.

• Use the horizontal scroll bar at the bottom of the left pane to shift the contents.

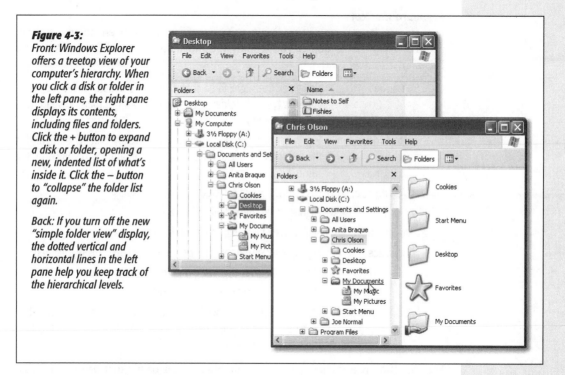

Figure 4-3:
Front: Windows Explorer offers a treetop view of your computer's hierarchy. When you click a disk or folder in the left pane, the right pane displays its contents, including files and folders. Click the + button to expand a disk or folder, opening a new, indented list of what's inside it. Click the – button to "collapse" the folder list again.

Back: If you turn off the new "simple folder view" display, the dotted vertical and horizontal lines in the left pane help you keep track of the hierarchical levels.

Viewing folder contents

To see what's in one of the disks or folders listed at the left side of the Explorer window, you can use any of these techniques. (See the box on page 115 for details on simple folder view.)

• *With simple folder view turned on:* In the left pane, click the icon, name, or + button of a disk or folder. The branch of your folder tree expands in the left pane, while the right pane displays its contents.

- *With simple folder view turned off:* In the left pane, click a folder or disk; the contents appear in the right pane. To expand the listing for a disk or folder, double-click its name, double-click its icon, or single-click the + button beside it.

- Right-click a folder in the left pane and select Open from the shortcut menu. A new window opens, displaying the contents of the folder you clicked. (To open a *program or document* appearing in either side of the window, double-click it as usual.)

The right-side pane of the Explorer window behaves exactly like any folder window. Don't forget that you can change it to an icon view or list view, for example, using the View menu as usual.

Keyboard shortcuts

If you arrive home one day to discover that your mouse has been stolen, or if you just like using the keyboard, you'll enjoy the shortcuts that work in the Windows Explorer window:

left arrow	Collapses the highlighted folder, or if it's already collapsed, highlights its "parent" folder. (The + key on your numeric keypad does the same thing.)
right arrow	Expands a highlighted folder, or if it's already expanded, highlights the first folder inside it. (The – key on your numeric keypad does the same thing.)
* (on number pad)	Displays *all* of the selected folder's subfolders.
F6 or Tab	Highlights the other half of the window.
Alt+left arrow	Highlights whichever folder you last highlighted.
Backspace	Highlights the "parent" disk or folder of whatever is highlighted.
Ctrl+Z	Undoes whatever you just did in this Explorer window.
Home, End	Highlights first or last icon in the folder list.
A, B, C…	Highlights the first visible file or folder in the left-pane hierarchy that matches the letter you typed. Type the same letter again to highlight the *next* matching icon.

You can also press the letter keys to highlight a folder or file that begins with that letter, or the up and down arrow keys to "walk" up and down the list.

Life with Icons

Both of the navigational schemes described so far in this chapter have only one goal in life: to help you manage your icons. You could spend your entire workday just mastering the techniques of naming, copying, moving, and deleting these icons—and plenty of people do.

Here's the crash course.

Renaming Your Icons

To rename a file, folder, printer, or disk icon, you need to open up its *renaming rectangle*. You can do so with any of the following methods:

- Highlight the icon and then press the F2 key at the top of your keyboard.

- Click carefully, just once, on a previously highlighted icon's name.

- Right-click the icon and choose Rename from the shortcut menu.

Tip: You can even rename your hard drive, so that you don't go your entire career with a drive named "Local Disk." Just rename its icon (in the My Computer window) as you would any other. You're not allowed to rename important system folders like Documents and Settings, Recycle Bin, Windows, WINNT, and System32, however.

In any case, once the renaming rectangle has appeared around the current name, simply type the new name you want, and then press Enter. Feel free to use all the standard text-editing tricks while you're typing: Press Backspace to fix a typo, press the left and right arrow keys to position the insertion point, and so on. When you're

---

POWER USERS' CLINIC

Long Names and DOS Names

Windows XP permits long filenames, but DOS—the ancient operating system that used to lurk beneath Windows—doesn't.

PC pros refer to the folder DOS naming system as the "eight dot three" system, because the actual name of the folder or file can't be any longer than eight characters, and it requires a file suffix that's up to three letters long. To accommodate DOS rules, Windows XP creates an 8.3 version of every long filename. As a result, every file on your computer actually has two *different* names—a long one and a short one.

Every now and then, you'll run up against DOS filename limitations. For example, this quirk explains why the actual name of an application is a cryptic, shortened form of its full name (WINWORD instead of Microsoft Word, for example).

Windows creates the shortened version by inserting the tilde character (~), followed by sequential numbers, after the sixth character of the filename—plus the original extension. For example, the *My Documents* folder shows up as *My Docu~1* when you view it in a DOS window. If you

name a file *letter to mom.doc,* it appears in DOS as *letter~1.doc.* If you then name a file *letter to dad.doc,* it appears in DOS as *letter~2.doc,* and so on.

This naming convention only becomes important if you work in DOS, or you exchange files with someone who uses Windows 3.1 or DOS.

Even when working in DOS, however, you can still use the long filenames of Windows XP if you wish. The trick is to enclose the names in quotation marks. For example, if you want to see what's in the My Documents folder, type *cd\"my documents" (cd* is the command to change folders). (You also need quotation marks if there's a space in the file or folder's name.)

To copy, delete, or rename files from the DOS command line, just use the same trick. (Renaming files is usually much easier in DOS than in Windows because you can change batches of files at once.) When you enter the *dir* command, you see *both* the DOS filename and the long filename, thus making it easy to use either the 8.3 or long filename (using quotes, of course).

---

finished editing the name, press Enter to make it stick. (If another icon in the folder has the same name, Windows beeps and makes you choose another name.)

A folder or file name can be up to 255 characters long, including spaces and the *filename extension* (the three-letter suffix that identifies the file type). Because they're reserved for behind-the-scenes use, Windows doesn't let you use any of these symbols in a folder or filename: \ / : * ? " < > |

Tip: If you highlight a bunch of icons at once and then open the renaming rectangle for any *one* of them, you wind up renaming *all* of them. For example, if you've highlighted folders called Cats, Dogs, and Fish, renaming one of them *Animals* changes the original names to Animals (1), Animals (2), and Animals (3).

If this new Windows XP feature hits you unexpectedly, press Ctrl+Z repeatedly until you've restored all the original names.

If you like, you can give more than one file or folder the same name, as long as they're not in the same folder. For example, you can have as many files named "Letter to Smith" as you wish, as long as each is in a different folder.

Note: Windows XP comes factory set not to show you filename extensions. That's why you sometimes might *think* you see two different files called, say, Quarterly Sales, both in the same folder.

The explanation is that one filename may end with *.doc* (a Word document), and the other may end with *.xls* (an Excel document). But because these suffixes are hidden (page 173), the files look like they have exactly the same name.

Icon Properties

As you may have read in Chapter 1, *properties* are a big deal in Windows. Properties are preference settings that you can change independently for every icon on your machine.

To view the Properties dialog box for an icon, choose from these techniques:

- Right-click the icon; choose Properties from the shortcut menu.

- While pressing Alt, double-click the icon.

- Highlight the icon; press Alt+Enter.

These settings aren't the same for every kind of icon, however. Here's what you can expect when opening the Properties dialog boxes of various icons (see Figure 4-4).

My Computer

This Properties dialog box is packed with useful information about your machine.

- The **General** tab tells you what kind of processor is inside, how much memory (RAM) your PC has, and what version of Windows you've got.

- The **Hardware** tab (shown in Figure 4-4) includes a link to the Device Manager, which breaks down your equipment even more specifically—it provides the manufacturer and model name of each component on your machine (modem, monitor, mouse, and so on).

- The **Computer Name** tab is where you set up your computer's name, as it will appear to other people on an office network.

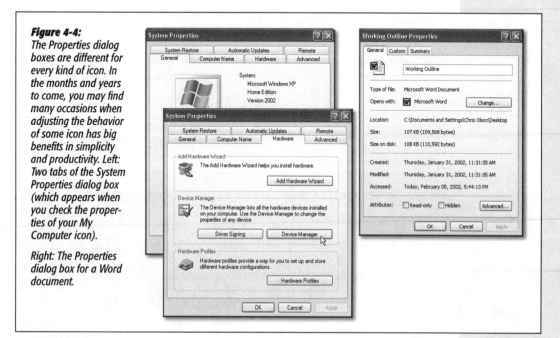

Figure 4-4:
The Properties dialog boxes are different for every kind of icon. In the months and years to come, you may find many occasions when adjusting the behavior of some icon has big benefits in simplicity and productivity. Left: Two tabs of the System Properties dialog box (which appears when you check the properties of your My Computer icon).

Right: The Properties dialog box for a Word document.

- The **Advanced** tab offers buttons that serve as rabbit holes into ever more technical dialog boxes. They include **Performance** (see the box on page 122), **User Profiles** (see page 525), and **Startup and Recovery** (advanced controls related to dual-booting [page 620] and what happens when the system crashes).

Tip: One button on the Advanced tab is actually not advanced at all—the Error Reporting button. You may have noticed that whenever a program crashes, freezes, or abruptly quits, Windows XP offers to email a report of the event to Microsoft for the benefit of its debugging teams. Using the Error Reporting dialog box, you can turn off this frequent attempt to contact the mother ship—or limit the attempts to certain programs.

- See page 457 for details on the **System Restore** tab, page 300 for information on **Automatic Updates**, and page 143 for details on the **Remote** tab.

Disks

In a disk's Properties dialog box, you can see all kinds of information about the disk itself:

- **General.** This tab shows you the disk's name (which you can change), its capacity (which you can't change), and how much of it is full.

- **Tools.** Offers quick access to such disk-maintenance tools as ScanDisk and Defrag (see Chapter 16).

- **Hardware.** Lists the individual drives—hard drives, CD drives, and so on—connected to your machine, complete with troubleshooting and Properties buttons.

- **Sharing.** Controls who can access the disk, in person or by network (Chapter 20).

- **Security.** Not only can you share certain folders or files with other people (either across a network or when they log into your PC using their own accounts), but you can also specify exactly who is allowed how much access to each file or folder. More about security in Chapter 17.

Note: If you don't see the Security tab, it's probably because *simple file sharing* is turned on (see page 574). If you turn it off, the Security tab reappears (*if* you've formatted your hard drive using the NTFS file system, as described on page 620).

GEM IN THE ROUGH

Performance Options

It's a funny quirk of people in the computer industry that they can't bring themselves to use English. They say *form factor* when they means size, *the user* when they mean you, and *price point* when they mean price.

As the System Properties dialog box illustrates, they also say *performance* when they mean speed.

For example, if you click the Advanced tab and then the Setting button in the Performance section of the box, you get to the Visual Effects tab of the Performance Options dialog box. It offers a long list of checkboxes that control the little animations and visual accents that define the more modern look and feel of Windows XP. For example, "Animate windows when minimizing and maximizing" makes Windows animate the shrinking of a window onto the taskbar when you minimize it. "Show shadows under mouse pointer" produces a tiny shadow beneath your cursor, as though it were floating a quarter-inch above the

surface of your screen.

All these little animations and shadows look cool, but each saps away a tiny scrap of speed and power from your processor. Using this dialog box, you can turn off the checkboxes of features you can do without. Turning all of them off often produces a PC that feels snappier and more responsive, although a bit less Macintosh-esque. (Leave "Use visual styles on windows and buttons" turned on, however, if you like the new, softened look of Windows XP.)

The Advanced tab of this dialog box is a far less casual business. It controls how Windows XP uses your processor power and memory, and provides a button that opens the Virtual Memory control center for your machine. These are extremely technical settings that you should adjust only with the guidance of a licensed geek.

- **Quota.** If different people use this PC, each with a different account, you can limit the amount of disk space each person is allowed to use. Details are on page 454.

Data files

The Properties for a plain old document depend on what kind of document it is. You always see a General tab, but other tabs may also appear (especially for Microsoft Office files).

- **General.** This screen offers all the obvious information about the document— location, size, modification date, the program that opens the document (which you can change with a click of the Change button), and so on—along with a few interesting-looking checkboxes. For example, the **read-only** checkbox locks the document. In the read-only state, you can open the document and read it, but you can't make any changes to it.

Note: If you make a *folder* read-only, it affects only the files already inside. If you add additional files later, they remain editable.

Hidden turns the icon invisible. (It's a great way to prevent something from being deleted. Of course, because the icon becomes invisible, you may find it a bit difficult to open it *yourself,* unless you've turned off "Do not show hidden files and folders" in the Folder Options dialog box, as described on page 89.)

The Advanced button offers a few additional options. **File is ready for archiving** means, "Back me up." This message is intended for the Backup program described in Chapter 16, and indicates that this document has been changed since the last time it was backed up (or that it's never been backed up). **For fast searching, allow Indexing Service to index this file** lets you indicate that this file should, or should not, be part of the quick-search database created by Indexing Service (described on page 54). **Compress contents to save disk space** and **Encrypt contents to secure data** are both described later in Chapter 15.

- **Security.** The Security tab shows who's allowed to open this file or folder and how much freedom they have to mess with its contents (Chapter 17). You can use this tab to delete or add groups, users, or permission.

- **Custom.** As explained below, the Properties window of Office documents includes a Summary tab that lets you look up a document's word count, author, revision number, and many other statistics. But you should by no means feel limited to these 21 properties—nor to Office documents.

Using the Custom tab, you can create properties of your own—Working Title, Panic Level, Privacy Quotient, or whatever you like. Just type the property name into the Name text box (or choose one of the canned options in the Type drop-down menu) and then click Add. You can then fill in the Value text box for the individual file in question (so that its Panic Level is Red Alert, for example). Especially technical people can later use Indexing Service (see page 54) to perform query-language searches for these values.

- The **Summary** tab tells you how many words, lines, and paragraphs are in a particular Word document. For a graphics document, the Summary tab indicates the graphic's dimensions, resolution, and color settings.

Folders

The Properties boxes for folders reveal the same checkbox options as found for data files. But now there's a separate tab called **Sharing,** which makes the folder susceptible to invasion by other people—either in person, when they log into this machine, or from across your office network (see Chapters 18 and 20).

Program files

There's not much here that you can change yourself, but you certainly get a lot to look at. For starters, there are the General, Security, and Summary tabs described earlier. But wait—that's not all:

- **Version.** This tab offers a considerable wealth of detail about the program's version number, corporate parent, language, and so on.

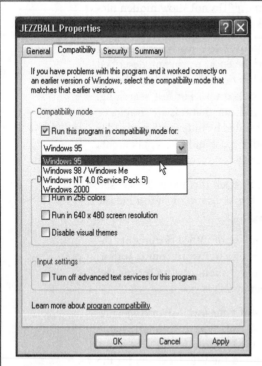

Figure 4-5:
By turning on "Run this program in compatibility mode for" and choosing the name of a previous version of Windows from the drop-down list, you can fool that program into thinking that it's running on Windows 95, Windows Me, Windows NT, or whatever. While you're at it, you can also specify that this program switch your screen to certain settings required by older games–256 colors, 640 x 480 pixel resolution, and so on–or without the new Windows XP look (turn on "Disable visual themes").

- **Compatibility.** There may come a day when you're more grateful for this tab than just about any other new Windows XP feature. The idea is to provide you with a way out of an uncomfortable situation. An example might be when you try to run a pre-2002 program on Windows XP, and (because it's never heard of Windows XP) it doesn't work right, or doesn't work at all. Figure 4-5 illustrates the magic in action.

Shortcuts

You can read about these useful controls later in this chapter.

Changing Your Icons' Icons

You can change the inch-tall illustrations that represent the little icons replete in your electronic world. You can't, however, pick a single method to do so, because Microsoft has divided up the controls among three different locations.

For example, one approach is to change the icon used by *all* files of a certain type. If you're French, for example, you might want to change the big W on a Word document to a big M (for *Mot*). Instructions appear on page 177.

You can also change the icon for some of the important Windows desktop icons: the Recycle Bin, My Documents, and so on. Open the Display program in the Control Panel (see Chapter 9), click the Desktop tab, then click Customize Desktop. You'll see a sliding collection of those important Windows icons. Click one, and then click Change Icon to choose a replacement from a collection Microsoft provides. (You haven't *lived* until you've made your Recycle Bin look like a green, growing tree.)

Finally, if you're sneaky, you can replace the icons for individual folder and shortcut icons on your PC. Here's how:

1. **Right-click the folder or shortcut whose icon you want to change. From the short-cut menu, choose Properties.**

   The Properties dialog box appears.

2. **Click the Customize tab (for a folder) or the Shortcut tab (for a shortcut). At the bottom of the dialog box, click the Change Icon button.**

   Yet another dialog box, filled with prefab replacement icons, appears. If you see one that suits your fancy, click it; otherwise, continue.

3. **Click Browse.**

   Windows XP now lets you hunt for icons on your hard drive. These can be icons that you've downloaded from the Internet, icons embedded inside program files and .dll files, or icons that you've made yourself using a freeware or shareware icon-making program like AX-Icons (available at *www.missingmanuals.com*, among other places).

4. **Click OK twice.**

   You should see your new replacement icon happily in place.

Copying and Moving Folders and Files

Windows XP offers two different techniques for moving files and folders from one place to another: dragging them, and using the Copy and Paste commands.

Whichever method you choose, you must start by showing Windows which icons you want to copy or move—by *highlighting* them.

Highlighting Icons

To highlight (that is, select) one icon, just click it once. But you don't have to move, copy, or delete one icon at a time; you can select a number of icons in the same folder or disk window. You may want to employ this technique, for example, when moving a bunch of documents from one folder to another, or copying them onto a backup disk en masse.

Tip: It's easiest to work with multiple icons in Details view (page 85), where every icon appears in a single column.

To highlight multiple files in preparation for moving, copying, or deleting, use one of these techniques:

To highlight all the icons

To select all the icons in a window, press Ctrl+A (the keyboard equivalent of the Edit→Select All command).

To highlight several icons

You can drag across file and folder names to highlight a group of consecutive icons. Start with your cursor above and to one side of the icons, then drag diagonally. As you drag, you create a temporary dotted-line rectangle. Any icon that falls within this rectangle darkens to indicate that it's been selected.

Alternatively, click the first icon you want to highlight, and Shift-click the last file. All the files in between are automatically selected, along with the two icons you clicked. (These techniques work in any folder view: Details, Thumbnails, or whatever.)

Tip: If you include a particular icon in your diagonally dragged group by mistake, Ctrl-click it to remove it from the selected cluster.

To highlight only specific icons

Suppose you want to highlight only the first, third, and seventh icons in the list. Start by clicking icon No. 1, then Ctrl-click each of the others. (If you Ctrl-click a selected icon *again*, you *de*select it. A good time to use this trick is when you highlight an icon by accident.)

Tip: The Ctrl key trick is especially handy if you want to select *almost* all the icons in a window. Press Ctrl+A to select everything in the folder, then Ctrl-click any unwanted subfolders to deselect them.

Copying by Dragging Icons

As you know, you can drag icons from one folder to another, from one drive to another, from a drive to a folder on another drive, and so on. (When you've selected several icons, drag any *one* of them and the others will go along for the ride.)

Here's what happens when you drag icons in the usual way (using the left mouse button):

- Dragging to another folder on the same disk *moves* the folder or file.

- Dragging from one disk to another *copies* the folder or file.

- Pressing the Ctrl key while dragging to another folder on the same disk *copies* the icon. (If you do so within a single window, Windows creates a duplicate of the file called "Copy of [filename].")

- Pressing Shift while dragging from one disk to another *moves* the folder or file (without leaving a copy behind).

- Pressing Alt while dragging an icon creates a shortcut of it.

Tip: You can move or copy icons by dragging them either into an open window or directly onto a disk or folder icon.

The right-mouse-button trick

Think you'll remember all of those possibilities every time you drag an icon? Probably not. Fortunately, you never have to. One of the most important tricks you can learn is to use the *right* mouse button as you drag. When you release the button, the menu shown in Figure 4-6 appears, so that you can either copy or move the icons.

Figure 4-6:
Thanks to this shortcut menu, right-dragging icons is much easier and safer than left-dragging when you want to move or copy something.

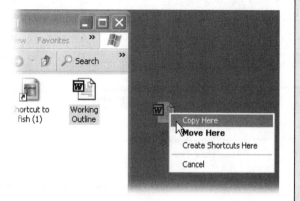

Tip: Press Esc to cancel a dragging operation at any time.

Dragging icons in Windows Explorer

You may find it easier to copy or move icons in Windows Explorer, since the two-pane display format makes it easier to see where your files are and where they're going. (See page 116 for a list of the ways to open the Explorer window.) Here's how to do it:

1. **Make the destination folder visible by clicking the + buttons next to your folder names, expanding your folder "tree" as necessary.**

   For example, to copy an icon into a certain folder, click the Local Disk (C:) icon to see its list of folders. If the destination is a folder *within* that folder, expand its parent folder as necessary.

2. **In the left pane, click the icon of the disk or folder that contains the icon you want to manipulate.**

   Its contents appear in the right pane.

3. **Locate the icon you want to move in the right pane, and drag it to the appropriate folder in the left pane (see Figure 4-7).**

   Windows copies the icon.

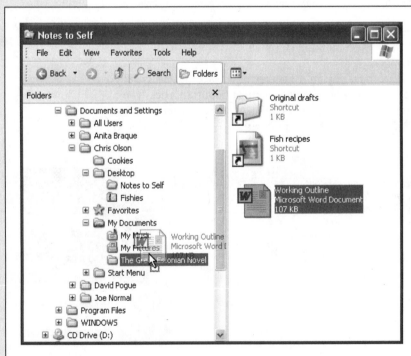

Figure 4-7:
The file Working Outline, located in the Notes to Self folder on the desktop, is being dragged to the folder named The Great Estonian Novel (in the My Documents folder). As the cursor passes each folder in the left pane, the folder's name darkens to show that it's ready to receive the drag-and-dropped goodies. Let go of the mouse button when it's pointing to the correct folder or disk.

Copying by Using Copy and Paste

Dragging icons to copy or move them feels good because it's so direct. You actually see your arrow cursor pushing the icons into the new location.

But you also pay a price for this satisfying illusion. That is, you may have to spend a moment or two fiddling with your windows, or clicking buttons in the Explorer folder hierarchy, so that you have a clear "line of drag" between the icon to be moved and the destination folder.

Fortunately, there's a better way: You can use the Cut, Copy, and Paste commands to move icons from one window into another. The routine goes like this:

POWER USERS' CLINIC

Secrets of the Send To Command

If you find yourself copying or moving certain icons to certain folders or disks with regularity, it's time to exploit the File→Send To command that lurks in every folder window (and in the shortcut menu for almost every icon).

This command offers a quick way to copy and move highlighted icons to popular destinations. For example, you can teleport a copy of a highlighted file directly to a floppy disk by choosing File→Send To→3 1/2 Floppy, or to a blank CD by choosing Send To→CD Burner. You're spared the tedium of choosing Copy, selecting the floppy drive, and choosing Paste.

Another useful command is Send To→"Desktop (create shortcut)," which dumps a shortcut icon onto your desktop background. Then there's the Send To→Mail Recipient, which bundles the highlighted icon as an email attachment that's ready to send. You can also zip up a folder (see Chapter 15) by choosing Send To→"Compressed (zipped) Folder."

But the real power of the Send To command is its ability to accommodate your *own* favorite or frequently used folders. Lurking in your My Computer→Local Disk (C:)→Documents and Settings→[Your Name] folder is a folder called SendTo. Any shortcut icon you place here shows up instantly in the Send To menus within your desk-

top folders and shortcut menus.

Alas, this folder is among those that Microsoft considers inappropriate for inspection by novices. As a result, the SendTo folder is *hidden* in Windows XP.

To make it appear, open any folder window. Choose Tools→ Folder Options, click the View tab, turn on "Show hidden files and folders", and click OK. Now, when you open your own account folder, you'll see the SendTo folder.

Most people create shortcuts here for folders and disks (such as your favorite backup disk). When you highlight an icon and then choose Send To→Backup Zip, for example, Windows XP copies the icon to that disk. (And if you simultaneously press Shift, you *move* the icon to the other disk or folder.)

You can even add shortcuts of *applications* (program files) to the SendTo folder. By adding WinZip to this Send To menu, for example, you can drop-kick a highlighted icon onto the WinZip icon (for decompressing) just by choosing Send To→WinZip. You can even create shortcuts for your printer or fax modem, so that you can print or fax a document just by highlighting its icon and choosing File→Send To→[printer or fax modem's name].

---

1. **Highlight the icon or icons you want to move or copy.**

   You can use any of the tricks described on page 126.

2. **Right-click one of the icons. Choose Cut or Copy from the shortcut menu.**

   Alternatively, you can choose Edit→Cut or Edit→Copy, using the menu bar at the top of the window. (Eventually, you may want to learn the keyboard short-cuts for these commands: Ctrl+C for Copy, Ctrl+X for Cut.)

   The Cut command makes the highlighted icons show up dimmed; you've now stashed them on the invisible Windows Clipboard. (They don't actually disappear from their original nesting place until you paste them somewhere else.)

   The Copy command also places copies of the files on the Clipboard, but doesn't disturb the originals.

3. **Right-click the window, folder icon, or disk icon where you want to put the icons. Choose Paste from the shortcut menu.**

   Once again, you may prefer to use the appropriate menu bar option—Edit→Paste. *Keyboard equivalent:* Ctrl+V.

   Either way, you've successfully transferred the icons. If you pasted into an open window, you'll see the icons appear there. If you pasted onto a closed folder or disk icon, you need to open the icon's window to see the results. And if you pasted right back into the same window, you get a duplicate of the file called "Copy of [filename]."

The Recycle Bin

The Recycle Bin is your desktop trash basket. This is where files and folders go when they've outlived their usefulness, like a waiting room for data oblivion. Your files stay here until you *empty* the Recycle Bin—or until you rescue them by dragging them out again.

While you can certainly drag files or folders onto the Recycle Bin icon, it's usually faster to highlight them and then perform one of the following options:

• Press the Delete key.

• Choose File→Delete.

• Right-click a highlighted icon and choose Delete from the shortcut menu.

Windows XP asks if you're sure you want to send the item to the Recycle Bin. (You don't lose much by clicking Yes, since it's easy enough to change your mind, as noted on the facing page.) Now the Recycle Bin icon looks like it's brimming over with paper.

Tip: To turn off the "Are you sure?" message that appears when you send something Bin-ward, right-click the Recycle Bin. Then choose Properties from the shortcut menu, and turn off "Display delete confirmation dialog." Turning off the warning isn't much of a safety risk. After all, files aren't really being removed from your drive when you put them in the Recycle Bin.

You can put unwanted files and folders into the Recycle Bin from any folder window, from within Windows Explorer, or even inside the Open File dialog box of many Windows applications (see Chapter 6).

Note: All of these methods put icons from your *hard drive* into the Recycle Bin. But deleting an icon from a removable drive (floppy or Zip drives, for example), or other computers on the network, does *not* involve the Recycle Bin, giving you no opportunity to retrieve them. (Deleting anything with the DOS *del* or *erase* commands bypasses the Recycle Bin, too.)

Restoring Deleted Files and Folders

If you change your mind about sending something to the software graveyard, open the Recycle Bin by double-clicking it. A window like the one in Figure 4-8 opens.

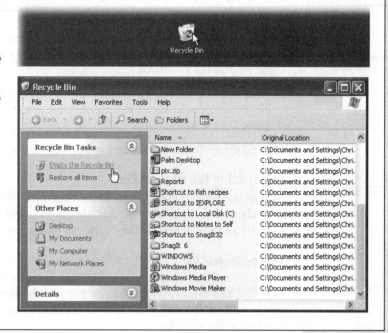

Figure 4-8:
When you double-click the Recycle Bin (top), its window (bottom) displays information about each folder and file that it holds. To sort its contents in Details view, making it easier to find a deleted icon, click the gray column heading for the type of sort you need.

To restore a selected file or a folder—or a bunch of them—click the "Restore the selected items" link in the task pane, or choose File→Restore, or right-click any one of the selected icons and then choose Restore from the shortcut menu.

Restored means returned to the folder from whence it came—wherever it was on your hard drive when deleted. If you restore an icon whose original folder has been deleted in the meantime, Windows XP even re-creates that folder to hold the restored file(s).

Tip: You don't have to put icons back into their original folders. By *dragging* them out of the Recycle Bin window, you can put them into any folder you like.

Emptying the Recycle Bin

While there's an advantage to the Recycle Bin (you get to undo your mistakes), there's also a downside: The files in the Recycle Bin occupy as much disk space as they did when they were stored in folders. Deleting files doesn't gain you additional disk space until you *empty* the Recycle Bin.

That's why most people, sooner or later, follow up an icon's journey to the Recycle Bin with one of these cleanup operations:

- Right-click the Recycle Bin icon, or a blank spot in the Recycle Bin window, and choose Empty Recycle Bin from the shortcut menu.

- Click the "Empty the Recycle Bin" link on the task pane in the Recycle Bin window.

- In the Recycle Bin window, highlight only the icons you want to eliminate, and then press the Delete key. (Use this method when you want to nuke only *some* of the Recycle Bin's contents.)

- Wait. When the Recycle Bin accumulates so much stuff that it occupies a significant percentage of your hard drive space, Windows empties it automatically, as described in the next section.

The first three of these procedures produce an "Are you sure?" message.

Customizing the Recycle Bin

You can make two useful changes to the behavior of the Recycle Bin. To investigate these alterations, right-click the Recycle Bin icon and choose Properties from the shortcut menu. The Recycle Bin Properties dialog box appears (see Figure 4-9).

Skip the Recycle Bin

If you, a person of steely nerve and perfect judgment, never delete a file in error, then your files can bypass the Recycle Bin entirely when you delete them. Furthermore, you'll reclaim disk space instantly when you press the Delete key to vaporize a highlighted file or folder.

To set this up, turn on the "Do not move files to the Recycle Bin" checkbox (shown in Figure 4-9). And voilà: Your safety net is gone. (Especially if you *also* turn off the checkbox shown at bottom in Figure 4-9—then you're *really* living dangerously.)

If that suggestion seems too extreme, consider this safety/convenience compromise: Leave the Recycle Bin safety net in place most of the time, but bypass the Recycle Bin on command only when it seems appropriate.

The trick to skipping the Recycle Bin on a one-shot basis is to press the Shift key while you delete a file. Doing so—and then clicking Yes in the confirmation box— deletes the file permanently, skipping its layover in the Recycle Bin. (The Shift-key trick works for every method of deleting a file: pressing the Delete key, choosing Delete from the shortcut menu, and so on.)

Figure 4-9:
Use the Recycle Bin Properties dialog box to govern the way the Recycle Bin works, or even if it works at all. If you have multiple hard drives, the dialog box offers a tab for each of them so you can configure a separate and independent Recycle Bin on each drive. To configure the Recycle Bin separately for each drive, select the "Configure drives independently" option.

Auto-emptying the Recycle Bin

The Recycle Bin has two advantages over the physical trash cans behind your house: First, it never smells. Second, when it's full, it can empty itself automatically.

To configure this self-emptying feature, you specify a certain fullness limit as a percentage of the hard drive capacity. When the Recycle Bin contents reach that level, Windows begins deleting files (permanently) as new files arrive in the Recycle Bin. Files that arrived in the Recycle Bin first are deleted first.

Unless you tell it otherwise, Windows XP reserves 10 percent of your drive to hold Recycle Bin contents. To change that percentage, just move the slider on the Properties dialog box (Figure 4-9). Keeping the percentage low means you're less likely to run out of the disk space you need to install software and create documents. On the other hand, raising the percentage means you'll have more opportunity to restore files you later want to retrieve.

Note: Every disk has its own Recycle Bin, which holds files and folders you have deleted from that disk. As you can see in the Recycle Bin Properties dialog box, the factory setting for automatic trash-deletion is 10 percent for *all* of your drives. If you click "Configure drives independently," you can use the separate dialog-box tabs for each of your hard drives. Accordingly, each hard drive will then have its own trash-limit slider and "Do not move files to the Recycle Bin" checkbox. (None of this affects the "Display delete confirmation dialog" checkbox on the Global tab, which you can't change on a disk-by-disk basis.)

Shortcut Icons

A *shortcut* is a link to a file, folder, disk, or program (see Figure 4-10). You might think of it as a duplicate of the thing's icon—but not a duplicate of the thing itself. (A shortcut takes up almost no disk space.) When you double-click the shortcut icon, the original folder, disk, program, or document opens. You can also set up a keystroke for a shortcut icon, so that you can open any program or document just by pressing a certain key combination.

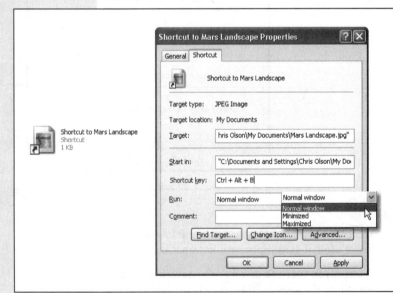

Figure 4-10:
You can distinguish a desktop shortcut (left) from its original in two ways. First, the tiny arrow "badge" identifies it as a shortcut. Second, its name contains the word shortcut (unless you've renamed it or an application has created its own shortcut on the desktop).

The Properties dialog box for a shortcut (right) indicates which actual file or folder this one "points" to. The Run drop-down menu lets you control how the window opens when you double-click the shortcut icon.

Shortcuts provide quick access to the items you use most often. And because you can make as many shortcuts of a file as you want, and put them anywhere on your PC, you can effectively keep an important program or document in more than one folder. Just create a shortcut of each to leave on the desktop in plain sight, or drag their icons onto the Start button or the Quick Launch toolbar. In fact, everything listed in the Start→Programs menu *is* a shortcut—even the My Documents folder on the desktop is a shortcut (to the actual My Documents folder).

Tip: Don't confuse the term *shortcut,* which refers to one of these duplicate-icon pointers, with *shortcut menu,* the context-sensitive menu that appears when you right-click almost anything in Windows. The shortcut *menu* has nothing to do with the shortcut icons feature. Maybe that's why it's sometimes called the *context* menu.

Creating and Deleting Shortcuts

To create a shortcut, right-drag an icon from its current location (Windows Explorer, a folder window, or even the Search window described on page 41) to the desktop. When you release the mouse button, choose Create Shortcut(s) Here from the menu that appears.

Tip: If you're not in the mood for using a shortcut menu, just left-drag an icon while pressing Alt. A shortcut appears instantly. (And if your keyboard lacks an Alt key—yeah, right—drag while pressing Ctrl+Shift instead.)

You can delete a shortcut the same as any icon, as described in the Recycle Bin discussion earlier in this chapter. (Of course, deleting a shortcut *doesn't* delete the file it points to.)

Unveiling a Shortcut's True Identity

To locate the original icon (program, folder, document, or whatever) from which a shortcut was made, right-click the shortcut icon and choose Properties from the shortcut menu. As shown in Figure 4-10, the resulting box shows you where to find the "real" icon—and offers you a quick way to jump to it, in the form of the Find Target button. When you click Find Target, you jump to the folder that stores the icon, which shows up highlighted.

Shortcut Keyboard Triggers

Even after reading all of this gushing prose about the virtues of shortcuts, efficiency experts may still remain skeptical. Sure, shortcuts let you put favored icons everywhere you want to be, such as your Start menu, Quick Launch toolbar, the desktop, and so on. But they still require clicking to open, which means taking your hands off the keyboard—and that, in the grand scheme of things, means slowing down.

Lurking within the Shortcut Properties dialog box is another feature with intriguing ramifications: the Shortcut Key text box. By clicking here and then pressing a key combination, you can assign a personalized keystroke for the shortcut. Thereafter, by pressing that keystroke, you can summon the corresponding file, program, folder, printer, networked computer, or disk window to your screen (no matter what you're doing on the PC).

Three rules apply when choosing keystrokes to open your favorite icons:

• The keystrokes work only on shortcuts stored *on your desktop or in the Start menu.* If you stash the icon in any other folder, the keystroke stops working.

• Your keystroke can't incorporate the Space bar or the Backspace, Delete, Esc, Print Screen, or Tab keys.

• There are no one- or two-key combinations available here. Your combination must include at least two of these three keys—Ctrl, Shift, and Alt—*and* another key.

Windows XP enforces this rule rigidly. For example, if you type a single letter key into the box (like *E*), Windows automatically adds the Ctrl and Alt keys to your combination (*Ctrl+Alt+E*). All of this is the operating system's attempt to prevent you from inadvertently duplicating one of the built-in Windows keyboard shortcuts and thoroughly confusing both your computer and yourself.

Tip: If you've ever wondered what it's like to be a programmer, try this. In the Shortcut Properties dialog box (Figure 4-10), use the Run drop-down menu at the bottom of the dialog box to choose Normal window, Minimized, or Maximized. By clicking OK, you've just told Windows what kind of window you want to appear when opening this particular shortcut. (See page 74 for a discussion of these window types.)

OK, controlling your Windows in this way isn't exactly the same as programming Microsoft Access, but you are, in your own small way, telling Windows what to do.

Burning CDs from the Desktop

In the old days (two years ago), every PC came with a CD-ROM drive. Nowadays, most new PCs come with a CD *burner*, a drive that can record new CDs that contain your own stuff.

If your PC has such a drive—either a CD-R drive (CD *recordable*, which means you can record each disc only once) or a CD-RW drive (CD *rewritable*, for which you can buy CD-RW discs that you can erase and re-record as many times as you like), you're in for a treat. For the first time, Windows XP lets you burn your own CDs full

---

FREQUENTLY ASKED QUESTION

Nothing to Lose

I'm burning a CD, and I get a message that I'm losing information. Why on earth would I want to click Yes?

When attempting to burn picture and music files onto a CD—not an uncommon task—you may be shown an error message that says, "This file has extra information attached to it that might be lost if you continue copying."

Windows is pointing out that some of the many informational tidbits it stores for *pictures and music files* (pixel dimensions of pictures, band name for music files, and so on) won't survive the transfer to a CD (whose more limited file format has only so much capacity for this kind of file trivia). This information won't be "lost" from the originals on your hard drive, of course—just in the CD copies.

Your best bet is to turn on "Repeat my answer each time this occurs" and then click Yes. (The alternative—clicking Skip so that Windows doesn't back up the file at all—is like throwing out the baby with the bathwater.)

---

of files and folders without having to buy a program like Roxio's Easy CD Creator (*http://www.roxio.com/en/products/ecdc*).

That's because Windows XP *includes* Easy CD Creator (pieces of it, anyway). That's a great feature for making backups, emailing people, or exchanging files with a Macintosh (the resulting CDs are cross-platform).

If your PC does, in fact, have a CD burner, start by inserting a blank CD. Windows offers to open a special CD-burning window, which will be the temporary waiting room for files that you want to copy to the CD (Figure 4-11, top left).

Note: If you've turned off this feature, you can open the CD window yourself: Open My Computer, and then double-click the CD icon.

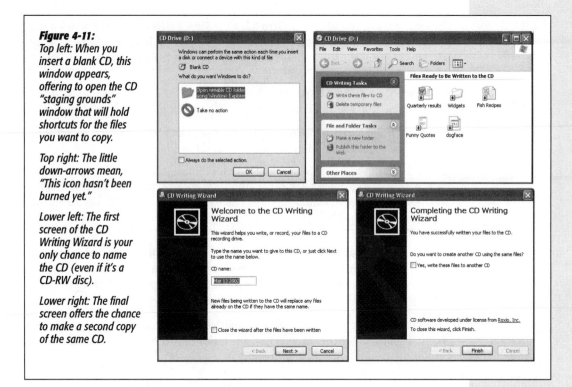

Figure 4-11:
Top left: When you insert a blank CD, this window appears, offering to open the CD "staging grounds" window that will hold shortcuts for the files you want to copy.

Top right: The little down-arrows mean, "This icon hasn't been burned yet."

Lower left: The first screen of the CD Writing Wizard is your only chance to name the CD (even if it's a CD-RW disc).

Lower right: The final screen offers the chance to make a second copy of the same CD.

Now tell Windows which files and folders you want copied onto it, using one of these three methods:

- Scurry about your hard drive, locating the files and folders you want on the CD. Drag their icons into the open CD window, or onto the CD icon in the My Computer window.

- Highlight the files and folders you want burned onto the CD. Choose File→Copy. Click in the CD's window, and then choose File→Paste to copy the material there.

• Explore your hard drive. Whenever you find a file or folder you'd like backed up, right-click it. From the shortcut menu, choose Send To→CD Drive.

Note: All of this pertains to copying everyday computer files onto a CD. If you want to burn *music* CDs, don't use this method. Use Windows Media Player instead. (See page 234 for details.)

In any case, Windows now copies the files and folders into a temporary, invisible holding-tank folder. (If you're scoring at home, this folder is in the Local Disk C:)→Documents and Settings→[Your Name]→Local Settings→Application Data→Microsoft→CD Burning folder.) In other words, you need plenty of disk space before you begin burning a CD, at least double the size of the CD files themselves.

Tip: Remember that a standard CD can hold only about 650 MB of files. To ensure that your files and folders will fit, periodically highlight all the icons in the My Computer→CD window (choose Edit→Select All). Then inspect the Details box in the task pane to confirm that the Total File Size is within the legal limit.

At last, when everything looks ready to go, click the "Write these files to CD" link in the task pane (top right in Figure 4-11), or choose File→Write these files to CD.

The CD Writing Wizard appears, as shown at bottom in Figure 4-11, to guide you through the process of naming the new CD and burning the disc.

Note: When using a CD-RW disc (that is, one that you can erase and re-record), you can't change the disc's name once it's been recorded for the first time. You can still replace its contents using the techniques described here, though.

Hard-core Windows power users, of course, sneer at all this. Only with a commercial CD-burning program, they point out, can you burn MP3 music CDs, create *mixed-mode* CDs (containing both music and files), create Video CDs (low-quality video discs that play on DVD players), and so on.

Still, if you use your burner primarily for quick backups, long-term storage, or transferring big files to other computers, a little bit of free software goes a long way.

Getting Help

A s you've no doubt noticed, each version of Windows gets bigger and more capable, but seems to come with fewer pages of printed instructions. In Windows XP, Microsoft has relegated more of its wisdom than ever to online help screens—or, even less conveniently, to Web pages on the Internet.

On the other hand, Microsoft has improved the Help window by incorporating links to various diagnostic and repair tools, troubleshooting wizards, and help sources on the Web. It may take all weekend, but eventually you should find written information about this or that Windows feature or problem.

Navigating the Help System

To open the help system, choose Start→Help and Support, or press F1. The Help and Support window appears, as shown in Figure 5-1. From here, you can home in on the help screen you want using any of three methods: clicking your way from the Help home page, using the index, or using the Search command.

Help Home Page

The home page shown in Figure 5-1 contains three basic areas. In the left column: Frequently sought help topics, such as "Music, video, games, and photos" and "Printing and faxing." In the right column: buttons that take you to specialized interactive help systems and utility software. Finally, at the lower right, Microsoft treats you each day to a different "Did you know?" headline.

If one of the broad topics on the left side corresponds with your question, click any topic to see a list of subtopics. The subtopic list will lead you to another, more focussed list, which in turn leads you to an even narrower list. Eventually you'll arrive at a list that actually produces a help page.

Tip: If you seem to have misplaced your contact lenses, simply adjust the type size used by the Help Center. Click Options on the toolbar, and then click "Change Help and Support Center options" at the left side of the window. In the right pane, under "Font size used for Help content," you'll see the "Font size" buttons—Small, Medium, or Large.

Frequently sought topics   Special help features

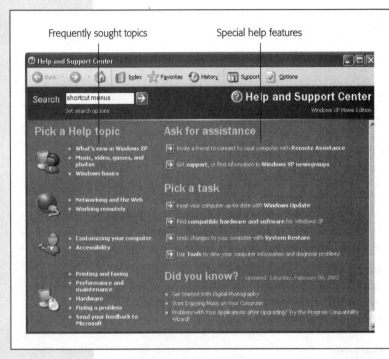

Figure 5-1:
When working in the Help and Support Center window, you can use the Back, Forward, Home, Favorites, and History buttons on the toolbar. They may look like the corresponding buttons in a Web browser, but these buttons refer only to your travels within the help system. The Favorites button here represents your favorite help pages—they're not the same favorites you see in Internet Explorer.

Search the Help Pages

By typing a phrase into the Search text box at the top of the main page and then clicking the green arrow (or pressing Enter), you instruct Windows XP to rifle through its 10,000 help pages to search for the phrase you typed.

Here are a few pointers:

- When you enter multiple words, Windows XP assumes that you're looking for help screens that contain *all* of those words. For example, if you search for *video settings,* help screens that contain both the words "video" and "setting" (although not necessarily next to each other) will appear.

- If you would rather search for an exact phrase ("video settings"), click the "Set search options" link underneath the Search text box. The search options page appears; at the bottom, you'll find a "Search for" drop-down menu. Choose "The exact phrase" and then repeat the search.

Tip: This same drop-down menu offers choices like "Any of the words," which means that if you type *video settings,* you'll find help pages that have *either* of those words. Choosing "The Boolean phrase" from this drop-down menu means that you intend to use the phrases *or, and,* or *not* in your search phrase for further specificity. For example, entering *video not settings* would yield all help pages concerning "video" that don't discuss "settings."

- Windows displays only the first fifteen topics it finds in each of its help databases. If you'd rather see more or fewer "hits," you'll find an adjustment control on, once again, the "Set search options" page. (That page also lets you turn off the *search highlight,* the dark rectangle shown in Figure 5-2 that appears around your search phrase on the resulting help pages.)

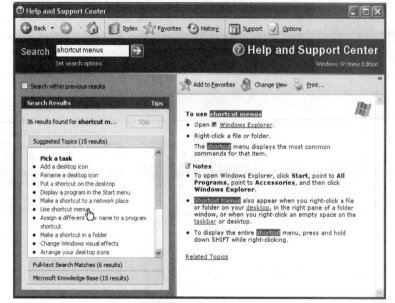

Figure 5-2:
Each document title in the list on the left is a link that opens up a help page on the right side of the menu. (The dark highlighting shows matches for your search phrase.) The results are divided into three different categories— Suggested Topics (fast but limited), Full-text Search Matches (slower but more complete), and Microsoft Knowledge Base (Internet-based). Click the appropriate category name.

After each search, the left-side list shows three different categories of help topics:

- **Suggested Topics** reveals help pages whose *keywords,* invisibly assigned by Microsoft, match your search phrase. Of course, if you and Microsoft don't happen to use the same terminology, you won't find what you're seeking listed in this group.

- **Full-text Search Matches** are help pages on which your search phrase actually appears in the help page text.

- **Microsoft Knowledge Base** refers to the massive collection of technical articles on the Microsoft Web site. If you're not online, you can't read them.

Tip: When you're on a laptop at 39,000 feet, you probably don't have an Internet connection. In that case, you may prefer that Windows not attempt to search the Microsoft Knowledge Base on the Internet. Click "Set search options" just beneath the Search text box, and then turn off the Microsoft Knowledge Base checkbox.

Help Index

The success of the Search command boils down to your using the same terminology Microsoft does. Sometimes, you may have better luck unearthing a certain help article by clicking the Index button on the toolbar.

Doing so produces a massive list of almost every help topic in the Windows repertoire, sorted alphabetically (Figure 5-3). Double-click a topic's name to see its corresponding help page Help window's right pane.

If you type a few letters into the Search box, the Index scrolls to the closest match. But if that doesn't produce a matching entry, you can still scroll through the index manually.

Figure 5-3:
As you type, Windows XP matches each character by highlighting successive index listings to correspond with the characters you've typed so far. Most of the entries in the index are indented—these are the links to actual help pages. Don't waste your time trying to double-click the category headings (the entries that aren't indented, but that have indented entries underneath them.) They don't do anything when double-clicked, since you're supposed to open one of the indented subentries.

Tip: Ordinarily, the Help window fills most of your screen, so it may cover up whichever steps you're trying to follow. However, clicking the Change View button (above the help text in the right pane) hides the list of topics and shrinks the help page so it fills a much smaller window. Click the button again to return to the two-pane view.

"What's This?": Help for Dialog Boxes

If you're ever facing a dialog box (like the one shown in Figure 5-4) while scanning a cluster of oddly worded options, Windows XP's "What's This?" feature can come to the rescue. It makes pop-up captions appear for text boxes, checkboxes, option buttons, and other dialog box elements.

You can summon these pop-up identifiers (see Figure 5-4) in either of two ways:

• Right-click something in the dialog box. In the world's shortest shortcut menu that now appears, click What's This?

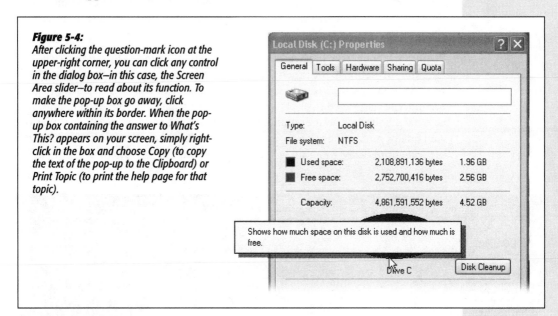

Figure 5-4:
After clicking the question-mark icon at the upper-right corner, you can click any control in the dialog box—in this case, the Screen Area slider—to read about its function. To make the pop-up box go away, click anywhere within its border. When the pop-up box containing the answer to What's This? appears on your screen, simply right-click in the box and choose Copy (to copy the text of the pop-up to the Clipboard) or Print Topic (to print the help page for that topic).

• Click the question mark in the upper-right corner of the dialog box, and then click the element you want identified.

Remote Assistance

You may think you've experienced stress in your lifetime: deadlines, breakups, downsizing. But absolutely nothing approaches the frustration of an expert trying to help a PC beginner over the phone—for both parties. The expert is flying blind, using

Windows terminology that the beginner doesn't know. Meanwhile, the beginner doesn't know what to look for and describe to the expert on the phone. Every little operation takes 20 times longer than it would if the expert were simply seated in front of the machine. Both parties are likely to age ten years in an hour.

Fortunately, that era is at an end. One of Windows XP's biggest big-ticket features is something called Remote Assistance. It lets somebody having trouble with the computer extend an invitation to an expert, via the Internet. Through Remote Assistance, the expert can actually see the screen of the flaky computer, and even take control of it by remotely operating the mouse and keyboard. The guru can make even the most technical tweaks—running utility software, installing new programs, adjusting hardware drivers, even editing the Registry (page 492)—by long distance remote control. Remote Assistance really *is* the next best thing to being there.

Remote Assistance: Rest Assured

Of course, these days, most people react to the notion of Remote Assistance with stark terror. What's to stop some troubled teenager from tapping into your PC in the middle of the night, rummaging through your files, and reading your innermost thoughts?

Plenty. First of all, you, the help-seeker, must begin the process by sending a specific electronic invitation to the expert. The invitation has a time limit: If the helper doesn't respond within, say, 10 minutes, the electronic door to your PC slams shut again. Second, the remote-control person can only see what's on your screen. She can't actually manipulate your computer unless you grant another specific permission. And finally, you must be present *at your machine* to make this work. The instant you see something fishy going on, a quick tap on your Esc key disconnects the interloper.

GEM IN THE ROUGH

Troubleshooters

When a PC feature isn't working the way you'd hope, or isn't working at all, Windows XP offers a special kind of wizard called a *troubleshooter*—a series of help screens specifically designed to solve problems.

If you follow all the steps the troubleshooter suggests, and you're unable to fix the problem, the troubleshooter apologizes and sug- gests another resource for more help.

Do you have a problem with your sound card?

If you receive an audio error message, or if you have general sound problems, you might have a problem with your sound card or sound card driver. Go to the Sound troubleshooter for more assistance.

Can you play DVDs after you fix a problem with your sound card?

- ○ No, my sound card is fine, but I still receive an error message.
- ○ Yes, this solves the problem.
- ○ I want to skip this step and try something else.

[Next] [Back] [Start Over]

You won't find troubleshooters for every conceivable problem; Microsoft created only a few. To see a list of them, open the main Help and Support window. Then type *troubleshooter* in the Search text box and press Enter. You can double-click a troubleshooter's name in the resulting list.

Tip: If, despite all of these virtual locks and chains, you absolutely can't stand the idea that there's a tiny keyhole into your PC from the Internet, choose Start→Control Panel. Click "Switch to Classic View," if necessary, and then double-click the System icon. In the System dialog box, click the Remote tab, and turn off "Allow Remote Assistance invitations to be sent from this computer." Click OK. Now you've effectively removed the use of the Remote Assistance feature from Windows XP.

Remote Assistance via Windows Messenger

Windows Messenger is a little program that lets two people communicate across the Internet—by typing in a chat window, speaking into their microphones, or even watching each other via a video camera. It's all detailed in Chapter 11.

For now, it's enough to note that the Remote Assistance process is much simpler and more streamlined if both the helper and the helpee use Windows Messenger. Here's how it works.

Instructions for the novice

Suppose you're the person who needs help. If you suspect that your expert may need to install software or fiddle with your network settings while fooling around with your machine, sign into your PC with an *Administrator account* (page 501). Then connect to the Internet, and proceed like this:

1. **Open Windows Messenger.**

   For example, click Start→All Programs→Windows Messenger.

2. **Choose Actions→Ask for Remote Assistance (Figure 5-5).**

   Now the Ask for Remote Assistance dialog box appears.

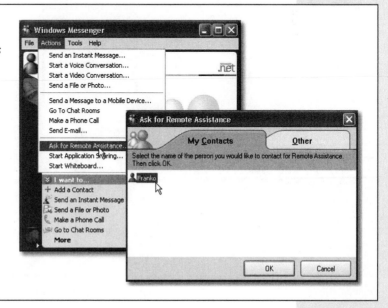

Figure 5-5:
Getting going in Remote Assistance is easiest in Windows Messenger (left). Just specify who's going to be the lucky one to troubleshoot your machine (right).

3. **Specify who's going to help you.**

If the email address of your personal guru is listed on the My Contacts screen, just click the corresponding address (Figure 5-5, right). Otherwise, click the Other tab and type the guru's email address into the appropriate box.

4. **Click OK.**

Windows Messenger sends an invisible invitation to your good Samaritan, who sees—thousands of miles away, perhaps—something like the top illustrations of Figure 5-6. If your buddy accepts the invitation to help you, then the message shown at bottom in Figure 5-6 appears, asking if you're absolutely, positively sure you want someone else to see your screen.

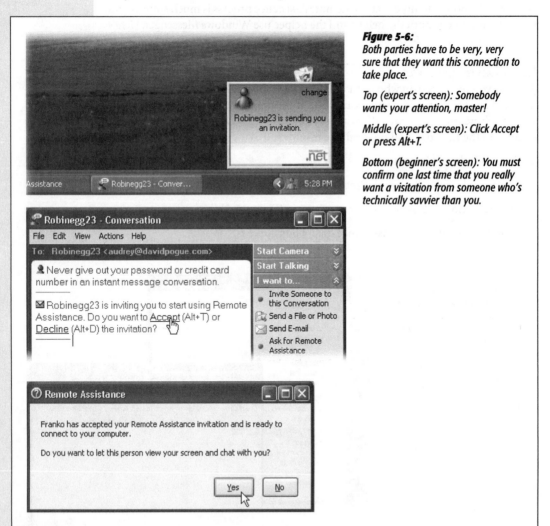

Figure 5-6:
Both parties have to be very, very sure that they want this connection to take place.

Top (expert's screen): Somebody wants your attention, master!

Middle (expert's screen): Click Accept or press Alt+T.

Bottom (beginner's screen): You must confirm one last time that you really want a visitation from someone who's technically savvier than you.

5. Click Yes.

You're in good shape. Let the help session begin (Figure 5-7).

The only further action that's required on your part comes when the expert asks for permission to take charge of your machine. You'll see a request like the one shown in Figure 5-8. Click Yes, and then watch in amazement and awe as your cursor begins flying around the screen, text types itself, and windows open and close by themselves. That's just your friendly neighborhood computer wizard fixing your machine.

Figure 5-7:
If the victim's screen isn't exactly the same size as yours, you have two options. If you click Actual Size, the other person's screen is represented at full size, although you may have to scroll around to see all of it. If you click Scale to Window, Windows compresses (or enlarges) the other person's screen image to fit inside your Remote Assistance window, even though the result can be distorted and ugly.

Take Control button

Scale/Actual buttons

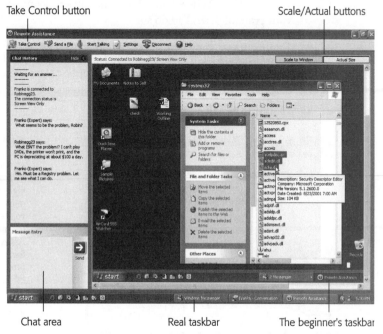

Chat area

Real taskbar

The beginner's taskbar

As noted earlier, if the expert's explorations of your system begin to unnerve you, feel free to slam the door by clicking the Stop Control button on the screen—or just by pressing the Esc key. Your friend can still see your screen, but can no longer control it. (To close the connection completely, so that your screen isn't even visible anymore, click the Disconnect button.)

Instructions for the expert

When your less-fortunate comrade sends you an electronic invitation to help, a little message on your Notification Area pops up, as shown in Figure 5-6 at top. Furthermore, the Windows Messenger on your taskbar changes color to signal the invitation. Bring Windows Messenger to the front, and then click Accept or press Alt+T (Figure 5-6, middle). Assuming that the hapless novice is skilled enough to click Yes to grant final permission (Figure 5-6, bottom), you're in.

At this point, you observe a strange sight: the other person's screen in a special Remote Assistance window (Figure 5-7). To communicate with your troubled comrade, use any of the Windows Messenger communications tools described in Chapter 11 (chat, microphone, video, sending files back and forth)—or just by chatting on the telephone simultaneously.

When you want to take control of the distant machine, click the Take Control button on the toolbar at the top of your Remote Assistance screen. Of course, all you've actually done is just ask *permission* to take control (Figure 5-8). If it's granted, you can now use your mouse, keyboard, and troubleshooting skills to do whatever work you need to do. When your job is done, click Disconnect on the toolbar—or wait for your grateful patient to do so.

Tip: Once you've taken control of the other person's screen, your first instinct might be to close the gargantuan Remote Assistance window that's filling most of the screen. Don't. If that window closes, the connection closes, too. What you really want is to *minimize* it, so it's out of your way but not closed.

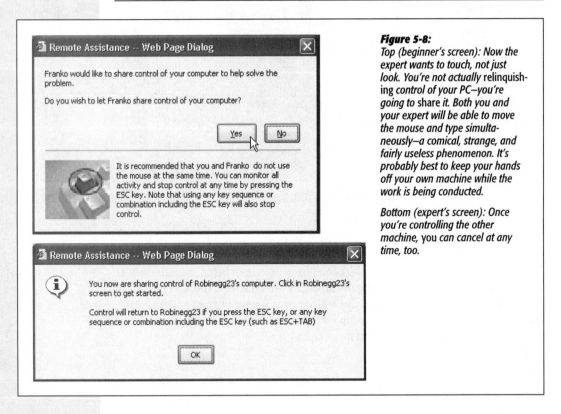

Figure 5-8:
Top (beginner's screen): Now the expert wants to touch, not just look. You're not actually relinquishing *control of your PC—you're going to* share *it. Both you and your expert will be able to move the mouse and type simultaneously—a comical, strange, and fairly useless phenomenon. It's probably best to keep your hands off your own machine while the work is being conducted.*

Bottom (expert's screen): Once you're controlling the other machine, you *can cancel at any time, too.*

Remote Assistance without Windows Messenger

As noted earlier, using Remote Assistance is most efficient and satisfying when both participants fire up the Windows Messenger program. That's not technically necessary, however. Although more steps are involved, anybody with Windows XP can help anyone else with Windows XP, even if neither person has a Passport nor uses Windows Messenger.

Instructions for the novice

If you're the one who wants help, send an invitation like this:

1. **Choose Start→Help and Support.**

   The Help and Support Center appears, as described earlier in this chapter.

2. **Click "Invite a friend to connect to your computer with Remote Assistance." On the next screen, click "Invite someone to help you."**

   The Remote Assistance Wizard is guiding you through the process of sending an invitation. You're offered two ways of sending it: using Windows Messenger, exactly as described in the previous section, and using email. Of course, since the entire purpose of this exercise is to seek the help of someone who *doesn't* have Windows Messenger, proceed like this:

3. **Type your guru's email address into the "Type an email address" box, and then click "Invite this person" (or press Enter).**

   This works only if you've already set up your PC for email, as described in Chapter 12.

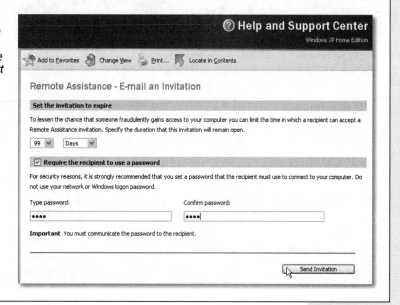

Figure 5-9:
Speaking of security, you can also set up a password here for even more protection. The guru won't be able to connect to your machine without the password. (Of course, you need to find some way of telling him what the password is—maybe calling on the phone or sending a separate email.)

Now the screen changes again.

Note: If you click "Save invitation as a file (Advanced)," instead, Windows saves a little invitation ticket (with the unusually long filename extension *.MsRcIncident)* as a file on your hard drive. You can transfer this little file—the actual invitation to inhabit your PC—via disk or via network instead of emailing it.

---

4. **In the From box, type the name you want to appear on the invitation. In the Message box, add a description of the problem, and then click Continue.**

   On this screen, Windows wants to know how long you want to keep your electronic invitation alive (Figure 5-9). If your guru doesn't respond within, say, an hour, you may want the invitation to expire quietly, for security reasons.

Tip: On the other hand, if the expert is a friend or family member who rescues you frequently, you may as well change the settings to the maximum—30 days—so that he can tap into your machine whenever it's convenient. (In fact, in the Control Panel program called System [page 295], you can crank up the maximum to 99 days by clicking the Remote tab and then Advanced.) You save several connection steps this way.

---

5. **Set up your security options. Make sure you're online, and then click the Send Invitation button.**

   A little dialog box may appear, warning you that a program is attempting to send an email message on your behalf. (This dialog box is designed to be a safeguard against viruses that transmit themselves without your knowledge.)

TROUBLESHOOTING MOMENT

Making Remote Assistance Work

If you can't get Remote Assistance to work, the first thing to check is the master on/off switch—the "Allow Remote Assistance..." checkbox described in the Tip on page 145.

If that box is indeed turned on, the next issue to investigate is the *IP address*—the string of four numbers, such as 24.226.23.1, that identifies every single computer that's on the Internet at a given moment. Whenever you invite an expert to visit your PC using Remote Assistance, you're transmitting your IP address to the expert's computer behind the scenes.

Suppose, then, that you dial into the Internet using a standard phone line. In that case, your Internet service provider

probably assigns you a different IP address each time you're online. Clearly, if your guru tries to "call you back" the day after you issue the invitation, it won't work, since you'll have a different IP address when you go online the next day. That's a good argument for prearranging the help session with your expert—so that you issue the invitation and actually *conduct* the session all during a single online session.

Other complications might arise if you have a cable modem or DSL connection that you share among several PCs using a piece of equipment called a router. Fortunately, most of these problems go away if you use the Windows Messenger method described in this chapter, rather than the email-an-invitation method.

---

6. Click the Send button.

Finally, the Remote Assistance wizard tells you, "Your invitation has been sent successfully."

Instructions for the expert

When the novice sends you an email invitation, it arrives in your email program with an attachment—a tiny file called rcBuddy.MsRcIncident (see Figure 5-10). This is your actual invitation, a Remote Assistance ticket.

When you open it, a little electronic message goes back to the novice, where a message like the one shown at bottom in Figure 5-6 appears. The online help session can now begin.

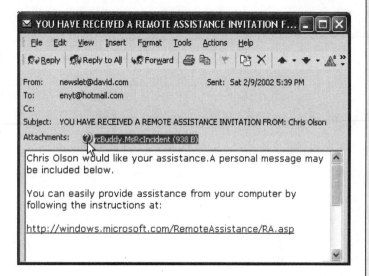

Figure 5-10:
You, the guru, have just received a .MsRcIncident ticket—an invitation to help somebody whose PC needs troubleshooting. Lucky you!

And by the way: If the novice, a trusting individual, has sent you a Remote Assistance ticket that doesn't expire for a very long time (99 days, for example), keep it around on your desktop or in your Start menu. From now on, both of you can skip all of the invitation-and-response rigamarole. Now, whenever he needs your help, he can just call you up or email you. And all you have to do is double-click your ticket and wait for the OK from the other side.

Getting Help from Microsoft

If you run into trouble with the installation—or with any Windows XP feature—the world of Microsoft is filled with sources of technical help. For example, you can consult:

- **The Microsoft Help Web pages.** Direct your Web browser (if, indeed, your computer works) to *www.microsoft.com/support*. There you'll find a long list of help resources that handle many of the most common questions: a database of help articles that you can search, a list of known glitches that Microsoft has published, newsgroups (Internet bulletin boards) where you can post questions and return later to read the answers, and so on.

• **Free phone help.** If you bought Windows XP (that is, it didn't come on your computer), you can call Microsoft for free phone help during business hours. The company is especially interested in helping you get Windows XP installed and running correctly—you can call as often as you like for help getting Windows going this way.

After that, you can call for everyday Windows questions for free—twice. You'll be asked to provide your 20-digit product ID number, which you can look up by right-clicking My Computer in your Start menu and clicking the Properties tab. The not-toll-free number is (425) 635-3311.

(If Windows XP came preinstalled in your machine, on the other hand, you're supposed to call the computer company with your Windows questions.)

• **Expensive phone help.** Once you've used up your two free calls, you can still call Microsoft with your questions—but it will cost you $35 per incident. (They say "per incident" to make it clear that if it takes several phone calls to solve a particular problem, it's still just one problem.) This service is available 24 hours a day, and the U.S. number is (800) 936-5700.

Tip: If you're not in the United States, direct your help calls to the local Microsoft office in your country. You'll find a list of these subsidiaries at *www.microsoft.com/support.*

Part Two:
The Components of
Windows XP

2

Programs and Documents

W hen you get right down to it, an operating system like Windows is nothing more than a home base from which to launch *applications* (programs).
And you, as a Windows person, are particularly fortunate, since more
programs are available for Windows than any other operating system on earth.

But when you launch a program, you're no longer necessarily in the world Microsoft
designed for you. Programs from other software companies work a bit differently,
and there's a lot to learn about how Windows XP handles programs that were born
before it was.

This chapter covers everything you need to know about installing, removing, launching, and managing programs; using programs to generate documents; and understanding how documents, programs, and Windows communicate with each other.

Launching Programs

Windows XP lets you launch (open) programs in many different ways:

- Choose a program's name from the Start→All Programs menu.

- Click a program's icon on the Quick Launch toolbar (page 103).

- Double-click an application's program-file icon in the My Computer→Local Disk
  (C:)→Program Files→application folder, or highlight the application's icon and
  then press Enter.

- Press a key combination you've assigned to the program's shortcut (page 135).

- Choose Start→Run, type the program file's name in the Open text box (page 38), and then press Enter.

- Let Windows launch the program for you, either at startup (page 34) or at a time you've specified (see Task Scheduler, page 473).

- Open a document using any of the above techniques; its "parent" program opens automatically. For example, if you used Microsoft Word to write a file called Last Will and Testament.doc, double-clicking the document's icon launches Word and automatically opens that file.

What happens next depends on the program you're using (and whether or not you opened a document). Most present you with a new, blank, untitled document. Some, such as FileMaker and Microsoft PowerPoint, welcome you instead with a question: Do you want to open an existing document or create a new one? And a few oddball programs, like Adobe Photoshop, don't open any window at all when first launched. The appearance of tool palettes is the only evidence that you've even opened a program.

Switching Programs

In these days where PCs with 256, 512 or more megs of RAM are common, it's the rare PC user who doesn't regularly run several programs *simultaneously*.

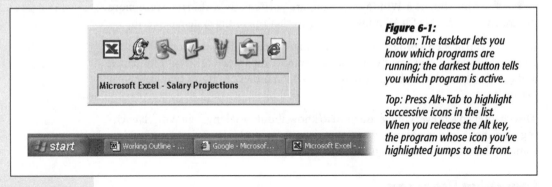

Figure 6-1:
Bottom: The taskbar lets you know which programs are running; the darkest button tells you which program is active.

Top: Press Alt+Tab to highlight successive icons in the list. When you release the Alt key, the program whose icon you've highlighted jumps to the front.

The key to juggling open programs is the taskbar, which lists all open programs (Figure 6-1). As explained at the end of Chapter 2, the taskbar also offers controls for arranging all the windows on your screen, closing them via the shortcut menu, and so on.

To bring a different program to the front, you can use any of these four tricks:

- **Use the Taskbar.** Clicking a button on the taskbar makes the corresponding program pop to the front, along with any of its floating toolbars, palettes, and so on.

  If you see a parenthetical number on a taskbar button, however, then button *grouping* is under way (page 98). In that case, clicking the taskbar button *doesn't* bring the program's windows forward. You must actually click a selection in the taskbar button's menu of open windows.

- **Click the window.** You can also switch to another program by clicking the part of its window that's visible in the background.

- **The relaunch technique.** Repeat the technique you used to initially launch the program (choose its name from the Start→All Programs menu, press its keystroke, and so on).

- **Alt+Tab.** Finally, you can bring a different program to the front without using the mouse. If you press Tab while holding down the Alt key, a floating palette displays the icons of all running programs, as shown at the top in Figure 6-1. Each time you press Tab again (still keeping the Alt key down), you highlight the next icon; when you release the keys, the highlighted program jumps to the front, as though in a high-tech game of Duck Duck Goose.

To move *backward* through the open programs, press *Shift*+Alt+Tab.

Tip: For quick access to the desktop, clear the screen by clicking the Desktop button on the Quick Launch toolbar (its icon looks like an old desk blotter)—or just press the Windows logo key+D. Pressing that keystroke again brings all the windows back to the screen exactly as they were.

UP TO SPEED

"Multiple Document Interface" Programs

The world of Windows programs is divided into two camps. First, there are *single-document interface* (SDI) programs, where the entire program runs in a single window. By closing that window, you also exit the application. (WordPad, Notepad, Internet Explorer, and Palm Desktop work this way.)

Second, there are *multiple-document interface* (MDI) programs, where the application itself is a mother ship, a shell, that can contain lots of different document windows. Word, Excel, and PowerPoint work like this. As shown here, you may see two sets of upper-right window controls, one just beneath the other. The top one belongs to the *application;* the one below it belongs to the *document.* Here, if you close a document window, you *don't* also quit the program.

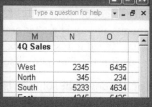

To help you navigate your various open windows, MDI programs usually offer commands that arrange all open windows to fit neatly on the screen, each occupying an even fraction of the screen space. (These commands work much like the Tile and Cascade commands in desktop windows.)

In Microsoft Word, for example, the Windows menu offers a command called Arrange All.

Getting to know which way a program deals with windows is important for a couple of reasons. First, it explains why the taskbar sometimes displays only one button for an entire *program* (such as Word), but sometimes displays a button for each open *window* in a program (such as Internet Explorer). Second, it explains why closing a window sometimes exits the application (when it's a *single*-document interface program), and sometimes doesn't (when it's an MDI program).

Exiting Programs

When you exit, or quit, an application, the memory it was using is returned to the Windows pot for use by other programs.

If you use a particular program several times a day, like a word processor or calendar program, you'll save time in the long run by keeping it open all day long. (You can always minimize its window to get it out of the way when you're not using it.)

But if you're done using a program for the day, exit it, especially if it's a memory-hungry one like, say, Photoshop. Do so using one of these techniques:

• Choose File→Exit.

• Click the program window's Close box, or double-click its Control-menu icon (at the upper-left corner of the window).

• Right-click the program's taskbar button and choose Close from the shortcut menu.

• Press Alt+F4 to close the window you're in. (If it's a program that disappears entirely when its last document window closes, you're home.)

• Press Atl+F, then X.

If you haven't yet saved the changes you've made to your document, the program offers the chance to do so before it shuts down all the way. Finally, after this step, the program's windows, menus, and toolbars disappear, and you fall "down a layer" into the window that was behind it.

When Programs Die

Windows XP itself may be a revolution in stability (at least if you're used to Windows Me), but that doesn't mean that *programs* never crash or freeze. They crash, all right—it's just that in XP, you rarely have to restart the computer as a result.

When something goes horribly wrong with a program, your primary interest is usually exiting it in order to get on with your life. But when a programs locks up (the cursor moves, but menus and tool palettes don't respond) or when a dialog box tells you that a program has "failed to respond," exiting may not be so easy. After all, how do you choose File→Exit if the File menu itself doesn't open?

As in past versions of Windows, the solution is to invoke the "three-fingered salute": Ctrl+Alt+Delete. What happens next depends on whether or not your PC is part of a domain network (page 23):

• **Part of a domain.** Ctrl+Alt+Delete summons the Windows Security dialog box, a special window shown in Figure 6-2. Click the Task Manager button. The Applications tab on the resulting dialog box provides a list of every open program. Furthermore, the Status column should make clear what you already know: that one of your programs is ignoring you.

- **Part of a workgroup (or not networked).** You save a step. Ctrl+Alt+Delete brings you directly to the Windows Task Manager dialog box.

Tip: You can also run Task Manager by right-clicking the taskbar and then selecting Task Manager from the shortcut menu. Doing this bypasses the Windows Security dialog box and brings you directly to Windows Task Manager, with the Applications tab selected.

As shown in Figure 6-2, shutting down the troublesome program is fairly easy; just click its name and then click the End Task button. (If yet another dialog box appears, telling you that "This program is not responding," click the End Now button.)

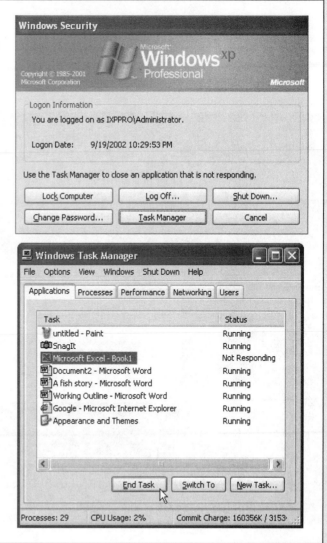

Figure 6-2:
Top: Click the Task Manager button on the Windows Security dialog box to check on the status of a troublesome program.

Bottom: As if you didn't know, one of these programs is "not responding." Highlight its name and then click End Task to slap it out of its misery. Once the program disappears from the list, close the Task Manager and get on with your life. You can even restart the same program right away—no harm done.

When you jettison a recalcitrant program this way, Windows XP generally shuts down the troublemaker gracefully, even offering you the chance to save unsaved changes to your documents.

Tip: If even this treatment fails to close the program, you might have to slam the door the hard way. Click the Processes tab, click the name of the program that's giving you grief, and then click the End Process button. (The Processes list includes dozens of programs, including many that Windows XP runs behind the scenes. Finding the abbreviated short name of the program may be the hardest part of this process.)

Any unsaved changes to your documents will be lost using this method—but at least the frozen program is finally closed.

Saving Documents

In a few programs, such as the Calculator or Solitaire, you spend your time working (or playing) in the lone application window. When you close the window, no trace of your work remains.

Sending an Error Report to Microsoft

Whenever Windows XP discovers that you have terminated one program or another in some eccentric way—for example, by using the Task Manager (see Figure 6-2)—a dialog box that says, "Please tell Microsoft about this problem" appears.

If you click the Send Error Report button, your PC connects to the Internet and sends an email report back to Microsoft, the mother ship, providing the company with the technical details about whatever was going on at the moment of the freeze, crash, or premature termination. (To see exactly what information you're about to send, click the "click here" link.)

Microsoft swears up and down that it doesn't do anything with this information except to collate it into gigantic electronic databases, which it then analyzes using special soft-

ware tools. The idea, of course, is to find trends that emerge from studying hundreds of thousands of such reports. "Oh, my goodness, it looks like people who own both Speak-it Pro 5 and Beekeeper Plus who right-click a document that's currently being printed experience a system lockup," an engineer might announce one day. By analyzing the system glitches of its customers en masse, the company hopes to pinpoint problems and devise software patches with much greater efficiency than before.

If you're worried about privacy, click Don't Send (or press Enter) each time this happens—or turn off this error-sending feature completely, as described on page 121. (On the other hand, if you're truly concerned about privacy and Windows XP, this particular feature is probably the least of your worries.)

WordPad MFC Application

You chose to end the nonresponsive program, WordPad MFC Application.

The program is not responding.

Please tell Microsoft about this problem.
We have created an error report that you can send to help us improve WordPad MFC Application. We will treat this report as confidential and anonymous.

To see what data this error report contains, click here.

[Send Error Report] [Don't Send]

Most programs, however, are designed to create *documents*—files that you can re-open for further editing, send to other people, back up on another disk, and so on.

That's why these programs offer File→Save and File→Open commands, which let you preserve the work you've done, saving it onto the hard drive as a new file icon so that you can return to it later.

The Save File Dialog Box

When you choose File→Save for the first time, the computer shows you the dialog box shown in Figure 6-3, in which you're supposed to type a file name, choose a folder location, and specify the format for the file you're saving. Using the controls in this dialog box, you can specify exactly where you want to file your newly created document.

Figure 6-3:
Top: These buttons vary by application, but the basics always help you navigate and view your files and folders.

Bottom: The buttons at the left side of the Save As dialog box provide quick access to the folders where you're most likely to stash newly created documents: the My Documents folder, the desktop itself, and so on. But by using the "Save in:" drop-down list at the top of the screen, you can choose any folder you like.

Back   New Folder

Up One Level   Views

Saving into My Documents

The first time you use the File→Save command to save a file, Windows proposes your My Documents folder as the new home of the document you've just created (Figure 6-3). Now you're free to navigate to some other folder location, as described in the next section. But the My Documents folder will suggest itself as the new-document receptacle every time.

Tip: Many programs let you specify a different folder as the proposed location for saved (and reopened) files. In Microsoft Word, for example, click Tools→Options→File Locations tab to change the default folders for the documents you create, where your clip art is stored, and so on.

What's the benefit? First, using the My Documents folder ensures that your file won't fall accidentally into some deeply nested folder where you'll never see it again (a common occurrence among first-time computer users). Instead, the newly minted document will be waiting for you in the My Documents folder, which itself is very difficult to lose.

Second, it's now very easy to make a backup copy of your important documents, since they're all in a single folder (which you can drag onto a backup disk in one swift move).

There's a third advantage, too: Whenever you use a program's File→Open command, Windows once again displays the contents of the My Documents folder. In other words, the Documents folder saves you time both when *creating* a new file and when *retrieving* it.

Tip: If the Documents folder becomes cluttered, feel free to make subfolders inside it to hold your various projects. You could even create a different default folder in My Documents for each program.

GEM IN THE ROUGH

Why You See Document Names in Black

In the Save dialog box, Windows XP displays a list of both folders *and documents* (documents that match the kind you're about to save, that is).

It's easy to understand why *folders* appear here: so that you can double-click one if you want to save your document inside it. But why do *documents* appear here? After all, you can't very well save a document into another document.

Documents are listed here so that you can perform one fairly obscure stunt: If you click a document's name, Windows XP copies its name into the "File name" text box at the bottom of the window. That's a useful shortcut if you

want to *replace* an existing document with the new one you're saving. By saving a new file with the same name as the existing one, you force Windows XP to overwrite it (after asking your permission, of course).

This trick also reduces the amount of typing needed to save a document to which you've assigned a different version number. For example, if you click the Thesis Draft 3.1 document in the list, Windows copies that name into the "File name" text box; doing so keeps it separate from earlier drafts. To save your new document as *Thesis Draft 3.2,* you only need to change one character (change the 1 to 2) before clicking the Save button.

Navigating in the Save As Dialog Box

If the My Documents method doesn't strike your fancy, use the Save As dialog box's various controls to navigate your way into any folder. That's the purpose of the "Save in:" drop-down list at the top of the dialog box. It lists, and lets you jump to, any disk or folder on your PC—or the desktop level, if that's a more familiar landscape.

To save a new document onto, say, a Zip disk or floppy, choose the drive's name from this drop-down list before clicking the Save button. To save it into a *folder* within a disk, simply double-click the successive nested folders until you reach the one you want.

Use the toolbar icons shown in Figure 6-3 to help you navigate, like this:

- **Back** shows you the contents of the last folder you browsed. Click its tiny black down-triangle button to see a drop-down list of folders you've opened recently within this program.

UP TO SPEED

Dialog Box Basics

To the delight of the powerful Computer Keyboard lobby, you can manipulate almost every element of a Windows XP dialog box by pressing keys on the keyboard. If you're among those who feel that using the mouse takes longer to do something, you're in luck.

The rule for navigating a dialog box is simple: Press Tab to jump from one set of options to another, or Shift+Tab to move backward. If the dialog box has multiple *tabs,* like the one shown here, press Ctrl+Tab to "click" the next tab, or Ctrl+*Shift*+Tab to "click" the previous one.

Each time you press Tab, the PC's *focus* shifts to a different control or set of controls. Windows reveals which element has the focus using text highlighting (if it's a text box or drop-down menu) or a dotted-line outline (if it's a button). In the illustration shown here, the "Different odd and even" checkbox has the focus.

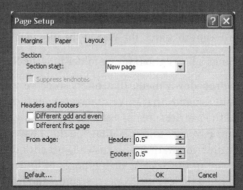

Once you've highlighted a button or checkbox, simply press the Space bar to "click" it. If you've opened a drop-down list or set of mutually exclusive *option buttons,* or *radio buttons,* press the up or down arrow key. (Tip: Once you've highlighted a drop-down list's name, you can also press the F4 key to open it.)

Each dialog box also contains larger, rectangular buttons at the bottom (OK and Cancel, for example). Efficiency fans should remember that tapping the Enter key is always the equivalent of clicking the *default* button—the one with the darkened or thickened outline (the OK button in the illustration here). And pressing Esc almost always means Cancel (or "Close this box").

Finally, remember that you can jump to a particular control or area of the dialog box by pressing the Alt key along with the corresponding underlined letter key.

Tip: In Microsoft Office, if you point to this button without clicking, a tooltip identifies the previous folder by name.

- **Up One Level** moves you up one level in your folder hierarchy (from seeing the My Documents contents to the hard drive's contents, for example). *Keyboard shortcut:* the Backspace key.

- **Create New Folder** creates a new folder in the current list of files and folders. Windows asks you to name it.

- **Views** changes the way file listings look in this dialog box. Each time you click the icon, you get a different view: List, Details, Thumbnails, and so on. (To choose one of these views by name, use the drop-down list rather than clicking the icon repeatedly.)

  The list of view options here depends on the program you're using. In general, they closely correspond to the View menu options described on page 82. But in some programs, including Microsoft Office programs, you may receive a few additional options—a choice of Large Icons or Small Icons, for example, or a Properties view that divides the window in half, with the list of files and folders on the left, and the properties (file size, date modified, and so on) of the highlighted icon on the right.

In some programs (such as Microsoft Office), you may find a few additional buttons across the top of the Save As dialog box, including:

- **Search the Web** closes the Save As dialog box, opens your browser, connects to the Internet, and prepares to search the Internet. (Next assignment: To figure out *why* you'd want to search the Web at the moment of saving your document.)

- **Delete** flings a highlighted file or folder into the Recycle Bin.

- **Tools** is drop-down menu that offers some very useful commands, including **Delete** and **Rename**, that let you manage your files right from within this dialog box. **Add to Favorites** creates a shortcut of the highlighted disk, server, folder, or file in your Favorites folder, so that you don't have to burrow through your folders every time you want access; instead, just click the Favorites folder icon, which also appears in the Save As dialog boxes of Office programs, to see everything you've stashed there. The **Properties** command lets you see an icon's description and stats.

  Map Network Drive lets you assign a drive letter (such as *G:*) to a folder that's on another PC of your network. Having that folder appear on your screen as just another disk makes it much easier to find, open, and manage. (See Chapter 20 for more on sharing networked folders.)

Navigating the List by Keyboard

When the Save As dialog box first appears, the "File name" text box is automatically selected so that you can type a name for the newly created document.

But as noted earlier in this chapter, a Windows dialog box is elaborately rigged for keyboard control. In addition to the standard Tab/Space bar controls, a few special keys work only within the list of files and folders. Start by pressing Shift+Tab (to shift Windows' attention from the "File name" text box to the list of files and folders) and then:

- Press various letter keys to highlight the corresponding file and folder icons. To highlight the Program Files folder, for example, you could type *PR*. (If you type too slowly, your key presses will be interpreted as separate initiatives—highlighting first the People folder and then the Rodents folder, for example.)

- Press the Page Up or Page Down keys to scroll the list up or down. Press Home or End to highlight the top or bottom item in the list.

- Press the arrow keys (up or down) to highlight successive icons in the list.

- When a folder (or file) is highlighted, you can open it by pressing the Enter key (or double-clicking its icon, or clicking the Open button).

The File Format Drop-Down Menu

The Save As dialog box in many programs offers a menu of file formats (usually referred to as the file *type*) below the "File name" text box. Use this drop-down menu when preparing a document for use by somebody whose computer doesn't have the same software.

For example, if you've typed something in Microsoft Word, you can use this menu to generate a Web page document or a Rich Text Format document that you can open with almost any standard word processor or page-layout program.

Closing Documents

You close a document window just as you'd close any window, as described in Chapter 3: by clicking the close box (marked by an X) in the upper-right corner of the window, by double-clicking the Control-menu icon just to the left of the File menu,

UP TO SPEED

Playing Favorites

Most people think of Favorites as Internet Explorer's version of "bookmarks"—a list of Web sites that you've designated as worth returning to. But Windows XP lets you designate *anything* as a favorite—a folder you open often, a document you consult every day, a program, and so on.

You can designate a particular icon as a Favorite in any of several ways. For example, in the Save As or Open dialog box of Microsoft Office programs, you can use the Add to Favorites command. In a desktop window (Windows Ex-

plorer, for example), you can highlight an icon and then choose Favorites→Add to Favorites.

Later, when you want to open a Favorite icon, you can do so using an equally generous assortment of methods: choose from the Start→Favorites menu (if you've created it as described on page 64); choose File→Open (from within a program) and click the Favorites folder or icon; choose from the Favorites menu of any desktop window; and so on.

or by pressing Alt+F4. If you've done any work to the document since the last time you saved it, Windows offers a "Save changes?" dialog box as a reminder.

As described on page 80, sometimes closing the window also exits the application, and sometimes the application remains running, even with no document windows open. And in a few *really* bizarre cases, it's possible to exit an application (such as Outlook Express) while a document window (an email message) remains open on the screen, lingering and abandoned!

The Open Dialog Box

To reopen a document you've already saved and named, you can pursue any of these avenues:

- Open your My Documents folder (or whichever folder contains the saved file). Double-click the file's icon.

- If you've opened the document recently, choose its name from the Start→My Recent Documents menu. (If you don't see this command, simply install it as described on page 59.)

- If you're already in the program that created the document, choose File→Open— or check the bottom of the File menu. Many programs add a list of recently opened files to the File menu, so that you can choose its name to re-open it.

- Type (or browse for) the document's path and name into the Start→Run box or into a folder window's Address toolbar.

The Open dialog box looks almost identical to the Save As dialog box. The big change: The navigational drop-down list at the top of the window now says "Look in" instead of "Save in."

Once again, you start out by perusing the contents of your My Documents folder. Here, you may find that beginning your navigation by choosing Look In→My Computer offers a useful overview of your PC when you're searching for a particular file. Here, too, you can open a folder or disk by double-clicking its name in the list, or by pressing the keystrokes described in the previous section. And once again, you can press Backspace to back *out* of a folder that you've opened.

When you've finally located the file you want to open, double-click it or highlight it (from the keyboard, if you like), and then press Enter.

In general, most people don't encounter the Open dialog box nearly as often as the Save As dialog box. That's because Windows offers many more convenient ways to *open* a file (double-clicking its icon, choosing its name from the Start→My Documents command, and so on), but only a single way to *save* a new file.

Moving Data Between Documents

You can't paste a picture into your Web browser, and you can't paste MIDI music information into your word processor. But you can put graphics into your word processor, paste movies into your database, insert text into Photoshop, and combine a surprising variety of seemingly dissimilar kinds of data. And you can transfer text from Web pages, email messages, and word processing documents to other email and word processing files; in fact, that's one of the most frequently performed tasks in all of computing.

Cut, Copy, and Paste

Most experienced PC users have learned to quickly trigger the Cut, Copy, and Paste commands from the keyboard—without even thinking. Figure 6-4 provides a recap.

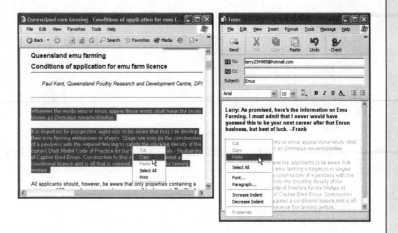

Figure 6-4:
Suppose you want to email some text on a Web page to a friend.

Left: Start by dragging through it and then choosing Copy from the shortcut menu (or choosing Edit→Copy). Now switch to your email program and paste it into an outgoing message (right).

Bear in mind that you can cut and copy highlighted material in any of three ways: First, you can use the Cut and Copy commands in the Edit menu; second, you can press Ctrl+X (for Cut) or Ctrl+C (for Copy); and third, you can right-click the highlighted material and choose Cut or Copy from the shortcut menu.

When you do so, the PC memorizes the highlighted material, socking it away on an invisible storage pad called the Clipboard. If you choose Copy, nothing visible happens; if you choose Cut, the highlighted material disappears from the original document.

At this point, you must take it on faith that the Cut or Copy command actually worked. (Windows XP no longer automatically pops open the Clipboard Viewer, as did previous Windows versions.)

Pasting copied or cut material, once again, is something you can do either from a menu (choose Edit→Paste), by right-clicking and choosing Paste from the shortcut menu, or from the keyboard (press Ctrl+V).

The most recently cut or copied material remains on your Clipboard even after you paste, making it possible to paste the same blob repeatedly. Such a trick can be useful when, for example, you've designed a business card in your drawing program and want to duplicate it enough times to fill a letter-sized printout. On the other hand, whenever you next copy or cut something, whatever was previously on the Clipboard is lost forever.

POWER USERS' CLINIC

ClipBook Viewer: The Missing Manual

The ClipBook Viewer of previous Windows versions is still available in Windows XP Pro; it's just hidden. To open it, choose Start→Run, type *Clipbrd.exe,* then press Enter.

As you cut or copy information (from a word processor, Web page, or whatever), it shows up in the Clipboard window within the ClipBook Viewer. Normally, cutting or copying anything new *replaces* what was on the Clipboard before—but that's where the ClipBook Viewer comes into play. It lets you *save* the current Clipboard contents for re-use later.

The instructions depend on what kind of network you're on (if at all); here goes:

Domain networks: Once ClipBook Viewer is open, choose Window→Local ClipBook window, and then choose Edit→Paste. When the Paste dialog box appears, type a name for the page of information stored in the Clipboard. Click OK to save this information to a file. You can go on with your work this way, pasting and saving each newly copied scrap of text.

Workgroup networks (or no network): In ClipBook Viewer, choose File→Save As. Name and save the scrap of information you've copied, and then click Save. You can save as many files as you want and then retrieve then later (as long as you remember the name of the folder where you stored them).

Of course, the purpose of saving them isn't just to give your fingers some exercise; the whole point is to retrieve them later to use in your documents. Here again, the instructions vary.

Domain networks: Bring the Local ClipBook window to the front again. If a list of your file names doesn't appear in this window, click View→Table of Contents. Double-click the file name you need. Make sure that the text or graphic is the one you're looking for, and then choose Edit→Copy. Voilà! You've put the information from the Local ClipBook window *back* into the Clipboard window, ready for pasting into a document just as you normally would (using Ctrl+V, right-clicking anywhere within your document and then selecting Paste from the shortcut menu, or choosing Edit→Paste).

Workgroup networks (or no network): In the ClipBook Viewer, choose File→Open. Locate the scrap you saved earlier, open it, and OK the vaporization of the *current* clipboard. Switch back into any other program; you're ready to paste the retrieved material.

Drag-and-Drop

As useful and popular as it is, the Copy/Paste routine doesn't win any awards for speed; after all, it requires four steps. In many cases, you can replace that routine with the far more direct (and enjoyable) drag-and-drop method. Figure 6-5 illustrates how it works.

Tip: To drag highlighted material offscreen, drag the cursor until it approaches the top or bottom edge of the window. The document scrolls automatically; as you approach the destination, jerk the mouse away from the edge of the window to stop the scrolling.

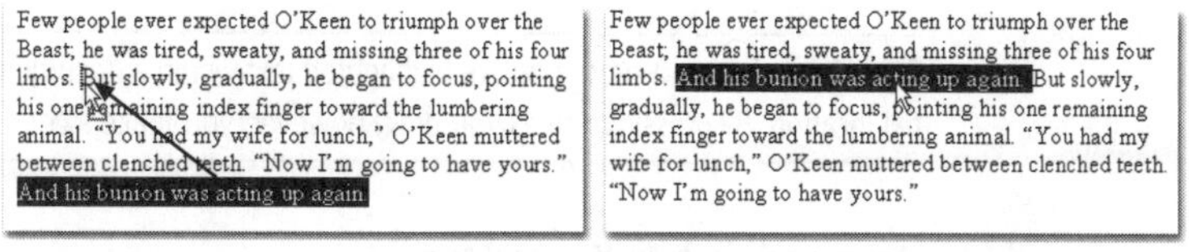

Figure 6-5:
Click in the middle of some highlighted text (left) and drag it into another place within the document—into a different window or program (right).

FREQUENTLY ASKED QUESTION

When Formatting Is Lost

How come pasted text doesn't always look the same as what I copied?

When you copy text from Internet Explorer, for example, and then paste it into another program, such as Word, you may be alarmed to note that the formatting of that text (bold, italic, font size, font color, and so on) doesn't reappear intact. In fact, the pasted material may not even inherit the current font settings in the word processor. There could be several reasons for this problem.

For example, not every program *offers* text formatting—Notepad among them. And the Copy command in some programs (such as Web browsers) doesn't pick up the formatting along with the text. So when you copy something from Internet Explorer and paste it into Word or WordPad, you may get plain unformatted text. (There is some good news along these lines, however. Word XP maintains formatting pasted from the latest Internet Explorer.)

Finally, a note on *text wrapping.* Thanks to limitations built into the architecture of the Internet, email messages aren't like word processor documents. The text doesn't flow continuously from one line of a paragraph to the next, such that it reflows when you adjust the window size. Instead, email programs insert a press of the Enter key at the end of each line *within* a paragraph.

Most of the time, you don't even notice that your messages consist of dozens of one-line "paragraphs"; when you see them in the email program, you can't tell the difference. But if you paste an email message into a word processor, the difference becomes painfully apparent—especially if you then attempt to adjust the margins.

To fix the text, delete the invisible carriage return at the end of each line. (Veteran PC users sometimes use the word processor's search-and-replace function for this purpose.) Or, if you just need a quick look, reduce the point size (or widen the margin) until the text no longer wraps.

Several of the built-in Windows XP programs work with the drag-and-drop technique, including WordPad and Outlook Express. Most popular commercial programs offer the drag-and-drop feature, too, including email programs and word processors, America Online, Microsoft Office programs, and so on.

As illustrated in Figure 6-5, drag-and-drop is ideal for transferring material between windows or between programs. It's especially useful when you've already copied something valuable to your Clipboard, since drag-and-drop doesn't involve (and doesn't erase) the Clipboard.

Its most popular use, however, is rearranging the text in a single document. In, say, Word or WordPad, you can rearrange entire sections, paragraphs, sentences, or even individual letters, just by dragging them—a terrific editing technique.

Tip: Using drag-and-drop to move highlighted text within a document also deletes the text from its original location. By pressing Ctrl as you drag, however, you make a *copy* of the highlighted text.

Drag-and-drop to the desktop

Figure 6-6 demonstrates how to drag text or graphics out of your document windows and directly onto the desktop. There your dragged material becomes an icon— a *Scrap file*.

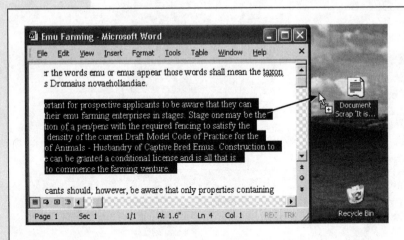

Figure 6-6:
A Scrap file will appear when you drag material out of the document window and onto the desktop. Its icon depends on the kind of material contained within, as shown here at left. You can view a clipping just by double-clicking it, so that it opens into its own window (right).

When you drag a clipping from your desktop *back* into an application window, the material in that clipping reappears. Drag-and-drop, in other words, is a convenient and powerful feature; it lets you treat your desktop itself as a giant, computer-wide pasteboard—an area where you can temporarily stash pieces of text or graphics as you work.

Tip: You can drag a Scrap file onto a document's taskbar button, too. Don't release the mouse button yet. In a moment, the corresponding document window appears, so that you can continue your dragging operation until the cursor points to where you want the Scrap file to appear. Now release the mouse; the Scrap material appears in the document.

In Microsoft Office applications, this works with entire document icons, too. You can drag one Word file into another's window to insert its contents there.

Insert Object (OLE)

Here's yet another relative of the Copy and Paste duo: the Insert Object command, which is available—although usually ignored—in many Windows programs. (You may hear it referred to as Object Linking and Embedding technology, or OLE, or even "oh-LAY.")

Using this feature, you can insert material from one OLE-compatible program (like Paint) into a document running in another (like Word). When you click the painting, in this example, Word's menus change to those of the campaign program, so that you can edit the graphic. When you click off the graphic, the familiar Word menus return.

In general, OLE never became the hit that Microsoft hoped, probably because it can be flaky if you don't have a fast machine with a lot of memory. Still, if the idea of self-updating inserted material intrigues you, here's how to try it:

1. **Create a document in a program that offers OLE features.**

   Some programs that do: Excel, Word, WordPad, PowerPoint, and Paint.

2. **Click to indicate where you want the inserted object to appear. Choose Insert→Object.**

   (Insert→Object is the menu wording in Microsoft Office programs; its location may differ in other programs.)

   Now an Object dialog box appears, offering two tabs: Create New, which creates a *new* graph, picture, spreadsheet, or other embedded element; and Create from File, which imports a document you've *already* created (using, for example, Excel, Paint, Graph, or Imaging).

   If you choose Create from File, a "Link to file" checkbox appears (Figure 6-7). It determines whether the inserted material will be *embedded* or (if you turn on the checkbox) *linked.* If you choose to link the inserted material, the fun begins. Now you can make changes in the original document and watch the revision appear automatically in any documents to which it's been linked.

3. **Choose the kind of data you want to create, and click OK.**

   You've successfully embedded or linked new information. To edit the document, just double-click it; the menus and palettes you need to modify this info reappear. (If you're linked to a separate document, double-clicking the embedded object actually opens that other document.)

Export/Import

When it comes to transferring large chunks of information from one program to another—especially address books, spreadsheet cells, and database records—none of the data-transfer methods described so far in this chapter do the trick. For these purposes, use the Export and Import commands found in the File menu of almost every database, spreadsheet, email, and address-book program.

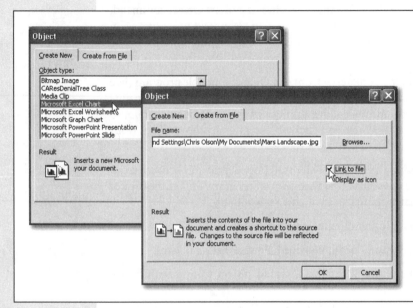

Figure 6-7:
Top: You can insert many kinds of "objects" into a Word or WordPad document: a Paint file ("Bitmap Image"), Image Document (something you've scanned), an Excel spreadsheet ("Work-sheet"), and so on.

Bottom: You may prefer to slap an entire existing file into the middle of the one you're now editing. Do that using the Create from File tab. Turn on "Link to file" if you want the data to update itself when the source file is edited separately.

These Export/Import commands aren't part of Windows, so the manuals or help screens of the applications in question should be your source for instructions. For now, however, the power and convenience of this feature are worth noting: Because of these commands, your four years' worth of collected names and addresses in, say, an old address-book program can find its way into a newer program, such as Palm Desktop, in a matter of minutes.

Filename Extensions

Every operating system needs a mechanism to associate documents with the applications that created them. When you double-click a Microsoft Word document icon, for example, Word launches and opens the document.

In Windows, every document comes complete with a normally invisible *filename extension* (or just *file extension)*—a period followed by a suffix that's usually three letters long. Here are some common examples:

When you double-click this icon ...	... this program opens it
Fishing trip**.doc**	Microsoft Word
Quarterly results**.xls**	Microsoft Excel
Home page**.htm**	Internet Explorer
Agenda**.wpd**	Corel WordPerfect
A home movie**.avi**	Windows Media Player
Animation**.dir**	Macromedia Director

Tip: For an exhaustive list of every file extension on the planet, visit *www.whatis.com*; click the link for "Every File Format in the World."

Behind the scenes, Windows maintains a massive table that lists every extension and the program that "owns" it. To see this list, choose Tools→Folder Options from the menu bar of any folder window. When the Folder Options box appears, simply click the File Types tab (Figure 6-8).

Figure 6-8:
Each software program you install must register the file types it uses. The link between the file type and the program is called an association. This dialog box displays the icon for each file type and an explanation of the selected listing. In this example, the box tells you that sound files with the suffix .aiff open in Windows Media Player when double-clicked.

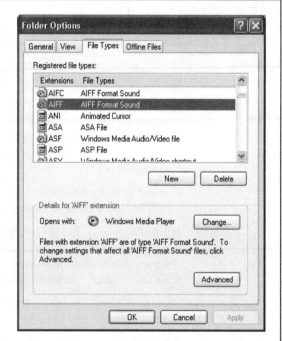

Displaying Filename Extensions

It's possible to live a long and happy life without knowing much about these extensions. Indeed, because file extensions don't feel very user-friendly, Microsoft designed Windows to *hide* the suffixes on most icons (see Figure 6-9). If you're new to Windows, and haven't poked around inside the folders on your hard drive much, you may never even have seen them.

Some people appreciate the way Windows hides the extensions, because the screen becomes less cluttered and less technical-looking. Others make a good argument for the Windows 3.1 days, when every icon appeared with its suffix.

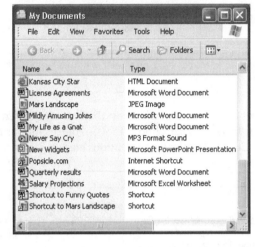

Figure 6-9:
Windows lets you see the filename extensions only when it doesn't recognize them.

Right: If Windows recognizes the filename extension on an icon, it hides the extension (look closely at the filenames).

Left: You can ask Windows to display all extensions, all the time.

For example, in a single Desktop window, suppose one day you discover that three icons all seem to have exactly the same name: PieThrower. Only by making filename extensions appear would you discover the answer to the mystery: that is, one of them might be called PieThrower.ini, another is an Internet-based software updater called PieThrower.upd, and the third is the actual PieThrower program, PieThrower.exe.

One way to make sense of such situations is simply to look at the window in Details view (right-click in the window and choose View→Details from the shortcut menu).

But that's too easy. To fully breathe in Windows technology, you can instruct Windows to reveal the file suffixes on *all* icons. To do so, choose Tools→Folder Options from any folder window's menu bar. In the Folder Options dialog box, click the View tab. Turn off "Hide extensions for known file types," and then click OK.

Now the filename extensions for all icons appear.

Tip: Even if you prefer to hide most file extensions, you may still want one particular type of document to appear on the screen with file extensions. For example, when working on a Web site, you may want to check whether the suffixes of your Web page documents are *.htm* or *.html.*

In these situations, choose Tools→Folder Options in any Desktop window. Click the File Types tab (see Figure 6-8). Scroll down to the file extension you want to make visible, click it, click the Advanced button, and—in the Edit File Type dialog box—turn on "Always show extension." Click OK, and then click the Close button.

Hooking up a File Extension to a Different Program

Windows XP comes with several programs (Notepad and WordPad, for example) that can open text files with the extension *.txt*. And Windows also comes with several programs (Paint, Imaging, Internet Explorer) that can open JPEG picture files with the extension *.jpg*. So how does it decide *which* program to open when you double-click a .txt or .jpg file?

Windows comes with its own extension-to-application pairing list, as depicted in Figure 6-8. But at any time, you can reassign a particular file type (file extension) to a different application. Having just bought Photoshop, for example, you might want it to open up your JPEG files, rather than Windows Picture and Fax Viewer.

The long way to perform this reassignment surgery is to use the File Types tab of the Folder Options dialog box shown in Figure 6-8. Click the file type you want to change, click the Change button, and then proceed as shown in Figure 6-10.

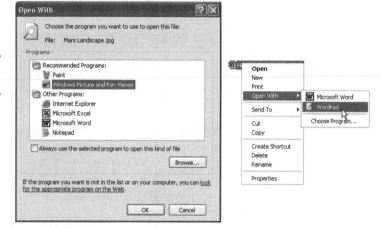

Figure 6-10:
Left: Windows is prepared to show you a list of every program that can open the mystery file. Scroll through the list of installed programs to select the one you want. By turning on the checkbox at the bottom of the dialog box, you create a file association that will handle similar files (those with the same file extension) in the future.

Right: A shortcut to the dialog box shown at left is the Open With→Choose Program shortcut menu.

Here's the short way: Right-click the icon of the file that needs a new parent program. In the shortcut menu, you'll see a command called Open With. As shown at right in Figure 6-10, it may offer a submenu that lists the programs capable of opening the file. If the submenu isn't offered—or if you bypass these proposals and select Choose Program from the submenu—Windows presents the Open With dialog box shown at left in Figure 6-10. Just find, and double-click, the name of the program you now want to open this kind of file.

As you do so, be sure to check the status of the checkbox below the list, which says, "Always use the selected program to open this kind of file." If that checkbox is on, then *all* files of this type (.jpg, for example) will open in the newly selected application from now on. If the checkbox is off, then the new application will open only *this* .jpg file—just this once.

Tip: This technique is an effective cure if you've made a file association by mistake, or when a newly installed program performs the dreaded Windows Power Grab, claiming a particular file type for itself without asking you.

Creating Your Own File Associations

Every now and then, you might try to open a mystery icon—one whose extension is missing, or whose extension Windows doesn't recognize. In that case, the dialog box shown in Figure 6-11 will appear. Maybe you've tried to double-click a document sent to you by a Macintosh fan (many Macintosh files lack file extensions), or maybe you're opening a document belonging to an old DOS program that doesn't know about the Windows file-association feature.

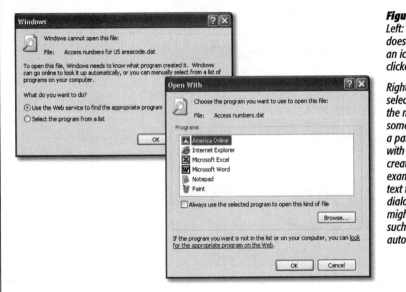

Figure 6-11:
Left: Sometimes Windows doesn't know what to do with an icon you've just double-clicked.

Right: Use this window to select a program for opening the mystery file. It's sometimes useful to associate a particular document type with a program that didn't create it, by the way. For example, if you double-click a text file, and the Open With dialog box appears, you might decide that you want such documents to open automatically into WordPad.

In any case, Windows offers you two different buttons:

- **Select the program from a list.** Windows displays a dialog box that looks a lot like the one at right in Figure 6-11. Click the name of the program you want, and then turn on "Always use the selected program to open this kind of file," if you like.

- **Use the Web service to find the appropriate program.** In other words, Windows will take your PC onto the Internet and look up the mystery file extension on the Microsoft Web site.

Fun with File Associations

The File Types tab on the Folder Options dialog box shown in Figure 6-8 provides an excellent display of the icons, file extensions, and descriptions of your various file types. As noted earlier, it also offers the New button, which lets you tell Windows about new file types, and the Change button, which lets you reassign an existing file type to a different program.

At the bottom of the box, though, is an Advanced button. When you click it, the dialog box shown at top left in Figure 6-12 appears. This box contains a few tweaky settings that could come in handy someday. For example:

- **Change the icon.** By itself, Windows doesn't let you change the icon for just one file. But you *can* change the icon for a particular file *type* (JPEG files, for example).

  To do so, click Change Icon. Windows offers you a handful of replacement icons for the kind of file you're editing (Figure 6-12, top right). If you don't see a good one, click Browse. You'll be offered a Change Icon dialog box, which you can use to navigate to the folder containing a program that may contain better icons (details on page 125).

- **Make it open after downloading.** If you turn on "Confirm open after download," files of this type will automatically open, as though magically double-clicked, whenever you download one from the Internet. You might want to turn this option on for compressed file types (*.zip,* for example), so that they unpack themselves automatically. (But avoid turning on this option for file types that may contain viruses, such as *.exe, .vbs,* or *.bat.*)

- **Change what happens when you double-click it.** In the Actions list, you'll see a list of things that might happen when you double-click an icon: *open* (open) and *printto* (print), for example.

  Of course, icons almost always *open* when you double-click them. But by highlighting one of the other Actions listed here (if, indeed, Windows gives you a choice for this file type) and then clicking Set Default, you can establish a new behavior for the file that you double-click. For example, you might want the JPEG files to print automatically when double-clicked. (Well, maybe that's not such a great example.)

- **Edit its shortcut menu.** When you right-click an icon, Windows displays a shortcut menu containing commands like Open, Print, and so on. If you click the New button, you get the New Action dialog box, where you can add a new command to the shortcut menu of files of this type.

  You can't exactly go wild here, adding shortcut-menu commands like Email to Uncle Joe, Backdate 30 Days, and so on. In fact, all you can really do is add commands—for example, Open in Photoshop—that *open* the selected file in a certain program. Figure 6-12 (bottom left) illustrates how it's done.

Tip: Placing an ampersand (&) symbol into the shortcut-menu command, as shown at lower left in Figure 6-12, creates an underlined shortcut key, as shown at lower right.

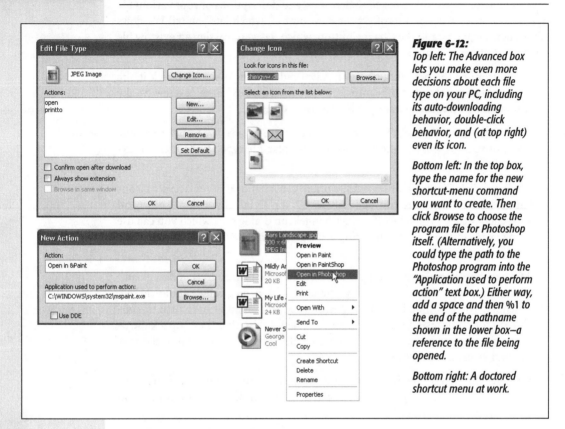

Figure 6-12:
Top left: The Advanced box lets you make even more decisions about each file type on your PC, including its auto-downloading behavior, double-click behavior, and (at top right) even its icon.

Bottom left: In the top box, type the name for the new shortcut-menu command you want to create. Then click Browse to choose the program file for Photoshop itself. (Alternatively, you could type the path to the Photoshop program into the "Application used to perform action" text box.) Either way, add a space and then %1 to the end of the pathname shown in the lower box—a reference to the file being opened.

Bottom right: A doctored shortcut menu at work.

Installing Software

Today, almost all new software comes to your PC from one of two sources: a CD or the Internet. The era of floppy-disk installers is over; you'd need a wheelbarrow to hold all the floppies required to install the average program these days.

Modern software usually comes with an installer program that's designed to transfer the software files to the correct places on your hard drive. The installer also adds the new program's name to the Start→All Programs menu, tells Windows about the kinds of files (file extensions) it can open, and makes certain changes to your *registry* (page 492).

The Pre-Installation Checklist

You can often get away with blindly installing some new program without heeding the checklist below. But for the healthiest PC and the least time on hold with tech support, answer these questions before you install anything:

- **Are you an administrator?** Windows XP derives part of its security and stability by handling new software installations with suspicion. For example, you can't install most programs unless you have an *administrator account* (see page 501). (The exception: You may be able to install new software if you upgraded your PC from a copy of Windows 2000 on a corporate network, and your account was in the *Power Users* group.)

  If you have only a normal account, most attempts to install new software crash and burn with some kind of error message. (If it's a relatively new program, the message might make sense: "To install this program, you must be an administrator or have administrator approval." Programs that predate Windows XP, on the other hand, may chug along happily for about a minute before conking out with some bizarre message of confusion.)

- **Does it run in Windows XP?** Windows XP is compatible with far more programs than Windows 2000 was—but far fewer than, say, Windows 98 or Windows Me.

  If the software or its Web site specifically says it's compatible with Windows XP, great. Install away. Otherwise, consult the Microsoft Web site, which includes a list—not a complete one, but a long one—of all XP-compatible programs. (The easiest way to get there is to choose Start→Help and Support, then click the "Find compatible hardware and software for Windows XP" link.)

Who Gets the Software?

As you're probably becoming increasingly aware, Microsoft designed Windows XP from Day 1 to be a *multi-user* operating system, in which each person who logs in enjoys an independent environment—from the desktop pattern to the email In Outlook Express. The question arises: When someone installs the new program, does every account holder have equal access to it?

In general, the answer is yes. If an administrator (page 501) installs a new program, a shortcut winds up in the Local Disk (C:)→Documents and Settings→All Users→Start Menu→Programs folder. In other words, a newly installed program generally shows up on the Start→All Programs menu of *every* account holder.

Occasionally, a program's installer may offer you a choice: Install the new software so that it's available *either* to everybody *or* only to you, the currently logged-in account holder.

Also occasionally, certain programs might just install software into your own account, so that nobody else who logs

in even knows that the program exists.

In that case, you can proceed in either of two ways. First, you can simply log in to each account, one after another, reinstalling the program for each account.

Second, you may be able to get away with moving the program's shortcut from your own personal account folder to the corresponding location in the All Users folder. As page 525 makes clear, Windows XP actually maintains two different types of Programs folders: one that's shared by everybody, and another for each individual account holder.

Here's where that information pays off: Open your Start→All Programs menu; right-click the name of the program you want everyone to be able to access, and choose Copy from the shortcut menu. Now right-click the Start menu; from the shortcut menu, choose Open All Users. In the window that appears, right-click the Programs folder and choose Paste from the shortcut menu. The program now appears on the Start menu of everybody who uses the machine.

- **Is the coast clear?** Exit all your open programs. (One quick way: Right-click the buttons on the taskbar, one at a time, and choose Close from the shortcut menu.) You should also turn off your virus-scanning software, which may take the arrival of your new software the wrong way.

- **Am I prepared to backtrack?** If you're at all concerned about the health and safety of the software you're about to install, remember that the System Restore feature (page 457) takes an automatic snapshot of your Windows system just before any new software installation. If the new program you've installed turns out to be a bit hostile, you can rewind your system to its current happier working condition, in the process wiping out every trace of damage (and software) that you've introduced.

Installing Software from a CD

Most commercial software these days comes on a CD. On each one is a program called Setup, which, on most installation CDs, runs automatically when you insert the disk into the machine. You're witnessing the *AutoPlay* feature at work.

If Autoplay is working, a few seconds after you insert the CD into your drive, the hourglass cursor appears. A few seconds later, the Welcome screen for your new software appears, and you may be asked to answer a few onscreen questions (for example, to specify the folder into which you want the new program installed). Along the way, the program may ask you to type in a serial number, which is usually on a sticker on the CD envelope or the registration card.

If the last installer window has a Finish button, click it. The installation program transfers the software files to your hard drive. When it's all over, you may be asked to restart the machine. In any case, open the Start menu; a yellow "New programs have been installed" balloon appears next to the All Programs button. If you click there, the program's name appears highlighted in orange, and your Start→All Programs menu is now ready for action.

FREQUENTLY ASKED QUESTION

Microsoft InstallShield?

I'm a bit confused. I bought a program from Infinity Workware. But when I run its installer, the Welcome screen says InstallShield. Who actually made my software?

Most of the time, the installer program isn't part of the software you bought or downloaded, and doesn't even come from the same company. Most software companies pay a license to installer-software companies. That's why, when you're trying to install a new program called, say, JailhouseDoctor, the first screen you see says InstallShield. (InstallShield is the most popular installation software.)

Installing software using "Add or Remove Programs"

Windows XP offers a second, more universal installation method: the greatly improved, but still ingeniously named, "Add or Remove Programs" program. To see it, open Start→Control Panel→Add or Remove Programs.

As shown in Figure 6-16, this listing shows every program on your PC—well, at least those that were installed using a standard Windows installer. Click the name of one to expand its "panel," a thick gray bar that shows you how much disk space the program takes, when you last used it, and so on.

Tip: Some programs include a "Click here for support information" link, which produces a little window revealing the name, Web site, and sometimes the phone number of the software company responsible for the software in question.

Use "Add or Remove Programs" whenever the usual auto-starting CD installation routine doesn't apply—for example, when the CD hasn't been programmed for AutoPlay, when the installer comes on floppy disks (remember those?), or when the installer is somewhere else on your office network.

To make it work, insert the floppy disk or CD that contains the software you want to install. Then click the Add New Programs button at the left side of the window. Finally, click the CD or Floppy button to make Windows look around for the Setup program on the disk or CD you've inserted. If the technology gods are smiling, the installation process now begins, exactly as described above.

Figure 6-13:
You can find thousands of Windows programs (demos, free programs, and shareware) at Web sites like downloads.com, tucows.com, or computingcentral.msn.com.

Top: When you click a link to download something, this box appears. Click the Save button.

Bottom: To avoid losing the download in some deeply nested folder, choose Desktop from the "Save in:" drop-down list at the top of this box. After the download is complete, quit your browser. Unzip the file, if necessary, and then run the downloaded installer.

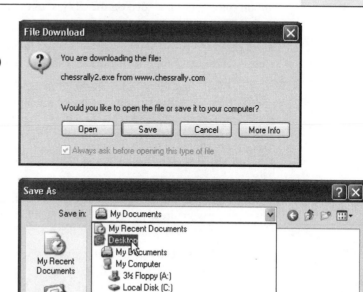

Installing Downloaded Software

The files you download from the Internet (see Figure 6-13) usually aren't ready-to-use, double-clickable applications. Instead, almost all of them arrive on your PC in the form of a *compressed* file, with all the software pieces crammed together into a single, easily downloaded icon. The first step in savoring your downloaded delights is restoring this compressed file to its natural state, as described on page 452.

After unzipping the software (if it doesn't unzip itself), you'll usually find, among the resulting pieces, an installer, just like the ones described in the previous section.

Installing Pre-Loaded Software

As you probably know, Microsoft doesn't actually sell PCs (yet). Therefore, you bought your machine from a different company, which probably installed Windows on it before you took delivery.

Many PC companies sweeten the pot by preinstalling other programs, such as Quicken, Microsoft Works, Microsoft Office, more games, educational software, and so on. The great thing about preloaded programs is that they don't need installing. Just double-click their desktop icons, or choose their names from the Start→All Programs menu, and you're off and working.

Installing Windows Components

The Windows XP installer may have dumped over a gigabyte of software onto your hard drive, but it was only warming up. Plenty of second-tier programs and features are left behind on the CD—stuff that Microsoft didn't want to burden you with right off the bat, but included on the CD just in case.

To see the master list of software components that you have and haven't yet installed, choose Start→Control Panel→"Add or Remove Programs." Click the Add/Remove Windows Components button at the left side of the window.

You've just launched the Windows Components Wizard—basically a list of all the optional Windows software chunks. Checkmarks appear next to some of them; these are the ones you already have. The checkboxes that aren't turned on are the options you still haven't installed. As you peruse the list, keep in mind the following:

- To learn what something is, click its name once. A description appears below the list.

- Turn on the checkboxes for software bits you want to install. Clear the checkboxes of elements you already have, but that you'd like Windows to delete in order to create more free space on your hard drive.

- To the right of the name of each software chunk, you can see how much disk space it uses when it's installed. Keep an eye on the "Space available on disk" statistic at the bottom of the dialog box to make sure you don't overwhelm your hard drive.

- Windows may ask you to insert your Windows CD.

- Some of these checkboxes' titles are just titles for bigger groups of independent software chunks (see Figure 6-14).

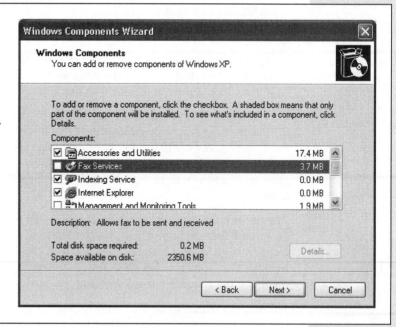

Figure 6-14:
Most of the optional installations involve networking and administrative tools designed for corporate computer technicians. One in particular, however, can be useful to just about anybody: Fax Services. This optional installation is the software that turns your PC into a fax machine.

As you click the name of a software component, the Details button may spring to life, "waking up" from its faded look. When you click it, another list of elements appears—the ones that make up the software category.

The truth is, most people find this list more useful for its ability to *remove* nonessential Windows files (including wallpaper, sounds, screen savers, and so on), saving multimegabytes of disk space on the process. (Some ideas: the 12 MB of games and the 13 MB of MSN Explorer [an America Online-like Web browser].) Just turn off the corresponding checkboxes, click OK, and then restart your machine.

Setting Program Access and Defaults

Software is never finished—especially Microsoft's. That's why, in the fall of 2002, Microsoft released a 330 MB software updater called Service Pack 1. (If your PC didn't come with SP1 already installed, you can download the installer from *www.microsoft.com/WindowsXP/pro/downloads/servicepacks/sp1/default.asp*. The same Web site includes instructions for ordering the SP1 on a CD for $10.)

Tip: To find out if you already have SP1, right-click My Computer and choose Properties. You'll see "Service Pack 1" beneath the other System details.

SP1 doesn't change XP's looks, features, or speed. It's mostly what Automatic Update (page 300) has been feeding you all along: bug fixes, security patches for your Internet programs, and so on. But it also offers a few changes like these:

- It makes Windows recognize USB 2.0, a faster kind of add-on equipment connector that's available on new PCs.

- It installs Java (page 338).

- If you make substantial changes to your PC's guts—surgery so dramatic that you have to reactivate XP (page 18)—you now have a three-day grace period before Windows locks you out of your own machine.

The real raison d'être for SP1, though, is satisfying the U.S. Department of Justice. In its agreement, Microsoft promised to give its competitors a fighting chance at equal footing. For the first time, Windows offers you the chance to hide Internet Explorer, Outlook Express, and a few other standard Microsoft programs, which is presumably a benefit to people who prefer Netscape, Eudora, and Microsoft's other rivals.

You can view this new dialog box by choosing Start→All Programs→Set Program Access and Defaults (a new command). (The long way: Open the Add or Remove Programs icon in the Control Panel, and then click the new "Set Program Access and Defaults" icon at the left side.) You see the display shown at top in Figure 6-15, where you can choose from among these options:

- **Microsoft Windows** means, "Use all of Microsoft's utility programs, just as Windows XP has been doing from Day One." You're saying that you prefer Microsoft's Web browser (Internet Explorer), email program (Outlook Express), Media Player (Windows Media Player), and instant messaging program (Windows Messenger).

Selecting this option doesn't *prevent* you from using other browsers, email programs, and so on—you'll still find them listed in the Start→All Programs menu. But this option does put the Internet Explorer and Outlook Express icons, for example, into prime positions at the upper-left section of your Start menu for quick and easy access.

- **Non-Microsoft** means, "Use *anything* but Microsoft's programs! Instead, use Netscape Navigator, Eudora, RealPlayer, Sun's Java, or whatever—just nothing from Microsoft."

You should install your preferred alternate programs *before* selecting this option. Otherwise, the only programs this feature "sees" are Microsoft programs, which would make selecting this option a tad pointless.

As with the "Microsoft" option, choosing this option places your preferred programs' icons into the upper-left section of your Start menu. Unlike the "Microsoft" option, however, this option *removes access* to the corresponding Microsoft programs. If you choose a non-Microsoft program as your email program, for example, Outlook Express disappears completely from the All Programs menu and its folder (in C:→Program Files). Figure 6-15 shows the idea.

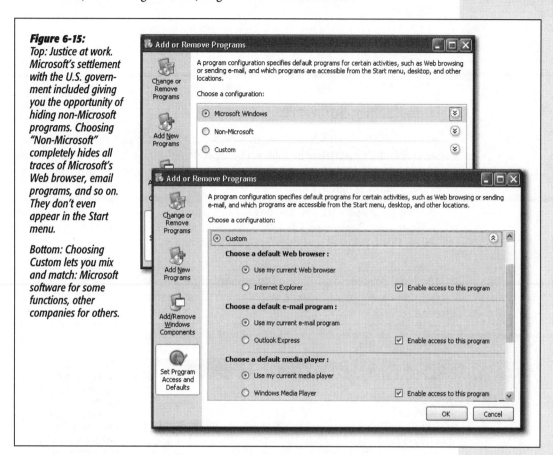

Figure 6-15:
Top: Justice at work. Microsoft's settlement with the U.S. government included giving you the opportunity of hiding non-Microsoft programs. Choosing "Non-Microsoft" completely hides all traces of Microsoft's Web browser, email programs, and so on. They don't even appear in the Start menu.

Bottom: Choosing Custom lets you mix and match: Microsoft software for some functions, other companies for others.

Of course, Microsoft's programs aren't really gone—they're just hidden. They pop right back when you choose the "Microsoft" option, or when you choose Custom (described below) and then click the associated "Enable access to this program" checkbox. Just remember to click OK to apply your changes.

- **Computer Manufacturer** means, "Use whatever programs are recommended by Dell" (or whoever made the PC and signed deals with AOL, Real, and so on). This option doesn't appear on all PCs.

- **Custom** lets you choose each kind of program independently, whether it comes from Microsoft or not. For example, you can choose Netscape, Internet Explorer, or your current Web browser as your default browser.

During your selection process, make sure that you've turned on "Enable access to this program" for each program you want to access (whether or not you're choosing it as the *default* program). Otherwise, Windows may deny access to that program.

Note: Not all non-Microsoft programs show up here—only versions that have been released since SP1 became available.

Uninstalling Software

When you've had enough of a certain program, and want to reclaim the disk space it occupies, don't just delete its folder. The typical application installer tosses its software components like birdseed all over your hard drive; therefore, only some of it is actually in the program's folder.

Instead, ditch software you no longer need using the "Add or Remove Programs" program described above. Click the Change or Remove Programs button at the top left, and then proceed as shown in Figure 6-16.

Tip: If your computer is a member of a workgroup and you're using Fast User Switching (see page 520), don't delete a program until you've ensured that isn't running in somebody else's account behind the scenes.

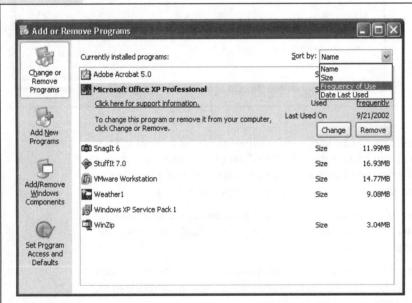

Figure 6-16:
Use the "Sort by" drop-down menu to sort the list by Frequency of Use. This view lets you see which programs have been eating up disk space unnecessarily— programs you hardly ever use. To vaporize a program, click its name to reveal its gray, highlighted panel, as shown here, and then click the Change/Remove button.

Even after you uninstall a program, the folder that contained it may still exist, especially if it contains documents that you created while the program was still alive. If you're sure you won't need those documents, it's safe to remove the folder, along with the remaining files inside it.

Tip: If the program you want to jettison isn't listed in the Add/Remove Programs dialog box, contact the manufacturer for removal instructions, if possible. You'll probably be advised to delete the software the low-tech way: by dragging the program's folder to the Recycled Bin.

Running Pre-XP Programs

As any Windows 2000 user can tell you, stability has its price. For years, people who ran Windows 2000 enjoyed far fewer system crashes than Windows Me people did—but they were limited to a much smaller set of compatible programs. (Barney the Dinosaur CDs, for example, simply wouldn't run on Windows 2000.)

Although it's based on Windows 2000, Windows XP isn't quite as limiting to your software library. Microsoft has pulled every trick in the book to make older, pre–Windows XP programs run successfully. For example:

16-Bit Programs

A 16-bit program is one that's so old, it was written when Windows 3.1 roamed the earth and George Bush Sr. was president. (Programs written for Windows 95 and later are known as *32-bit* programs.)

Amazingly enough, even Windows XP can run most of these programs. It does so in a kind of software simulator—a DOS-and-Windows 3.1 PC impersonation called a *virtual machine.*

As a result, these programs don't run very fast, they don't understand the long filenames of the modern-day Windows, and they may crash whenever they try to "speak" directly to certain components of your hardware (the simulator stands in their way, in the name of keeping Windows XP stable). Furthermore, if just one of your 16-bit programs crashes, *all* of them crash, because they all live in the same memory bubble.

FREQUENTLY ASKED QUESTION

This File Is in Use

Hey, I tried to uninstall a program using Add or Remove Programs, like you said. But during the process, I got this scary message saying that one of the deleted program's files is also needed by other programs. It asked me if I was sure I wanted to delete it! Heck, I wouldn't have the *faintest idea. What should I do?*

Don't delete the file. Leaving it behind does no harm, but deleting it might render one of your other applications non-runnable.

Even so, it's impressive that they run at all, ten years later.

DOS Programs

These programs are 16-bit programs, too, and therefore they run just fine in Windows XP, even though DOS no longer lurks beneath the operating system.

To open the black, empty DOS window that's familiar to longtime PC users, choose Start→All Programs→Accessories→Command Prompt. (See page 199 for more on this program.)

Programs Written for Windows 95, 2000, Etc.

In principle, programs that were written for recent versions of Windows should run fine in Windows XP, even if they don't specifically say so. Unfortunately, some of them contain software code that deliberately sniffs around to find out what Windows version you have. Because these programs were written before Windows XP existed, these programs (or even their installer programs) may say, in effect, "Windows *what?*"—and refuse to run.

Microsoft is way ahead of them on this one. The Properties box of every program (or program shortcut) now offers you the opportunity to fool such programs into

---

Not Your Father's Keyboard

Keyboards built especially for using Windows contain some extra keys on the bottom row:

- On the left, between the Ctrl and Alt keys, you may find a key bearing the Windows logo (⊞). No, this isn't just a tiny Microsoft advertising moment; you can press this key to open the Start menu without having to use the mouse. (On desktop PCs, the Windows key is usually on the bottom row; on laptops, it's sometimes at the top of the keyboard.)

- On the right, you may find a duplicate Windows key, as well as a key whose icon depicts a tiny menu, complete with a microscopic cursor pointing to a command. Press this key to simulate a right-click at the current location of your cursor.

Even better, the Windows logo key offers a number of useful functions when you press it in conjunction with other keys. For example:

⊞+**D** hides or shows all of your application windows (ideal for jumping to the desktop for a bit of housekeeping).

⊞+**E** opens the My Computer window in Windows Explorer view (page 116).

⊞+**F** opens the Search window (page 41).

⊞+**Ctrl**+**F** opens the Search–Computers window .

⊞+**M** minimizes all open windows, revealing the desktop. (Windows key+D is better, however, since the same keystroke also returns the windows.)

⊞+**Shift**+**M** restores all minimized windows.

⊞+**R** opens the Run command (see page 37).

⊞+**V** turns your speaker on and off.

⊞+**Tab** switches through all the application buttons on the taskbar.

⊞+**Break** opens the System Properties dialog box.

---

believing that they're running on a Windows 95 machine, Windows 2000 machine, or whatever. Figure 6-17 details the process.

Despite the fact that this sneaky trick often works, a few footnotes are in order:

- You're much better off securing an updated version of the program, if it's available. Check the program's Web site to see if an XP-compatibility update is available.

- Don't try this trick with utilities like virus checkers, backup programs, CD burning software, and hard drive utilities. Installing older versions of these with Windows XP is asking for disaster.

- If the program you're trying to run is on a CD or on a hard drive elsewhere on the network, you won't be able to change its properties using the steps described in Figure 6-17. Instead, choose Start→All Programs→Accessories→Program Compatibility Wizard. A series of wizard screens explains the concept of compatibility-fooling, and then lets you choose the program you'd like to fool.

Figure 6-17:
If you've successfully installed an older program that doesn't seem to work in Windows XP, find its application icon as described on page 67. Right-click the icon and choose Properties from the shortcut menu. In the Properties dialog box, click the Compatibility tab, turn on "Run this program in compatibility mode for," and then, using the drop-down menu of past Windows versions, choose the version you suspect will make your program happiest. When you click OK, Windows XP will try to fake out the program, making it run. Your dialog box may differ slightly from the one you see here, depending on the program you are trying to run.

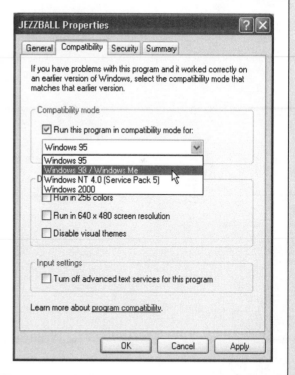

The Freebie Software

Even after a fresh installation of Windows XP, a glance at your Start→All Programs menu reveals a rich array of preinstalled Windows XP applications— as an infomercial might put it, they're your *free bonus gift*. This chapter offers a crash course in these programs, a few of which could probably merit Missing Manuals of their own.

The Windows XP Accessories

Microsoft calls many of these built-in programs *accessories*. They have two things in common. First, they're all smallish, single-purpose programs that you'll probably use only occasionally. Second, you get to them from the Start→All Programs→Accessories menu.

Accessibility Features

If you have trouble using your keyboard or making out small text on the screen, the programs in the Start→All Programs→Accessories→Accessibility menu may be just what you need.

Accessibility Wizard

Windows XP is one of the most disability-friendly operating systems on earth. It includes a long list of features that enables the PC to magnify, speak, or otherwise boost the elements of the screen.

The Accessibility Wizard offers these features to you, one feature at a time. Its screens invite you to enlarge all kinds of things: the type in dialog boxes and menus, scroll bars and window borders, desktop icons, the arrow cursor itself, and so on.

Tip: Not all of these features are useful only to the disabled. If you have a flat-panel screen, for example, you may have noticed that everything on the screen is smaller than it might be on a traditional CRT screen. The result is that the cursor is sometimes hard to find and the text is sometimes hard to read.

Finally, the wizard offers specialized accessibility features for the hearing-impaired and people with trouble using the keyboard. All of these visibility options are duplicated in Windows XP's various Control Panel programs (see Chapter 9). Microsoft just hoped that by putting them all in a single wizard, in interview format, these features would be easier to find.

Magnifier

Magnifier is like a software magnifying glass—a floating rectangular window that enlarges whatever your cursor touches (see Figure 7-1). Using the Magnifier Settings dialog box shown in Figure 7-1, you can specify how much magnification you want (1 to 9 times), which area of the screen gets magnified, and so on.

On-Screen Keyboard

If you're having trouble typing, keep the On-Screen Keyboard program in mind. It lets you type just by clicking the mouse (Figure 7-1)—an option you may find useful in a pinch.

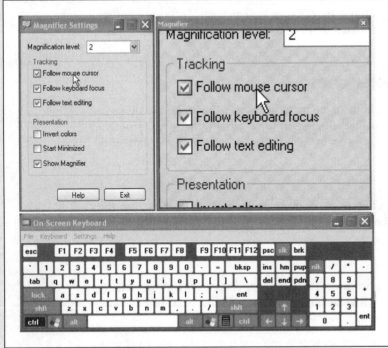

Figure 7-1:
Top: Open Magnifier by choosing Start→All Programs→Accessories→ Accessibility→Magnifier. You can drag the large magnified window (top right) around to a more convenient spot on the screen, and even resize it by dragging the lower-right corner. If you like, use the Magnifier Settings dialog box (top left) to choose the Invert Colors option–a color scheme with higher contrast.

Bottom: The On-Screen Keyboard may be just the ticket if your keyboard keys (or your hands) aren't fully functional.

Narrator

As the little welcome screen tells you, Narrator is a program that reads aloud whatever text appears on the screen—dialog boxes, error messages, menus, text you've typed, and so on. Narrator doesn't work in all programs, and it sounds a little bit like a Norwegian who's had a few beers. Still, if you have trouble reading text on the screen, or if you just like to hear your email read back to you, it's better than nothing.

Tip: By closing or moving the Welcome dialog box, you'll discover a second dialog box hiding squarely behind it—one that lets you control what Narrator reads, and when. For example, you might want to turn on "Move mouse pointer to the active item," so that Windows doesn't read anything to you until you've actually pointed to it.

Utility Manager

This strange little program is designed to control the three accessibility programs just described. The first time you open it, a strange little error message warns you that some of Utility Manager's features are available only if you start and stop the program using its keyboard shortcut (Windows logo key+U). That's good advice.

Once you're in, you'll find the same controls for Magnifier, Narrator, and On-Screen Keyboard: Start and Stop buttons, plus three checkboxes—one of which lets you start any of these accessibility programs automatically when you log into Windows XP.

Communications Menu

The Start→All Programs→Accessories→Communications menu contains several shortcuts:

- **HyperTerminal** is an old-time, text-only terminal program—the sort people once used to dial into BBS (bulletin board) systems in the pre-Web era. Even today, however, you may find this program useful for connecting to *telnet* systems—the text-only display system used by many public libraries.

  You can also use HyperTerminal to set up a PC-to-PC, modem-to-modem link—a useful setup when somebody wants to shoot a file over to you directly, completely bypassing the Internet. The most important thing to remember is that both computers must use precisely the same HyperTerminal settings. (The world is full of programs that are designed for this kind of file transfer, but this one is free.) If you yearn for additional details, see "To receive a file from a remote computer" in HyperTerminal Help.

- **Network Connections** is a shortcut to the Network Connections program in the Control Panel, a window that lists every connection you've established to the Internet or to an office network. See Chapter 18 for details.

- **Network Setup Wizard** and **New Connection Wizard** are shortcuts to the setup programs described in Chapter 18.

- **Remote Desktop Connection.** As described in the Introduction, one of the differences between the Professional and Home editions of Windows XP is something called Remote Desktop connection—a feature that lets you dial into your PC from the road, bringing to your screen everything you'd see if you were sitting in front of the home PC.

For this to work, only the machine you're dialing into (the *host* computer) needs to be running XP Pro. The PC doing the actual dialing (the *client* computer) can be running Windows 95, 98, Me, NT 4.0, 2000 or, of course, XP. Page 604 has the details.

Entertainment Menu

The truth is, you probably won't find the programs in the Entertainment menu particularly entertaining (unless there's *very* little going on in your life). A better name for this menu (Start→All Programs→Accessories→Entertainment) might be Multimedia, since all the programs in it relate to video and sound. They're described in Chapter 8, which is, by happy coincidence, called "Pictures, Sounds, and Movies."

System Tools Menu

This menu (Start→All Programs→Accessories→System Tools) is designed to be a toolbox for basic Windows administration, maintenance, and troubleshooting programs. These programs, including Disk Cleanup, Disk Defragmenter, Scheduled Tasks, System Information, and System Restore, are all described in Chapter 16.

Three of this submenu's contents, however, have nothing to do with PC health and fitness, and were stashed here perhaps because Microsoft couldn't find a more logical place to stash them. The items in question are Activate Windows, Character Map, and the Files and Settings Transfer Wizard.

Activate Windows

As noted on page 18, few Windows features are more controversial than the activation scheme, a form of copy protection that prevents the installation of a single copy of Windows XP onto more than one PC.

If you're not ready to join the Windows XP generation, there's no need to activate your copy when the installer prompts you. In fact, you have 30 days to evaluate Windows XP and decide whether you want to leave it in place.

During that time, reminder balloons appear at the lower-right corner of your screen with all the subtlety of a blinking neon sign. If you ultimately decide to activate your copy, either click that reminder balloon or open this little program, which will walk you through the activation process. (Once you've activated your copy, you won't need this program anymore. Feel free to delete it from your Start menu.)

Character Map

Your computer is capable of creating hundreds of different typographical symbols—the currency symbols for the yen and British pound, diacritical markings for French and Spanish, various scientific symbols, trademark and copyright signs, and so on. Obviously, these symbols don't appear on your keyboard; to provide enough keys, your keyboard would have to be the width of Wyoming. You *can* type the symbols, but they're hidden behind the keys you do see.

The treasure map that reveals their locations is the Character Map. When first opening this program, use the Font drop-down list to specify the font you want to use (because every font contains a different set of symbols). Now you see every single symbol in the font. As you hold your mouse down on each symbol, a magnified version of it appears to help you distinguish them. See Figure 7-2 for details on transferring a particular symbol to your document.

Figure 7-2:
Top: Double-click a character to transfer it to the "Characters to copy" box, as shown here. (Double-click several in a row, if you want to capture a sequence of symbols.) You may have to scroll down quite a bit in some of today's modern Unicode fonts, which contain hundreds of characters. Click Copy, then Close.

Bottom: When you've returned to your document, choose Edit→Paste to insert the symbols.

Tip: In general, Internet email can't handle the fancy kinds of symbols revealed by the Character Map. Don't be surprised if your copyright symbol turns into a gibberish character when received by your lucky correspondent.

Files and Settings Transfer Wizard

This handy utility is designed to simplify the process of moving your life from an older PC to a new one. Page 630 has instructions.

Address Book

The Address Book (Start→All Programs→Accessories→Address Book) is a central Windows directory for phone numbers, email addresses, and mailing addresses.

Once you've launched the program (see Figure 7-3), choose File→New Contact. You're shown a dialog box with seven tabbed panels for various categories of contact information. Now you're supposed to type the name, email address, phone number, and other information for each person in your social or business circle. After you've gone to the trouble of typing in all of this information, Windows XP repays your efforts primarily in two places:

- **In Outlook or Outlook Express.** As Chapter 12 makes clear, a well-informed address book is extremely useful when sending an email message. There's no need to remember that Harold Higgenbottom's email address is *hhiggenbottom@crawl-sapce.ix.net.de;* instead, you only need to type *hhig.* The program fills in the email address for you automatically.

- **In the Search dialog box.** As noted in Chapter 2, you can quickly look up somebody's number by choosing Start→Search→"Printers, computers or people." (If you're not part of a corporate domain, the command says "Computers or people" instead.) This function searches your address book and pulls up the requested name and number.

FREQUENTLY ASKED QUESTION

When Alt+0169 Is Faster

I use the copyright symbol quite a bit, so I figured I would just memorize the keystroke for it instead of having to open Character Map every time I need it. When I click the symbol in Character Map, the lower-right corner of the window says "Keystroke: Alt+0169." But when I try to enter that key sequence into my word processor, I don't get the copyright symbol!

That's absolutely right. You're leaving out two critical steps: First, you can't type those Alt+number codes unless you're in NumLock mode. If the NumLock light (usually at the top of your keyboard) isn't illuminated, press the NumLock key first.

Second, even once you're in NumLock mode, you must type the numbers using the numeric keypad at the right side of your keyboard, not the numbers on the top row. (If you're on a laptop without a numeric keypad, God help you.) Remember to keep the Alt key pressed continuously as you type the suggested numbers.

Tip: To import address book information from another program, choose File→Import→Address Book (WAB) or File→Import→Other Address Book. Windows can inhale the information from any of several popular address book programs.

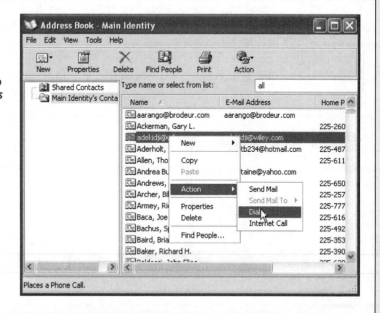

Figure 7-3:
Left column: Generally you can ignore this business of identities, a system of separating the address books and email collections of several people who share the same PC. The Windows XP user accounts feature described in Chapter 17 is a far superior method of keeping everybody's stuff separate.

Lower right: Right-clicking a name in your address book produces a shortcut menu that offers such useful commands as Send Mail and Dial.

Calculator

At first glance, this calculator (Start→All Programs→Accessories→Calculator) looks like nothing more than a thinner version of every pocket calculator you've ever seen (Figure 7-4). You can operate it either by clicking the buttons with your mouse or by pressing the corresponding keys on your keyboard.

Tip: Choosing View→Digit Grouping instructs the Calculator to display numbers with commas (123,456,789), making large numbers (123456789) a lot easier to read.

Most of the buttons look just like the ones on the plastic calculator that's probably in your desk drawer at this very moment, but several require special explanation:

- **/.** The slash means "divided by" in computerese.

- ***.** The asterisk is the multiplication symbol.

- **sqrt.** Click this button to find the square root of the currently displayed number.

- **%.** Type in one number, click the * button, type a second number, and then click this button to calculate what percentage the first number is of the second.

Tip: This calculator may appear to have almost every feature you could desire, but, in fact, it lacks a paper-tape feature—and we all know how easy it is to get lost in the middle of long calculations.

The solution is simple: Type your calculation, such as *34+(56/3)+5676+(34*2)=*, in a word processor. Highlight the calculation you've typed, choose Edit→Copy, switch to the Calculator, and then choose Edit→Paste. The previously typed numbers fly into the Calculator in sequence, finally producing the grand total on its screen. (You can then use the Edit→Copy command to copy the result back out of the Calculator, ready for pasting into another program.)

But by choosing View→Scientific, you turn this humble five-function calculator into a full-fledged scientific number cruncher, as shown in Figure 7-4.

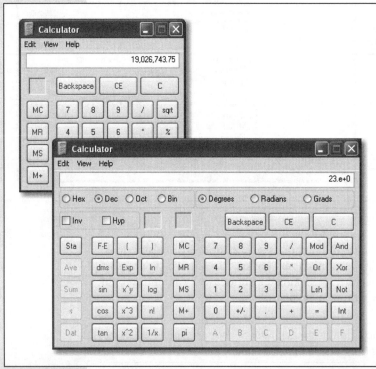

Figure 7-4:
After ducking into a phone booth, the humble Calculator (left) emerges as Scientific Calculator (right), which contains a hexadecimal/ decimal/octal/binary converter for programmers, mathematical functions for scientists, and enough other buttons to impress almost anyone. To learn a particular button's function, right-click it and choose What's This? from the shortcut menu. Don't miss the online help, by the way, which reveals that you can control even the scientific mode from the keyboard.

FREQUENTLY ASKED QUESTION

Clipboard Viewer

Hey, what happened to the Clipboard Viewer? It used to be in the System Tools group of my Start→Programs→ Accessories menu, and now it's gone. It used to be a cool little program for seeing the material I'd most recently copied.

It's still around; it's just hidden. Choose Start→Run, type *Clipbrd.exe,* and press Enter. See page 168 for details.

If that seems like a hassle, you could always replace it with a shareware equivalent like AccelClip (available from *www.missingmanuals.com,* among other places).

Command Prompt

This program summons the MS-DOS window—the black, empty screen that's familiar to longtime PC users. At the C:> prompt, you can type any of hundreds of DOS commands; when you press Enter, the PC executes your typed instruction.

You may need to use this DOS mode to run certain older programs that aren't Windows-compatible; masters of DOS also extol its ability to manipulate (rename, for example) many files at once, to poke and prod a network (using DOS utilities such as *ping.exe* and *netstat.exe*), and so on.

Tip: To learn a few of the hundreds of DOS commands at your disposal, consult the Internet, which is filled with excellent lists and explanations. To find them, visit a search page like *www.google.com* and search for *DOS command reference*. You'll find numerous ready-to-study Web sites that tell you what to type at the MS-DOS prompt.

Notepad

Notepad is a bargain-basement *text editor*, which means it lets you open, create, and edit files that contain plain, unformatted text, like the Read.txt files that often accompany new programs. You can also use Notepad to write short notes or edit text that you intend to paste into your email program after editing it.

Notepad basics

Notepad opens automatically when you double-click text files (those with the file extension *.txt*, as described in the previous chapter). You can also open Notepad by choosing Start→All Programs→Accessories→Notepad.

You'll quickly discover that Notepad is the world's most frill-free application. Its list of limitations is almost longer than its list of features.

For example, Notepad can't open large files. If you double-click a text file icon that contains more than about 50 KB of text, Windows XP automatically opens the file in WordPad (described next) instead of Notepad. Furthermore, the Notepad window has no toolbar and can only work with one file at a time.

What's more, the Print command on the File menu doesn't even open the Print dialog box. Instead, it sends the file directly to your printer, so you can't specify which pages you want, or how many copies of them.

Above all, Notepad is a *text* processor, not a *word* processor. That means that you can't use any formatting at all—no bold, italic, centered text, and so on. That's not necessarily bad news, however. The beauty of text files is that any word processor on any kind of computer—Windows, Mac, Unix, whatever—can open plain text files like the ones Notepad creates.

About word wrap

In the old days, Notepad didn't automatically wrap lines of text to make everything fit in its window. As a result, chunks of text often went on forever in a single line of text or got chopped off by the right side of the window, which could produce disastrous results when you were trying to follow, say, a soufflé recipe.

In Windows XP, lines of text wrap automatically, exactly as they do in a word processor. But you're still seeing nothing more than the effects of the Format→Word Wrap command—an option you can turn off, if you like, by choosing the command again. (You can tell when Word Wrap is on by the presence of a checkmark next to the command in the Format menu.)

Tip: When you print from Notepad, the text automatically wraps to the size of your printer's default paper, regardless of whether Word Wrap is on or off. Choose File→Page Setup from the Notepad menu bar to configure different margins for printing.

Paint

You can use Paint to "paint" simple artwork or to edit graphics files from other sources. You might say that Paint, in other words, is something like Adobe Photoshop (well, in the same way that you'd say that the local Cub Scout newsletter is like the *New York Times*). Common tasks for this program include making quick sketches, fixing dust specks on scanned photos, and entertaining kids for hours on end.

Launch Paint by choosing Start→All Programs→Accessories→Paint, and then:

1. **Choose Image→Attributes to specify the dimensions of the graphic you want to create. Click OK.**

GEM IN THE ROUGH

Notepad Log Files

As stripped-down as it is, Notepad has one surprising feature not available in any other text processor or word processor: automated log files. Every time you open a certain file, Notepad can automatically insert the current date and time at the bottom of the file, creating a tidy record of when you last worked on it—a nifty way to keep any type of a log, like a record of expenditures or a secret diary.

To set this up, create a new Notepad document (choose File→New). Then type the phrase *.LOG* at the top of the new document. (Capitalize LOG, and put nothing, not even a space, before the period.)

Now save the document (File→Save) and give it a name. (Notepad adds the extension *.txt* automatically.)

When you next open the file, Notepad types out the date and time automatically, and puts your cursor on the next line. Now you're ready to type the day's entry.

To make your log file easier to read, press the Enter key to insert a blank line after each entry before saving the file.

Later in your life, you may want to peruse the other commands in this menu, which let you stretch or flip your graphic.

2. **Click a tool on the palette at the left side.**

   If you need help identifying one of these tools, point to it without clicking. A tooltip identifies the icon by name, while a help message appears at the bottom of the window.

3. **If you've selected a painting tool, like the paintbrush, pencil, or line tool, click a "paint" color from the palette at the bottom of the window.**

   You may also want to change the "brush" by choosing from the options located below the tool palette, like the three spray-paint splatter sizes shown in Figure 7-5.

4. **If you've selected one of the enclosed-shape tools at the bottom of palette, *right*-click a swatch to specify the color you want to fill the *inside* of that shape.**

   These tools all produce enclosed shapes, like squares and circles. You can specify a different color for the border of these shapes and for the fill color inside.

5. **Finally, drag your cursor in the image area (see Figure 7-5).**

   As you work, don't forget that you can use the Edit→Undo command up to three times in a row, "taking back" the last three painting maneuvers you made. (Just don't screw up *four* times in a row.)

   For fine detail work, click the magnifying-glass icon and then click your painting. You've just enlarged it so that every dot becomes easily visible.

Figure 7-5:
The Paint tools include shapes, pens for special uses (straight lines and curves), and coloring tools (including an airbrush). The top two tools don't draw anything. Instead, they select portions of the image for cutting, copying, or dragging to a new location.

Paint can open and create several different file formats, including .bmp, .jpg, and .gif—every file format you need to save graphics for use on a Web site.

Tip: Paint also offers a nifty way to create wallpaper (see page 264). After you create or edit a graphic, choose File→Set as Background (Tiled) or File→Set as Background (Centered) to transfer your masterpiece to your desktop immediately.

Program Compatibility Wizard

This program is nothing more than an interview-style version of the dialog box described on page 124—the one that lets you trick an older, XP-incompatible program into believing that it's actually safely nestled on an old Windows 95 computer, for example. Fire it up if some older program is giving you grief in XP.

Scanner and Camera Wizard

Once your XP-compatible camera or scanner is turned on and hooked up, this command walks you through the process of downloading photos or triggering the scan. You'll find more detail on page 211.

Synchronize

You're supposed to use this command in conjunction with the *offline Web-page* feature described on page 335. It forces your machine to go download the latest ver-

---

UP TO SPEED

Text-Selection Fundamentals

Before doing almost anything to text in a word processor, like making it bold, changing its typeface, or moving it to a new spot in your document, you have to *highlight* the text you want to affect. For millions of people, this entails dragging the cursor extremely carefully, perfectly horizontally, across the desired text. And if they want to capture an entire paragraph or section, they click at the beginning, drag very carefully diagonally, and release the mouse button when they reach the end of the passage.

That's all fine, but because selecting text is the cornerstone of every editing operation in a word processor, it's worth learning some of the faster and more precise ways of going about it. For example, double-clicking a word highlights it, instantly and neatly. In fact, by keeping the mouse button pressed on the second click, you can now drag horizontally to highlight text in crisp one-word chunks—a great way to highlight text faster and more precisely. These tricks work anywhere you can type.

In most programs, including Microsoft's, additional shortcuts await. For example, *triple*-clicking anywhere within a paragraph highlights the entire paragraph. (Once again, if you *keep* the button pressed at the end of this maneuver, you can then drag to highlight your document in one-paragraph increments.)

In many programs, including Word and WordPad, you can highlight exactly one sentence by clicking within it while pressing Ctrl.

Finally, here's a universal trick that lets you highlight a large blob of text, even one that's too big to fit on the current screen. Start by clicking to position the insertion point cursor at the very beginning of the text you want to capture. Now scroll, if necessary, so that the ending point of the passage is visible. Shift-click there. Windows instantly highlights everything that was in between your click and your Shift-click.

---

sions of the Web sites you've "subscribed" to. (This feature is great for laptop owners who want to take work home from the office network, or network domain members want to keep working on documents even if the server that houses them goes down.)

Tour Windows XP

This command gives you a multimedia advertisement for the new features of Windows XP. Try to contain your excitement.

Windows Explorer

See page 116 for details on this navigational tool.

Windows Movie Maker

Chapter 8 has the details on this bare-bones video editor.

WordPad

Think of WordPad as Microsoft Word Junior, since it looks much the same as Word (see Figure 7-6) and creates files in exactly the same file format. That's a great feature if you don't *have* Microsoft Word, because WordPad lets you open (and edit) Word files sent to you by other people. (WordPad can open only one file at a time, however.)

If Microsoft Word isn't on your PC, then any icon with the file extension .doc opens into WordPad when double-clicked. (If you install Microsoft Word, however, it takes over the .doc extension.) WordPad can also open and create plain text files, Rich Text Format (RTF) documents, and Microsoft Write documents.

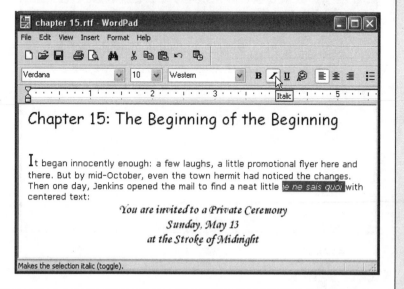

Figure 7-6:
WordPad has menu bars, toolbars, rulers, and plenty of other familiar Windows features. Unlike Notepad, WordPad lets you use bold and italic formatting to enhance the appearance of your text. You can even insert graphics, sounds, movies, and other OLE objects (see Chapter 6).

Using WordPad

When WordPad first opens, you see an empty sheet of electronic typing paper. Just above the ruler, you'll find drop-down menus and buttons that affect the formatting of your text, as shown in Figure 7-6. As in any word processor, you can apply these formats (like bold, italic, or color) to two kinds of text:

- Text you've highlighted by dragging the mouse across it.

- Text you're *about* to type. In other words, if you click the I button, the next characters you type will be italicized. Click the I button a second time to "turn off" the italics.

The rightmost formatting buttons affect entire paragraphs, as shown in Figure 7-7.

WordPad doesn't offer big-gun features like spell checking, style sheets, or tables. But it does offer a surprisingly long list of core word processing features. For example:

- **Edit→Find, Edit→Replace.** Using the Find command, you can locate a particular word or phrase instantly, even in a long document. The Replace command takes it a step further, replacing that found phrase with another one (a great way to change the name of your main character throughout an entire novel, for example).

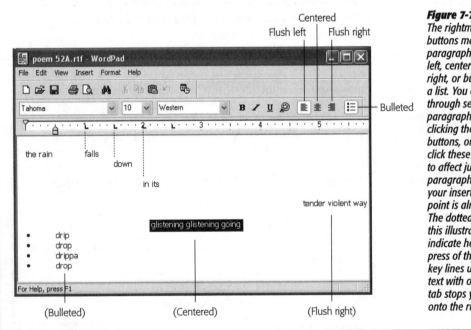

Figure 7-7:
The rightmost buttons make paragraphs flush left, centered, flush right, or bulleted as a list. You can drag through several paragraphs before clicking these buttons, or you can click these buttons to affect just the paragraph where your insertion point is already. The dotted lines in this illustration indicate how each press of the Tab key lines up the text with one of the tab stops you click onto the ruler.

- **Indents and Tab stops.** As shown in Figure 7-7, you click on the ruler to place Tab stops there. Each time you press the Tab key, your insertion point cursor jumps in line with the next tab stop.

- **Object Linking and Embedding.** As described in the previous chapter, this feature (Insert→Object) lets you create or insert a picture, graph, chart, sound, movie, spreadsheet, or other kind of data into your WordPad document.

- **Drag-and-drop editing.** Instead of using the three-step Copy and Paste routine for moving words and phrases around in your document, you can simply drag highlighted text from place to place on the screen. See page 169 for details.

Windows XP Games

Although the central concept of Windows XP—merging what were once separate Windows versions for corporations and homes—is a noble and largely successful one, a few peculiar juxtapositions result. If you're a corporate user, for instance, you may wonder what to make of things like Movie Maker (for editing home movies), Outlook Express (a stripped-down, free version of Outlook)—and games. Yes, Windows XP even includes eleven games for your procrastination pleasure.

More interesting still, several of them let you play against other people on the Internet. At the Microsoft Game Center (*www.zone.com*), players from all over the world gather to find worthy opponents. When you choose one of the Internet-enabled games, your PC connects automatically with this Game Center. An automated matchmaker searches for someone else who wants to play the game you chose, and puts the two of you together, albeit anonymously.

The game board that opens, like the one in Figure 7-8, provides more than just the tools to play; there's even a pseudo-chat feature. By choosing from the canned list of phrases, you can send little game exclamations to your opponent ("Good move," "King me!" "Bad luck," and so on).

Tip: The list of utterances available in your chat session is completely canned. For example, you can't type in, "That was uncalled-for, you sniveling roach!" Still, its canned nature has a virtue of its own: You can exchange platitudes with players anywhere in the world. Your quips show up automatically in the language of your opponent's copy of Windows, be it Korean, German, or whatever.

Here's the Windows XP complement of games, all of which are listed in the Start→All Programs→Games submenu.

Tip: Complete instructions lurk within the Help menu of each game. That's fortunate, since the rules of some of these card games can seem elaborate and quirky, to say the least.

- **FreeCell.** You might think of this card game as solitaire on steroids. When you choose Game→New Game, the computer deals eight piles of cards before you.

The goal is to sort them into four piles of cards—one suit each and sequentially from ace to king—in the spaces at the upper-right corner of the screen. (To move a card, click it once and then click where you want it moved to.)

You can use the upper-left placeholders, the "free cells," as temporary resting places for your cards. From there, cards can go either onto one of the upper-right piles or onto the bottom of one of the eight piles in the second row. However, when moving cards to the eight piles, you must place them alternating red/black, and in descending sequence.

Tip: When you're stuck, move your cursor back and forth in front of the little king icon at top center. Watch his eyes follow your arrow as though hypnotized.

- **Hearts, Internet Hearts.** The object of this card game is to get rid of all the hearts you're holding by passing them off to other players. At the end of each round, all players counts up their points: one point for each heart, and thirteen points for the dreaded queen of spades. The winner is the person with the fewest points when the game ends (which is when somebody reaches 100).

What makes it tricky is that even while you're trying to ditch your hearts, somebody else may be secretly trying to collect them. If you can collect *all* of the hearts

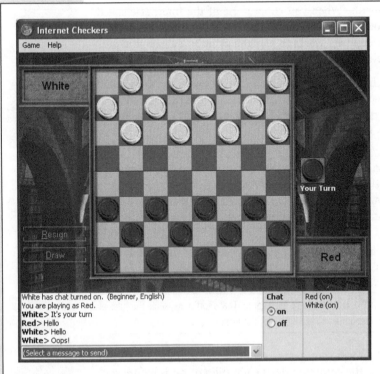

Figure 7-8:
It may look like a simple game of checkers, but you're actually witnessing a spectacular feature of Windows XP: instantaneous anonymous Internet gaming. Two Internet visitors in search of recreation have made contact, a game board has appeared, and the game is under way. The Chat window sits below the game board. You can even turn Chat off if you're planning to play a cutthroat game and don't want to fake having friendly feelings toward your opponent.

and the queen of spades, you win big-time; everybody else gets 26 big fat points, and you get off scot-free.

You can play Classic Hearts either against Windows, which conjures up names and hands for three other fictional players to play against you, or against people on your network. And if you open Internet Hearts, you can play against other similarly bored Windows PC owners all over the world.

- **Internet Backgammon.** This is classic backgammon, but with a twist: Now you're playing against people you've never met, via the MSN Gaming Zone.

- **Internet Checkers.** It's just checkers; once again, though, you can now play against random players on the Internet (see Figure 7-8).

- **Internet Reversi.** Like Othello, you play this strategy game on a chess-type board against another player from the MSN Gaming Zone.

- **Internet Spades.** Here's yet another card game, again designed for Internet playing.

- **Minesweeper.** Under some of the grid cells are mines; under others, hints about nearby mines. Your goal: Find the mines without blowing yourself up.

  When clicking random squares, you run the risk of getting blown up instantly. If that happens, you lose; them's the breaks. But if you get lucky, you uncover little numbers around the square you clicked. Each number reveals how many mines are hidden in the squares surrounding it. Using careful mathematical logic and the process of elimination, you can eventually figure out which squares have mines under them. (To help keep track, you can right-click the squares to plant little flags that mean, "Don't step here.") You win if you mark all the mine squares with flags.

- **Pinball.** To start this noisy, animated, very realistic pinball machine (Figure 7-9), choose Game→New Game. You get three balls; launch the first one by tapping the Space bar. (For a more powerful launch, hold the Space bar down longer before releasing.)

Tip: The game becomes a lot more fun when it fills the screen. Press F4 to make it so.

- **Solitaire.** Here it is: The program that started it all, the application that introduced millions of people to the joys of a graphic interface like Windows. (Ask the advanced-beginner Windows fan to identify a good program-file code to type into the Start→Run dialog box, and he might not know *winword* or *msconfig*—but he'll probably know *sol.*)

  In Solitaire, the object is to build four piles of cards, one for each suit, in ascending order (starting with aces). To help achieve this, you maintain seven smaller stacks of cards in the second row. You can put cards onto these piles as long as you alternate red and black, and as long as the cards go in descending order (a four of hearts can be placed on a five of spades, for example). Click a face-down card on one of these piles to turn it over. If it helps you to continue the red/black/red/black sequence you've started, remember you can drag around stacks of face-up cards on these piles. And when you can't find any more moves to make, click the deck in the upper-left corner to reveal more cards.

If you win, an animated simulation of what's euphemistically called "52 Pickup" appears for your viewing pleasure.

Tip: You can't play Solitaire over the Internet. Even Microsoft hasn't yet figured out a way to turn Solitaire into a multiplayer game.

Figure 7-9:
Once the Pinball ball is in orbit around the screen, you twitch the flippers by pressing the Z and / keys. (Put your pinkies there—this feels much more logical than it reads. Even so, you can reassign these functions to other keys by choosing Options→Player Controls.) You can even "bump the table" by pressing the X, period, or up arrow key.

- **Spider Solitaire.** If your spirit needs a good game of solitaire, but you just don't have the time or patience for Solitaire or FreeCell, this kinder, gentler, *easier* game may be just the ticket. Thanks to the built-in cheat mechanism, which suggests the next move with no penalty, you can blow through this game with all of the satisfaction and none of the frustration of traditional solitaire games.

  You play with 104 cards. You get ten stacks across the top of the screen, and the rest in a pile in the lower-right corner of the screen. By dragging cards around, all you have to do is create stacks of cards in descending order, from king down to ace. As soon as you create such a stack, the cards fly off the playing board. The goal is to remove *all* of the cards from the playing board.

In the easiest level, there's no need to worry about color or suit, because the game gives you *only* spades. If you run out of imagination, just press the letter M key to make the program propose a move, accompanied by a heavenly sounding harp ripple. And if even the game can't find a legal move, simply click the deck in the lower-right corner to distribute another round of cards, which opens up a new round of possibilities.

Sticking with the game to the very end delivers an animated confetti/fireworks display—and a tiny, budding sense of achievement.

Everything Else

The rest of the programs listed in the Start→All Programs menu (at least the ones that come with Windows XP) are covered elsewhere in this book. Internet Explorer is cover in Chapter 11, Outlook Express is described in Chapter 12, Remote Assistance in Chapter 5, and Windows Media Player in Chapter 8.

Tip: There's much more free Microsoft software available to Windows XP gluttons. For example, you'll have a lot of fun trying out the popular PowerToys package (programs produced after the operating system's release), the Windows Media Bonus pack, and additional screen savers. You'll find them all here: *http://www.microsoft.com/windowsxp/pro/downloads/default.asp.*

Pictures, Sounds, and Movies

Windows XP is the most advanced version yet when it comes to playing and displaying multimedia files—photos, sounds, and movies. New features make it easier than ever for your PC to control your digital camera or scanner, play movies and sounds, and play radio stations from all over the world as you work on your PC (thanks to your Internet connection).

In this chapter, you'll find guides to all of these features.

Digital Photos in XP

The new stability of XP is nice, and the new task pane can save you time. But if you have a digital camera, few of the new features in Windows XP are quite as useful as its ability to manage your digital photos. Microsoft has bent over backward to simplify and streamline a process that was once a chain of pain: transferring photos from your camera to the PC, and then trying to figure out what to do with them.

Hooking Up Your Camera

If your digital camera is less than a few years old, it probably came with a USB cable designed to plug into your PC. Fortunately, if your PC is young enough to run Windows XP, it probably has a USB jack, too.

Furthermore, Windows XP comes preloaded with drivers for hundreds of current camera models, generally sparing you the standard installation process described in Chapter 14. That's why, for most people, the instructions for transferring photos from the camera to the PC are as follows:

1. **Connect the camera to the PC, using the USB cable.**

That's it—there is no step 2. As shown in Figure 8-1, Windows XP automatically opens the Camera and Scanner Wizard, a series of screens that guides you through the process of selecting and then transferring the photos you want.

Note: If hooking up the camera produces the dialog box shown at the top of Figure 8-1, then you've installed some photo-management software of your own (maybe some that came with the camera). In that case, you have a choice: Either select that program to download and manage your photos or click Cancel to let XP do the job as described in these pages. Then open your My Pictures folder (Start→My Pictures) and, at the left side of the window, click "Get pictures from camera or scanner."

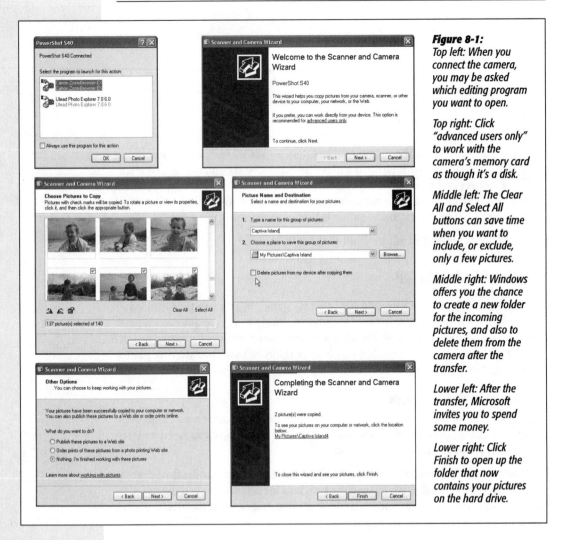

Figure 8-1:
Top left: When you connect the camera, you may be asked which editing program you want to open.

Top right: Click "advanced users only" to work with the camera's memory card as though it's a disk.

Middle left: The Clear All and Select All buttons can save time when you want to include, or exclude, only a few pictures.

Middle right: Windows offers you the chance to create a new folder for the incoming pictures, and also to delete them from the camera after the transfer.

Lower left: After the transfer, Microsoft invites you to spend some money.

Lower right: Click Finish to open up the folder that now contains your pictures on the hard drive.

The various screens of the Camera Wizard take you through these steps:

- **Welcome screen.** If you're the kind of person who prefers to let others do your grunt work, just click Next.

  Note, however, the "advanced users only" link (Figure 8-1, top right). If you click it, Windows XP opens up a new folder window that shows you the contents of the camera's memory card. Each photo is represented as a file icon. At this point, you can copy these photos to your hard drive by dragging them. Use this technique if you want to file them into different folders, for example, rather than using the wizard to dump them all into a single place.

- **Choose Pictures to Copy.** On this screen (Figure 8-1, middle left), you can look over slide-sized versions of the pictures currently on the camera and, by turning on the checkboxes above them, tell Windows which ones you want to copy to your hard drive.

Tip: To straighten a photo that's turned 90 degrees, click it and then click one of the two tiny Rotate buttons at the lower-left corner of the dialog box.

- **Picture Name and Destination.** On this screen (Figure 8-1, middle right), Windows asks you to type the name of the group of pictures to be imported. If you name this group *Robin's Party,* for example, Windows will put the downloaded photos into a My Pictures→Robin's Party folder. (It will, that is, unless you intervene by clicking the Browse button to choose a different folder.)

TROUBLESHOOTING MOMENT

When the Wizard Doesn't Show Up

If the wizard doesn't appear when you hook up your camera, you may be one of the unlucky ones whose camera driver didn't come installed with XP. Technically speaking, the Camera Wizard gets triggered only by cameras whose manufacturers promise *WIA (Windows Image Acquisition)* compatibility. Almost all cameras sold since the year 2000 *are* WIA-compatible.

If the wizard doesn't appear even though you have a compatible camera, you may have to install the driver yourself, using the CD-ROM that came with your camera, as described in Chapter 14. If the camera is reasonably new, it should thereafter work just as described on these pages.

If your camera is too old for Windows XP's tastes, you won't be able to use any of the automated downloading features described in this chapter. You can still get your pictures onto the PC, however, either by using the software provided with the camera (or an updated version—check the camera maker's Web site) or by buying a *card reader,* an inexpensive external "disk drive" that accepts the memory card from your camera. Once inserted, Windows treats the memory card exactly as though it's a giant floppy disk. Opening the card (from within the My Computer window) lets you manually drag the photos to your hard drive.

Tip: This screen offers one of the most useful options: a checkbox called "Delete pictures from my device after copying them." If you turn on this checkbox, then you'll find your memory card freshly erased after the photo transfer, ready for more picture taking.

- **Other Options.** When the transfer process is over, the next screen (Figure 8-1, lower left) offers you direct links to publishing the photos to a Web site, ordering prints by mail via the Web, or Nothing—which is almost always what you want to do here.

- **Completing the Scanner and Camera Wizard.** The final screen (Figure 8-1, lower right) completes the process by offering you a link that opens the folder currently containing the pictures (on your hard drive). Click either the link or the Finish button, which does the same thing.

Fun with Downloaded Pictures

Once you've transferred pictures to your hard drive, you can enjoy a long list of photo-manipulation features, new in Windows XP. These features put to shame the national photo-management system: shoving drugstore prints into a shoebox, which then goes into a closet.

POWER USERS' CLINIC

Bypassing the Wizard

The Camera Wizard is user-friendly to the extreme, but it isn't the most efficient method of transferring your pictures to the hard drive. Plenty of people would rather have Windows just shut up and automatically copy all photos to the hard drive each time the camera is connected. Once the photos are there, *then* you can take the time to select which ones you want, rotate them, and so on. You don't need no stinkin' wizard.

To make it so, connect your camera and turn it on. Choose Start→Control Panel, then open the Scanners and Cameras icon. In the resulting window, you'll see an icon for your camera. Right-click it and choose Properties from the shortcut menu.

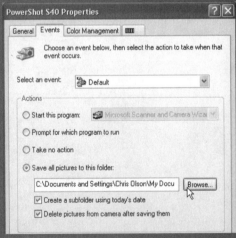

When you click the Events tab, shown here, you'll see that the Actions section options let you govern what happens when you plug in the camera. For example, use the drop-down list at the top to choose a different "digital shoebox" program to start automatically (instead of the Microsoft Scanner and Camera Wizard).

But by turning on "Save all pictures to this folder," you tell Windows to copy all pictures from the camera each time the camera is connected—no muss, no fuss. Using the associated checkboxes, you can also direct it to create a new folder (bearing the date) and, if you like, to erase the camera's memory card after the transfer.

Suppose you've opened a folder of freshly downloaded pictures. (As noted above, they're usually in a folder in your My Pictures folder, which itself is in your My Documents folder. Unless you've deliberately removed My Pictures from your Start menu, just choose its name from the Start menu to get going. Or you can put a shortcut icon for My Pictures right on your desktop, as described on page 134.)

Here are some of the ways you can manage your pictures after their safe arrival on your PC.

Download more photos

When a camera or scanner is turned on and connected to the PC, the first link in the task pane of your My Pictures folder is, "Get pictures from camera or scanner." Click it to launch the Camera and Scanner Wizard all over again.

Look them over

Windows XP comes with two folder window views especially designed for digital photos: Thumbnail and Filmstrip. You can read about them on page 82; for now, it's enough to note that Filmstrip view (Figure 8-2) is ideal for reviewing a batch of freshly transferred pictures at the size that's big enough for you to recognize them.

Remember to press the F11 key to maximize the window and hide a lot of the ancillary toolbar junk that eats into your photo-displaying space. (Press F11 again to restore the window size when you're done.) Also remember to rotate the photos that

Figure 8-2:
In filmstrip view, the enlarged image shows the currently selected photo. You can select a different one for enlargement by clicking another image icon (bottom row) or by clicking the Previous and Next buttons beneath the selected photo. Don't miss the special tasks listed in the task pane at the left side—or the options in the menu that appear when you right-click the central enlarged image.

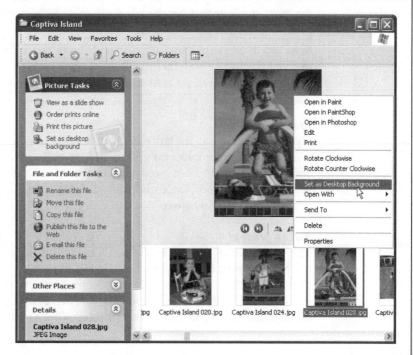

were taken with the camera turned sideways, especially if you plan to use the slide show, Web page, or email features described in the following paragraphs.

Tip: When rotating a photo in Filmstrip view (Figure 8-2), Windows sometimes announces: "Because of the dimensions of this picture, rotating it might permanently reduce its quality. Do you want to proceed?"

This scary message pops up only when you're trying to rotate a photo whose dimensions (measured in pixels) aren't an even multiple of sixteen. Windows is letting you know that, thanks to a quirk in the science of JPEG compression, it must *recompress* the graphic in order to rotate it. Microsoft says that the "quality loss" is imperceptible to the human eye, and you'll probably agree. But if you're worried about it, make a copy of the original photo file before you rotate it.

Start a slide show

When you click "View as a slide show" in the task pane, your screen goes dark, thunder rumbles somewhere, and your entire monitor fills with a gorgeous, self-advancing slide show of the pictures in the folder. If you then move the mouse, a tiny palette appears in the upper-right corner with buttons of control buttons that correspond to Play, Pause, Previous, Next, and Stop.

The beauty of a slide show like this is that everyone at your presentation (or, if this is your home computer, in your family) can see it at once. It beats the pants off the ritual of passing out individual 4 x 6 drugstore prints to each person.

To stop the slide show, press the Esc key on your keyboard (or click the X button in the floating palette that appears when you move your mouse).

Note: Why do photo-related tasks appear on the task pane only in the My Pictures folder? Because Microsoft has applied the Pictures or Photo Album *folder template* to it. You can make these tasks appear in any other folder, however, just by applying the same folder template; see page 82.

Order prints online

If you click this link in the task pane, Windows XP presents a wizard that helps you select photos in your folder for uploading to an online photo processor, like Kodak, Shutterfly, or Fuji. You can specify how many copies you want of each print, and at what sizes (Figure 8-3). Once you've plugged in your credit card number, the prints arrive by mail in about a week.

Make a printout

This task-pane link, too, opens a wizard. This time, it guides you through a selection of photos in your folder to print, a selection of printers to use, and the layout of photos on each 8½ x 11 sheet (four 3 x 5 inch prints, 9 wallet-sized prints, and so on). Note that many of these layouts chop off parts of your pictures to make them fit the page; the layout previews will reveal exactly which parts of the image you'll lose.

Install new wallpaper

The "Set as desktop background" link (which appears whenever you've highlighted a picture) plasters the currently selected photo across the entire background of your screen, turning your PC into the world's most expensive picture frame. (For instructions on changing or removing this background, use the Display program described on page 263.)

Figure 8-3:
The price for prints via Web is usually 50 cents for 4 x 6 prints, and up to $20 for a 20 x 30 inch poster. Be especially careful when you see the red minus symbol shown here. It lets you know that the resolution of that photo is too low to make a good quality print at that size. A 640 x 480–pixel shot, for example, will look grainy when printed at 5 x 7 inches.

Low-resolution warning

Post the photos on the Web

In the old days, creating and posting Web pages was a task fit only for geeks. In Windows XP, however, anybody can create a gallery of photos that hangs on the Web for everyone in the world to see.

Start by clicking "Publish this file ([folder] if no file is selected) to the Web" in the task pane at the left side of your pictures folder window. Yes, it's the Web Publishing Wizard, whose screens walk you through this process:

• Choosing the photos (from the assortment in the current folder) that you want to put online.

• Choosing a Web-hosting company that will provide the disk space for your pictures on the Internet. Note that this means paying money—*unless* you choose MSN Groups from the selection on the third wizard screen.

Although it's free to let Microsoft host your Web page in this way, there are two downsides. First, it limits you to 3 MB of storage—and that's not very many pictures (maybe a dozen). Second, using MSN requires that you have a Microsoft *Passport*. See page 436 for instructions and privacy considerations.

- Choosing an MSN Group (Web page) for displaying your new photos. The first time you do this, you'll want to select "Create a new MSN Group to share your files." Microsoft will name your first Web page for you, tell you the URL (Web address), and offer to add the URL to your list of Favorites. When you create subsequent pages, you'll be asked to type a name for each, enter your email address, and type a description. Whether you're creating new or additional Web pages, the wizard then asks you to indicate whether or not you want the Internet at large to be able to find this page.

- The next wizard screen provides the URL (Web address) for your finished Web page gallery: *www.msnusers.com/*[whatever name you provided for your Web page]. You can distribute this address to friends, family, or whomever you'd like to invite to view your masterpieces online.

- Another wizard screen tells you exactly where your Web-page document and graphics files have been stored online. Unless you're some kind of Web-savvy HTML guru, you probably won't care.

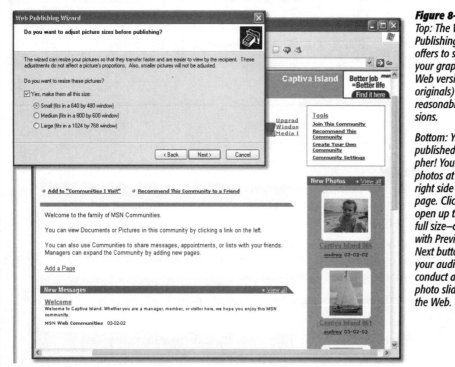

Figure 8-4:

Top: The Web Publishing Wizard offers to scale down your graphics (the Web versions, not the originals) to reasonable dimensions.

Bottom: You're a published photographer! You'll find your photos at the lower-right side of the Web page. Click one to open up that photo at full size—complete with Previous and Next buttons that let your audience conduct a full-sized photo slide show on the Web.

- Most digital cameras create enormous photo files, containing enough resolution for high-quality prints. Unfortunately, those files are much too large for use as Web-page graphics, which feature far lower resolution than printouts do. As a remedy, the wizard screen shown in Figure 8-4 offers to scale the photos down to reasonable dimensions, so that you won't tie up the modems of your potential audience all day.

At last, Windows uploads your reduced-size photos to the Internet, which can take some time. The final wizard screen offers you the chance to go online, opening your browser automatically to the new Web page.

Email photos

Photo files destined for *printing* are much too massive for *emailing*. A single digital photo can occupy 2 MB of disk space or more, which would take until Thanksgiving to send by email. Even then, a photo file might never reach your recipient. If it overflows her email account's storage limit (typically 5 or 10 MB), it will just bounce back to you. Then you'll be forced to sit and wait while it downloads right back to you—a fitting punishment for uploading such a big file to begin with!

The solution is the "E-mail this file" link in the task pane of your pictures folder, which appears whenever you've highlighted at least one picture. Clicking this link produces the dialog box shown in Figure 8-5, which offers to smoothly reduce the dimensions of your pictures in the process of emailing them.

Once you click OK, Windows automatically launches your email program and opens a new, outgoing email message, with the photo files (reduced in size, if that's what you specified) already attached. All you need to do is indicate the address, a subject line, and some comments (in the body of the message), if you like.

Tip: At this point, you can drag the reduced-size picture attachments directly out of the email and *back* to your desktop, or to a waiting folder, without ever addressing or sending the message. Doing so capitalizes on the photo-shrinking power of the "E-mail this file" feature—without actually emailing anything.

POWER USERS' CLINIC

Grabbing Screenshots

Screenshots—illustrations of the computer screen—are a staple of articles, tutorials, and books about computers (including this one). Windows XP has a built-in feature that lets you make them.

Press the Print Screen (PrntScrn) key to capture the entire screen, or Alt+ Print Screen to grab only the front (active) window. You've just stored the image on your invisible Windows Clipboard, and now it's ready for pasting into a graphics program—like Paint. Once it's there, you can print

it, save it, email it, or go into the computer-book writing business on your own.

If you're really serious about capturing screenshots, you should opt instead for a program like SnagIt *(www.techsmith.com).* This versatile program can capture virtually anything on the screen—even neatly snipping open menus out of the background image—and save it into your choice of graphics format.

Create a photo screen saver

There's no "Create photo screen saver" link in the task pane of a photo folder, but Windows XP can still turn your favorite pictures into an automatic slide show whenever your computer isn't in use. Just right-click the desktop, choose Properties from the shortcut menu, click the Screen Saver tab in the resulting dialog box, and then choose My Pictures Slideshow from the "Screen saver" drop-down list.

Tip: The screen saver is composed of photos in your My Pictures folder. If you'd like to choose a different folder as fodder for the slide show, click the Settings button, and then click the Browse button. You'll be offered the chance to choose any folder on your hard drive.

From now on, whenever your PC has gone untouched for five minutes (or whatever interval you specify here), your pictures will fill the screen, complete with special transition effects between images, if you so choose.

Tip: If you're the impatient sort, simply press the right and left arrow keys on your keyboard to summon the next or previous photo while the screen saver is playing.

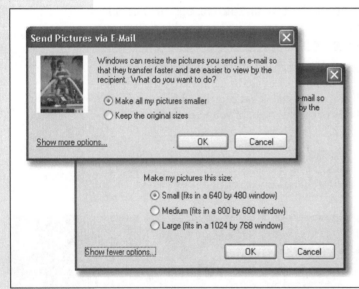

Figure 8-5:
Top: If you just click OK, the selected photos will get emailed at 640 x 480 pixel resolution—just right for satisfactory viewing (and fairly speedy transferring) by email.

Bottom: Clicking the "Show more options" link offers you the opportunity to specify which reduced size you want.

View them bigger

If you double-click a picture or scan a file whose file type you haven't assigned to open in a particular graphics program (page 175), it opens up in a program called Windows Picture and Fax Viewer. WPFV, as Windows veterans don't call it, is a strange, phantom little program. It doesn't show up in your Start menu and you can't find it by searching for it. You can only open it by double-clicking a graphic or by right-clicking a picture's icon and choosing Preview from the shortcut menu.

The result is a simple preview window (Figure 8-6). At the bottom edge, you'll find buttons that do exactly the kinds of things you've been reading about: Show the previous or next image, start a slideshow, rotate the graphic, print it, email it, and so on.

Figure 8-6:
To learn what each button does, point to it without clicking. The Zoom In and Zoom Out buttons magnify or reduce the image on the screen, and the Delete button deletes the file from your hard drive (or, rather, flings it into the Recycle Bin).

POWER USERS' CLINIC

Special Pictures for Special Folders

Filmstrip view, illustrated in Figure 8-2, isn't the only way to view pictures in Windows XP. Thumbnails view has charms of its own—including the ability to display folders like the ones illustrated here, complete with miniature photos on the folder icon to show you what's inside.

If you open your My Pictures folder and set it to Thumbnails view, for example, you'll see that Windows XP has already dressed up the icons of any picture folders inside.

Captiva Island   Captiva Island2

It's worth knowing that, if the collection of pictures inside one of these folders changes, their miniatures on the folder icon itself don't change—at least not until you right-click the folder icon and choose Refresh Thumbnail from the shortcut menu.

Bear in mind that you're not stuck with seeing *four* tiny photos on the folder icon. If you prefer, you can choose a *single* photo to represent the folder contents, as shown here at right. Just right-click any folder in Thumbnails view, choose Properties from the shortcut menu, and click the Customize tab. Finally, click the Choose Picture button and, in the resulting dialog box, double-click the photo you want to plaster onto the folder's icon—and then click OK.

Or, when time is of the essence, try this wacky tip: Just put a graphics file named *folder.jpg* into a folder. That picture instantly becomes the folder's icon!

Scanning

As far as Windows XP is concerned, a scanner is just another kind of digital camera. When an XP-compatible scanner is turned on and connected to the PC, for example, the Camera and Scanner Wizard starts up automatically. (If it doesn't, open your My Pictures folder. You'll see that the first link in the task pane is, "Get pictures from camera or scanner." Clicking launches—you guessed it—the Scanner and Camera Wizard.)

The options you see during the march of the wizard screens are very similar to the ones described in the previous pages. The chief difference is the Choose Scanning Preferences screen, where you're supposed to indicate what kind of scan you want to make (color, grayscale, or black and white) and what portion of the page you want scanned (by dragging the little square handles on the preview of the page).

To view and manipulate your scanned images, use the commands in the My Pictures task pane. You'd be nuts to order prints of something you've just scanned, however. Instead, you'll probably want to use the software provided by the manufacturer to open and edit your image files. Or, if you haven't installed such a program, you can just double-click the scanned document's icon to open it in the Windows Picture and Fax Viewer (page 220).

Windows Media Player

You can use Windows Media Player—one of the most useful freebie features of Windows XP—to play sounds, play digital movies, or tune in to Internet radio stations. It's the Grand Central Station for digital music and movies, as well as the junction for your hard drive, CD player, CD burner, MP3 player, and the Internet (from which you can download new music files and movie clips).

It's easy to see how excited Microsoft is about version 8, since shortcuts connecting you to it are everywhere. It appears in two different Start menu locations (including

Scanning Text—and Then Editing It

I scanned an article from a magazine. How do I copy a couple of paragraphs from it into my word processor?

When you scan an article or book, you're not capturing *text*. You're just taking a *picture* of text. You can no more copy and paste a paragraph out of the resulting graphic file than you could copy text out of a photograph. Your PC sees everything on the scanned page as one gigantic graphic.

If you do want to edit text that you've scanned, then you need *optical character recognition (OCR)* software, which comes free with certain scanners. This kind of software analyzes the patterns of dots in each scanned graphics file, and does a fairly good job of turning it into a word processor document that contains the original text. When businesses decide to convert old paper documents into computer files (insurance company policies, research papers, and so on), OCR software is what they use.

the Start→All Programs→Accessories→Entertainment submenu) and on the Quick Launch toolbar. In any case, you can use a different method for opening Windows Media Player every other day.

Windows Media.com

The first time you launch Media Player, it connects to the Internet in order to bring you to WindowsMedia.com, a Web site dedicated to pop culture in all its commercial forms: rock albums, movies, music videos, and so on.

Tip: If you'd rather stifle Media Player's innate urge to go online every time you open it, choose Tools→Options. (If you don't see the Tools menu at all, press the Alt key, as described below.) Click the Player tab, turn off "Start player in Media Guide," and then click OK.

The Lay of the Land

Before using Windows Media Player, you must first understand the peculiarities of its top edge and its left side.

The top edge, as you may have noticed, isn't rectangular like most windows. Instead, it's the shape of—well, a non-rectangle, which leaves no room for the standard menu bar. You can make it reappear either by pressing the Alt key, moving your mouse to where the menu bar *should* be, or by clicking the tiny double arrow in the upper-left corner (see Figure 8-7). You'll need to do just that, in fact, in order to take advantage of some of the features described in the following sections.

The left edge of the window reveals seven important buttons that correspond to some of the most important Media Player features. The buttons aren't necessarily clearly labeled, however. They're described in more detail in the following pages, but here's a quick overview:

- **Now Playing.** Click this button while music or sound is playing from any source. This is where you can see a list of songs on the CD, a graphic equalizer, and a wild, psychedelic screen saver that pulses in time to the music.

- **Media Guide.** This button takes you online to WindowsMedia.com, a veritable fan magazine for pop culture. It offers links that let you download movie clips, listen to music, and read up on what's what in the movie and pop music worlds.

- **Copy from CD.** Use this screen to copy songs from one of your music CDs onto your hard drive, as described later in this chapter.

- **Media Library.** This screen is like a Windows Explorer display—a folder tree on the left side, and the contents of a selected folder listed on the right—that lists every piece of music or video your copy of Media Player has ever encountered. This is also where you can sort your songs into subsets called *playlists*.

- **Radio Tuner.** As long as you're connected to the Internet, you can use Media Player as the front panel of the world's most powerful radio, capable of picking up stations all over the world.

• **Copy to CD or Device.** After transferring some songs to your hard drive—from the Internet or your own music CD collection—you can then burn your own CDs (if your PC has a CD burner) or copy them to a portable music player. This screen is the loading dock.

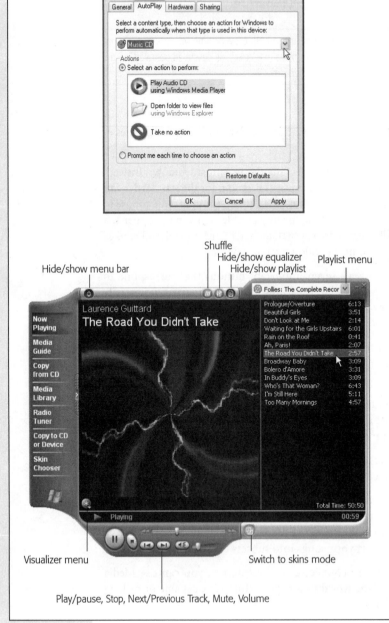

Figure 8-7:
Top: Windows politely asks what you want it to do with a music CD.

Bottom: In the right pane, Media Player displays the album title and the titles of each track, if that information was encoded onto your music CD—or if you have an Internet connection and Windows was able to find the name of your CD on the Internet's massive database of CDs and track names. (If you don't see this list of tracks, click the Show Playlist button, or choose View→Now Playing Tools→Show Playlist.) Beneath the psychedelic screen saver, you see the name of the current song and the elapsed time. Double-click a song name to listen to it.

Hide/show menu bar

Shuffle
Hide/show equalizer
Hide/show playlist
Playlist menu

Visualizer menu

Switch to skins mode

Play/pause, Stop, Next/Previous Track, Mute, Volume

- **Skin Chooser.** Even though it sounds like a complexion cream, this screen lets you choose any of several wacky, even inscrutable new "faceplates" for the look of Media Player.

Playing Music CDs

For its first trick, Media Player can simulate a $100 CD player, capable of playing your music CDs while you're working at your computer. To fire it up, just insert an audio CD into your computer's CD or DVD drive. As shown at top in Figure 8-7, Windows now wants to know how it should respond:

- **Play Audio CD.** If you accept this option by clicking OK or pressing Enter, Windows Media Player opens automatically and begins to play the songs on your CD.

- **Open folder to view files.** If you click this option (or press the down arrow key and then the Enter key), no music plays. Instead, a standard desktop window appears, displaying the icons for the songs on the CD (named things like Track 1, Track 2, and so on). At this point, you can double-click a particular track icon to listen to it, drag certain icons to copy them to your hard drive, and so on. (Note, however, that it's easier to perform most of these tasks in Media Player, as described in the following sections.)

- **Take no action.** The music CD sits in your PC, silent and forgotten.

UP TO SPEED

Which Disks Play Automatically?

As shown in Figure 8-7, inserting a music CD into a brand new Windows XP computer inspires Windows to ask what you want to do with it–play it, show you its contents, or do nothing. Similar choices appear when you insert a DVD, a CD containing pictures, a CD containing files, and so on.

If you'd rather avoid the appearance of this questionnaire dialog box every time you insert a disc, then visit the AutoPlay control center and make your selections all at once. Start by choosing Start menu→My Computer. In the My Computer window, right-click your CD drive's icon. From the shortcut menu, choose Properties. In the resulting dialog box, click the AutoPlay tab shown here.

From the drop-down list at the top of the box, choose the kind of disc you want to affect. Choose "Music files" (a CD filled with MP3 files), "Music CD" (standard audio CDs), "DVD Movie," or whatever.

Then click one of the icons in the Actions list. Apart from Play, the most useful options here are "Open folder to view files" (the CD or DVD's contents window will simply open when you insert it) or "Take no action" (nothing will happen when you insert this kind of disk). The factory setting is, of course, "Prompt me each time to choose an action," which produces the dialog box that began this whole adventure, shown in Figure 8-7.

If you accept the proposed option—to play the music—Media Player opens and, sure enough, begins to play the music (Figure 8-7, bottom). As the music plays, you get to watch psychedelic screen-saver-like displays—called *visualizations* by Microsoft—that bounce and shimmer to the music.

Tip: If all these fancy dancing-to-the-music graphics are slowing down your machine as you try to work in other programs, you can always turn them off (choose View→Now Playing Tools→Show Visualizations to eliminate the checkmark in front of the menu command).

Fun with Media Player

When the work you're supposed to be doing leaves you uninspired, here are a few of the experiments you can conduct on the Media Player screen design:

- **Switch visualizations.** To try a different visualization, click the Next Visualization or the Previous Visualization arrow (the tiny arrow buttons just below the shimmery display), or press Tab+Enter and then click the Video Settings button, or choose View→Visualizations. And if you tire of the displays built into Windows, then just download more of them from the Internet by choosing Tools→Download Visualizations.

Tip: One of the most interesting choices is Album Art, which displays a picture of the album cover for whichever song is now playing.

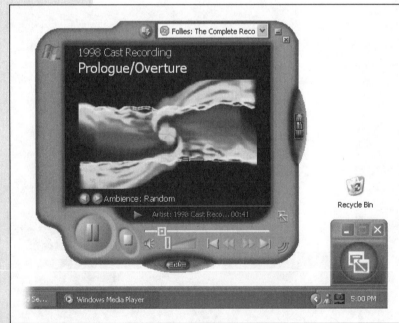

Figure 8-8:
At full size, the Media Player window occupies a large chunk of your screen (Figure 8-7), and shows off Microsoft's fledgling tendency to move beyond the rectangular window. In Skin Mode (left), it takes up less space on your screen and can use any of dozens of radical new design schemes. Skin Mode also produces a small control window (right), which appears in the lower-right corner of your desktop. Clicking this compact window produces a menu that offers, among other commands, "Switch to full mode."

- **Shrink the window to show some skin.** If the Media Player window is taking up too much screen space, making it harder for you to work on that crucial business plan as you listen to *NSync, press Ctrl+2 (or click the Skin Mode button in either the center or lower-right corner of the Media Player window, depending on whether the right playlist pane is open) to shrink the window (see Figure 8-8). Press Ctrl+1 to return the Media Player window to its full-sized glory. (Of course, you can also just minimize Media Player, as you would any window.)

- **Expand the window.** On the other hand, if your PC is briefly serving as a glorified stereo system at a cocktail party, choose View→Full Screen (or press Alt+Enter). The screen-saver effect now fills the entire screen, hiding all text, buttons, and controls. If you have an available coffee table and a laptop to put it on, you've got yourself a great atmospheric effect. (When the party's over, just click the mouse, or press Alt+Enter again, to make the standard controls reappear.)

- **Change the skin.** In hopes of riding the world's craze for MPEG Audio Layer-3 (MP3) files (compact, downloadable, CD-quality sound files), Microsoft has helped itself to one of MP3-playing software's most interesting features: *skins*. A skin is a design scheme that completely changes the look of Windows Media Player (see Figure 8-9).

To choose a new skin, click the Skin Chooser button on the left side of the Media Player window. Then click each of the available skins to see a preview of its appearance. When you click the Apply Skin button (at the top left corner of the window), your player takes on the look of the skin you chose *and* shrinks down into the compact Skin mode, as described in the previous tip.

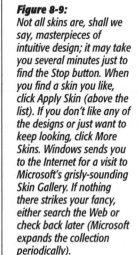

Figure 8-9:
Not all skins are, shall we say, masterpieces of intuitive design; it may take you several minutes just to find the Stop button. When you find a skin you like, click Apply Skin (above the list). If you don't like any of the designs or just want to keep looking, click More Skins. Windows sends you to the Internet for a visit to Microsoft's grisly-sounding Skin Gallery. If nothing there strikes your fancy, either search the Web or check back later (Microsoft expands the collection periodically).

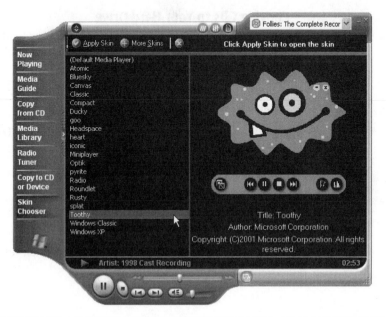

• **Fool around with the playback sequence.** You can make the songs on the CD play back in a random order, just as though you'd pushed the Shuffle button on a CD player. To do this, just click the Shuffle button or press Ctrl+H—the shortcut for the Play→Shuffle command. And if you love a particular CD so much that you'd like to hear it over and over again (instead of stopping at the end), press Ctrl+T—the shortcut for Play→Repeat.

Tip: These tricks work for whatever *playlist* you've currently selected—not just an audio CD. (Playlists are described later in this chapter.)

• **Fool around with the sound.** The View→Now Playing Tools submenu offers all kinds of options for summoning special-effects displays. Some of these options, including Captions and Lyrics, are available only if you've typed them in yourself.

Don't miss, however, the graphic equalizer, a little row of sliders that lets you adjust the bass, treble, and other frequencies of the music to suit your particular speakers and your particular ears. And SRS WOW (another one of these menu options) simulates a 3-D sound experience through nothing more than stereo speakers or headphones (press Ctrl+Enter).

• **Read the "CD booklet."** The large buttons at the left edge of Media Player include a button called "Copy from CD," which can be extremely useful even if you have no intention of copying songs from the CD. For example, it provides the most useful display of information from the CD you're listening to—song titles, track links, singer names, and album information (that even includes a little review and, needless to say, an opportunity to buy another copy of the CD online).

Copying CDs to Your Hard Drive

You can copy an album, or selected tracks, to your hard drive in the form of stand-alone music files that play when double-clicked. Having CD songs on your hard drive affords you the following benefits:

• You can listen to the songs you like, without having to hunt for the CDs they came from.

• You can listen to music even if you're using the CD-ROM drive for something else (such as a CD-based game).

• You can build your own *playlist* (set of favorite songs) consisting of cuts from different albums.

• You can compress the file in the process, so that each song takes up very little disk space.

• You can transfer the songs to a portable music player or burn them onto a home-made CD.

If you're sold on the idea, here's how you go about it:

1. **Insert the music CD. Click the "Copy from CD" button on the left side of the Media Player window.**

   The list of songs on the CD appears. See the box below for information on ensuring that the album name and track names are correct.

2. **Turn off the checkbox of any track you *don't* want to copy.**

   You've waited all your life for this: At last, you have the power to eliminate any annoying songs and keep only the good ones.

   And while you're playing record-company executive, take a moment to drag the names of the songs up or down the list to rearrange them.

3. **Choose Tools→Options. In the resulting dialog box, click the Copy Music tab.**

   The dialog box shown in Figure 8-10 appears. Unless you intervene by clicking the Change button near the top, Windows will copy your song files into the My Documents→My Music folder.

GEM IN THE ROUGH

Filling in Track Names

Most audio CDs don't come programmed to know their own names (and song names). To this day, millions of people insert music CDs into their computers and see the songs listed as nothing more than "Track 1," "Track 2," and so on—and the album itself goes by the catchy name Unknown Album.

If your PC is online when you insert a certain music CD—you lucky thing—you'll bypass that entire situation. Windows takes a quick glance at your CD, sends a query to *www.allmusic.com* (a massive database on the Web containing information on over 200,000 CDs), and downloads the track list and a picture of the album cover for your particular disc.

If *allmusic.com* draws a blank, as it often does for classical recordings, no big deal. Media Player makes it easy to search the Web for this information at a later time. Just insert the CD, connect to the Internet, click "Copy from CD" at the left edge of the screen, and then click the Get Names button at the top of the screen. A wizard appears at the bottom of the screen to walk you through the process of finding your CD in the online database and, if you like, editing the track information that the Web site finds.

If the online database still doesn't know about your CD, you'll be offered the chance to upload your information to the Web database for the benefit of future generations.

You can also type in the names of your songs manually. Once again, click "Copy from CD" at the left side of the screen to view the list of tracks. Now right-click the track and, from the shortcut menu, choose Edit. A little text box opens so that you can type in the track information manually.

No matter how the track names and album art gets onto your PC, Windows XP saves this information in your music library (see "Copying Music to Your Hard Drive" later in this chapter). Therefore, the next time you insert this CD, the Media Player will recognize it and display the track names and album information automatically.

Tip: While you're in this dialog box, consider clicking the Advanced button. It opens a dialog box that lets you specify which information gets added to the names of the files that you're about to copy. By turning on Track Number, Title, Artist and Album, for example, you'll ensure that your files wind up with names like "01 Back in the USSR Beatles White Album."

That's not especially useful when you're just looking at the files on your hard drive, because in Tiles or Details view, Windows displays this information anyway. Instead, this option is provided for the benefit of portable music players that only show a single line of information—the song name—while playing. By tacking this supplementary information onto each song's name, you ensure that you'll see a little more data when you glance at your music player screen.

What you're really interested in here, however, is the "Copy Music at this quality" slider. See Figure 8-10 for details.

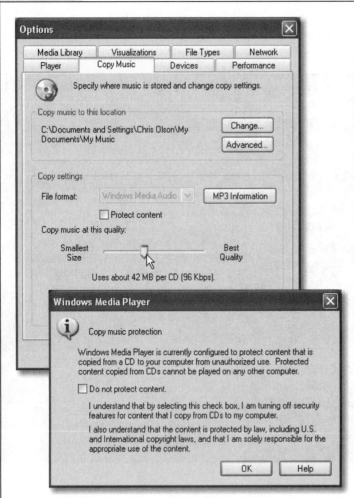

Figure 8-10:
Top: Music files take up a lot of space on the hard drive. By adjusting this slider, you can specify how much Windows compresses the song files, with the understanding that you sacrifice sound quality as you make the file smaller. In general, the 96 K setting offers an excellent trade-off— the resulting files sound just like a CD, but the entire CD consumes only about 42 MB on the hard drive. Experiment with the other settings to accommodate your ears and speakers.

Bottom: This is what happens when lawyers get involved in software design. Windows is offering you the chance to copy-protect your own music so that you can't transfer the songs to other computers or portable music players. Unless you're a particularly self-destructive person, turn on "Do not protect content" and then click OK.

4. **Adjust the quality slider and then click OK.**

   You return to Windows Media Player.

5. **Click Copy Music.**

   You'll find this button in the narrow strip above the list of songs.

   Clicking it displays the message shown at bottom in Figure 8-10 (but just the first time you ever copy songs).

6. **Turn on "Do not protect content" and then click OK.**

   Windows begins to copy the songs onto your hard drive. The Copy Music button changes to Stop Copy, which you can click to interrupt the process.

Organizing Your Music Library

Every CD transferred to your hard drive winds up with an entry in the *playlist* menu, identified in Figure 8-7. Whenever you want to play back some music, just choose its name from this menu—there's no need to hunt around in your shoeboxes for the original CD the songs came from.

But that's just the beginning of Media Player's organizational tools; see Figure 8-11.

Transferring CD songs to your hard drive isn't the only way to log your files in the Media Player database. You can also add sound and video files to this master list using any of these methods:

FREQUENTLY ASKED QUESTION

MP3, Microsoft, and You

Hey! What are these files Windows Media Player is copying to my hard drive? They're not MP3 files! I want MP3 files!

Microsoft, as you may have noticed, is expending a good deal of effort on becoming the controlling party for as many technology standards as possible (the Internet is one example). With Windows XP, Microsoft has shown that it would also like to take over the music-file business. To that end, it has designed Windows Media Player to generate files in Microsoft's own proprietary format, something called Windows Media Audio (WMA) format (.wma). However, it can't create the infinitely more popular MP3 files—at least not out of the box.

But some people prefer, and even require, MP3 files. For example, most recent CD players and portable music play-

ers can play back MP3 files—but won't know what to do with WMA files.

If you really want Windows Media Player to create MP3 files, Microsoft has provided a way—for a fee. In Windows Media Player, choose Tools→Options. In the resulting dialog box, click the Copy Music tab, and then the MP3 Information button. Windows takes you onto the Internet, to a special Web page that offers you the opportunity to buy any of several MP3 plug-in software modules that add MP3-creating abilities to Windows Media Player for about $10.

There are, however, plenty of ways to create MP3 files from your CDs without sending Microsoft more money. The Web is filled with free MP3-creation and playback programs, including MusicMatch Jukebox (*www.musicmatch.com*).

- Use the Tools→Search for Media Files command (or press F3).

- Drag sound or video files directly from your desktop or folder windows into the right side of Media Player.

- Choose File→Add to Media Library. From the submenu, choose Add Currently Playing Track, Add File, or (for files on the Web) Add URL.

- The Internet is crawling with Web sites that harbor downloadable music files that you can make part of your music library. To find them, click the Media Guide button at the left side of the Media Player window. You're shown a list of Microsoft Web sites, where you'll find lists, search engines, and other methods for finding music.

Once you've created a well-stocked fridge of music, you can call up a particular song by clicking the Search button (at the top of the Media Library list), by navigating the folder tree (at the left side of the Media Library list), or by using the playlist drop-down list (at the top right of the Media Player window).

Playlists

As noted above, each CD that you transfer to your hard drive becomes a *playlist* in Windows Media Player: a group of songs, listed in the folder tree at the left side, that you can play back with a single click. Media Player automatically turns your CDs into playlists, but you can also create your own, mixing and matching songs from different albums for different purposes (which you might name Work Music, Downer Tunes, Makeout Music, or whatever).

To create a new playlist, make sure you've selected the Media Library button at the left side of the screen. Then click the "New playlist" button above the list of folders. Type a name for the new playlist, click OK, and take satisfaction in the fact that it now appears on the left side of the screen (in the "folder" called My Playlists). To

---

WORKAROUND WORKSHOP

You, the DJ

You're not allowed to change the playback order of songs you've copied to your PC from a CD (the ones in playlists that Windows created automatically). Actually, there is one built-in way to affect their playback order—just click the column headers (Title, Artist, Album, and so on) to sort them accordingly—but it's not very flexible. And besides, Media Player forgets this kind of change the next time you start it up.

If you want the freedom to rearrange the songs on a CD

you imported, there's only one thing to do: Create a new playlist of your own. Then find the original CD playlist that Windows created, click its name, and then drag all of the songs from that CD into your homemade playlist. (Dragging names around in this way does not actually duplicate any files on your hard drive.)

Yes, you now have two different playlists for the same CD, but at least you have the freedom to rearrange the playback order of the songs in your homemade one.

---

stock this playlist with songs from your entire collection, just drag their names from the song list on the right side, shown in Figure 8-11.

Once you've created a playlist of your own, you can rearrange its playback sequence just by dragging the songs up or down the right-side list.

Deleting things

Whenever you want to delete a song, a playlist, or anything else, the key is to right-click it. You'll find the Delete command in the shortcut menu.

Note: When you choose the command Delete from Library, Media Player doesn't obey immediately. Instead, it works like the Recycle Bin, moving the songs to a folder called Deleted Items (located in the playlist of the Media Library screen) so that you can restore them to another playlist if you change your mind. They're not really gone until you click the All Deleted Media "playlist," select the song names in the right-side list, right-click one of them, and then choose Delete from Library from the shortcut menu.

Figure 8-11:
Top: Clicking the Media Library button at the left side of the screen reveals a Windows Explorer-like display that lets you access your music in a number of ways: by album, by artist, by musical style (genre), and so on. You can even manage video clips with these controls—if you're one of the six people who collect them. You can add songs to custom playlists just by dragging, as shown.

Bottom: Behind the scenes, Windows builds a set of nested folders in the My Documents →My Music folder. Within the My Music folder, you'll find a folder for each performer. Within the performer folder, there's a folder for each CD, and within that folder, you'll find icons representing the tracks you copied.

Burning Your Own CDs

The beauty of a CD burner is that it finally frees you from the stifling restrictions put on your musical tastes by the record companies. You can create your own "best of" CDs that play in any CD player—and that contain only your favorite songs in your favorite order.

The easiest way to create a CD like this in Media Player is to assemble the songs you want in a custom playlist, as described in the previous section. Then, at the left edge of the Media Player window, click the "Copy to CD or Device" button. A screen that looks something like Figure 8-12 appears next.

Note: To burn a CD without creating a playlist first, scamper through your media library, right-clicking each song you want and choosing Copy to Audio CD from the shortcut menu. Media Player copies each song name into a special playlist called Send To (it's listed in the My Playlists "folder" at the left side of the window). At that point, you have, in effect, created a playlist that you can treat just like the one described in these instructions.

Figure 8-12:
Remember that a music CD can only hold so much music. (Just how much it holds depends on the quality setting you've specified for your music files.) If some of your songs say, "Will not fit," as shown here, turn off some songs (by clearing their checkboxes) until everything fits.

Once you've assembled the audio CD-to-be, insert a blank CD into your burner, and then click the Copy Music button at the upper-right side of the window. The transfer process takes quite a bit of time and quite a bit of hard drive space, so budget appropriately for both. When the process is complete, your PC spits out the CD automatically.

Copying Music to a Portable Player

If you have a pocket gizmo that's capable of playing music, such as a Diamond Rio or a Pocket PC, the process for loading your favorite songs onto it is exactly the same as the process for burning your own CD. Just make sure that it's hooked up to your PC and that its name appears in the drop-down list of devices at the upper-right corner of the screen.

Internet Radio

The 2000s' twist on listening to the radio as you work is listening *without a radio*. Nowadays, the computer itself is used as a radio, one that can tune in to hundreds of radio stations all over the world, each brought to you by the Internet.

The first step in transforming your computer into a "radio" is to open Windows Media Player. Next, click the Radio Tuner button at the left to connect to the Internet, where you can select the stations you want to hear (see Figure 8-13). Click the green arrow next to a station's name to listen in. (You may have to wait for 30 seconds or so before the station "tunes in," and, of course, you can only listen when you're actually connected to the Internet.)

To create your own list (that will replace Microsoft's Featured Stations list), find your favorite stations by using the search features in the right pane. In the Search Keyword text box, type in the name of the show, a host, a city name, or whatever.

Figure 8-13:
The left side of the Radio Tuner window lists your preset stations. (Microsoft starts you off with several popular stations in a collection named Featured Stations.) The right side provides search features to help you find stations you want to add to this canned list.

When you find a radio station you like, select it and then click the Add to My Stations link that appears below its name. (To remove a station from your preset list, select it and then click Remove from My Stations.)

Tip: You need the Radio Tuner screen only to *set up* your list of favorite stations. After that, the radio stations appear in the "folder" labeled Radio Tuner Presets, located within your Media Library (Figure 8-11). You can play radio stations from the Media Library screen—the same screen you use to play everything else in your multimedia world.

Video Clips

Media Player can also play movie files, such as those you've downloaded from the Internet, made yourself, or grabbed from a CD-ROM. The standard Windows movie-file format is *.avi*, but Media Player can also play files with the extensions .wmv, .wvx, .avi, .mpeg, .mpg, .mpe, .m1v, .mp2, .mpa, and .ivf.

Tip: Media Player doesn't recognize two of the most popular video-file formats: QuickTime and RealVideo. To play these files, you'll need QuickTime Player (available free from *www.apple.com/quicktime*) or RealPlayer (from *www.real.com*), respectively.

DVD Movies

If your PC has a drive that's capable of playing DVDs, you're in for a treat. Media Player can play rented or purchased Hollywood movies on DVD as though it was born to do so—a new feature in Windows XP.

Watching movies on your screen couldn't be simpler: Just insert the DVD. Windows XP automatically detects that it's a video DVD—as opposed to, say, one that's just filled with files. Then, depending on the settings you made in the dialog box shown in Figure 8-7, it either opens Media Player automatically or offers to do so. (If not, no problem: Open Media Player yourself and then choose Play→DVD or CD Audio→[your DVD drive's name].)

Media Player starts out playing your movie in a relatively small window—but you didn't come this far, and pay this much, just to watch movies on a *slice of* your screen. Your first act, therefore, should be to enlarge the picture to fill the screen. Pressing Alt+Enter is the easiest way, but you can also choose View→Full Screen or click the Full Screen button (see Figure 8-14).

After you enlarge the screen, a slider appears for a few seconds at the lower-left corner of the screen, permitting you to speed backward or forward through the movie, and then fades away so as not to obscure Arnold Schwarzenegger's face. It's joined by the Rewind, Fast Forward, and other buttons identified in Figure 8-14. To pause the movie, jump around in it, or advance one frame at a time, just twitch the mouse to make the controls (and the playlist of DVD chapters) reappear.

Tip: For real fun, turn on *English* subtitles but switch the *soundtrack* to a foreign language. No matter how trashy the movie you're watching, you'll gain much more respect from your friends and family when you tell them that you're watching a foreign film.

Figure 8-14:
Once the DVD is playing, you control the playback using the standard Media Player controls (at the bottom-left edge of the window). To switch to a different "chapter," use the list at right (choose View→Now Playing Tools→Show Playlist if you don't see it). To change language or subtitle options, open the DVD→ View menu, as shown here. When you're playing the movie full screen, a "remote control" appears only when you move the mouse a bit. Then the variable-speed slider appears, along with the Rewind, Play/Stop, and other controls labeled here. It fades away again a few seconds after you stop moving the mouse.

Rewind   Play/Stop   Fast forward   Chapter list
                                                             (double-click)

Ditching the Remote Control

When the remote control is hidden, you can always return it to the screen just by moving your mouse. But the true DVD master would never bother with such a sissy technique. The secret keystrokes of Media Player are all you really need to know:

Function	Keystroke
play	Ctrl+P
stop	Ctrl+S
fast forward	Ctrl+Shift+F
rewind	Ctrl+Shift+B
louder	F10
quieter	F9
mute	F8
next/previous "chapter"	Ctrl+F, Ctrl+B
full-screen mode	Alt+Enter
eject	Ctrl+E

Tip: Watching a movie while sitting in front of your PC is not exactly the great American movie-watching dream. To enhance your viewing experience, you can always connect the video-output jacks of your DVD-equipped PC (most models) to your TV.

Just be sure to connect the cables from the PC's video-output jacks *directly* to the TV. If you connect them to your VCR instead, you'll get a horrible, murky, color-shifting picture—the result of the built-in copy-protection circuitry of every VCR.

Making WAVs with Sound Recorder

Windows XP comes with a generous assortment of sound files that you can use as error beeps, as described in Chapter 9. But no error beep is as delightful as one that you've made yourself—of your two-year-old saying, "Nope!" for example, or your own voice saying, "Dang it!"

Using Sound Recorder (Figure 8-15) requires a sound card, speakers, and a microphone. If your PC is appropriately equipped, you can use this little program to record various snippets of your life, which can serve a number of purposes, including error beeps.

Recording a New Sound

Here's how to do it:

1. **Choose Start→All Programs→Accessories→Entertainment→Sound Recorder.**

   The window shown at top in Figure 8-15 appears.

   At this point, you may want to take a detour by choosing File→Properties. In the resulting dialog box, click Convert Now to specify the sound quality of the recording you're about to make. The choices in the Name drop-down list— Radio Quality, CD Quality, and so on—indicate not only the sound quality, but also how much disk space the file will consume. (Better quality takes up more disk space.) Click OK twice after you've made your selections.

2. **Click the Record button, make the sound, and then click Stop as soon as possible thereafter.**

   If you see animated sound waves in the Sound Recorder window, great; that's your VU (sound level) meter. It tells you that the PC is hearing you. If you don't see these yellow lines, however, then the sound isn't getting through. Most likely, the problem is that your PC control panel isn't set to record the appropriate sound source. Choose Edit→Audio Properties, and then use the Default Device drop-down list in the Sound Recording section to choose your microphone's name.

   If it's impossible to capture a clean sound, free of dead space—because you're recording babies or animals who refuse to perform on cue, for example—you're not out of luck. You can always edit out the dead space. Use the scroll bar to position the handle just before the dead space at the end of the sound, and then choose Edit→Delete After Current Position. (To get rid of dead space *before* the good part, position the handle and then choose Edit→Delete *Before* Current Position.)

At this point, click the Play button to see what you've got. If it isn't quite what you had hoped, repeat this step; your first take is automatically obliterated.

Tip: Don't miss the good times that await you in the Effects menu. You can increase or decrease your recording speed, add an echo effect, or even play it backward—great for finding subliminal messages in your own speech.

When you've got something worth keeping, go on:

3. **Choose File→Save As. Type a name for your sound file in the "File name" text box, choose a folder for it, and then click the Save button.**

You've just created a *.wav* file, a standard Windows sound file.

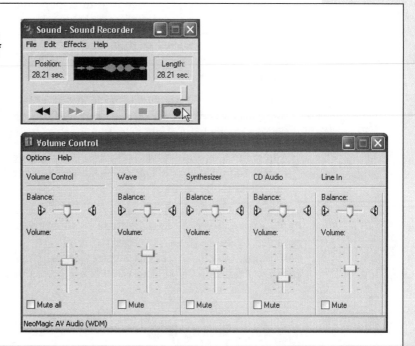

Figure 8-15:
Sound Recorder (top) lets you capture the sounds of your world—digitally. Volume Control (bottom) offers left-to-right stereo balance controls and volume adjustments for every sound-related component of your PC.

What to Do with Sounds

When you double-click a *.wav* file that you've saved to your desktop, the file opens in Windows Media Player and plays back immediately. (Press Esc to interrupt playback.) Sound files are also ideal for emailing to other Windows users, posting on Web sites, transferring over the network, and so on. Many a Bart Simpson sound clip proliferates via the Internet in exactly this way.

Finally, if you put a *.wav* file into your my Computer→Local Disk (C:)→ Windows→ Media folder, it joins the other sound files that Windows uses for its various error beeps. You can then use the instructions on page 294 to replace Windows XP's sound effects with ones you've created.

Volume Control

This program has perhaps the most understated name of all time. As you can see by Figure 8-15 at bottom, the program looks more like a 747 cockpit than a simple volume knob.

In any case, the controls here govern the volume and balance levels of the speakers, microphones, and sound-card elements of your PC. Every PC's sound card and other features are different, so not all of the controls may be operational on your machine…but you get the idea.

Here are a few things you might want to do with Volume Control:

- **Shut your PC up.** Clicking "Mute all" at the lower-left corner of the window completely silences your PC—a handy feature, for example, when you don't want an errant beep or squawk to let everyone in church know you're using a laptop.

- **Adjust the stereo balance of your PC speakers.** If one of the speakers is farther away from your head, you might want to drag the Balance sliders so that the distant speaker plays a little bit louder.

- **Fine-tune Musical Instrument Digital Interface (MIDI) playback.** If your sound card can play back MIDI files (a compact file format for instrumental music), use the Synthesizer balance and volume controls to tweak its sound.

- **Adjust the bass and treble.** These knobs don't appear on the Volume Control screen. You must choose Options→Advanced Controls, and then click the Advanced button to see these sliders.

Tip: If you rarely use certain Volume Control features, or if some of them don't apply to your system, or if your system has features (like a microphone) that *don't* have corresponding controls, you can hide or show individual panels. To do that, choose Options→Properties. Then in the Properties dialog box, a scrolling list of checkboxes lets you independently hide or show each of the volume controls—Synthesizer, CD Audio, Line In, Microphone, and so on.

Windows Movie Maker 2

Movie Maker 1.0 was Microsoft's first effort at video-editing software. It let camcorder owners edit the boring parts out of their footage, add crossfades, and save the result as a digital file for emailing to friends or saving onto a disk.

Otherwise, though, it was pretty disappointing, offering only a single kind of transition between clips, no special effects, no way to add credits and titles, and no way to send your masterpiece back out to the camcorder for playback on a TV.

Movie Maker 2, released at the end of 2002, is another story. It remedies every one of those problems and more. Unfortunately, version 2 probably didn't come with your copy of Windows XP Pro. You have to download it from Microsoft's Web site (*www.microsoft.com/windowsxp/moviemaker*), or use the Windows Update feature described on page 259.

Movie Maker 2 has been so dramatically improved that, frankly, you'd be silly to use the copy of Movie Maker 1 that came with Windows. If you plan to do any video editing at all—and to be sure, this may not be an everyday activity for you if you use XP Pro in some humming hive of a corporation—download the new version and enjoy its flexibility. The following discussion covers only version 2.

Equipment List

Editing is the easy part. The hard part is getting equipped to do so, since there's nowhere to plug a camcorder into a standard PC. To use Movie Maker, proceed in any of these three ways:

- **Use analog equipment.** In other words, use a standard camcorder or VCR, and play your footage into your PC from standard VHS, 8mm, or Hi-8 tapes.

  A quick inspection of the back of your computer, however, should make clear that it has no connector for a VCR. Therefore, you also need to buy a *video capture card* or one of those inexpensive USB capture boxes designed to let you pour video into your PC. The quality might be grainy, though, since Movie Maker achieves its goal of creating emailable movie files by heavily compressing your video.

- **Use digital equipment.** If you prefer better quality, use Movie Maker with a *digital* (DV) camcorder. A digital camcorder ($600 and up) uses special tapes called MiniDV cassettes. (Sony Digital8 models are the exception, as they record onto ordinary Hi-8 tapes—saving you money in the process.)

Note: Although the new, shockingly tiny Sony MicroMV camcorders are indeed digital, their signal is incompatible with Movie Maker. Sony says that it's working with Microsoft on revising Movie Maker for MicroMV compatibility. In the meantime, you can use the software that comes with the camcorder–MPEG Movie Shaker–to grab the footage from the camera. You can then import the resulting files into Movie Maker.

  Next, you need a *FireWire card* (about $60). You insert this kind of add-on circuit board, sometimes called an *IEEE-1394* or *i.link card*, directly into your PC. On the side of almost every digital camcorder model is a special connector, a FireWire port, that connects to the FireWire card with a special FireWire *cable*. This single cable communicates both sound and video, in both directions, between the PC and the camcorder.

- **Use existing pictures or movies.** You can use Movie Maker to edit existing movie files you've downloaded from the Internet or copied from CD-ROMs, or even to splice together still photos that you've scanned or captured from a digital camera for the purpose of creating a living photo album.

***

Note: If you're working with a digital camcorder, you need a *lot* of hard drive space. Digital video footage takes up 3.6 MB *per second* of video—enough to fill up 10 GB in about 40 minutes.

***

See Chapter 14 for tips on installing cards. And be sure to ask about Movie Maker 2/ Windows XP compatibility before you buy any cards.

Getting Started with Movie Maker 2

After you've downloaded and installed Movie Maker, you open the program by choosing Start→All Programs→Accessories→Windows Movie Maker. The Windows Movie Maker screen appears, shown in Figure 8-16. Its left-side task pane indicates the three major steps you'll take to putting a movie together: Capture Video, Edit Movie, and Finish Movie.

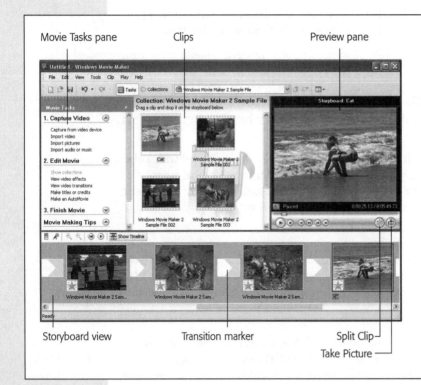

Movie Tasks pane   Clips   Preview pane

Storyboard view   Transition marker   Split Clip   Take Picture

Figure 8-16:
Windows Movie Maker 2 sports a new Movie Tasks pane that provides quick access to the most-used menu options. The other major working areas of the program are all identified here. You'll do most of your work in the Storyboard or Timeline view at the bottom of the screen.

Behind the scenes, Windows XP creates a folder in your My Documents folder called My Videos. This is where you'll find icons representing the various video clips that you capture from your camcorder. (You'll also find a few sample video clips there to fool around with until you get your equipment-buying act together.)

How you transfer footage into Movie Maker for editing depends on what kind of equipment you've got—analog, digital, or none.

Capturing footage

To capture footage, hook up your VCR or camcorder to the PC. Then:

1. **Choose File→Capture Video, press Ctrl+R, or click "Capture from video device" in the Movie Tasks pane.**

   The Video Capture Device Wizard screen appears, shown at top in Figure 8-17.

2. **Click the icon for your camera or capture card.**

   If it has multiple input connections, like an S-video connection and a composite video connection, use the "Video input source" drop-down list to select the one you want to use. You can also take this opportunity to specify which connection the sound will be coming from, using the "Audio input source" drop-down list.

3. **Click Next. On the Captured Video File screen (second from top in Figure 8-17), type a name for the video file you're about to create, and choose a folder for saving it. Click Next.**

   The Video Setting screen appears, shown third from top in Figure 8-17.

4. **Choose the video quality you want.**

   The bigger the resulting movie (in terms of its onscreen dimensions when played back), the more disk space it will take up. A movie that fills your screen may look great on your PC, but you'll never be able to email it to anyone; the video file will be too huge.

   If you plan to show your movie only on the computer, "Best quality for playback on my computer" is a good choice. If you hope to export the result to your camcorder (for playback on TV), though, choose the "Digital device format (DV-AVI)" option (which is offered only if you have a digital camcorder). That's an extremely disk space–hungry format, but it preserves 100 percent of the original DV quality.

5. **Click Next.**

   If you're capturing from a digital camcorder, the Capture Method screen now appears. Here, you can specify whether you want to capture the *entire* tape (in which case the camcorder automatically rewinds and then starts playing back as the PC captures) or just selected scenes (in which case you're supposed to use the onscreen playback controls to stop and start the tape). Click Next.

6. **On the Capture Video screen (bottom in Figure 8-17), adjust your options.**

   If you turn on "Create clips when wizard finishes," Movie Maker will automatically chop up the incoming video into individual *clips*—icons, each representing one shot you made with your camcorder. If you don't select this option, Movie Maker will treat all the footage you import as one big video chunk.

7. Click Start Capture.

If you have a digital camcorder, Movie Maker automatically commands it to be-gin playing; you're essentially controlling the camcorder by remote control. If you're using a non-digital camcorder or a VCR, it's up to you to push Play on the equipment. Either way, you can inspect the video as it arrives on your hard drive by watching it in the Preview window.

8. When the recording is complete, click Stop Capture, and then click Finish.

You may be asked to wait while Movie Maker processes the incoming footage.

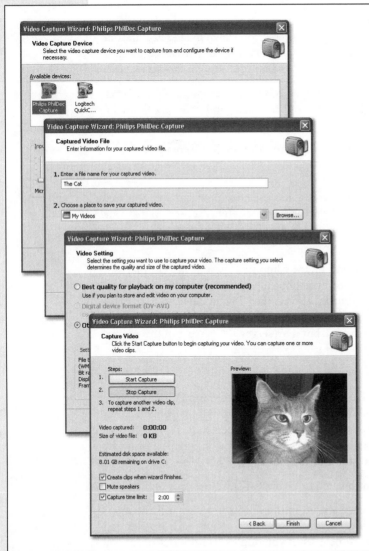

Figure 8-17:
Top: You select the video capture device, audio device, video input source, and audio input source in the Video Capture Device screen.

Second from top: In the Captured Video File screen, you name your captured video and select a folder to store it.

Third from top: Select one of three settings you want to use to capture your video in the Video Settings screen, and then verify the selected settings in the information boxes at the bottom of the screen.

Bottom: Finally, you and your tape are both ready to roll. Use the Start Capture and Stop Capture buttons to control the transfer of footage to your hard drive. (If you use a digital camcorder, you'll see Play, Stop, and Rewind buttons that let you control the camcorder right from the screen.)

9. To capture another clip, find it on your tape, and then repeat from step 6 on.

Repeat this process until you've captured all the pieces needed to create your masterpiece.

Importing pictures and movies

You don't necessarily need fancy equipment to fool around with Movie Maker. You can also bring any movie or picture file on your hard drive into your Movie Maker project by choosing File→Import into Collections (or clicking "Import video" or "Import pictures" in the Movie Tasks pane). Movie Maker turns the file into a clip, which you can edit, chop up, or manipulate, as described in the following paragraphs.

For example, while waiting for your video-capture card to arrive by mail order, you can try your hand at editing one of the existing movies that comes with Windows XP. In your My Documents→My Videos folder, you'll find a sample video file (called Windows Movie Maker 2 Sample File). After opening it, double-click one of the clip icons to watch a convincing home movie of a Microsoft employee's family romping at the zoo.

Tip: To the ancient question, "What is the sound of one hand clapping?" you can now add, "What is the duration of a still picture?" As far as Windows is concerned, the answer is, "Two seconds." When you drag a still-image clip into your Timeline, as described below, Windows gives it a two-second proposed duration. To make a still image stay on the screen for a longer or shorter interval, however, simply drag its right-hand triangle on the ruler, as shown in Figure 8-18.

Editing Video

Once you've accumulated a few clips, it's time to conduct some general organization—rearranging the clips; trimming off excess footage from the ends; adding credits, music, and effects, and so on.

Phase 1: Organize your clips

Icons for the clips you've imported gather in the Collection area at the center of the screen. (Behind the scenes, they're really in your My Documents→My Videos folder.)

If you choose View→Collections, the task pane disappears, replaced by an area where you can create virtual folders to hold your clips (choose Tools→New Collection Folder). Rename or delete these folders by right-clicking them. (You can bring back the Movie Tasks pane by choosing View→Task Pane.)

Whenever you click one of these folders, the middle part of the window shows you the clips it contains. To play one of these clips, double-click its icon, or click it and then press the Space bar. (To stop playback before the end of the clip, press Space again.)

Phase 2: Drag them into the storyboard

The clip-assembly area at the bottom of the Movie Maker screen can appear in either of two ways, depending on your current selection in the View menu (see Figure 8-18):

- **Storyboard.** In this view, each clip appears as an icon, like a slide on a slide viewer. Each is the same size, even if one is eight minutes long and the next is only two.

- **Timeline.** In this view, each clip is represented by a horizontal bar that's as wide as the clip is long. Short clips have short bars; long clips stretch across your screen. Additional parallel "tracks" represent soundtracks playing simultaneously, titles and credits, and transition effects.

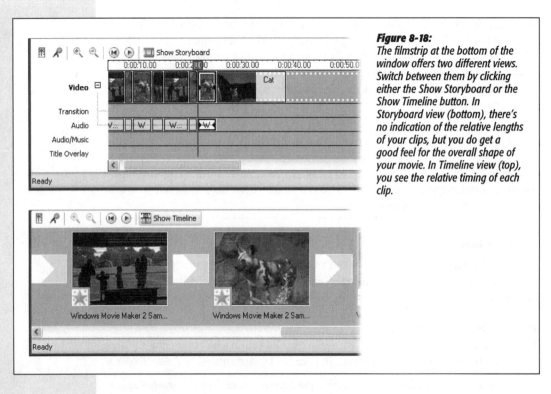

Figure 8-18:
The filmstrip at the bottom of the window offers two different views. Switch between them by clicking either the Show Storyboard or the Show Timeline button. In Storyboard view (bottom), there's no indication of the relative lengths of your clips, but you do get a good feel for the overall shape of your movie. In Timeline view (top), you see the relative timing of each clip.

Either way, this is where you'll organize the scenes of your movie. Drag the clips from the Clips area (shown in Figure 8-16) down into this area to place them in the order you want. You can rearrange them once they're there, too, just by dragging. You can also trim unwanted material off the beginning or end of each clip by dragging the triangles in each icon.

As you go, you can preview your film in progress by choosing Play→Play Storyboard (or Timeline, depending on which window you're working with). To interrupt playback, click the Pause button in the Preview pane, click Play→Pause Clip, or click Play→Stop.

Tip: Choose View→Full Screen (or press Alt+Enter) to make the movie fill your monitor as it plays back. Unless you're working with digital video, the blotchy, blurry enlargement may trigger your innate demand-your-money-back instincts. But this trick is useful, for example, when showing your finished movie to a group of people in a room. From a few feet away, the poor picture quality isn't as noticeable.

Phase 3: Chop up the clips

As you work, you may frequently find it useful to cut your clips into smaller pieces, thereby eliminating boring material. You can do this in either of two ways:

- **Split a clip.** After aligning the scroll bar underneath the Preview pane with the spot where you want the clip chopped, choose Clip→Split, press Ctrl+L, or click the "Split the clip" button (shown in Figure 8-16). Movie Maker turns the single clip into two different clips, adding a number to the name of the second one.

Tip: You can do the opposite, too. After arranging a few clips into a satisfying sequence, you can merge them into a single, new uni-clip for easier manipulation. To do that, click the first one in the Storyboard or the Timeline window and then Shift-click successive clips. Finally, choose Clip→Combine.

- **Trim a clip.** Sometimes you just want to trim off unwanted footage from either *end* of a clip—a task Movie Maker lets you perform only after you've added a clip to the Timeline. Then just drag the triangle handles, which you can see in Figure 8-17.

Phase 4: Add video transitions

To create a *cross-dissolve* transition from one clip to another instead of just cutting, switch to the Timeline view shown at top in Figure 8-18. Then drag a clip in the Timeline slightly to the left, so that it overlaps the preceding clip. The amount of overlap determines how long the crossfade lasts; adjust this amount by dragging the clip again. (Dragging the clip all the way to the right, so that it no longer overlaps, eliminates the crossfade altogether.)

For fancier transitions, click Tools→Video Transitions (or click "View video transitions" in the Movie Tasks pane). The available transitions—60 of them—appear in the Video Transitions pane, shown in Figure 8-19. You can double-click any of these icons to see what the transition looks like. To use one in your movie, drag its icon down between two clips in either the Storyboard or the Timeline window.

Tip: It's easiest to drag transition icons when you're in the Storyboard view, because you have such a big target: the big square between the clips shown in Figure 8-18.

Phase 5: Add video effects

A video effect is a special effect: a color filter, frame rotation, slow motion, artificial zooms (in or out), and so on. As with transitions, using them with abandon risks making your movie look junky and sophomoric—but every now and then, a special effect may be just what you need for videographic impact.

To view your choices, choose Tools→Video Effects (or click "View video effects" in the Movie Tasks pane). You can apply a video effect in either of two ways:

- Drag its icon from the Video Effects pane directly onto the desired clip. (You can drag more than one onto the same clip.)

- Right-click the clip icon in either the Storyboard or the Timeline window, then choose Video Effects from the shortcut menu. The Add or Remove Video Effects dialog box appears. If you promise to use good taste, you can even pile up multiple effects on a single clip and rearrange the order in which they're applied.

Note: When you apply an effect, Movie Maker 2 applies it to the entire clip. When you split, move, cut, or copy a clip or picture, its effects remain attached to it (or all of its parts). On the other hand, if you combine two clips, the first clip's effects retain control, and the second clip's effects are vaporized.

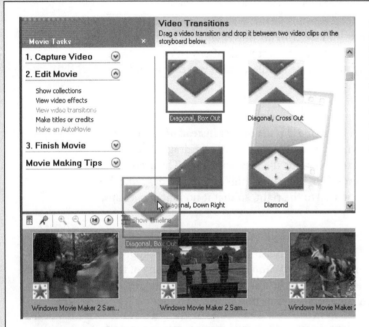

Figure 8-19:
Microsoft has provided 60 video transitions for your movies. Use them to soften transitions from one clip to the next—but use discretion. Going hog-wild with different nutty transitions in one movie will brand you as an amateur. Professional filmmakers rarely use anything beyond a simple cut or a cross-dissolve.

Phase 6: Add titles and credits

Text superimposed over footage is incredibly common in the film and video worlds. You'd be hard-pressed to find a single movie, TV show, or commercial that doesn't have titles, captions, or credits. In fact, it's the *absence* of superimposed text that pegs most camcorder videos as amateur efforts.

To add this kind of text in Movie Maker 2, begin by choosing Tools→Titles and Credits (or click "Make titles or credits" in the task pane).

As shown in Figure 8-20, you're offered five places to put text: at the beginning of the movie, at the end of the movie, before a clip, on a clip, or after a clip. Note that in Movie Maker terminology, text that appears before or after a movie is called *credits,* and it must take the form of name/job pairs (like "Director: Chris Olson"). Text that appears just before, after, or superimposed on a clip is just called a *title.*

Once you've clicked your choice, you're offered the chance to type the actual text. This screen also offers "Change the title animation" and "Change the text font and color" links, which affect how the titles or credits drift across the screen (and in what type style). The animation effects duplicate just about every common TV title style: letters flying onto the screen, spinning onto the screen, scrolling across the screen, and so on.

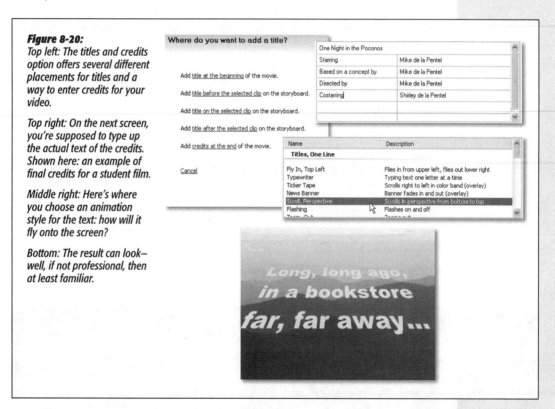

Figure 8-20:
Top left: The titles and credits option offers several different placements for titles and a way to enter credits for your video.

Top right: On the next screen, you're supposed to type up the actual text of the credits. Shown here: an example of final credits for a student film.

Middle right: Here's where you choose an animation style for the text: how will it fly onto the screen?

Bottom: The result can look— well, if not professional, then at least familiar.

When you click Done, the program switches to Timeline view and adds your text to the film in progress (Figure 8-20, bottom). On the Timeline, text gets its own block, which you can double-click to edit. You can also drag its ends to change the beginning or ending points. In Storyboard view, superimposed text doesn't show up at all; text inserted between clips appears as a separate clip.

Phase 7: Add background music

If you're lucky, you may someday get a chance to watch a movie whose soundtrack isn't finished yet. At that moment, your understanding of the film medium will take an enormous leap forward. "Jeez," you'll say, "without music and sound effects, this $100 million Hollywood film has no more emotional impact than…my home movies!"

And you'll be right. Without music, sound effects (called SFX for short), and sound editing, even the best Hollywood movie will leave you cold and unimpressed. Fortunately, Movie Maker can use any MP3 or WMA file on your hard drive as a musical soundtrack. Just choose File→Import into Collections. The music file appears among your clips with a special musical-note icon.

Now, in Timeline view, drag the music clip onto the track marked Audio/Music. You can drag the appropriate rectangular strip left or right to control where it starts and ends. Using the Tools→Audio Levels command, you can also adjust its volume relative to the camcorder sound. Unfortunately, you can't create variations along the music's length (to make it softer during dialog, for example).

Tip: Even if you don't own a camcorder, one of the nicest things you can do with Movie Maker is produce a slide show with sound. After importing still images as described earlier, import a pop song to lay underneath it. You'll be surprised at how much impact the result has.

Phase 8: Save the movie

When your flick looks and sounds good, you can save it as a stand-alone file on your hard drive, which you can then double-click to play or send to potential investors.

To do so, Choose File→Save Movie File (Ctrl+P), or click "Save movie file" in the task pane. In the Movie Location screen (Figure 8-21), specify where you want to save the movie. You have five options:

• **My Computer.** Choose this option if you want to preserve the complete movie as a file on your hard drive.

GEM IN THE ROUGH

The Narrator Speaks

If your PC has a microphone, you can narrate your own "voice-over" soundtrack as the video plays—a great way to create a reminiscence or identify the scene. Unfortunately, you can't add *both* music *and* narration; Movie Maker can tolerate only one added audio track.

In Timeline view, then choose Tools→Narrate Timeline; the Narrate Timeline pane appears. Drag the playback in-

dicator to an empty point on the Audio/Music track and then click the Start Narration button. You can watch the video play as you speak into your microphone.

Click Stop Narration to wrap it up. You're asked to name and save your narration file (it gets a .wma filename extension). At this point, you can adjust the volume or starting/ending points of the narration track just as you would a music track: by adjusting its bar in the Audio/Music track.

- **Recordable CD.** A wizard appears to walk you through the process of saving a lower-resolution movie onto a blank CD, so you can distribute it to friends for playback on their PCs. (These disks will also play back on CD and DVD players that bear Microsoft's "High M.A.T." logo—of which there are very few.)

- **E-mail, The Web.** Video really isn't a good match for Internet distribution methods; video files are huge and slow to download. This wizard, then, guides you through making a very low-quality, small-framed, slightly jittery movie whose file size is small enough to transmit via the Internet.

- **DV camera.** For many people, this is the most important new feature of Movie Maker 2. While you're editing your movie, you watch your work-in-progress on the screen—but that's only a low-res representation of the spectacular clarity of digital video. Fortunately, behind the scenes, every shred of crisp, clear, smooth-motioned video is intact on your hard drive. To see it, you must export the movie *back* to your DV camcorder, where it appears with all of its high-resolution glory.

Once the final production is back on a DV tape, you can play it on a TV with incredible quality, or copy it onto your VCR (at much lower quality) for distribution to family, friends, and Los Angeles agents.

Figure 8-21:
You choose where you want to save or send your video from the Movie Location screen. You can save the video to your computer, to a recordable CD, email, the Web, or a DV camera. The wizard walks you through the process.

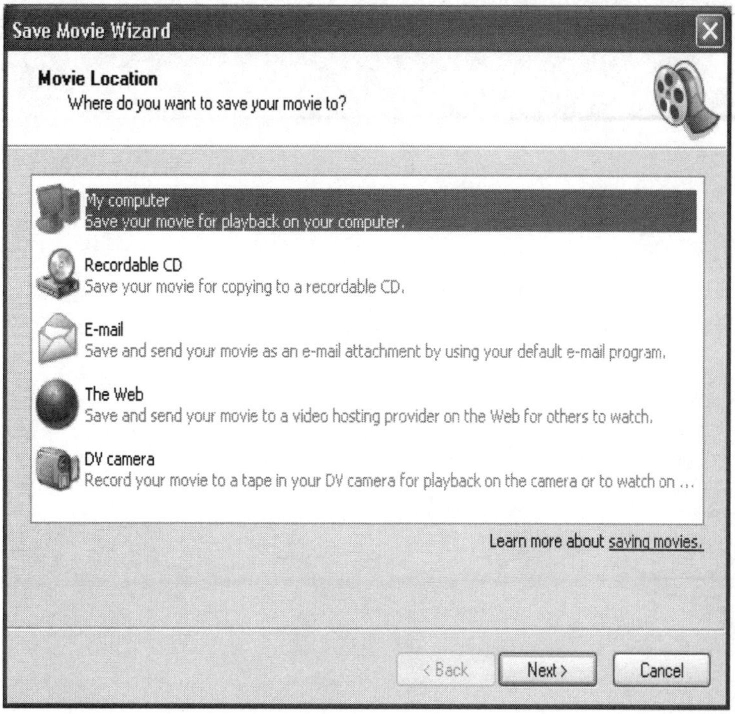

Tip: You can turn any individual frame from your movie into a still picture (a JPEG file). In the Preview pane (shown in Figure 8-16), watch the footage until you see the frame you want to capture, and then click the round Take Picture button (also in Figure 8-16). Windows asks you to name your newly created graphics file and save it.

ROUGH IN THE ROUGH

AutoMovie

AutoMovie might sound like a synonym for "drive-in theatre," but it really means "automatically assembled movie." This feature, new in Movie Maker 2, purports to do all of the editing for you. You just show it which clips or clip collections you want assembled, and the program does the rest.

"The rest," in this case, primarily consists of adding transitions and a few video effects between the clips. Don't expect the software to add a narrative arc and develop characters.

To use AutoMovie, choose Tools→AutoMovie (or click "Make an AutoMovie" in the Movie Tasks pane). A box appears, listing several canned style choices: Flip and Slide,

Highlights Movie, Music Video, Old Movie, and so on—and links that let you insert a title or choose a soundtrack.

Unfortunately, there's no way to preview these canned editorial decisions. You have no choice but to click "Done, edit movie," take a look at the result, and then choose Edit→Undo AutoMovie if you'd like to try a different variation.

The truth is, you probably won't use AutoMovie very often. Video editing is an art, and letting a computer do the editing usually isn't any more successful than letting a computer write your term paper for you. But it sure looks good at trade show demos.

The Control Panel

The Control Panel is an extremely important window in Windows XP. It's teeming with miniature applications that govern every conceivable setting for every conceivable component of your computer. Some are so important, you may use them (or their corresponding notification area controls) every day. Others are so obscure, you'll wonder what on earth inspired Microsoft to create them. This chapter covers them all.

Category View: The Big XP Change

To see your PC's collection of Control Panel programs, open the Control Panel window by choosing Start→Control Panel.

The first time you see the XP Control Panel, you may be in for a shock. Instead of the list of two dozen programs that used to be there, there are now only nine gigantic icons under the headline, "Pick a category" (Figure 9-1).

Microsoft developed this new design to be friendlier to novices. First click the category heading that you think contains the settings you want to change, such as Appearance and Themes. Now you'll see a second screen (Figure 9-1, bottom) that lists a few common tasks in that category: "Change the desktop background," "Choose a screen saver," and so on.

At this point, if you so desire, open the relevant Control Panel program by clicking its icon at the bottom of the screen (Display, in this example). But by clicking the name of the task instead, you're spared a bit of hunting around, since Windows XP takes you directly to the appropriate *tab* of the appropriate program.

Tip: If you install software that comes with a Control Panel program of its own, it may not be smart enough to place itself into the correct category. In that case, you'll find it by clicking the link (in the task pane) called Other Control Panel Options (see Figure 9-1).

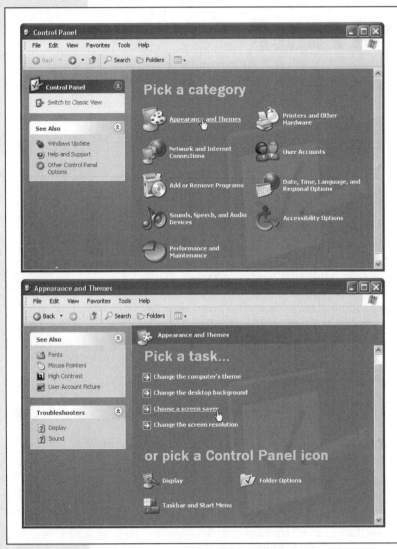

Figure 9-1:
Top: This new design is Microsoft's attempt to make the Control Panel look less overwhelming to first-timers. This arrangement groups the existing control panels into functional categories. When you click one of these headings, you're taken to another new screen.

Bottom: The next screen lists the corresponding control-panel icons at the bottom—but, perhaps more useful to the novice, it also lists the useful tasks that those control panels handle.

Restoring the Old Control Panel

If you're a veteran Windows user, the new arrangement of the Control Panel may strike you as just another drag on your efficiency. After all, it places another layer of red tape between you and familiar control panels.

Fortunately, it's easy enough to eliminate the "Pick a category" display forever: Just click "Switch to Classic View" in the task pane (Figure 9-1, top). Now your programs appear just as they always have, as a tidy collection of individual icons (Figure 9-2).

Category View:
The Big XP Change

The rest of this chapter assumes that you're looking at the list in Classic view—the one that presents an alphabetical arrangement.

Tip: If you're really a speed freak, even the Classic View method of accessing a particular Control Panel program is fairly inefficient. First you have to choose Start→Control Panel and wait for the window to open, then you have to double-click the individual program you want.

To save time, turn on the feature that lets you choose a certain program's name *directly* from the Start menu, as described on page 63.

Figure 9-2:
If you're used to the old way of accessing the Control Panel programs, shown here, a single click on "Switch to Classic View" (Figure 9-1) does the trick. Even the standard Control Panel list (shown here in Details view) attempts to be helpful, though—the Comments column describes the function of each program, and tooltips appear when you point to programs without clicking.

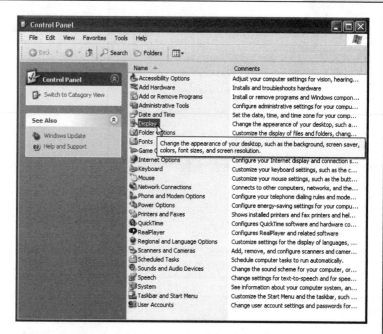

Accessibility Options

Most of the options here are designed to make computing easier for people with disabilities, though some options can benefit almost anyone (Figure 9-3).

Keyboard Tab

The Keyboard adjustments make it easier for some people to type without errors.

StickyKeys

StickyKeys is for people who have difficulty pressing two keys (such as Ctrl, Alt, and Shift key combinations) at once.

Once this feature has been turned on, you can press a single key of a specified combination one at a time instead of simultaneously. To do so, press the first key (Ctrl, Alt, or Shift) *twice*, which makes it "stick." Then press the second key (usually a letter key). Windows responds exactly as though you had pressed the two keys simultaneously.

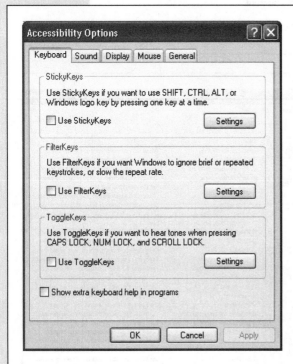

Figure 9-3:
Double-click the Accessibility Options icon in the Control Panel to open the dialog box shown here. You start out looking at the Keyboard tab, which offers useful ways to adjust keyboard behavior. Clicking any of the Settings buttons allows you to fine-tune many of these features, making it even easier to accommodate special computing needs.

If you click the Settings button, Windows displays a dialog box offering several useful options. One of them, for example, makes Windows XP beep when a key is double-pressed and "stuck"—a confirmation that you're about to trigger a keyboard shortcut.

FilterKeys

In Windows, holding down a key for longer than a fraction of a second produces repeated keystrokes (such as TTTTTTT). When you turn on the FilterKeys option, Windows XP treats a repeated key as a *single* keystroke, which can be useful if you have trouble pressing keys lightly and briefly.

The Settings button lets you access options like these:

- **Use shortcut.** Requires that you also press the right-side Shift key for eight to sixteen seconds as the on/off switch for the filtering mode.

- **Show FilterKey status on screen.** Puts a stopwatch-like icon in the Notification Area when you're in FilterKeys mode.

ToggleKeys

When you turn on this option, the computer beeps whenever you press the CapsLock, NumLock, or ScrollLock key.

You don't have to be disabled to find this option attractive, since the confirmation beep prevents you from looking up after five minutes of typing to find a page of text tHAT lOOKS lIKE tHIS.

Sound Tab

Turning on SoundSentry instructs Windows XP to make your screen flash or blink when a sound occurs—a useful feature if you have trouble hearing. Use the "Choose the visual warning" drop-down list to select which part of the screen you want to use as a warning: the title bar of the active window, the active window itself, or the desktop.

Turn on ShowSounds if you'd like your applications to display an explanatory caption every time a sound is generated. (Not all programs do, although those specifically advertised as being Windows XP–compatible generally do.)

Display Tab

If your sight is going, you may find that Use High Contrast makes text easier to read. Use the Settings button to choose white lettering on black, black on white, or any color combination that works for you.

You can also use this dialog box to make your blinking insertion point (which appears when you're editing text) easier to see. Use the associated slider to change the blink rate, the width of the blinker, or both. (Making it fatter comes in especially handy on older laptops whose screens aren't the greatest.)

Tip: One of the simplest and most powerful aids to people with failing vision is the "Windows Standard (large)" and "Windows Standard (extra large)" *Desktop Themes.* You'll find these controls in the Display program's Appearance tab, as described later in this chapter. With a single click, you can make Windows enlarge the font used in all of its dialog boxes, menus, icon names, tooltips, and so on.

Don't miss the Mouse program (page 279), either, where you can select much larger arrow cursors.

Mouse Tab

If you find using the mouse difficult, or if you'd like more precision when using graphics programs, consider turning on the MouseKeys feature (by turning on the "Use MouseKeys" checkbox on this tab, and then pressing the NumLock key to turn

MouseKeys mode on and off). It lets you use the number keypad to control the arrow cursor. Pressing the 2, 4, 6, and 8 keys on this pad moves the mouse around your screen—down, left, up, and right. (Check your keyboard for the corresponding directional arrows on these keys.)

In MouseKeys mode, the other numeric-keypad keys also have new assignments:

- Turn on "Hold down Ctrl to speed up and Shift to slow down" to do just what it says: make the cursor jump in larger or smaller increments when you press Ctrl or Shift, respectively.
- Use the 5 key to simulate a mouse click (left-click).
- Use the minus-sign key to simulate a right-click.
- Use the + key to simulate a double-click.

To fine-tune the MouseKeys behavior, click the Settings button. Here's one useful fine-tuning option: If you'd like to require that the left-side Alt and Shift keys be pressed in addition to NumLock (to prevent accidental MouseKeys triggering), turn on the "Use shortcut" checkbox. If you prefer to use both your numeric-keypad keys *and* MouseKeys, set "Use MouseKeys when NumLock is" to Off.

MouseKeys also offers a way to drag, so you can select text or move objects on the screen without using the mouse:

1. **Use the keypad arrows to position the cursor on the highlighted text, icon, or whatever you want to drag.**

2. **Press Ins (the zero key on your numeric keypad).**

   To "right-drag," press the minus-sign key, *then* Ins.

3. **Use the keypad arrows to drag to the target location.**

4. **Press Del on the keypad to "drop" the object.**

General Tab

Using the settings on the General tab, you can set Windows XP to turn *off* accessibility options if it's been awhile since you've used them. This setup is also useful when several people share the same PC on the same account (see Chapter 17), and only one of them requires these options. You can also ask Windows XP to play a sound or a message to notify you when you turn options on or off.

The General tab also has an option to recognize *SerialKey* devices: special equipment (usually keyboard and mouse replacements) for people with disabilities.

Add New Hardware

This icon isn't really a Control Panel program at all; it's a wizard, and it's described in Chapter 14.

Add or Remove Programs

This program, freshly overhauled in Windows XP, is described at length in Chapter 6. It offers three or four panels that offer important software-management functions.

Change or Remove Programs

This tab displays a list of every program you've installed onto your PC. To remove one from your system, click its name and then click the Remove or the Change/Remove button. Some program packages (like Microsoft Office) offer a Change button, too, so that you can add or remove individual components—*just* Excel, for example. When you click the Change button, have your installation CD handy, because the program may ask you to insert it into your drive.

Add New Programs (and Windows Update)

You won't need the first option here ("Add a program from CD-ROM or floppy disk") very often, because most software programs come with their own installers. Using the CD or Floppy button is just a roundabout way of launching the installer on the disk you've inserted.

Windows Update

The Windows Update button here, however, is useful indeed—it takes you directly to the Microsoft Web page that displays updates, bug fixes, and patches that Microsoft has released for your version of Windows XP. You'll soon find out just how much of Windows XP is a work in progress: it seems like Microsoft releases another one of these fixes, patches, or updates every week or so.

Most people will never have to fool around with this Windows Update feature, because Windows's *Automatic* Updates feature (page 300) generally delivers the relevant software updates right to your PC.

The Windows Update button is for people who have turned off the Automatic business—or for anyone who'd like to see a list of the updates that have been installed so far. Each time you click it, your PC goes online, and your browser opens to a Web page that lists only the updates that apply to your machine.

Tip: You can save yourself a few mouse clicks on your way to the Windows Update site by clicking Start→All Programs→Windows Update.

The first time you click the Windows Update button, a Security Warning dialog box may appear, inviting you to install and run "Windows Update Control V4," distrib-

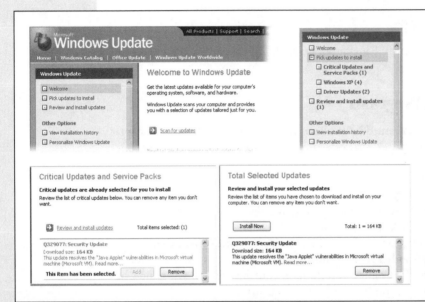

Figure 9-4:
Top left: Clicking "Scan for updates" makes Windows check to see which updates you've already installed.

Top right: Click a category name to see the exact updates Microsoft is recommending for you.

Bottom left: Each update bears an Add and Remove button.

Bottom right: Click Install Now to launch the update installation for your computer.

Trust Microsoft?

Whenever you download and try to install software straight from the Internet, you generally see a dialog box like the one shown here. It represents an effort by Microsoft to protect you from headaches like viruses and Trojan horses. It identifies the software company responsible for the program, and asks you whether or not you trust this company for its software's purity.

Of course, the whole thing is a little silly—how are you supposed to know whether or not the company is trustworthy?

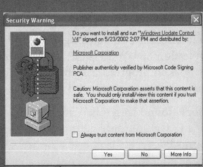

If you do believe the company to be trustworthy, then you can turn on the "Always trust content from XYZ Corporation" checkbox at the bottom of the dialog box. Thereafter, you won't see this dialog box for that particular company anymore.

On the other hand, you should decline to install programs when this dialog box states that the authenticity verification has expired, or when there's no mention of authenticity verification in this type of dialog box (you may see a sentence something like "Publisher authenticity verified by" with no additional information following).

uted by Microsoft. (V4 is the version number. Each time Microsoft updates this software, the number increases.) Click Yes. For some unexplained reason, Microsoft wants you to see this dialog box at least twice; click the Yes button each time.

After the installation is complete, a dialog box invites you to restart your computer, so that the new changes will take effect. (Save your open documents first, of course.)

After your computer restarts, open the Add or Remove Programs program again. Click the Windows Update button again to return to the Update Web site. This time, the site greets you with a Welcome to Windows Update page (see Figure 9-4, top left). Click the "Scan for updates" link.

After a moment, the left pane lets you know how many updates are available for your PC in each of three categories: Critical Updates and Services Packs, Windows XP, and Driver Updates (Figure 9-4, top right). Clicking a category link displays the list of the updates themselves, complete with not-very-helpful descriptions (Figure 9-4, lower left). (Most of them just patch security holes to make Windows and Internet Explorer more hacker-proof.)

Click the Add or Remove button for each software chunk you want to install. After you've selected the updates you want to install, click "Review and install updates."

On the Total Selected Updates page (Figure 9-4, lower right), the program gives you one last chance to remove any item from the list that you don't want to install. Click Install Now when you're ready for the installation. A license agreement dialog box appears; click Accept.

Finally, Windows copies the update files to a temporary folder on your hard drive and then installs them. When the installation is over, a dialog box invites you to restart your PC. Whether you click OK to restart it immediately or Cancel to restart it later, your newly updated operating system will be ready to go the next time it starts up.

Add/Remove Windows Components

Think of this tab as a miniature version of the Windows XP Installer described in Appendix A. It affords you the opportunity to install (or remove) a new Windows XP software component without having to reinstall all of Windows.

Set Program Access and Defaults

You see this option only if your PC has the Windows XP Service Pack 1 (SP1) installed. It's described in detail on page 183.

Administrative Tools

This icon isn't a program, either. It's nothing more than a folder containing a handful of very technical diagnostic utilities—in fact, only shortcuts to them. You'll find brief descriptions of these tools in Chapter 16.

Date and Time

Your PC's conception of what time it is can be very important. Every file you create or save is stamped with this time, and every email you send or receive is marked with it. When you drag a document into a folder that contains a different draft of the same thing, Windows warns that you're about to replace an older version with a newer one (or vice versa)—but only if your clock is set correctly.

Tip: Double-clicking the time in the taskbar notification area (or right-clicking the time and then selecting Properties from the shortcut menu) also displays the Date and Time Properties dialog box. Upon first examination, only two of the three tabs show up: the Date & Time and the Time Zone tabs. If you let the dialog box remain open on the desktop for a few seconds longer, however, the Internet Time tab will mysteriously make its appearance in the dialog box. ("Sorry I'm late. Did I miss anything?")

This program offers three different tabs:

- **Date & Time.** To set the date, choose the month and year from the drop-down lists, and then click the correct calendar day square. To set the time, see Figure 9-5.

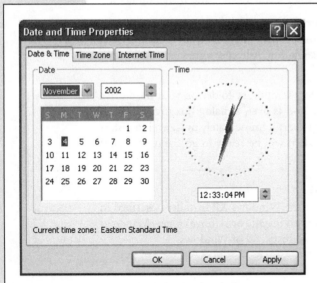

Figure 9-5:
To specify the current time, don't bother dragging the hands of the clock–they're just for decoration. Instead, click numbers in the time box, and then change it by typing numbers, pressing the up or down arrow keys on your keyboard, or by clicking the tiny up or down arrow buttons. To jump to the next number for setting, press the Tab key.

- **Time Zone.** This tab presents a world map—one that might tempt you to click to indicate your location on the planet. This display, too, is just for decoration; use the drop-down list above it to specify your time zone.

- **Internet Time.** By "Internet Time," Microsoft isn't referring to the recent, fanciful notion of a single, global timekeeping system (in which each day is divided into 1,000 equal time units). Instead, this tab lets you teach your PC to set its own clock by consulting a highly accurate scientific clock on the Internet. To activate this feature, turn on "Automatically synchronize with an Internet time server," choose one of the time server Web sites listed in the Server drop-down list, make sure you're online, and then click the Update Now button. (No need to worry about Daylight Savings Time, either, as the time servers take that into account.)

Note: Your PC will set its clock again once a week—*if* it's connected to the Internet at the time. If not, it will give up until the following week. If you have a dial-up modem, in other words, you might consider connecting to the Internet every now and then, and then using the Update Now button to compensate for all the times your PC unsuccessfully tried to set its own clock.

Display

Have you ever admired the family photo or Space Shuttle photo plastered across a co-worker's monitor desktop? The Display icon—one of the most important programs on your PC—is your ticket to such interior decoration stunts, and many others.

This icon opens into a window (see Figure 9-6) whose controls are then divided into five tabs: Themes, Desktop, Screen Saver, Appearance, and Settings.

Figure 9-6:
Lower right: Here's a tool chest filled with everything you need to change the look of your desktop. In addition to redecorating the desktop, you can even redo the design scheme used for the windows you open as you work.

Middle: The Desktop tab lets you choose a picture to plaster onto your desktop backdrop.

Upper left: Some screen savers are animated; they move, grow, or appear with fade-in effects. The My Pictures Slideshow shown here, for example, offers an endless slide show.

Tip: Here's a quick way to open the Display program: Right-click any blank spot on the desktop and choose Properties from the shortcut menu.

Themes Tab

Past versions of Windows let you change the background picture for your desktop, but that's kid stuff. This tab, new to Windows XP, lets you radically change the look and emotional tenor of your entire PC with a single click (see Figure 9-6, lower right).

Each of the themes listed here comes with a color scheme, font selection for your menus and dialog boxes, pictures for use as desktop icons, sounds, cursor shapes, and a desktop picture. (These special desktop pictures, by the way, are bonus back-drops that aren't listed in the Desktop tab, described next.) Now you know why it's so easy for people who don't care for the new, blue Windows XP graphic-design look to switch back to the old design—since each look is nothing more than a Theme.

Note: Choosing "More themes online" from the Theme drop-down list does indeed take you to a Microsoft Web page where you can download additional themes—as well as additional screen savers, games, and so on. But these aren't free. In fact, they're part of the $40 Microsoft Plus pack. (Operators are standing by.)

It's easy enough to design a new Theme of your own, however. Just use the other tabs in this program to set up the desired appearance of your PC screen, complete with your choice of desktop background, menu and window fonts, icons, and so on, exactly as described in the following pages. (Visit the Mouse and Sound programs in the Control Panel, too, to select cursor shapes and beep sounds.)

Then return to the Themes tab and click the Save As button. Finally, give your new theme a name, so that you can call it up whenever you like.

Desktop Tab

Your desktop's background surface doesn't have to show a sunlit hillside forever. You can very easily decorate it with a picture, pattern, or solid color.

Applying wallpaper

Wallpaper, in Windows lingo, is a picture that you can "hang" on your screen back-drop. Click one of the names in the Background list box (Figure 9-6, middle) to see how it looks on the miniature monitor in the dialog box. You'll quickly discover that Windows XP is blessed with some of the most spectacular full-screen photos ever amassed, including close-ups of flowers, the moon, spacey-looking ripples, Stonehenge, and several desert shots that some photographer must have sweat a lot to capture.

Tip: Not everything in the Background list box is a photo, however. Many of them are repeating patterns. Choosing one of these leaves a bit more memory in the PC pot for use by your programs.

If nothing in the list excites you, use one of your own graphic files as wallpaper, such as a scanned photo of your family or your family dog. Then click the Browse button to find the file you want. You can use any graphics file with one of these extensions: .bmp, .gif, .jpg, .jpeg, .png, .dib, .htm, or .html.

If the graphic is a small picture, you can specify how you want Windows to handle it by choosing one of these commands from the Position drop-down list:

- **Center** puts the graphic right smack in the middle of the screen, surrounded by a margin of whatever color you choose from the Color drop-down menu.

- **Tile** multiples the image, repeating it over and over, until it fills the entire desktop.

- **Stretch** distorts and expands the single image to fill the desktop, sometimes with extremely coarse and grainy results.

After selecting a backdrop you like, click OK to apply it and close the dialog box. Or, to preview the wallpaper on your desktop, click the Apply button, leaving the dialog box open so that you can make another choice if the first one looks hideous.

To remove wallpaper, return to the Display Properties dialog box and select (None) at the top of the Background list box. Whatever color you've chosen in the Color drop-down menu reappears on your desktop in place of the wallpaper.

Solid colors

To change the color of your desktop without actually putting a picture there, click (None) in the Background list box, and then choose the color you want from the Color drop-down menu.

The "Customize Desktop" Button

Clicking the Customize Desktop button at the bottom of the Display Properties dialog box takes you into an absolutely enormous world of additional options, in-

GEM IN THE ROUGH

Webby Wallpaper

If there's a graphic on the Web that strikes your fancy, *it* can become wallpaper, too. Right-click the image—right there in your Web browser—and choose Set as Background from the shortcut menu. The graphic moves immediately to the middle of your desktop. (You'll probably have to close or minimize your browser window to see it.)

Windows XP saves the file in your Documents and Settings→[your name]→Application Data→Microsoft→ Internet Explorer folder, naming it *Internet Explorer Wallpaper.bmp*. (If you use a Netscape browser, the file is called *Netscape Wallpaper.bmp* and lands in your Windows folder.) If you find another Web graphic you like and want to repeat the steps to turn it into wallpaper, be aware that Windows XP will save the new file with the same name, *replacing* the original file. To have access to both files, change the filename of the previous wallpaper file before grabbing a new image.

cluding the famous Active Desktop feature that turns your entire desktop into a Web browser.

The first thing you see after clicking the Customize Desktop button is the General tab.

General tab

A better name for this tab might have been "Desktop icons," since all of its options pertain to the icons that sit, or don't sit, on your desktop.

- **Desktop icons.** Microsoft is on a crusade to clean up the desktop. "The Start menu," its designers seem to say, "is the proper launching bay for opening files, programs, and folders. The desktop, meanwhile, is just supposed to be your placemat—so keep it clean."

  That's why most of the desktop icons that appeared in previous versions of Windows no longer appear on the desktop in Windows XP. This is Phase I of Microsoft's campaign to keep the desktop clean.

  If you want My Documents, My Computer, My Network Places, and Internet Explorer to sit out on your desktop, you must put them there yourself—by turning on the corresponding checkboxes here. (They also return to the desktop automatically when you switch the Start menu to its "Classic" view, as described on page 64.)

- **Change Icon.** The middle section of the dialog box lets you change the pictures that Windows uses for the important desktop icons. If, say, you can't stand the

---

POWER USERS' CLINIC

Check Before You Sweep

When using Windows XP's *user accounts* feature (Chapter 17), keep in mind that the desktop icons you're sweeping away might not necessarily be *your* desktop icons. They might be *everybody's* desktop icons.

In other words, before you wildly nuke a bunch of desktop icons, it would be courteous to inspect them to make sure you're not deleting some shared icons that other people, when they log in, expect to find. To do so, right-click the desktop icon; from the shortcut menu, choose Properties. In the resulting dialog box, check the Location. Does the folder path display just your name, or "All Users"?

If it is, indeed, a shared desktop icon (All Users), you might want to leave it alone. Or, if you've already allowed the Desktop Cleanup Wizard to move the icon into the Unused Desktop Shortcuts folder, you can move it back manu-

ally to "everybody's" desktop by dragging them into the My Computer→Local Disk (C)→Documents and Settings→All Users→Desktop folder.

Conversely, if you fire up the PC one day and discover that someone else has cleared away shortcuts from *your* desktop, you can get them back. (Note that this trick requires you to use a local Administrator account, as described on page 501.)

Start by locating the Unused Desktop Shortcuts folder. It's in the Documents and Settings→[name of whoever deleted the icons]→Desktop→Unused Desktop Shortcuts folders. Once you find the missing icons, you can either move them back to the All Users→Desktop folder, or copy them back only to *your* Desktop folder.

---

look of the Recycle Bin icon, click it in this scrolling list and then click the Change Icon button. You'll be shown an assortment of potential replacement images. And if you've created or downloaded additional miniature pictures, you can use one of those by clicking the Browse button and navigating to the folder that contains them.

- **Desktop cleanup.** Phase II of Microsoft's clean-up-your-desktop campaign involves the Desktop Cleanup Wizard. Every two months, a message pops up on your screen, offering to sweep away any desktop icons that you haven't used in a while (Figure 9-7).

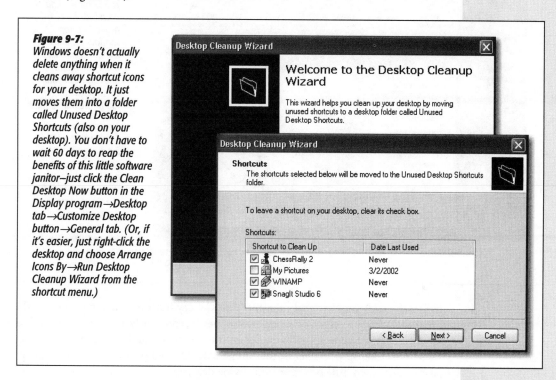

Figure 9-7:
Windows doesn't actually delete anything when it cleans away shortcut icons for your desktop. It just moves them into a folder called Unused Desktop Shortcuts (also on your desktop). You don't have to wait 60 days to reap the benefits of this little software janitor—just click the Clean Desktop Now button in the Display program→Desktop tab→Customize Desktop button→General tab. (Or, if it's easier, just right-click the desktop and choose Arrange Icons By→Run Desktop Cleanup Wizard from the shortcut menu.)

Web tab

You use the Web tab to turn on *Active Desktop,* a feature that presents information from the Web directly on your desktop, live and self-updating. If you want to keep an eye on an approaching tornado, the stock market, or a live Webcast, this is the feature for you.

Of course, receiving live, continuous Internet information requires a live, continuous Internet *connection.* It's great if you have a cable modem or DSL line, for example, but less practical if you dial the Internet using a modem.

Once the Web tab is in front of you, turn on a checkbox in the Web Pages list box (such as "My Current Home Page").

These checkboxes represent the various Web pages you'd like to see plastered across your desktop. To add to this list, click the New button, type the URL (Web address), and click OK.

You can add any kind of Web information to your Active Desktop. Frequently updated pages like stock tickers are popular, but you can also use Web pages that don't change much.

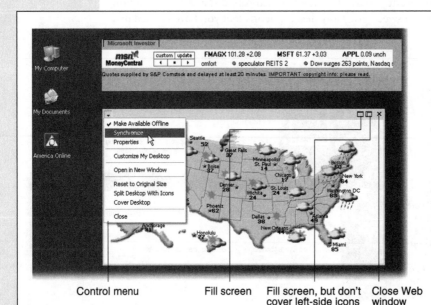

Figure 9-8:
The Control menu of each individual Active Desktop window contains useful commands. To make the menu appear, push your cursor close to the top of the mini-page.

The Investor ticker (top) works a little bit differently. Click Custom to type in stock symbols you want to track; click the tiny square to pause the motion of the text. This item doesn't offer the usual mini-menu bar.

Control menu   Fill screen   Fill screen, but don't   Close Web
                                  cover left-side icons   window

In fact, by clicking New and then the Visit Gallery button, you can check out the Microsoft Web site, which offers an array of newsy, constantly updating Active Desktop elements—such as sports, weather, or travel news—that have been specially designed for desktop use. That is, they aren't actually Web pages, but blurbs that appear in their own little boxes on your living desktop.

And if you click the Browse button in the New Desktop Item dialog box, you can choose a graphics file or HTML (Web page document) on your hard drive for displaying on the desktop.

Tip: Here's something to tuck away for future Web-browsing sessions. Whenever you stumble onto a Web page that might make a good Active Desktop display, right-click its page–right there in Internet Explorer–and choose Set as Desktop Item from the shortcut menu. You've just added a new option without fiddling around in the Display program.

No matter how you select your desktop Web material, however, the process always ends with an "Add item to Active Desktop" confirmation box. It identifies both the name and the URL (Web address) of the page you've selected. It also contains a

Customize button, which lets you specify how often you want your PC to update the Web page information with fresh data from the Internet. (Later, you can always adjust the schedule using the Properties button on the Web tab *of* the Desktop tab *of* the Display program in the Control Panel.)

When you click OK, a strange thing happens: Your entire desktop becomes a Web browser. Here's what you can do now:

- **Click links.** Web page material now appears directly on your desktop, complete with pictures, text—and links. Clicking one of these links takes you to a new Web

---

Active Desktop for Modem Fans

While Active Desktop works best with a full-time Internet connection, using it with a dial-up modem isn't impossible. Just set up your PC to connect at a certain time of day (just before you arrive at your desk, for example), update the Web page on your desktop, and then hang up. That way, a recent (but detached-from-the-Internet) Web page greets you each morning.

To arrange this, open the Desktop tab of the Display program, click the Customize Desktop button, and then click the Web tab. Click the name of the Web page you want to self-update, and then click the Properties button.

A special Properties dialog box appears. On the Web-Document tab, turn on "Make this page available offline," and then click the Schedule tab. Turn on "Using the following schedule(s)"; click Add; use the controls to indicate the time of day you want your desktop updated; name the schedule, if you like; and turn on the "automatically connect for me" checkbox at the bottom of the window.

Before you click OK, though, consider this. At the specified time, your PC will dial the Internet and update the Web page on your desktop. But what then? You can read what's on the page, but you can't very well click one of the links on it. The Web page is frozen onto your desktop, disconnected from the Internet. As a result, if you click one of its links, you'll get only an error message.

That's the virtue of the final tab, the Download tab shown here. The "Download pages ___ links deep from this page" option instructs your PC to download not just the specified Web page, but also all Web pages *connected* to it. If you change the number here to 2, then you'll also be able to click links on *those* pages, as well. In essence, you'll have the freedom to explore the links on your Active Desktop Web page to the extent of the pages-from-pages you specify. (All of these additional downloaded Web pages take up disk space, however, which is why there's a "Limit hard-disk usage" checkbox, too.) You can also conserve disk space by clicking the Advanced button and then omitting certain file types from the downloaded Web page, like graphics, sound, and video.

When you're finished setting up your automatic download, click OK.

---

page, exactly as in a Web browser—in fact, it *will* be in your Web browser, which opens automatically. You can actually surf the Web using the pages plastered to your desktop.

- **Move the page.** By pushing your cursor to the top of the Web page area, you can even make a little title bar/menu bar appear. Just drag it like a handle to move these little Web windows around the screen. (If you right-click *outside* the Web page portion of your desktop, you can choose Arrange Icons By→Lock Web Items on Desktop from the shortcut menu. You've just frozen the size and position of your Active Desktop windows. Repeat this process to unlock the positions.)

- **Enlarge the page.** To make a little Web snippet fill your entire screen, or only the part unoccupied by icons, simply click one of the Fill Screen buttons shown in Figure 9-8. Of course, you can also drag the lower-right corner of a Web window to make it larger or smaller.

- **Update the page.** Unless you've set up a schedule, as described in the box on page 269, your Active Desktop windows don't automatically update themselves to reflect the *latest* stocks, weather, and so on. To update the information, open the drop-down menu shown in Figure 9-8 and choose Synchronize.

Tip: The usual Internet Explorer menu bar doesn't appear when your desktop is a browser. Therefore, you won't find standard commands like Back, Forward, Add to Favorites, and so on.

But if you right-click the desktop, a special shortcut menu appears that contains all of these important Web-browsing commands.

To turn off a particular Active Desktop window, choose Close from its drop-down menu (shown in Figure 9-8). You can also turn it off in the Display program, of course.

Screen Saver Tab

You don't technically *need* a screen saver to protect your monitor from burn-in. Today's energy-efficient monitors wouldn't burn an image into the screen unless you left them on continuously, unused, for at least two years, according to the people who actually design and build them.

No, screen savers are mostly about entertainment, pure and simple—and Windows XP's built-in screen saver is certainly entertaining.

The idea is simple: A few minutes after you leave your computer, whatever work you were doing is hidden behind the screen saver; passers-by can't see what's on the screen. To exit the screen saver, move the mouse, click a mouse button, or press a key.

Tip: Moving the mouse is the best way to get rid of a screen saver. A mouse click or a key press could trigger an action you didn't intend—such as clicking some button in one of your programs or typing the letter whose key you pressed.

Choosing a screen saver

To choose a Windows XP screen saver, use the Screen Saver drop-down list. A miniature preview appears in the preview monitor on the dialog box (see Figure 9-6, top).

Tip: If you have graphics files in the Start→Documents→My Pictures folder, select the My Pictures Slideshow. Windows XP puts on a slide show that features your My Pictures images one at a time, bringing each to the screen with a special effect (flying in from the side, fading in, and so on). You can also click the Browse button to choose a different folder full of pictures.

To see a *full-screen* preview, click the Preview button. The screen saver display fills your screen and remains there until you move your mouse, click a mouse button, or press a key.

The Wait box determines how long the screen saver waits before kicking in, following the last time you moved the mouse or typed. Click the Settings button to play with the chosen screen saver module's look and behavior. For example, you may be able to change its colors, texture, or animation style.

At the bottom of this tab, click the Power button to open the Power Options Properties dialog box described later in this chapter.

Appearance Tab

Windows XP includes a number of *schemes*: predesigned accent-color sets that affect the look of all the windows you open. (Don't confuse schemes with *Themes*, of which schemes are just one portion.) These color-coordinated design schemes affect the colors of your window edges, title bars, window fonts, desktop background, and so on. They also control both the size of your desktop icons and the font used for their names (as shown in Figure 9-9), and even the fonts used in your menus.

The factory setting, called "Windows XP style," creates the sunlit blue look of window title bars, the new rounded shape of OK and Cancel buttons, and so on. By

---

POWER USERS' CLINIC

Password-Protecting Screen Savers

When you password-protect a screen saver, the act of "awakening" the PC by clicking the mouse or pressing a key merely produces a password dialog box. Until somebody types the correct password, the screen saver remains on the screen. This setup protects the data that's currently on your screen from prying eyes and also prevents anyone from using your computer.

To activate password protection, turn on "On resume, password protect" (if your PC belongs to a network domain) or

"On resume, display Welcome screen" (if not). (Actually, the workgroup-PC wording depends on whether or not Fast User Switching is turned on, as described on page 520.)

A determined ne'er-do-well may think he can bypass this obstacle by unplugging the computer and turning it back on again. Of course, that tactic won't get him far, because he'll wind up right at the login dialog box, where once again, he'll need a password to get in.

---

choosing "Windows Classic style" from the "Windows and buttons" drop-down list (Figure 9-9, left), you return your PC to the visual look of Windows Me/Windows 2000. The top half of the dialog box provides a preview of the effect.

You, the interior designer

The real fun, however, awaits when you choose "Windows Classic style" (Figure 9-9, left) and *then* click the Advanced button. Now you find yourself in a dialog box that lets you change every single aspect of this scheme independently (Figure 9-9, right).

Note: Microsoft put a lot of work into the new look of XP, and doesn't want people diluting it with their own random changes. "If you want the XP look," the company is saying, "it's all or nothing."

The bottom line: If "Windows XP style" is selected in the "Windows and buttons" list (Figure 9-9, left), the changes you make in the Advanced box (Figure 9-9, right) generally have no effect whatsoever.

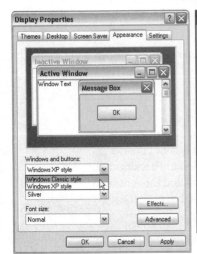

Figure 9-9:
Left: For the full arsenal of design-scheme controls, choose "Windows Classic style," as shown here, before clicking the Advanced button.

Right: As you click parts of the view pane, the Item list identifies what you clicked (such as Desktop, Scrollbar, and so on). Then use the drop-down lists to choose colors and type sizes for the chosen interface element.

Proceed with your interior decoration crusade in either of two ways:

- Change the elements of the scheme one at a time. Start by choosing from the Item drop-down list (or by clicking a piece of the view pane, as shown in Figure 9-9). Then use the Size, Color 1, and Color 2 drop-down lists to tailor the chosen element—such as Desktop or Scrollbar—to suit your artistic urges.

- Some of the screen elements named in the Item drop-down list have text associated with them: Icon, Inactive Title Bar, Menu, Message Box, ToolTip, and so on. When you choose one of these text items, the Font drop-down list at the bottom of the dialog box comes to life. Using this menu, you can change the typeface (font, color, and size) used for any of these screen elements. If you have trouble reading the type used in tooltips, wish your icon names showed up a little more boldly, or would prefer a more graceful font in your menus, these controls offer the solution.

If you create an attractive combination of colors and type sizes, remember that you can preserve it for future generations. Click OK to return to the Appearance tab, click the Themes tab, and then click Save As. You'll be asked to name your creation. Thereafter, you'll see its name listed alongside the "official" Microsoft themes.

Effects

Effects is the other button on the Appearance Tab. It takes you to a dialog box that lets you control what Microsoft calls *special effects* in Windows XP. These aren't exactly the kind of special effects they make at Industrial Light and Magic for use in *Star Wars* movies. On the contrary, they're so subtle, they're practically invisible. Nevertheless, they exist—sometimes slowing down your PC in the process—and you can control them in this dialog box. Here's what you'll find:

- **Use the following transition effect for menus and tooltips.** When this box is checked, menus, lists, and tooltips don't just pop open when clicked; instead, they gracefully *slide* open—an attractive, but time-wasting, effect. (Try it on your Start menu.) The drop-down list allows you to specify whether you want them to *fade* into view or *scroll* into view.

  If the checkbox is filled in with a solid color rather than a checkmark, then the transitions are turned on for some elements (like menus), but not for others (like tooltips).

- **Use the following method to smooth edges of screen fonts.** When fonts are enlarged, they become ragged on the curves. But when you turn on this option, Windows XP softens the curves, making all text look more professional (or slightly blurrier, depending on your point of view; see Figure 9-10).

Figure 9-10:
Using the drop-down list, you can choose a smoothing technology that's new in Windows XP—something called ClearType. It's designed especially for flat-panel screens, including the ones on laptops. By changing the colors of the individual pixel on the edges of certain letters, it makes the type appear to be smoother than it really is.

Chapter XIV: The Big Break

In which Tom finds his true talent

By January 1975, Tom Cruise was growing increasingly unhappy with his job at the gas station. His hands were calloused, the work was monotonous, and the fumes were getting to him.

But it wasn't until the sleek, white stretch limo pulled in for five gallons of Premium and a check under the hood that Tom knew his life would change. For inside the limousine was no ordinary passenger. It was prominent Hollywood casting scout Gerber "Slats" McGibbons.

Chapter XIV: The Big Break

In which Tom finds his true talent

By January 1975, Tom Cruise was growing increasingly unhappy with his job at the gas station. His hands were calloused, the work was monotonous, and the fumes were getting to him.

But it wasn't until the sleek, white stretch limo pulled in for five gallons of Premium and a check under the hood that Tom knew his life would change. For inside the limousine was no ordinary passenger. It was prominent Hollywood casting scout Gerber "Slats" McGibbons.

- **Use large icons.** This checkbox refers to desktop icons. If you're having trouble seeing your desktop icons, turn on this option to produce jumbo icons. *Factory setting:* Off.

- **Show shadows under menus.** Take a look: In Windows XP, open menus actually seem to cast faint, light gray drop shadows, as though the menu is floating an eighth of an inch above the surface of the window behind it. It's a cool, but utterly superfluous special effect that saps a tiny bit of speed from the proceedings. This checkbox is the on/off switch. *Factory setting:* On, if your PC belongs to a network domain; Off otherwise.

- **Show window contents while dragging.** If this option is off, when you drag a window, a faint outline of its border is visible; you don't see all the items *in* the window coming along for the ride. As soon as you stop dragging, the contents reappear. If it's on, however, as you drag a window across your screen, you see all its contents, too—which can slow the dragging process on slower machines. *Factory setting:* On.

- **Hide underlined letters for keyboard navigation until I press the Alt key.** This option refers to the small underlines that appear on certain letters in menus and dialog boxes, something like this. These are designed to help you remember the keyboard shortcuts for those menu commands. It's reminding you that by pressing the Alt key along with the underlined letter, you can choose the corresponding menu command without even using the mouse.

Figure 9-11:
All desktop screens today, and even most laptop screens, can make the screen picture larger or smaller, thus accommodating different kinds of work. Conducting this magnification or reduction entails switching among different resolutions (the number of dots that compose the screen).

In Windows XP, however, these underlined letters are hidden. They don't appear until you actually press the Alt key (or the Tab key, or an arrow key), which tells Windows XP: "I'd like to use my keyboard for navigating now, please."

The factory setting is On. If you turn off this checkbox, the underlines appear all the time, exactly as in older editions of Windows.

Settings Tab

The Settings tab (Figure 9-11) is where you can ensure that Windows XP is getting the most out of your video hardware.

Screen resolution

The "Screen resolution" slider snaps to the various possible *resolution* settings that your monitor's software driver makes available: 800 x 600, 1024 x 768, and so on.

When using a low-resolution setting, such as 640 x 480, the size of the pixels (dots) that comprise your screen image increase, thus enlarging the picture—but showing a smaller slice of the page. This setting is ideal, for example, when playing a small movie so that it fills more of the screen. At higher resolutions (such as 800 x 600 or 1024 x 768), the pixels decrease, reducing the size of your windows and icons, but showing more overall area. Use this kind of setting when you want to see as much screen area as possible: when working on two-page spreads in a page-layout program, for example.

Color quality

Today's monitors offer different *color depth* settings, each of which permits the screen to display a different number of colors simultaneously. This drop-down list varies by video driver, but generally offers settings such as Medium (16-bit), which was called High Color in previous versions of Windows; High (24-bit), once known as True Color; and Highest (32-bit).

In the early days of computing, higher color settings required a sacrifice in speed. Today, however, there's very little downside to leaving your screen at its highest setting. Photos, in particular, look best when you set your monitor to higher quality settings.

FREQUENTLY ASKED QUESTION

Blurry Flat-Panel Screens

Yucko! I tried the 800 x 600 setting on my laptop, and everything got all blurry and fuzzy! How do I fix it?

On any flat-panel screen—not just laptop screens—only one resolution setting looks really great: the maximum one. That's what geeks call the *native* resolution of that screen.

At lower resolutions, the PC does what it can to blur together adjacent pixels, but the effect is fuzzy and unsatisfying. (On a traditional bulky monitor, the electron gun can actually make the pixels larger or smaller, but on flat-panel screens, every pixel is a fixed size.)

The Low (8-bit) option—if you even have it—makes photos look blotchy. It displays only 256 colors on the screen, and is therefore useful only for certain computer games that, having been designed to run on ancient PCs, require the lower color setting. (In any case, you shouldn't set your whole system to 256 colors just to run these older games. Instead, you should use the new compatibility mode described on page 124.)

Multiple monitors

By installing two or more graphics cards, or one graphics card with multiple connections, you can hook up two or more monitors to your PC simultaneously, creating a gigantic virtual desktop. As you work, you can move icons or toolbars from one monitor to another, or stretch windows across multiple screens. This setup also enables you to keep an eye on Web activity on one monitor while you edit data on another. It's a glorious arrangement, even if it does make the occasional family member think you've gone off the deep end with your PC obsession.

When you have multiple monitors attached, the controls on the Settings tab change; it now displays individual icons for each monitor. By dragging them around, you can arrange the icons in this dialog box to reflect the way Windows "thinks" of them: beside one another, or stacked vertically, for example. That is, you can indicate which edge of your primary monitor permits your cursor to travel beyond the glass and onto the next monitor.

One monitor is considered the *primary* monitor. This is the screen that will display your opening Windows XP screen, the Login dialog box (if you use one), and so on. When configuring the monitor settings, be sure to assign your primary monitor to monitor icon #1.

Tip: Don't have the cash for three more monitors? Then try the next best thing: a software version, courtesy of PowerToys for Windows XP, Microsoft's free goody bag of extra features (available from *www.missingmanuals.com*).

PowerToys includes Virtual Desktop Manager, a new taskbar toolbar that gives you four side-by-side *virtual* monitors. Each screenful can have its own background picture and holds its own set of open programs and windows. You can switch from one desktop to the next by pressing a keystroke of your choice, or by clicking the 1, 2, 3, or 4 buttons on the Desktop Manager toolbar.

Advanced settings

If you click the Advanced button on the Settings tab, you're offered a collection of technical settings for your particular monitor model. Depending on your video driver, there may be tab controls here that adjust the *refresh rate* to eliminate flicker, install an updated adapter or monitor driver, and so on. In general, you'll rarely need to adjust these controls—except on the advice of a consultant or help-line technician.

Folder Options

This program offers three tabs—General (pages 76 and 87), View (page 87), and File Types (page 175)—all of which are described elsewhere in this book.

Fonts

This icon is a shortcut to a folder; it's not a program. It opens into a window that reveals all of the typefaces installed on your machine, as described in Chapter 13.

Gaming Options

If you're a serious gamer, the Game Controllers program may interest you. You use it to configure and control the joysticks, steering wheels, game pads, flight yokes, and other controllers you've attached to your PC. After all, if your joysticks and controllers aren't installed and configured properly, you can't pulverize aliens to full capacity.

To get started, install the driver software that came with your gaming device. If it's a modern, USB, Windows XP–compatible gadget, you may not even need to do that much. Just plug in the device and watch the notification area for a message that Windows XP has detected it and installed the correct driver. (See Chapter 14 for more on installing gadgetry.)

Next, open the Game Controllers program, where you should see the newly installed controller listed. Click it and then click OK. If your device isn't listed, click the Add button. In the Add Game Controller dialog box, specify the kind of controller you intend to install—"Gravis GamePad Pro (GamePort)," "6-button joystick w/two POVs and throttle," or what have you, and then click OK.

Once you've selected the device, highlight its name in the Controller list box and then click the Properties button to test and set up its various buttons, wheels, and knobs.

Note: Game controllers generally work only in games that recognize them—not within Windows itself. That USB steering wheel you've installed, for example, will almost certainly work in your racing car simulator game, but don't expect it to help you drive around the icons on your desktop.

Internet Options

A better name for this program would have been "Web Browser Options," since all of its settings apply to Web browsing—and, specifically, to Internet Explorer. Its tabs break down like this:

• **General, Security, Privacy, and Content.** These tabs control your home page, cache files, and history list. They also let you define certain Web pages as off-limits to your kids. Details on these options are in Chapter 11.

- **Connections.** Controls when your PC modem dials; see page 316 for details.

- **Programs.** Use these drop-down lists to indicate which Internet programs you generally prefer for email, creating Web pages, and so on. For example, the email program you specify here is the one that will open automatically whenever you click an "email me!" link on a Web page. The checkbox at the bottom of the dialog box warns Windows to watch out for the day when you install a browser other than Internet Explorer. At that time, you'll be asked which program—IE or the new one—you want to use as your everyday browser.

- **Advanced.** On this tab, you'll find dozens of checkboxes, most of which are useful only in rare circumstances and affect your Web experience only in minor ways. For example, "Enable Personalized Favorites Menu" shortens your list of bookmarks over time, as Internet Explorer hides the names of Web sites you haven't visited in a while. (A click on the arrow at the bottom of the Favorites menu makes them reappear.) Turning off the "Show Go button in Address bar" checkbox hides the Go button at the right of the Address bar. After you've typed a Web address (URL), you must press Enter to open the corresponding Web page instead of clicking a Go button on the screen. And so on.

For a relatively coherent description of each checkbox, click the question-mark button in the upper-right corner of the window and then turn on the checkbox in question.

Keyboard

You're probably too young to remember the antique known as a *typewriter*. On some electric versions of this machine, you could hold down the letter X key to type a series of XXXXXXXs—ideal for crossing something out in a contract, for example.

On a PC, *every* key behaves this way. Hold down any key long enough, and it starts spitting out repetitions, making it easy to type, "No WAAAAAY!" or "You go, grrrrl!" for example. (The same rule applies when you hold down the arrow keys to scroll through the text document, hold down the = key to build a separator line between paragraphs, hold down Backspace to eliminate a word, and so on.) The Speed tab of this dialog box (Figure 9-12) governs the settings.

- **Repeat delay.** This slider determines how long you must hold down the key before it starts repeating (to prevent triggering repetitions accidentally).

- **Repeat rate.** The second slider governs how fast each key spits out letters once the spitting has begun.

After making these adjustments, click in the "Click here and hold down a key" test box to try out the new settings.

- **Cursor blink rate.** The "Cursor blink rate" slider actually has nothing to do with the *cursor,* the little arrow that you move around with the mouse. Instead, it governs the blinking rate of the *insertion point,* the blinking marker that indicates where typing will begin when you're word processing, for example. A blink rate that's too slow makes it more difficult to find your insertion point in a window filled with data. A blink rate that's too rapid can be distracting.

Figure 9-12:
How fast do you want your keys to repeat? This control panel also offers a Hardware tab, but you won't go there very often. You'll use it exclusively when you're trying to troubleshoot your keyboard or its driver.

Mouse

All of the icons, buttons, and menus in Windows make the mouse a very important tool. And the Mouse program is its configuration headquarters (Figure 9-13).

TROUBLESHOOTING MOMENT

Sharing a Computer Between a Lefty and Righty

If a right- and left-hander share a computer, confusion and marital discord may result. If the mouse is set for the righty, nothing works for the lefty, who then may assume that the PC is broken or cranky.

If you're using individual user accounts (see Chapter 17), Windows XP can solve the problem by switching the left- and right-button modes automatically when each person logs on.

But if you're not using user accounts, you probably need a quick way to switch the mouse buttons between lefties and righties. The easiest way is to create a shortcut to the Mouse control panel. Be sure to put it on the desktop or the Quick Launch toolbar, as described on page 103, so that the button-switching checkbox is only a click away.

Buttons Tab

This tab offers three useful controls: button configuration, double-click speed, and ClickLock.

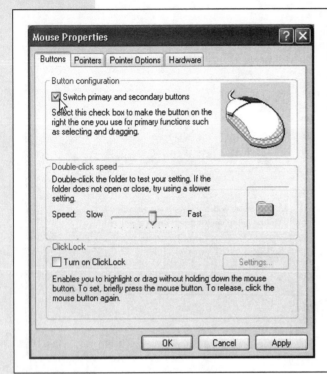

Figure 9-13:
If you're a southpaw, you've probably realized that the advantages of being left-handed when you play tennis or baseball were lost on the folks who designed the computer mouse. It's no surprise, then, that most mice are shaped poorly for lefties–but at least you can correct the way the buttons work.

Button configuration

This checkbox is for people who are left-handed and keep their mouse on the left side of the keyboard. Turning on this checkbox lets you switch the functions of the right and left mouse buttons, so that your index finger naturally rests on the primary button (the one that selects and drags).

Double-click speed

Double-clicking isn't a very natural maneuver. If you double-click too slowly, the icon you're trying to open remains stubbornly closed. Or worse, if you accidentally double-click an icon's name instead of its picture, Windows sees your double-click as two single clicks, which tells Windows that you're trying to rename the icon.

The difference in time between a double-click and two single clicks is usually well under a second. That's an extremely narrow window, so let Windows XP know what you consider to be a double-click by adjusting this slider. The left end of the slider bar represents 0.9 seconds, and the right end represents 0.1 seconds. If you need more time between clicks, move the slider to the left; by contrast, if your reflexes are highly tuned (or you drink a lot of coffee), try sliding the slider to the right.

Each time you adjust the slider, remember to test your adjustment by double-clicking the little folder to the right of the Speed slider. If the folder opens, you've successfully double-clicked. If not, adjust the slider again.

ClickLock

ClickLock is for people blessed with large monitors or laptop trackpads who, when dragging icons onscreen, get tired of keeping the mouse button pressed continually. Instead, you can make Windows XP "hold down" the button automatically, avoiding years of unpleasant finger cramps and messy litigation.

When ClickLock is turned on, you can drag objects on the screen like this:

1. **Point to the item you want to drag, such as an icon. Press the left mouse or trackpad button for the ClickLock interval.**

   Specify this interval by clicking the Settings button in this dialog box.

2. **Release the mouse button.**

   The button acts as though it's still pressed.

3. **Drag the icon across the screen by moving the mouse (or stroking the trackpad) without holding any button down.**

   To release the button, hold it down again for your specified time interval.

Pointers Tab

If your fondness for the standard Windows arrow cursor begins to wane, you can assert your individuality by choosing a different pointer shape.

Selecting a pointer scheme

Windows has many more cursors than the arrow pointer. At various times, you may also see the hourglass cursor (which means, "wait; I'm thinking" or "wait; I've crashed"), the I-beam cursor (which appears when you're editing text), the little pointing-finger hand made famous by Microsoft's advertising (which appears when you point to a Web page link), and so on.

All of these cursors come prepackaged into design-coordinated sets called *schemes*. To look over the cursor shapes in a different scheme, use the Scheme drop-down list; the corresponding pointer collection appears in the Customize list box. Some are cute: Dinosaur, for example, displays an animated marching cartoon dinosaur instead of the hourglass cursor. Some are functional: The ones whose names include "large" offer jumbo, magnified cursors ideal for very large screens or failing eyesight. When you find one that seems like an improvement over the Windows Default (system scheme) set, click OK.

Select individual pointers

It's worth noting that you don't have to change to a completely different scheme; you can also replace just one cursor. To do so, click the pointer you want to change, and then click the Browse button. You're shown the vast array of cursor-replacement icons (which are in the Local Disk (C:)→Windows→Cursors folder). Click one to see what it looks like; double-click to select it.

Create your own pointer scheme

Once you've replaced a cursor shape, you've also changed the scheme to which it belongs. At this point, either click OK to activate your change and get back to work, or save the new, improved scheme under its own name, so you can switch back to the original when nostalgia calls. To do so, click the Save As button, name the scheme, and then click OK.

Tip: The "Enable pointer shadow" checkbox at the bottom of this tab is pretty neat. It casts a shadow on whatever's beneath the cursor, as though it's skimming just above the surface of your screen.

Pointer Options Tab

This tab offers a few more random cursor-related functions.

Pointer speed

It comes as a surprise to many people that the cursor doesn't move five inches when the mouse moves five inches on the desk. Instead, you can set things up so that moving the mouse one *millimeter* moves the pointer one full *inch*—or vice versa—using the Pointer speed slider.

It may come as even greater surprise that the cursor doesn't generally move *proportionally* to the mouse's movement, regardless of your "Pointer speed" setting. Instead, the cursor moves farther when you move the mouse faster. How *much* farther depends on how you set the "Select a pointer speed" slider.

The Fast setting is nice if you have an enormous monitor, since it prevents you from needing an equally large mouse pad to get from one corner to another. The Slow setting, on the other hand, can be frustrating, since it forces you to constantly pick up and put down the mouse as you scoot across the screen. (You can also turn off the disproportionate-movement feature completely by turning off "Enhance pointer precision.")

Snap To

A hefty percentage of the times when you reach for the mouse, it's to click a button in a dialog box. If you, like millions of people before you, usually click the *default* (outlined) button—such as OK, Next, or Yes—the Snap To feature can save you the effort of positioning the cursor before clicking.

When you turn on Snap To, every time a dialog box appears, your mouse pointer jumps automatically to the default button, so that all you need to do is click. (And to click a different button, such as Cancel, you have to move the mouse only slightly to reach it.)

Visibility

The options available for enhancing pointer visibility (or invisibility) are mildly useful under certain circumstances, but mostly, they're just for show.

- **Display pointer trails.** *Pointer trails* are ghost images of your mouse pointer that trail behind the pointer like a bunch of little ducklings following their mother. In general, this stuttering-cursor effect is irritating. On rare occasions, however, you may find that it helps locate the cursor if you're making a presentation on a low-contrast LCD projector.

- **Hide pointer while typing.** Hiding the mouse pointer while you're typing is useful if you find that it sometimes gets in the way of the words on your screen. As soon as you use the keyboard, the pointer disappears; just move the mouse to make the pointer reappear.

- **Show location of pointer when I press the CTRL key.** If you've managed to lose the cursor on an LCD projector or a laptop with an inferior screen, this feature helps gain your bearings. When you press and release the Ctrl key after turning on this checkbox, Windows displays an animated concentric ring each time you press the CTRL key to pinpoint the cursor's location.

Hardware tab

The Mouse program provides this tab exclusively for its Troubleshoot and Properties buttons, for use when your mouse, or its driver, is acting up.

Network Connections

This icon opens up into a window containing icons representing the various network connections you've configured—for America Online, your Internet provider, your network (the Local Area Connection icon), and so on. See Chapter 18 for details.

Phone and Modem Options

You'll probably need to access these settings only once: the first time you set up your PC or laptop to dial out. Details in Chapter 10.

Power Options

The Power Options program manages the power consumption of your computer. That's a big deal when you're operating a laptop on battery power, of course, but it's also important if you'd like to save money (and the environment) by cutting down on the juice consumed by your *desktop* PC.

The options available in this program depend on your PC's particular features. Figure 9-14 displays the Power Options Properties dialog box for a typical laptop computer.

Power Schemes Tab

The Power Schemes tab lets you select, change, or create *power schemes*. A power scheme defines which components of your PC shut down since you last used your keyboard, mouse, or processor. Much like a screen saver, power schemes are designed to save power, but they offer a greater variety of tricks:

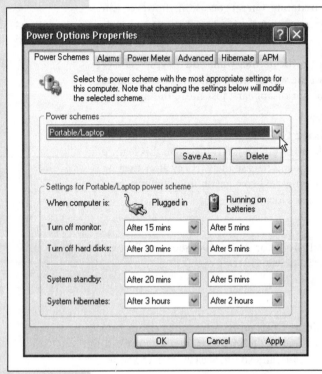

Figure 9-14:
The Power Options program is a shape-shifter, meaning which set of tabs it has, and which controls are available on each one, vary from one PC to the next. Some of these tabs appear only if you have a laptop (or an uninterruptible power supply). Others depend on how new the PC is, and which version of the standard power-management circuitry it contains.

- **Turn off monitor.** Your monitor goes dark, and its power light changes from green to yellow.

- **Turn off hard disks.** The hard drives stop spinning.

- **System standby.** The computer goes into *standby mode*, which is similar to being asleep. The monitor, fan, hard drive, and other components go dark and still. (Only a trickle of electricity is required to keep alive what's stored in memory.) When you press a key or click the mouse, the PC wakes up in less than five seconds, returning to the screen everything you were doing before the computer dozed off. (The one downside of standby mode: If the power goes out, you lose any unsaved changes in the documents on the screen.)

- **System hibernates.** As described in more detail on page 33, a PC that's about to hibernate copies everything in its memory into a file on the hard drive (a process that takes a minute or so). Then the computer completely shuts down, requiring no power at all. Even if the power goes out, everything you had open is safely preserved.

Later, when you "awaken" the computer again (by pressing the power button), you're returned to the same open documents and programs. Copying all of this information from the hard drive back into memory takes 30 or seconds or so, but that's still a lot faster than the computer would have taken to turn on from its Off condition.

Use the "Power schemes" drop-down list to choose from Windows XP's built-in power schemes: Home/Office Desk, Portable/Laptop, Presentation, Always On, and so on. Each of these schemes calls up certain canned settings to match the situation. For example:

- **Home/Office Desk** is designed for desktop computers. The factory settings put the monitor into low-power mode first, then the hard drive, then the computer itself. (In other words, it goes into standby or hibernate mode.)

- **Always On** puts your monitor and hard drive to sleep after ten minutes or an hour, but never invokes standby for the PC itself.

- **Portable/Laptop** puts the monitor, hard drive, and computer to sleep sooner than the desktop schemes in order to save battery power.

You're welcome to change the settings for any of these schemes. Once you've done so, click the Save As button to preserve your new settings under a new scheme name. Finally, click OK to close the Power Options Properties dialog box and activate the selected power scheme.

___

Tip: You might want to set up your power scheme so that the PC goes into standby mode after, say, ten minutes, and then hibernates after 30. That way, if you're only away from your desk for a minute, you can get back to work immediately—but if you get called away longer, or even overnight, everything that was open on the screen is safe—and you're not using electricity while you're away.

___

Waking up your PC

To bring your computer out of standby mode, just move the mouse or press a key. The PC can wake itself up, too, when you've programmed something to happen (such as setting up your email program to check for new messages) or when a fax call comes in (if you've set up your PC to receive faxes). When the task or the phone connection ends, the computer returns to standby automatically.

To bring the computer back from hibernation, you generally have to press the power key.

Alarms and Power Meter Tabs: For Laptops

Notebook computers offer additional power options, which help them conserve power when running on batteries.

Alarms tab

When your battery starts running out of juice, your laptop displays a warning message. When there are only a few seconds of power left, you get another, more urgently worded message. Both messages are designed to alert you that *now* is a good time to save whatever document you've been working on; the laptop is about to go to sleep until you've plugged the power cord into the wall.

The controls on this tab let you specify when (or whether) these messages appear, what kind of notification you want (a message, a sound, or both), and what the laptop does as a result (such as going into standby mode).

Power Meter tab

This tab is your laptop battery's fuel gauge. If your computer has two batteries, turn on "Show details for each battery." You'll see an icon for each battery, which slowly "empties" as your power runs down.

Advanced Tab

The "Always show icon on the taskbar" option puts a tiny power-plug icon (or battery icon, if you're using a laptop that's unplugged) in the notification area of the taskbar. Click this icon to produce a menu listing the power *schemes* you've established (see page 284), making it easy for you to switch among them. And if you right-click this icon, you're offered commands that take you directly to the Power Options program or its Power Meter tab.

If you select "Prompt for password when computer resumes from standby," you're asked to enter your login password (if you have one—see Chapter 17) each time you awaken the computer. That's handy protection when you wander away from the desk for some coffee or a candy bar.

Tip: Despite the name of this checkbox, Windows XP also demands a password in order to awaken from *hibernation* mode (not just standby).

On some PCs, this tab contains a third option, which lets you specify what happens when you press the power button on your computer. You may prefer that the power button put your computer into standby or hibernate modes, instead of turning the computer off. This feature is an ingenious hedge against a potentially disastrous situation: The computer is in standby mode but, upon seeing that your monitor is dark, you assume that it's turned off. You hit the power button to turn it *on*—but actually cut the power, obliterating any unsaved documents and possibly causing other file damage.

Tip: If you've assigned the power button to the Standby or Hibernate functions, you can still use it to turn off the computer completely. Just hold the button down for a few seconds.

On a laptop, you can choose two different sets of settings, one for when the laptop is plugged in and one—presumably a more power-stingy configuration—for when it's running on batteries.

Laptops may also let you specify what happens when you close the lid (standby, hibernate, or do nothing) or press the sleep button (standby, hibernate, shut down, do nothing, or ask you what to do).

Hibernate Options

If you have a Hibernate tab—which is likely, since most computers young enough to run Windows XP are also young enough to include this relatively recent feature— you can use it to set up the *hibernation* feature (see page 33). Turning on "Enable hibernation" does the following:

• The Power Schemes tab displays a new power-scheme option called System Hibernates. Now you can specify the duration of idle time before your PC hibernates automatically. On some older PCs, you may not see the System Hibernates option until you turn on the "Enable Advanced Power Management Support" checkbox on the APM tab.

• The Shut Down dialog box (Start→Turn Off Computer) displays a Hibernate option (in addition to Shut Down and Restart). See page 33 for details.

Note: Because the hibernation feature saves everything in memory as a file, it consumes a lot of disk space—in fact, as much disk space as your PC has RAM. (Note for techies: When the PC hibernates, it copies everything that was in RAM into a file on the hard drive called *Hiberfil.sys*.)

The Hibernate tab displays the amount of free disk space, along with the amount of disk space that's required for the PC to hibernate.

Troubleshooting Standby and Hibernation

Both standby and hibernation modes can cause glitches. For example:

Standby doesn't save data

When your computer is in standby mode, any unsaved documents on the screen remain unsaved. In fact, your computer is in the same state it would be if you walked away without using standby—the only difference is that the PC is consuming less power. During hibernation, by contrast, everything in memory—that is, everything on the screen, including all open documents and programs—is saved to a file on your hard drive.

If you shut off the computer, or if power fails, any documents you forgot to save are gone forever. Therefore, it's a good idea to choose File→Save for any documents you're working on before putting the computer into standby mode or leaving your computer unattended (which triggers standby mode automatically).

Your disks don't work right away

Because standby mode affects every hardware device in your system, moving your mouse to wake up your computer from standby mode doesn't make every device available to you in a nanosecond. Some add-on gear, notably removable-disk drives like Jaz, Zip, and CD-ROM drives, require several seconds to "warm up" after your PC awakens.

Computer fails to enter hibernate or standby mode

Standby and hibernate modes work only with the cooperation of all the gear attached to your system. Behind the scenes, Windows notifies the device drivers that power is being reduced. Those drivers are supposed to respond with a message indicating they're capable of *awakening* from standby or hibernate mode. If a device driver doesn't indicate that it can be awakened, the PC stays on.

In such cases, an error message appears telling you that your system can't enter standby/hibernate mode because "*<name of device driver>* failed the request." The exact wording of the message depends on whether you're trying to enter standby or hibernate mode, and on the specific hardware problem. The most common culprits are video-controller drivers and sound-card drivers.

Until you update the hardware driver (or replace the component with one that has a standby-capable driver), you won't be able to put the PC into standby or hibernate mode at all.

APM Tab

This tab appears only on older PCs that don't meet a Microsoft standard called ACPI (Advanced Configuration and Power Interface).

Note: If your computer is ACPI-compatible—or OnNow-compatible, as it may be labeled—it offers a few extra power-management enhancements. Some examples include separate battery-level displays (if you have more than one), the ability to add and remove PC cards without restarting the computer, and the ability to wake up for network activity.

APM (Advanced Power Management), in other words, isn't quite so advanced by today's standards. Still, if you have this tab, be sure to turn on "Enable Advanced Power Management support" to receive the features it does offer—the very features described in these pages.

UPS Tab

This tab has nothing to do with the United Parcel Service, even if that's how your PC was delivered. It refers instead to an uninterruptible power supply—a box (about $120) capable of generating a few minutes of battery power in the event of a blackout. This short reprieve provides just enough time for you to save your documents before the lights go out.

The truth is that this tab is designed to accommodate older UPS devices that plug into your PC's serial port. Using the controls here, you can check the battery in the UPS, click Configure to specify when you want its battery-low alarm to sound, and so on.

More recent UPS products, on the other hand, connect to your PC's USB port. Ironically, hooking it up to your computer makes the UPS Tab *disappear* from the Power Options program. In its place, you get the two tabs—Alarms and Power Meter—that usually show up only on laptops. After all, these dialog boxes are designed to let you monitor and configure battery power—and in effect, your desktop PC is now battery-powered.

Printers and Faxes

This one isn't a program at all; it's a shortcut to your Printers and Faxes folder, described in Chapter 13.

Regional and Language Options

Windows XP is by far the most internationally oriented version of Windows to date. It can accommodate any conceivable arrangement of date, currency, and number formats; comes with fonts for dozens of Asian languages; lets you remap your keyboard to type non-English symbols of every ilk; and so on.

For the first time in Windows, you can install multiple input languages on your computer and easily switch between them when the mood strikes (see page 104 for

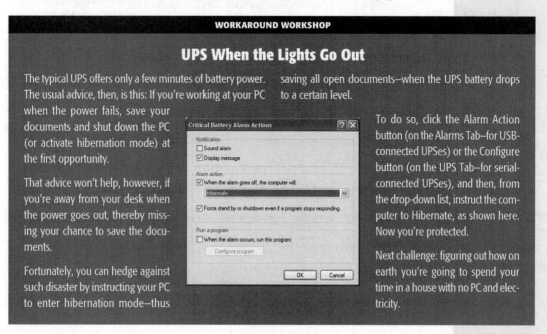

WORKAROUND WORKSHOP

UPS When the Lights Go Out

The typical UPS offers only a few minutes of battery power. The usual advice, then, is this: If you're working at your PC when the power fails, save your documents and shut down the PC (or activate hibernation mode) at the first opportunity.

That advice won't help, however, if you're away from your desk when the power goes out, thereby missing your chance to save the documents.

Fortunately, you can hedge against such disaster by instructing your PC to enter hibernation mode—thus

saving all open documents—when the UPS battery drops to a certain level.

To do so, click the Alarm Action button (on the Alarms Tab—for USB-connected UPSes) or the Configure button (on the UPS Tab—for serial-connected UPSes), and then, from the drop-down list, instruct the computer to Hibernate, as shown here. Now you're protected.

Next challenge: figuring out how on earth you're going to spend your time in a house with no PC and electricity.

details about the Language bar). The key term here is *input language*; the language for the operating system doesn't change. If you installed Windows XP in English, you'll still see the menus and dialog boxes in English. But when you switch the input language, your keyboard will type the characters necessary for the selected language.)

Regional Options Tab

If you think that 7/4 means July 4 and that 1.000 is the number of heads you have, skip this section.

But in some countries, 7/4 means April 7, and 1.000 means one thousand. If your PC isn't showing numbers, times, currency symbols, or dates in a familiar way, click the Customize button to rearrange the sequence of date elements (see Figure 9-15).

Tip: The Customize Regional Options box (Figure 9-15, left) is where you can specify whether you prefer a 12-hour clock ("3:05 PM") or a military or European-style, 24-hour clock ("1505").

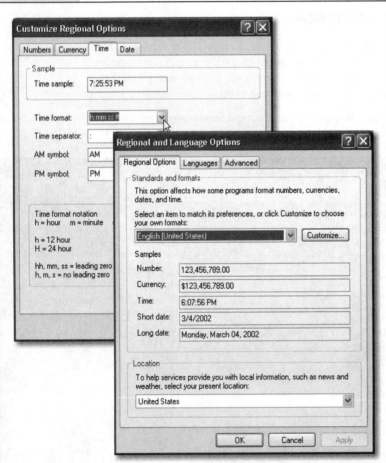

Figure 9-15:
Lower right: The Regional Options tab is a summary of the crazy settings that you can change by clicking the Customize button—which opens the Customize Regional Options dialog box, shown at top left.

Top left: The changes you make here are reflected in the date and time stamps on your files located in list-view folder windows, and in Microsoft Excel (in the case of your Currency-tab choices).

Languages Tab

The symbols you use when you're typing in Swedish aren't the same as when you're typing in English. Microsoft solved this problem by creating different *keyboard layouts,* one for each language. Each keyboard layout rearranges the letters that appear when you press the keys. For example, using the Swedish layout, pressing the semicolon key produces an ö—not a semicolon (;).

For a choice of keyboard layouts, use the Settings tab of this dialog box to install the appropriate driver. Click Details, click Add, and, in the resulting window, choose the languages you want (see Figure 9-16).

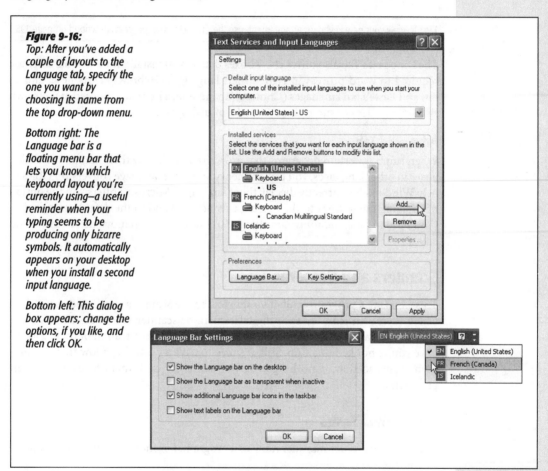

Figure 9-16:
Top: After you've added a couple of layouts to the Language tab, specify the one you want by choosing its name from the top drop-down menu.

Bottom right: The Language bar is a floating menu bar that lets you know which keyboard layout you're currently using—a useful reminder when your typing seems to be producing only bizarre symbols. It automatically appears on your desktop when you install a second input language.

Bottom left: This dialog box appears; change the options, if you like, and then click OK.

After installing more than one keyboard layout, you can switch between them in either of two ways:

- Use the Language bar, as shown in Figure 9-16. It's a floating, ghostly menu that lets you switch keyboard layouts no matter what you're doing on the PC (Figure 9-16, bottom).

Note: The Language bar also appears if you've turned on or installed handwriting-recognition systems, Microsoft speech-recognition systems, or additional input languages, including special input software designed to let you type Asian language characters.

- You can also switch from one keyboard layout to the next by simultaneously pressing the left-side Alt and Shift keys. Clicking the Key Settings button at the bottom of the dialog box shown at top left in Figure 9-16 lets you change this key combination, or set up individual key combinations for each language layout you've installed.

Tip: To view your new keyboard arrangement, use the Character Map program described on page 195.

The Languages Tab also offers checkboxes that let you install the additional software required to word process in right-to-left languages (Hebrew, Vietnamese, and so on) and East Asian languages (Chinese, Japanese, and Korean). Proceed at your own risk—these files consume about 250 MB of disk space.

Advanced Tab

When running certain programs that are written to display their menus and dialog boxes in other languages, you can, in theory, use these language conversion tables to help Windows XP correctly display those languages. Microsoft offers you the option of applying the settings to the current user account and to the default user profile. (You have to be an *administrator* [page 501] to install or remove these conversion tables.)

Scanners and Cameras

This icon isn't a program at all; it's a shortcut to the Scanners and Cameras window, where there's an icon for each digital camera or scanner you've installed. As described in Chapter 8, Windows XP largely automates the operation of these gadgets once you've hooked them up. Still, it's nice to have a central window that contains their icons, so that, if nothing else, you can right-click them to examine their properties.

Scheduled Tasks

Here's another folder masquerading as a program. For more on scheduled tasks, see Chapter 16.

Sounds and Audio Devices

The five tabs within this panel control every aspect of your microphone, speakers, and associated software.

Volume Tab

These controls govern the speaker volume for your system, but you'd be crazy to open the Control Panel and this program every time you want to adjust your PC speakers. Fortunately, the "Place volume icon in the taskbar" checkbox puts a speaker icon in your notification area, near the time display. Click that icon to open a much more convenient volume slider.

This dialog box also offers these buttons:

- **Advanced.** Opens the Volume Control program described on page 240.

- **Speaker Volume.** Produces sliders that let you set the left and right channel volumes of your PC's audio independently. (This essentially duplicates the function of the Balance slider in the Volume Control program, but at least you can't claim you're unable to adjust your speaker balance.)

- **Advanced** (yes, there's a second Advanced button, this one at the bottom of the dialog box, in the Speaker settings section). If you're an audiophile whose PC is the center of the sound system, this one is for you. It opens an Advanced Audio Properties dialog box that lets you specify exactly what kind of speakers are connected to your PC—5.1 surround sound, quadraphonic, monitor-mounted stereo speakers, and so on. Its Performance tab lets you specify how much of the PC's energy should be put into sound generation.

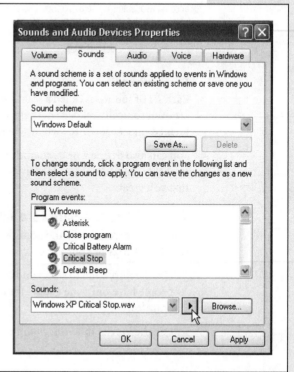

Figure 9-17:
The Program Events list box presents every conceivable category in which a sound is played: Windows, NetMeeting, Windows Explorer, and so on. (The installers for some programs—America Online, for example—may add categories of their own.)

Sounds Tab

Windows plays little sound effects—beeps, musical ripples, and chords—all the time: when you turn on the PC, trigger an error message, empty the Recycle Bin, and so on. And if you like, you can hear them on many other occasions, such as when you open or exit a program, open a menu, restore a window, and so on. This tab lets you specify which sound effect plays for which situation (Figure 9-17).

Program events

A speaker icon denotes the occasions when a sound will play. If you click the name of some computer event, you can:

- Remove a sound from the event by choosing (None) from the Sounds drop-down list.

- Change an assigned sound, or add a sound to an event that doesn't have one, by clicking the Browse button and choosing a new sound file from the list in the Open dialog box.

When you select a sound, its filename appears in the Sounds drop-down list box. Click the triangular Play button to the right of the box to hear the sound.

Tip: When you click the Browse button, Windows XP opens the Local Disk (C:)→Windows→Media folder, which contains the *.wav* files that provide sounds. If you drag *.wav* files into this Media folder, they become available for use as Windows sound effects. Many people download *.wav* files from the Internet and stash them in the Media folder to make their computing experience quirkier, more fun, and richer in *Austin Powers* sound snippets.

Sound scheme

Each set of sounds is called a sound *scheme*. Sometimes the sound effects in a scheme are even sonically related (perhaps the collection is totally hip-hop, classical, or performed on a kazoo). To switch schemes, use the "Sound scheme" drop-down list.

You can also define a new scheme of your own. Start by assigning individual sounds to events, and then click the Save As button to save your collection under a name that you create.

Audio, Voice, and Hardware Tabs

The other three tabs on the Sounds and Audio Devices Properties dialog box control the settings of your various multimedia gadgets.

- Use the Audio tab to select and configure your microphones and speakers. (Most people have only one gadget for each purpose, so making a choice isn't exactly a brainteaser.)

- Use the Voice tab to select and configure your microphone.

- The Hardware tab offers a subset of the Device Manager (see page 431). It presents a list of the sound, video, and movie-related hardware components on your PC, and identifies them by brand and model.

Speech

This little program, new in Windows XP, lets you set up all the speech-related features of Windows.

Unfortunately, Windows XP doesn't *have* any speech-related features.

Think of this program instead as the front end for the speech features of other software. For example:

Speech Recognition Tab

This tab isn't even visible unless you've installed the limited speech-recognition feature of Microsoft Office XP. Use the controls here to retrain the system, configure the microphone, set the pronunciation sensitivity level, and so on.

Tip: In the end, if you decide that voice dictation is destined to be a productive part of your work regimen, you'd be well advised to invest in a far superior, more mature program like NaturallySpeaking. However, such programs don't have anything to do with this control-panel program.

Text To Speech Tab

Here's where you configure the voice of Windows—the robotic voice, called Microsoft Sam—that you hear any time Windows reads text aloud.

The catch here is that Windows never *does* read text aloud, except when you're using Narrator (page 193)—and Narrator has its own set of voice-selection controls. Microsoft Word XP *can* read text to you, however, and for that reason, you may be happy to know that you can specify Sam's rate of speaking (or Michael's, or Michelle's) using this dialog box.

System

This advanced control panel is the same one that appears when you right-click your My Computer icon and choose Properties from the shortcut menu (or press Windows logo key+Break key). Its various tabs identify every shred of circuitry and equipment inside, or attached to, your PC.

General Tab

You can't change anything on this screen, but that doesn't mean it's not useful. Here you can learn:

- Which version of Windows XP you have (don't be surprised if the version number contains far more decimal points than you were taught is legal).

CHAPTER 9: THE CONTROL PANEL   **295**

- The model name and speed of your PC's processor chip (such as Pentium 4, 2.6 GHz).

- How much memory your PC has—a very helpful number to know, particularly when it comes time to sell your old computer.

Computer Name

You personally will never see whatever you type into the "Computer description" box here. If you're on a network, however, the blurb you type here is what others see from across the wires. You might use the "Computer description" box to inform your fellow network citizens as to the operating system your PC uses, or what its contents are.

Likewise, the computer description isn't the same thing as your computer *name*, which once again comes into play primarily when you, or your co-workers, view your network connections. (Click the Change button to change the computer's name.)

Hardware Tab

This dialog box is nothing more than a portal. Its four buttons lead to these four other dialog boxes:

- **Add Hardware Wizard.** The best way to install the software for a new piece of equipment—a scanner, printer, camera, or whatever—is to use the installation CD that came with it. If you've downloaded a driver from the Internet, however, or in certain other circumstances, you can use this wizard to walk you through the installation.

Figure 9-18:
If you're confident about the hardware add-ons that you install—and the stability of their drivers—instruct Windows XP to stop warning you every time an unsigned driver attempts to infiltrate your hard drive (click the top option button). On the other hand, if you want to guarantee the continued stability of Windows XP, click the Block option button, so that such software is never allowed to enter your system.

- **Driver Signing.** After years of grief from its customers for having written an "unstable" operating system, Microsoft went to the root of the problem: buggy software drivers. In response, it created the driver *signing* program, in which the makers of various hardware add-ons can pay Microsoft to test and certify the safety and stability of their drivers. Whenever you install a driver that hasn't received this Microsoft blessing, a frightening dialog box appears to warn you, as described on page 430.

  By clicking this button, you can specify just how sensitive you want your PC to be when it encounters an installer putting an unsigned driver onto your system, as shown in Figure 9-18.

- **Device Manager.** This very powerful dialog box (see Figure 9-19) lists every component of your PC: CD-ROM, Modem, Mouse, and so on. Double-clicking a component's name (or clicking the + symbol) discloses the brand and model of that component. Many of these items are *controllers*—the behind-the-scenes chunks of electronics that control the various parts of your computer, with a technical-looking name to match. For much more on the Device Manager, see page 431.

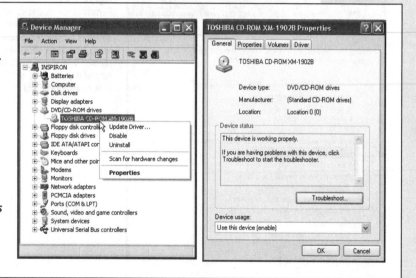

Figure 9-19:
Left: The Device Manager dialog box shows you where every dollar of your PC's purchase price went. Click a + sign to see exactly which CD-ROM drive, floppy circuitry, or other hardware you currently have.

Right: Double-clicking a component (or right-clicking it and choosing Properties, as shown at left) lets you read about its specs.

- **Hardware Profiles.** If you're a laptop owner, your add-on equipment list probably changes from location to location. For example, when you're at the office, you may connect your laptop to a docking station—and when you're at 39,000 feet, you probably don't. The hardware profiles feature lets you switch between these configurations relatively easily. See page 435 for details.

Advanced Tab

Here's another dialog box that's nothing more than a nesting place for five buttons that open other dialog boxes—some of which aren't "advanced" in the least. Three of these buttons are called Settings, and here's what they cover:

Performance

The Visual Effects tab of the Performance Options dialog box (Figure 9-20) offers a long list of checkboxes that control the little animations and visual accents that define the more modern look and feel of Windows XP. For example, "Animate windows when minimizing and maximizing" makes Windows present a half-second animation showing your window actually shrinking down onto the taskbar when it's minimized. "Show shadows under mouse pointer" produces a tiny shadow beneath your cursor, as though it were floating a quarter-inch above the surface of your screen.

All these little animations and shadows look cool, but each saps away a tiny scrap of speed and power. Using this dialog box, you can freely turn off the checkboxes for the features you could do without (see Figure 9-20).

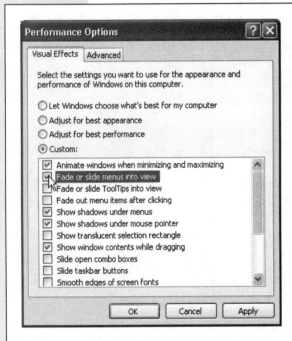

Figure 9-20:
Performance *means speed. Depending on the speed and age of your machine, you may find that turning off all of these checkboxes produces a snappier, more responsive PC—if a bit less Macintosh-esque. (Leave "Use visual styles on Windows and buttons" turned on, however, if you like the new, softened look of Windows XP.)*

The Advanced tab of this dialog box is far less casual. It controls how Windows XP uses your processor power and memory, and provides a button that opens the Virtual Memory control center for your machine. These are extremely technical settings that you should adjust only with the guidance of a licensed geek.

User Profiles

This screen displays the master list of user profiles. See page 525 for details.

Startup and Recovery

This dialog box contains advanced options related to *dual-booting*—see page 620—and what happens when the system crashes. It also lets you edit the startup options file (boot.ini, beloved by tech-heads everywhere) by clicking the Edit button.

Environment Variables

This button opens a dialog box that's intended solely for the technically minded. It identifies, for example, the path to your Windows folder and the number of processors your PC has. If you're not in the computer-administration business, avoid making change here.

Error Reporting

You may have noticed that whenever a program crashes, freezes, or abruptly quits, Windows XP offers to email a report of the event to Microsoft for the benefit of its debugging teams. Using the Error Reporting dialog box (click the Error Reporting button), you can turn off this frequent attempt to contact the mother ship—or limit the attempts to certain programs.

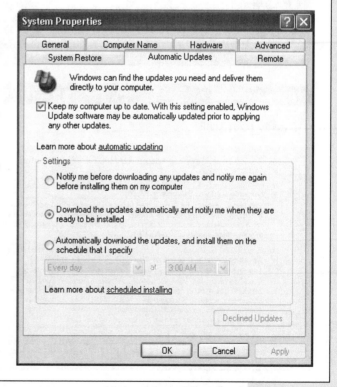

Figure 9-21:
If you turn off Windows XP's new auto-update-installation feature (by turning off the "Keep my computer up to date" checkbox), you can get your updates directly from the Microsoft Web site by choosing Start→All Programs→Windows Update. If you prefer automatic updates, you can ask to be notified either before the software patch is downloaded (top choice) or after it's been downloaded and is ready to install (middle choice). You can also permit the updates to be updated and then installed automatically, on a schedule that you specify (bottom choice).

System Restore Tab

This dialog box is the control center for the Windows XP System Restore feature, which lets you rewind a balky computer to an earlier date when it was working fine. Details in Chapter 16.

Automatic Updates

Thanks to this feature, you no longer have to be a *PC World* subscriber to find out when Microsoft comes up with bug fixes or security patches for Windows—an event that, these days, seems to occur about every eight minutes. If you access the Internet with any regularity, the Automatic Updates feature will *tell* you about these inevitable software patches (Figure 9-21). In fact, such updates flew thick and fast in the first six months of Windows XP's release.

This tab lets you control how (and whether) you're notified about such new features.

The first time Windows discovers an update, it puts an Automatic Update icon on your taskbar (Figure 9-22). Click the icon to begin the installation process for a

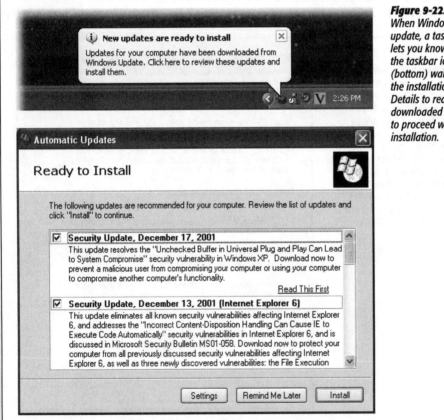

Figure 9-22:
When Windows finds an update, a taskbar note (top) lets you know. If you click the taskbar icon, a wizard (bottom) walks you through the installation process. Click Details to read about all downloaded files, or Install to proceed with the installation.

particular software patch. You'll be shown a description of the fix and offered the opportunity to install it (which may require that you restart the computer).

If Windows XP reveals that an update is ready to be installed, but you choose not to install it (by clicking the Remind Me Later button shown in Figure 9-22), Windows makes the updater invisible on your hard drive (if it has space). If, later in life, you decide that you really *would* like to have that particular update, just click the Restore Declined Items button on the Automatic Update tab. Then, the next time you install an update, those choices become available once again.

Tip: All of the software updates detailed by Windows XP are also available for do-it-yourself download and installation at *http:// windowsupdate.microsoft.com* (you can also get to this site by choosing Start→All Programs→Windows Update). This site also reports exactly which bugs are fixed in each update.

Furthermore, you can find a record of the updates you've installed (and even uninstall them, if you want) in the Add or Remove Programs program.

Remote Tab

To read about Remote Assistance—the feature that lets a technical help person connect to your PC (via the Internet) to help you troubleshoot—turn to page 143. This tab contains its master on/off switch, and lets you specify how long one of your "invitations" to such geniuses should remain open.

This tab also offers the on/off switch for Remote Desktop, which lets someone at another computer take control of yours. For the full story, see Chapter 21.

Taskbar and Start Menu

This program controls every conceivable behavior of the taskbar and Start menu. You can read all about these options—the same ones that appear when you right-click the taskbar or the Start button and choose Properties from the shortcut menu—in Chapters 2 and 3.

User Accounts

This control panel is the master switch and control center for the user-accounts feature described in Chapter 17. If you're the only one who uses your PC, you can (and should) ignore it.

WINDOWS XP PRO: THE MISSING MANUAL

Part Three:
Windows Online

3

Hooking Up to the Internet

Plenty of people buy a PC to crunch numbers, scan photos, or cultivate their kids' hand-eye coordination. But for millions of people, Reason One for using a PC is to access the Internet. Few computer features have the potential to change your life as profoundly as the World Wide Web and email.

To join the Internet party already in progress, you need three components: a *connection*, such as a modem, cable modem, DSL, or corporate network; an Internet *account*; and Internet *software*, like the Web browsers and email programs described in the next chapter.

Five Degrees of Online Readiness

If you have any intention of making your PC a citizen of the Internet, you probably fall into one of these categories:

- **Your PC can already get online.** This is the case if, for example, you upgraded to Windows XP Professional from an earlier version of Windows. (The XP installer is thoughtful enough to preserve your old Internet settings.) If you can already access the Internet, you don't need the advice in this chapter, which explains how to set up an account yourself. Just skip to the following chapter.

- **You have an Internet account on another PC that you want to transfer.** In this case, consider using the Files and Settings Transfer Wizard, described on page 630. It teaches your new Windows XP machine all about the settings that worked on the old machine.

Alternatively, if you know all the configuration details for your existing account—your account name, local access number, password, and so on—you can use the New Connection Wizard described on page 312.

- **You want to sign up for a new America Online account.** Microsoft, an AOL rival, no longer includes the America Online starter software with Windows. You'll need to secure the AOL installer on your own—using one of the several billion AOL starter CDs that come with magazines, in cereal boxes, and sometimes out of the faucet.

- **You want to sign up for a new MSN account, or a standard Internet account (EarthLink, AT&T, Sprint, or whatever).** In this case, use the New Connection Wizard described on page 293.

- **You want to access the Internet, but don't yet know the best way to do it.** In this case, read on.

How to Get Online

Most people connect to the Internet using a *modem,* a device that connects your PC to a standard voice phone line. Almost every modern computer comes with a built-in, preinstalled modem.

Cable Modems and DSL

On the other hand, a growing minority of computer fans connects to the Internet with much faster gear called *cable modems* and *DSL.* These contraptions offer several gigantic advantages over dial-up modems. For example:

- **Speed.** These modems operate at 5 to 50 times the speed of a traditional dial-up modem. For example, you might wait 5 minutes to download a 2 MB file with a standard modem—a job that would take about 10 *seconds* with a cable modem. And complex Web pages that take almost a minute to appear in your browser with a standard modem will pop up almost immediately with a cable modem or DSL.

POWER USERS' CLINIC

Installing a Modem

If you're among the six people whose PC didn't come with a built-in modem, you can install one yourself.

You can choose between an internal modem (a small circuit board that you push into a slot inside the PC, saving some desktop clutter, a power socket, and a few dollars) or an external one (which is easier to transfer from machine to machine). An external modem connects to the

back of the PC via a cable, or takes the form of a PC Card that slips into your laptop.

After completing the physical installation of your modem, you must install the modem's software—its *drivers.* The instructions that accompany the modem should guide you through the process.

- **No dialing.** These fancier connection methods hook you up to the Internet permanently, full time, so that you don't waste time connecting or disconnecting—ever. You're *always* online.

- **No weekends lost to setup.** Best of all, there's no need to do any of the setup yourself. A representative from the phone company or cable company generally comes to your home or office to install the modem and configure Windows XP to use it. If you sign up for a cable modem, the cable TV company pays you a visit, supplies the modem, installs a network card into your PC, and sets up the software for you.

- **Possible savings.** At this writing, cable modems and DSL services cost about $30 to $50 a month. That includes the Internet account for which you'd ordinarily pay $20 if you signed up for a traditional ISP. And since you're connecting to the Internet via cable TV wires or unused signal capacity on your telephone lines, you may be able to save even more money by canceling your second phone line.

Not all cable TV companies offer cable modem service, but the list is quickly growing. Unfortunately, you can't get DSL unless the phone company has a central office within 18,000 feet (about three miles) of your home.

It's also worth noting that cable modems and DSL modems aren't *always* blazing fast. The speed of your cable modem decreases slightly when too many people in your area use their cable modems simultaneously. And DSL modems are slower the farther away you are from the telephone company. Even so, these devices are always faster than a dial-up modem.

Tip: Actually, neither cable modems nor DSL modems are *modems,* since they don't *mo*dulate or *de*modulate anything. (That's where the term modems comes from: they convert data into bursts of sound.) Still, we need to call them something, so most people call them modems anyway.

ISP vs. Online Service

After choosing a method of connecting to the Net, you need an Internet *account.* You can get one in either of two ways: by signing up for an *online service,* such as America Online or MSN, or through a direct Internet account with an Internet service provider (or *ISP,* as insiders and magazines inevitably call them).

National ISPs like EarthLink and AT&T have local telephone numbers in every U.S. state and many other countries. If you don't travel much, you may not need such broad coverage. Instead, you may be able to save money by signing up for a local or regional ISP. Either way, dialing the Internet is a local call for most people.

Tip: The Internet is filled with Web sites that list, describe, and recommend ISPs. To find such directories, visit a search page like *www.google.com* and search for *ISP listings.* One of the best Web-based listings, for example, can be found at *www.boardwatch.com.* (Of course, until you've actually got your Internet account working, you'll have to do this research on a PC that *is* online, like the free terminals available at most public libraries.)

Each route to the Internet (online services or ISP) has significant pros and cons.

- Most national ISPs charge $22 a month for unlimited Internet use; America Online costs $24 per month.

Tip: Free Internet access is also available—if you can tolerate an ad window that sits on your desktop and can limit your time online to ten hours each month. (To investigate these services, visit *www.juno.com* and *www.netzero.com.*) Some stores even offer gigantic discounts on new computers if you commit to paying for several years of service with one online service or another.

- Online services strike many people as easier to use, since a single program operates all Internet functions, including email and Web surfing. When using an ISP, on the other hand, you fire up a different application for each function: Internet Explorer for surfing the Web, Outlook Express for email, and so on.

- Some online services, notably America Online, disconnect automatically if you haven't clicked or typed for several minutes. ISPs don't hang up on you nearly as quickly, if at all.

- Some online services are screened to block out pornography. The Internet itself, of course, isn't sanitized in this way. (Of course, you can get *to* the Internet from any online service, which makes this point less relevant.)

- Online services provide proprietary, members-only features like games and chat rooms.

- Because online services are slightly easier to use than ISP accounts, you'll run into people who look down on MSN and America Online members.

Establishing a Brand-new Internet Account

If you'd like to sign up for Microsoft's Internet service, called MSN (and by the way, Microsoft would *love* you to sign up for MSN), or a traditional ISP, you're ready for the New Connection Wizard.

1. **Choose Start→All Programs→Accessories→Communications→New Connection Wizard.**

   If you managed to mouse across that labyrinth of menus, the New Connection Wizard appears (Figure 10-1).

2. **Click Next. On the next screen, click Connect to the Internet, and then click the Next button.**

   Now you reach an important juncture: the Getting Ready screen (third from top in Figure 10-1).

3. **Click "Choose from a list of Internet service providers (ISPs)," and then click Next.**

Here's where you tell the wizard whether you want to sign up for the pricier, but sanitized, world of MSN, or a standard Internet service provider.

4. **Click either "Get online with MSN" or "Select from a list of other ISPs," and then click Finish.**

If you choose MSN, the graphic design scheme of the wizard changes—suddenly you're in pastel land. This, of course, is the MSN Signup Wizard. Over the next few minutes, you'll be guided through the process of signing up for a new account. You'll be asked for your name, address, birthday, occupation, credit card number, and so on. You'll also be offered the chance to preserve your existing Microsoft-service email address (anything ending with *@hotmail.com* or *@msn.com*). (During the process, the computer will dial a toll-free number to connect with MSN.)

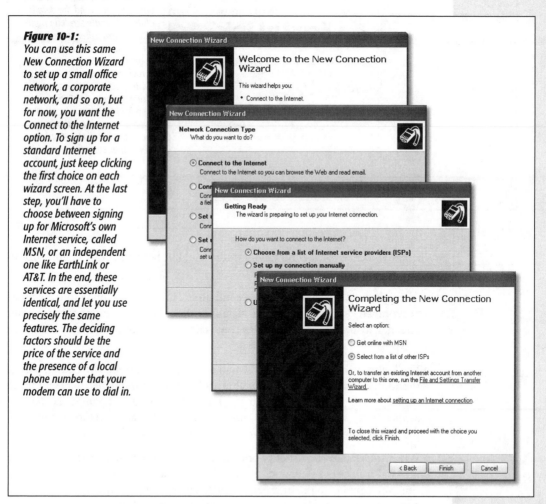

Figure 10-1:
You can use this same New Connection Wizard to set up a small office network, a corporate network, and so on, but for now, you want the Connect to the Internet option. To sign up for a standard Internet account, just keep clicking the first choice on each wizard screen. At the last step, you'll have to choose between signing up for Microsoft's own Internet service, called MSN, or an independent one like EarthLink or AT&T. In the end, these services are essentially identical, and let you use precisely the same features. The deciding factors should be the price of the service and the presence of a local phone number that your modem can use to dial in.

If you choose "Select from a list of other ISPs," the wizard disappears, and Windows deposits you into a folder window containing two shortcuts: "Get online with MSN" (which opens the same wizard described in the previous paragraph) and "Refer me to more Internet Service Providers." Use the latter shortcut to sign up for traditional Internet accounts, as shown in Figure 10-2.

Figure 10-2:
In the U.S., the ISP Signup Wizard starts by calling a toll-free number to retrieve a list of Internet service providers that have deals with Microsoft in "your area" (in general, this means "in your country"). Click one, and then read the details of its deal in the scrolling right-side window. After settling on one, click the Next button to begin the signup process (providing your name, address, credit card number, and so on). Along the way, you'll probably be asked to select a local telephone number (that your modem will call to get online) from an existing list.

Whether you choose MSN or a more traditional ISP, however, both signup wizards share a few things in common:

- Along the way, the wizard dials a second time. This time, it's contacting the Internet company you've selected. The details of the service plan now appear on your screen. If you agree with the ISP's rules, click the Accept button, and then click Next.

- You'll also be asked to invent an email address for yourself. The ending part of the address is determined by your choice of ISP—*@earthlink.net,* for example, or *@msn.com.* The first part is up to you, but keep in mind that names like *Bob* and *Seinfeld* were snapped up some time in the Reagan era. Therefore, if the email name you type in isn't unique, you'll be asked to try a different one.

- When you're shown a list of phone numbers, choose one that's local. If there are no local numbers listed, and you'd rather not pay long distance charges every time you connect to the Internet, consider canceling this entire signup operation and spending some time researching smaller, regional ISPs.

The Connection Icon

When it's all over, Windows XP stores your ISP information, your name, your password, and so on, into a single icon called a *connection*. To see the one you've just created, choose Start→All Programs→Accessories→Communications→Network Connections, as shown in Figure 10-3. There are dozens of ways to get online, and one way is to double-click this special icon.

Doing so produces the dialog box shown in Figure 10-3 at right. This box will soon become extremely familiar, since it appears every time your computer attempts to access the Internet for any reason.

Once you've set up your connection, skip ahead to "Connecting to the Internet." You're now ready to explore the Net.

Figure 10-3:
Right: This particularly well-endowed individual has four different ways to get to the Internet. The New Connection Wizard created two of them—the ones represented by the MSN Explorer and EarthLink icons. One of the many ways to go online is to double-click this icon.

Left: Double-clicking one of these icons produces this dialog box, where you can click Dial to go online. (Turning on "Save password" eliminates the need to type your password each time—in general, a great idea.)

Manually Plugging in Internet Settings

Although the New Connection Wizard does an admirable job of trying to simplify the hairy process of accessing the Internet, it's not always appropriate. Here are a few cases when you may want to arrange your settings manually:

- You already have an Internet account.

- You have a cable modem or DSL connection.

- The New Connection Wizard didn't find any ISPs with local phone numbers for you, but you've heard about a local service—offered by your local PC user group, for example—that sounds just right.

• Your PC is connected to a network through which your company provides Internet service.

In each of these cases, you can still use the New Connection Wizard; however, a good deal more typing is required.

Via Dial-up Modem

If you connect to the Internet via telephone jack, like most of the world, choose Start→All Programs→Accessories→Communications→New Connection Wizard. Make sure that your computer is plugged into a phone jack.

Click Next, "Connect to the Internet," Next, "Setup my Internet connection manually," and Next. Now click "Connect using a dial-up modem," and then Next.

On the following several screens, you'll be asked to type in a few pieces of information that only your ISP can provide: the local phone number that connects your PC to the Internet, your user name, and your password. (You can call your ISP for this information, or consult the literature delivered by postal mail when you signed up for an ISP account.)

You'll also be offered these three important checkboxes:

• **Use this account name and password when anyone connects to the Internet from this computer.** This option refers to the Windows XP *user accounts* feature described in Chapter 17, in which various people who share the same computer keep their worlds of information and settings separate by signing in each time they use the machine. It's asking you: "Is this the Internet account you want this PC to use no matter who's logged in at the moment?"

• **Make this the default Internet connection.** Some people have more than one way to access the Internet. Maybe you connect your laptop to a cable modem when you're at home but dial out using the modem when you're on the road. Turn on this checkbox if the account you're setting up is the one you want it to use most often.

Tip: You can always change your mind. In the Network Connections window (Figure 10-3), right-click a connection icon and choose Set as Default Connection from the shortcut menu. On the other hand, if you're a laptop-toting traveler, you might want to specify a different connection in each city you visit. In that case, right-click the default icon (shown by the checkmark at right in Figure 10-3) and choose Cancel as Default Connection from the shortcut menu. This way, your laptop will never dial away automatically, using some hopelessly irrelevant access number for the city you're in.

• **Turn on Internet Connection Firewall for this Connection.** Windows XP offers a certain degree of protection from incoming hacker attacks in the form of a personal firewall (see the facing page). Turn this off only if you've equipped your PC with other firewall software (or if you have a *router*, as described in Chapter 18).

When it's all over, you'll find that you've given birth to a *connection icon*, as shown at right in Figure 10-3. Once you've correctly typed in all of the necessary information, you should be ready to surf.

GEM IN THE ROUGH

The Windows XP Internet Firewall

One of Windows XP's most popular new features is its built-in firewall software. It's designed to protect against hackers and the automatic sniffing software that they use—either of which could theoretically sneak into your PC over its Internet connection, exposing your files to ne'er-do-wells or causing other damage.

You can turn on the built-in firewall in any of several ways. First of all, as noted earlier in this chapter, the New Connection Wizard offers it as an option when you set up a new Internet account. Second, you can right-click your connection icon (Figure 10-3), choose Properties from the shortcut menu, and, in the resulting dialog box, click the Advanced tab. Turn on the "Protect my computer and network" checkbox and then click OK—that's all there is to it. There's little downside to turning on this free bit of protection.

It's important to note, however, that this firewall software blocks only *incoming* tentacles of evil. If a virus manages to infiltrate your PC by other means (from an attachment that you opened in your email program, for example), the Windows firewall does nothing to block *outgoing* mischief. (Some viruses, for example, are designed to attach themselves to every outgoing email message you send; some even send out email to everyone in your address book.)

If you prefer something more secure—software that blocks both incoming and outgoing malice, for example—consider using a free piece of firewall software like ZoneAlarm instead (*www.zonealarm.com*).

Furthermore, if you've set up several PCs to share one Internet connection (page 486), turn on the XP firewall option only for the *first* computer—the one that's connected directly to the Internet. Otherwise, the firewall software will prevent your *own* computers from talking to each other. Similarly, leave the firewall software turned off if your computers are connected to a *router*—a piece of equipment that lets several PCs share the same Internet connection (Chapter 18).

Techie note: The firewall works by blocking all unsolicited data from the Net. If you click Settings in this box, you can tell the firewall software to permit *certain* kinds of incoming, unsolicited queries—a useful feature if your PC hosts a Web site, for example. The Settings button in the Advanced tab, meanwhile, lets you turn on *logging*, which creates a text file that contains a list of every piece of Internet traffic the firewall tried to block. If you're a TCP/IP sleuth, this information could theoretically be a useful starting point for tracking down hackers foolish enough to take you on.

Tip: If you carry a laptop from city to city—each of which requires a different local Internet number—you might want to create more than one connection icon by plugging in a different local access number each time. (Alternatively, just create one connection icon—and then, in the Network Connections window, right-click it and choose Create Copy.) Another helpful hint: Name each of these connections after the appropriate location ("EarthLink Cleveland," "EarthLink Stamford," and so on), so you'll remember which one to use for which city.

Via Cable Modem, Network, or DSL

As noted earlier in this chapter, you're usually spared the hassle of setting up these so-called broadband accounts. The installation person generally handles it for you.

If you ever need to set up such an account yourself for some reason, here's the procedure:

1. **Choose Start→Control Panel. In Classic view (page 253), double-click Network Connections.**

   (That's an alternate route to the Network Connections window shown in Figure 10-3.) If your PC does, in fact, have an Ethernet adapter—a requirement for a cable modem, DSL modem, or network Internet account—you'll see an icon for it in this window.

2. **Right-click the Local Area Connection icon; from the shortcut menu, choose Properties.**

   You get the dialog box shown at left in Figure 10-4.

3. **Double-click the listing that says Internet Protocol (TCP/IP).**

   An even more intimidating dialog box now appears, as shown at right in Figure 10-4.

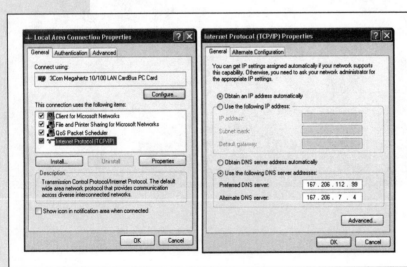

Figure 10-4:
Left: In this dialog box, double-click the Internet Protocol (TCP/IP) item that corresponds to your Ethernet card.

Right: Your cable or phone company generally configures these settings for you. But if a freak solar eclipse wipes out all of your settings, you can re-enter them here. When you click OK, you should be back online.

4. **With your cable company, DSL company, or network administrator on the phone, type in your account information.**

   Most of the time, you'll be instructed to turn on "Obtain an IP address automatically" and "Obtain DNS server address automatically." You don't know how lucky you are—you've been saved from typing in all the other numbers in this dialog box. Otherwise, turn on "Use the following IP address" and type in the appropriate numbers. Do the same with "Use the following DNS server addresses."

5. **Click OK.**

   As a courtesy, Windows XP doesn't make you restart the computer in order for your new network settings to take effect.

Upon completing this task, you won't wind up with a connection icon, as you would if you intended to connect to the Internet using a dial-up modem. Instead, you're online all the time, 24 hours a day—or at least whenever your cable/DSL/network is working correctly.

Connecting to the Internet

If you enjoy a full-time Internet connection like a cable modem or DSL, you're constantly connected to the Internet. Skip to the next chapter.

If you have a dial-up modem, however, you should now have a connection icon in your Network Connections window.

Manual Connections

Double-click the connection's icon in the Network Connections window (Figure 10-3). The Connect To dialog box appears, as shown at left in that figure. Just press Enter, or click Dial, to go online.

But that's just the beginning. If you crave variety, here are a few other ways of opening the connection:

UP TO SPEED

IP Addresses and You

Every computer connected to the Internet, even temporarily, has its own exclusive *IP address* (IP stands for Internet Protocol). When you set up your own Internet account, as described on these pages, you'll be asked to type in this string of numbers. As you'll see, an IP address always consists of four numbers separated by periods.

Some PCs with high-speed Internet connections (cable modem, DSL) have a permanent, unchanging address called a *fixed* or *static* IP address. Other computers get assigned a new address each time they connect (a *dynamic* IP address). That's always the case, for example, when you connect via a dial-up modem. (If you can't figure out whether your machine has a static or fixed address, ask your Internet service provider.)

If nothing else, dynamic addresses are more convenient in some ways, since you don't have to type numbers into the Internet Protocol (TCP/IP) Properties dialog box shown in Figure 10-4.

- Right-click your connection icon, and then choose Connect from the shortcut menu.

- If you've added the "Connect to" submenu to your Start menu, as described in the box on page 302, just choose the name of the connection you want.

- Create a desktop shortcut for your connection icon (the icon in the Network Connections window) by right-dragging it out of the window and onto the desktop. When you release the mouse button, choose Create Shortcut(s) Here from the shortcut menu. Now just double-click the shortcut whenever you feel the urge to surf.

- Drag your connection icon shortcut onto the Quick Launch toolbar (page 97), so that you can now get to the Internet with just one click.

The Notification Area Icon

While you're connected to your ISP, Windows XP puts an icon in the notification area (Figure 10-5), reminding you that you're online. You can watch the icon light up as data zooms back and forth across the connection. And if you point to it without clicking, you'll see a yellow tooltip showing your speed and how much data has been transmitted. (If this little taskbar icon isn't visible, take a moment to turn it back on, as directed in Figure 10-5. You'll find it to be an important administrative center for going online and offline.)

GEM IN THE ROUGH

Faster Access to Connection Icons

In the following pages, you'll quite frequently work your way to the Network Connections window and the connection icons inside it. With just a little Start-menu surgery, however, you can directly access this folder, or the connection icons inside it, without burrowing through the Control Panel window first.

To do so, right-click the Start button. From the shortcut menu, choose Properties. Click the Customize button, and then click the Advanced tab.

Finally, scroll down until you see Network Connections. Here you have a couple of useful options. "Display as Connect to menu" adds a submenu—directly to your Start menu—listing the various

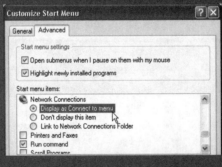

connections available. If you're a laptop owner, for example, and you've established connection icons for several different cities, this submenu makes it extremely easy to get online using the correct local phone number.

"Link to Network Connections Folder," meanwhile, adds a command to the right side of the Start menu called Network Connections. It opens the Network Connections window, once again saving you the intermediate step of opening Control Panel first.

When you're finished, click OK twice. Use the new spare time you've just won yourself to take up hang gliding or learn French.

Automatic Dialing

It's important to understand that when your PC dials, it simply opens up a connection to the Internet. But aside from tying up the phone line, your PC doesn't actually *do* anything until you then launch an Internet program, such as an email program or a Web browser. By itself, making your PC dial the Internet is no more useful than dialing a phone number and then not saying anything.

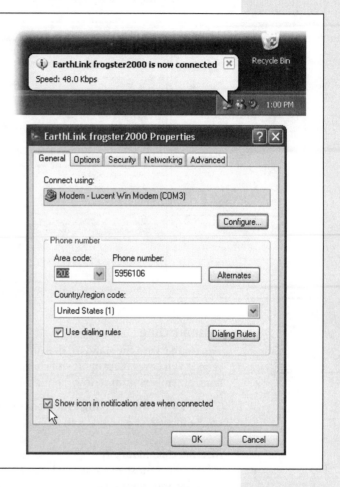

Figure 10-5:
Top: To make the notification area icon appear, right-click the icon for your connection (Figure 10-3). From the shortcut menu, choose Properties.

Bottom: At the bottom of the General tab, you'll see the key feature, "Show icon in notification area when connected." Turn on this option, and then click OK.

Therefore, using the Internet is generally a two-step procedure: First, open the connection; second, open a program.

Fortunately, Windows offers a method of combining these two steps. You can make the dialing/connecting process begin automatically whenever you launch an Internet program. This way, you're saved the trouble of fussing with the connection icon every time you want to go online.

To turn on this option, just open your Web browser and try to Web surf. When the PC discovers that it's not, in fact, online, it will display the Dial-up Connection dialog box at left in Figure 10-6. Turn on the "Connect automatically" checkbox, and then click Connect.

From now on, whenever you use a feature that requires an Internet connection, your PC dials automatically. (Examples: specifying a Web address in a window's Address bar, clicking the Send and Receive button in your email program, clicking a link in the Windows Help system, and so on.)

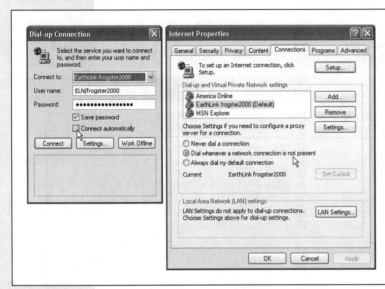

Figure 10-6:
Left: "Connect automatically" makes your PC dial whenever any of your programs tries to go online.

Right: If you can't seem to get online despite taking this step, open the Internet Options program in the Control Panel (page 265). Click the Connections tab. Make sure that "Never dial a connection" isn't selected; choose one of the other options. (That's an option for people who like to establish the Internet connection manually before opening an Internet program like a Web browser.)

Disconnecting

The trouble with the standard dial-up Internet connection is that, unless you intervene, it will never hang up. It will continue to tie up your phone line until the other family members hunt it down, hours later, furious and brandishing wire cutters.

Therefore, it's worth taking a moment to configure your system so that it won't stay online forever.

Disconnecting manually

When you're finished using the Internet, end the phone call by performing one of the following steps:

- Right-click the little connection icon on your taskbar. Choose Disconnect from the shortcut menu (Figure 10-7, top).

- Double-click the little connection icon on the taskbar. Click the Disconnect button in the Status dialog box that appears (Figure 10-7, bottom), or press Alt+D.

- Right-click the connection icon in your Network Connections window. Choose Disconnect from the shortcut menu.

Disconnecting automatically

You can also set up your PC to hang up the phone automatically several minutes after your last activity online.

To find the necessary controls, right-click your connection icon (page 297); from the shortcut menu, choose Properties. In the resulting dialog box, click the Options tab. Near the middle of the box, you'll see a drop-down list called "Idle time before hanging up." You can set it to 1 minute, 10 minutes, 2 hours, or whatever.

Figure 10-7:
Top: The quickest way to hang up is to use the notification-area icon. Right-click it and choose Disconnect from the shortcut menu that appears.

Bottom: You can also double-click the icon to view statistics on your session so far, and to produce a Disconnect button for hanging up.

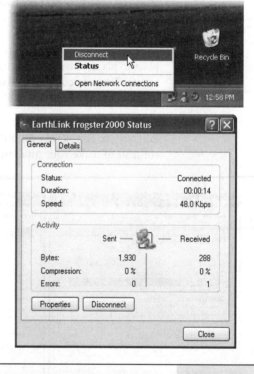

Laptop's Lament: Away from the Cable Modem

When I'm home, I connect my laptop to my cable modem. But when I'm on the road, of course, I have to use my dial-up ISP. Is there any way to automate the switching between these two connection methods?

If there weren't, do you think your question would have even appeared in this book?

The feature you're looking for is in the Internet Options program in Control Panel (page 265). Open it, click the Connections tab, and then turn on "Dial whenever a network connection is not present."

From now on, your laptop will use its dial-up modem only when it realizes that it isn't connected to your cable modem.

Advanced Modem Settings

Because so many people consider the Internet such an important PC feature, Windows XP lets you fine-tune its dialing, modem, and Internet settings to within an inch of their lives. You should consider the rest of this chapter optional—or power-user—reading.

To adjust the settings for your modem's dialing patterns, choose Start→Control Panel. In Classic view (see page 243), double-click Phone and Modem Options. (See Chapter 9 for more on the Control Panel window.) The resulting dialog box (Figure 10-8, left) consists of three major tabs, each serving important functions.

Dialing Rules Tab

The Dialing Rules tab (Figure 10-8, left) is made for travelers. As you move from place to place, you may wind up in locations that have very different dialing requirements. The area code may change, not to mention the requirement to dial 9 for an outside line, the availability of touch-tone dialing, and so on.

To set up the dialing rules for your current location, click its name and then click the Edit button. The New Location box appears (Figure 10-8, right), bristling with enough controls to make your modem sing, dance, and stand on its head.

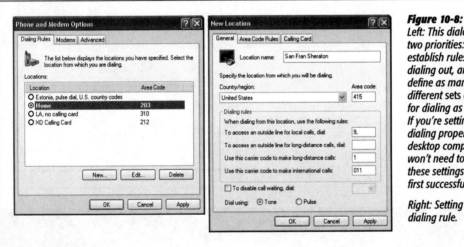

Figure 10-8:
Left: This dialog box has two priorities: to establish rules for dialing out, and to define as many different sets of rules for dialing as you need. If you're setting up dialing properties for a desktop computer, you won't need to change these settings after the first successful call.

Right: Setting up a new dialing rule.

General tab

Here are the guidelines for filling out this dialog box:

- **Location name, Country, Area code.** These boxes inform Windows where you're presently located. When your modem dials another city or country, Windows XP will know when to dial a 1 (and a country or area code, when necessary) before dialing.

- **To access an outside line for local/long distance calls.** In many offices and hotels, you must dial a number (usually 8 or 9) to get an outside line. If you enter numbers into these text boxes, Windows will dial them before the regularly scheduled Internet number.

- **Use this carrier code to make long distance/international calls.** These options specify the codes that you have to dial, even before the area code, when dialing internationally. For example, in the United States, the long distance carrier code is 1. For international calls, the carrier code consists of the digits you dial before the country code—to make international calls from the United States, for example, the carrier code is 011.

- **To disable call-waiting.** If you have call-waiting service, that little beep that announces another incoming call can scramble your Internet connection. Fortunately, Windows XP will be delighted to automatically disable call-waiting whenever you use the modem. Turn on this checkbox; from the drop-down list to its right, choose from the list of the common call-waiting disabling key sequences (*70, 70#, and 1170). (If you don't know which sequence works for your local phone company, check the front of your phone book.)

  When the modem disconnects from the Internet after your online session, call-waiting automatically returns to the phone line.

- **Tone or pulse dialing.** Specify whether your telephone service is touch-tone (push-button) or pulse (as on old-fashioned rotary-dial phones).

Area Code Rules tab

It used to be easy to dial the telephone in America. For local calls, you dialed a seven-digit number. Calls to other area codes started with 1 and then the area code.

Not any more. Many metropolitan areas now utilize *ten-digit dialing*—an insidious system that requires you to dial the full area code even for your next-door neighbor. Worse, some cities have several *different* area codes—not all of which require a 1+ area code dialing pattern. To confuse things further, in some cases, you dial *only* the area code plus the seven-digit number.

To clue your modem in on the vagaries of your own area's area code practices, click the Area Code Rules tab. From there, set up the dialing sequences for certain locations by clicking the New button to open the New Area Code Rule dialog box. The resulting options (Figure 10-9) let you specify the area code and three-digit prefixes. Click OK to return to the New Location dialog box.

Calling Card tab

If you, the shrewd traveler, feel that there's a better use for your money than paying most of it to your hotel's $3-per-minute long distance scheme, this dialog box is for you. It lets you train your modem to bill its calls to a calling card (Figure 10-10).

Note: Creating a calling card profile doesn't mean you must use it every time you use your modem. In fact, you can choose whether or not to use the calling card each time you dial out.

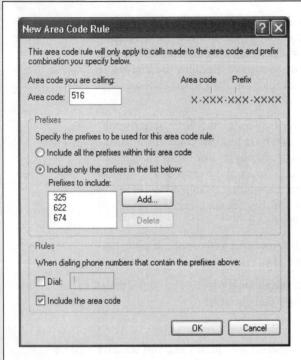

Figure 10-9:
This dialog box can handle any weird and convoluted area code rule in your town. (If there aren't special rules yet in your area, it's only a matter of time.) When your local phone company changes the rules, don't forget to open this dialog box and explain the changes to your modem.

If your calling card isn't listed, you can create a setup for it yourself, which Windows then adds to the list. Armed with the instructions from your calling card company, click the New button. In the resulting dialog box, specify the card name, account number, PIN, and so on.

By clicking the Long Distance tab in the New Calling Card dialog box, you can specify the steps needed to use the card for long distance. For instance, you may need to dial a number and then wait for a tone that confirms that the number has been accepted. In this dialog box, you can specify the number of seconds you want Windows to wait. (You can set up the same kinds of rules for international and local calls by clicking the appropriate tabs.)

Once you've set up a calling card, it becomes part of one of these dialing rules. Now when you want to go online, you'll be able to bill your modem calls to your calling card on a case-by-case basis.

To do so, start by double-clicking your connection icon (Figure 10-3). When the dialog box shown at left in Figure 10-3 appears, use the "Dialing from" drop-down list to choose the name of the dialing-rule setup that contains your calling card configuration. Now click Dial to start your call.

Modems Tab

All the preceding discussion concerns only the first of the three tabs in the Phone
and Modem Options program. The second tab, called Modems, is simply a list of
the modems currently connected to your PC. (Most people not in Oprah's tax bracket,
of course, see only one modem listed here.)

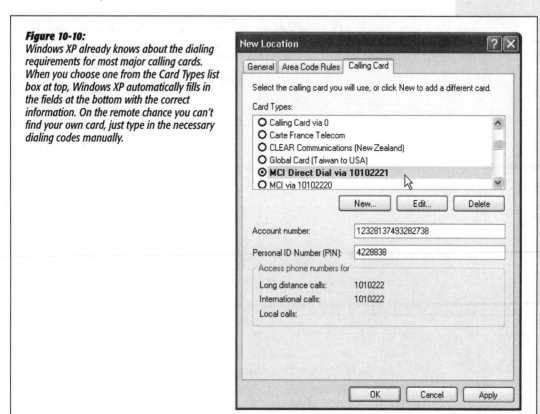

Figure 10-10:
*Windows XP already knows about the dialing
requirements for most major calling cards.
When you choose one from the Card Types list
box at top, Windows XP automatically fills in
the fields at the bottom with the correct
information. On the remote chance you can't
find your own card, just type in the necessary
dialing codes manually.*

Double-clicking the name of your modem opens its Properties dialog box, which
bursts with technical parameters for your modem. In general, you'll need to visit
these dialog boxes only when troubleshooting, following the instructions of some
telecommunications geek from your modem company. Two of them, however, are
more generally useful:

- **Change the speaker volume.** The modern modem may have revolutionized computer communications, but the squealing sounds it makes could wake the dead—
or, worse, the spouse. To turn the speaker off, so that you no longer hear the
shrieks every time you dial, click the Modem tab (Figure 10-11), and then drag
the Speaker volume slider to Off.

Tip: The slider affects the speaker volume only while it's dialing and making a connection to another computer. After the connection is established, the speaker *always* goes silent, so you don't have to listen to all the squawking noises that indicate data transmission.

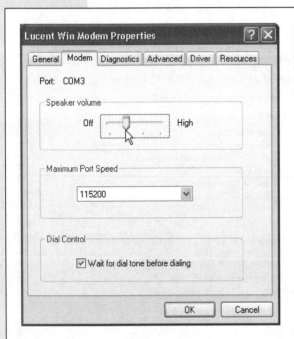

Figure 10-11:
The Modem tab of the Modem Properties dialog box. Many people, perhaps thinking wishfully, set a speed higher than the modem's rated speed. Unfortunately, the speed doesn't actually improve as a result.

- **Wait for the dial tone before dialing.** This checkbox (also on the Modem tab, as shown in Figure 10-11) is normally turned on. If you travel abroad with your laptop, however, you may experience trouble connecting if the foreign country's dial tone doesn't sound the same as it does back home. Turning off this checkbox often solves the problem.

Advanced Tab (of Phone and Modem Options)

These controls, too, are extremely advanced options that you'll never need to adjust except in times of intense troubleshooting.

Web, Chat, and
Videoconferencing

Microsoft has gone to great lengths to integrate the Internet into every nook and cranny of Windows XP. Links and buttons that spur your modem into a dialing frenzy are everywhere: on the Help screens, in the Search window, and even in the "Send error report to Microsoft?" dialog boxes that appear after program crashes. Once you've got your Internet connection working (Chapter 10), you may find that it's easier to go online than it is *not* to.

The Internet offers dozens of different features, most of them graced with such unhelpful, invented-by-government-scientists-in-the-sixties names as FTP, Telnet, Gopher, and so on. But a few of the most popular Internet services are both easy to understand and easy to use: the World Wide Web, email, online chatting, videoconferencing, and free phone calls.

You can use whichever software you prefer for these functions. To connect to the Web, for example, use Netscape Navigator or any of several less-famous Web browsers. To check your email, use Eudora, Lotus Notes, and so on.

But most Windows XP users wind up using the Internet programs that are built right into the operating system: Internet Explorer or MSN Explorer for Web browsing; Outlook Express for email; and Windows Messenger or NetMeeting for chatting, free long-distance "phone" calls, and teleconferencing. This chapter covers all of these programs except Outlook Express, which is described in Chapter 12.

Internet Explorer 6

Internet Explorer (or IE, as it's often abbreviated) is the most famous Web browser on earth, thanks to several years of Justice-department scrutiny and newspaper headlines. The initial release of Windows XP comes with IE version 6, which you can open in a number of ways:

- Choosing its name from the Start menu (either the left column or the All Programs menu).

- Clicking its shortcut on the Quick Launch toolbar.

- Choosing a Web site's name from your Start→Favorites menu (that is, if you've put favorites there).

- Typing a Web address—sometimes called its *URL* (*Uniform Resource Locator*) into a window's Address bar. A Web page URL usually begins with the prefix *http://*, but you can leave that part off when typing into the Address bar.

- Clicking a blue, underlined link on a Windows Help screen.

…and so on.

As you can see in Figure 11-1, the Internet Explorer window is filled with tools that are designed to facilitate a smooth trip around the World Wide Web.

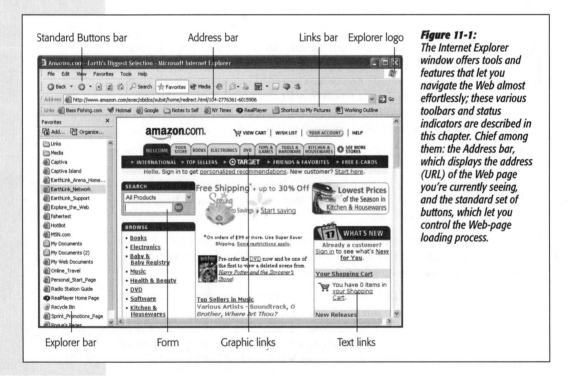

Standard Buttons bar   Address bar   Links bar   Explorer logo

Explorer bar   Form   Graphic links   Text links

Figure 11-1:
The Internet Explorer window offers tools and features that let you navigate the Web almost effortlessly; these various toolbars and status indicators are described in this chapter. Chief among them: the Address bar, which displays the address (URL) of the Web page you're currently seeing, and the standard set of buttons, which let you control the Web-page loading process.

Browsing Basics and Toolbars

Navigating the Web requires little more than clicking buttons or those underlined blue phrases, as shown in Figure 11-1.

When you click an underlined *link* (or *hyperlink*), you're transported from one Web page to another. One may be the home page of General Motors; another may contain critical information about a bill in Congress; another might have baby pictures posted by a parent in Omaha. Several hundred million Web pages await your visit.

Around the edges of any Web page, as well as within it, you'll encounter standard Internet features. For example:

- **Explorer logo.** When this globe is spinning, your PC is still downloading (receiving) the information and graphics on the Web page. In other words, you're not seeing everything yet.

- **Button and picture links.** Clicking a picture or a button generally takes you to a new Web page.

- **Text links.** Clicking a link takes you to a different Web page (or a different place on the same Web page).

Tip: Text links aren't always blue and underlined. In fact, modern Web designers sometimes make it very difficult to tell which text is clickable, and which is just text. When in doubt, just move your cursor over some text. If the arrow changes to a pointing-finger cursor, you've found yourself a link.

Actually, you can choose to hide *all* underlines, a trick that makes Web pages look cleaner and more attractive. Underlines appear only when you point to a link (and wait a moment). If that arrangement appeals to you, open Internet Explorer. Choose Tools→Internet Options, click the Advanced tab, scroll down to "Underline links," select the Hover option, then click OK.

- **Graphics worth saving.** When you see a picture you'd like to keep, right-click it and choose Save Picture As from the shortcut menu. After you name the picture and then click the Save button, the result is a new graphics file on your hard drive containing the picture you saved. (You can also choose Set as Background, which makes the picture part of your desktop image itself.)

- **Scroll bars.** Use the scroll bar to move up and down the page—or to save mousing, press the Space bar each time you want to see more. Press Shift+Space bar to scroll *up*. (The Space bar has its traditional, space-making function only when the insertion point is blinking in a text box or the Address bar.)

You can also press your up and down arrow keys to scroll. Page Up and Page Down scroll in full-screen increments, while Home and End whisk you to the top or bottom of the current Web page.

Tip: If you have an IntelliMouse mouse from Microsoft, you can use your roller wheel (and use similar scrolling tricks) to scroll the page, too.

Internet Explorer Toolbars

Many of Internet Explorer's most useful controls come parked on toolbars exactly like those described in Chapter 3. You summon or hide these toolbars the same way,

---

too: by choosing their names from the View→Toolbars submenu. Here's what you'll find on each.

Tip: Drag the tiny "grab bar" at the left end of a toolbar up or down to rearrange the bars' vertical stacking order. You can even drop this grab bar halfway across *another* toolbar, thus placing two toolbars side-by-side on the same horizontal strip.

The Standard Buttons toolbar

This toolbar, identified in Figure 11-1, contains the buttons that most people use for browsing most of the time. Some of them lack text labels, but all offer tooltip labels:

- **Back button, Forward button.** Click the Back button to revisit the page you were just on. (*Keyboard shortcut:* Backspace, or Alt+left arrow.)

  Once you've clicked Back, you can then click the Forward button (or press Alt+right arrow) to return to the page you were on *before* you clicked the Back button. Click the tiny black triangle for a drop-down list of *all* the Web pages you've visited during this online session.

- **Stop button.** Click to interrupt the downloading of a Web page you've just requested (by mistake, for example). (*Keyboard shortcut:* Esc.)

- **Refresh.** Click if a page doesn't look or work quite right, or if you want to see the updated version of a Web page (such as a stock ticker) that changes constantly. This button forces Internet Explorer to redownload the Web page and reinterpret its text and graphics.

- **Home button.** Click to bring up the Web page you've designated as your home page (see page 337).

Tip: You can rearrange these buttons, delete some, or add additional function buttons, by choosing View→Toolbars→Customize. For details on operating Microsoft's toolbar-rearrangement window, see page 93.

The Address bar

When you type a new Web page address (URL) into this strip and press Enter, the corresponding Web site appears. (If only an error message results, then you may have mistyped the address, or the Web page may have been moved or dismantled—a relatively frequent occurrence.)

Because typing out Internet addresses is so central to the Internet experience and such a typo-prone hassle, the Address bar is rich with features that minimize keystrokes. For example:

- You don't have to click in the Address bar before typing; just press Alt+D.

- You don't have to type out the whole Internet address. You can omit the *http:// www* and *.com* portions by pressing Ctrl+Enter—which makes Internet Explorer fill in those standard address bits for you. To visit Amazon.com, for example, a speed freak might press Alt+D to highlight the Address bar, type *amazon,* and then press Ctrl+Enter.

- Even without the Ctrl+Enter trick, you can still omit the *http://* from any Web address, since Internet Explorer adds it automatically. (Most of the time, you can omit the *www,* too.) To jump to today's Dilbert cartoon, type *dilbert.com* and then press Enter.

- When you begin to type into the Address bar, the AutoComplete feature compares what you're typing against a list of Web sites you've recently visited. IE displays a drop-down list of Web addresses that seem to match what you're typing. To spare yourself the tedium of typing out the whole thing, just click the correct complete address with your mouse, or use the down arrow key to reach the desired listing and then press Enter. The complete address you selected then pops into the Address bar.

  (To make Windows *forget* one of the Web sites you've visited recently, highlight it in the drop-down AutoComplete list and then press your Delete key. Or, to make Windows forget *all* of the sites you've seen, choose Tools→Internet Options, click the General tab, and then click the Clear History button.)

Tip: IE can also remember user names, passwords, and other information you type into Web page text boxes *(forms).* You can turn on this feature by choosing Tools→Internet Options, clicking the Content tab, clicking AutoComplete, and turning on the appropriate checkboxes. Or you can just wait for Internet Explorer to *invite* you to turn it on, via a little dialog box that appears when you first type something into such a form. Having your browser remember the names and passwords for your various Web sites is a great time and memory saver, even though it doesn't work on all Web sites.

When you want Internet Explorer to "forget" your passwords—for security reasons, for example—choose Tools→Internet Options, click the Content tab, click the AutoComplete button, and then click Clear Forms and Clear Passwords.

- Press F4 (or use the drop-down list at the right end of the Address bar) to view a list of URLs you've visited during this browsing session. (The list drops down from the Address bar.) Once again, you can click the one you want—or press the up or down arrow keys to highlight one, and the Enter key to select it.

You can also type a plain English phrase into the Address bar. When you press Enter, IE does a Web search for that term and opens up the first Web page that seems to contain what you're looking for. At the same time, the Search pane appears at the left side of the browser window, offering a list of other Web sites that seem to match your query.

Tip: For more control over which search site Internet Explorer uses, download TweakUI, a free Microsoft utility that comes with Powertoys (which you can download from *www.missingmanuals.com*). After installing the Powertoys, choose Start→All Programs→Powertoys for Windows XP→TweakUI. Click Internet Explorer in the list at left, and then click Search.

You're offered the chance to create little keywords that, when they precede your search term, will direct Windows to a certain search page. You could set up *ggl* to mean Google, for example. Thereafter you could type *ggl llamas* into the Address bar to make Internet Explorer search for "llamas" at *www.google.com.*

The Links toolbar

The Favorites menu described on page 640 is one way to maintain a list of Web sites you visit frequently. But opening a Web page listed in that menu requires two mouse clicks—an exorbitant expenditure of energy. The Links toolbar, on the other hand, lets you summon a few, very select, *very* favorite Web pages with only *one* click.

Figure 11-2 illustrates how to add buttons to, and remove them from, this toolbar. It's also worth noting that you can rearrange these buttons simply by dragging them horizontally.

Tip: As shown in Figure 11-2, you can drag a link from a Web page onto your Links toolbar. But you can also drag it directly to the desktop, where it turns into a special Internet shortcut icon. To launch your browser and visit the associated Web page, just double-click this icon whenever you like.

Better yet, stash a few of these icons in your Start menu or Quick Launch toolbar for even easier access. (If you open your My Computer→C: drive→Documents and Settings→[Your Name]→Favorites folder, moreover, you'll see these shortcut icons for *all* your favorite links. Feel free to drag them to the desktop, Quick Launch toolbar, Links toolbar, or wherever you like.)

Figure 11-2:
Once you've got a juicy Web page on the screen, you can turn it into a Links icon just by dragging the tiny Explorer-page icon from the Address bar directly onto the Links bar, as shown here. (You can also drag any link, like a blue underlined phrase, from a Web page onto the toolbar.) To remove a button, right-click it and choose Delete from the shortcut menu.

Status Bar

The status bar at the bottom of the window tells you what Internet Explorer is doing (such as "Opening page…" or "Done"). When you point to a link without clicking, the status bar also tells you which URL will open if you click it.

If you consult this information only rarely, you may prefer to hide this bar, thus increasing the amount of space actually devoted to showing you Web pages. To do so, choose View→Status Bar. (A checkmark appears next to its name in the View menu to indicate that the status bar is showing.)

Explorer Bar

From time to time, the *Explorer bar* appears at the left side of your browser window. Choosing commands from the View→Explorer Bar menu triggers a number of helpful lists: Search, Favorites, History, and so on. They're described in greater detail on page 77.

Ways to Find Something on the Web

There's no tidy card catalog of every Web page. Because Web pages appear and disappear hourly by the hundreds of thousands, such an exercise would be futile.

The best you can do is to use a *search engine:* a Web site that searches *other* Web sites. The best of them, such as *www.google.com,* consist of little more than a text box where you can type in your desired subject. Then, when you click the Search button (or press Enter), you're shown a list of Web site links that contain the information you want.

Other popular search pages include *yahoo.com, altavista.com, infoseek.com,* and *hotbot.com.* Using the Search panel of the Explorer bar, you can even search several of these simultaneously. That's handy, because no single search engine "knows about" every Web page on earth.

UP TO SPEED

More Web Pages Worth Knowing

The Web can be an overwhelming, life-changing marketplace of ideas and commerce. Here are some examples of Web pages that have saved people money, changed their ways of thinking, and made history:

www.dilbert.com—A month's worth of recent Dilbert cartoons.

www.clicktv.com or *tvguide.com*—Free TV listings for your exact area or cable company.

www.shopper.com, www.dealtime.com, www.mysimon .com—Comparison-shopping sites that produce a list of Web sites that sell the particular book, computer gadget, PalmPilot, or other consumer good you're looking for. This quick, simple research can save you a *lot* of money.

www.efax.com—A free service that gives you a private fax number. When someone sends a fax to your number, it's automatically sent by *email.* You read it on your screen with a free fax-viewer program. You're saved the costs of a fax machine, phone line, paper, and ink cartridges—plus you can receive faxes anywhere in the world.

http://terraserver.microsoft.com—Satellite photographs of everywhere (your tax dollars at work). Find your house!

www.yourdictionary.com—A web of online dictionaries.

www.homefair.com/homefair/cmr/salcalc.html—The International Salary Calculator.

Tips for Better Surfing

Internet Explorer is filled with shortcuts and tricks for better speed and more pleasant surfing. For example:

Full-screen browsing

All of the toolbars and other screen doodads give you plenty of surfing control, but also occupy huge chunks of your screen space. The Web is supposed to be a *visual* experience; this encroachment of your monitor's real estate isn't necessarily a good thing.

But if you press F11 (or choose View→Full Screen), all is forgiven. The browser window explodes to the very borders of your monitor, hiding the Explorer bar, status bar, stacked toolbars, and all. The Web page you're viewing fills your screen, edge to edge—a glorious, liberating experience. Whatever toolbars you had open collapse into a single strip at the very top edge of the screen, their text labels hidden to save space.

You can return to the usual crowded, toolbar-mad arrangement by pressing F11 again—but you'll be tempted never to do so.

Bigger text, smaller text

You can adjust the point size of a Web page's text using the View→Text Size commands (and then pressing F5 to refresh the screen, if necessary). When your eyes are tired, you might like to make the text bigger. When you visit a Web site designed for Macintosh computers (whose text tends to look too large on PC screens), you might want a smaller size.

Tip: If you have an IntelliMouse mouse, you can also enlarge or reduce the type on the page by pressing the Ctrl key as you turn the mouse's wheel.

Enlarge or shrink online photos

Internet Explorer has always offered a number of great features when it comes to graphics found online. Right-clicking an image, for example, produces a shortcut menu that offers commands like Save Picture As, E-mail Picture, Print Picture, Set as Background (that is, wallpaper), and Set as Desktop Item (that is, an Active Desktop item, as described in Chapter 9). There was only one problem: Most people never knew these features existed.

In Internet Explorer 6, therefore, Microsoft tries to make it more obvious that this browser has some smarts with regards to pictures. Whenever your cursor moves over a graphic, a small *image toolbar* appears, as shown in Figure 11-3. And if it's a big picture—too big to fit in your browser window—Internet Explorer automatically shrinks it so that it does fit, also as shown in Figure 11-3.

Tip: To turn off IE's picture toolbar and picture-shrinking feature, choose Tools→Internet Options. Click the Advanced tab, scroll down to the Multimedia heading, and turn off "Enable Automatic Image Resizing" and "Enable Image Toolbar (requires restart)." Click OK, and (if you turned off the toolbar) quit and reopen IE.

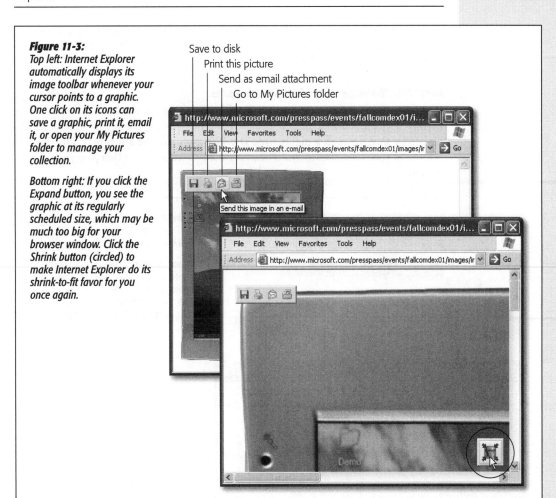

Figure 11-3:
Top left: Internet Explorer automatically displays its image toolbar whenever your cursor points to a graphic. One click on its icons can save a graphic, print it, email it, or open your My Pictures folder to manage your collection.

Bottom right: If you click the Expand button, you see the graphic at its regularly scheduled size, which may be much too big for your browser window. Click the Shrink button (circled) to make Internet Explorer do its shrink-to-fit favor for you once again.

Save to disk
Print this picture
Send as email attachment
Go to My Pictures folder

Faster browsing without graphics

Of course, graphics are part of what makes the Web so compelling. But they're also responsible for making Web pages take so long to arrive on the screen. Without them, Web pages appear almost instantaneously. You still get fully laid-out Web pages; you still see all the text and headlines. But wherever a picture would normally be, you see an empty rectangle containing a generic "graphic goes here" logo, usually with a caption explaining what that graphic would have been.

To turn off graphics, choose Tools→Internet Options, which opens the Internet Options dialog box. Click the Advanced tab, scroll down halfway into the list of checkboxes, and turn off "Show pictures" (in the Multimedia category of checkboxes; see Figure 11-5). Now try visiting a few Web pages; you'll feel a substantial speed boost.

And if you wind up on a Web page that's nothing without its pictures, you can choose to summon an individual picture. Just right-click its box and choose Show Picture from the shortcut menu.

Favorites: "Bookmarking" favorite Web sites

When you find a Web page you might like to visit again, press Ctrl+D. That's the keyboard shortcut for Favorites→Add to Favorites—but it's better, because it doesn't make you slog through a dialog box. The Web page's name appears instantly at the bottom of your Favorites menu. The next time you want to visit that page, just choose its name.

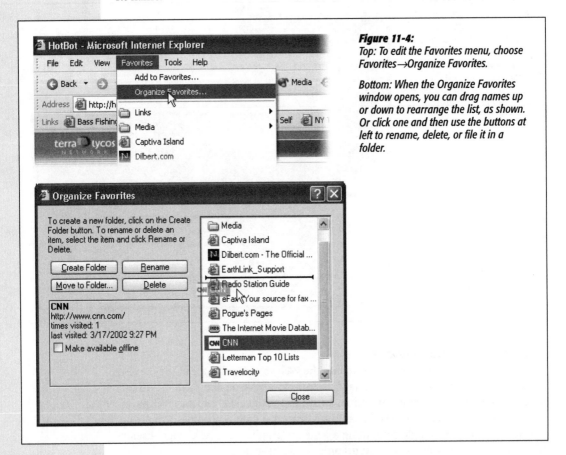

Figure 11-4:
Top: To edit the Favorites menu, choose Favorites→Organize Favorites.

Bottom: When the Organize Favorites window opens, you can drag names up or down to rearrange the list, as shown. Or click one and then use the buttons at left to rename, delete, or file it in a folder.

You can rearrange the commands in your Favorites menu easily enough: Just drag them up and down the open menu (something that doesn't occur to most Web fans.) If your Favorites *pane* is open at the left side of the window, you can rearrange them there, too, just by dragging with the Alt key pressed.

For more dramatic management tasks—to edit, rename, or delete your favorites, for example—see Figure 11-4.

Viewing Web pages offline

You don't have to be connected to the Net to read a favorite Web page. Using the Offline feature, you can make Internet Explorer *store* a certain Web page on your hard drive so that you can peruse it later—on your laptop during your commute, for example.

The short way is to choose File→Save As. For greatest simplicity, choose "Web Archive, single file (*.mht)" from the "Save as Type" drop-down list. (The other options here save the Web page as multiple files on your hard drive—a handy feature if you intend to edit them, but less convenient if you just want to read them later.) Name the file and click the Save button. You've just preserved the Web page as a file on your hard drive, which you can open later by double-clicking it or by choosing File→Open from within Internet Explorer.

That sweet, simple technique isn't quite what Microsoft has in mind when it refers to Offline Browsing, however. This more elaborate feature adds more options, such as automatic *updating* of the page you've saved and the ability to click *links* on that same page.

To store a Web page in this way, follow these steps:

1. **Add the Web page to your Favorites menu or Links toolbar, as described earlier in this chapter.**

   Before saving a Web page for offline viewing, you must first designate it as a Link or Favorite.

2. **Right-click the Web page's name in the Favorites menu or on the Links toolbar; from the shortcut menu, choose "Make available offline."**

   The Offline Favorite Wizard appears.

3. **Answer the questions posed by the wizard, clicking Next after each answer.**

   You'll be asked, for example, whether or not you want IE to store pages that are *linked* to the page you're saving—and how many "levels deep" you want this page-to-linked-page storage to proceed. In other words, if you're storing a World News page, you'll probably find nothing but headlines on its home page. When you're sitting on the train to work with your laptop, you'll appreciate the ability to click the headlines to open the attached article pages, which are one link "deep."

   On the other hand, be careful. Links to links exponentially increase the amount of disk space IE uses. Increasing the "Download pages __ links deep from this page" number too high could fill your hard drive with hundreds of Web pages and thousands of graphics you never intended to download.

The wizard also asks how often you want this stored page updated when you *are* connected to the Internet. (If you decline to specify a schedule, you can always update the stored page manually by choosing Tools→Synchronize.)

4. **When you want to look at the pages you've stored offline, choose File→Work Offline. Then use the Favorites menu or Links toolbar to choose the name of the Web page you want.**

It springs instantly to the screen—no Internet connection required.

Ditching Pop-Unders

The ad banners at the top of every Web page are annoying enough—but nowadays, they're just the beginning. The world's smarmiest advertisers have begun inundating us with *pop-up* and *pop-under* ads: nasty little windows that appear in front of the browser window, or, worse, behind it, waiting to jump out the moment you close your browser. They're often deceptive, masquerading as error messages or dialog boxes; they'll do absolutely anything to get you to click inside them.

If this kind of thing is driving you crazy, you can either use the free solution—turning off all graphics, and features such as Flash, Java, and JavaScript, thereby missing out on half the fun of the Web itself—or the software solution. That involves installing a program like Guidescope (*www.guidescope.com*, free) or AdSubtract Pro (*www.adsubtract.com*, $30).

These programs do an excellent job of blocking *all* kind of ads. Note, by the way, that advertisers are constantly working on new, ever more intrusive methods. That's why it's important to keep your ad-blocking software current with updates and patches. That's also why even the best ad-blocking software can't stop every single ad that might come your way.

Even so, these programs do a remarkable job of keeping most ads out of your face. As a result, your Web browser will feel much faster; with the ads stripped out, many pages load in half the time. Yes, it's a war out there—but at least you now have some ammunition.

UP TO SPEED

What You Need to Know about Plug-Ins

Most Web pages contain text and pictures. A few, however, offer sound, movies, or animation. By itself, Internet Explorer doesn't know how to play this kind of onscreen show. It needs assistance from a software add-on called a *plug-in*. Once installed on your PC, a plug-in teaches Explorer how to play a specific kind of sound, movie, or animation. Plug-ins are free; most are available at *www.plugins.com*. (The ones you'll need most often are Flash, Shockwave, QuickTime, and RealPlayer.)

Setting Basic IE Options

By spending a few minutes adjusting Internet Explorer's settings, you can make it more fun (or less annoying) to use. To see the most important options, choose Tools→Internet Options (see Figure 11-5).

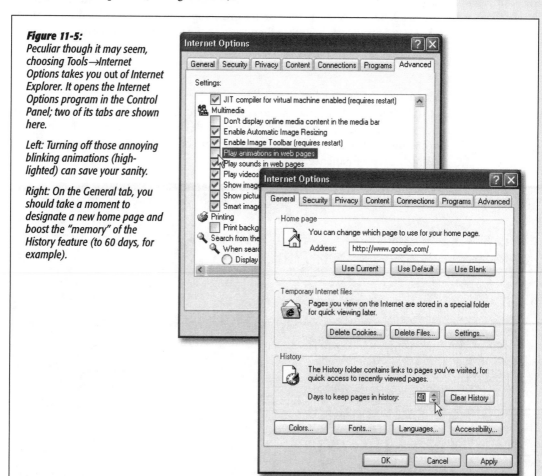

Figure 11-5:
Peculiar though it may seem, choosing Tools→Internet Options takes you out of Internet Explorer. It opens the Internet Options program in the Control Panel; two of its tabs are shown here.

Left: Turning off those annoying blinking animations (high-lighted) can save your sanity.

Right: On the General tab, you should take a moment to designate a new home page and boost the "memory" of the History feature (to 60 days, for example).

Designate your home page

The first Web site you encounter when IE connects to the Internet is a Microsoft Web site (or Dell, or EarthLink—the point is, *you* didn't choose it). This site is your *home page*. Unless you actually work for Microsoft, Dell, or EarthLink, however, you'll probably find Web browsing more fun if you specify your *own* favorite Web page as your home page.

In the Home Page section of the General tab (Figure 11-5, right), enter the Internet address of a favorite Web site. You might consider one of the Web sites described in the previous section, for example, or a search engine like *http://www.google.com*.

Tip: Instead of typing in a URL into the Address box to specify a new home page, you can also click Use Current. This button means: "Use the Web page I'm looking at *right now* as my home page in the future."

If you can't decide on a home page, or your mood changes from day to day, click the Use Blank button. Some people prefer this setup, which makes IE load very quickly when you first launch it. Rather than wasting time loading some home page you've specified, it displays an empty window instead. Once this window opens, *then* you can tell the browser where you want to go today.

Set storage options for temporary files

Most Web pages take a long time to appear in your browser window because they're crammed with *pictures*, which, on the great scale of computer files, are big and slow to download. If you use a modem, moving from one Web page to the next can be an agonizing test of patience.

WORKAROUND WORKSHOP

Missing in Action: Java

Many Web sites—especially electronic banking, stock trading, and game sites—rely on a programming language called *Java* to make them look less like ordinary Web sites and more like actual software, complete with stock tickers, interactive animation, and so on.

You can't see these goodies unless your Web browser understands the Java language. Technically, you need a blob of software called a *Java virtual machine*. Previous versions of Windows came with this software—but not Windows XP.

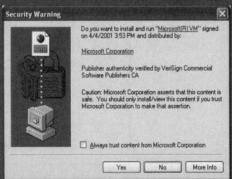

As it turns out, Microsoft has had a long-running feud with Sun Microsystems, the company that created the Java language. Sun sued Microsoft, accusing the bigger company of making changes to the Java language. But as everybody knows, it's not nice to anger Mother Microsoft. Bill Gates's revenge was swift and terrible: he and his team simply removed Java from Internet Explorer. The original version of Windows XP Pro didn't let you access Java-based Web sites at all.

Fortunately, Service Pack 1 (page 183) restores Java, although Microsoft says that it may remove it in a future update. Furthermore, if you upgraded your PC from an earlier version of Windows, you have nothing to worry about—your previous installation of the Java virtual machine will continue to work just fine in Windows XP. Just forget everything you've read here.

On the other hand, if you have a new PC, or if you performed a clean installation of Windows XP, you'll have to download the Java virtual machine yourself. There's not much to it: The first time you visit a Java Web site, you'll see a message like the one shown here, offering to send you the Java virtual machine software. Just click Yes.

The download is 5 MB, which can take some time if you're on a dial-up modem. But after the Java virtual machine has been installed, the Java Web sites should be available to you once again.

Every now and then, you might decide to return to a Web page you've already visited, perhaps during a recent Internet session. To help speed the process of loading pages you've already seen, Internet Explorer constantly saves the contents of *every* page visited onto your hard drive. When you revisit a site, the saved file is opened—fast—thus eliminating the time-consuming process of downloading the contents again.

You can test this mechanism for yourself. Direct IE to a page you've never seen before. (Go to *www.google.com,* type in, say, *electric drapes,* and then click the "I'm Feeling Lucky" button.) You wind up on something we'll call Page A.

Click a link on it to visit Page B. When you click the Back button at the top of the browser, you return to Page A *very* quickly. That's because IE doesn't have to download all those graphics a second time. Having already stored them on your hard drive during Page A's first appearance, IE now whips them onto your screen almost instantaneously.

These saved-up Web page files are called *cache* files. (Cache, pronounced "cash," is French for "hide.") IE stashes its cache in the Local Disk (C:)→Documents and Settings→[Your Name]→Local Settings→Temporary Internet Files folder. (The Local Settings folder is generally hidden; see page 89.) This folder has a limited, albeit adjustable, capacity (see Figure 11-6). Windows XP deletes older files automatically to make room for new files.

Figure 11-6:
To change the size of your cache folder, click the Settings button in the General tab of the Internet Options dialog box (Figure 11-5), and then adjust the number shown here. Enlarging the number makes it possible to store more files, enhancing the odds that when you revisit a Web site you've seen before, it will pop up onto the screen quickly. To see the temporary files (if you can even think of a reason to do so), click the View Files button. To view a list of programs you've downloaded, click the View Objects button.

Set options to check for changes

The cache-file scheme is great when it comes to speeding up the reappearance of Web pages you've seen before. Unfortunately, it has one significant drawback: If you decide to visit a Web page you've seen before, and IE blasts it onto your screen from its saved temporary files folder, then you're seeing *an old version* of that page—as it was the last time you visited. Therefore, if that Web page has been updated in the meantime, you're looking at old news—a particular hazard if it's a news Web site.

Fortunately, the dialog box shown in Figure 11-6 offers a great deal of control regarding when IE checks a particular Web page for changes made since your last visit. Here are your options:

- **Every visit to the page.** This option forces IE to check *every* Web page to see if its contents have changed since you last visited. If so, IE loads the updated page from the Internet. Of course, this option slows the process of reopening Web pages, since IE must download all of those pages' contents anew. Select this option only if you consistently visit Web sites with rapidly changing contents (stock ticker pages, news pages, Madonna hairstyle pages).

- **Every time you start Internet Explorer.** This option divides your Web browsing into two categories: sites you've visited during *this session* of using IE, and sites you visited in previous sessions.

  When you select this option, IE checks for new contents only on pages you visited in previous sessions. Revisiting any pages you viewed in the *current* session (which, of course, are less likely to have changed) produces the stored file. If you think the contents of the Web page may have changed, click the Refresh button on the IE toolbar to reload the page from the Internet.

- **Automatically.** This option, the factory setting, is similar to the previous one, but smarter. It instructs IE to keep an eye on your Web activity, in order to determine a pattern for the type of pages you visit. *Most* of the time, IE reloads pages from the Internet exactly as described in the previous paragraph—that is, only when you visit a site you'd visited in a previous session. But this time, IE pays attention to individual Web sites: When reloading them from the Internet, what percentage of the time have they actually changed? Eventually, IE stops checking for updates on sites that change infrequently.

- **Never.** This option instructs IE to load the stored, hard drive–based cache files for any Web site you're revisiting. The program never checks the site's contents to see if they've changed. (Of course, you can always click the Refresh button on your IE toolbar to force the browser to download the latest version of the page.)

Configure and view the History folder

This *history* is a list of the Web sites you've visited. It's the heart of three IE features: AutoComplete, described at the beginning of this chapter; the drop-down list at the right side of the Address bar; and the History list found in View→Explorer Bar (it also appears when you click the unlabeled icon to the right of the Media button). These are all great features if you can't remember the URL for a Web site that you remember having visited, say, yesterday.

You can configure the number of days for which you want your Web visits tracked. To do so, choose Tools→Internet Options (Figure 11-5); click the General tab. The more days IE tracks, the easier it is for you to refer to those addresses quickly. On the other hand, the more days you keep, the longer the list becomes, which may make it harder to use the list easily and efficiently.

Tip: Some people find it creepy that Internet Explorer maintains a complete list of every Web site they've seen recently, right there in plain view of any family member or co-worker who wanders by. If you're in that category, then turn the history feature off completely. Just click the Clear History button in the General tab, then set the "Days to keep pages in history" to 0. (After all, you might be nominated to the Supreme Court some day.)

Figure 11-7:
The History panel (left) appears when you click the tiny History button (the unlabeled button to the right of the Media button) on the Standard toolbar. It offers more details than the History list displayed in the Address bar. Click one of the time-period icons to see the Web sites you visited during that era. Click the name of a Web site to view a list of each visited page within that site—information you don't get from the drop-down list on the Address bar. You can sort the sites by clicking the View button in the History pane and choosing one of these sorting schemes: Date, Site, Most Visited, Order Visited Today.

To delete an individual Web site from the list, right-click its name and choose Delete from the shortcut menu.

Turn off animations

If blinking ads make it tough to concentrate as you read a Web-based article, choose Tools→Internet Options, click the Advanced tab, and then scroll down to the Multimedia heading (Figure 11-5). Turn off "Play animations in web pages" to stifle animated ads. (Take a moment, too, to look over the other annoying Web page elements that you can turn off, including sounds.)

The Content Advisor

The IE Content Advisor is designed to give parents a way to control what their children view on the Web—an especially important feature for home computers. You can specify sites you approve, as well as sites you want to block. If somebody tries to visit a Web site that you've declared off-limits using this feature, he'll see a message saying that the site isn't available.

To activate the Content Advisor, choose Tools→Internet Options. Click the Content tab, and then click the Enable button. The Content Advisor dialog box, shown in Figure 11-8, presents four tabs, called Ratings, Approved Sites, General, and Advanced.

Figure 11-8:
The Internet represents ultimate freedom of expression for anybody, causing some parents to think of it as a wild frontier town where anything goes. To protect young eyes, you can use the options in the Content Advisor to control what's available to your copy of IE. You can also password-protect these settings so nobody else can make changes to them.

Ratings tab

In theory, you can click a raunchiness category (like Language, Nudity, or Sex) and then move the slider bar to the left or right to loosen or tighten the restrictions. (Hint: You can't actually drag the slider's handle. You must click a notch on the slider with your mouse.)

This slider works by looking for the ratings associated with each Web page, as defined by the Internet Content Rating Association (*www.icra.org*). Unfortunately, the Content Rating Association doesn't actually rate Web sites; Web sites are supposed to rate *themselves*. As you can well imagine, the resulting Ratings feature isn't exactly a foolproof (or even half-finished) system.

FREQUENTLY ASKED QUESTION

Cookie Control

Help! I'm afraid of cookies!

Cookies are something like Web page preference files. Certain Web sites—particularly commercial ones like Amazon.com—deposit them on your hard drive like little bookmarks, so that they'll remember you the next time you visit. Most cookies are perfectly innocuous—and, in fact, are extremely helpful, because they help Web sites remember you. Cookies spare you the effort of having to type in your name, address, credit card number, and so on, every single time you visit these Web sites.

But fear is on the march, and the media fans the flames with tales of sinister cookies that track your movement on the Web. If you're worried about invasions of privacy, Internet Explorer is ready to protect you.

Once the browser is open, choose Tools→Internet Options→Privacy tab. As you'll see, the slider in this dialog box is like a paranoia gauge. If you drag it all the way to the top, you create an acrylic shield around your PC. No cookies can come in, and no cookie information can go out. You'll probably find that the Web is a very inconvenient place, because you'll have to re-enter your information upon every visit, and some Web sites may not work properly.

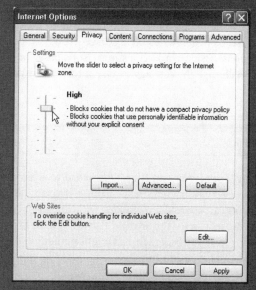

As you drag the slider down, Windows becomes more permissive. For example, it may welcome only cookies with a published privacy policy (which, presumably, contains a promise not to use your information for secret commercial purposes).

But here's a simpler, quicker method of disposing with the cookie threat. On the Privacy tab shown here, click the Advanced button, and then turn on "Override automatic cookie handling." You can now choose how you want the browser to handle two kinds of cookies: *first-party* cookies (those given to you from the Web site you're actually viewing) and *third-party* cookies (those deposited on your hard drive by sites you're not actually visiting—maybe given to you by an especially evil banner ad, for example).

For best results, then, choose Accept for first-party cookies, and Block for third-party cookies. Or, if you're especially paranoid, you can choose the Prompt option, in which case Internet Explorer will ask for individual permission to download every single cookie that comes your way.

Finally, note that the Web is crawling with more flexible and more powerful cookie-control programs, including CookieWall. (You can download it from *www.missing manuals.com*, among other places.)

Tip: The Content Advisor feature comes set to block *all* Web sites that don't have a rating—which is to say, 99.99 percent of them. If you do decide to turn on this feature, therefore, consider clicking the General tab and turning on "Users can see sites that have no rating." Otherwise, Internet Explorer will "protect" you and your kids from virtually the entire Internet—including perfectly innocent sites.

Approved Sites tab

Use the Approved Sites tab to enter the addresses of particular sites you either want to permit or block. (It's normal for this list to show up empty, since it's designed to list Web pages *you* specify.) After you enter a URL, select Always to make the site available to your Web browser, or choose Never to make it unavailable.

The listings in the Approved Sites tab take precedence over the Ratings tab. If you type in a Web address and then click the Always button, your kids will be able to view that site regardless of where it falls in the ratings scheme.

General tab

It wouldn't do you much good to declare certain Web sites off-limits to your kids if, after you've gone to bed, they could simply open the dialog box in Figure 11-8 and declare those Web sites available again. Fortunately, you can use the Change Password button to assign yourself a supervisor's password. Once that's accomplished, nobody can change the settings or visit a forbidden Web site without knowing the password.

Caution: Don't lose this password. There's no way to recover it, and no way to change your security settings without it.

Turning on "Supervisor can type a password to allow users to view restricted content" makes every restricted site available—if you type in the correct password. For example, you can share the password with the adults in your household. You may also want to use it so that your children will have to explain why they need access to a restricted site. If you buy their explanation, then type the supervisor's password to permit one-time access to the site.

Advanced tab

The Advanced tab is the place to add new rating systems and rating rules as Internet citizens invent them.

Note: Programs like Symantec's Norton Internet Security and McAfee's Internet Guard Dog give you finer control over what your browser can supervise on the Web. These products don't rely on Content Ratings, and they let you define different standards for different users on the computer.

Windows Messenger

You might argue that you'll have plenty to do at your desk, what with all of the games and programs included with Windows XP (oh, yeah…and *work*). But if you've got even more time to kill, Microsoft invites you to "chat" with other people on the Internet by typing live comments into a little window. For millions of people, chat is a big deal. It offers the immediacy of a phone call, with the privacy, transcript-keeping features, and price ($0) of email.

Better yet, you don't have to *type* all of your witty comments. If your PC has a microphone and speakers (or a headset), you can also *speak* to your friends, using the Internet as a free long-distance service. It's not quite as handy as a phone—you and your conversation partner must arrange to be online at a specified time—but the price is delightful. And adding an inexpensive Web camera means that you can actually turn your PC into a cheapo videophone, Dick Tracy–style.

The software you need is Windows Messenger (which was called MSN Messenger Service in previous versions of Windows). The quickest way to open it is by double-clicking the icon that appears in your notification area (see Figure 11-9). If you don't see it, just choose Start→All Programs→Windows Messenger (although you may also find the icon listed in the left-side column of your Start menu).

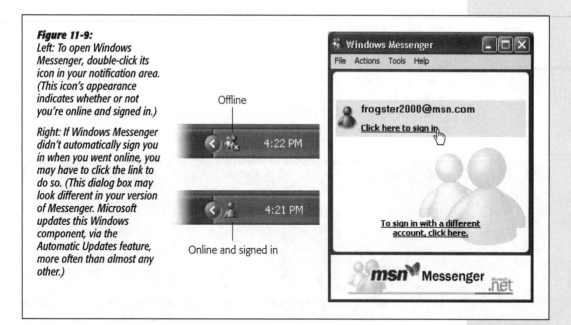

Figure 11-9:
Left: To open Windows Messenger, double-click its icon in your notification area. (This icon's appearance indicates whether or not you're online and signed in.)

Right: If Windows Messenger didn't automatically sign you in when you went online, you may have to click the link to do so. (This dialog box may look different in your version of Messenger. Microsoft updates this Windows component, via the Automatic Updates feature, more often than almost any other.)

Offline

Online and signed in

Note: At the moment, Windows Messenger can communicate only with other people who use Windows Messenger. People who use the extremely popular AOL Instant Messenger (AIM) are off-limits, separated from you by a great invisible wall of incompatibility.

That situation may change, however. With Windows XP, Microsoft has adopted a new, universal standard for chat programs. And if America Online decides to adopt the same standard, it will be a great day in the land of chatters, who will now be united in a single, unified, global standard of chatting love.

Getting a .NET Passport

Windows Messenger is one of several Windows XP features that require a *.NET Passport*—a fancy way of saying that you need to enter yourself into Microsoft's database of Internet users. It's free, and it doesn't require you to expose any more information than your email address. (It doesn't even require that you have a Hotmail or MSN email address, as in previous versions of Windows.)

It's certainly not difficult to figure out how to sign up for this passport. From the first day you use Windows XP, a balloon in the notification area begins to nag you to sign up for one (Figure 11-10, top). To start the Passport sign-up wizard, you can click that balloon, double-click the Windows Messenger icon in the notification area, or launch the wizard yourself. To do so, open the Control Panel. Double-click the User Accounts icon, and click the green arrow button called "Set up my account to use a .NET Passport" (see Figure 11-10, bottom).

Note: Once you've signed up for a passport, Microsoft's software robot sends a message to the email address you specified. Your Passport account isn't official until you reply to it. You'll be able to use Windows Messenger in the meantime, but everybody you correspond with will see your name stamped with "E-mail Address Not Verified." All of this is Microsoft's way of saying, "It's not worth providing a bogus email address when you sign up for a Passport, buddy."

WORKAROUND WORKSHOP

Antisocialites' Corner

Windows XP comes set up to run the Windows Messenger software every time you turn on the computer. Its icon always appears in the notification area of the taskbar, whether you intend to use it or not.

Difficult though it may be to believe, there are actually people here and there who have no particular use for Windows Messenger. There exists a tiny minority that doesn't feel the need to start up chat sessions online, and who, perhaps, could do without the Windows Messenger icon appearing every day on the notification area.

To delete it, double-click that icon to open Windows Messenger. In the resulting window, choose Tools→Options. Click the Preferences tab, turn off "Run this program when Windows starts," and then click OK.

You can also eliminate the "Bob Smith has just signed in" notification that pops up in the lower-right corner of your screen every time somebody on your buddy list goes online. Within Windows Messenger, choose Tools→Options, click the Preferences tab, and turn off "Display alerts when contacts come online." Now click OK.

Your Buddy List

After creating a Passport account, you must build a list of people who have Passport accounts. To do that, open Windows Messenger, log in and then click the Add a Contact link. As you probably could have predicted, the result is something called the Add a Contact Wizard, which offers you the chance to add people to your list whose email address you know.

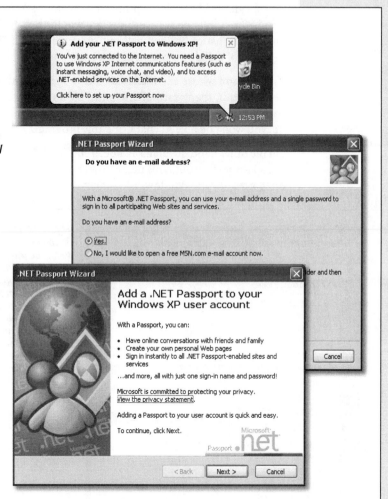

Figure 11-10:
Top: The instant you access the Internet for the first time, Windows XP invites you to become a part of the great Passport database.

Bottom: The .NET Passport Wizard invites you to provide your existing email address—or to create a free MSN.com email account in the process of signing up for the Passport. Either way, you need a .NET Passport to use Windows XP online features like Windows Messenger. If you feel like it, you can also pay a visit to www.passport.com to create a Passport wallet, meaning that you can input your credit card numbers and other personal information, to save you time when buying stuff on Passport-compatible Web sites.

In general, there's no need to bother with the "Search for a contact" option. It can search only part of your Outlook Express address book (it doesn't search addresses that the program added to the address book automatically), and part of the online Hotmail.com member registry (it doesn't search people who have declined to be listed in the registry). Furthermore, it finds a match only if you have typed the entire name precisely.

Tip: You can also turn someone in your Outlook Express address book into a Windows Messenger "buddy." To do so, right-click a name in the Contacts pane at the lower-left corner of the Outlook Express window (see Figure 12-1 in the next chapter). From the shortcut menu, choose Set as Online Contact. Once again, however, you won't be able to add the person to your Messenger buddy list unless she already has a Passport.

As a slender reed of privacy protection, Windows Messenger requires your permission before somebody else can declare you his buddy. Likewise, you can't add anyone to *your* list of buddies without *his* permission. (The permission request takes the form of a dialog box that appears on your screen the next time you go online.)

If the person whose email address you've specified hasn't yet signed up for a Passport account, the wizard offers to fire off an email message to that person—from you—with instructions on how to acquire one. Until both of you are fully signed up, you won't be able to chat using this program.

On the other hand, if you have indeed specified the email address of somebody who has a Passport account, his name now shows up in either the Online or Not Online categories of your Windows Messenger display (Figure 11-11).

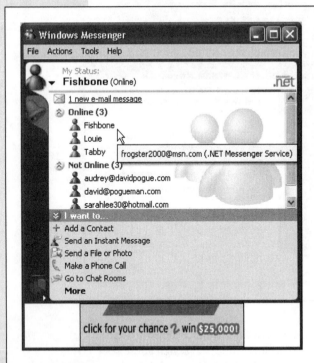

Figure 11-11:
To commence with some high-tech communications, you can proceed in either of two ways. First, you can double-click somebody in your Online list to open up a chat window. From there, you're able to start a voice conversation, window-sharing session, videoconferencing session, and so on. Second, you can click one of the "I want to…" links shown here at bottom and then specify with whom you'd like to do it. Note that if you have a Hotmail account, the top of the window reveals how many email messages you have waiting.

Beginning a Chat

To start a conversation, connect to the Internet. Then double-click somebody's name in your Online list, also as shown in Figure 11-11. (You can't conduct a very meaningful chat with somebody who *isn't* online.)

Chances are pretty good that your colleague is, in fact, running Windows Messenger in the background; the program comes set to run automatically whenever you connect to the Internet. If that's the case, a special alert box appears at the lower-right corner of his screen, as shown in Figure 11-12 (top right).

If he's interested in accepting your invitation to chat, he can click the words in that little box. And suddenly, you're chatting—whatever you type is transmitted to his Windows Messenger window as soon as you press Enter, and vice versa. Figure 11-12 shows the effect.

Figure 11-12:
Top: You're being invited to chat. (You also hear a chime, and a Windows Messenger taskbar button, shown here, blinks and changes color to get your attention.) Clicking the words in the square invitation box opens Windows Messenger.

Bottom: Now you can type away. A chat session is like a teleprompter transcript that rolls down the screen. You type into the bottom box, pressing Enter after each comment, and inserting little "emoticons" (smiley faces, frowny faces, and so on) by choosing them from the drop-down list.

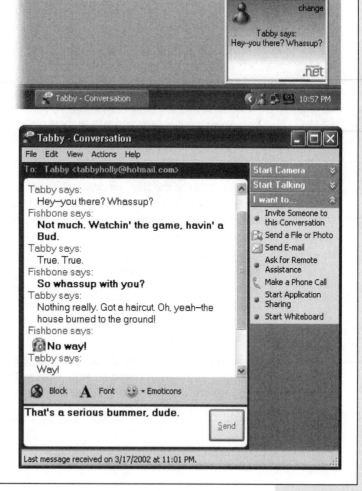

Tip: You might find it easier to distinguish your words of brilliance from the drivel of your correspondents by changing the font for your own comments. To do so, choose Tools→Options; on the Personal tab, click the Change Font button. Choose a new font, size, style, or color in the resulting dialog box, and then click OK twice. (Both of you will see the change, assuming you have similar fonts installed.)

Fun Things to Do While Chatting

As the conversation goes on, you can spice things up, as well as add more controlling features, like this:

Screen out the riffraff

If some idiot keeps bothering you for a chat, turn on the blocking feature for that person. There are a number of different ways to go about it:

- Right-click the person's name in your contact list and, from the shortcut menu, choose Block.

- Choose Tools→Options; on the Privacy tab, click the name of the person you want to block and then click the Block button. This is the quickest way to block a whole bunch of people at once.

- If you're already chatting with someone, just click the Block button in the chat window.

Of course, you were already given the opportunity to perform a preemptive strike. Remember, people can't add you to their buddy lists unless you first give your permission by clicking OK in the dialog box that appears the first time they try to do so.

Grin, sob, or stick out your tongue

At the bottom of the chat window, you'll find a drop-down list of little smiley-face icons. Some find them adorable, others find them insufferable—but they're there if you want a little graphic expression of, well, your expression. Choose one at any time, and then press Enter or click Send, to pop it into your chatter.

Tip: In the heat of chat, it's sometimes inconvenient to take your hands off the keyboard to select a smiley face from the little drop-down list. Fortunately, any of these symbols can be triggered right from the keyboard. Type :) to make a smiley face, :D to make a laughing face, :P to "stick out your tongue," (Y) to give a thumbs-up, (N) for thumbs-down, and so on. Then press Enter or click the Send button to see them in the actual chat window.

(If you really want to delve into this, check out the complete list of keystroke equivalents for Windows Messenger's 30 *emoticons,* as they're known, by choosing Help→Help Topics from within Windows Messenger, and then typing *emoticons* in the "For help on Windows Messenger" box. Click "Use Emoticons in messages to show feelings" on the resulting Help Topics page.)

Duck out for a moment

Windows Messenger offers a list of Status messages: Online, Busy, Be Right Back, On The Phone, and so on. Whatever status you choose appears next to your name on the screens of your conversation partners.

To hang out one of these little "Do not disturb" signs, choose from the File→My Status submenu, or right-click the Windows Messenger icon in the notification area and choose from the My Status submenu there. (To duck out for good, sign out. Do that by right-clicking the Messenger icon in the notification area and choosing "Sign out" from the shortcut menu.)

Send a text message to a phone

To send a message to somebody's pager or cellphone, just right-click the person's name, and then choose Send a Message to a Mobile Device from the shortcut menu. (If it's a text pager, you can even type up a little message to send.)

Exchange files

As the conversation proceeds, you can send a photo, Word document, or any other file to your chat partner. There are two ways to do so:

- Drag the icon of the file you want to send right into the chat window (from the desktop or a folder, for example).

- Click the Send a File or Photo link at the right side of the screen. A "Send a File" window appears, so that you can navigate to and double-click a file that you want to send.

Either way, your buddy sees an invitation to accept the file (Figure 11-13), and then a stern warning to be careful of doing so, for fear of viruses and other nasty surprises.

Tip: This feature is especially welcome if you've grown frustrated transmitting files via email. Some programs, notably Microsoft Outlook, refuse to accept files—like application programs (*.exe* files)—that could conceivably harbor viruses. Messenger imposes no such restriction. Nor will you encounter "mailbox full" problems when you send files back and forth using Messenger, the way you sometimes do when sending them as email attachments.

Add another chatter

You can include another person in your chat by choosing Actions→Invite Someone to this Conversation. You'll be offered a list of other people in your buddy list who are already online. (Up to five people can participate in a typed chat, although only two of you can use the video or phone features described in the following sections.)

Get help

As you can see by Figure 11-13, "Ask for Remote Assistance" is another link on the task pane. Clicking it initiates a *Remote Assistance* session, in which some helpful geek on the other end of the line takes control of your computer, and sees what's on your screen, in order to troubleshoot a specified problem. Complete details in Chapter 5.

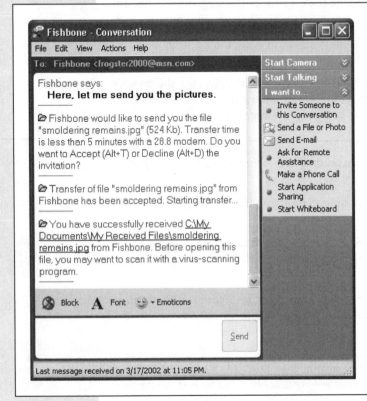

Figure 11-13:
You can send a file from your hard drive to your conversation partner—a great way to turn this time-wasting feature into a useful collaboration tool. (Your partner will find the file in her My Documents→My Received Files folder. She can change the folder location for file deposits by choosing Tools→Options, clicking the Preferences tab, and then clicking the Browse button in the File Transfer section.)

Add features

As time goes by, Microsoft adds new features to Windows Messenger without telling you. You can already send short text messages to your friends' cellphones, see how many new Hotmail email messages are waiting for you, create and edit your own online profile, and so on—but only by first going to the Microsoft Add-In Web page and downloading the necessary software modules.

To do so, choose Tools→Add-In Web Site. Your browser opens to a Microsoft Web site that lists whatever new modules are available; click "Click here to download this add-in!" to add them to your copy of Windows Messenger. (Windows: It's not just an operating system—it's a lifestyle!)

Preserve your brilliance for future generations

If you'd like a written record of your chat session, choose File→Save As. You'll be offered the chance to save a transcript as a text file to your hard drive.

Tip: Of course, a text file has no formatting, so the Windows Messenger transcript will not display any of the fonts, styles, and colors that liven up the chat session. If you'd rather preserve some of that formatting, choose Edit→Select All to highlight all the text, and then copy and paste the text into a word processor like WordPad or Microsoft Word. You still won't get the little smiley icons, but at least you'll get the colors and fonts.

PC as Telephone

If both you and your friend have PCs with microphones and speakers (or a USB headset), the two of you can switch into live, spoken conversation, exactly like using a low-quality telephone. Your friend hears everything you say into the microphone, and you hear everything she says into hers. You'll both hear a slight delay, as though you're on a long-distance call to Estonia, but otherwise, it's the equivalent of an unlimited, free, long-distance calling plan.

Tip: This free feature covers computer-to-computer calling only. You can also make calls from your computer to an actual phone number, which will ring an actual telephone (that's what the Make a Phone Call link in the task pane is for)—but it's no longer free in Windows XP. You have to sign up for it and pay for it. (To sign up, choose Actions→Make a Phone Call and then, in the Phone window, click Get Started Here.)

To start a voice "call," begin a chat as described above. But once the window is open, click the Start Talking tab in the task pane at the right side of the window. (The very

---

TROUBLESHOOTING MOMENT

When Video and Phone Features Don't Work

This note is exclusively for people whose PCs are part of an office network.

In this arrangement, all of the computers often share a single Internet connection. In short, they all plug into a single box called a router, which is itself connected to the Internet.

Routers generally double as *firewalls* that protect the network from hacker attacks—and that's where the problem with Windows Messenger multimedia comes in. You can use the Windows Messenger voice and videoconferencing features *within* your office network (behind the firewall),

but you may find yourself unable to connect to people in the outside world.

The reasons for this breakdown are very technical, but the bottom line is this: Routers bought in the pre–Windows XP era block the signal going to and from Windows Messenger. More recent routers—specifically those billed as having "Universal Plug and Play" or "SIP (Session Initiation Protocol)" compatibility—don't have this problem.

If your router is one of the older ones, you're not necessarily condemned to buying a new one. Many router manufacturers offer downloadable updaters that give existing routers Universal Plug and Play compatibility.

first time you do this, Windows will ask you to test the quality of your microphone and speakers.)

Your friend sees a typed invitation to join you in a spoken voice conversation ("Fishbone would like to have a voice conversation with you. Do you want to Accept [Alt+T] or Decline [Alt+D] the invitation?"). If she clicks Accept (or presses Alt+T), the two of you are in business: Simply begin talking—even if you're in San Francisco and she's in Turkey. Clearly, phone company executives aren't thrilled with the development of this technology (at least, not until they go home at night and fire up Windows Messenger themselves).

During the conversation, each participant can adjust the microphone or speaker levels using the sliders, or "hang up" by clicking Stop Talking.

PC as Videophone

The videophone feature requires that you and your online chat partner each have a video camera (some cheap Webcam will do just fine) and corresponding software already installed. By the way, "video" is a generous term: You may find that the picture is extremely jerky and grainy, more like a series of still images than a TV broadcast. (Obviously, a high-speed connection like a cable modem or DSL is extremely helpful in this regard.)

Click the Start Camera button (Figure 11-14) to begin transmitting; click Stop Camera when you've had enough. (If only one of you has a video camera, no problem—only one of you receives a video picture. The other person just hears the sound.)

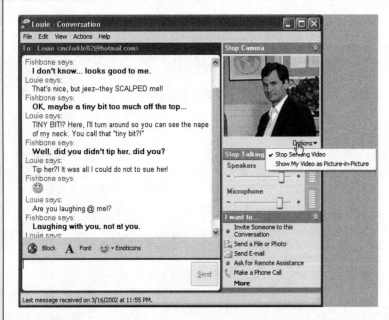

Figure 11-14:
During the video conversation, don't miss the Options drop-down menu. Use the Stop Sending Video command when, for example, you'd like to pick your nose in privacy. Turn on Show My Video as Picture-in-Picture if you want to see your own image in the lower-right corner of the larger one, in order to see both participants at once.

It's crude, sure, but there are times when a little video goes a long way—when you're on the road with your laptop for three weeks and miss seeing the kids, for example; or when you want to show a prototype to a client without having to buy a plane ticket.

Sharing a Program

Amazingly enough, the other person in your little online meeting can use *your programs*—editing one of your Word documents, typing numbers into your Excel spreadsheet, and so on—even if he doesn't have Word or Excel on his machine.

It works like this:

1. **Launch the program you want everyone to use. Then click the Start Application Sharing link in the task pane at the right side of the window (Figure 11-15).**

   Your recipient sees a message that says: "Fishbone is inviting you to start using Application Sharing. Do you want to Accept (Alt+T) or Decline (Alt+D) the invitation?" Obviously, your colleague should click Accept (or press the corresponding keystroke).

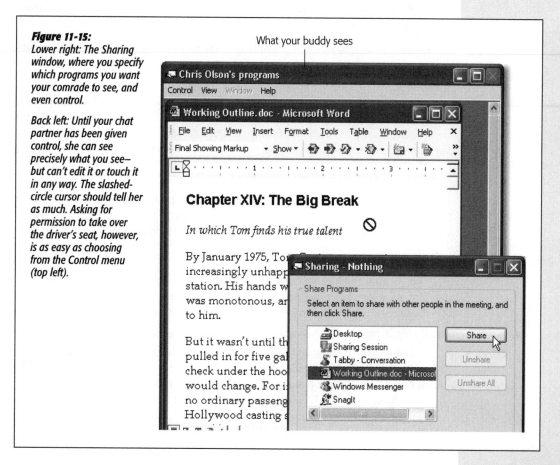

Figure 11-15:
Lower right: The Sharing window, where you specify which programs you want your comrade to see, and even control.

Back left: Until your chat partner has been given control, she can see precisely what you see— but can't edit it or touch it in any way. The slashed-circle cursor should tell her as much. Asking for permission to take over the driver's seat, however, is as easy as choosing from the Control menu (top left).

What your buddy sees

Now a little palette appears at the upper-left corner of both screens to keep you posted on the status of the sharing feature. It says "waiting," and then says "connecting;" finally you see the list of programs shown in Figure 11-15.

2. **Click the name of the program or document you want to share, and then click Share.**

Note, in particular, the desktop, which is always listed in the Share Programs window. If you share it, then everybody else in the meeting can see what you see as you work in Windows. As far as Windows Messenger is concerned, the desktop is simply another program that you can share. (This effect is essentially the same thing as the new Remote Assistance feature described on page 143, except that it's slower and lets you limit what your comrade sees. Otherwise, it's equally effective for securing troubleshooting help from some guru elsewhere on the Internet.)

Shortly after you click the Share button, something strange and weird happens: A new window appears on your conversation partner's screen, showing exactly what you see in *your* copy of the program. When you move your cursor, it moves on her screen; when you open a dialog box, she sees it, too; and so on. (This means, by the way, that your colleague can see *all* open documents in whatever program you're using—not just the front one.)

Because your microphone is working at the same time, you can use this feature to collaborate on documents, to teach somebody a new program, to help somebody troubleshoot a PC, and so on.

Note: If your correspondent sees a bizarre checkerboard pattern superimposed on the shared document window, there's no need to worry. That simply means that the program you're sharing is partly covered up by a window from some other program. (The likeliest culprit: the Sharing dialog box itself, shown in Figure 11-15.)

Under most circumstances, the other people in the meeting can just *look* at the program you're using. But if you'd like the other person to *control* the application—to edit the documents, use the menus, and so on—then proceed like this:

3. **Click Allow Control.**

Just clicking the Allow Control button, however, is not enough to transfer control of a program to one of your collaborators. He must also choose Control→Request Control from his shared-program window, and you must grant permission.

A dialog box appears on your screen, saying: "Harry Potter would like to take control of your shared programs." (Actually, it probably says, "*default* would like to take control." Your collaborator's actual name rarely shows up, because Windows Messenger displays whatever name appears in the Options dialog box of a completely different program—NetMeeting. See page 359 for details.)

4. **Click Accept.**

Only now can your colleague edit your documents, manipulate your desktop, and so on. Conversely, *you* can't do anything in that program. Moving the mouse doesn't even move the cursor in that program. It may take you some time to get used to this effect—a process psychologists call *learned helplessness.*

If the feelings of helplessness become overwhelming, you can reclaim control by clicking the mouse or pressing any key on your keyboard. In fact, by pressing the Esc key, you resume control *and* prevent your colleague from attempting to take any further control.

If you've shared your desktop, by the way, relinquishing control means that other people can even manipulate your computer files and folders! They can open folders, rename files, make backup copies, delete files, and so on, from wherever on the Internet they happen to be.

Tip: If you're truly collaborating, you'll probably want to turn on "Automatically accept requests for control," so that your collaborator won't have to request control (and you won't have to grant permission) over and over again during the work session. On the other hand, turn on "Do not disturb with requests for control right now" if you don't want to be interrupted by even your collaborator's requests for control. The answer is always no.

It's worth noting, by the way, that all of this controlling and sharing requires Windows to shuttle an enormous amount of data over the wires. As a result, the cursor may seem jerky, and everything will feel very slow. That's normal, especially if you're connecting via standard dial-up modem.

Whiteboard

When you click the Start Whiteboard link in the task pane, Windows Messenger opens up a graphics window (Figure 11-16) that looks, at first glance, like the Paint program described in Chapter 7. The difference: Anything you draw or paste into this window appears instantly on your colleague's screen—and vice versa. Using the various graphics tools and colors, you can draw maps for each other, propose design changes, or just play tic-tac-toe.

Note: Application Sharing and Whiteboard cannot be used at the same time. In fact, you can't start one without first quitting the other. You should also note that closing the tiny Sharing Session window terminates both features.

Here are a few of the special collaboration tools that you won't find in Microsoft Paint:

• **Highlighter.** Draws over whatever is there with transparent "ink"—exactly like a felt-tip highlighting marker.

• **Remote Pointer.** As you move this hand around the screen, your buddy sees exactly what you're pointing to. Because he can also hear what you're saying (thanks to your microphone), this is a great way to comment on something—say, a photo you've pasted into this window.

- **Lock Contents.** Freezes the picture as it is right now, so that nobody can alter it (at least until you click the same button again to unlock it).

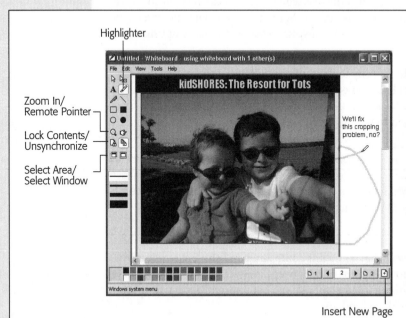

Highlighter

Zoom In/
Remote Pointer

Lock Contents/
Unsynchronize

Select Area/
Select Window

Insert New Page

Figure 11-16:
The Whiteboard lets you and a colleague mark up a diagram, sketch, or anything else you can paste into this window. It's a lot like Paint, except that you're not editing individual pixels—it's a drawing program. *Each shape, text box, or line you draw, and each object you paste in, remains a distinct object that you can drag around, independent of the background. You can also make objects go in front of or behind the other ones using the Bring to Front and Send to Back commands in the Edit menu, and you can edit text at any time.*

- **Unsynchronize.** In general, if your collaborator "turns the page" by clicking one of the page buttons, you see the page change, too. To unlink your screen, so that it's no longer tied to what your colleague sees, simply click this button. (Click again to restore synchronization.)

- **Select Area.** When you click this tool, a message invites you to drag across an area of the screen—even outside of the Whiteboard window. You can use this feature, for example, to capture an error message, tool palette, or some other element of Windows or one of your programs. As soon as you release the mouse, Windows pastes the area you covered into the upper-left corner of the Whiteboard window, ready for comment and annotation by your partner.

- **Select Window.** This tool is exactly like the Select Area tool except that it grabs an entire window (from some other program, from the desktop, or whatever) elsewhere on your screen for pasting into the Whiteboard window.

Tip: This tool never captures the *title bar* of the window you click—only the parts of the window beneath it. If you want to capture the complete window, click the title bar instead of inside the window.

- **Insert New Page.** Click this button to create a new page for further annotations. Once you've created several pages, you can move among them using the arrow buttons.

Windows
Messenger

NOSTALGIA CORNER

Microsoft NetMeeting

Windows Messenger is all the rage, but it's not the only videoconferencing game in town. In previous versions of Windows, its functions were assumed by something called Microsoft NetMeeting. And as we all know, Microsoft never actually takes away a feature—it only adds new ones. As a result, NetMeeting is still available in Windows XP.

In many ways, Windows Messenger is a superior program. For example, Windows Messenger looks better, is easier to figure out, and is better integrated with Windows.

Still, in its own obsolete way, NetMeeting has its charms. For example, it's the only way you can carry on voice or videoconferencing sessions, collaborate on documents, or use the whiteboard feature with people who don't have Windows Messenger. Furthermore, you need NetMeeting if you want to use the whiteboard or program-sharing features with more than two people—Windows Messenger's limit.

To fire it up, choose Start→Run. In the resulting dialog box, type *conf* and press Enter. During the NetMeeting startup wizard, you'll be asked for your name, email ad-

dress, and connection speed. The wizard also offers to create a shortcut for NetMeeting on your desktop and on your Quick Launch toolbar, so that you won't have to use that Start→Run business in subsequent sessions.

Once the program is running, click the little phone book button near the upper-right corner to see your list of Windows Messenger contacts. To begin a chat session, click somebody's name in the Contacts Currently Online. (NetMeeting no longer uses the Internet Locator Service used by previous versions.) Your colleague's copy of Windows Messenger intercepts the invitation and fires up his own copy of NetMeeting. Now you're ready to begin.

Windows Messenger also assumes the duties of the old Phone Dialer program. Once again, however, that program is still around—and remains the only way to carry on voice or videoconferencing sessions involving more than two people. You can open it by choosing Start→Run, typing *dialer*, and pressing Enter—or by locating (and making a desktop shortcut of) its icon in the My Computer→Local Disk (C:)→Program Files→Windows NT folder. It's called *Dialer.exe*.

Outlook Express 6

Email is a fast, cheap, convenient communication medium; these days, it's almost embarrassing to admit that you don't have an email address. To spare you that humiliation, Windows XP includes Outlook Express 6, a program that lets you receive and send email messages and read *newsgroups* (Internet bulletin boards). (Incidentally, don't confuse Outlook Express with Outlook, a far bigger and more complex corporate email program that's sold as part of the Microsoft Office software suite.)

Note: Outlook Express doesn't work with online services like America Online or Prodigy. Instead, you're supposed to check and send your email using the software you got when you signed up for these services.

To use Outlook Express, you need several technical pieces of information: an email address, an email server address, and an Internet address for sending email. Your Internet service provider or your network administrator is supposed to provide all of these ingredients.

Setting Up Outlook Express

The first time you use Outlook Express (which you can open from the Start menu), the Internet Connection Wizard appears to help you plug in the necessary Internet addresses and codes that tell the program where to find your email.

Note: If you used the New Connection Wizard (page 312) to establish your Internet account, then your settings are probably already in place. In that case, you probably won't see this Internet Connection Wizard; skip to the next section.

Click Next on each wizard window to step through the process, during which you'll provide the following information:

- **Display Name.** The name that will appear in the "From:" field of the email you send.

- **Email Address.** The email address you chose when you signed up for Internet services, such as *billg@microsoft.com.*

- **Mail Servers.** Enter the information your ISP provided about its mail servers: the type of server, the name of the incoming mail server, and the name of the outgoing mail server. Most of the time, the incoming server is a *POP3 server* and its name is connected to the name of your ISP, such as *popmail.mindspring.com.* The outgoing mail server (also called the *SMTP server*) usually looks something like *mail.mindspring.com.*

- **Logon Name and Password.** Enter the name and password provided by your ISP.

If you wish, turn on "Remember password," so that you won't have to enter it each time you want to collect mail. (But turn on Secure Password Authentication [SPA] only if instructed by your ISP or network administrator.)

Click the Finish button to close the wizard and open Outlook Express.

UP TO SPEED

POP, IMAP, and Web-based Mail

When it comes to email, there are three flavors of accounts (not counting America Online Mail, which is a mutant breed and not something that Outlook Express can talk to): POP (also known as POP3), IMAP (also known as IMAP4), and Web-based. Each has its own distinct feeling, with different strengths and weaknesses.

POP accounts are the most common kind. A POP server transfers your incoming mail to your hard drive before you read it, and then deletes its Internet-based copy. From now on, those messages are stored on your computer, and it's up to you to save them, back them up, or delete them. (You can configure Outlook Express not to delete the messages from the server, but most ISPs don't give you much disk space. If your mailbox gets too full, the server may begin rejecting your incoming messages.)

IMAP servers are newer than, and have more features than, POP servers, but as a result they don't enjoy as much popularity or support. IMAP servers are Internet computers that store all of your mail for you, rather than making you down-

load it each time you connect, so you can access the same mail regardless of the computer you use. IMAP servers remember which messages you've read and sent, too.

One downside to this approach, of course, is that you can't work with your email except when you're online, because all of your mail is on an Internet server, not on your hard drive. Another is that if you don't conscientiously manually delete mail after you've read it, your online mailbox eventually overflows. Sooner or later, the system starts bouncing fresh messages back to their senders, annoying your friends and depriving you of the chance to read what they had to say.

Free, Web-based servers like Hotmail also store your mail on the Internet. You can use a Web browser on any computer to read and send messages—or, if it's Hotmail, Outlook Express (because both are Microsoft products). They're also slower and more cumbersome to use than "regular" email accounts.

Tip: If you want to add a second email account for someone else who uses this PC (assuming you're *not* using the User Accounts feature described in Chapter 16), choose Tools→ Accounts in Outlook Express. In the resulting dialog box on the Mail tab, click Add→Mail; the Internet Connection Wizard will reappear.

Figure 12-1:
The four panes of Outlook Express. Click a folder in the upper-left pane to see its contents in the upper-right pane. When you click the name of a message in the upper-right pane, the message itself appears in the lower-right pane.

Lower left: your list of MSN Messenger Service "buddies," as described in the previous chapter.

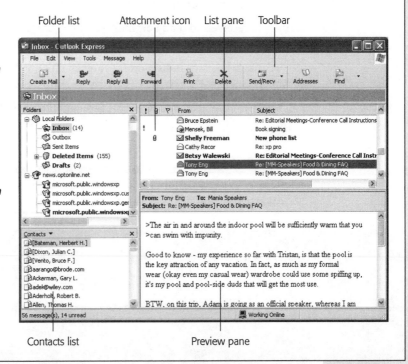

Folder list   Attachment icon   List pane   Toolbar

Contacts list   Preview pane

Checking a Specific Email Account

You don't have to check *all* of your email accounts whenever you want to get mail. Suppose, for example, that you want to send a message to *yourself*—from your work account to your home account. In that case, you'd want to send/receive mail only from your office account. (If, in the same pass, Outlook Express also downloaded messages *from* your home account, you'd wind up with the same message in your office PC's copy of Outlook Express, defeating the whole purpose of the exercise.)

Excluding an account (or several accounts) from the "Send and Receive All" routine is easy enough. Open the Accounts window (Tools→Accounts), double-click the account's name, turn off "Include this account when receiving Mail or synchronizing," click OK, and close the Accounts window.

Now suppose you *usually* want to check all accounts, but *occasionally* want to check only one of them. On such an occasion, choose that account's name from the drop-down list that appears when you click the down-arrow black triangle beside the Send/Recv button. (Alternatively, choose the account name from the Tools→Send and Receive submenu.)

Sending Email

When you finally arrive at the main Outlook Express screen, you've got mail; the Inbox contains a message for you. The message is a welcome from Microsoft, but it wasn't actually transmitted over the Internet; it's a starter message just to tease you. Fortunately, all your future mail will come via the Internet.

In order to receive and send new mail, you must use the Send & Receive command. You can trigger it in any of several ways:

- Click the Send/Recv button on the toolbar. (It's identified in Figure 12-1, which depicts Outlook Express after you've been living in it for a while.)

- Choose Tools→Send and Receive→Send and Receive All.

- Press Ctrl+M.

Tip: Outlook Express can be set up to check your email accounts automatically according to a schedule. Just choose Tools→Options. On the General tab, you'll see the "Check for new messages every __ minutes" checkbox, which you can change to your liking.

The Mighty Morphing Interface

You don't have to be content with the factory-installed design of the Outlook Express screen; you can control which panes are visible, how big they are, and which columns show up in list views.

To change the size of a pane, drag its border to make it larger or smaller, as shown here. You can also hide or show the toolbar, folder list, or preview pane using the View→Layout command. For example, to hide the toolbar, choose View→ Layout; turn off Toolbar; and click OK.

The View→Layout command also lets you control where the preview pane appears: under the message list, as usual, or to its right—a great arrangement if you have a very wide screen.

Outlook Express lets you decide what columns are displayed in the list pane; for example, if you don't particularly care about seeing the Flag column for your email, you can hide it, leaving more space for the Subject and Received columns. To switch columns on or off, choose from the list in the View→Columns dialog box.

You can also *rearrange* the columns, which can be handy if you'd rather see the Subject column first instead of the sender, for example. Just drag the column's name *header* horizontally and release when the vertical dotted line is where you want the column to wind up. To make a column wider or narrower, drag the short black divider line between column names horizontally, much the way you'd resize a folder window list-view column.

Now Outlook Express contacts the mail servers listed in the account list, retrieving new messages and downloading any files attached to those messages. It also sends any outgoing messages and their attachments.

In the list on the right side of your screen, the names of new messages show up in bold type; folders containing new messages show up in bold type, too (in the Folders list at the left side of the screen). The bold number in parentheses after the word "Inbox" represents how many messages you haven't read yet.

Finally, after messages are downloaded, Outlook Express applies its *mail filters—* what it calls *rules*—to all new messages (to screen out junk mail, for example). More on rules on page 377.

Mail folders in Outlook Express

Outlook Express organizes your email into *folders* at the left side of the screen. To see what's in a folder, click it once:

• **Inbox** holds mail you've received.

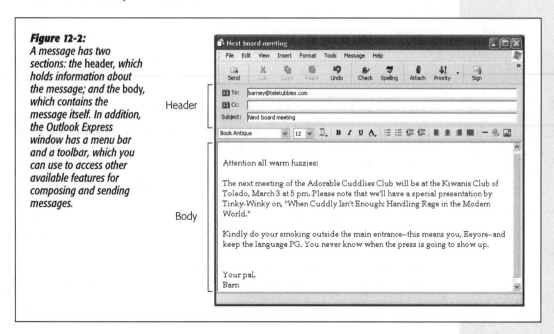

Figure 12-2:
A message has two sections: the header, *which holds information about the message; and the* body, *which contains the message itself. In addition, the Outlook Express window has a menu bar and a toolbar, which you can use to access other available features for composing and sending messages.*

• **Outbox** holds mail you've written but haven't sent yet.

• **Sent Items** holds copies of messages you've sent.

• **Deleted Items** holds mail you've deleted. It works a lot like the Recycle Bin, in that messages placed there don't actually disappear. Instead, they remain in the Deleted Items folder, awaiting rescue on the day you retrieve them. To empty this folder, right-click it and choose "Empty 'Deleted Items' Folder" from the shortcut menu (or just choose Edit→Empty 'Deleted Items' Folder).

- **Drafts** holds messages you've started but haven't finished—and don't want to send just yet.

You can also add to this list, creating folders for your own organizational pleasure— Family Mail, Work Mail, or whatever. See page 374.

Composing and sending messages

To send email to a recipient, click the Create Mail icon on the toolbar (or press Ctrl+N, or choose Message→New Mail). The New Message form, shown in Figure 12-2, opens so you can begin creating the message.

Composing the message requires several steps:

1. **Type the email address of the recipient into the "To:" field.**

   If you want to send a message to more than one person, separate their email addresses using semicolons, like this: *bob@earthlink.net; billg@microsoft.com; steve@apple.com.*

   There's no need to type out all those complicated email addresses, either. As you begin typing the person's plain-English name, the program attempts to guess who you mean (if it's somebody in your address book)—and fills in the email address automatically, as described in the next section. If it guesses the correct name, great; press Tab to move on to the next text box. If it guesses wrong, just keep typing; the program quickly retracts its suggestion and watches what you type next. (You can also double-click somebody's name in your address book.)

   As in most Windows dialog boxes, you can jump from blank to blank in this window (from the "To:" field to the "CC:" field, for example) by pressing the Tab key.

2. **To send a copy of the message to other recipients, enter the additional email address(es) in the "CC:" field.**

   CC stands for *carbon copy.* There's very little difference between putting all your addressees on the "To:" line (separated by semicolons) and putting them on the "CC:" line; the only difference is that your name in the "CC:" line implies, "I sent you a copy because I thought you'd want to know about this correspondence, but I'm not expecting you to reply."

Once again, use the address book to quickly type in these names, and be sure to separate email addresses with semicolons. Press Tab when you're finished.

3. **Type the topic of the message in the "Subject:" field.**

Some people, especially those in the business world, get bombarded with email. That's why it's courteous to put some thought into the Subject line (use "Change in plans for next week" instead of "Hi," for example).

Press the Tab key to move your cursor into the large message-body area.

4. **Choose a format (HTML or plain text), if you like.**

When it comes to formatting a message's body text, you have two choices: *plain text* or *HTML* (Hypertext Markup Language).

Plain text means that you can't format your text with bold type, color, specified font sizes, and so on. HTML, on the other hand, is the language used to create Web pages, and it lets you use formatting commands (such as font sizes, colors, and bold or italic text). But there's a catch: Some email programs can't read HTML-formatted email, and HTML mail is much larger (and therefore slower to download) than plain-text messages.

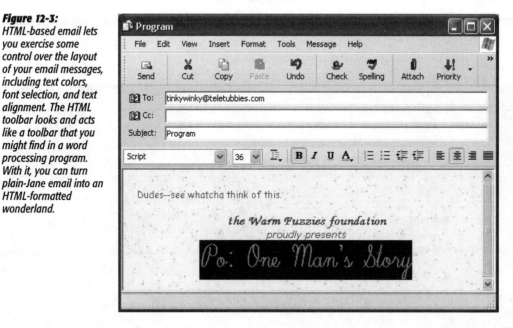

Figure 12-3:
HTML-based email lets you exercise some control over the layout of your email messages, including text colors, font selection, and text alignment. The HTML toolbar looks and acts like a toolbar that you might find in a word processing program. With it, you can turn plain-Jane email into an HTML-formatted wonderland.

So which should you choose? Plain text tends to feel a little more professional, never irritating anybody—and you're guaranteed that the recipient will see exactly what was sent. If you send an HTML message to someone whose email program can't handle HTML, all is not lost—your message appears in a friendly, plain-text format at the top, and then again at the bottom, cluttered with HTML codes.

To specify which format Outlook Express *proposes* for all new messages (plain text or HTML), choose Tools→Options. Click the Send tab. Then, in the section labeled Mail Sending Format, choose either the HTML or Plain Text button, and then click OK.

No matter which setting you specify there, however, you can always switch a particular message to the opposite format. Just choose Format→Rich Text (HTML), or Format→Plain Text.

If you choose the HTML option, clicking in the message area activates the HTML toolbar, whose various buttons control the formatting, font, size, color, paragraph indentation, line spacing, and other word processor–like formatting controls.

One thing to remember: Less is more. If you go hog-wild formatting your email, the message may be difficult to read. Furthermore, since most *junk* email is formatted using HTML codes, using HTML formatting may route your message into some people's Junk Mail folders.

5. **Enter the message in the message box (the bottom half of the message window).**

   You can use all standard editing techniques, including Cut, Copy, and Paste, to rearrange the text as you write it.

UP TO SPEED

Blind Carbon Copies

A *blind carbon copy* is a secret copy. This feature lets you send a copy of a message to somebody secretly, without any of the other recipients knowing. The names in the "To:" and "CC:" fields appear at the top of the message for all recipients to see, but nobody can see the names you typed into the BCC: box. To view this box, choose View→All Headers.

You can use the "BCC:" field to quietly signal a third party that a message has been sent. For example, if you send your co-worker a message that says, "Chris, it bothers me that you've been cheating the customers," you could BCC your boss or supervisor to clue her in without getting into trouble with Chris.

The BCC box is useful in other ways, too. Many people send email messages (containing jokes, for example) to a long list of recipients. You, the recipient, must scroll through a very long list of names the sender placed in the "To:" or "CC:" field.

But if the sender used the "BCC:" field to hold all the recipients' email addresses, you, the recipient, won't see any names but your own at the top of the email. (Unfortunately, spammers—the miserable cretins who send you junk mail—have also learned this trick.)

Tip: If Microsoft Word is installed on your PC, you can also spell-check your outgoing mail—just choose Tools→Spelling (or press F7) in the new message window.

6. **Add a signature, if you wish.**

Signatures are bits of text that get stamped at the bottom of outgoing email messages. They typically contain a name, a mailing address, or a Monty Python quote. (In fact, some signatures are longer than the messages they accompany.)

To create a signature, choose Tools→Options, click the Signatures tab, and then click the New button. The easiest way to compose your signature is to type it into the Edit Signatures text box at the bottom of the window. (If you poke around long enough in this box, you'll realize that you can actually create multiple signatures—and assign each one to a different outgoing email account.)

Once you've created a signature (or several), you can tack it onto your outgoing mail for all messages (by turning on "Add signatures to all outgoing messages" at the top of this box) or on a message-by-message basis (by choosing Insert→Signature in the New Message window).

7. **Click the Send button.**

Alternatively, press Alt+S, or choose File→Send Message. Your PC connects to the Internet and sends the message.

If you'd rather have Outlook Express place each message you write in the Outbox folder instead of connecting to the Net each time you click the Send button, see "Send tab," on page 381. There you'll discover how to make Outlook Express quietly collect your outgoing mail—until you click the Send/Recv button on the toolbar, that is.

Using the Address Book
Accumulating names in an address book—the same one described on page 196—eliminates the need to enter complete email addresses whenever you want to send a message. Click the Addresses button on the toolbar; then, to begin adding names and email addresses, click New.

Tip: Outlook Express offers a convenient timesaving feature: the Tools→Add Sender to Address Book command. Whenever you choose it, Outlook Express automatically stores the email address of the person whose message is on the screen. (Alternatively, you can right-click an email address in the message and choose "Add to Address Book" from the shortcut menu.)

Attaching files to messages
Sending little text messages is fine, but it's not much help when you want to send somebody a photograph, a sound recording, a Word or Excel document, and so on. Fortunately, attaching such files to email messages is one of the world's most popular email features.

To attach a file to a message, use either of two methods:

- **The long way.** Click the Attach button on the New Message dialog box toolbar. When the Insert Attachment dialog box opens, navigate the folders on your drive to locate the file and select it. (In the resulting navigation window, Ctrl-click multiple files to attach them all at once.)

  When you click the Attach button, the name of the attached file appears in the message in the Attach text box. (In fact, you can repeat this process to send several attached files with the same message.) When you send the message, the file tags along.

Note: If you have a high-speed connection like a cable modem, have pity on your recipients if they don't. A big picture or movie file might take you only seconds to send, but tie up your correspondent's modem for hours. If you intend to send a photo, for example, use the technique described on page 219, and take advantage of XP's offer to scale down the image to emailable size before sending it.

- **The short way.** If you can see the icon of the file you want to attach—in its folder window behind the Outlook Express window—then attach it by *dragging* its icon directly into the message window. That's a handy technique when you're attaching many different files.

Tip: To remove a file from an outgoing message before you've sent it, right-click its icon and choose Remove from the shortcut menu—or just left-click it and then press the Delete key.

Reading Email

Just seeing a list of the *names* of new messages in Outlook Express is like getting wrapped presents; the best part is yet to come. There are two ways to read a message: using the preview pane, and opening the message into its own window.

To preview a message, click its name in the list pane; the body of the message appears in the preview pane below. Don't forget that you can adjust the relative sizes of the list and preview panes by dragging the gray border between them up or down.

To open a message into a window of its own, double-click its name in the list pane. An open message has its own toolbar, along with Previous and Next message buttons.

Regardless of your viewing preference, any attached pictures, sounds, or movies *also* appear in the body of the message; what's more, these sounds and movies can be played in the email message itself.

Once you've read a message, you can view the next one in the list either by pressing Ctrl +right arrow (for the next message) or Ctrl +U (for the next *unread* message), or by clicking its name in the list pane. (If you're using preview mode, and haven't opened a message into its own window, you can also press the up or down arrow key to move from one message to the next.)

Tip: To mark a message that you've read as an *unread* message, so that its name remains bolded, right-click its name in the list pane and choose Mark as Unread from the shortcut menu.

Here's another timesaver: To hide all the messages you've already read, just choose View→Current View→Hide Read Messages. Now, only unread messages are visible in the selected folder. To bring the hidden messages back, choose View→Current View→Show All Messages.

How to Process a Message

Once you've read a message and savored the feeling of awe brought on by the miracle of instantaneous electronic communication, you can process the message in any of several ways.

Deleting messages

Sometimes it's junk mail, sometimes you're just done with it; either way, it's a snap to delete a message. Just click the Delete button on the toolbar, press the Delete key, or choose Edit→Delete. (You can also delete a batch of messages simultaneously by highlighting the entire group and then using the same button, menu command, or keystroke.)

Either way, the message or messages don't actually disappear, just as moving a file icon to the Recycle Bin doesn't actually delete it. Instead, these commands move the messages to the Deleted Items folder; if you like, click this folder to view a list of the messages you've deleted. You can even rescue some simply by dragging them into another folder (such as right back into the Inbox).

Outlook Express doesn't truly vaporize messages in the Deleted Items folder until you "empty the trash." You can empty it in any of several ways:

UP TO SPEED

Selecting Messages

In order to process a group of messages simultaneously—to delete, move, or forward them, for example—you must first master the art of multiple message selection.

To select two or more messages that appear consecutively in your message list, click the first message, then Shift-click the last. Known as a *contiguous selection*, this trick selects every message between the two that you clicked.

To select two or more messages that *aren't* adjacent in the list (that is, skipping a few messages between selected ones), Ctrl-click the messages you want. Only the messages you click get selected—no filling in of messages in between, this time.

After using either technique, you can also *deselect* messages you've managed to highlight—just Ctrl-click them again.

- Right-click the Deleted Items folder. Choose "Empty 'Deleted Items' Folder" from the shortcut menu.

- Click a message, or a folder, within the Deleted Items Folder list and then click the Delete button on the toolbar (or press the Delete key). You'll be asked to confirm its permanent deletion.

- Set up Outlook Express to delete messages automatically when you quit the program. To do so, choose Tools→Options. On the Maintenance tab, turn on "Empty messages from the 'Deleted Items' folder on exit." Click OK.

Replying to Messages

To reply to a message, click the Reply button in the toolbar, or choose Message→Reply to Sender, or press Ctrl+R. Outlook Express creates a new, outgoing email message, preaddressed to the sender's return address.

To save additional time, Outlook Express pastes the entire original message at the bottom of your reply (complete with the > brackets that serve as Internet quoting marks); that's to help your correspondent figure out what you're talking about. (To turn off this feature, choose Tools→Options, click the Send tab, and turn off "Include message in reply.") Outlook Express even tacks *Re:* ("regarding") onto the front of the subject line.

Your cursor appears at the top of the message box; now begin typing your reply. You can also add recipients, remove recipients, edit the subject line or the message, and so on.

Tip: Use the Enter key to create blank lines within the bracketed original message in order to place your own text within it. Using this method, you can splice your own comments into the paragraphs of the original message, replying point by point. The brackets preceding each line of the original message help your correspondent keep straight what's yours and what's hers.

Note, by the way, that there are three kinds of replies, each represented by a different icon on the toolbar:

UP TO SPEED

About Mailing Lists

During your email experiments, you're likely to come across something called a mailing list—a discussion group conducted via email. By searching Yahoo *(www.yahoo.com)* or other Web directories, you can find mailing lists covering just about every conceivable topic.

You can send a message to all members of such a group by sending a message to a single address—the list's address. The list is actually maintained on a special mail server. Everything sent to the list gets sent to the server, which forwards the message to all of the individual list members. That's why you have to be careful when you think you're replying to *one person* in the discussion group; if you reply to the list and not to a specific person, you'll be sending your reply to every address on the list—sometimes with disastrous consequences.

- A **standard reply** goes to the sender of the message (click the Reply button). If that sender is a mailing list (see the sidebar box below), then the message gets sent to the *entire* mailing list, which has gotten more than one unsuspecting novice PC fan into trouble.

- **Reply Group** (available only when you're reading newsgroup messages) creates a reply intended for the entire Internet—that is, everyone who reads this newsgroup. (By contrast, click Reply to shoot a private note to only one person: the person who typed the message.)

- The **Reply To All** button addresses a message to all recipients of the original message, including any CC recipients. This is the button to use if you're participating in a group discussion of some topic. For example, six people can simultaneously carry on an email correspondence, always sending each response to the other five in the group.

Forwarding Messages

Instead of replying to the person who sent you a message, you may sometimes want to *forward* the message—pass it on—to a third person.

To do so, click the Forward button in the toolbar, choose Message→Forward, or press Ctrl+F. A new message opens, looking a lot like the one that appears when you reply. Once again, before forwarding the message, you have the option of editing the subject line or the message itself. (For example, you may wish to precede the original message with a comment of your own, along the lines of: "Frank: I thought you'd be interested in this joke about Congress.")

All that remains is for you to specify who receives the forwarded message. Just address it as you would any outgoing piece of mail.

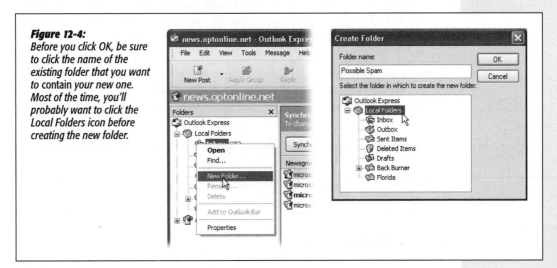

Figure 12-4:
Before you click OK, be sure to click the name of the existing folder that you want to contain your new one. Most of the time, you'll probably want to click the Local Folders icon before creating the new folder.

Printing Messages

Sometimes there's no substitute for a printout of an email message—an area where Outlook Express shines. Just click the Print button in the toolbar, choose File→Print, or press Ctrl+P. The standard Windows Print dialog box pops up, so that you can specify how many copies you want, what range of pages, and so on. Finally, click the Print button to begin printing.

Filing Messages

Outlook Express lets you create new folders in the Folders list; by dragging messages from your Inbox onto one of these folder icons, you can file away your messages into appropriate storage cubbies. You might create one folder for important messages, another for order confirmations when shopping on the Web, still another for friends and family, and so on. In fact, you can even create folders *inside* these folders, a feature beloved by the hopelessly organized.

To create a new folder, choose File→Folder→New, or right-click the Local Folders icon (in the folder list), and choose New Folder from the shortcut menu (Figure 12-4, left). Either way, a Create Folder window appears, providing a place to name the new folder (Figure 12-4, right).

Tip: To rename an existing folder, right-click it and choose Rename from the shortcut menu.

To move a message into a folder, proceed like this:

- Drag it out of the list pane and onto the folder icon. You can use any part of a message's "row" in the list as a handle. You can also drag messages en masse onto a folder, after first selecting them using the tips on page 371.

- Control-click a message (or one of several that you've highlighted). From the resulting shortcut menu, choose Move to Folder. In a dialog box, the folder list appears; select the one you want, then press Enter or click OK.

Tip: When you click a + button in the Folder list, you see all folders contained within that folder, exactly as in Windows Explorer. You can drag folders inside other folders, nesting them to create a nice hierarchical folder structure. (To drag a nested folder back into the list of "main" folders, just drag it to the Local Folders icon.)

You can also drag messages between folders; just drag one from the message list onto the desired folder at the left side of the screen.

This can be a useful trick when applied to a message in your Outbox. If you decide to postpone sending it, drag it into any other folder; Outlook Express won't send it until you drag it *back* into the Outbox.

Flagging Messages

Sometimes, you'll receive an email message that prompts you to some sort of action, but you may not have the time (or the fortitude) to face the task at the moment.

("Hi there… it's me, your accountant. Would you mind rounding up your expenses for 1993 through 2001 and sending me a list by email?")

That's why Outlook Express provides the Flag commands, which let you *flag* a message, positioning a little red flag in the corresponding column next to a message's name. These little red flags are simply visual indicators that you place for your own convenience, meaning whatever you want them to mean. You can bring all flagged messages to the top of the list by choosing View→Sort By→Flag.

To flag a message in this way, select the message (or several messages) and choose Message→Flag Message. (Use the same command again to clear a flag from a message.)

Figure 12-5:
Top: One way to rescue an attachment from an email message is to click the paper clip icon and choose Save Attachments.

Bottom: Dragging an attachment's icon onto your desktop takes the file out of the Outlook Express world and into your standard Windows world, where you can file it, trash it, open it, or manipulate it as you would any file.

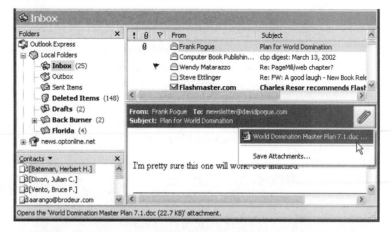

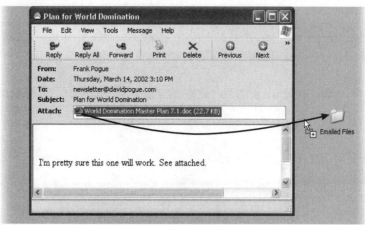

Opening Attachments

Just as you can attach files to a message, people can also send files to you. You know when a message has an attachment because a paper clip icon appears next to its name in the Inbox.

Outlook Express doesn't store downloaded files as normal file icons on your hard drive. All your messages *and* all the attached files are part of one big, specially encoded mail file. To extract an attached file from this mass of software, use one of the following methods:

- Click the attachment icon (Figure 12-5), select Save Attachments from the shortcut menu, and then specify the folder in which you want the file saved.

- Click the attachment icon. A shortcut menu appears, from which you can either choose the name of the attachment to open the file directly (in Word, Excel, or whatever), or Save Attachments to save it to the disk.

- If you've double-clicked the message so that it appears in its own window, then drag the attachment icon out of the message window and onto any visible portion of your desktop, as shown in Figure 12-5.

- Again if you've opened the message into its own window, you can double-click the attachment's icon in the message. Once again, you'll be asked whether you want to open the file or save it to the disk.

Note: Whenever you open an attachment directly from within the email (rather than saving it to the disk first), *use the File→Save As command* to save the file into a folder! Otherwise, you won't be able to open the file again except from within Outlook Express—and any changes you make to that document will appear only when you open it from within Outlook Express, too.

Not Everyone Has the Same Software

People send me documents in Microsoft Word, but I use WordPerfect. I write back and tell them to paste the text into the email message itself, but they don't like to do that. Do I have to buy tons of software I don't want just to open attachments?

No. There's often a way to open attachments even if you don't own the program used to create them. Microsoft Word documents, for instance, automatically open in WordPad if you don't have Microsoft Word on your system.

Word processors and spreadsheet programs can usually *import* documents created by other applications, complete with formatting. To try this approach, open the email message that contains the attachment. Then right-click the icon for the attachment. From the shortcut menu, choose Save As and save the file in a folder (the My Documents folder is a good choice).

Finally, launch your own equivalent application (word processor, spreadsheet program, or whatever), and then choose File→Open or File→Import. Locate the file you moved into your My Documents folder. You'll be pleased at how often this trick opens a document that was created by a program that you don't have…using a program that you do.

Message Rules

Once you know how to create folders, the next step in managing your email is to set up a series of *message rules*. Message rules are filters that can file, answer, or delete an incoming message *automatically* based on its subject, address, or size. Message rules require you to think like the distant relative of a programmer, but the mental effort can reward you many times over. In fact, message rules can turn Outlook Express into a surprisingly smart and efficient secretary.

Setting up message rules

Now that you're thoroughly intrigued about the magic of message rules, here's how to set one up:

1. **Choose Tools→Message Rules→Mail.**

   The New Mail Rule dialog box appears, as shown in Figure 12-6 at top left.

2. **Use the top options to specify how Outlook Express should select messages to process.**

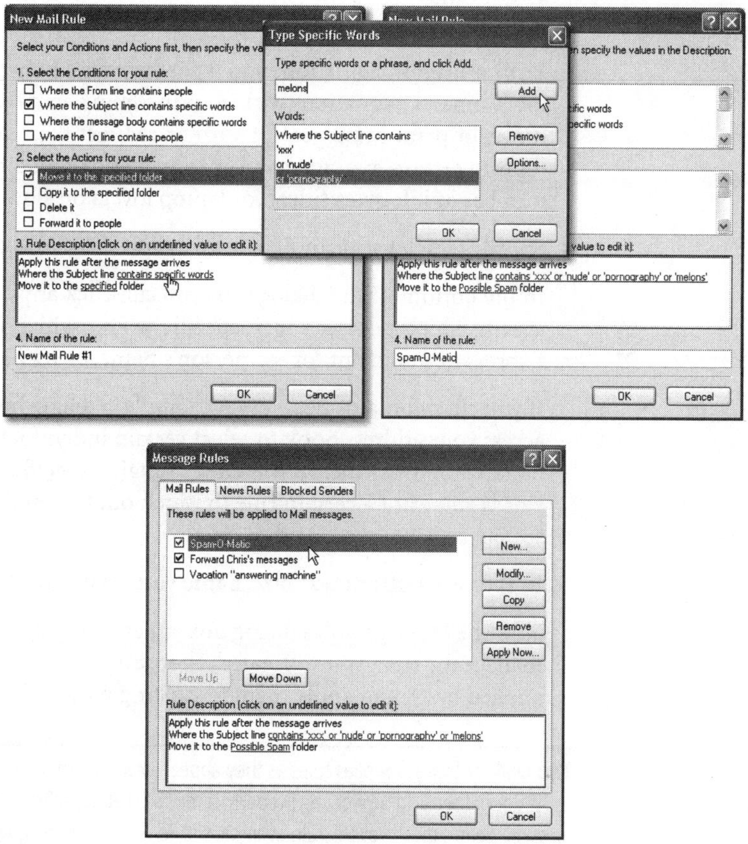

Figure 12-6:
Top left: Building a message rule entails specifying which messages you want Outlook Express to look for—and what to do with them. By clicking the underlined words, as shown here, you specify what criteria you're looking for.

Top middle: Let the rule know which words it's supposed to watch for.

Top right: The completed message rule (note the summary at the bottom).

Bottom: All mail message rules you've created appear in the Message Rules dialog box. Select a rule to see what it does, and use the Move Up and Move Down buttons to specify the order in which rules should be run. Double-click a rule to open the Edit Rule dialog box, where you can specify what the rule does.

For example, if you'd like Outlook Express to watch out for messages from a particular person, you would choose, "Where the From line contains people."

To flag messages containing *loan, $$$$, XXXX, !!!!,* and so on, choose, "Where the Subject line contains specific words."

If you turn on more than one checkbox, you can set up another condition for your message rule. For example, you can set up the first criterion to find messages *from* your uncle, and a second that watches for subject lines that contain "humor." Now, only jokes sent by your uncle will get placed in, say, Deleted Items.

(If you've set up more than one criterion, you'll see the underlined word <u>and</u> at the bottom of the dialog box. It indicates that the message rule should apply only if *all* of the conditions are true. Click the <u>and</u> to produce a little dialog box, where you have the option to apply the rule if *any* of the conditions are met.)

3. **Using the second set of checkboxes, specify what you want to happen to messages that match the criteria.**

   If, in step 2, you told your rule to watch for junk mail containing *$$$$* in the Subject line, here's where you can tell Outlook Express to delete or move the message into, say, a Spam folder.

   With a little imagination, you'll see how these checkboxes can perform absolutely amazing functions with your incoming email. Outlook Express can delete, move, or print messages; forward or redirect them to somebody; automatically reply to certain messages; and even avoid downloading files bigger than a certain number of kilobytes (ideal for laptop lovers on slow hotel room connections).

4. **Specify *which* words or people you want the message rule to watch out for.**

   In the bottom of the dialog box, you can click any of the underlined phrases to specify which people, which specific words, which file sizes you want Outlook Express to watch out for—a person's name, or *XXX*, in the previous examples.

   If you click <u>contains people</u>, for example, a dialog box appears in which you can access your address book to select certain individuals whose messages you want handled by this rule. If you click <u>contains specific words</u>, you can type in the words you want a certain rule to watch out for (in the Subject line, for example; see Figure 12-6, top). And so on.

5. **In the very bottom text box, name your mail rule. Click OK.**

   Now the Message Rules dialog box appears (Figure 12-6, bottom). Here, you can manage the rules you've created, choose a sequence for them (those at the top get applied first), and apply them to existing messages (by clicking Apply Now).

Tip: Outlook Express applies rules as they appear—from top to bottom—in the Message Rules window; if a rule doesn't seem to be working properly, it may be that an earlier rule is intercepting and processing the message before the "broken" rule even sees it. To fix this, try moving the rule up or down in the list by selecting it and then clicking the Move Up or Move Down buttons.

Two sneaky message-rule tricks

You can use message rules for many different purposes. But here are two of the best:

- **Create a spam filter.** When a spammer sends junk email, he usually puts your address on the "BCC:" (blind carbon copy) line, to prevent you from seeing who else received the message. This characteristic makes it easy to screen out such mail, and create a message rule that looks for messages where the "To:" or "CC:" line contains *your* address—and files them into the Inbox as usual.

Figure 12-7:
The Options dialog box has ten tabs, each loaded with options. Most tabs have buttons that open additional dialog boxes. Coming in 2006: Outlook Express Options: The Missing Manual.

But then create another message rule for "For all messages" that puts messages into a folder that you've created—called, for example, Possible Spam. Because the second rule doesn't kick in until *after* the first one has done its duty, the second rule affects only messages in which your name appeared on the "BCC:" line (which is almost always spam). Once a week, it's wise to look through the Possible Spam folder in case a legitimate message found its way there.

- **The email answering machine.** If you're going on vacation, turn on "For all messages" in step 2, and then "Reply with message" in step 3. In other words, you can turn Outlook Express into an email answering machine that automatically sends a canned "I'm away until the 15th" message to everyone who writes you.

Tip: Be sure to unsubscribe from, or turn off, any email mailing lists before you turn on "For all messages"; otherwise, you'll incur the wrath of the other Internet citizens by littering their email discussion groups with copies of your auto-reply message.

Configuring Outlook Express

Outlook Express has enough features and configuration options to fill a very thick book. You can see them for yourself by choosing Tools→Options from the Outlook Express window (see Figure 12-7). Here's an overview of some of the features you'll find.

General tab

Most of the controls on the General tab govern what Outlook Express does when you first launch it. Take note of the options for configuring automatic connection to your ISP. You can select the option to check for messages every few minutes, and

---

FREQUENTLY ASKED QUESTION

Canning Spam

Help! I'm awash in junk email! How do I get out of this mess?

Spam is a much hated form of advertising that involves sending unsolicited emails to thousands of people. While there's no instant cure for spam, you can take certain steps to protect yourself from it.

1. If you have more than one email account, consider using one each for online shopping, Web site and software registration, and newsgroup posting. Spammers have automated software robots that scour every public Internet message and Web page, automatically locating and recording email addresses they find. These are the primary sources of spam, so at least you're now restricting the junk mail to one secondary mail account. (Reserve a separate email account for person-to-person email.)

2. Whenever you receive a piece of junk mail, choose Message→Block Sender from the Outlook Express toolbar. Outlook Express will no longer accept email from that sender.

3. When filling out forms or registering products online, always look for checkboxes requesting permission for the company to send you email or share your email address with its "partners." Just say no.

4. When posting messages in a newsgroup, insert the letters NOSPAM somewhere into the email address you've specified in the News Account dialog box (page 384). Anyone replying to you via email must manually remove the NOSPAM from your email address, which is a slight hassle; meanwhile, the spammers' software robots (which aren't very bright) will lift a bogus email address from newsgroup posts.

5. Create *message rules* to filter out messages containing typical advertising words such as *casino, guaranteed, loan,* and so forth. (You'll find instructions in this chapter.)

6. If you *really* have a spam problem, get a new email address. Give it to people you trust; use the old address only for junk mail, and check it for messages only infrequently.

---

then use the drop-down list to tell Outlook Express how, and whether, to connect at that time—if you're not already online.

Read tab

Use these options to establish how the program handles messages in the Inbox. One of these options marks a message as having been read—changing its typeface from bold to non-bold—if you leave it highlighted in the list for five seconds or more, even without opening it. That's one option you may want to consider turning off. (This is also where you choose the font you want to use for the messages you're reading, which is an important consideration.)

Receipts tab

You can add a *return receipt* to messages you send. When the recipient reads your message, a notification message (receipt) is emailed back to you under two conditions: *if* the recipient agrees to send a return receipt to you, and *if* the recipient's email program offers a similar feature. (Outlook Express, Outlook, and Eudora all do.)

Send tab

The options on the Send tab govern outgoing messages. One option to consider turning *off* here is the default option, "Send messages immediately." That's because as soon as you click the Send button, Outlook Express tries to send the message, even if that means triggering your modem to dial. All of this dialing—and *waiting* for the dialing—drives some people crazy, especially in households with only one phone line.

If you turn this option off, then clicking the Send button simply places a newly written message into the Outbox. As you reply to messages and compose new ones, the Outbox collects them. They're not sent until you choose Tools→Send and Receive (or click Send/Recv on the toolbar, or press Ctrl+M). Only at that point does Outlook Express command your modem to dial the Internet. It then sends all the waiting outgoing mail at once.

Tip: To see the messages waiting in your Outbox, click the Outbox icon at the left side of the screen. At this point, you can click a message's name (in the upper-right pane of the screen) to view the message itself in the *lower*-right pane, exactly as with messages in your Inbox.

Don't bother to try *editing* an outgoing message in this way, however, since Outlook Express won't let you do so. Only by double-clicking a message's name (in the upper-right pane), thus opening it into a separate window, can you make changes to a piece of outgoing mail.

The Send tab also includes features for configuring replies. For example, you can disable the function that puts the original message at the bottom of a reply.

Finally, the "Automatically put people I reply to in my Address Book" can be a real timesaver. Each time you reply to somebody, his email address is automatically saved in your address book, so that the next time you want to write him a note, you won't need to look up the address—just type the first few letters of it in the "To:" box.

Compose tab

Here's where you specify the font you want to use when writing messages and newsgroup messages.

This is also the control center for stationery; it houses custom-designed templates, complete with fonts, colors, backgrounds, borders, and other formatting elements that you can use for all outgoing email. Needless to say, sending a message formatted with stationery means that you're using HTML formatting, as described earlier, complete with its potential downsides.

To choose a stationery style for all outgoing messages, turn on the Mail checkbox and then click the Select button. You're offered a folder full of Microsoft stationery templates; click one to see its preview. You can also click the Create New button on the toolbar, which launches a wizard that walks you through the process of designing your own background design.

Tip: You don't have to use one particular stationery style for all outgoing messages. When sending a message, instead of clicking the Create Mail button on the Outlook Express toolbar, just click the tiny down-arrow triangle *next* to it. Doing so opens a window that lists several stationery styles, letting you choose one on a message-by-message basis.

Signatures tab

As noted earlier in this chapter, you use this tab to design a *signature* for your messages. By clicking the New button and entering more signature material in the text box, you can create several *different* signatures: one that's for business messages, one for your buddies, and so on. (Outlook Express calls them Signature #1, Signature #2, and so on. To rename a signature, click its name and then click the Rename button.)

To insert a signature into an outgoing message, choose Insert→Signature, then choose the one you want from the list that appears.

Spelling tab

The Spelling tab offers configuration options for the Outlook Express spell-checking feature (which requires that you have Microsoft Word). You can even force the spell checker to correct errors in the *original* message when you send a reply (although your correspondent may not appreciate it).

Security tab

This tab contains options for sending secure mail, using digital IDs, and encryption. If you're using Outlook Express in a business that requires secure email, the system administrator will provide instructions. Otherwise, you'll find that most of these settings have no effect.

Tip: One of these options is very useful in the modern age: "Warn me when other applications try to send mail as me." That's a thinly veiled reference to virus programs that, behind the scenes, send out hundreds of infected emails to everybody in your address book. This option ensures that if some software—not you— tries to send messages, you'll know about it.

Connection tab

You change options for making and sustaining the connection to your ISP in the Connection tab. For example, you can tell Outlook Express to hang up automatically after sending and receiving messages (and reconnect the next time you want to perform the same tasks). As noted in the dialog box, though, Outlook Express otherwise uses the same Internet settings described in Chapter 10.

Maintenance tab

This tab is your housekeeping center. These options let you clear out old deleted messages, clean up downloads, and so on.

Newsgroups

Newsgroups have nothing to do with news; in fact, they're Internet bulletin boards. There are at least 50,000 of them, on every conceivable topic: pop culture, computers, politics, and every other special (and *very* special) interest; in fact, there are several dozen just about Windows. Use Outlook Express to read and reply to these messages almost exactly as though they were email messages.

Furthermore, Outlook Express lets you use multiple *news servers* (bulletin-board distribution computers), subscribe to individual newsgroups, filter messages in your newsgroups using rules, and post and read messages complete with attachments.

Note: If a news server (not an individual newsgroup) is selected in the Folders list, then the rightmost portion of the Outlook Express interface displays a list of newsgroups available on that server.

UP TO SPEED

Newsgroups Explained

Newsgroups (often called *Usenet*) started out as a way for people to conduct discussions via a bulletin-board-like system, in which a message is posted for all to see and reply to. These public discussions are divided into categories called newsgroups, which cover the gamut from miscellaneous photographic techniques to naval aviation.

These days, Usenet has a certain seedy reputation as a place to exchange questionable pictures, pirated software, and MP3 files with doubtful copyright pedigrees. Even so, there are tens of thousands of interesting, informative discussions going on, and newsgroups are great places to get help with troubleshooting, exchange recipes, or just to see what's on the minds of your fellow Usenet users.

Setting Up an Account

Setting up a new news account is similar to setting up a new email account; the adventure begins by contacting your Internet service provider and finding out its *news server address*, along with your user name and password.

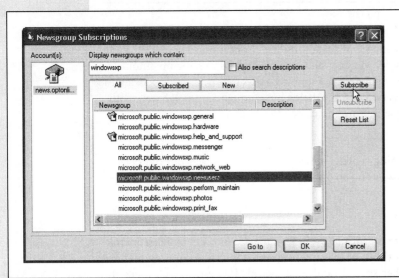

Figure 12-8:
In the text box at the top, enter the text you want to look for in the newsgroup's title (such as windowsxp, *as shown here—in cyberspace, there are no spaces between words). If you turn up an appealing-sounding topic in the gigantic list beneath, click its name and click the Subscribe button to subscribe to it. Now Outlook Express will download the latest messages on that topic each time you connect.*

Next, choose Tools→Accounts; click the News tab, click the Add button, and then click News.

Now a wizard steps you through the process of creating a news account in Outlook Express; it involves entering your email address and the address of your news server. (Sometimes you get newsgroup access with your regular Internet account. If your ISP doesn't provide newsgroup access, you'll have to subscribe to a news service. The price depends on how much you download each month; visit *www.easynews.com, www.supernews.com,* or *www.newsguy.com* for more information.)

Download the List of Newsgroups

When you're finished with the wizard, Outlook Express invites you to download a list of newsgroups available on your server. Click the Yes button, and then wait patiently for a few minutes.

Outlook Express goes to work downloading the list, which can be quite long—more than 50,000 entries, in many cases—and takes several minutes if you connect to the Internet with a dial-up modem. Once that's done, though, you won't have to do it again.

You wind up with the dialog box shown in Figure 12-8. (You can always get to this master list of newsgroups by choosing Tools→Newsgroups, or by pressing Ctrl+W.)

Finding Newsgroups and Messages

If you're looking for a particular topic, such as Windows XP, you can view a list of matching discussions by typing a phrase into the text box that's labeled, however ungrammatically, "Display newsgroups which contain" at the top of the window. Outlook Express hides any newsgroups that *don't* match that text (see Figure 12-8).

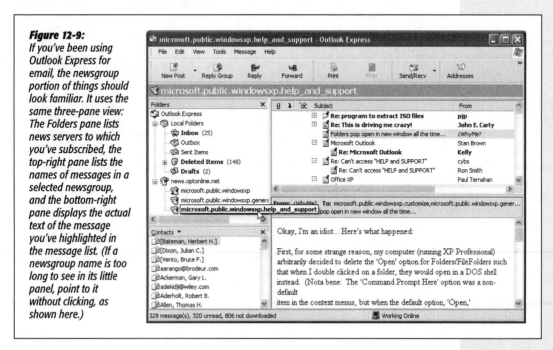

Figure 12-9:
If you've been using Outlook Express for email, the newsgroup portion of things should look familiar. It uses the same three-pane view: The Folders pane lists news servers to which you've subscribed, the top-right pane lists the names of messages in a selected newsgroup, and the bottom-right pane displays the actual text of the message you've highlighted in the message list. (If a newsgroup name is too long to see in its little panel, point to it without clicking, as shown here.)

Reading Messages

Once Outlook Express has downloaded a list of available newsgroups, it's up to you to sift through them and select the discussions you want to monitor.

Fortunately, Outlook Express makes it easy to follow the raging Internet discussions with a feature called *subscriptions*. To subscribe to a newsgroup, select its name in the list, and then click the Subscribe button. When you click OK, an icon for that discussion topic appears under the server's name in the Folder list, acting as though it's a nested folder.

The next time you connect to the Internet, Outlook Express downloads all of the message summaries in the discussions to which you've subscribed. (There may be just a few messages, or several hundred; they may go back only a few days or a couple of weeks, depending on the amount of "traffic" in each discussion and the amount of storage space available on the news server.) These are not the messages themselves, just the *headers*—the author's name, the subject, and the date the message was sent.

To read the actual messages in a newsgroup, either click an entry in the list of messages to download the contents of the message and display it in the preview window (Figure 12-9), or double-click an entry to open the list of messages in a new window.

Some particularly large attachments in newsgroups are automatically divided into multiple segments, in part to accommodate those with slow Internet connections. If you're having trouble saving a multipart attachment to your hard drive, make sure that you've selected the message that contains the *first* part. (Even then, you may find that joining multipart newsgroup messages isn't one of Outlook Express's strongest features.)

Tip: You can set up message rules to screen out messages from certain people, messages with certain phrases in their Subject lines, and so on. It works exactly like the message rules for email, as described earlier in this chapter.

Replying, Composing, and Forwarding Messages

Working with newsgroup messages is very similar to working with email messages, except that you must be conscious of whether you're replying to the individual sender of a message or to the entire group. Otherwise, you can reply to messages, forward them, or compose them exactly as described earlier in this chapter. As with email, you can use plain text or (if you don't mind annoying the other Internet citizens) HTML formatting, and include file attachments, too (use the Attach toolbar button, for example).

Tip: Aside from posting advertisements and HTML-formatted messages, the best way to irritate everyone on a newsgroup is to ask a question that has already been answered recently on the newsgroup. Before asking a question, spend five minutes reading the recent newsgroup messages to see whether someone has already answered your question. Also consider visiting the Groups tab at *www.google.com,* a Web site that lets you search all newsgroups for particular topics.

Part Four:
Plugging into Windows XP

4

Printing, Fonts, and Faxing

Technologists got pretty excited about "the paperless office" in the eighties, but the PC explosion had exactly the opposite effect: Thanks to the proliferation of inexpensive, high-quality PC printers, we generate far more printouts than ever. There's not much to printing from Windows XP, so this is a short chapter.

Installing a Printer

A printer is designed to follow computer instructions called *printer codes* from your PC. These codes tell the printer what fonts to use, how to set margins, which paper tray to use, and so on.

But the codes aren't identical for every printer. Therefore, every printer requires a piece of software—the *printer driver*—that tells the printer how to interpret what it "hears" from your computer.

Windows XP comes with hundreds of printer drivers built right in; your printer also came with a set of drivers on a CD or floppy. You can often find more recent driver software for your printer on the manufacturer's Web site, such as *www.epson.com* or *www.lexmark.com,* or from a central driver repository like *www.windrivers.com.*

Existing Printers

Did you upgrade your PC to Windows XP from an earlier version—one that worked fine with your printer? In that case, Windows XP automatically notices and inherits your existing settings. If it's a fairly recent printer with a fairly recent driver, it'll probably work fine with Windows XP.

But if the printer is especially elderly, the printer software may be incompatible with Windows XP. In that case, your first activity after dinner should be to search the printer company's Web site for an updated version, or check Microsoft's master Windows XP compatibility list at *www.microsoft.com/hcl.*

If you just bought a new computer or a new printer, however, you'll have to hook it up yourself and install its software. In general, there's not much to it.

Note: Only people with Administrator accounts can install a new printer to a Windows XP machine (see Chapter 16).

USB Printers

If you're like most people at home these days, you use an inkjet printer that connects to your PC's USB (Universal Serial Bus) port. As a technology, USB has lots of advantages: USB gadgets are easy to connect and disconnect, are very fast, conserve space, can be plugged and unplugged while the PC is running, and so on.

Just the act of connecting a USB printer to your PC, for example, inspires Windows XP to dig into its own bag of included driver modules to install the correct one (Figure 13-1). See Chapter 14 for more on this process.

Figure 13-1:
You got lucky. Windows recognizes your printer, has the appropriate driver, and has put the software into place. Let the printing begin.

Network Printers

If you work in an office where numerous people on the network share a single laser printer, the printer usually isn't connected directly to your computer. Instead, it's elsewhere on the network; the Ethernet cable coming out of your PC connects you to it indirectly.

In general, there's very little involved in ensuring that your PC "sees" this printer. Its icon simply shows up in the Start→Control Panel→Printers and Faxes folder. (If you don't see it, run the Add Printer Wizard described in the following section. On its second screen, you'll be offered the chance to look for "A network printer, or printer attached to another computer." That's the one you want.)

Parallel, Serial, and Infrared Printers

Although USB printers are the world's most popular type today, there was, believe it or not, a time before USB. In those days, most home printers fell into one of these categories:

- **Parallel.** Before USB changed the world, most printers connected to PCs using a printer cable or *parallel cable.* The cable connects to your PC's parallel port, which Microsoft's help screens call the LPT1 port—a 25-pin, D-shaped jack. (On many PCs, this connector is marked with a printer icon on the back panel.)

- **Serial.** Other older printers use a cable connected to one of your computer's *serial* (or *COM*) ports, the connectors that often accommodate an external modem. The primary advantage of a serial connection is the extended cable length: Parallel cables must be no more than nine feet long, while serial cables up to 50 feet long work fine.

Tip: To protect its innards, turn off the PC before connecting or disconnecting a parallel or serial cable.

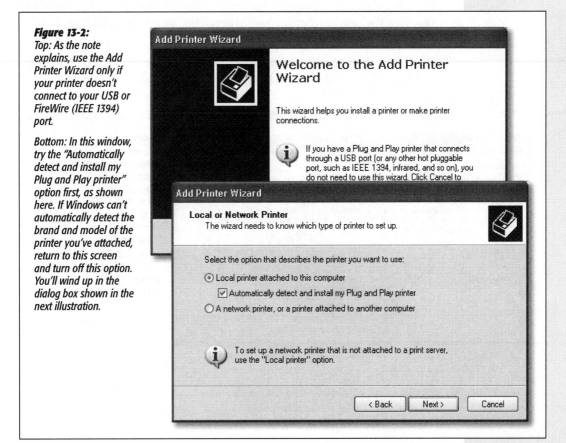

Figure 13-2:
Top: As the note explains, use the Add Printer Wizard only if your printer doesn't connect to your USB or FireWire (IEEE 1394) port.

Bottom: In this window, try the "Automatically detect and install my Plug and Play printer" option first, as shown here. If Windows can't automatically detect the brand and model of the printer you've attached, return to this screen and turn off this option. You'll wind up in the dialog box shown in the next illustration.

- **Infrared.** Certain printers from HP, Canon, Citizen, and other companies print using *infrared* technology—that is, there's no cable at all. Instead, if your PC has an infrared lens (as many laptops do), it can communicate with the printer's similar lens wirelessly, as long as the printer and PC are within sight of, and relatively close to, each other.

If the technology gods are smiling, you can just connect the printer, turn on your Windows XP machine, and delight in the "Found new hardware" message that appears on your taskbar. You're ready to print.

But if Windows doesn't "know about" the printer model you've hooked up, it can't install its drivers automatically. In that case, the Add Printer Wizard appears (Figure 13-2)—or you can always open it. (Choose Start→Control Panel→Printers and Faxes; click the Add Printer link.) Click Next to walk through the questions until you've correctly identified your printer and installed the appropriate software.

Here are the guidelines for using the next screen:

- Try the "Automatically detect and install my Plug and Play printer" checkbox first (see Figure 13-2 at bottom). If it doesn't succeed in locating your printer and installing the software, run the wizard again, this time turning that option off.

- If the "Automatically detect" option didn't work, you'll be asked to specify which PC port your printer's connected to. You'll then be asked to indicate, from a gigantic scrolling list of every printer Microsoft has ever heard of, your exact brand and model (Figure 13-3).

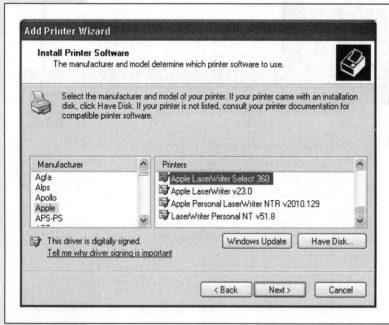

Figure 13-3:
The left pane lists every printer manufacturer Microsoft has ever heard of. Once you've selected your printer's manufacturer, a list of all the printer models from that manufacturer (that Windows XP knows about) appears in the right pane. Click the Have Disk button if your printer's driver software is on a disk supplied by the manufacturer.

At this point, you must lead Windows by the nose to the printer's driver software. On the Add Printer Wizard screen, select your printer from the list of printers. If Windows doesn't list your printer there, or if its manufacturer supplied the Windows XP driver on a disk, click the Have Disk button, and then navigate to the CD, floppy disk, or downloaded Internet installation file that contains the driver.

Either way, subsequent wizard screens will invite you to type a short name for your printer, in order to make it available to other computers on the network (yes, Windows can even share, for example, a USB inkjet, even though it's not technically a network printer), to print a test page, and so on. (If the test page doesn't print out correctly, Windows XP launches its printer *troubleshooter*—a specialized wizard that offers you one troubleshooting suggestion after another until either you or Windows quits in frustration.)

The Printer Icon

If your driver-installation efforts are ultimately successful, you're rewarded by the appearance of an icon that represents your printer.

This icon appears in the *Printers and Faxes* window—an important window that you'll be reading about over and over again in this chapter. Exactly how you arrive there depends on how you've set up Windows XP:

- If you've set up your Start menu to display a submenu for the Control Panel (page 63), just choose Start→Control Panel→Printers and Faxes.

- If you view your Control Panel in *Classic* view (page 253), choose Start→Control Panel, and then open the Printers and Faxes icon.

- If you view your Control Panel in *Category* view, choose Start→Control Panel, click the Printers and Other Hardware link, and finally click the "View installed printers or fax printers" link.

The Printers and Faxes window should be listed in your Start menu, which saves you some burrowing if you use this feature a lot. If it's not there, for some reason,

TROUBLESHOOTING MOMENT

If Your Printer Model Isn't Listed

If your printer model isn't in the list of printers (Figure 13-3), then Windows XP doesn't have a driver for it. Your printer model may be very new (more recent than Windows XP, that is) or very old. You have two choices for getting around this roadblock:

First, you can contact the manufacturer (or its Web site) to get the drivers. Then install the driver software as described in the previous section.

Second, you can use the *printer emulation* feature. As it turns out, many printers work with one of several standard drivers that come from other companies. For example, many laser printers work fine with the HP LaserJet driver. (These laser printers are not, in fact, HP LaserJets, but they *emulate* one.)

The instructions that came with your printer should have a section on emulation; the manufacturer's help line can also tell you which popular printer yours can impersonate.

right-click the Start button. From the shortcut menu, choose Properties. On the Start Menu tab, click Customize, then click the Advanced tab. Scroll down in the list of checkboxes, and finally turn on "Printers and Faxes." Click OK twice.

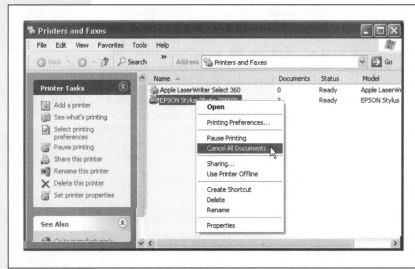

Figure 13-4:
At first, the task pane in the Printers and Faxes window offers only two commands. But when you click a printer icon, a long list of useful options appears, as shown here. Many of them duplicate the options that appear when you right-click a printer icon—something you'd be wise to remember the day your right mouse button breaks.

GEM IN THE ROUGH

Installing Fake Printers

If your printer has two paper trays, switching to the secondary one is something of a hassle. You must spend time making the changes in the Print dialog box, as described later in this chapter. Similarly, switching the printout resolution from, say, 300 dpi to 600 dpi when printing important graphic documents is a multi-step procedure.

That's why you may find it useful to create several different icons for *the same printer*. The beauty of this stunt is that you can set up different settings for each of these icons. One might store canned settings for 600 dpi printouts from the top paper tray, another might represent 300 dpi printouts from the bottom one, and so on. When it comes time to print, you can switch between these virtual printers quickly and easily.

To create another icon, just run the Add Printer Wizard a second time, as described on the preceding pages. At the point in the installation where you name the printer, in-

vent a name that describes this printer's alternate settings, like *HP6-600 dpi* or *Lexmark-Legal Size.*

When the installation process is complete, you'll see both printer icons—the old and the new—in the Printers and Faxes window. Right-click the new "printer" icon, choose Printing Preferences from the shortcut menu, and change the settings to match its role.

To specify which one you want as your *default* printer—the one you use most of the time—right-click the appropriate icon and choose Set as Default Printer from the shortcut menu.

But thereafter, whenever you want to switch to the other set of printer settings—when you need better graphics, a different paper tray, or other special options for a document—just select the appropriate printer from the Printer Name drop-down list in the Print dialog box (see Figure 13-5 at top). You've just saved yourself a half-dozen additional mouse clicks and settings changes.

Tip: If you're using your Start menu in Classic view (page 253), you get to your Printers and Faxes window by clicking Start→Settings→Printers and Faxes.

In any case, the Printers and Faxes window now contains an icon bearing the name you gave it during the installation (Figure 13-4). This printer icon comes in handy in several different situations, as the rest of this chapter clarifies.

Printing

Fortunately, the setup described so far in this chapter is a one-time-only task. Once it's over, printing is little more than a one-click operation.

Figure 13-5:
Top: The options in the Print dialog box are different on each printer model and each application, so your Print dialog box may look slightly different.

For example, here are the Print dialog boxes from Microsoft Word and WordPad. Most of the time, the factory settings shown here are what you want (one copy, print all pages). Just click OK or Print (or press Enter) to close this dialog box and send the document to the printer.

Bottom: During printing, the tiny icon of a printer appears in your notification area. Pointing to it without clicking produces a pop-up tooltip like this that reveals the background printing activity.

Printing from Applications

After you've created a document you want to see on paper, choose File→Print (or press Ctrl+P). The Print dialog box appears, as shown in Figure 13-5.

This box, too, changes depending on the program you're using—the Print dialog box in Microsoft Word looks a lot more intimidating than the WordPad version—but here are the basics:

- **Select Printer.** If your PC is connected to several printers, or if you've created several differently configured icons for the same printer, choose the one you want from this drop-down list or scrolling panel of printer icons.

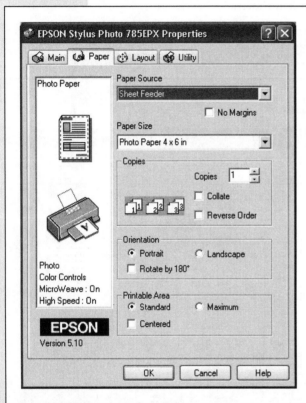

Figure 13-6:
When you choose Properties from the Print dialog box, you can specify the paper size you're using, whether you want to print sideways on the page ("Landscape" orientation), what kind of photo paper you're using, and so on. Here, you're making changes only for a particular printout; you're not changing any settings for the printer itself. (The specific features of this dialog box depend on the program you're using.)

- **Preferences/Properties.** Clicking this button opens a version of the printer's Properties dialog box, as shown in Figure 13-6.

- **Page range.** These controls specify which pages of the document you want to print. If you want to print only some of the pages, click the Pages option and type in the page numbers you want (with a hyphen, like *3-6* to print pages 3 through 6).

Tip: You can also type in individual page numbers with commas, like *2, 4, 9* to print only those three pages—or even add hyphens to the mix, like this: *1-3, 5-6, 13-18.*

Click Current Page to print only the page that contains the blinking insertion point. Click Selection to print only the text you selected (highlighted) before opening the Print dialog box. (If this option button is dimmed, it's because you didn't highlight any text—or because you're using a program that doesn't offer this feature.)

- **Number of copies.** To print out several copies of the same thing, use this box to specify the exact amount. You'll get several copies of page 1, then several copies of page 2, and so on—*unless* you also turn on the Collate checkbox, which produces complete sets of pages, in order.

- **Print.** The Print drop-down list in the lower-left section of the dialog box offers three options: "All pages in range," "Odd pages," and "Even pages."

  Use the Odd and Even pages options when you have to print on both sides of the paper, but your printer has no special feature for this purpose. You'll have to print all the odd pages, turn the stack of printouts over, and run the pages through the printer again to print even page sides.

- **Application-specific options.** The particular program you're using may add a few extra options of its own to this dialog box. Figure 13-7 shows a few examples from Internet Explorer's Print dialog box.

When you've finished making changes to the print job, click OK or Print, or press Enter. Thanks to the miracle of *background printing*, you don't have to wait for the document to emerge from the printer before returning to work on your PC. In fact, you can even exit the application while the printout is still under way, generally speaking.

Tip: You'll probably never want to turn off background printing. But if you must for some technical reason, you'll find the on/off switch in the Advanced Properties dialog box for your printer (see Figure 13-10 for instructions on getting there). Select "Print directly to the printer" to turn off background printing.

POWER USERS' CLINIC

Printing from a DOS Program

Windows programs don't need any special setup steps to print. But if you want to print from a DOS application, you must first tell it which port your printer is connected to.

To do so, find the printing options menu. There you'll be able to tell the software the name of the port to which your printer is connected (usually LPT1).

Unfortunately, the commands required to print are unique to each DOS program; knowing them is up to you.

Printing from the Desktop

You don't necessarily have to print a document while it's open in front of you. You can, if you wish, print it directly from the desktop—via an open disk or folder window, or Windows Explorer, for example—in any of three ways:

- Right-click the document icon, and then choose Print from the shortcut menu. Windows launches the program that created it—Word or Excel, for example. The Print dialog box appears, so that you can specify how many copies you want and which pages you want printed. When you click Print, your printer springs into action, and then the program quits automatically (if it wasn't already open).

- If you've opened the Printers and Faxes window, you can drag a document's icon directly onto a printer icon.

- If you've opened the printer's own print queue window (Figure 13-8) by double-clicking the Printers icon in your Printers and Faxes window, you can drag any document icon directly into the list of waiting printouts. Its name joins the others on the list.

These last two methods bypass the Print dialog box, and therefore give you no way to specify which pages you want to print, nor how many copies. You just get one copy of the entire document.

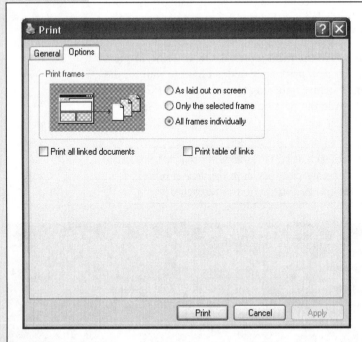

Figure 13-7:
The Web page about to be printed uses frames (individual, independent, rectangular sections). The Print dialog box in Internet Explorer recognizes frames, and lets you specify exactly which frame or frames you want to print. If the page contains links to other Web pages (and these days, what Web page doesn't?), you can print those Web pages, too, or just print a table of the links (a list of the URL addresses).

Printing from the Internet

If you use Internet Explorer to browse the Web (see Chapter 11), the Print dialog box offers a tab called Options, which contains a few special features for printing Web pages. Figure 13-7 illustrates a few of them.

Controlling Printouts

Between the moment when you click OK in the Print dialog box and the arrival of the first page in the printer's tray, there's a delay. When printing a complex document with lots of graphics, the delay can be considerable.

Fortunately, the waiting doesn't necessarily make you less productive, since you can return to work on your PC, or even quit the application and go watch TV. An invisible program called the *print spooler* supervises this background printing process. The spooler collects the document that's being sent to the printer, along with all the codes the printer expects to receive, and then sends this information, little by little, to the printer.

Note: The spooler program creates huge temporary printer files, so a hard drive that's nearly full can wreak havoc with background printing.

To see the list of documents waiting to be printed—the ones that have been stored by the spooler—open the Printers and Faxes window, and then double-click your printer's icon to open its window.

Tip: While the printer is printing, a printer icon appears in the notification area. As a shortcut to opening the printer's window, just double-click that icon.

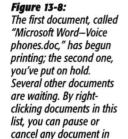

Figure 13-8:
The first document, called "Microsoft Word–Voice phones.doc," has begun printing; the second one, you've put on hold. Several other documents are waiting. By right-clicking documents in this list, you can pause or cancel any document in the queue–or all of them at once.

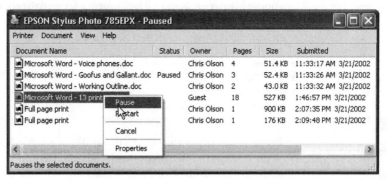

Document Name	Status	Owner	Pages	Size	Submitted
Microsoft Word - Voice phones.doc		Chris Olson	4	51.4 KB	11:33:17 AM 3/21/2002
Microsoft Word - Goofus and Gallant.doc	Paused	Chris Olson	3	52.4 KB	11:33:26 AM 3/21/2002
Microsoft Word - Working Outline.doc		Chris Olson	2	43.0 KB	11:33:32 AM 3/21/2002
Microsoft Word - 13 print		Guest	18	527 KB	1:46:57 PM 3/21/2002
Full page print		Chris Olson	1	900 KB	2:07:35 PM 3/21/2002
Full page print		Chris Olson	1	176 KB	2:09:48 PM 3/21/2002

EPSON Stylus Photo 785EPX - Paused

Printer Document View Help

Pause
Restart
Cancel
Properties

Pauses the selected documents.

The printer's window lists the documents currently printing and waiting; this list is called the *print queue* (or just the *queue*), as shown in Figure 13-8. (Documents in the list print in top-to-bottom order.)

You can manipulate documents in a print queue in any of the following ways during printing:

- **Put one on hold.** To pause a document (put it on hold), right-click its name and choose Pause from the shortcut menu. When you're ready to let the paused document continue to print, right-click its listing and reselect Pause to turn off the checkmark.

- **Put them all on hold.** To pause the printer, choose Printer→Pause Printing from the printer window menu bar. You might do this when, for example, you need to change the paper in the printer's tray. (Choose Printer→Pause Printing again when you want the printing to pick up from where it left off.)

Note: You can also pause the printer by right-clicking its icon in the Printers and Faxes window and choosing Pause Printing from the shortcut menu. (To undo this procedure, right-click the icon and choose Resume Printing.)

- **Add another one.** As noted earlier, you can drag any document icon directly *from its disk or folder window* into the printer queue. Its name joins the list of printouts-in-waiting.

- **Cancel one.** To cancel a printout, click its name and then press the Delete key—or, alternatively, right-click its name and choose Cancel from the shortcut menu. Either way, if you click Yes in the confirmation box, the document disappears from the queue; now it'll never print out.

- **Cancel all of them.** To cancel the printing of all the documents in the queue, choose Printer→Cancel All Documents. (Alternatively, right-click the printer icon itself in the Printers and Faxes window and choose Cancel All Documents from the shortcut menu, as shown in Figure 13-4.)

Note: A page or so may still print after you've paused or canceled a printout. The explanation: Your printer has its own memory (the *buffer*), which stores the printout as it's sent from your PC. If you pause or cancel printing, you're only stopping the spooler from sending *more* data to the printer.

- **Rearrange them.** If you're used to, say, Windows Me, it may take you a moment—or an afternoon—to figure out why you can't simply drag documents up or down in the list of waiting printouts to rearrange their printing order. In Windows XP, the procedure is slightly more involved.

Start by right-clicking the name of one of the printouts-in-waiting; from the shortcut menu, choose Properties. On the General tab, drag the Priority slider left or right (documents with higher priorities print first).

Fancy Printer Tricks

The masses of Windows users generally slog through life, choosing File→Print, clicking OK, and then drumming their fingers as they wait for the paper to slide out of the printer. But your printer can do more than that—much more. Here are just a few of the stunts that await the savvy PC fan.

Printing at 39,000 Feet

Printing any document is really a two-step procedure. First, Windows converts the document into a seething mass of printer codes in the form of a *spool file* on your hard drive. Second, it feeds that mass of code to the printer.

When you're not connected to your printer—for example, when you're sitting in seat 23B several miles over Detroit—you can separate these two tasks. You can do the time-consuming part of the printing operation (creating the spool files) right there on the plane. Then, later, upon your happy reunion with the printer, you can simply unleash the flood of stored spool files, which will print very quickly.

To set this up, right-click the icon for your printer in the Printers and Faxes window (Figure 13-4). From the shortcut menu, choose Pause Printing. That's all there is to it. Now you can merrily "print" your documents, 100 percent free of error messages. Windows quietly stores all the half-finished printouts as files on your hard drive.

When the printer is reconnected to your machine, right-click its icon once again—but this time, choose Resume Printing from its shortcut menu. You'll find that the printer springs to life almost immediately, spewing forth your stored printouts with impressive speed.

Sharing a Printer

If you have more than one PC connected to a network, as described in Chapter 18, they all can use the same printer. In the old days, this convenience was restricted to expensive Ethernet network printers like laser printers. But in Windows XP, you can share even the cheapest little inkjet that's connected to the USB port of one computer.

To begin, sit down at the computer to which the printer is attached. In the Printers and Faxes window, right-click the printer's icon and, from the shortcut menu, choose Sharing. Proceed as described in Figure 13-9.

Once you've *shared* the printer, other people on the network can add it to their own Printers and Faxes windows like this:

1. **In the Printers and Faxes window, click "Add a printer" in the task pane at the left side.**

   The Add a Printer Wizard appears, exactly as described earlier in this chapter.

2. **Click Next. On the second screen, click the bottom option: "A network printer, or a printer attached to another computer." Click Next.**

Now you're asked to locate the printer that's been shared. If you're like most people, you'll want to *browse* for it (choose it from a list). If you're a geek, you can click the second button and then type the printer's *UNC code* (page 566). And if you're geeky beyond belief, you can use the third option, which lets you send your printouts to a printer *somewhere else on the Internet.* (The downside: Bringing the printouts back to your desk can take days.)

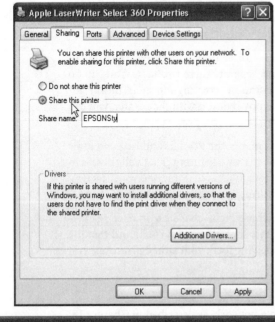

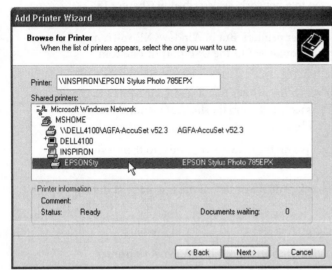

Figure 13-9:
Top: Turn on "Share this printer," and then give the printer a name in the Share name text box. (No spaces or punctuation allowed—and keep it short.) Click OK. The printer is now available on your network.

Bottom: Other people, seated at their own computers, can now bring your printer onto their own screens. (If the other PCs aren't running Windows XP, click the Additional Drivers button on the Sharing tab and turn on the checkboxes for the Windows versions they are using.)

3. Select "Connect to this printer (or browse for a printer)," and then click Next. On the screen that appears, click the name of the printer you want, as shown in Figure 13-9 at bottom.

On the final screens of the wizard, you'll be asked if you want this printer to be your default (primary) printer. After answering, click the Finish button to close the wizard. The shared printer now appears in your Printers and Faxes folder, even though it's not directly connected to your machine.

Printing to a File

When it comes to printing, most of the time you probably think of printing onto paper. In certain circumstances, however, you may not actually want a printout. Instead, you might want to create an electronic printer file on your hard drive, which can be printed later. You might want to do so, for example, when:

- You're working on a document at home, and you've got only a cheesy $49 inkjet printer. By creating a printer file, you can delay printing until tomorrow, in order to use the office's $4,000 color laser printer.

- You plan to send your finished work to a service bureau—that is, a professional typesetting shop. Sending a finished printer file avoids incompatibilities of applications, fonts, layout programs, and so on.

- You want to give a document to someone who doesn't have the program you used to create it, but has the same printer. If you email the *printer file* to her, she'll get to see your glorious design work slide out of her printer nonetheless.

Creating a printer file

To create such a printer file, choose File→Print, just as you would print any document. The Print dialog box appears; now turn on the "Print to file" option. When you then click OK or Print, the Print to File dialog box opens. It resembles the standard Save As dialog box, in that you can choose a drive, a folder, and a filename. The file type for a document printing to a file is a Printer File, which has the file extension *.prn*.

Printing a printer file

To print a printer file, choose Start→All Programs→Accessories→Command Prompt. You've just started an MS-DOS command session; your cursor is blinking on the command line.

Now type this:

copy *c:\foldername\filename*.prn lpt1: /b

Here's how this instruction breaks down:

- **Copy** is the name of the command you use to print the file—notice that it's followed by a space.

- **C:** is the letter of the drive that contains your printer file. Omit this part if the printer file is on the current drive (usually C:).

- **\foldername** is the name of the folder into which you saved the printer file.

- **\filename** is the name you gave the file.

- **.prn** is the filename extension (which Windows added to the file automatically when you saved the printer file).

- **lpt1:** is the port to which the printer is connected. Note the colon following the name, and also note there's a space *before* this part of the command. If the printer is attached to LPT2, substitute that port name.

- **/b** tells the Copy command that the file is *binary* (containing formatting and other codes), not simply text.

Note: A printer file (a *.prn* file) can only be printed on the same model that was selected in the Print dialog box when the file was generated. If you want to create a printer file for that color printer at work, in other words, be sure to first install its driver on your computer.

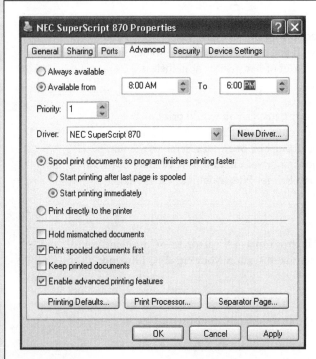

Figure 13-10:
Right-click your printer's icon in the Printers and Faxes window. From the shortcut menu, choose Properties, then click the Advanced tab, shown here. Select "Available from," and use the time setting controls to specify when your underlings are allowed to use this printer from across the network. Clicking OK renders the printer inoperable during off-hours.

Limiting Hours of Access

If it's just you, your Dell, and a color inkjet, then you're entitled to feel baffled by this feature, which lets you declare your printer off-limits during certain hours of the day. But if you're the manager of some office whose expensive color laser printer makes printouts that cost a dollar apiece, you may welcome a feature that prevents employees from hanging around after hours in order to print out 500 copies of their head shots.

To specify such an access schedule for a certain printer, follow the instructions in Figure 13-10.

POWER USERS' CLINIC

Color Management

As you may have discovered through painful experience, computers aren't great with color. That's because each device you use to create and print digital images "sees" color a little bit differently, which explains why the deep amber captured by your scanner may be rendered as brownish on your monitor, but come out as a bit or-angey on your Epson inkjet printer. Since every gadget defines and renders color in its own way, colors are often inconsistent as a print job moves from design to proof to press.

The Windows *color management system* (CMS) attempts to sort out this mess, serving as a translator among all the different pieces of hardware in your workflow. For this to work, each device (scanner, monitor, printer, copier, and so on) must be calibrated with a unique *CMS profile*—a file that tells your PC exactly how your particular monitor (or scanner, or printer, or digital camera) defines colors. Armed with the knowledge contained within the profiles, the CMS software can make on-the-fly color corrections, compensating for the various quirks of the different devices.

Most of the people who lose sleep over color fidelity do commercial color scanning and printing, where "off" colors are a big deal—after all, a customer might return a product after discovering, for example, that the actual product color doesn't match the photo on a Web site. Furthermore, not every gadget comes with a CMS profile, and not every gadget can even accommodate one (if yours does, you'll see a tab called Color Management in the Properties dialog box for your printer, as shown here).

If you're interested in this topic, open the Color Management tab for your printer. The Automatic setting usually means that Windows came with its own profile for your printer, which it has automatically assigned. If you click Manual, you can override this decision and apply a new color profile (that you downloaded from the printer company's Web site, for example).

Remember to follow the same procedure for the other pieces of your color chain—monitors, scanners, and so on. Look for the Color Management tab or dialog box, accessible from their respective Properties dialog boxes.

CHAPTER 13: PRINTING, FONTS, AND FAXING

405

Add a Separator Page

If your PC is on a network whose other members bombard a single laser printer with printouts, you might find *separator pages* useful—the printer version of fax cover sheets. A separator page is generated before each printout, identifying the document and its owner.

This option, too, is accessible from the Advanced tab of the printer's Properties dialog box (Figure 13-10). Click the Separator Page button at the bottom of the dialog box. In the Separator Page dialog box, click the Browse button to choose a *.sep* (separator page) file.

You'll see that Windows XP comes with four of them:

- **Sysprint.sep** is the one you probably want. Not only does this page include the name, date, time, and so on, but it also automatically switches the laser printer to PostScript mode—if it's not already in that mode.

- **Pcl.sep** is the same idea, except that it switches the laser printer to PCL mode— commonly found on HP printers—before printing. (PostScript and PCL are the two most common languages understood by office laser printers.)

- **Pscript.sep** switches the printer to PostScript mode, but doesn't print out a separator page.

- **Sysprtj.sep** prints a separator page, switches the printer to PostScript mode, and sets Japanese fonts, if they're available on your printer.

Save Printouts for Later

Ordinarily, each printout travels from your PC into a temporary holding file on the hard drive (the spool file), gets fed from there to the printer, and then disappears forever.

But sometimes it can be useful to keep the spool files on hand for use later. Maybe you print standard contracts all the time, or price lists, or restaurant menus. It's much faster to reprint something directly from the spool file than to open the original document and print it again from scratch.

The key to making Windows hang onto your already-printed documents is in the Advanced tab of the printer's Properties dialog box (see Figure 13-10). Just turn on "Keep printed documents."

From now on, every time you generate a printout, Windows maintains a copy of it in the printer's window (the one that appears when you double-click the printer icon in the Printers and Faxes window; see Figure 13-8). To reprint a document you've already printed, right-click its name in this list and choose Restart from the shortcut menu. (If you do this frequently, consider dragging the printer icon to your desktop, to the Start menu, or to the Quick Launch toolbar so that it will be easier to open the next time around.)

Tip: Behind the scenes, Windows XP stores these saved printouts in the Local Disk (C:)→Windows→ System32→Spool→Printers folder. Over time, all of your saved printouts can consume quite a bit of disk space. It's worth opening up that folder now and then to clean out the ones you no longer need.

Printer Troubleshooting

If you're having a problem printing, the first diagnosis you must make is whether the problem is related to *software* or *hardware*. A software problem means the driver files have become damaged. A hardware problem means there's something wrong with the printer, the port, or the cable.

Test the printer by sending it a generic text file from the command line. (Printing a regular printer disk file isn't an effective test, because if there's a problem with the driver, the codes in the file are likely to contain the problem.) To perform such a test, locate a text file, or create one in Notepad (page 199). Then choose Start→All Programs→Accessories→Command Prompt; send the file to the printer by typing *copy filename.txt prn* and then pressing Enter. (Of course, remember to type the file's actual name and three-letter extension instead of *filename.txt*.)

If the file prints, the printing problem is software-related. If it doesn't work, the problem is hardware-related.

For software problems, reinstall the printer driver by opening the Printers and Faxes window, right-clicking the printer's icon, and choosing Delete from the shortcut menu. Then reinstall the printer as described at the beginning of this chapter.

If the problem seems to be hardware-related, try these steps in sequence:

- Check the lights or the LED panel readout on the printer. If you see anything besides the normal "Ready" indicator, check the printer's manual to diagnose the problem.

- Turn the printer off and on to clear any memory problems.

- Check the printer's manual to learn how to print a test page.

- Check the cable to make sure both ends are firmly and securely plugged into the correct ports.

- Test the cable. Use another cable, or take your cable to another computer/printer combination.

Another way to check all of these conditions is to use the built-in Windows *trouble-shooter*—a wizard specifically designed to help you solve printing problems. To run, choose Start→Help and Support. In the Help center, click "Printing and faxing," and on the next screen, click "Fixing a printing problem." Finally, click "Printing Troubleshooter."

If none of these steps leads to an accurate diagnosis, you may have a problem with the port, which is more complicated. Or even worse, the problem may originate from your PC's motherboard (main circuit board), or the printer's. In that case, your computer (or printer) needs professional attention.

Fonts

Some extremely sophisticated programming has gone into the typefaces that are listed in the Fonts dialog boxes of your word processor and other programs. They use *OpenType* and *TrueType* technology, meaning that no matter what point size you select for these fonts, they look smooth and professional—both on the screen and when you print.

Figure 13-11:
All of your fonts sit in the Fonts folder (top); you'll frequently find an independent font file for each style of a font: bold, italic, bold italic, and so on. You can tell a TrueType font by its TT icon, or an OpenType font by its O icon. Those marked by an A may be PostScript fonts, which come with a phalanx of the printer font files that they require; others may look fine on the screen, but may not print out smoothly. Double-click a font's icon to see what the font looks like (bottom).

Managing Your Fonts

Windows XP comes with several dozen great-looking OpenType and TrueType fonts: Arial, Book Antiqua, Times New Roman, and so on. But the world is filled with additional fonts. You may find them on the CD-ROMs that come with PC magazines, on Windows software Web sites, or in the catalogs of commercial typeface companies. Sometimes you'll find new fonts on your system after installing a new program, courtesy of its installer.

To review the files that represent your typefaces, open the Fonts icon in the Control Panel.

Tip: The Fonts icon in your Control Panel window is only a shortcut to the *real* folder, which is in your Local Disk (C:)→Windows→Fonts folder.

When you open the Fonts folder, you'll see that for every font that appears in the Font menus of your various programs, there's an icon on your hard drive—or several. As Figure 13-11 illustrates, it's easy and enlightening to explore this folder.

To remove a font from your system, simply drag its file icon out of this window, right-click it and then choose Delete from the shortcut menu, or highlight it and then choose File→Delete. To install a new font, drag its file icon into this window (or choose File→Install New Font, and then navigate to, and select, the font files you want to install).

Either way, you'll see the changes immediately reflected in your programs' Font dialog boxes.

Tip: Some fonts appear in your menus, but *not* in your Fonts menu. These are the fonts that Windows uses in its menus, windows, and dialog boxes (Courier, MS Sans Serif, Small Fonts, Symbol, and so on). If you accidentally remove or move any of these fonts, Windows will substitute something that doesn't look right, and you'll wonder what the heck is going on with the typography of your programs. That's why, unless you've turned on the "Show hidden files" option (page 89), these files are invisible in the Fonts folder.

Faxing

It's a good thing you bought a book about Windows XP. If you hadn't, you might never have known about one of Windows XP's most spectacular features: its ability to turn your PC's built-in fax modem into a fax machine. This feature works like a charm, saves all kinds of money on paper and fax cartridges, and may even spare you the expense of buying a physical fax machine—but it isn't installed in the standard Windows installation.

Here's the basic idea: When faxes come in, you can opt to have them printed automatically, or you can simply read them on the screen. And sending a fax is even easier on a PC than on a real fax machine; you just use the regular File→Print command, exactly as though you're making a printout of the onscreen document.

If this sounds good to you, grab your Windows XP CD-ROM and read on.

Installing the Fax Software

To turn on the hidden fax feature, open your Printers and Faxes window (page 393), and then click "Set up faxing" on the task pane on the left side (Figure 13-12, left). After a moment, you'll be asked to insert your Windows XP Professional CD.

Tip: When the big blue "Welcome to Microsoft Windows XP" screen appears, just click its close button. It's obscuring the *real* action in the Configuring Components dialog box behind it.

When the installation is over, you'll find a new Fax icon in your Printers and Faxes folder (Figure 13-12, right). You'll also find a few fax utilities in your Start→All Programs→Accessories→Communications→Fax submenu, which you can read about in the following sections.

Note: Upgrading your PC to Windows XP from an earlier version of Windows enables you to import your old fax collection into the newer software. For instructions, choose Start→All Programs→Accessories→Communications→Fax→Fax Console. Choose Help→Help Topics, and read the help topics under the first headline ("Fax after upgrading to Windows XP").

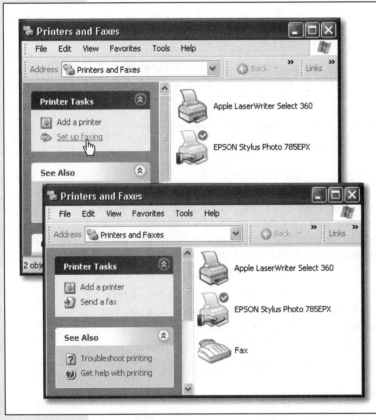

Figure 13-12:
Top: In the Printers and Faxes window, click the "Set up faxing" link on the task pane at the left side of the window. Insert the Windows XP Professional CD when the wizard asks you to do so.

Bottom: The Fax icon is added to the Printers and Faxes window, ready to use.

Getting Ready to Fax

Before you fax, choose Start→All Programs→Accessories→Communications→Fax→Fax Configuration Wizard (or choose Tools→Configure Fax from the Fax

Console window). You'll be treated to the Fax Configuration Wizard, whose screens walk you through these steps:

- **Filling in your own name, email address, fax number, address, and other information.** This information will appear on your fax cover sheet, so that the lucky recipient can contact you if the fax didn't come through. (*All* of this information is optional.)

- **Choosing the fax device.** This drop-down list is provided solely for the convenience of those rich people who actually have more than one fax modem on their PCs.

  There are two useful checkboxes here for everyone, however: Enable Send and Enable Receive. The ability to send faxes is a no-brainer. But not everybody wants their PC to *receive* faxes; see "Receiving a Fax" on page 414.

- **Specifying your own fax number.** Microsoft calls this the *TSID* (transmitting subscriber identification) information—the name and fax number that will appear on the screen of the receiving fax machine.

- **Specifying your fax number again.** You see this screen only if you indicated that you want your PC to receive faxes. Once again, you're supposed to enter your name and fax number, which will appear on the screen of the *sending* fax machine during transmission.

Figure 13-13:
If "Use dialing rules" is turned off, then just type the entire fax number, complete with the area code, the number 1 for long distance, and so on, into the second "Fax number" box. Commas, parentheses, and dashes are irrelevant. But if you turn on "Use dialing rules," you can choose one of the canned dialing setups—complete with calling card information, bizarre local area code dialing procedures, and so on— that you set up as described on page 320.

- **Choosing a fax destination.** Here again, you see this screen only if you've declared that you want your PC to receive faxes. Windows gives you the option of having incoming faxes automatically printed, or stored as graphics files in a certain folder. (This option stores a *second* copy of each fax as a file; each fax is automatically stored in the Inbox of Fax Console, which is described later.)

The final wizard screen displays a summary of the settings you've made. Click the Finish button, and you're all set. You can change the settings at any time, just by running the wizard again.

Sending a Fax

The one big limitation of PC-based faxing is that you can only transmit documents that are, in fact, *on the computer.* That pretty much rules out faxing notes scribbled on a legal pad, clippings from *People* magazine, and so on (unless you scan them first).

If you're still undaunted, the procedure for sending a fax is very easy. Just open up whatever document you want to fax. Choose File→Print. In the Print dialog box, click the Fax icon (or choose Fax from the Name drop-down list), and then click OK or Print.

Now the Send Fax Wizard appears. This is where you can type in the phone number of the fax machine you're trying to reach (Figure 13-13)—or click Address Book to select the fax machine of somebody in your address book.

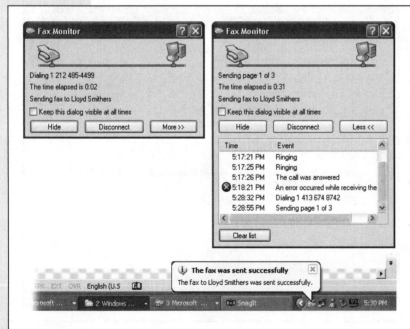

Figure 13-14:
Top left: The Fax Monitor keeps you posted during faxing. If you click More>>, you can see a log of all your fax activities (top right). The more you use the fax software, the less you may feel that you need this little window in your face—eventually, you may prefer to continue working while Windows does its faxing in the background. In that case, click Hide.

Bottom: After you've faxed successfully, you hear a tiny trumpet fanfare and see this message on your notification area.

Click Next. On the second wizard screen, you can opt to precede the fax with a cover page. This screen also gives you a place to type in a subject line and a little note, if you like, which will also appear on the cover page.

When you click Next again, Windows asks *when* you want the fax sent. Most of the time, of course, you'll just accept the proposed choice—Now—and click Next. But if you work in an office where the fax line is busy all the time, you can schedule your fax to go out at a specified time ("Specific time in the next 24 hours") or "When discount rates apply."

Cover Page Art Class

You don't have to be content with the handful of fax cover pages that Microsoft provides. The Fax Console program comes with its own little cover page design studio. To get started, choose Tools→Personal Cover Pages.

At this point, you could click the New button to call up a pure, empty, virginal cover page. But by far the easiest way to get going is to open one of the existing cover pages, make changes to it, and then save it under a different name.

To do so, click the Copy button now in front of you, and then open one of the four cover page templates that Windows presents. Windows puts it into what's now a one-item list in the Personal Cover Pages window. Click Rename to give it a new name, if you like, and then click Open to begin work on your redesign. (You'll see a "Did you know?" Tips window; read the tips, if you like, and then click OK.)

The design program works like any standard drawing program. In order to type text that won't change—a confidentiality notice, for example—click the Text tool on the toolbar (which looks like this: **ab|**), and then click on the page. Use the commands in the Insert menu to plop placeholder text boxes onto the page—special rectangles that, on the actual cover sheet, will be filled by your name, fax number, the number of pages, and so on. You can transfer your own company logo onto the page just by pasting it there (Edit→Paste).

Every item that you place on the page—a text block, a graphic, and so on—is a separate object that you can move around independently using the arrow tool. In fact, you can even move a selected object in front of, or behind, other objects, using the commands in the Layout menu.

When you're finished with your masterpiece, choose File→Save As, and type a new name for it. It gets saved into your My Documents→Fax→Personal Cover pages folder (meaning that only you have access to it—not other people who share the PC and log in with their own accounts).

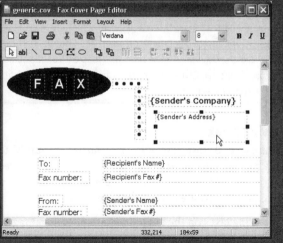

Note: "When discount rates apply" is a lame-duck holdover from the days when long distance companies charged more during business hours. If this still matters to you, however, you must first tell Windows *when* discount rates apply. To do so, right-click the Fax icon in your Printers and Faxes window; choose Properties. Click the Devices tab, click the Properties button, and use the "Discount rates start" and "Discount rates stop" controls to specify your window of opportunity.

On the final wizard screen, you can simply click Finish to send the fax. However, you may want to click the Preview Fax button to give it a final inspection before it goes forth over the airwaves. When you're finished looking it over, close the window and then click Finish.

After a moment, a little window appears called Fax Monitor (Figure 13-14). It keeps you posted on the progress of the fax.

Your recipient is in for a real treat. Faxes you send straight from your PC's brain emerge at the receiving fax machine looking twice as crisp and clean as faxes sent from a stand-alone fax machine. After all, you never scanned them through a typical fax machine's crude scanner on your end.

Tip: If you just have a few quick words to fax to somebody, you can use the Send Fax Wizard by itself, without first opening a document on your PC. Choose Start→All Programs→Accessories→Communications→Fax→Send a Fax. Fill in your recipient's phone number, click Next, and on the Preparing the Cover Page screen, type your memo to the recipient into the Note field. Windows will send only the cover page, complete with your note.

Receiving a Fax

There are several reasons why you may *not* want your PC to receive faxes. Maybe you already have a stand-alone fax machine that you use for receiving them. Maybe your house only has one phone line, whose number you don't want to give out to people who might blast your ear with fax tones.

But receiving faxes on the PC has a number of advantages, too. You don't pay a cent for paper or ink cartridges, for example, and you have a handy, organized software program that helps you track every fax you've ever received.

Exactly what happens when a fax comes in is up to you. As noted earlier, you can make this decision by running the Fax Configuration Wizard, or by opening the dialog box shown in Figure 13-15, to change its behavior at any time.

Here are your options (see Figure 13-15):

- **Manual.** This option is an almost-perfect solution if your PC and your telephone share the same phone line—that is, if you use the line mostly for talking, but occasionally receive a fax. From now on, every time the phone rings, a balloon in your notification area announces: "The line is ringing. Click here to answer this call as a fax call" (Figure 13-15, middle).

When you do so, the Fax monitor program appears and downloads the fax. To see it, open your Fax Console program, described on page 410.

- **Answer automatically.** Use this option if your PC has a phone line all to itself. In this case, incoming faxes produce a telephone-ringing sound, but there's otherwise no activity on your screen until the fax has been safely received (Figure 13-15, bottom). Once again, received faxes secrete themselves away in your Fax Console program.

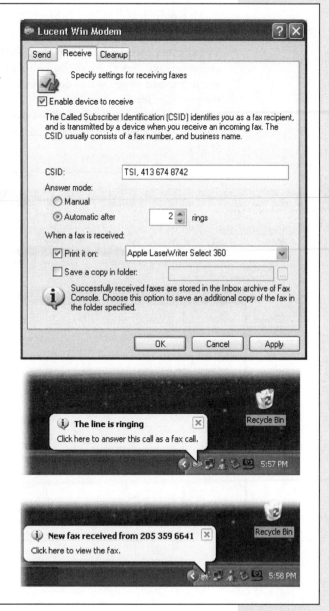

Figure 13-15:
Top: This dialog box offers all of the options for receiving faxes. Getting here, however, is no picnic. Right-click the Fax icon in your Printers and Faxes window; choose Properties. Click the Devices tab, and then click the Properties button. In the resulting dialog box, click the Receive tab.

Middle: If you have only one phone line that your telephone shares, this note will appear every time a call comes in. Most of the time, you'll just answer the phone, and this message goes away. If you click it, though, your PC treats the call as an incoming fax.

Bottom: Once a fax is safely snuggled into your Fax Console program, this note lets you know.

- **Print it out.** If you like, you can direct Windows to print out each incoming fax, using the printer you specify here. Of course, doing so defeats the environmental and cost advantages of viewing your faxes on the screen, but at least you've got something you can hold in your hand.

- **Save a copy in a folder.** Ordinarily, incoming faxes are transferred to your Fax Console program, as described next. If you turn on this option, however, you can direct Windows to place a *duplicate* copy of each one—stored as a graphics file—in a folder of your choice. (Either way, it's handy to know that these are standard TIFF graphics files that you can email to somebody else—or even edit.)

To look at the faxes you've received, you must first launch the Fax Console program. You can get to it by choosing Start→All Programs→Accessories→Communications→Fax→Fax Console, but your fingers will be bloody stumps by the time you're finished mousing that deeply into the menu. Fortunately, once you've opened the program for the first time, it appears in the lower-left quadrant of your Start menu. From there, you can drag its name to a more convenient location, like the desktop, the Quick Launch toolbar, or the more permanent top *left* portion of your Start menu.

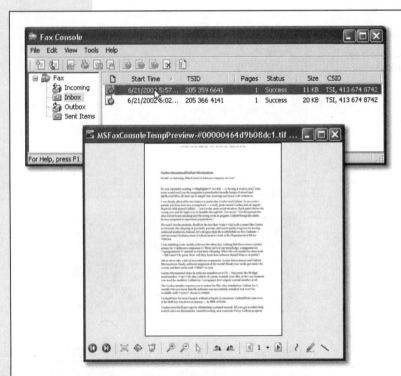

Figure 13-16:

Top: Until you delete them in Fax Console (by selecting them and then pressing the Delete key), your sent and received faxes stay here forever. Some of the toolbar buttons are useful, including Save (turns the fax into a graphics file on your hard drive) and Mail (sends the fax via email).

Bottom: Double-click a fax to open it into its own window. Click the little magnifying glass to enlarge your view, or just make the window bigger. Rotate it by clicking one of the two rotate buttons near the center of the toolbar. You can even add notes using the three tools on the far right side.

In any case, Fax Console looks something like an email program, as shown in Figure 13-16. Click the Inbox, for example, to see a list of faxes that have come in—and then double-click one to open it up (Figure 13-16, bottom).

Tip: Another great way to capitalize on the power of your PC for fax purposes is to sign up for J2 or eFax (*www.j2.com* and *www.efax.com*). These services issue you your own personal fax number. And here's the twist: All faxes sent to that number arrive at your PC as email attachments.

The brilliance of the system, of course, is that you don't need another phone line for this, and you can get these faxes anywhere in the world, even on the road. And here's the best part: As of this writing, both of these services are absolutely free. (You might consider reserving a separate email address just for your J2 or eFax account, however, since waves of junk mail are part of the "free" bargain.

Hardware

A PC contains several pounds of wires, slots, cards, and chips—enough hardware to open a TruValue store. Fortunately, you don't have to worry about making all of your PC's preinstalled components work together. In theory, at least, the PC maker did that part for you. (Unless you built the machine yourself, that is; in that case, best of luck.)

But adding *new* gear to your computer is another story. Hard drives, cameras, printers, scanners, network adapter cards, video cards, keyboards, monitors, game controllers, palmtop synchronization cradles, and other accessories can all make life worth living for the power user. When you introduce a new piece of equipment to the PC, you must hook it up and install its *driver*, the software that lets a new gadget talk to the rest of the PC.

UP TO SPEED

About Drivers

When a software program wants to communicate with your gear, Windows is the mediator. For example, when your word processor needs the printer, it says, "Yo, printer! Print this document, will ya?" Windows intercepts the message and gives the printer very specific instructions about printing, ejecting pages, making text bold, and so on. It speaks to the printer in "Printerese," a language it learns by consulting the printer's software driver.

Other hardware components work similarly, including sound cards, network interface cards (NICs), modems, scanners, and so on. All of them require specifically formatted instructions and driver software.

Fortunately, Microsoft has taken much of the headache out of such installation rituals by its invention of Plug and Play. This chapter guides you through using this feature—and counsels you on what to do when Plug and Play doesn't work.

Note: Chapter 13 contains additional hardware-installation details specific to printers.

The Master Compatibility List

Remember that Windows XP is based on Windows 2000. It's compatible with many more pieces of add-on equipment than Windows 2000 is, but nowhere near as broadly compatible as previous "home" versions of Windows (like Windows 98 and Windows Me). For anybody who's switching to Windows XP from an earlier version, discovering that a piece of equipment becomes flaky or nonfunctional is par for the course.

If you'd like to eliminate every glitch and every shred of troubleshooting inconvenience, limit your add-on gear to products on Microsoft's Hardware Compatibility List (HCL), which appears at *www.microsoft.com/hcl*. Each item on this list has been tested and certified to work flawlessly with Windows XP.

Now, this list doesn't include *everything* that works with Windows XP. Hundreds of products that work just fine with Windows XP don't appear on the list (perhaps because they haven't been submitted for Microsoft's certification process). If you have some cherished piece of gear that you're reluctant to replace and that doesn't appear on the compatibility list, try it out with Windows XP before giving up hope.

Tip: Many drivers that were certified for compatibility with Windows 2000 and Windows Me work with Windows XP. But if all you have for a particular gadget is Windows 98 (and earlier) driver software, you're probably out of luck.

Hardware Connections

Part of the installation process for a new piece of hardware is ensuring that it doesn't interfere with any of your *other* components (see the box on the facing page). Fortunately, Microsoft's Plug and Play technology is designed to avoid such conflicts.

Virtually every modern computer add-on is Plug and Play–compatible. (Look for a "Designed for Windows" logo on the box.) Chances are good that you'll live a long and happy life with Windows XP without ever having to lose a Saturday to manually configuring new gizmos you buy for it, as your forefathers did.

But gadgets that were designed before the invention of Plug and Play are another story. These so-called *legacy* devices often require manual configuration. Fortunately, Windows XP comes with wizards to walk you through this process, making it slightly less difficult.

Installing Cards in Expansion Slots

When installing a new piece of hardware, you either connect it to a *port* (a connector usually on the back of your computer) or insert it into an expansion slot on the *motherboard* (the computer's main circuit board).

Modems and adapter cards for video, sound, network cabling, disk drives, and tape drives, for example, generally take the form of circuit boards, or *cards*, that you install by inserting into an expansion slot inside your PC's case. These slots are connected to your PC's *bus,* an electrical conduit that connects all the components of the machine to the brains of the outfit: the processor and memory.

The two common (and mutually incompatible) kinds of slots are called *ISA* and *PCI.* The ISA bus (Industry Standard Architecture) has been around since the dawn of the PC in the early 1980s. PCI (Peripheral Component Interconnect) is comparatively new, and offers much better speed. Most of the computers in use today have both kinds of slots. There may be some museum pieces floating around that have only ISA slots inside; in fact some manufacturers have begun to eliminate ISA slots from their new computers, relying completely on PCI.

There's also a third type of slot in many of today's computers, called AGP (Accelerated Graphics Port). This slot is almost always occupied by a graphics card.

UP TO SPEED

Message Pathways

You're already familiar with one common routing system for messages: area codes and telephone numbers. Together, they pinpoint a unique location in the nation's telephone system.

To send instructional codes to your hardware, Windows needs a similar communication channel for each device. During installation, the operating system learns the location (phone number) of the hardware, plus the path (area code) its messages must take to arrive there.

But instead of area codes and phone numbers, PC components have unique channels called *IRQs* (Interrupt Request Lines), reserved areas of memory called *I/O addresses,* and other technical assignments that reserve their places in your system—or resources, as they're known in the geek business.

If your sound card occupies IRQ 11 and has an I/O address that starts at 6100, then Windows knows how to contact the card when your email software wants to play a

"You've got mail" sound, for example. If your printer also occupied those addresses, the operating system would send a sound code, the printer would become confused ("What am I supposed to do with this instruction? It has nothing to do with printing!"), and the sound card might not receive the "Wake up and make the music" command. And it's not enough to set just a hardware component to the right channels; their *drivers* must be tuned to those same channels, too, if they're to communicate.

Clearly, Windows needs a traffic cop to ensure that each hardware gadget receives the correct messages. That's one of the functions of Plug and Play technology.

After you install a Plug and Play device and start your computer, the new component tells Windows: "Hi, I'm new here. Here's my species, here's my name, here are the resources I'd like to use if they're free. If they're not free, please assign resources, and let me know what they are so I can listen for my orders on the right channel."

Knowing the characteristics of the different bus types isn't especially important. What is important is knowing what type of slots your computer has free, so you can purchase the correct type of expansion card. To do this, you'll have to open your PC's case to see which type of slots are empty:

- The plastic wall around an ISA slot is usually black. It has metal pins or teeth in the center and a small crossbar about two-thirds of the way down the slot. On some older computers, there may be shorter-length ISA slots with no divider.

- The plastic wall around a PCI slot is usually white or off-white, and shorter than an ISA slot. A PCI slot has a metal center and a crossbar about three-quarters of the way along its length.

Installing a card usually involves removing a narrow plate (the *slot cover*) from the back panel of your PC, which allows the card's connector to peek through to the outside world. After unplugging the PC and touching something metal to discharge static, unwrap the card and carefully push it into its slot until it's fully seated.

Note: Depending on the type of card, you may have to insert one end first and then press the other end down with considerable force to get it into the slot. A friendly suggestion, however: Don't press so hard that you flex and crack the motherboard.

External Attachments

When you buy a printer, scanner, digital camera, or something else that plugs into connectors on the PC, you're actually buying a *peripheral,* in the lingo of PC magazines and clubs everywhere. Over the years, various engineering organizations have devised an almost silly number of different connectors for these peripherals (Figure 14-1 shows a typical assortment). The back panel—or front, or even side panel—of your PC may include any of these connector varieties:

- **FireWire port.** You probably don't have the special, rectangle-with-one-V-shaped-end jack unless you special-ordered it with your PC, but it's a winner nevertheless. (Various companies may also call it IEEE-1394 or i.Link.) It's an extremely high-speed connector that's *hot-pluggable,* meaning that you don't have to turn the computer off when connecting or disconnecting it. At the moment, what most people plug into a FireWire port are digital camcorders (for video editing), and external hard drives.

- **USB (Universal Serial Bus) port.** This compact, thin, rectangular connector accommodates a huge variety of USB gadgets: scanners, mice, keyboards, printers, palmtop cradles, digital cameras, Zip drives, and so on. Most modern PCs come with two or more USB ports, often on both the front and back panels. If that's not enough to handle all your USB devices, you can also attach a USB *hub* (with, for example, four or eight additional USB ports), in order to attach multiple USB devices simultaneously. USB is the most modern type of connector and therefore gaining in popularity; all USB devices are Plug and Play–compatible and hot-pluggable, and feature a faster connection than their older counterparts.

Note: Some USB gadgets (and some PCs) offer faster, enhanced connectors called USB 2. The original version of Windows XP couldn't recognize them, but thanks to software patches, it does now. (Automatic Updates, described on page 300, should download the necessary software automatically, or you can just install it using the installation disk that comes with your USB 2.0 appliances.)

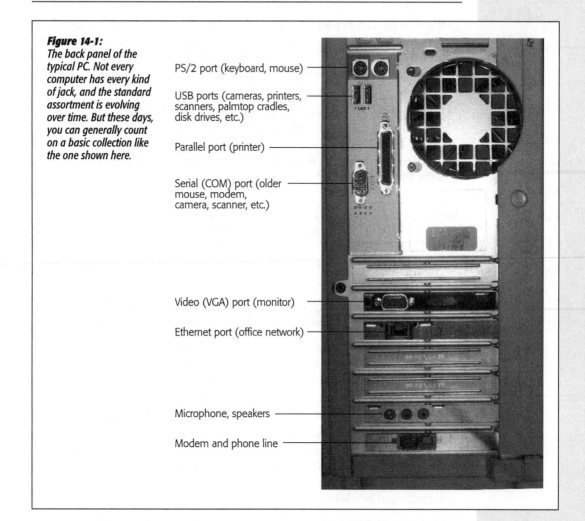

Figure 14-1:
The back panel of the typical PC. Not every computer has every kind of jack, and the standard assortment is evolving over time. But these days, you can generally count on a basic collection like the one shown here.

PS/2 port (keyboard, mouse)

USB ports (cameras, printers, scanners, palmtop cradles, disk drives, etc.)

Parallel port (printer)

Serial (COM) port (older mouse, modem, camera, scanner, etc.)

Video (VGA) port (monitor)

Ethernet port (office network)

Microphone, speakers

Modem and phone line

- **Bluetooth adapters.** Bluetooth is a fascinating new wireless technology. Don't think of it as a networking scheme—it's intended for the elimination of *cable clutter.* Once you've equipped your printer, PC, and Palm organizer with Bluetooth adapters, your computer can print to the printer, or HotSync with your Palm, from up to 30 feet away.

Note: The original version of Windows XP Pro didn't work with Bluetooth. Here again, however, Microsoft made XP Bluetooth-compatible via a software patch in late 2002. Once again, the Automatic Updates feature was supposed to notify you about it when it was ready—or you can just check *windowsupdate .microsoft.com* to see if it's available as a download.

- **Wireless (Infrared) port.** You'll find this kind of port most often on laptops. It lets your computer talk to similarly equipped gadgets (such as infrared-equipped printers, PalmPilots, and so on) through the air, via infrared or RF communication. An infrared port is a small, translucent plastic lens; RF ports look like little antennas.

- **PC card slot.** This kind of slot, too, is primarily found on laptops. It accommodates PC cards, which look like metal Visa cards. Each card adds a useful feature to your laptop: an Ethernet port, a modem, a wireless networking antenna, and so on. Expect this technology to be around for a while since there's currently no other alternative.

Tip: Because they're so new, *all* USB, FireWire, and PC card equipment is Plug and Play–compatible, meaning that you can install the necessary driver software simply by connecting a gadget to the PC.

- **Video (VGA) port.** A narrow female port with fifteen holes along three rows. Your monitor plugs in here.

- **Game Port.** This connector, which is usually part of a sound card, is a wide female port that accepts such gaming devices as joysticks and steering wheels.

- **SCSI port.** Here's another one that's fairly rare on everyday Windows workstation PCs (as opposed to industrial-strength *server* machines). You generally have an SCSI port only if it was installed as part of an add-on card. Unlike FireWire, though, its popularity is fading in the home market.

  SCSI is a high-speed internal and external bus that's more common on large servers than workstations. This kind of (there are various sizes and shapes) connector is designed to accommodate scanners, hard drives, CD-ROMs, magnetic tape drives, and so on. SCSI can be something of a diva technology, since setting up a chain of devices, connecting and disconnecting them, and configuring them correctly can be a fussy and temperamental business.

- **PS/2.** A small, round, female connector (known in PC circles as a *6-pin mini-DIN* connector). Not all PCs have PS/2 ports; but if yours does, it probably has two, one for the keyboard and the other for the mouse. As USB grows in popularity, these ports will vanish from new computers in the future.

- **Parallel (DB-25) port.** A wide female port with two rows of holes. It's usually connected to a printer (which is why it's sometimes called the printer port). You can plug some other kinds of equipment in here, including Zip or Jaz drives, tape drives, and other drives. Here again, parallel ports are dying out, having been replaced by the more popular (and much faster) USB ports.

- **Serial port.** A male connector with nine or 25 pins. It connects to a *serial device*, such as a mouse, modem, camera, scanner, or serial printer; it can also connect your PC to another one, port-to-port.

  Most computers have two serial ports, which are also called *COM* ports—but not for long. Serial ports, too, will probably also go the way of dinosaurs as USB ports take over the earth.

- **Keyboard port.** This round, 5-pin (DIN) female connector, similar to a PS/2 connector but larger, is becoming one of the rarest of all. It was designed to fit keyboards that don't use a PS/2 connection, and is yet another obsolete port in the USB era.

Connecting New Gadgets

In books, magazines, and online chatter about Windows, you'll frequently hear people talk about *installing* a new component. In many cases, they aren't talking about physically hooking it up to the PC—they're talking about installing its driver software.

The truth is that you generally have to install *both* the hardware and the software. The ritual goes like this:

1. **Run the installer on the setup disk, if one came with the new equipment.**

   Doing so copies the driver files to your hard drive, where Windows will be able to find it in the later steps of the installation.

2. **Physically connect the gadget.**

   That is, connect it to the inside or outside of the computer, according to the instructions that accompanied the equipment.

   The beauty of USB gadgets, FireWire gadgets, and PC cards is that they identify themselves to Windows XP the instant they're plugged in. For this kind of gizmo, there is no step 3.

   Other kinds of gear aren't so lucky. In general, you must turn off your PC before connecting or disconnecting components from other kinds of connectors. When you turn it on again (after hooking up the new gadget), Windows XP examines every connector, port, and slot on your machine, checking to see whether or not it's now occupied by a piece of equipment it hasn't seen before.

3. **Install the driver software into Windows.**

   If your new gear is Plug and Play–compatible (if its box bears a "Designed for Windows" logo, for example), then skip this step. The simple act of connecting the equipment inspires Windows to find the driver—either the one you copied to the drive in step 1, or one from its own database of drivers. (For *non*–Plug and Play gadgets, this step can require a considerable amount of effort, as described later in this chapter.)

Note: Windows XP comes with the driver software for thousands of different pieces of gear. It keeps many of these drivers, in compacted form, right there on your hard drive (in a file called Driver.cab). The Windows XP CD comes with hundreds of others.

All of these included drivers have been tested to work perfectly with Windows XP. Furthermore, Microsoft adds to this collection as new products appear, and sends you these new drivers via the Automatic Update feature described on page 300.

In either case, your gear is now completely installed—both its hardware and its software—and ready to use.

When Plug and Play Doesn't Work

If, when you connect a new component, Windows XP doesn't display a message like the one at top in Figure 14-2, it probably can't "see" your new device.

- If you've installed an internal card, make sure that it's seated in the slot firmly (after shutting down your computer, of course).

- If you attached something external, make sure that it has power and is correctly connected to the PC.

In either case, before panicking, try restarting the PC. If you still have no luck, try the Add New Hardware Wizard described in the next section. (And if even *that* doesn't work, call the manufacturer.)

If your new gadget didn't come with a disk (or maybe just a disk with drivers, but no installer), then hooking it up may produce the "Found New Hardware" balloon shown at top in Figure 14-2. Click the balloon to make the New Hardware Wizard appear (Figure 14-2, bottom). In that case, proceed like this:

- **If you have the drivers on a disk from the manufacturer.** Select the first option, "Install the software automatically," insert the driver disk if it's not already in the machine, and then click Next. Windows either finds the compatible driver and installs it automatically, or offers you a choice of several.

FREQUENTLY ASKED QUESTION

Using Manufacturer's Drivers for Plug and Play Devices

Windows XP finds my new Plug and Play device and installs it, but I don't want to use the Windows XP drivers. I have newer, better, drivers from the manufacturer. How can I stop the automated installation so I can use the better drivers?

You can't stop Plug and Play detection, but you *can* update the drivers after Windows XP has installed your new hardware. You do that in the Device Manager, described on page 431.

Tip: If you have drivers on a floppy, and this technique fails to find them, try the next option. The "Install from a list or specific location" option often works when the "Install the software automatically" choice doesn't.

• **If you've downloaded the driver from the Web.** Select the second option, "Install from a list or specific location," and click Next. You should now turn on both of the checkboxes shown in Figure 14-2, and then click the Browse button to navigate to, and select, the driver you downloaded.

Figure 14-2:
Top: You're halfway home. Windows XP has at least acknowledged that you've plugged something in. Click the balloon to proceed with the software installation (if you didn't install the software first, as you should have).

Bottom: The Found New Hardware Wizard. You'll rarely use the bottom option, "Don't search. I will choose the driver to install." It's primarily used to override Windows XP's own, preinstalled driver in favor of another one—for example, one that came from the original manufacturer that you've been told offers more features than the official Microsoft driver.

Note: If you run the Found Hardware Wizard but don't, in fact, have drivers of any kind to feed it, Windows offers you the opportunity to register a kind of electronic complaint—something like an emailed record of your unsuccessful driver search.

As the first screen of the Get Help with Your Hardware Device Wizard makes clear, receiving help entails sending details of your PC and its configuration to Microsoft. If enough people agree to send in reports in this way, Microsoft will put pressure on the negligent manufacturer, in hopes of one day producing an XP-compatible driver that will be sent back to your PC automatically (via the Automatic Updates feature).

Using the Add Hardware Wizard

The Add Hardware Wizard fulfills some of the functions of the Found New Hardware Wizard, but comes in handy in different circumstances. You can use it whenever Windows fails to notice that you've blessed it with new components, for example, or to update the original driver when a better one becomes available.

Begin by connecting the new gear (turning off the computer first, if necessary). Turn the machine on again and then open the Add Hardware Wizard program in the Control Panel (Chapter 9). Click Next to move past the Welcome screen.

The search for Plug and Play

The first thing the wizard wants to do is search for a Plug and Play device. You already know that it won't find one—after all, if the hardware you're trying to install were Plug and Play–compatible, Windows XP would have found it already.

Unfortunately, you can't stop the Hardware Wizard juggernaut. You have no choice but to click Next and proceed as outlined in the next section.

Add Hardware Wizard searches for non–Plug and Play devices

If the search for Plug and Play hardware fails, a new wizard window opens and asks you if the new equipment is already connected to the PC. If you answer no, the wizard closes—its subtle way of telling you that you were supposed to have connected the gadget before even opening the wizard.

FREQUENTLY ASKED QUESTION

Driver vs. Driver

Which is better: the drivers that come with Windows XP, or the drivers I've downloaded from the manufacturer's Web site?

In many cases, they're the same thing. The drivers included with Windows XP usually did come from the hardware's manufacturer, which gave them to Microsoft for inclusion with Windows. However, you should still use the drivers that came from your gadget's manufacturer whenever possible, especially if you got them from the manufacturer's Web site. They're likely to be newer versions than the ones that came with Windows XP.

If you select "Yes, I have already connected the hardware," on the other hand, you're taken to a list of every component that's already in your computer (Figure 14-3). Scroll to the very bottom of the list and select "Add a new hardware device." Click Next.

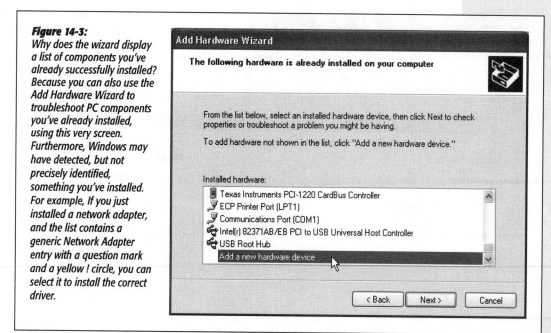

Figure 14-3:
Why does the wizard display a list of components you've already successfully installed? Because you can also use the Add Hardware Wizard to troubleshoot PC components you've already installed, using this very screen. Furthermore, Windows may have detected, but not precisely identified, something you've installed. For example, If you just installed a network adapter, and the list contains a generic Network Adapter entry with a question mark and a yellow ! circle, you can select it to install the correct driver.

Now the wizard asks you to make yet another decision:

- **Search for and install the hardware automatically.** If you choose this option and click Next, Windows makes yet another attempt to detect the new equipment and install its driver. If a happy little "Found New Hardware" balloon appears in your notification area, all is well; the wizard's work is done.

  If the search succeeds, you've saved a couple of keystrokes; if it fails, you move on to the second option anyway.

- **Install the hardware that I manually select from a list.** If you choose this option and click Next (or if the previous option fails), the wizard displays a list of device types (top left in Figure 14-4). From that list, find and select the type of hardware you want to install—"Imaging devices" for a digital camera or a scanner, for example, "PCMCIA adapters" for a PC card, and so on. (Click Show All Devices if you can't figure out which category to choose.)

  Then click Next. Now Windows XP opens a two-paned window like the one shown at bottom in Figure 14-4.

  To complete the installation, click Next to forge on through the wizard pages. You may be asked to select a port or configure other settings. When you click the

Finish button on the last screen, Windows transfers the drivers to your hard drive.
(Along the way, you may be instructed to insert the Windows XP Professional
installation CD.) As a final step, you may be asked to restart the PC.

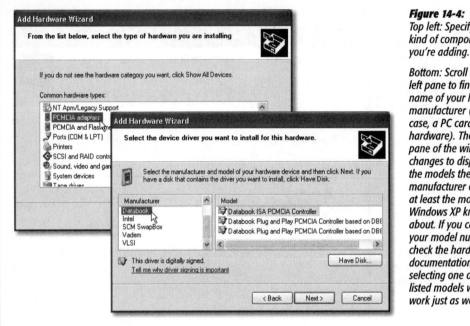

Figure 14-4:
*Top left: Specify which
kind of component
you're adding.*

*Bottom: Scroll down the
left pane to find the
name of your hardware
manufacturer (in this
case, a PC card is the
hardware). The right
pane of the window
changes to display all
the models the
manufacturer offers, or
at least the models that
Windows XP knows
about. If you can't find
your model number,
check the hardware's
documentation to see if
selecting one of the
listed models would
work just as well.*

Driver Signing

Every now and then, when you try to install the software for one new gadget or
another, you'll see the warning box shown in Figure 14-5. It's telling you that Microsoft has not tested this driver for Windows XP compatibility and programming
solidity. (Technically speaking, Microsoft has not put its digital signature on that
driver; it's an *unsigned driver*.)

If the message shown in Figure 14-5 appears before you, your first instinct should be
to contact the manufacturer or its Web site to find out if a newer XP-certified driver
is now available.

If not—for example, if the manufacturer has gone to that great dot-com in the sky—
you may as well try to install the driver anyway. If it seems to make your system
slower or less stable, you can always uninstall it, or rewind your entire operating
system to its condition before you installed the questionable driver. (You would use
System Restore for that purpose, which is described on page 457. Windows XP automatically takes a snapshot of your working system just before you install any unsigned driver.)

Tip: If you'd rather not contend with the "unsigned driver" message every time you install something, you can shut it up forever. Conversely, you can close up Windows like a vault, so that it will *never* accept unsigned drivers, for maximum, conservative safety. (Instead, you'll see a message declaring that the installation has been "blocked.") Instructions for setting up both scenarios are on page 297.

Figure 14-5:
The most stable and smoothly operating PC is one whose components use nothing but digitally signed drivers. On the other hand, just because a driver isn't signed doesn't mean it's no good; it may be that the manufacturer simply didn't pony up the testing fee required by Microsoft's Windows Hardware Quality Labs.

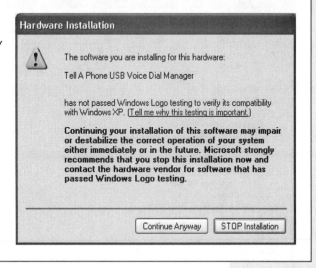

The Device Manager

The Device Manager is an extremely powerful tool that lets you troubleshoot and update drivers for gear you've already installed. It's a master list of every component that constitutes your PC: floppy drive, CD-ROM drive, keyboard, modem, and so on (Figure 14-6). It's also a status screen that lets you know which drivers are working properly, and which ones need some attention.

You can open the Device Manager in any of three ways:

- Right-click My Computer (in your Start menu or on the desktop); choose Properties from the shortcut menu. In the Systems Properties dialog box, click the Hardware tab, and then click the Device Manager button.

- Choose Start→Control Panel; open the System icon. Once again, click the Hardware tab to find the Device Manager button.

- Choose Start→Run. In the Run dialog box, type *devmgmt.msc* and press Enter.

In each of these cases, you now arrive at the screen shown in Figure 14-6.

Red X's and Yellow !'s: Resolving Conflicts

A yellow exclamation point next to the name indicates a problem with the device's driver. It could mean that either you or Windows XP installed the *wrong* driver, or that the device is fighting for resources being used by another component. It could also mean that a driver can't find the equipment it's supposed to control. That's what happens to your Zip-drive driver, for example, if you've detached the Zip drive.

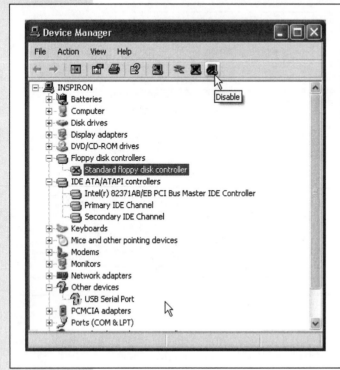

Figure 14-6:
The Device Manager lists types of equipment; to see the actual model(s) in each category, you must expand each sublist by clicking the + symbol. A device that's having problems is easy to spot, thanks to the red X's and yellow exclamation points.

A red X next to a component's name, meanwhile, indicates that it just isn't working, or that you've deliberately disabled it, as described in a moment. At other times, the X is the result of a serious incompatibility between the component and your computer, or the component and Windows XP. In that case, a call to the manufacturer's help line is almost certainly in your future.

Tip: To find out which company actually created a certain driver, double-click the component's name in the Device Manager. In the resulting Properties dialog box, click the Driver tab, where you'll see the name of the company, the date the driver was created, the version of the driver, and so on.

Duplicate devices

If the Device Manager displays icons for duplicate devices (for example, two modems), remove *both* of them. (Right-click each and then choose Uninstall from the shortcut menu.) If you remove only one, Windows XP will find it again the next time the PC starts up, and you'll have duplicate devices again.

If Windows XP asks if you want to restart your computer after you remove the first icon, click No, and then delete the second one. Windows XP won't ask again after you remove the second incarnation; you have to restart your computer manually.

When the PC starts up again, Windows finds the hardware device and installs it (only once this time). Open the Device Manager and make sure that there's only one of everything. If not, contact the manufacturer's help line.

Resolving resource conflicts

If the "red X" problem isn't caused by a duplicate component, double-click the component's name, and then click the Resources tab. Here you'll find an explanation of the problem, which is often a conflict in resources (see Figure 14-7).

Click the name of the resource that's having the conflict, and then click the Change Setting button. (If the Change Setting button is grayed out, turn off the "Use automatic settings" checkbox.)

Click the up/down control arrows next to the resource value, keeping an eye on the message in the Conflict Information box. When you select a value that has no conflict (as indicated by the Conflict Information box), move on to the next resource that indicates a conflict, and then click OK.

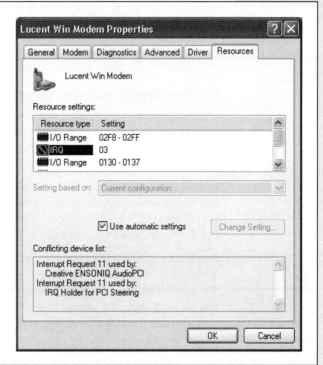

Figure 14-7:
The Resources tab should have all the information you need to resolve a problem. Any resource with a conflict is marked with a red X "not working" icon. Selecting a resource with a problem displays information about the conflict.

Note: When Windows XP installs a Plug and Play device, it can modify the settings for both the device and its driver in order to find a combination that works. Windows might even have to reconfigure other devices in the computer, so that the new device can function properly.

But when you're working with a *non*–Plug and Play device, Device Manager can change the hardware settings only for the driver, not the device itself. In some cases, the driver may not be able to work with the device's settings. In these cases, you have to modify the settings of the hardware device itself using a program supplied by its manufacturer—or for really old gadgets, you'll have to flip jumpers or DIP switches right on the device itself.

Or just sell the whole thing and move to the Amish country.

Turning Components Off

If you click to select the name of a component, the icons at the top of the Device Manager window spring to life. The one on the far right is the Disable button (Figure 14-6), which makes your PC treat the component in question as though it's not even there. (You'll be asked to confirm your decision.)

This feature is mostly used to create *hardware profiles* (see page 435), but you can also use this function to test device conflicts. For example, if a red X indicates that there's a resource conflict, you can disable one of the two gadgets, which may clear up a problem with its competitor.

When you disable a component, a red X appears next to the component's listing in the Device Manager. To undo your action, click the device's name and click the Enable button in the toolbar (formerly the Disable button).

Updating Drivers with the Device Manager

If you get your hands on a new, more powerful (or more reliable) driver for a device, you can use the Device Manager to install it. Newer isn't *always* better, however; in the world of Windows, the rule "If it ain't broke, don't fix it" contains a grain of truth the size of Texas.

In the Device Manager, click the + button for the appropriate type of equipment, and then double-click the component's name to open its Properties box. On the Driver tab (see Figure 14-8), click the Update Driver button. The Update Device Driver Wizard walks you through the process.

Along the way, the wizard will offer to search for a better driver, or display a list of drivers in a certain folder so you can make your own selection. Ignore the "Install the software automatically (Recommended)" option; you *know* where the driver is, and it's faster to find it yourself. Select "Install from a list or specific location (Advanced)," and then click Next.

If the newer driver is on a disk, turn on the top checkbox ("Search removable media"), and then click Next. If you've downloaded it, turn on "Include this location in the search," and then click the Browse button to find and select it. In either case, you may have to restart the PC to put the newly installed driver into service.

Driver Rollback

Suppose that you, the increasingly proficient PC user, have indeed downloaded a new driver for some component—your scanner, say—and successfully installed it using the instructions in the previous paragraphs. Life is sweet—until you discover that your scanner won't scan except in black and white.

In this situation, you'd probably give quite a bit for the chance to return to the previous driver, which, though older, seemed to work better. That's the beauty of the Driver Rollback button. To find it, open the Device Manager (page 431), double-click the component in question, click the Driver tab in the resulting Properties dialog box, and then click the Roll Back Driver button (shown in Figure 14-8).

Windows XP, forgiving as always, instantly undoes the installation of the newer driver, and reinstates the previous driver.

Figure 14-8:
When you double-click a component listed in your Device Manager and then click the Driver tab, you find four buttons and a lot of information. The Driver Provider information, for example, lets you know who is responsible for your current driver—Microsoft or the maker of the component. Click the Driver Details button to find out where on your hard drive the actual driver file is, the Update Driver button to install a newer version, the Roll Back Driver button to reinstate the earlier version, or the Uninstall button to remove the driver from your system entirely—a drastic decision.

Hardware Profiles

Hardware profiles are canned sets of settings for particular equipment configurations. By switching from one profile to another, you can quickly inform your computer that you've got a different assortment of gear connected—a feature that, as you can probably tell, is primarily useful for laptop owners.

If your laptop has a bay that can hold either a CD-ROM drive or a floppy drive, for example, you might create two hardware profiles, one for each of the drives. Or maybe you connect your laptop to a docking station at work; in that case, you could create one hardware profile for the equipment available on the docking station (including a monitor), and another hardware profile for use when you're undocked.

To create a hardware profile, open the System Properties dialog box (see page 295). Then click the Hardware tab, and click the Hardware Profiles button (see Figure 14-9).

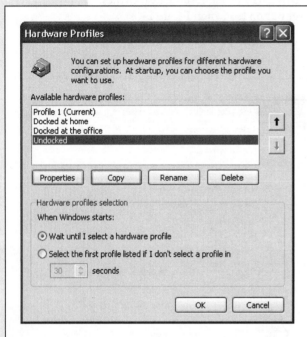

Figure 14-9:
Every computer is equipped with a hardware profile named Profile 1. Creating a new profile is simply a matter of copying the existing profile, creating a new name for the copy, and making changes to it. Use the option buttons at the bottom to specify how long you want Windows to display the menu of profiles at system startup time.

The quickest way to create a new profile is to duplicate an existing one, and then make changes to it. Proceed like this:

1. **Click the name of an existing profile, click the Copy button, name the new profile, and then click OK.**

   The new profile appears in the list shown in Figure 14-9.

2. **Click to select the new profile, and then click OK.**

   You return to the Hardware tab.

3. **Click the Device Manager button.**

   The Device Manager displays a list of all the various hardware gadgets you've installed into, or attached to, this machine.

4. **Click the + symbol, and then the name of the component you want to turn on or off in this profile.**

The Disable button on the Device Manager toolbar becomes available.

5. **Click the Disable button on the toolbar (see Figure 14-6). Click Yes when you're asked to confirm.**

After the Device Manager list collapses and expands, updating itself, you'll see a little red X on the icon of the component you've turned off. (That's what you'll see, that is, if the computer doesn't tell you that it first needs to be restarted.)

6. **Repeat steps 4 and 5 for any other devices you'd like to enable or disable for this profile, and then click OK.**

Hereafter, whenever you start your computer, you'll see, on a black, DOS-like screen, a list of the hardware profiles you've created. Only after you've selected one, following the instructions in Figure 14-10, does Windows XP finish its startup process.

Figure 14-10:
Every time you turn on your Windows PC, you'll be shown this listing of hardware profiles. Highlight the profile you want by pressing the up and down arrow keys; press the Enter key when you've highlighted the one you want. Windows loads only the drivers for the hardware you've turned on in the selected profile.

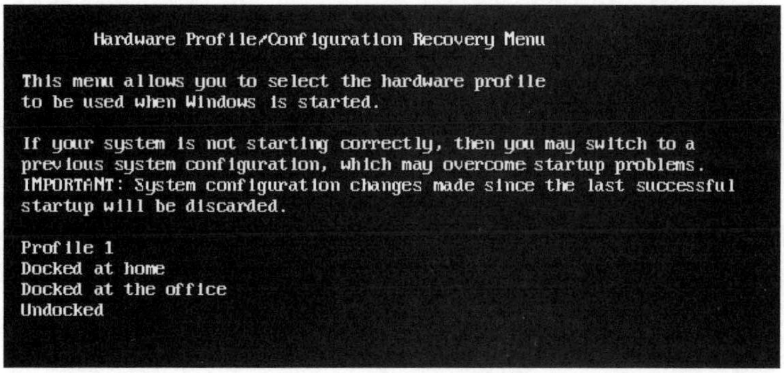

```
           Hardware Profile/Configuration Recovery Menu

This menu allows you to select the hardware profile
to be used when Windows is started.

If your system is not starting correctly, then you may switch to a
previous system configuration, which may overcome startup problems.
IMPORTANT: System configuration changes made since the last successful
startup will be discarded.

Profile 1
Docked at home
Docked at the office
Undocked
```

Joining, Compressing, and Encrypting Disks

iles and folders, as you've probably noticed, have a tendency to multiply. Creating new documents, installing new software, and downloading new files can fill up even the largest disk drives in no time—especially if, as Microsoft fervently hopes, you get heavily into music, pictures, and video. Fortunately, Windows XP Professional offers a number of ways to expand the amount of space on your drives: schemes called *dynamic disks* and *disk compression*.

For many people, security is another concern. Files on your drives may contain confidential financial data for your company, top-secret government research, or—worse—the holiday gift list for your family. Windows XP Professional has a solution for this problem too, called the Encrypting File System (EFS).

You can skip this entire chapter, if you wish, and get along quite well without using any of these features. They're strictly optional. But if you aspire to wear the Power User T-shirt, read on.

Note: Dynamic disks, disk compression, and EFS all require the *NTFS file system* on your computer's disk drives; they're absent if you've chosen the FAT 32 file system instead. To find out the benefits and drawbacks of NTFS, as well as how to convert FAT 32 drives to NTFS, see Appendix A.

Dynamic Disks

Suppose you've run out of space on your first hard drive, and have installed a second one to collect the overflow. Thanks to a Windows XP Pro feature called *dynamic disks,* you don't have to move files to the new drive or reorganize your folder scheme.

Instead, you can make the new drive fold its space seamlessly with the first's, so that you suddenly have more disk space on your "one" combo drive.

How Dynamic Disks Work

If this setup intrigues you, a bit more technical explanation is required.

When you (or your PC maker) first installed Windows XP, it configured each drive as a *basic disk*—a disk with its own drive letter. But before you can combine two actual drives into one volume, you must first convert them into a more flexible format that Microsoft calls a *dynamic disk*.

The good news is that you can convert a basic disk into a dynamic disk without losing any data on the drive. (The actual steps, as you'll find out shortly, are easy indeed.) The bad news is that you can't change a dynamic disk *back* to a basic disk, unless you erase all of the data stored there.

And why would you want to? Because dynamic disks, for all their flexibility, also have some limitations. Before you proceed with converting basic disks to dynamic disks, assume a reclining position and read the following fine print:

- Once you've combined two physical disks into an über-disk (technically called a *spanned volume*), a fatal problem on *one* of the two hard drives will make you lose all of the data on *both* drives—an event that can ruin your whole morning. Keeping regular backups of your spanned volume is critically important (see Chapter 16).

- Dynamic disks are a specialty of Windows XP Pro only. No other version of Windows can read them (not even Windows XP Home Edition).

UP TO SPEED

Volumes Defined

You won't get far in this chapter, or at PC user group meetings, without understanding a key piece of Windows terminology: *volume*.

For most people, most of the time, volume means "disk." But technically, there's more to it than that—a distinction that becomes crucial if you explore the techniques described in this chapter.

If you open your My Computer window, you'll see that each disk in your PC has its own icon and drive letter (C:, for example). But each icon isn't necessarily a separate disk. It's possible that you, or somebody in charge of your PC, has split a single drive into multiple *partitions* (Appendix A), each with a separate icon and drive letter. Clearly, the world needs a term for "an icon/drive letter in My Computer, whether it's a whole disk or not." That term is *volume*.

In Windows XP Pro, you can do more than partition one hard drive into multiple volumes—you can also do the reverse, as described in this chapter. If you've installed more than one hard drive, you can actually request that Windows represent them on the screen as *one* volume. This way, you can have as many hard disk drives in your computer as you want and combine their storage space into a unit, represented by one icon and drive letter.

- A dynamic disk can contain only one operating system. You can't *dual boot* (choose which of two operating systems to use each time you turn on the PC), as you can with basic disks.

- To convert a hard drive to a dynamic disk, it must set aside an invisible storage area to hold a *dynamic disk database*. If you partitioned the drive using Windows 2000 or XP Professional, then Windows already reserved enough space for this purpose. But if the drive was partitioned with another operating system, you may have to erase it before converting it to a dynamic disk.

- Dynamic disks don't work on laptops, removable disks, disks connected by USB cables or IEEE 1394 (FireWire) cables, or disks connected to shared SCSI buses. If your disks fall into any of these categories, Windows XP won't let you convert them to dynamic disks.

Converting a Basic Disk to a Dynamic Disk

If you haven't yet been scared off by all of these cautions, and are ready to convert your basic disks to dynamic disks, the procedure is simple. First, back up the disk you plan to convert. You probably won't need it, but it's a good idea to back up a disk before performing any kind of traumatic surgery to it.

Next, log on to the computer as its Administrator (page 501), and exit any programs that might be running on the disk you plan to convert.

You convert disks and manage the dynamic volumes on them using a special window called the Disk Management console. To open it, use any of these methods:

- Choose Start→Control Panel→Administrative Tools→Computer Management. In the resulting Computer Management window, double-click Disk Management in the list at the left side.

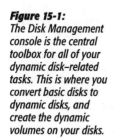

Figure 15-1:
The Disk Management console is the central toolbox for all of your dynamic disk–related tasks. This is where you convert basic disks to dynamic disks, and create the dynamic volumes on your disks.

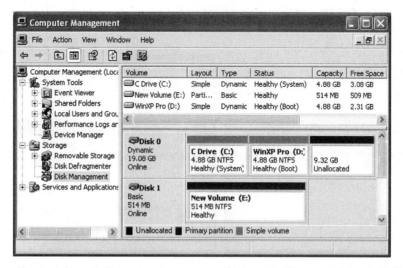

- In the Start menu, right-click My Computer. From the shortcut menu, choose Manage. Once again, double-click Disk Management in the list at the left side.

- Choose Start→Run; type *diskmgmt.msc* and press Enter.

Once this window is before you, follow these steps:

1. **Click the Disk Management icon under Storage in the left pane of the Computer Management console.**

   You see a display of your drives and the partitions on them, as shown in Figure 15-1.

   The top part of the window lists the partitions on your computer. The bottom part contains a horizontal box representing each drive on your computer, with smaller boxes inside indicating the partitions on each drive. Notice that the header box for each drive indicates the number of the drive in your system, its capacity, whether or not it's online, and the word "Basic" (indicating that it's currently a basic disk).

2. **Right-click the header box for the drive, as shown in Figure 15-2; from the shortcut menu, choose Convert to Dynamic Disk.**

   A Convert to Dynamic Disk dialog box appears (Figure 15-2, bottom left), in which you select the disk(s) you want to convert.

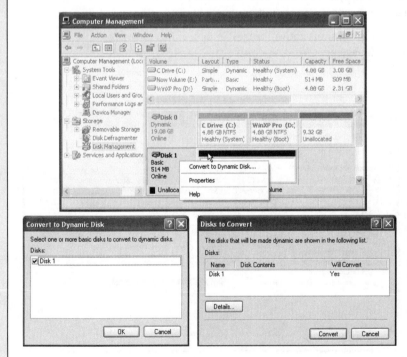

Figure 15-2:
Top: To convert a basic disk to a dynamic disk, right-click the header box for the drive and choose Convert to Dynamic Disk from the shortcut menu. Don't right-click one of the partitions—you must click the header box.

Bottom left: The Convert to Dynamic Disk dialog box lists the drives that are eligible for conversion to dynamic disks. You can even select and convert several disks at once.

Bottom right: The Disks to Convert dialog box lists the dynamic volumes that Windows XP will automatically create on your newly converted drives.

3. **Click OK.**

If you're converting a disk that contains basic partitions, a Disks to Convert dialog box appears (Figure 15-2, bottom right).

If you click a disk and then click Details, a Convert Details dialog box appears, listing the dynamic volumes that you're about to create. (All of the standard partitions on the drive are converted into *simple* dynamic volumes—that is, they aren't yet combined into *spanned* volumes. That step comes later.)

4. **Click the Convert button.**

If Windows XP detects other operating systems on your disk, you'll be warned that they won't be able to start up the PC after the conversion. If you're converting the disk that contains Windows XP Pro itself, you'll have to restart the PC.

Otherwise, though, the conversion process takes only a few seconds. After restarting (if necessary), log on and open the Disk Management console again. As shown in Figure 15-3, the conversion is complete.

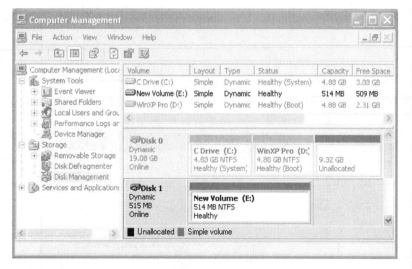

Figure 15-3:
Now the header box for your disk says "Dynamic" rather than "Basic," and what used to be partitions on the disk (with blue header bars) are now simple volumes (with red header bars).

Three Uses for Unallocated Space

If you've installed a new hard drive, you'll see, in the Disk Management window, that it consists of *unallocated space*—disk space that doesn't belong to any volume yet. It's just sitting there, unaccounted for, unusable, waiting for you to make it part of one volume or another.

Whenever you find yourself with unallocated space, you get to discover the flexibility of dynamic disks. If you right-click an unallocated area in one of the disk boxes and choose New Volume from the shortcut menu, you'll see that you can choose any of three options: Simple, Spanned, or Striped (see Figure 15-4). Here's a rundown of each:

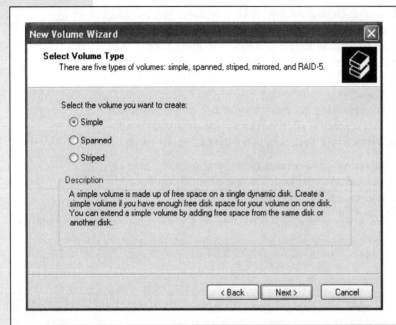

Figure 15-4:
The Select Volume Type screen of the New Volume Wizard displays the dynamic volume types that you can create on your computer. Click one to read a description at the bottom of the dialog box.

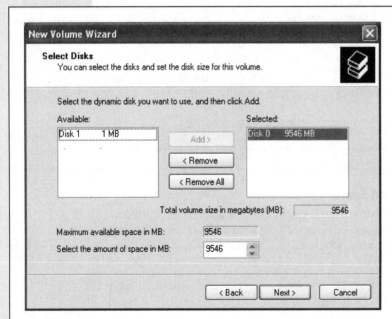

Figure 15-5:
On the Select Disks screen, you specify where you want to get the unallocated space that the wizard will use to create the dynamic volume. When creating a simple volume, you can only select one disk, but for spanned or striped volumes, you can select up to 32.

Creating a simple volume

A *simple volume,* on a dynamic disk, is a lot like a partition on a basic disk. It's a subdivision of the hard drive that looks and acts exactly like a separate disk, complete with its own drive letter and icon in your My Computer window.

To make one, follow these steps, beginning with the New Volume Wizard screen shown in Figure 15-4:

1. **Click Simple (Figure 15-4) and then click Next.**

   The Select Disks screen appears (Figure 15-5).

2. **Specify the size of the volume you want to create (in megabytes) in the "Select the amount of space in MB" box.**

   Often, you'll want to leave the maximum number here, so that you turn *all* of the unallocated space into a single new volume—but you don't have to. You can chop up the space into a number of different volumes, if you like.

POWER USERS' CLINIC

Extending a Volume

One big advantage of dynamic disks is that you can extend an existing volume whenever you feel like it, just by allocating additional disk space to it. If, for example, you run out of space on a volume you've named Data, and you still have some unallocated space on some other disk, you can simply add it to the Data volume to make it bigger. The unallocated space you specify becomes a permanent part of the Data volume. (Note that this is a one-way trip. Once you've added free space to a dynamic volume, it becomes part of that volume permanently, or at least until you delete the volume—and its data—and re-create it.)

The disk space you use to extend the volume can come from either the same disk or another dynamic disk (in which case you create a *spanned* volume). Note, though, that you can't extend the *system* volume, nor any volume that was

originally a partition created by another operating system.

To extend an existing dynamic volume, right-click it in the

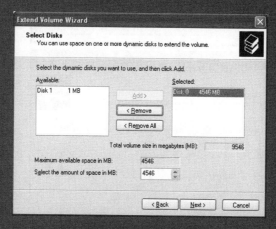

Disk Management window; choose Extend Volume from the shortcut menu. The Extend Volume Wizard appears, consisting of nothing but a Select Disks screen shown here. When you've made your selections, click Next and then Finish to complete the wizard.

When you look at the Disk Management display, the new space you've allocated appears at first to be an entirely new volume, with a separate box in the drive display. Look more carefully, however, and you'll see that both the original volume and the new one have the same drive letter. Furthermore, when you look at the drive list at the top of the window, the volume appears only once, with the capacity reflecting the total of the original volume and the extension you just created.

---

3. **Click Next.**

The Assign Drive Letter or Path screen appears (Figure 15-6, top).

4. **Specify the drive letter you want to assign to the volume.**

If you like, you can also turn the volume into a sub-folder of an existing NTFS folder (a technical trick described on page 472).

5. **Click Next. On the Format Volume screen (Figure 15-6, bottom), specify the NTFS file system. Type a name for your new volume into the "Volume label" box. Click Next, and then Finish.**

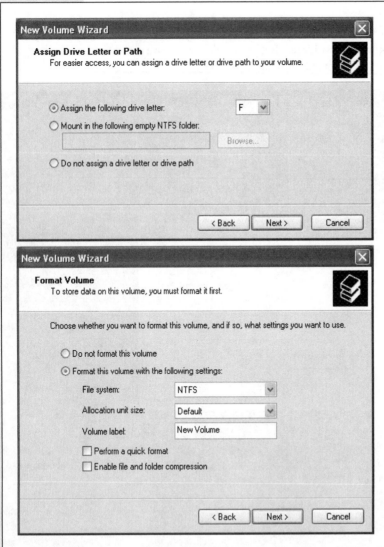

Figure 15-6:
Top: On the Assign Drive Letter or Path screen, you specify what drive letter you want to use for the new volume. Alternatively, you can mount it as a folder on an NTFS drive.

Bottom: The Format Volume screen lets you format your new dynamic volume as soon as it's created, as well as specify a volume name and turn on disk compression. Because this is a dynamic disk, NTFS is the only file system available for formatting.

Presto: What used to be unallocated space (denoted by a black header bar in the Disk Management window) is now a simple volume (with a red header bar). The new volume now appears in your My Computer window—and everywhere else—with the drive letter you assigned to it. It's ready to store data.

Tip: You can delete a dynamic volume as easily as you created it. Just right-click it in the Disk Management window and select Delete Volume from the shortcut menu. Doing so deletes the entire volume, erasing all the data on it and removing its space from any spanned or striped space on other disks.

Creating a spanned volume

Suppose you've managed to shoehorn every byte of data you possibly can onto your PC's one hard drive. You decide to install a second hard drive, to give you more space.

But then what? You don't want to spoil the carefully organized folder structure on your old hard drive by moving parts of it to the new drive; you just want to continue to build on your folders as they are.

The solution, as you know if you read the beginning of this chapter, is to create a *spanned volume,* a single disk icon (and drive letter) that's actually composed of the space from both your old and new drives.

The first order of business (after restarting the computer) is to make sure that Windows XP has recognized the new drive. Messages inform you that the operating system has located a new hardware device and identified it as a hard drive. When you launch the Disk Management console, a new drive appears in the list, with a great big block of unallocated space for you to fill, as shown in Figure 15-7.

Figure 15-7:
When you install a new hard drive in your computer, it appears in the Disk Management console as a large block of unallocated space. Of course, you quickly notice that the new drive is a basic drive; therefore, all you can do is create a basic partition on it.

Before you can use the new drive to enlarge your existing volume, you must convert it to a dynamic disk, just as described on page 441. At that point, you're free to right-click your original volume (in the Disk Management window) and open the Extend Volume Wizard.

When the Select Disks screen appears (Figure 15-8, top), you'll see that the only available unallocated space in your computer is on your new drive. Select it in the Available column and click Add to add it to the Selected column. Specify how much of the new drive you want to add to the volume (or, to add *all* of it to your original drive, do nothing). Finally, click Next and then Finish.

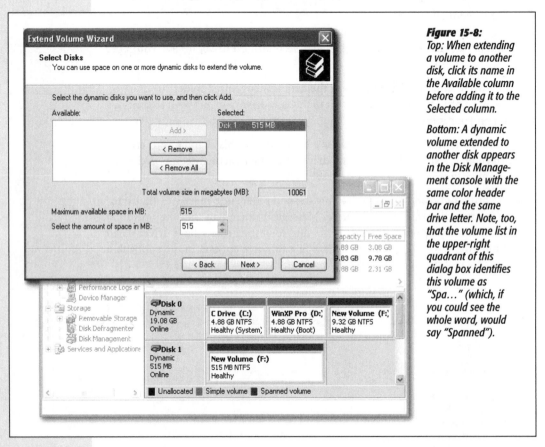

Figure 15-8:
Top: When extending a volume to another disk, click its name in the Available column before adding it to the Selected column.

Bottom: A dynamic volume extended to another disk appears in the Disk Management console with the same color header bar and the same drive letter. Note, too, that the volume list in the upper-right quadrant of this dialog box identifies this volume as "Spa..." (which, if you could see the whole word, would say "Spanned").

Notice now that your original volume and your new drive both have a purple header bar and use the same drive letter, as shown at bottom in Figure 15-8. You now have a spanned volume using space on both of your hard drives. Your hard drive is now effectively bigger, and you can continue to amass new files at your accustomed rate.

Creating a striped volume

As you now know, a *spanned volume* is like a virtual hard drive made up of storage space from two to 32 dynamic disks. When Windows XP saves data onto a spanned volume, it completely fills up the allotted space on one drive, then proceeds to the next drive in the volume, until the allotted space on all of the drives is full.

A *striped volume* is similar, in that it's a single volume made up of space from several actual disks, but the way Windows XP saves data to the drives is different. Instead of filling up one drive and proceeding to the next one, Windows XP saves pieces of each file on more than one disk. Because more than one hard drive is saving and reading data in parallel, a speed benefit can theoretically result.

The truth is, though, that the differences are measured in milliseconds—thousandths of a second—so it's generally not worth creating striped volumes on everyday PC workstations. (On corporate file servers that handle hundreds or thousands of file access requests per minute, it's a different story. The cumulative savings in access times can be significant.)

If you're still tempted to create a striped-volume set, the process is nearly identical to creating a new *spanned* volume (see the box below). The only difference is that you must use the same amount of space on each of the drives you select. For example, if you have one gigabyte of unallocated space on Disk 0 and five gigabytes of unallocated space on Disk 1, your striped volume can be no larger than two gigabytes, one from each drive.

Compressing Files and Folders

Although the hard drives made these days have greater capacities than ever, programs and files are much bigger, too. Running out of disk space is still a common problem. Fortunately, Windows XP Pro is especially effective at compressing files and folders to take up less disk space.

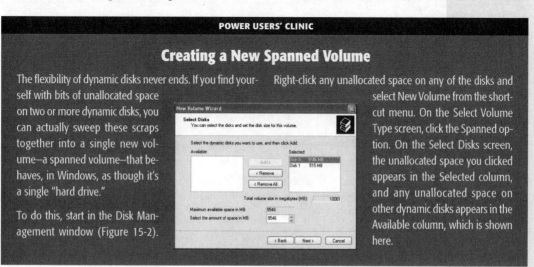

POWER USERS' CLINIC

Creating a New Spanned Volume

The flexibility of dynamic disks never ends. If you find yourself with bits of unallocated space on two or more dynamic disks, you can actually sweep these scraps together into a single new volume—a spanned volume—that behaves, in Windows, as though it's a single "hard drive."

To do this, start in the Disk Management window (Figure 15-2).

Right-click any unallocated space on any of the disks and select New Volume from the shortcut menu. On the Select Volume Type screen, click the Spanned option. On the Select Disks screen, the unallocated space you clicked appears in the Selected column, and any unallocated space on other dynamic disks appears in the Available column, which is shown here.

Compressing files and folders can also be useful when you want to email files to someone without dooming them to an all-night modem-watching session. That's why Microsoft has endowed Windows XP with two different schemes for compressing files and folders: *NTFS compression* for storing files on your hard drive, and *zipped folders* for files that might have to be transferred.

NTFS Compression

If Windows XP Pro was installed on your PC when you bought it, or if you upgraded your PC from Windows 2000, or if you erased your hard drive before installing Windows XP, then your hard drive is probably formatted using a file system called *NTFS* (short for *NT file system;* see page 620 for details).

Most people can live a long and happy life without knowing anything about NTFS. If you work in a corporation, you might be grateful for the additional security it offers to Windows XP Pro fans (Chapter 17), and leave it at that. Now and then, however, you'll read about other features that are available *only* if your hard drive was prepared using NTFS—and this is one of those cases.

Tip: To find out whether or not your hard drive uses NTFS formatting, choose Start→My Computer. Right-click the hard drive icon; choose Properties from the shortcut menu. In the resulting dialog box, you'll see either "File system: NTFS" or "File system: FAT 32." (If it says FAT 32, you probably upgraded your PC from Windows 98 or Windows Me.) Unfortunately, special NTFS features like automatic compression aren't available to you, but you can upgrade your drive formatting to NTFS without having to erase it. See page 622 for instructions.

The NTFS compression scheme is especially likable because it's completely invisible to you. Windows XP Pro automatically compresses and decompresses your files, almost instantaneously. At some point, you may even forget you've turned it on.

UP TO SPEED

Data Compression

Data compression is the process of replacing repetitive material in a file with shorthand symbols. For example, if a speech you've written contains the phrase *going forward* 21 times, a compression scheme like the one in NTFS may replace each occurrence with a single symbol, making the file that much smaller. When you reopen the file later, the operating system almost instantaneously restores the original, expanded material.

The degree to which a file can be compressed depends on what kind of data the file contains and whether it's already been compressed by another program. For example, programs (executable files) often shrink by half when com-

pressed. Bitmapped graphics like TIFF files squish down to as little as one-seventh their original size, saving a great deal more space.

The GIF and JPEG graphics files so popular on the Web, however, are already compressed (which is why they're so popular—they take relatively little time to download), and so they don't get much smaller if you try to compress them manually. That's one of the main rules of data compression: data can only be compressed once.

In short, there's no way to predict just how much disk space you'll save by using NTFS compression on your drives. It all depends on what you have stored there.

Consider:

- Whenever you open a compressed file, Windows quickly and invisibly expands it to its original form so that you can read or edit it. When you close the file again, Windows instantly recompresses it.

- If you send compressed files (via disk or email, for example) to a PC whose hard drive doesn't use NTFS compression, Windows XP once again decompresses them, quickly and invisibly.

- Any file you copy into a compressed folder or disk is compressed automatically. (If you only *move* it into such a folder from elsewhere on the disk, however, it stays compressed or uncompressed—whichever it was originally.)

Compressing files, folders, or disks

To turn on NTFS compression, right-click the icon for the file, folder, or disk whose contents you want to shrink. Choose Properties from the shortcut menu. Click the Advanced button, and in the resulting dialog box, turn on "Compress contents to save disk space" (Figure 15-9). If you have selected a folder for compression, you are prompted as to whether you also want to compress the files and subfolders within it.

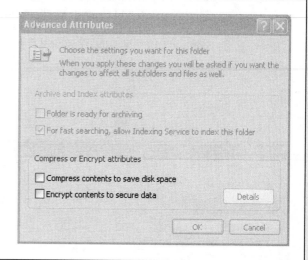

Figure 15-9:
If you don't see the "Compress contents to save disk space" checkbox (highlighted here), then your hard drive probably doesn't use the NTFS formatting scheme.

Many Windows veterans wind up turning on compression for the entire hard drive. It can take Windows XP several hours to perform the initial compression of every file on the drive. (If you plan to go see a movie while Windows is working, though, quit all your programs first. Otherwise, the compression process will halt whenever it encounters an open file—waiting for you to close the file or tell Windows to ignore it—and you'll find the job only half done when you return.)

When Windows is finished compressing, the compressed file and folder icons appear in a different color, a reminder that Windows is doing its part to maximize your disk space. (If they don't change color, somebody—maybe you—must have turned off the "Show encrypted or compressed NTFS files in color" option described on page 91.)

When you look at the Properties dialog box for a compressed file (right-click the file and choose Properties from the shortcut menu), you can see two file sizes. The Size value indicates the actual (uncompressed) size of the file, and the Size On Disk value is the compressed size of the file, that is, the amount of disk space it is occupying.

Zipped Folders

As noted above, NTFS compression is great for freeing up disk space while you're working at your PC. But when you email your files to somebody else or burn them to a CD, Windows XP always decompresses them right back to their original sizes first. And, of course, NTFS compression isn't even an option if your hard drive doesn't *use* NTFS formatting (page 620).

Fortunately, there's another way to compress files: Zip them. If you've ever used Windows before, you've probably encountered Zip files. Each one is a tiny little suitcase, an *archive*, whose contents have been tightly compressed to keep files together, to save space, and to transfer them online faster (see Figure 15-10). Use Zip files when you want to email something to someone, or when you want to pack up a completed project and remove it from your hard drive to free up space.

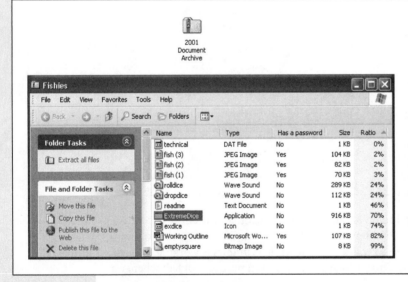

Figure 15-10:
Top: A Zip archive looks like an ordinary folder–except for the tiny zipper.

Bottom: Double-click one to open its window and see what's inside. Notice (in the Ratio column) that JPEG graphics and GIF graphics usually don't become much smaller than they were before zipping, since they're already compressed formats. But word processing files, program files, and other file types reveal quite a bit of shrinkage.

Creating zipped folders

In Windows XP, you don't even need a shareware program like PKZip or WinZip to create or open Zip files. You can create a Zip archive in either of two ways:

- Right-click any blank spot on the desktop or an open window. From the shortcut menu, choose New→Compressed (zipped) Folder. Type a name for your newly created, empty archive, and then press Enter.

  Now, each time you drag a file or folder onto the archive's icon (or into its open window), Windows automatically stuffs a *copy* of it inside.

  Of course, you haven't actually saved any disk space, since now you have two copies of the original material (one zipped, one untouched). If you'd rather *move* a file or folder into the archive—in the process deleting the full-size version and saving disk space—right-drag the file or folder icon onto the archive icon. Now from the shortcut menu, choose Move Here.

- To turn an existing file or folder *into* a zipped archive, right-click its icon. (To zip up a handful of icons, select them first, then right-click any *one* of them.) Now, from the shortcut menu, choose Send To→Compressed (zipped) Folder. You've just created a new archive folder *and* copied the files or folders into it.

Tip: At this point, you can right-click the zipped folder's icon and choose Send To→Mail Recipient. Windows automatically whips open your email program, creates an outgoing message ready for you to address, and attaches the zipped file to it—which is now set for transport.

Working with zipped folders

In many respects, a zipped folder behaves just like any ordinary folder. Double-click it to see what's inside.

If you double-click one of the *files* you find inside, however, Windows opens up a *read-only* copy of it—that is, a copy you can view, but not edit. To make changes to a read-only copy, you must use the File→Save As command and save it somewhere else on your hard drive.

Note: Be sure to navigate to the desktop or the My Documents folder, for example, before you save your edited document. Otherwise, Windows will save it into an invisible temporary folder, where you may never see it again.

HISTORY CLASS

PKZip

The Zip archive format was developed in the late 1980s by Phil Katz, a pioneer of PC compression technology. Katz's original product, PKZip, was a DOS-based archiving program that soon became an industry standard.

There have been many other archive compression standards over the years, but none of them became as ubiquitous as the Zip format. Every program today that creates or manipulates Zip files, including Windows XP, owes a debt of thanks—if not a free T-shirt or two—to Phil Katz.

To decompress only some of the icons in a zipped folder, just drag them out of the archive window; they instantly spring back to their original sizes. Or, to decompress the entire archive, right-click its icon and choose Extract All from the shortcut menu (or, if its window is already open, click the "Extract all files" link on the task pane). A wizard asks you to specify where you want the resulting files to wind up.

Encrypting Files and Folders

If your My Documents folder contains nothing but laundry lists and letters to your mom, data security is probably not a major concern for you. But if there's some stuff on your hard drive that you'd rather keep private—you know who you are—Windows XP Professional can help you out. The Encrypting File System (EFS) is an NTFS feature that stores your data in a coded format that only you can read.

POWER USERS' CLINIC

Disk Quotas

Does one of your account holders have a tendency to become a bit overzealous about downloading stuff from the Web, threatening to overrun your hard drive with shareware junk and MP3 files? Fortunately, it's easy enough for you, the wise administrator, to curb such behavior among holders of Limited accounts (if your drive uses NTFS formatting, as described on page 620).

Just choose Start→My Computer. Right-click the hard drive icon; in the Properties dialog box, click the Quota tab (shown here). Turn on "Enable quota management" to un-dim the other options.

You might start by turning on "Deny disk space to users exceeding quota limit." This, of course, is exactly the kind of muzzle you were hoping to place on out-of-control downloaders. The instant they try to save or download a file that pushes their stuff over the limit, an "Insufficient disk space" message appears. They'll simply have to delete some of their other files to make room.

Use the "Limit disk space to ___" controls to specify the cap you want to put on each account holder. Using these con-

trols, you can specify a certain number of kilobytes (KB), megabytes (MB), gigabytes (GB)—or even terabytes (TB), petabytes (PB), or exabytes (EB). (Then write a letter to *PC World* and tell the editors where you bought a multi-exabyte hard drive.)

You can also set up a disk-space limit ("Set warning level to ___") that will make a *warning* appear—not to the mad downloader, but to you, the administrator. By clicking the Quota Entries button, you get a little report that shows exactly how much disk space each of your account holders has used up. (This is where you'll see the warning, as a written notation.)

You may have noticed that Windows lets you set a space limit (and a warning) even if "Enable quota management" *isn't* turned on. You'd set things up that way if you just want to track your underlings' disk usage without actually limiting them.

When you click OK, Windows warns you that it's about to take some time to calculate just how much disk space each account holder has used so far.

The beauty of EFS is that it's effortless and invisible to you, the authorized owner. Windows XP automatically encrypts your files before storing them on the drive, and decrypts them again when you want to read or modify them. Anyone else who logs on to your computer, however, will find these files locked and off-limits.

If you've read ahead to Chapter 17, of course, you might be frowning in confusion at this point. Isn't keeping private files private the whole point of XP's *accounts* feature? Don't XP Pro's *NTFS permissions* (page 528) keep busybodies out already?

Yes, but encryption provides additional security. If, for example, you are a top-level agent assigned to protect your government's most closely guarded egg salad recipe, you can use NTFS permissions to deny all other users access to the file containing the information. Nobody but you can open the file in Windows XP.

However, a determined intruder from a foreign nation could conceivably boot the computer using *another* operating system—one that doesn't recognize the NTFS permissions system—and access the hard drive using a special program that reads the raw data stored there. If, however, you had encrypted the file using EFS, that raw data would appear as gibberish, foiling your crafty nemesis.

Using EFS

You use EFS to encrypt your folders and files in much the same way that you use NTFS compression. To encrypt a file or a folder, you open its Properties dialog box, click the Advanced button, turn on the Encrypt Contents To Secure Data checkbox, and click OK (see Figure 15-11).

Depending on how much data you've selected, it may take some time for the encryption process to complete. Once the folders and files are encrypted, they appear in a different color from your compressed files (unless, once again, you've turned off the "Show encrypted or compressed NTFS files in color" option).

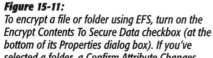
Figure 15-11:
To encrypt a file or folder using EFS, turn on the Encrypt Contents To Secure Data checkbox (at the bottom of its Properties dialog box). If you've selected a folder, a Confirm Attribute Changes dialog box appears, asking if you want to encrypt just that folder or everything inside it, too.

Note: You can't encrypt certain files and folders: system files, or any files in the system *root folder* (usually the WINNT or Windows folder). You can't encrypt files and folders on FAT 32 drives, either.

Finally, note that you can't both encrypt *and* compress the same file or folder. If you attempt to encrypt a compressed file or folder, Windows XP will decompress it first. You can, however, encrypt files that have been compressed using another technology, such as Zip files or compressed image files.

After your files have been encrypted, you may be surprised to see that, other than their color change, nothing seems to have changed. You can open them the same way you always did, change them, and save them as usual. Windows XP is just doing its job: protecting these files with minimum inconvenience to you.

Still, if you're having difficulty believing that your files are now protected by an invisible force field, try logging off and back on again with a different user name and password. When you try to open an encrypted file now, a message cheerfully informs you that you don't have the proper permissions to access the file. (For more on Windows XP security, see Chapter 17.)

EFS Rules

Any files or folders that you move *into* an EFS-encrypted folder get encrypted, too. But dragging a file *out* of it doesn't un-protect it; it remains encrypted as long as it's on an NTFS drive. A protected file loses its encryption only when:

- You manually decrypt the file (by turning off the corresponding checkbox in its Properties dialog box).

- You move it to a FAT 32 drive.

- You transmit it via network or email—an important point. It means that if somebody can access your hard drive from across the network, they can open your encrypted files, even without knowing your account password! To protect files from prying eyes across the network, you must *also* use NTFS permissions, as described on page 528.

By the way, EFS doesn't protect files from being deleted. Even if passing evildoers can't *open* your private file, they can still *delete* it—unless you've protected it using XP's permissions feature (Chapter 17). Here again, truly protecting important material involves using several security mechanisms in combination.

GEM IN THE ROUGH

Recovering Encrypted Data

Every now and then, encrypted data becomes inaccessible. Maybe a hard-drive crash nukes your password, and therefore your ability to open your own encrypted files. Or maybe a disgruntled employee quits, deliberately refusing to divulge his password or decrypt his important files first.

Fortunately, Windows XP has a fallback mechanism—a back door. The local Administrator account on a certain PC generally has exclusive access to this feature, although, using *group policies* (page 18), it's possible to designate other account holders as recover agents, too.

Maintenance, Backups, and Troubleshooting

L ike you, its human sidekick, your computer requires periodic checkups and preventive maintenance. Fortunately, Microsoft has put quite a bit of effort into equipping Windows XP with special tools, all dedicated to the preservation of what Microsoft calls PC Health. Here's a crash course in keeping your PC—and its hard drive—humming.

System Restore

As you get more proficient on a PC, pressing Ctrl+Z—the keyboard shortcut for Undo—eventually becomes an unconscious reflex. In fact, you can sometimes spot veteran Windows fans twitching their Ctrl+Z fingers even when they're not near the computer—after knocking over a cup of coffee, locking the car with the keys inside, or blurting out something inappropriate in a meeting.

Windows XP offers one feature in particular that you might think of as the mother of All Undo commands: System Restore. This feature alone can be worth hours of your time and hundreds of dollars in consultant fees.

The pattern of things going wrong in Windows usually works like this: The PC works fine for a while, and then suddenly—maybe for no apparent reason, but most often following an installation or configuration change—it goes on the fritz. At that point, wouldn't it be pleasant to be able to tell the computer: "Go back to the way you were yesterday, please"?

System Restore does exactly that: It "rewinds" your PC back to the condition it was in before you, or something you tried to install, messed it up.

Of course, some people will say that this is what backups are for. But System Restore isn't the same thing; it takes only your *operating system* back to its previous condition. It doesn't touch your email, Internet Explorer History or Favorites lists, Web cookies, files in your Windows→Downloaded Program Files folder, My Documents folder, or any standard document types (*.doc*, *.xls*, graphics files, and so on).

And if you don't like your PC after restoring it, you can always restore it to the way it was *before* you restored it—back to the future.

Tip: If your PC manages to catch a virus, System Restore can even rewind it to a time before the infection— sometimes. Unfortunately, you can't count on your PC having that function. By the time you discover it, the virus may have infected your documents, which System Restore doesn't touch. An up-to-date antivirus program is a much more effective security blanket.

About Restore Points

System Restore works by taking snapshots of your operating system. In fact, your copy of Windows XP has been creating these memorized snapshots, called *restore points*, ever since you've been running it. When the worst comes to pass, and your PC starts acting up, you can use the System Restore calendar (see Figure 16-2) to rewind your machine to its configuration the last time you remember it working well.

As Figure 16-2 illustrates, Windows XP automatically creates landing points for your little PC time machine at the following times:

• The first time you boot up Windows XP.

• After every 10 hours of operation.

• After every 24 hours of real-world time (unless your PC is turned off all day; then you get a restore point the next time it's turned on).

• Every time you install a new program (provided it uses a recent version of the Microsoft Windows Installer or InstallShield).

• Every time the Automatic Update feature (see page 300) updates a component of your operating system.

• Whenever you feel like it—for instance, just before you install some new component. (To create one of these *manual* checkpoints, choose Start→Help and Support. Click "Undo changes to your computer with System Restore." On the next screen, click "Create a restore point," and then click Next; name your new checkpoint and click OK.)

Note: When your hard drive is running low on space, System Restore turns off automatically, without notice. It turns itself back on when you free up some space.

As you can well imagine, storing all of these copies of your Windows configuration consumes quite a bit of disk space, especially since the factory setting for the amount of space that System Restore can use is 12 percent of every hard drive. That adds up quickly—on a 60 GB hard drive, that's 7.2 GB.

Fortunately, you can control exactly how much disk space is dedicated to this function—or turn the function off entirely—as described in Figure 16-1. (Note that turning off System Restore, even momentarily, wipes out all existing restore points.)

Tip: Ever wonder where Windows is storing this backup copy of your operating system? It's in a folder called System Volume Information that sits in your Local Disk (C:) window. Inside are individual folders for each restore point. (System Volume Information is generally an invisible folder, but you can make it visible following the instructions on page 89. You still won't be allowed to move, rename, or delete it, however—thank goodness.)

That's why Windows XP automatically begins *deleting* restore points after 90 days (or when it's running out of disk space)—as well as any chance of rewinding your system back that far. That's also why the System Restore feature stops working if your hard drive is very full.

And that's *also* why you should run the System Restore feature promptly when your PC acts strangely.

Figure 16-1:
To specify how much disk space System Restore is allowed to use (and therefore how many "rolling back" opportunities you have), open the System program in Control Panel. Click the System Restore tab, and then drag the slider to change the amount of disk space you're willing to sacrifice for this feature. (If you have several hard drives, you get a Settings button that lets you individually change the limit—or turn off System Restore—for each.) Click Apply and then OK.

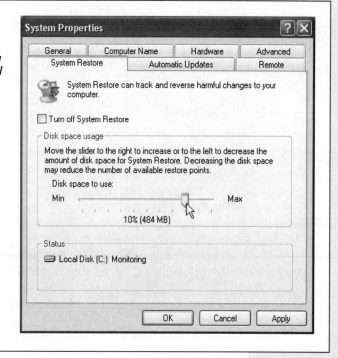

Tip: When you value hard drive space more than the opportunity to return your PC to a distant moment of health, you can use an obscure button (Figure 16-3), to delete all but the *most recent* system restore point. To get there, choose Start→All Programs→Accessories→System Tools→Disk Cleanup. Click the More Options tab, and then click the "Clean up" button in the System Restore section.

Performing a System Restore

If something goes wrong with your PC, here's how to roll it back to the happy, by-gone days of late last week:

1. **Choose Start→Help and Support.**

   The Help center appears.

2. **Click "Undo changes to your computer with System Restore." On the next screen, confirm that "Restore my computer to an earlier time" is selected, and then click Next.**

   Now you see the System Restore calendar (Figure 16-2). The calendar squares containing boldface numbers indicate the days on which Windows memorized your operating system condition.

GEM IN THE ROUGH

Automatic System-File Replacement

One of Windows XP's best PC-health features has no control panel, no window, and no icon of its own. It's a behind-the-scenes, automatic feature that may have already saved your PC's hide a time or two without your knowledge. It's System File Protection.

Ordinarily, you can't see the icons of extremely important Windows system files. Years of calls to Microsoft's help center have taught the company to keep these files hidden from the inexperienced, the curious, and the mischievous.

But if you make these files visible again (see page 89) *and* drag one of the vital files in the Local Disk (C:)→Windows folder to the Recycle Bin, you won't even get the satisfaction of seeing your machine crash. Instead, even before you can close and open the Windows folder again, the operating system replaces the deleted system file with a perfect, fresh copy.

This feature also solves the age-old "My-application's-installer-replaced-an-important-system-file-with-an-older-version-and-now-nothing-works!" snafu. Simply put, Windows XP won't allow an application to replace a Windows XP file with an older version. True, this means that some older programs won't run—but better to do without them than your entire PC.

Incidentally, Windows XP uses a similar technique to keep your system updated with *Service Pack* files. (Service Packs are periodic updates that Microsoft releases to address problems in the operating system.)

In the old days of Windows NT, if you installed some new operating system feature after installing a Service Pack, you had to install the Service Pack again to ensure that the new feature was using all the latest files. Windows XP saves you this hassle by storing the Service Pack files right on your hard drive. Whenever applications need new versions of the operating system files, Windows installs them automatically, using the downloaded Service Pack files for reference.

---

3. Click the boldface calendar square closest to the last day you remember your PC working correctly.

   Now you see, in the right pane, the restore points that were created on that day, complete with a description.

4. Click one of the checkpoints listed on the right side, and then click Next.

   You're now warned to close all your documents and programs. Right-click each window button on your taskbar (except the System Restore button, of course), choosing Close from each shortcut menu until System Restore is the only program left running.

Figure 16-2:
Top: To change the month, click the < or > button at either end of the calendar. When you click a calendar square containing a bold number, the pane on the right shows the restoration points available for that date. You may find "Manual Checkpoint," which is one that you created yourself; "System Checkpoint," which is one that Windows XP created automatically (a "just in case" restore point); "Update to an unsigned driver," which means you installed software that Microsoft hasn't inspected (as described on page 430); "Automatic Updates Install," which is a Windows patch that XP downloaded and that you approved for installation; and so on.

Bottom: After a restart, you're back in business. This message reminds you that you can even rewind the rewinding, if it didn't produce the results you were seeking.

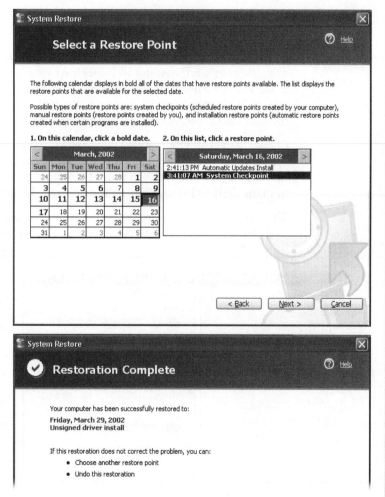

5. **Click Next.**

Now Windows goes to town, reinstating your operating system to reflect its condition on the date you specified. Leave your PC alone while this occurs.

When the process is complete, the computer restarts automatically, and the message shown in Figure 16-2 (bottom) appears. Welcome back to the past.

Tip: If rewinding your system to the golden days actually makes matters worse, you can always reverse the entire Restore process. To do so, open Start→Help and Support again. Once again, click "Undo changes to your computer with System Restore"–but this time, select "Undo my last Restoration." Click Next, click OK, click Next, and wait for the process to reverse itself.

Disk Cleanup

As you use your computer, Windows places numerous temporary files on your hard drive. Programs, utilities, and Web sites litter your hard drive with disposable files. Trouble is, Windows doesn't always clean them up when they're no longer needed. If you could see your hard drive surface, it would eventually look like the floor of a minivan whose owners eat a lot of fast food.

Choose Start→All Programs→Accessories→System Tools→Disk Cleanup to open Windows XP's built-in housekeeper program. (Or, if you find it faster, right-click the icon for your hard drive in your My Computer window, and choose Properties from the shortcut menu. Then, on the General tab, click the Disk Cleanup button.)

The program dives right in, inspecting your drive and reporting on files you can safely remove (Figure 16-3). It's like getting a bigger hard drive for free.

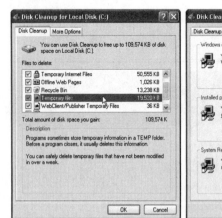 

Figure 16-3:
Left: Disk Cleanup announces how much free space you stand to gain. Click View Files to see the individual file icons in their native folders, for more selective deletion.

Right: Links on the More Options tab lead to several uninstall functions, for quick removal of programs, Windows parts, and restore points.

Start by selecting the drive you want to clean, and then wait while Disk Cleanup examines various files. The Disk Cleanup dialog box shown in Figure 16-3 (at left) appears when the inspection is over. Turn on the checkboxes of the file categories you'd like to have cleaned, and then click OK to send them to the digital landfill.

Tip: The More Options tab of this dialog box (Figure 16-3, right) provides links to three other Cleanup programs of Windows XP. Its three "Clean up" buttons take you to the Add or Remove Windows Components window (which lets you delete Windows modules you don't use), the main Add and Remove Programs window (which reveals which programs you haven't used in a while) and a confirmation box that lets you delete all but the latest *restore point,* described earlier in this chapter.

Disk Defragmenter

When you save a new file, Windows records its information onto the hard drive in small pieces called *blocks*. On a new PC, Windows lays the blocks end-to-end on the hard drive surface. Later, when you type more data into a document (thus enlarging it), the file no longer fits in the same space. Windows XP puts as much of the file in the original location as can fit, but may have to store a few of its blocks in the next empty spot on the hard drive.

Ordinarily, you'll never even notice that your files are getting chopped up in this way, since they open promptly and seamlessly. Windows keeps track of where it has stored the various pieces, and reconstitutes them when necessary.

As your drive fills up, the free space that's left is made up of smaller and smaller groups of blocks. Eventually, a new file may not fit in a single "parking place" on the hard drive surface, since there are no free spaces left that are large enough to hold it. In fact, Windows may have to store a file in several different areas of the disk, or even hundreds.

When you later try to open such a *fragmented* file, the drive heads (which read the disk) must scamper all over the disk surface, rounding up each block in turn, which is slower than reading contiguous blocks one after the other. Over time, this *file fragmentation* gets worse and worse and may eventually result in noticeable slowdowns when you open or save files.

The solution: Disk Defragmenter, a program that puts together pieces of files that have become fragmented (split into pieces) on your drive. The "defragger" also rearranges the files on your drives to make the operating system and programs load more quickly. Although Disk Defragmenter takes some time to do its thing, a freshly defragged PC feels faster and more responsive than a heavily fragmented one.

Tip: Fragmentation doesn't become noticeable except on hard drives that have been very full for quite a while. Don't bother defragmenting your drive unless you've actually noticed it slowing down. The time you'll spend waiting for Disk Defragmenter to do its job is much longer than the fractions of seconds caused by a little bit of file fragmentation.

Defragmenting a Drive

Before you run Disk Defragmenter, exit all programs, disable your antivirus software, empty the Recycle Bin, and plan some time away from the PC—remember, defragging is time-consuming. Depending on the size of your drive, the number of files on it, how fragmented it is, and especially how much free space is available, the Disk Defragmenter can take all day to run.

Defragmenting also puts your hard drive into a temporarily delicate condition. Therefore, don't defragment if your hard drive is ailing, if there's a thunderstorm, when your laptop is running on battery, or when you've set up the Task Scheduler (see page 473) to trigger automatic tasks.

Tip: During the defragmentation process, Windows picks up pieces of your files and temporarily sets them down in a different spot, like somebody trying to solve a jigsaw puzzle. If your hard drive is very full, defragmenting will take a lot longer than if you have some empty space available—and if there's less than fifteen percent free, Windows can't do the job completely. Before you run Disk Defragmenter, then, use Disk Cleanup and make as much free disk space as possible.

To open the Disk Defragmenter program, log on using an Administrator account (page 501), and then use any of these techniques:

- Choose Start→All Programs→Accessories→System Tools→Disk Defragmenter.

- Choose Start→My Computer. Right-click the icon of a hard drive; from the shortcut menu, choose Properties. In the Properties window, click the Tools tab, and then click Defragment Now.

- Choose Start→Run. Type *dfrg.msc* and press Enter.

Tip: Throughout Windows, and throughout its book and magazine literature, disks are referred to as *volumes.* Usually, volume means disk. But technically, it refers to *anything with its own disk icon* in the My Computer window—including disk *partitions* (page 470), Zip disks, DVDs, and so on. Page 440 has details.

The Disk Defragmenter window opens, listing your hard drives.

1. **Click the drive you want to work on.**

   Unless you have multiple hard drives, the C: drive is already selected.

2. **Click Analyze.**

   The program takes a minute to study the condition of the files on your hard drive. If, in its considered opinion, defragmenting is worth the time and effort, a message will tell you so (see Figure 16-4).

3. **Click Defragment.**

   Disk Defragmenter works by juggling file segments, lifting some into memory and depositing them elsewhere on the drive, then moving smaller files into the newly created free space. This shuffling process goes on for some time, as file fragments and whole files are moved around until every file lies on the drive in one piece.

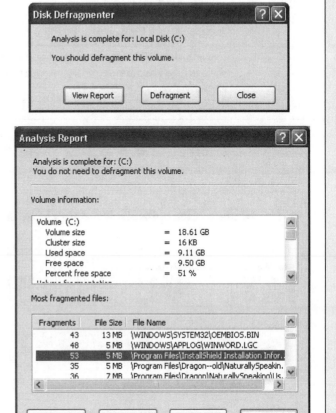

Figure 16-4:
Windows lets you know whether or not you'll gain anything by defragmenting your hard drive (top). If you're terminally curious, click View Report. A dialog box then appears (like the one here at bottom), listing each individual file on your hard drive and revealing the extent of its fragmentation.

Technically, in fact, Defragmenter doesn't rejoin file fragments randomly. In restoring them, Disk Defragmenter tries to organize the files better on the hard drive surface, using logic to position them so that applications will open up as quickly as possible.

A progress bar at the bottom of the window lets you know how far along it is. You can wander away to watch TV—or, if you're fascinated by this kind of thing, you can watch the colorful graphs (Figure 16-5).

For best results, leave your PC alone while the defragmenting process is going on. If you absolutely must perform a task at your computer during the defragging process, click Pause.

If you save a file while the drive is being defragmented (whether you pause the program or not), Disk Defragmenter starts the process over from the beginning.

Note: Disk Defragmenter isn't the only tool for this job. Programs like Norton Utilities include additional features. For example, because they track how often you use the various files on your drive, they can store the most frequently used files at the beginning of the disk for quicker access. In some programs, you can even *choose* which files go at the beginning of the disk.

Do these additional features actually produce a measurable improvement over Windows XP's built-in defragger? That's hard to say, especially when you remember the biggest advantage of Disk Defragmenter: it's free.

Figure 16-5:
A detailed view of the defragmentation process helps you understand what Disk Defragmenter is doing. The color of each little square shows what's going on, as the program juggles software files, system files, and data files to put each file in the best possible place. At that point of perfection, Disk Defragmenter announces victory over fragmentation and asks if you want to close the program. Say Yes unless you have another hard drive that needs defragging.

Hard Drive Checkups

Every time you shut down the computer, Windows tidies up, ensuring all files are saved properly on the drive. When all is well, Windows turns off the machine (or, on older computers, displays a message on your screen telling you it's OK to shut off your computer manually). The time that elapses between your Turn Off Computer command and the actual power-down moment is the "tidying up" period.

But sometimes, thanks to a system crash, power outage, or toddler playing with your surge suppressor, your computer gets turned off without warning—and without the usual shutdown checks. In the days before Windows XP, restarting the PC after such a *dirty shutdown* would automatically run a program called ScanDisk, a utility designed to detect and, when possible, repair drive damage that may have occurred as a result of an improper shutdown.

ScanDisk doesn't exist in Windows XP, but its functions have been reincarnated. You get to this feature by right-clicking the icon of the hard drive you want to check (in the My Computer window). From the shortcut menu, choose Properties; click the Tools tab, and click Check Now (Figure 16-6, top).

As shown in the middle of Figure 16-6, a dialog box appears that offers two optional checkboxes:

- **Automatically fix file system errors.** Clearly, you want this option turned on, so that any problems Windows finds are taken care of automatically. If you're checking the system drive (the drive on which Windows XP is installed), you'll see the dialog box shown at bottom in Figure 16-6. Click Yes to defer the actual scan until the next time you restart the computer. (Other drives get scanned immediately.)

- **Scan for and attempt recovery of bad sectors.** If you turn on this option, whenever the scan finds a damaged section of a drive, it'll move any files located there elsewhere on the drive. Then the program surrounds that hard-disk area with the digital equivalent of a yellow "Police Line—Do Not Cross" tape, so that Windows won't use the damaged area for storing files in the future.

When Good Drives Go Bad

I was surprised when the Check Disk dialog box found some problems with my hard drive. I don't understand what could have gone wrong. I treat my PC with respect, talk to it often, and never take it swimming. Why did my hard drive get flaky?

All kinds of things can cause problems with your hard drive, but the most common are low voltage, power outages, voltage spikes, and mechanical problems with the drive controller or the drive itself.

An inexpensive gadget called a *line conditioner* (sold at computer stores) can solve the low-voltage problem. A more expensive gizmo known as an *Uninterruptible Power Supply* (UPS) maintains enough backup battery power to keep your computer going when the power goes out completely—for a few minutes, anyway, so that you can shut down the computer properly. The more expensive models

have line conditioning built in. A UPS is also the answer to power outages, if they're common in your area.

Voltage spikes are the most dangerous to your PC. They frequently occur during the first seconds when the power comes back on after a power failure. A surge suppressor is the logical defense here. But remember that the very cheap devices often sold as surge suppressors are actually little more than extension cords. Furthermore, some of the models that do provide adequate protection are designed to sacrifice themselves in battle. After a spike, you may have to replace them.

If you care about your computer (or at least about the money you spent on it), buy a good surge suppressor, at the very least. The best ones come with a guarantee that the company will replace your equipment (up to a certain dollar value) if the unit fails to provide adequate protection.

Before you begin the scan, quit all other open programs; otherwise, Windows will report that it was "unable" to complete the scan. Finally, click the Start button in the Check Disk dialog box to begin the scan. When all phases of the check are complete ("Phase 1, Phase 2"...), a dialog box lets you know how things turned out.

Note: If you elected to format your hard drive with the *NTFS file system,* described on page 620, you'll find hard-drive glitches fixable by ScanDisk and its descendant to be extremely rare, because NTFS drives are designed to be self-repairing.

If you still use the *FAT 32* formatting scheme, however, it's a good idea to perform this kind of check once every few months, so that it can check your hard drive for any nascent problems.

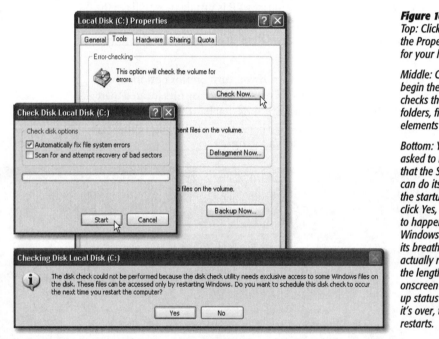

Figure 16-6:
Top: Click Check Now in the Properties dialog box for your hard drive.

Middle: Click Start to begin the scan, which checks the file structure, folders, files, and other elements on your drive.

Bottom: You may be asked to restart the PC, so that the Son of ScanDisk can do its thing during the startup process. If you click Yes, nothing seems to happen at all. Windows is just holding its breath until you actually restart. During the lengthy procedure, onscreen messages serve up status reports. When it's over, the computer restarts.

Disk Management

"Disk management" isn't just a cool, professional-sounding skill—it's the name of yet another built-in Windows XP maintenance program, one that may be familiar to Windows 2000 veterans, but is completely new to people who are used to Windows Me and its predecessors.

To open this technical database of information about your disks and drives, you can use any of three methods:

- Choose Start→Control Panel→Administrative Tools→Computer Management. In the resulting Computer Management window, double-click Disk Management in the list at the left side.

- In the Start menu, right-click My Computer. From the shortcut menu, choose Manage. Once again, double-click Disk Management in the list at the left side.

- Choose Start→Run; type *diskmgmt.msc* and press Enter.

In any case, you arrive at the window shown in Figure 16-7. At first glance, it appears to be nothing more than a table of every disk (and *partition* of every disk) currently connected to your PC. In truth, the Disk Management window is a software toolkit that lets you *operate* on these drives, too. For example, Chapter 15 describes in detail how you can use this window to slice and dice the free space on your drives into new, combined "virtual disks" (volumes).

Figure 16-7:
The Drive Management window is part of the much bigger, much more technical entity known as the Computer Management console. You access it by clicking Disk Management (in the left-side pane). Then you can operate on your drives by right-clicking them. Don't miss the View menu, by the way, which lets you change either the top or the bottom display. For example, you can make them display all of your disks instead of your volumes (there's a difference).

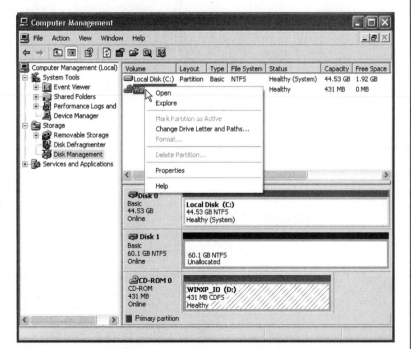

Change a Drive Letter

As you've probably noticed, Windows assigns a drive letter to each disk drive associated with your PC. The floppy disk drive is always A:, the primary internal hard drive is generally C:, and so on. Among other places, you see these letters in parentheses following the names of your drives, as when you choose Start→My Computer.

Windows generally assigns these letters in the order that you install new drives to your system. You're not allowed to change the drive letter of your floppy drive or primary hard drive (usually the C: drive). You can, however, override the standard, unimaginative Windows letter assignments easily enough, as shown in Figure 16-8.

Note: If Windows XP is currently using files on the disk whose drive letter you're trying to change, Disk Management might create the new drive letter assignment but leave the old one intact until the next time you restart the computer. This is an effort not to pull the rug out from under any open files.

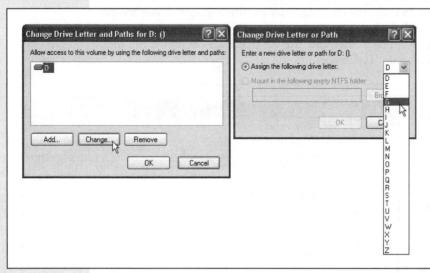

Figure 16-8:
Right-click a drive icon as shown in Figure 15-7. From the shortcut menu, choose Change Drive Letter and Paths.

Left: In this dialog box, click Change.

Right: Then choose a letter that hasn't already been assigned. Click OK, and then approve your action in the confirmation box.

Partition a New Drive

The vast majority of Windows PCs have only one hard drive, represented in the My Computer window as a single icon.

Plenty of power users, however, delight in *partitioning* the hard drive—dividing its surface so that it appears on the screen as two different icons with two different names. At that point, you can live like a king, enjoying the following advantages just like people who have two separate hard drives:

• You can keep Windows XP on one of them and Windows Me (for example) on the other, so that you can switch between the two at startup time. (You may hear this feature called *dual booting,* a procedure described on page 620.)

• Life is much easier if you frequently install and reinstall the operating system, or different versions of it. Doing so allows you to keep all your files safely on one partition, confining all the installing/uninstalling activity to the other.

• You can use multiple partitions to keep your operating system(s) separate from folders and files. In this way, you can perform a *clean install* of Windows (page

617) onto one partition without having to worry about losing any of your important files or installation programs.

Unfortunately, partitioning a hard drive using the tools built into Windows XP requires first *erasing the hard drive completely.* And that, of course, involves copying all of your files and programs onto some kind of backup disk first—and then copying them back onto the hard drive when the process is over. Ponder this compromise, weighing it against the advantages of partitioning.

Tip: You *can* partition your hard drive without having to erase everything on it—just not for free. Commercial programs like PartitionMagic *(www.powerquest.com)* create, resize, merge, and convert partitions without disturbing any of your files.

The Disk Management program included with Windows XP, therefore, is best suited for creating new partitions on *new or empty* hard drives. Ditto for FDISK, a DOS utility that can also do the job (as described in Appendix A).

In the Disk Management window, free space (suitable for turning into a partition of its own) shows up with a black bar and the label Unallocated. Figure 16-7, for example, depicts a brand new hard drive that hasn't yet been named or sliced up into partitions. The whole thing is still "unallocated."

To create a new partition, right-click one of these unallocated segments. From the shortcut menu, choose New Partition. A wizard appears, whose screens ask you:

- What kind of partition you want to create. (You'll usually want Primary.)

- How big you want the partition to be. If you're dividing up a 60 GB drive, for example, you might decide to make the first partition 20 GB and the second 40 GB. You'd begin by creating the 20 GB partition (right-clicking the big "Unallocated" bar in Figure 16-7); when that was over, you'd see a smaller "Unallocated" chunk still left in the Disk Management window. You'd right-click it and choose New Partition *again,* this time accepting the partition size the wizard proposes (which is *all* the remaining free space).

- What drive letter you want to assign to it.

- What disk-formatting scheme you want to apply to it (you'll usually choose NTFS—see page 620).

When the wizard is through with you, it's safe to close the window. A quick look at your My Computer window will confirm that you now have new "disks" (actually partitions of the same disk), which you can use for different purposes.

Note: Partitioning and disk management can go even farther. You can resize your disk volumes, combine the space from multiple disks into one large volume, and perform other advanced stunts, as described in Chapter 15.

Turn a Drive into a Folder

Talk about techie: Most people could go their entire lives without needing this feature, or even imagining that it exists. But Microsoft loves power users, and this one's for them.

Using the Paths feature of Disk Management, you can actually turn a hard drive (or partition) into a *folder* on another hard drive (or partition). Each of these disks-disguised-as-folders is technically known as a *mounted volume, junction point,* or *drive path.* See Figure 16-9 for details.

This arrangement affords the following unique possibilities:

• In effect, you can greatly expand capacity of your main hard drive—by installing a second hard drive that masquerades as a folder on the first one.

• You can turn a burned CD into a folder on your main hard drive, too—a handy way to fool your programs into thinking that the files they're looking for are still in the same old place on your hard drive. (You could pull this stunt in a crisis—when the "real" folder has become corrupted or has been thrown away.)

• If you're a *power* power user with lots of partitions, disks, and drives, you may feel hemmed in by the limitation of only 26 assignable letters (A through Z). Turning one of your disks into a mounted volume bypasses that limitation, however. A mounted volume doesn't need a drive letter at all.

• A certain disk can be made to appear in more than one place at once. You could put all your MP3 files on a certain disk or partition—and then make it show up as a folder in the My Music folder of everyone who uses the computer.

Note: You can only create a mounted volume on an *NTFS-formatted* hard drive (see page 620).

To bring about this arrangement, visit the Disk Management window, and then right-click the icon of the disk or partition that you want to turn into a mounted volume. From the shortcut menu, choose Change Drive Letter and Paths.

In the Change Drive Letter and Paths dialog box, click Add; in the next dialog box, click Browse. Navigate to and select an empty folder—the one that will represent the disk. (Click New Folder if you didn't create one in advance, as shown at right in Figure 16-9.) Finally, click OK.

Once the deed is done, take time to note a few special characteristics of a mounted volume:

• The mounted volume may behave just like a folder, but its icon is a dead giveaway, since it still looks like a hard drive (or CD drive, or DVD drive, or whatever).

Still, if you're in doubt about what it is, you can right-click it and choose Properties from the shortcut menu. You'll see that the Type information says "Mounted Volume," and the Target line identifies the disk from which it was made.

- Avoid circular references, in which you turn two drives into folders on *each other.* Otherwise, you risk throwing your programs into a spasm of infinite-loop thrashing.

- To undo your mounted-drive effect, return to the Disk Management program and choose View→Drive Paths. You're shown a list of all the drives you've turned into folders; click one and then click Remove. You've just turned that special, "I'm really a drive" folder into an ordinary empty folder.

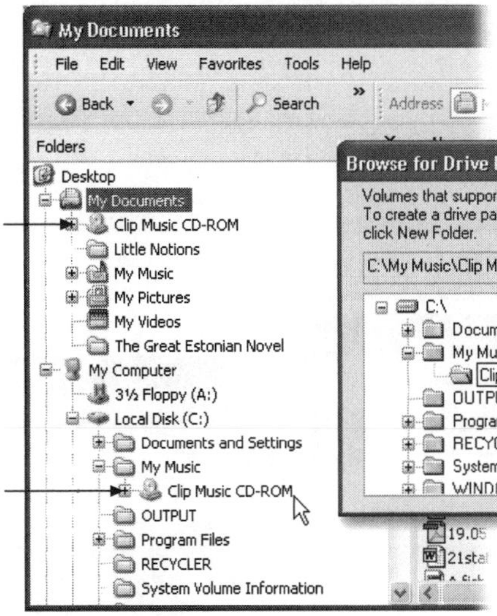

Figure 16-9:
Left: Man, how many CD drives does this guy have? Just one. But through the miracle of mounted volumes, it's appearing in as many different folders as the owner likes. You could do the same thing with a hard drive—make it appear as a folder icon on any other drive.

Right: Here's how to do it: Designate an empty folder to be the receptacle—a metaphysical portal—for the drive's contents.

Task Scheduler

The Scheduled Tasks window lets you set up Windows XP to open certain programs, utilities, and documents according to a schedule that you specify. Unfortunately, all it can do is *open* programs and documents on cue. Unless you're prepared to type in the special codes, called *switches,* the Scheduled Tasks window can't actually make them *do* anything once they're open. The tutorial on page 476 offers more information about switches.

To open the Task Scheduler (see Figure 16-10), choose Start→All Programs→Accessories→System Tools→Scheduled Tasks. The Scheduled Tasks window opens, at first containing only a single icon (unless a program you've installed has already scheduled a task), called Add Scheduled Task.

Adding a Task to the Scheduler

To add a task to the schedule, double-click the Add Scheduled Task icon. A wizard appears; click Next. A list of programs now appears on your PC (Figure 16-10, bottom left). If the one you want to schedule is listed, click it. If not, click Browse, find and open its folder, and double-click its icon.

Now you're asked how often you want the new task to run: every day, every week, and so on. Make a selection, then follow the wizard's prompts to schedule your task. For example, if you chose Monthly, you can tell the wizard which *day* of the month, and at which time (Figure 16-10, bottom right).

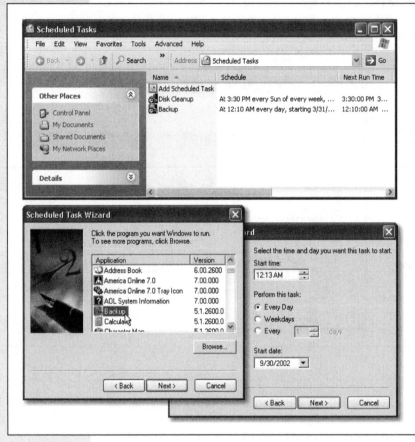

Figure 16-10:
Top: The Task Scheduler keeps a calendar for Windows XP. Tasks appear in the schedule when you enter them manually, or when other programs (such as the Maintenance Wizard) set them up. You can use the Task Scheduler window to add, modify, or remove tasks. (Make sure your computer is turned on during the time any task is supposed to run.)

Bottom: The wizard asks you what you want to open, and how often.

Finally, because Windows XP can accommodate multiple user accounts (see the next chapter), and can even run *your* tasks while somebody *else* is logged in and using the computer, you'll have to enter your user name and password.

Completing the wizard means you've successfully added a new icon to the Scheduled Tasks window (Start→Control Panel→Scheduled Tasks). If the window is in Details view, tidy little columns tell you what each task's schedule is and when it will run next.

Changing Scheduled Tasks

Double-clicking a task's listing in the Task Scheduler window opens its Properties dialog box (Figure 16-11), where you can make several kinds of changes:

- **Cancel a scheduled task.** You can, of course, stop a certain scheduled task from running just by deleting the task entirely—throwing away its icon from the Scheduled Tasks window. In many cases, however, you might find it more flexible to simply turn off its Enabled checkbox (on the Task tab of the Properties dialog box). The latter method leaves the task in the Task Scheduler window, so that you can turn it back on at a later date.

- **Change the schedule for a task.** Click the Schedule tab of the Properties dialog box to change the schedule for a task.

- **Change the settings for a scheduled task.** Using the Settings tab of a task's Properties dialog box, you can design certain automated tasks to run, or not, according to certain conditions (see Figure 16-11). For example, you might want to turn on "Only start the task if the computer has been idle for at least __ minutes," so that your processor-intensive task doesn't fire itself up when somebody else (using another account) is rendering 3-D movie scenes.

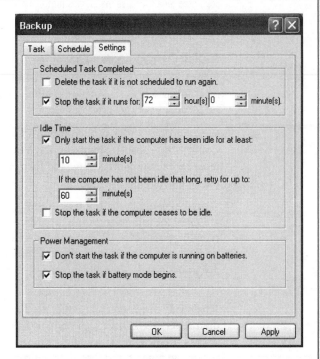

Figure 16-11:
Some of the factory settings for scheduled tasks are a bit ridiculous. For example, it's probably a good idea to stop a task if it runs longer than 4 or 5 hours, not 72 hours. In fact, except for defragging the hard drive, most scheduled tasks should take less than an hour. The bottom section of the dialog box applies to laptop computers.

Start a Task Immediately

To trigger one of the listed programs right now, right-click its listing in the Scheduled Tasks window and choose Run from the shortcut menu. (The task will run again at its next scheduled time.)

Pause All Scheduled Tasks

If a schedule-triggering event is taking place on your PC while you're trying to work, thus slowing down the proceedings, you can suspend those background operations until your work is complete. Just open the Scheduled Tasks window and choose Advanced→Pause Task Scheduler.

When you think it's OK for those background-scheduled tasks to carry on, "unpause" the scheduler by choosing Advanced→Continue Task Scheduler.

Stop Using Task Scheduler

If you don't want any tasks to run, ever, open the Scheduled Tasks window and choose Advanced→Stop Using Task Scheduler. Doing so prevents the scheduler from starting up when you turn on the computer. (Choose Advanced→Start Using Task Scheduler to turn it back on.)

Note: You can request that Windows XP notify you, the next time you log on, when a task didn't run at its appointed time (because the PC was turned off, for example). To set this up, open the Scheduled Tasks window and then choose Advanced→Notify Me of Missed Tasks.

A Disk Defragmenter Example

Before the invention of the mouse, menus, and icons, computer geeks operated their machines solely at the *command line*—a black window where you had to type cryptic commands to get anything done.

Windows XP still has a command line (Start→All Programs→Accessories→ Command Prompt). Most everyday Windows fans don't even know it's there—but it comes in handy every now and then. You need the command line, in fact, to use the Task Scheduler.

To make matters even less user-friendly, remember that Windows doesn't call programs by the same names you do. (Microsoft Word, for example, is really a program called *winword.exe*.) To run a program from the command line, you have to call it by the same name Windows uses. You can find what that is by right-clicking the program's icon in the Start menu, choosing Properties from the shortcut menu, and looking at the Target field in the Properties dialog box.

That's only one ingredient you'll need to run a program from the command line— the others are command parameters called *switches*. These are usually dashes or slashes followed by letter and number combinations, like the second part of the command *ping –t*, and they tell the program what to *do* once you've opened it. Task Scheduler runs programs by executing command line strings like this.

Putting together the correct switches to trigger the activity you want is not for the technically timid. But if you'd like to know what you're getting into, here's an example that demonstrates how to schedule Disk Defragmenter to run at a specific time (when you're sleeping, for example, and won't care that it's slowing down your

PC). In fact, this is one of the most common uses of the Task Scheduler: using it to trigger common maintenance tasks without your involvement.

Programming Disk Defragmenter

To schedule a program like Disk Defragmenter, you must first learn what switches it understands.

To discover which switches are available in a Windows XP program, open a Command Prompt window (Start→All Programs→Accessories→Command Prompt). Then type the name of the program, followed by either the *-h* or *-?* switch. (Both of these mean "help.") For example, you can find out which switches drive Disk Defragmenter by typing this:

```
Defrag -?
```

When you press Enter, a help screen like this appears:

```
Usage:
Defrag <volume> [-a] [-f] [-v] [-?]
volume  Drive letter or mount point d:\ or d:\vol\mountpoint
-a Analyze only
-f Force defragmentation even if free space is low
-v Verbose output
-? Display this help text
```

From this, you might discern that the command necessary to run the Disk Defragmenter on your hard drive (C:) is this:

```
Defrag C:\ -f
```

which means, "Use the *defrag* command on my C: drive; defragment it even if I don't have much free space."

Always test your command line before you schedule it to run unattended. If the command behaves itself while you're watching, you can be confident that it will do the same when Task Scheduler runs unattended.

To schedule the command, open the Scheduled Tasks program in the Control Panel. Double-click the Add Scheduled Task icon. The Scheduled Task Wizard appears; click Next to see the list of programs that the Task Scheduler offers to trigger.

However, Disk Defragmenter isn't listed, so you must click Browse and navigate to the Local Disk (C:)→Windows→System32 folder, where you'll find it (the program's real name is defrag.exe). Double-click it, and then proceed with the wizard screens that let you specify a schedule and record your account password. You can schedule the program to run once or at regular intervals, and even create multiple schedules for the same task. (If your user account doesn't *have* a password assigned, you'll have to create one, following the instructions on page 503.)

On the final wizard screen, don't click Finish until you've first turned on "Open advanced properties for this task when I click Finish." After you click Finish, a special summary window appears, listing the program to be run: *C:/WINDOWS/SYS-TEM32/defrag.exe.* Click in the Run box at the end of the command, press the Space bar, and then type *C:*, another space, and then *-f*, as shown in Figure 16-12. Click OK.

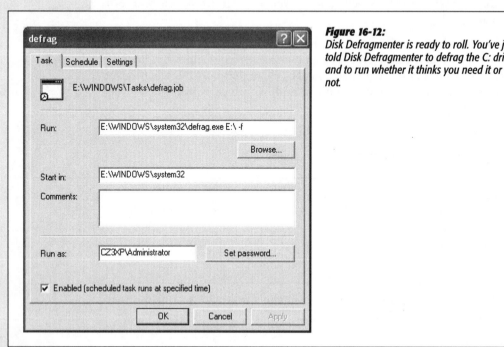

Figure 16-12:
Disk Defragmenter is ready to roll. You've just told Disk Defragmenter to defrag the C: drive, and to run whether it thinks you need it or not.

Finally, you're asked to type in your password—twice. When you click OK, your work is done. An icon for your scheduled task appears on the screen for the Disk Defragmenter schedule that you've just added, and it's prepared to run automatically at the times you specified.

Interpreting Results

If you switch the Scheduled Tasks window into Details view by choosing View→ Details, the Last Result column is supposed to tell you whether or not the tasks you scheduled were completed. Unfortunately, Task Scheduler doesn't translate the numerical result codes into English, so what you see in this column is typically a cryptic hexadecimal value like *0x0*.

All you have to know about such *exit codes* is that, in most cases, a value of 0 (or 0x0) means that the program ran without a hitch. Anything else represents some kind of error message. If that's what you get, you, or somebody who knows about this kind of thing, should try running the command in the Command Prompt window in hopes of discovering why it's not working correctly.

Microsoft Backup

Consider this: The proximity of your drive's spinning platters to the head that reads them is roughly the same proportion as the wheels of an airliner flying at 500 miles per hour, twelve inches off the ground. It's amazing that hard drives work as well, and as long, as they do.

Still, because a hard drive is nothing more than a mass of moving parts in delicate alignment, every now and then disaster strikes. That's why backing up your data (making a safety copy) on a regular basis is an essential part of using a PC. Even if computers aren't your career, there's probably a lot of valuable stuff on your hard drive: all of your digital photos, the addresses and phone numbers you've spent hours typing into your Contacts list, a lifetime's worth of email, the Web sites in your Favorites folder, and so on.

Now, if you use XP Pro in a corporation—a distinct possibility, considering its target audience—you probably don't even have to think about backing up your stuff. A network administrator generally does the backing up for you and your co-workers. (You're probably instructed to save your files on a network server PC instead of your own, so that the administrator can back up all of the employees' files in one swift move.) In that case, you can flip ahead to more interesting sections of this chapter.

If you use Windows XP at home, or in a smaller company that doesn't have network nerds running around to ensure your files' safety, you might be grateful for Microsoft Backup, a very simple backup program that comes with Windows XP. It lacks some of the specialized features of commercial backup programs, but at least it lets you back up entire drives or selected files and folders, at times and under the conditions you specify, to other disks or tapes. You can even schedule it to run at regular intervals (using the Task Scheduler program), so that you always have a recent copy of your data on hand.

Backup Hardware

An external hard drive makes an extremely convenient backup system, since it spares you the hassle of inserting and tracking multiple removable disks (like Zips or CDs).

Still, removable disks are the safest disks of all, because you can store them somewhere else: in a fireproof box, a safe deposit box at the bank, or the trunk of your car—anywhere but in your office, making your data safe even in the case of fire or burglary.

Here's a rundown of popular removable backup disks:

- **Floppy disks.** Forget it. Unless you work with nothing more than a few text files, your stuff will never fit onto floppies.

- **Zip, Jaz, Peerless.** When it comes to removable cartridge drives like these from Iomega, consider capacity and expense. The older Zip cartridges, which hold 100 or 250 MB, may be too small for most backup purposes. The newer 750 MB drives are a better bet.

Jaz and Peerless cartridges can hold a lot more, but they're expensive. Divide the number of megabytes by the cartridge price to figure out which is the most cost-effective.

- **Recordable CD.** Burning your backups onto blank CD-R and CD-RW disks is another viable alternative—especially since blanks are dirt cheap. Unfortunately—and incredibly—the Windows XP Backup program doesn't recognize CD-ROM drives as backup devices.

  Many other backup programs do, however. Your CD burner may even have come with one. As long as you don't have many gigabytes of files to back up, this system can work well.

- **Tape cartridges.** Magnetic tapes are economical, retain their data for years, and offer huge capacity in a compact package. Better yet, Microsoft's Backup program works with them. Tape drives are available in either external USB versions or internal units that you install yourself.

  The main drawback of a tape system is that you can't use it for anything *other* than backups. You can't get to a file at the end of the tape without fast forwarding through all of the data that precedes it, so you wouldn't want to use these as everyday disks.

Creating a Backup Job

To launch the Backup program, choose Start→All Programs→Accessories→System Tools→Backup. A wizard walks you through the process of setting up a backup job, like this:

Backup or restore?

The first wizard screen (Figure 16-13, top) wants to know whether you want to *back up* your files (because you're a shrewd, confident, happy person in a time of PC health) or *restore* them (because you're a desperate, unhappy person whose files have somehow been deleted or corrupted).

To back up your files, of course, click "Backup files and settings" and then click Next.

Create a backup job

The next wizard window asks what you want to back up:

- **My documents and settings, Everyone's documents and settings.** These options assume that you're using a PC shared by several people, each with a separate account (see the next chapter). It's asking whether you want to back up just *your* files and settings, or those of every account holder. (If you're the sole proprietor of your machine, just use the first option.)

- **All information on this computer.** This option tells Backup to copy every single file and folder on your drive(s), including almost two gigabytes of Windows itself. This is a massive project—and, in general, an unnecessary one. After all, you already have a backup of Windows itself (on your Windows CD) and of your programs (on the original software disks), so there may not be much point in making another copy.

- **Let me choose what to back up.** This option leads to a Windows Explorer–like display (see Figure 16-13, bottom) that lets you choose the specific folders and files to be backed up.

Tip: If you choose this option, don't miss the System State icon. Selecting this icon backs up the Windows XP *registry* (page 492) and other vital system components that are otherwise inaccessible because they're in use while the backup is running. In case of disaster, only people who backed up the System State will be able to *completely* restore their PCs to their original conditions.

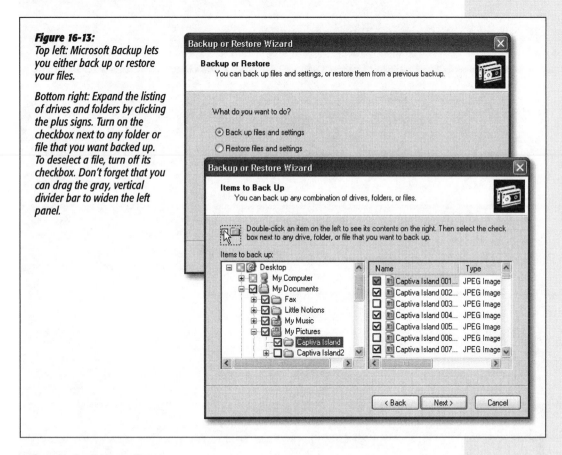

Figure 16-13:
Top left: Microsoft Backup lets you either back up or restore your files.

Bottom right: Expand the listing of drives and folders by clicking the plus signs. Turn on the checkbox next to any folder or file that you want backed up. To deselect a file, turn off its checkbox. Don't forget that you can drag the gray, vertical divider bar to widen the left panel.

Select the backup medium

The next screen asks where you want to store the backup files you're about to create. The drop-down list starts out suggesting that you back up your hard drive onto *floppy disks*—not exactly a forward-thinking choice. Considering the massive size of today's hard drives, you'll be inserting blank floppies for the next three presidential administrations.

Instead, if your PC does, in fact, have a backup disk connected (a magnetic tape drive, for example, or a Zip drive), choose its name from this drop-down list.

The other option, available on all computers, is to back up the selected data to a file on your hard drive. You can use this option to create CD-sized backup files for burning onto CDs later, to back up your data to another hard drive in the same computer, or to back up to another computer on the network. (To use the latter option, click Browse.) In any case, click Cancel if you're asked to insert a floppy disk.

Advanced Backup Types

As noted above, the Advanced wizard offers you a choice among several kinds of backups.

To understand the differences, it's important to understand that each time it backs up a file, backup programs manipulate an invisible switch on that file called the *archive bit*. It's a little note to itself, a flag that tells Windows whether or not that file needs backing up.

In a **Normal** backup, for example, the program copies all of the selected files to the backup drive, regardless of their archive bits. During the backup process, Windows changes each archive bit to Off, in effect marking it as having been backed up.

(If you later make changes to the file, Windows turn its archive bit back on. As a result, files whose archive bits are turned on are the ones that have been changed since the last Normal backup.)

If you choose **Copy,** Backup copies the files, but doesn't turn off their archive bits. In other words, you're simply using Backup as a glorified copying program.

An **Incremental** backup copies *only* files whose archive bits are set to On—that is, files that are new or have changed since the last Normal backup. After the backup, all archive bits get turned off again, denoting everything as having been backed up.

Incremental backups work much faster (and use less space) than full backups, since Windows copies only a few files each time. But they're less convenient if the worst should happen. When restoring your files to the PC from your backup disks, you must restore each backup file in chronological order, beginning with the Normal backup disks

and proceeding through all of the incrementals performed since that last Normal backup.

A **Differential** backup also copies only the files that have their archive bits turned on. So far, it's the same as an incremental backup. However, this type of job leaves the archive bits as they are instead of turning them off. Therefore, the *second* differential backup *also* backs up all the files that have been changed since the full backup, and so does the third. In other words, if you perform a full backup on Monday, the differential backups on Tuesday, Wednesday, and Thursday each back up *all* the files that have changed since Monday.

Of course, this system requires more backup disk space (or tapes), because you're actually making duplicate and triplicate copies of certain files. But the payoff comes when your hard drive dies. Instead of having to restore each day's backup job (as you would with an incremental backup), you need to restore only the last Normal backup and *one* differential backup set (the most recent one)—a relatively fast and simple procedure.

A typical backup cycle is to perform a Normal backup once a week or month, with incremental or differential backups in between.

This technical tradeoff between convenience at backup time and convenience in case of disaster should sound familiar to anyone who's ever had to choose between two insurance policies, one of which costs less but has a high deductible.

Finally, the **Daily** backup copies files you created or changed today. It doesn't change the archive bits.

The Save As dialog box that appears asks you to name the backup file you're creating (its filename extension is *.bkf*). Click Save when you've selected a location and typed a name.

Advanced backup options

The final wizard screen now appears (Figure 16-14). If you click Finish, the backup process begins—a process that may take several seconds or several hours, depending on how much you're copying. Your work here is done.

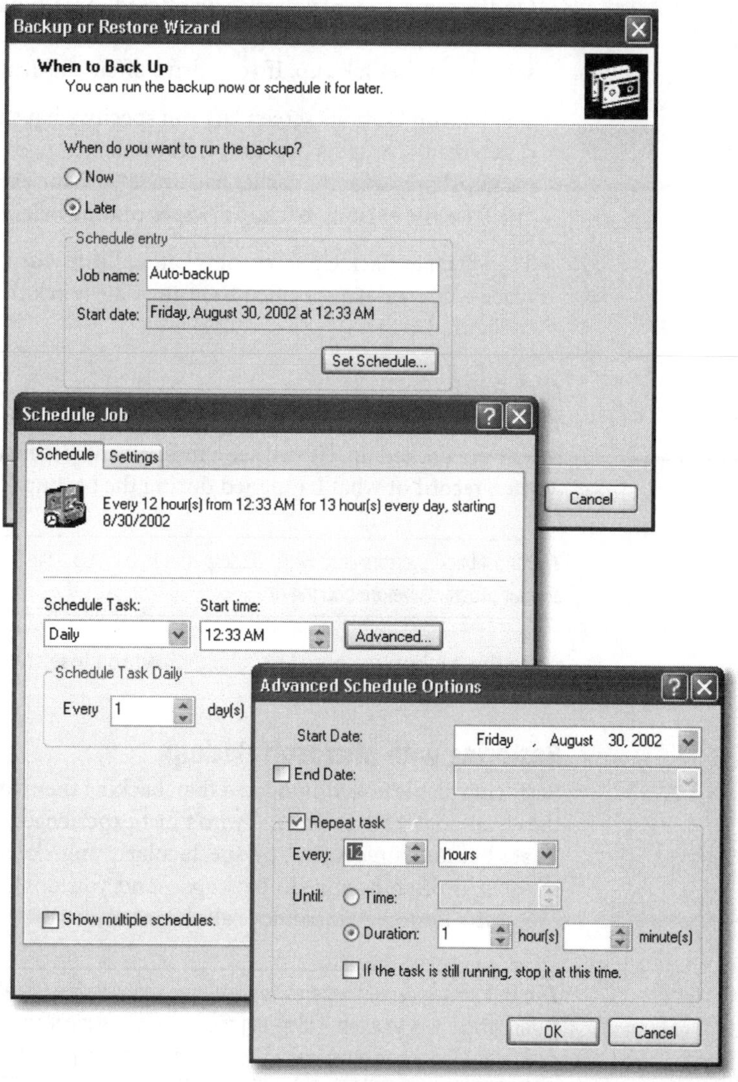

Figure 16-14:
Of all the Advanced options, this series of screens (click Set Schedule, then Advanced) may be the most useful, because it lets you establish a backup that runs automatically, without your involvement. (Behind the scenes, it creates a task in your Start→Control Panel→ Scheduled Tasks window, where you can manipulate it or adjust its schedule.)

On the other hand, if you click the Advanced button on the final wizard screen, you're treated to yet another wizard. Most people, most of the time, will never need these special-case options, but here's what the screens of the Advanced wizard offer:

- Choose the *type* of backup you want: Normal, Copy, Incremental, Differential, or Daily (see the box on page 482).

- The next part of the screen offers to *verify* each file that's backed up. In just a few seconds, you get a confirmation that the copy perfectly matches the original—a good idea.

  On the same screen, you may be offered something called Hardware Compression, a reference to circuitry inside a tape drive that condenses the amount of space your files take up. If your drive offers this feature, use it.

- The Backup Options screen lets you specify what should happen if your backup disk already contains previous backup files. "Append this backup to the existing backups" preserves the earlier backup set—at the expense of disk space, of course. "Replace the existing backups" wipes out the original backup.

- The When to Back Up screen lets you indicate when you want this backup to take place—now or at a specified time and date (click the Set Schedule button shown in Figure 16-14).

Click Finish

When Backup is finished backing up your files, a window shows how many files and bytes were backed up. (If you see a message indicating an error, click Report to see a written record of what happened during the backup.)

Tip: Most backup errors arise when Backup tries to back up a file that's open. To avoid this problem, exit all your programs before backing up.

After the backup is complete, click Close to close the Report window. Your data is safe—for now.

Restoring with Microsoft Backup

Restoring files is less complicated than backing them up—a good thing, considering the emotional state of anyone who's just experienced a total hard drive meltdown. That's because, unless you're a spectacularly unlucky individual, you don't perform restores as often as you do backups—and you don't schedule them. The Backup program's Restore Wizard does all the work for you.

Tip: Perform regular test restores, to make sure your data is retrievable from the backup disks. (Consider restoring your files to a test folder–not the folder where the files came from–so you don't wind up with duplicates.) There's no other way to be absolutely sure that your backups are working properly.

To restore files using the Restore Wizard, here's the plan (which assumes that, if your whole hard drive was trashed, you have already replaced it and reinstalled Windows XP):

1. **Click Start→All Programs→Accessories→System Tools→Backup.**

   The Backup or Restore Wizard Welcome screen appears.

2. **Click Next. On the second screen, click "Restore files and settings," and then click Next.**

   The What To Restore page contains the now-familiar expanding display that lists your PC's backup devices. The display lists a File icon, too, so that you can restore from a backup file (see "Select the backup medium" on page 481). Backup displays the date and time each backup file was made, making it easy to select the right file. If you use a tape drive or other device for your backups, the display lists the tapes or disks you have created.

   Click to select the items you want to restore, exactly as you did when selecting files to back up.

Tip: Clicking the + button expands a folder so that you can select an individual file inside it. This is also a great trick if you're restoring, from your backup file, a document that you've accidentally deleted from the hard drive.

---

3. **Select the tape or disk that contains your backup. Select the data to restore.**

   When you select the backup disk or tape, the right pane in the What to Restore screen contains an expandable list of its contents. Double-click the folders seen here for a list of individual files. Turn on the checkboxes of the files and folders you want to restore, as shown in Figure 16-15.

Note: Whenever Backup backs up your files, it remembers which files it put on which backup disks by creating a table of contents on the disk or tape that was in the drive when the job ended.

That's why, as you browse the files listed on a backup disk, you may be asked to insert that final disk or tape. Only then can Backup show you what's on it.

---

4. **On the Completing the Backup or Restore Wizard screen, click the Advanced button, if you like.**

   Ordinarily, Backup restores every backed-up file onto your hard drive in exactly the same folder from which it came. If the original file is still *in* that original folder, however, it doesn't bother copying the equivalent file from the backup disk. If that arrangement sounds good to you, skip to the next step.

   But suppose you'd like Backup to put the files in a *different* folder, or you want them to *replace* the duplicate files it encounters. In that case, the Advanced button is just the ticket. It lets you specify where you want the restored files to go: into the folders they came from or some other disk or folder.

If you choose "Alternate location," you can type in the path to (or Browse to) a different folder (like *C:\Rescued*). If there's no such folder, Backup will create it for you.

If you turn on "Single folder," Backup dumps all of the selected files directly into one specified folder, loose (not in a hierarchy of folders). Choose this option if you're simply trying to reclaim a few important files, rather than trying to rein- state your entire drive.

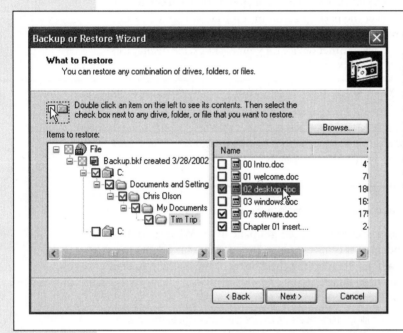

Figure 16-15:
The Restore Wizard's What to Restore page is similar in format to Windows Explorer, except that it displays only the contents of a particular backup tape or disk. You can select from the backup tapes, disks, or files you've created, or click Import File to read the contents of a backup file you created on another Windows XP system.

5. **Click Next. Indicate whether or not you want Backup to overwrite duplicate files.**

Backup's file-restoring feature isn't only useful when you've had to wipe out your hard drive completely. It can also be handy when something less drastic went wrong, like a folder accidentally being thrown out. All the rest of your files and folders are OK.

But suppose you've indicated that you want your My Documents folder restored from the backup disks. What should Backup do when it encounters files that are *still in* your My Documents folder, and in perfect shape? You can choose one of three options. **Leave existing files** means that Backup won't restore any file that's already on the hard drive. **Replace existing files if they are older than the backup files** makes Backup replace a file on your hard drive only if it's an *older version* than the backed-up copy. Finally, **Replace existing files** restores every file, replacing its equivalent on the hard drive, regardless of which is newer.

6. **Click Next.**

The options on this penultimate screen pertain to specialized security and system files.

You're free to click past them, but if curiosity gets the better of you, here's what these three very technical options do.

"Restore security settings" restores certain settings for each file and folder, including permissions and file ownership (see Chapter 17)—an option available only for files you backed up from a Windows XP, NTFS-formatted machine (and files that you're restoring to one).

The second option is "Restore junction points, but not the folders and file data they reference." Here, Microsoft is talking about *mounted drives* (page 622). Turn this option on if you're restoring a mounted drive; turn it off if you want to restore only the folder *containing* the mounted drive.

The third option, "Preserve existing volume mount points" requires that you understand *volume mount points,* described on page 472. Turn this option on if you want to restore data to a *replacement* drive, on which you've restored volume mount points yourself. Turn it off if you're restoring data to a reformatted partition or drive, and want to restore the old volume mount points from the backup.

7. **Click Next. If the restore summary page looks good, click Finish.**

Backup swings into action, asking you to insert backup disks or tapes as necessary, and restoring your backed-up files safely onto your hard drive.

UP TO SPEED

Floppy Disk Crash Course

Floppy disks are quickly becoming extinct, largely because sending files by email or over network wiring are much faster and more convenient ways of shuttling information between computers. But in a pinch, it's still useful to know the basics of using floppy disks: how to insert, erase, eject, and copy them.

Insert a floppy disk into your floppy drive label side up, metal side first. (If your floppy drive is mounted vertically, the label side faces away from the eject button.) To see what's on the disk, double-click your My Computer icon, and then double-click the "3 1/2 Floppy (A:)" icon. (If you

double-click this icon when there's no disk in the drive, you'll get nothing but an error message.)

To erase (format) a floppy, right-click the "3½ Floppy (A:)" icon and choose Format from the shortcut menu. To make a copy of the disk, right-click the icon and choose Copy from the shortcut menu. A little window appears like the one shown here, which you can use to specify where you want the copy made.

To remove the floppy from your machine, push the plastic eject button next to the drive slot, or right-click the floppy's icon and choose Eject from the shortcut menu.

The Briefcase

In its way, the Briefcase is a form of backup program, but for a very specific purpose: It's designed to help you keep your files straight when you transport them from desktop to laptop, or from home to work. If you learn to use the Briefcase, you'll be less likely to lose track of which copies of your documents are the most current.

To use the Briefcase, start by adding a briefcase icon on your desktop. To do so, right-click any spot on the desktop; from the shortcut menu, choose New→Briefcase. A new icon appears, called New Briefcase. (If you're feeling inspired, rename it as you would any folder.)

Now round up the icons of the documents you'll work on when away from your main PC. Drag them onto the My Briefcase icon. Windows XP copies the files into this special temporary holding tank.

Now connect your laptop to the desktop PC, if you haven't already. (See Chapter 18 for tips on connecting machines.) Or, if you plan to take your files with you on a disk (such as a floppy or Zip disk), insert the disk. Drag the My Briefcase icon onto the laptop or the disk.

You're ready to leave your office. When you get to wherever you're going, open and edit the documents in the copied Briefcase "folder" icon. Just don't move them.

When you return to your main PC, reconnect the laptop or reinsert the travel disk. Now all of your careful step-following is about to pay off. Open the disk or laptop window and double-click its My Briefcase icon. In the Briefcase window, click the "Update all items" link in the task pane. Windows copies the edited files back to their original folders on your desktop-PC hard drive, automatically replacing the older, original copies. (If you highlighted only some of the icons in the Briefcase window, you can instead click "Update the selected items." Windows copies only the highlighted icons back to the main PC.)

Safe Mode and the Startup Menu

PC troubleshooting is among the most difficult propositions on earth, in part because your machine has so many cooks. Microsoft made the operating system, another company made the computer, and dozens of others contributed the programs you use every day. The number of conflicts that can arise and the number of problems you may encounter are nearly infinite. That's why, if you were smart, you bought your PC from a company that offers a toll-free, 24-hour help line for life. You may need it.

If the problems you're having are caused by drivers that load just as the computer is starting up, turning them all off can be helpful, at least so that you can get into your machine to begin your troubleshooting pursuit. That's precisely the purpose of the Startup menu—a menu most people never even know exists until they're initiated into its secret world by a technically savvy guru.

Making the Startup menu appear is a matter of delicate timing. It goes like this:

1. **Restart the computer. Immediately after the *BIOS startup messages* disappear, press the F8 key (on the top row of most keyboards).**

   The BIOS startup messages—the usual crude-looking text on a black screen, filled with copyright notices and technical specs—are the first things you see after turning on the computer.

   If you press the F8 key after the Windows logo makes its appearance, you're too late. If you've done it right, on the other hand, you see a message that says, "Please select the operating system to start." Most people have only one option here— "Microsoft Windows XP Professional."

2. **At the "Please select the operating system" screen, press F8 again.**

   If all goes well, you'll see the Windows Advanced Options Menu (see Figure 16-16). Displayed against a black DOS screen, in rough lettering, is a list of options that includes Normal, Logged, Safe Mode, and so on.

3. **Select the startup option you want.**

   To make a selection, press the up or down arrow keys to "walk through" the list. Press Enter when you've highlighted the option you want.

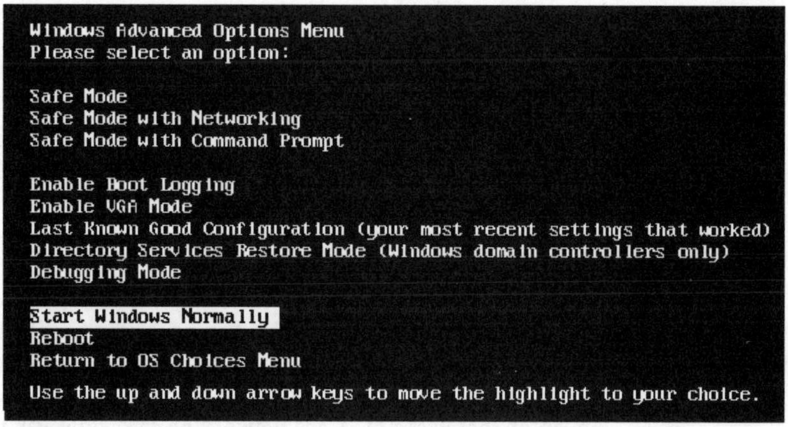

Figure 16-16:
The Startup menu (not to be confused with the Start menu) appears only when you press F8 a couple times as the computer is starting up. In times of deep trouble, it can be a lifesaver.

```
Windows Advanced Options Menu
Please select an option:

Safe Mode
Safe Mode with Networking
Safe Mode with Command Prompt

Enable Boot Logging
Enable VGA Mode
Last Known Good Configuration (your most recent settings that worked)
Directory Services Restore Mode (Windows domain controllers only)
Debugging Mode

Start Windows Normally
Reboot
Return to OS Choices Menu

Use the up and down arrow keys to move the highlight to your choice.
```

Here's what the Startup menu commands do:

• **Safe Mode.** Safe Mode starts up Windows in a special, stripped-down, generic, somewhat frightening-looking startup mode—with the software for dozens of hardware and software features *turned off.* Only the very basic components work: your mouse, keyboard, screen, and disk drives. Everything else is shut down and cut off. In short, Safe Mode is the tactic to take if your PC *won't* start up normally, thanks to some recalcitrant driver.

Once you've selected the Safe Mode option on the Startup menu, Windows asks which operating system you want to run—for most people, Windows XP Professional is the only choice, so just press Enter. Now you see a list, filling your screen, of every driver that Windows is loading. Eventually, you'll be asked to log in; a dialog box then appears, reminding you that you are in Safe Mode.

This dialog box offers two useful buttons. Yes proceeds with the startup process, taking you to the Windows desktop. Clicking No takes you directly to the System Restore screen shown in Figure 16-2, so that you can choose a date when your computer was running properly—and rewind to that happier time.

You'll probably discover that your screen looks like it was designed by drunken cave men, with jagged and awful graphics and text. That's because in Safe Mode, Windows doesn't load the driver for your video card. (It avoids that driver, on the assumption that it may be causing the very problem you're trying to troubleshoot.) Instead, Windows XP loads a crude, generic driver that works with *any* video card.

Tip: Note, by the way, how *fast* Windows is in this mode—a testimony to the dragging effect of all those modern graphic niceties.

The purpose of Safe Mode is to help you troubleshoot. If you discover that the problem you've been having is now gone, you've at least established that the culprit is one of the drivers that Windows has now turned off. Safe Mode also gives you full access to the technical tools of Windows XP, including System Restore (page 457), the Device Manager (page 431), the Registry Editor (page 492), Microsoft Backup (page 479), and the Help center. You might use the Device Manager, for example, to roll back a driver that you just updated (page 435), or System Restore to undo some other installation that seems to have thrown your PC into chaos.

If this procedure doesn't solve the problem, contact a support technician.

- **Safe Mode with Networking.** This option is exactly the same as Safe Mode, except that it also lets you load the driver software needed to tap into the network, if you're on one—an arrangement that offers a few additional troubleshooting possibilities, like being able to access files and drivers on another PC. (If you have a laptop that uses a PC-Card networking card, however, this option still may not help you, since the PC-Card driver itself is still turned off.)

- **Safe Mode with Command Prompt.** Here's another variation of safe mode, this one intended for ultra-power users who are more comfortable typing out text commands at the command prompt (page 199) than using icons, menus, and the mouse.

- **Enable Boot Logging.** This startup method is the same as Normal, except that Windows records every technical event that takes place during the startup in a log file named *ntbtlog.txt* (it's on the startup drive, in the Windows folder).

Most of the time, you'll use the Boot Logging option only at the request of a support technician you've phoned for help. After confirming the operating system startup, the technician may ask you to open ntbtlog.txt in your Notepad program and search for particular words or phrases—usually the word "fail."

- **Enable VGA Mode.** In this mode, your PC uses a standard VGA video driver that works with all graphics cards, instead of the hideously ugly generic one usually seen in Safe Mode. Use this option when you're troubleshooting video-display problems—problems that you are confident have less to do with drivers than with your settings in the Display control panel (which you're now ready to fiddle with).

- **Last Known Good Configuration.** Here's yet another method of resetting the clock to a time when your PC was working correctly, in effect undoing whatever configuration change you made that triggered your PC's current problems. It reinstates whichever set of drivers, and whichever Registry configuration, was in force the last time the PC was working right. (This option isn't as effective as the newer System Restore option, however, which also restores operating-system files in the process.)

- **Directory Services Restore Mode.** This extremely technical option is useful only in corporations with specialized *domain controller* computers running Windows .NET Server or Windows 2000 Server.

POWER USERS' CLINIC

The Recovery Console

Between System Restore and Safe Mode, everyday Windows users are well equipped to recover from most typical Windows snafus. But there are times—extremely rare ones, thank goodness—when the files of Windows itself are so corrupted that you can't even access these tools.

In those situations, technically proficient PC fans can take advantage of something called the Recovery Console. As in DOS or UNIX, this window displays nothing but text—no icons, menus, or other graphic niceties—but if you know the correct commands to type, Recovery Console can help get you out of some very tight scrapes. It lets you manipulate files and folders, turn off specific drivers or background services, perform certain hard drive repairs, and even erase (reformat) drives.

To prevent unscrupulous techies from exploiting this emergency tool, Recovery Console offers access only to the system files and folders of Windows itself—application and

document folders are off-limits—and doesn't let you copy files onto floppies, Zip disks, or other removable disks. Otherwise, however, Recovery Console looks and works much like the standard DOS command prompt. (Type *help*—and then press Enter—to see a list of all the commands you can use.)

To access Recovery Console, restart the PC from your Windows XP Professional CD-ROM. (On some computers, of course, you can't start up from a CD until you first adjust settings in the BIOS. Ask your PC's manufacturer for help.)

When you see the Welcome to Setup screen, press the R key, and then type and the number corresponding to the copy of Windows you want repaired. When you're asked for the password, just press Enter.

When you're finished making your repairs, type *exit* to get out of Recovery Console and restart the PC.

- **Debugging Mode.** Here's another extremely obscure option, this one intended for very technical people who've connected one PC to another via a serial cable. They can then use the second computer to analyze the first, using specialized debugger software.

- **Start Windows Normally.** This option starts the operating system in its usual fashion, exactly as though you never summoned the Startup menu to begin with. The Normal option lets you tell the PC, "Sorry to have interrupted you…go ahead."

- **Reboot.** Choose this command to restart the computer.

- **Return to OS Choices Menu.** Use this choice to back up to the "Please select the operating system to start" screen that first appeared when you pressed F8 during startup.

The Registry

Here and there, in books, articles, and conversations, you'll hear hushed references to something called the Windows *Registry*—usually accompanied by either knowing or bewildered glances.

Microsoft would just as soon you not even know about the Registry. There's not a word about it in the basic user guides, and the only information you'll find about it in the Help and Support center says, "It is strongly recommended that you do not edit Registry settings yourself. Incorrectly editing the Registry may severely damage your system."

If you're curious, however, read on.

The Registry is your PC's master database of preference settings, most of which are extremely technical. It keeps track of every program you install, every Plug and Play device you add, every multiple-user profile you create (Chapter 17), your networking configuration, and much more. If you've noticed that shortcut menus and Properties dialog boxes look different depending on what you're clicking, you have the Registry to thank. It knows what you're clicking and what options should appear as a result.

As you can well imagine, therefore, the Registry (Figure 16-17) is an extremely important cog in the Windows XP machine. That's why Windows marks your Registry files as invisible and non-deletable, and why it makes a Registry backup every single

---

---

day. If the Registry gets damaged or randomly edited, a grisly plague of problems may descend upon your machine. Windows XP's System Restore feature (described in this chapter) can extract you from such a mess, but at least you now know why the Registry is rarely even mentioned to novices.

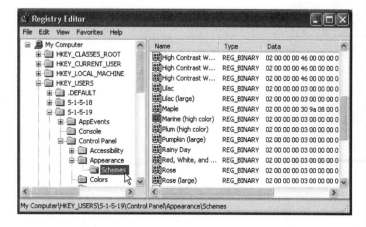

Figure 16-17:
The Registry's settings are organized hierarchically; RegEdit looks a lot like Windows Explorer. But there's no way to figure out which part of the Registry holds a particular setting or performs a particular function. It's like flying a plane that has no windows.

Still, the Registry is worth learning about. You shouldn't edit it arbitrarily, but if you get a step-by-step "recipe" from a book, magazine, Web site, or technical-help agent, you shouldn't fear opening the Registry to make a few changes. You can do so using a program called RegEdit, which appears when you choose Start→Run, type *regedit*, and press Enter. (There are dozens of other Registry-editing, Registry-fixing, and Registry-maintenance programs, too, from Symantec and other companies.)

You'll discover that the Registry uses cryptic abbreviations to describe the operating system's various components and settings. (You're generally shielded from all of this geekiness by friendlier front ends. For example, most of the programs in the Control Panel are nothing more than dialog boxes that modify settings in the Registry.)

If you think you're ready to dip into the programmery netherworld of Registry editing, a world of recipes awaits you on the Web. You might start with *www.regedit.com* and *www.winreg.com*, which provide dozens of useful tips and tricks for making your PC world a better place via Registry adjustments.

Tip: In the market for a cool-looking diagnostic tool that gives you the geeky rush of the Registry without any of the danger? Press Ctrl+Alt+Delete to open the Task Manager dialog box, and then click the Performance tab. These yellow-on-black graphs update themselves in real time, looking something like a lie detector's output—except that these peaks and valleys represent the efforts of your processor and virtual-memory manager. As you go about your work, opening programs, editing documents, and so on, you'll see these graphs respond to the load on your system.

(Close it when you're finished marveling, though, so the graph doesn't slow down your PC.)

Part Five:
Life on the Network

5

CHAPTER

17

Accounts, Permissions, and Logging On

For years, teachers, parents, tech directors, and computer lab instructors struggled to answer a difficult question: How do you rig one PC so that several different people can use it throughout the day, without interfering with each others' files and settings? And how do you protect a PC from getting fouled up by mischievous (or bumbling) students and employees?

Introducing User Accounts

Like the Windows 2000 under its skin, Windows XP is designed from the ground up to be a multiple-user operating system. On a Windows XP machine, anyone who uses the computer must *log on*—click (or type) your name and type in a password—when the computer turns on. And upon doing so, you discover the Windows universe just as you left it, including these elements:

- **Desktop.** Each person sees a different set of shortcut icons, folder icons, and other stuff left out on the desktop.

- **Start menu.** If you reorganize the Start menu, as described in Chapter 2, you won't confuse anybody else who uses the machine. No one else can even *see* the changes you make.

- **My Documents folder.** Each person sees only her own stuff in the My Documents folder (see Chapter 2).

- **Email.** Windows XP maintains a separate stash of email messages for each account holder—along with separate Web bookmarks, a Windows Messenger contact list, and other online details.

- **Favorites folder.** Any Web sites, folders, or other icons you've designated as Favorites (see page 642) appear in *your* Favorites menu, and nobody else's.

- **Internet cache.** You can read about *cached* Web pages in Chapter 11. This folder stores a copy of the Web pages you've visited recently for faster retrieval.

- **History and cookies.** Windows maintains a list of recently visited Web sites independently for each person; likewise a personal collection of *cookies* (Web site preference files).

- **Control Panel settings.** Windows memorizes the preferences each person establishes using the Control Panel (see Chapter 9), including keyboard, sound, screen saver, and mouse settings.

- **Privileges.** Your user account also determines what you're allowed to do on the network and even on your own computer: which files and folders you can open, which settings you can change in the Control Panel, and even which files and folders you can open.

Tip: Behind the scenes, Windows XP stores *all* of these files and settings in a single folder that techies call your *user profile*. It's in your My Computer→Local Disk (C:)→Documents and Settings→[Your Name] folder.

This feature makes sharing the PC much more convenient, because you don't have to look at everybody else's files (and endure their desktop design schemes). It also adds a layer of security, making it less likely for a marauding six-year-old to throw away your files.

Tip: Even if you don't share your PC with anyone and don't create any other accounts, you might still appreciate this feature because it effectively password-protects the entire computer. Your PC is protected from unauthorized fiddling when you're away from your desk (or when your laptop is stolen)—especially if you tell Windows to require your logon password any time after the screen saver has kicked in (page 271).

Since the day you first installed Windows XP or fired up a new Windows XP machine, you may have made a number of changes to your desktop—fiddled with your Start menu, changed the desktop wallpaper, added some favorites to your Web browser, downloaded files onto your desktop, and so on—without realizing that you were actually making these changes only to *your account*.

Accordingly, if you create an account for a second person, when she turns on the computer and signs in, she'll find the desktop exactly the way it was as factory installed by Microsoft: basic Start menu, Teletubbies-hillside desktop picture, default Web browser home page, and so on. She can make the same kinds of changes to the PC that you've made, but nothing she does will affect your environment the next time *you* log on. You'll still find the desktop the way you left it: *your* desktop picture fills the screen, the Web browser lists *your* bookmarks, and so on.

In other words, the multiple-accounts feature has two components: first, a convenience element that hides everyone else's junk; and second, a security element that protects both the PC's system software and other people's work.

If you're content simply to *use* Windows XP Pro, that's really all you need to know about accounts. If, on the other hand, you have shouldered some of the responsibility for *administering* XP Pro machines—if it's your job to add and remove accounts, for example—read on.

Windows XP: The OS With Two Faces

As you may remember from the beginning of Chapter 2, Windows XP Pro is designed to handle either of two different kinds of networks: workgroups (small, informal home or small-business networks) and domains (corporate, professionally and centrally administered).

This distinction becomes particularly important when it comes to user accounts.

- **A workgroup network.** In this smaller kind of network, each computer maintains its own security settings, such as user accounts, passwords, and permissions. You can't open files on another computer on the network unless its owner has created an account for you on *that* computer. Before you can access the files on the Front Desk PC and the Upstairs PC, for example, you must create an account for yourself on each of those machines. (Clearly, setting up an account on every PC for every employee would get out of hand in a huge company.)

  If you're part of a workgroup network (or no network), you'll find that Windows XP Pro gives you simplified, but less secure, access to user accounts and *permissions,* both of which are described in this chapter.

- **A domain network.** In a corporation, your files may not be sitting right there on your hard drive. They may, in fact, sit on a network server—a separate computer dedicated to dishing out files to employees from across the network. As you can probably imagine, protecting all this information is Job Number One for somebody or other.

  That's why, if your PC is part of a domain, you'll find Windows XP Pro more reminiscent of Windows 2000, with more business-oriented features and full access to the account maintenance and permissions management options.

This chapter tackles these two broad feature categories—the workgroup scenario and the domain scenario—one at a time.

Note: *After the Windows XP Pro installation is completed, you can modify the Windows configuration to use either the simple mode or the detailed one, no matter how your computer is equipped.*

Local Accounts on a Workstation

This section is dedicated to computers in a workgroup network—or no network at all. If your computer is a member of a domain, skip to "Local Accounts on a Domain Computer," later in this chapter.

To see what accounts are already on your PC, choose Start→Control Panel, and then open the User Accounts icon. You'll see a list of existing accounts (Figure 17-1).

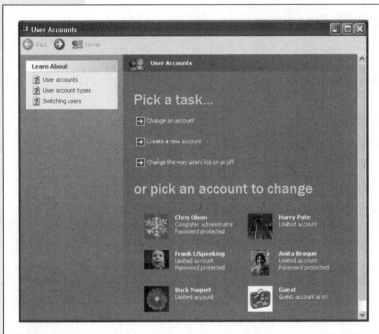

Figure 17-1:
This screen lists everyone for whom you've created an account. From here, you can create new accounts or change people's passwords. (Hint: To change account settings, just click the person's name on the bottom half of the screen. Clicking the "Change an account" link at top requires an extra, redundant click.)

If you see more than one account here—not just yours—then one of these situations probably applies:

- You created them when you installed Windows XP Pro, as described in Appendix A.

Tip: *All of the accounts you create when you first install Windows XP become* Administrator *accounts, as described in the following section.*

- You bought a new computer with Windows XP preinstalled, and created several accounts when asked to do so the first time you turned on the machine.

- You upgraded the machine from an earlier version of Windows. Windows XP gracefully imports all of your existing accounts.

Note: Upgrader beware: If you've upgraded from Windows 98 or Me, Windows XP (a) treats all of these imported accounts as Administrator accounts, described below, and (b) wipes out their passwords, which leaves open a security hole the size of Canada. Promptly after upgrading, therefore, you should take a moment to assign passwords and downgrade account types to Limited, as described below.

If you're new at this, there's probably just one account listed here: yours. This is the account that Windows XP created when you first installed it.

Administrator Accounts

It's important to understand the phrase that appears just under each person's name. On your own personal PC, the words "Computer administrator" probably appear underneath yours.

Because you're the person who installed Windows XP to begin with, the PC assumes that you're one of its *computer administrators*—the technical wizards who will be in charge of it. You're the teacher, the parent, the resident guru. You're the one who will maintain this PC and who will be permitted to make system-wide changes to it.

You'll find settings all over Windows XP Professional (and all over this book) that *only* people with "Computer administrator" accounts can change. For example, only an administrator is allowed to:

- Create or delete accounts and passwords on the PC.
- Install new programs (and certain hardware components).
- Make changes to certain Control Panel programs that are off-limits to non-administrators.
- See and manipulate *any* file on the machine.

As you go about creating accounts for other people who'll use this PC, you'll be offered the opportunity to make each one an administrator just like you. Needless to say, use discretion. Bestow these powers only upon people as responsible and technically masterful as you.

Limited Accounts

Anyone who isn't an administrator is an ordinary, everyday Limited account holder. "Limited" people have everyday access to certain Control Panel settings—the ones that pertain to their own computing environments. But most other areas of the PC are off-limits, including everybody else's My Documents folders, Windows system files, and so on.

If you're a Limited account holder, in other words, your entire world consists of the Start menu, your My Documents folder, the Shared Documents folder (page 111), and any folders you create.

Tip: If a Limited account holder manages to download a computer virus, its infection will be confined to his account. If an *administrator* catches a virus, on the other hand, every file on the machine is at risk.

That's a good argument for creating as few computer administrator accounts as possible. In fact, some Windows pros don't even use Administrator accounts *themselves.* Even they use Limited accounts, keeping one Administrator account on hand only for new software or hardware installations, account or password changing, and similar special cases.

Adding an Account

Once you've opened the User Accounts program in the Control Panel, it's easy to create a new account: just click the "Create a new account" link shown in Figure 17-1. (You see this link only if you are, in fact, an administrator.)

A wizard guides you through the selection of a name and an account type (see Figure 17-2).

When you're finished with the settings, click the Create Account button (or press Enter). After a moment, you return to the User Accounts screen (Figure 17-1), where the new person's name joins whatever names were already there. You can continue adding new accounts forever or until your hard drive is full, whichever comes first.

Figure 17-2:
Top left: If it's all in the family, the account's name could be Chris or Robin. If it's a corporation or school, you'll probably want to use both first and last names. Capitalization doesn't matter, but most punctuation is forbidden.

Bottom right: This is the master switch that lets you specify whether or not this unsuspecting computer user will be a computer administrator, as described above.

Tip: If you never had the opportunity to set up a user account when installing Windows XP—if you bought a PC with Windows XP already on it, for example—you may see an account named Owner already in place. Nobody can use Windows XP at all unless there's at least *one* Administrator account on it, so Microsoft is doing you a favor here.

Just use the User Accounts program in the Control Panel to change the name Owner to one that suits you better. Make that account your own using the steps in the following paragraphs.

Editing an Account

Although the process of creating a new account is swift and simple, it doesn't offer you much in the way of flexibility. You don't even have a chance to specify the new person's password, let alone the tiny picture that appears next to the person's name and at the top of the Start menu (rubber ducky, flower, or whatever).

That's why the next step in creating an account is usually *editing* the one you just set up. To do so, once you've returned to the main User Accounts screen (Figure 17-1), click the name or icon of the freshly created account. You arrive at the screen shown at the top in Figure 17-3, where—if you are an administrator—you can choose from any of these options:

- **Change the name.** You'll be offered the opportunity to type in a new name for this person and then click the Change Name button—just the ticket when one of your co-workers gets married or joins the Witness Protection Program.

- **Create a password.** Click this link if you'd like to require a password for access to this person's account (Figure 17-3, bottom). Capitalization counts.

  The usual computer book takes this opportunity to stress the importance of having a long, complex password, such as a phrase that isn't in the dictionary, something made up of mixed letters and numbers, and *not* "password." This is excellent advice if you create sensitive documents and work in a corporation.

  But if you share the PC only with a spouse or a few trusted colleagues in a small office, for example, you may have nothing to hide. You may see the multiple-users feature more as a convenience (for keeping your settings and files separate) than a way of protecting secrecy and security.

  In these situations, there's no particular need to dream up a convoluted password. In fact, you may want to consider setting up *no* password—leaving both password blanks empty. Later, whenever you're asked for your password, just leave the Password box blank. You'll be able to log on that much faster each day.

  If you do decide to provide a password, you can also provide a *hint* (for yourself or whichever co-worker's account you're operating on). This is a hint than anybody can see (including bad guys trying to log on as you), so choose something meaningful only to you. If your password is the first person who ever kissed you plus your junior-year phone number, for example, your hint might be "first person who ever kissed me plus my junior-year phone number."

Later, if you ever forget your password, you'll be offered an opportunity to view this hint at sign-in time to jog your memory (page 524).

***

Tip: When you're creating accounts that other people will use for the purpose of accessing their machines from across the network, set up the same passwords they use when logging onto their own computers. You'll save them time and hassle. Once they've logged onto another machine on the network, they'll be able to connect to their own without having to type in another name and password.

***

By the way, it's fine for you, an administrator, to create the *original* passwords for new accounts. But don't change their passwords later on, after they've been using the computer for a while. If you do, you'll wipe out various internal security features of their accounts, including access to their stored Web site passwords and stored passwords for shared folders and disks on the network (Chapter 20). See the box on page 507 for details.

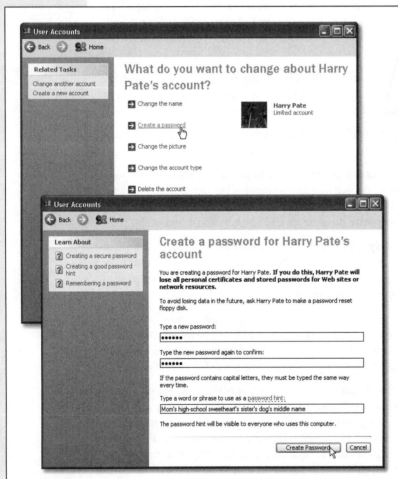

Figure 17-3:
Top: Here's the master menu of account changing options that you, an administrator, can see. (If you're a Limited account holder, you see far fewer options.)

Bottom: You're supposed to type your password twice, to make sure you didn't introduce a typo the first time. (The PC shows only dots as you type, to guard against the possibility that some villain is snooping over your shoulder.)

- **Make your files private.** The first time you make up a password *for your own account,* another screen asks: "Do you want to make your files and folders private?" If you're using the accounts feature more for convenience than for security—if you and your boss are married and have no secrets from each other, for example—click No.

Note: *The private-folder feature is available only on hard drives you've formatted using the NTFS scheme, as described on page 620.*

But if you click the button labeled "Yes, Make Private," Windows takes a minute to mark everything in your *user profile folder* off-limits to other account holders. (Your user profile folder is the one bearing your name in the Documents and Settings folder on your hard drive.) Henceforth, if anyone else tries to open any of your files or folders (when they're logged in under their own names), they'll get nothing but a curt "Access is denied" message.

(Technically, making a folder private even shields it from the eyes of the machine's Administrator account holders—but it's a pretty flimsy shield. A determined administrator can burrow past this wisp of protection to examine your files, if she's determined to do so, or even change your password late one night to gain full access to your stuff.)

Note that even if you *do* make your files and folders private, you'll still be able to share selected files and folders with other people. You just put them into the Shared Documents folder described on page 111.

Tip: *You can make any of your own folders private—or un-private, for that matter. Just right-click the folder; from the shortcut menu, choose Properties; click the Sharing tab; and turn "Make this folder private" on or off.*

To make your entire world un-private, for example, you'd perform this surgery on your user profile folder in the Documents and Settings folder (page 525).

- **Change the picture.** The usual sign-in screen (Figure 17-14) displays each account holder's name, accompanied by a little picture. When you first create the account, however, it assigns a picture to you at random—and not all of them are necessarily appropriate for your personality. Not every extreme-sport headbanger, for example, is crazy about being represented by a dainty flower or butterfly.

  If you like the selections that Microsoft has provided (drag the vertical scroll bar to see them all), just click one to select it as the replacement graphic. If you'd rather use some other graphics file on the hard drive instead—a digital photo of your own face, for example—you can click the "Browse for more pictures" link (Figure 17-4). You'll be shown a list of the graphics files on your hard drive so that you can choose one, which Windows then automatically scales down to postage stamp size (48 pixels square).

• **Change the account type.** Click this link to change a Limited account into an Administrator account, or vice versa. You might want to use this option, for example, after upgrading a Windows 98 or Windows Me computer to Windows XP—a process that otherwise leaves all existing user accounts as Administrator accounts.

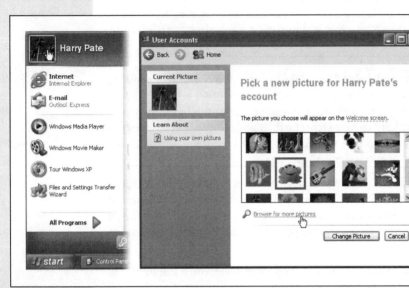

Figure 17-4:
Right: Here's where you change your account picture. If a camera or scanner is attached, you get an extra link here, "Get a picture from a camera or scanner"—instant picture. And here's a tip: If you like to change your picture with your mood, there's a shortcut to this dialog box. Just click your picture at the top of the open Start menu (left).

• **Delete the account.** See page 508.

You're free to make any of these changes to any account at any time; you don't have to do it just after first creating the account.

Tip: If the User Accounts program looks nothing like the illustrations in this chapter so far, it's probably because you have only a Limited account. In that case, opening User Accounts in the Control Panel offers only certain links: "Create a password" (or "Change my password"), "Change my picture," and "Set up my account to use a .NET Passport." Only a computer administrator can make the other kinds of changes described here.

The Forgotten Password Disk

As described later in this chapter, Windows XP contains a handy hint mechanism for helping you recall your password if you've forgotten it: the little ? icon that appears after you click your name on the Welcome screen. When you click that little icon, you're shown the hint that you provided for yourself—*if* you provided one—when setting up your account.

But what if, having walked into a low-hanging branch, you've completely forgotten both your password and the correct interpretation of your hint? In that disastrous situation, your entire world of work and email would be locked inside the computer forever. (Yes, an administrator could issue you a new password—but as noted in the box on page 507, you'd lose all your secondary passwords in the process.)

Fortunately, Windows XP offers a clever solution-in-advance: the Password Reset Disk. It's a floppy disk that you can use like a physical key to unlock your account, in the event of a forgotten password. The catch: You have to make this disk *now*, while you still remember your password.

To create this disk, choose Start→Control Panel. Open the User Accounts program. If you're an administrator, click your account name; if not, you can skip this step.

Either way, you should now see a link in the task pane called, "Prevent a forgotten password." Click that to open the Forgotten Password Wizard shown in Figure 17-5.

When the day comes that you can't remember your password, your attempts to get past the logon screen will be met by a "Use your Password Reset Disk" link. (If you've turned off the standard Welcome screen shown at top in Figure 17-14, you'll see a Reset button instead.)

When you click that link or button, Windows asks you to insert your Password Reset Disk, and then gives you the opportunity to create a new password (and a new hint to remind you of it). You're in.

UP TO SPEED

Passwords Within Passwords

The primary password that you or your administrator sets up in the User Accounts program has two functions. You already know that it lets you log on each day, so that you can enter your Windows world of desktop clutter, Start menu tailoring, Web bookmarks, and so on.

But what you may not realize is that it's also the master key that unlocks all the *other* passwords associated with your account: the passwords that Internet Explorer memorizes for certain Web sites, the passwords that get you into shared disks and folders on the network, the password that protects your .NET Passport (and its Wallet for electronic payments, if you set one up), and so on. The simple act of logging onto your account also unlocks all of these other secure areas of your PC life.

But remember that anyone with an Administrator account can *change* your password at any time. Does that mean that whoever has an Administrator account—your teacher, boss, or teenager, for example—has full access to your pri-

vate stuff? After you leave the household, company, or school, what's to stop an administrator from changing your password, thereby gaining access to your electronic-brokerage account (courtesy of its memorized Internet Explorer password), buying stuff with your Passport Wallet, and so on?

Fortunately, Microsoft is way ahead of you on this one. The instant an administrator changes somebody else's password, Windows XP *wipes out* all secondary passwords associated with the account. That administrator can log onto your account and see your everyday files, but not Web sites with memorized passwords, and so on.

Note that if you change your *own* password—or if you use a Forgotten Password Disk, described next—none of this applies. Your secondary passwords survive intact. It's only when *somebody else* changes your password that this little-known Windows XP security feature kicks in, sanitizing the account for your protection.

Even though you now have a new password, your existing Password Reset Disk will still be good. Keep it in a drawer somewhere, for use the next time you experience a temporarily blank brain.

Figure 17-5:
The screens of this wizard guide you through the process of inserting a blank floppy disk and preparing it to be your master skeleton key. If you forget your password—or if some administrator has changed your password—you can use this disk to reinstate it without the risk of losing all of your secondary passwords (memorized Web passwords, encrypted files, and so on).

Deleting User Accounts

It happens: Somebody graduates, somebody gets fired, somebody dumps you. Sooner or later, you may need to delete a user account from your PC.

To delete a user account, you, an administrator, must open the User Accounts program, click the appropriate account name, and then click "Delete the account."

Windows XP now asks you if you want to preserve the contents of this person's My Documents folder. If you click the Keep Files button, you'll find a new folder, named for the dearly departed, on your desktop. (As noted in the dialog box, only the documents, contents of the desktop, and the My Documents folder are preserved—but *not* programs, email, or even Web favorites.) If that person ever returns to your life, you can create a new account for him and copy these files into the appropriate folder locations.

If you click the Delete Files button, on the other hand, the documents are gone forever.

A few more important points about deleting accounts:

- You can't delete the account you're logged into.

- You can't delete the last Administrator account. One account must always remain.

- You can create a new account with the same name and password as one that you deleted earlier, but in Windows XP's head, it's still not the same account. As described in the box on page 507, it won't have any of the original *secondary* passwords (for Web sites, encrypted files, and so on).

- Don't manipulate accounts manually (by fooling around in the Documents and Settings folder, for example). Create, delete, and rename them only using the User Accounts program in the Control Panel. Otherwise, you'll wind up with duplicate or triplicate folders in Documents and Settings, with the PC name tacked onto the end of the original account name (Bob, Bob.MILLENNIA, and so on)—a sure recipe for confusion.

Tip: If you're an administrator, don't miss the Users tab of the Task Manager dialog box (press Ctrl+Alt+Delete to open it). It offers a handy, centralized list of everybody who's logged into your machine—even those who have dialed in from the road, as described in Chapter 21—and buttons that let you log them off, disconnect them, or even make a little message pop up on their screens. All of this can be handy whenever you need some information, a troubleshooting session, or a power trip.

FREQUENTLY ASKED QUESTION

Limited Unlimited

OK, OK, I get it: for maximum security, it's best to create Limited accounts for the people who use my PC. But I've got this program, Beekeeper Pro, that doesn't work right under a Limited account. Now what?

Unfortunately, you have only two alternatives, and neither is particularly convenient.

First, whenever a Limited account holder encounters a place where administrator powers are required, he doesn't actually have to log out so that you, the administrator, can log on and make changes. Instead, he can just call you over to the PC. He can then right-click the icon of the problem program and, from the shortcut menu, choose "Run as."

The dialog box shown here appears. You, the administrator, should click "The following user," and then fill in your own name and password—if, indeed, you feel comfortable permitting your peon limited user to proceed. As far as Windows (and the specific program in question) is concerned, that limited user is now officially an administrator.

That, of course, is a one-shot, temporary solution—a routine that will grow old fast if the limited user has to use that recalcitrant program every single day. In that case, you may have no alternative but to upgrade your colleague to an Administrator account, despite the security downsides.

Run As

Which user account do you want to use to run this program?

○ Current user (INSPIRON\Harry Pate)

☑ Protect my computer and data from unauthorized program activity

This option can prevent computer viruses from harming your computer or personal data, but selecting it might cause the program to function improperly.

● The following user:

User name: 🗐 Chris Olson

Password: ••••

OK   Cancel

The Administrator Account

It may come as a surprise to a workgroup user that Windows XP provides one more, very special account: an emergency, backup account with full administrator powers. Even if you delete all of your other accounts, this one will still remain, if only to give you some way to get into your machine. It's an account called Administrator, and it's ordinarily hidden.

In fact, you'll generally see it only in times of troubleshooting, when you start up your PC in Safe Mode (page 488). It's the ideal account to use in those situations. Not only does it come with no password assigned, but it's also not limited in any way. It gives you free powers over every file, which is just what you may need to troubleshoot your computer.

The Guest Account

Actually, Administrator and Limited aren't the only kinds of accounts you can set up on your PC.

The third kind, called the Guest account, is ideal for situations where somebody is just visiting you for the day. Rather than create an entire account for this person, complete with password, hint, little picture, and so on, you can just switch on the Guest account.

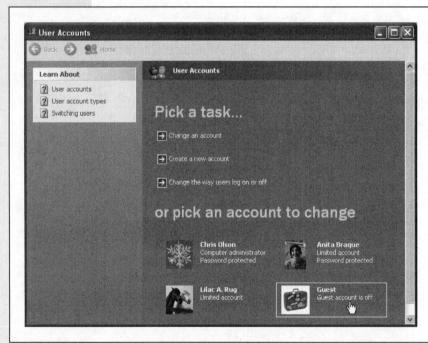

Figure 17-6:
There's not really much to learn about the Guest account; it's exactly the same thing as a Limited account, except that it requires no password at all.

To do so, open the User Accounts program in the Control Panel. If you're an administrator, you'll see an icon for the Guest account at the bottom of the screen (Figure 17-6). Click it; on the next screen, click the button labeled Turn On the Guest Account. That's all there is to it.

When the visitor to your office is finally out of your hair, healthy paranoia suggests that you turn off the Guest account once again. (To do so, follow precisely the same steps, except click Turn Off the Guest Account in the final step.)

Local Accounts on a Domain Computer

When your computer is a member of a corporate domain, the controls you use to create and manage user accounts are quite a bit different.

In this case, when you choose Start→Control Panel→User Accounts, you see the dialog box shown in Figure 17-7. The layout is different, but the idea is the same: You can see all of the accounts on the computer, including the Administrator account described above. (In a domain situation, it isn't hidden, as it is on a workgroup computer.)

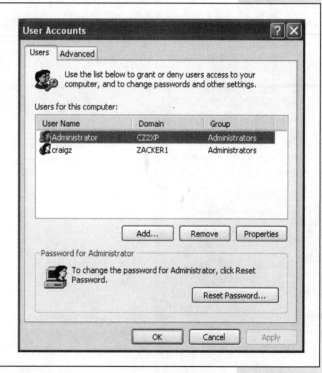

Figure 17-7:
A Windows XP Professional computer that's a member of a domain has a more detailed User Account dialog box. Instead of creating new accounts on your local machine, these controls let you give other people on your domain the ability to log onto your computer locally (that is, in person, rather than from across the network).

This dialog box lets you create *local* accounts—accounts stored only on your computer, and not on the corporate domain machine—for existing citizens of the domain. (Why would you need a local account, if all of your files and settings are actually stored elsewhere on the network? Because certain tasks, like installing drivers for new hardware, require you to log on using a *local* Administrator account.)

Note: This business of creating a local account that corresponds to an *existing domain account* isn't quite the same thing as creating a completely new account for a completely new person. For that purpose, see page 514.

Creating a Local Account for a Domain Member

When you click the Add button (Figure 17-7), an Add New User Wizard appears. It lets you specify the person's name and the name of the domain that already stores his account. (You can also click the Browse button to search your domain for a specific person.)

When you click Next, the wizard prompts you to specify what level of access you want to grant this person. You have three choices:

NOSTALGIA CORNER

The Windows 2000 User Accounts Control Panel

You're supposed to do most of your account-editing work in the User Accounts program of the Control Panel, which is basically a wizard that offers one option per screen. That requirement may not thrill veteran Windows 2000 fans, however, who are used to the much more direct—and more powerful—User Accounts screen.

Actually, it's still in Windows XP. To make it appear, choose Start→Run; type out *control Userpasswords2,* and then press Enter. You see the program shown here.

Most of the functions here are the same as what you'd find in the new XP User Accounts program—it's just that you don't have to slog through several wizard screens to get things done. Here you can add, remove, or edit accounts all in a single screen.

This older Control Panel program also offers a few fea-

tures that you don't get at all in the new one. For example, you can turn off the checkbox called, "Users must enter a user name and password to use this computer." When you do so, you get a dialog box called Automatically Log On, where you can specify a user name and password of one special person. This lucky individual won't have to specify any name and password at logon time, and can instead turn on the PC and cruise directly to the desktop. (This feature works only at *startup time.* If you choose Start→Log Off, the standard Logon dialog box appears, so that other people have the opportunity to sign in.)

This automatic-logon business is ordinarily a luxury enjoyed by solo operators whose PCs have only one account and no password. By using the secret User Accounts method, however, you can set up automatic logon even on a PC with several accounts, provided you appreciate the security hole that it leaves open.

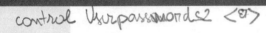

- **Standard user.** This person will be allowed to change certain system settings and install programs that don't affect the Windows XP system files.

- **Restricted user.** A restricted user can log in and save documents, but isn't allowed to install software or modify system settings.

- **Other.** If you choose this option, you'll be allowed to specify what local *group* this person belongs to, as described later in this chapter.

Once the account you selected appears in the user accounts list, that person is now ready to log into your PC using the local account.

Local Users and Groups

The simple control panels you've read about so far in this chapter are designed for simplicity and convenience, but not for power. Windows XP Pro offers a second way to create, edit, and delete accounts: an alternative window that, depending on your taste for technical sophistication, is either intimidating and technical—or liberating and flexible.

It's called the Local Users and Groups console.

Opening the Console

You can open up the Local Users and Groups window in any of several ways:

- Choose Start→Control Panel→Administrative Tools→Computer Management. Click the Local Users and Groups icon in the left pane of the window.

- Choose Start→Run, type *Lusrmgr.msc,* and click OK.

- *Domain PCs only:* Choose Start→Control Panel. Open User Accounts, click the Advanced tab , and then, under Advanced User Management, click the Advanced button.

In any case, the Local Users and Groups console appears, as shown in Figure 17-8.

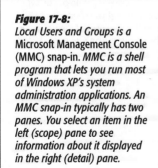

Figure 17-8:
Local Users and Groups is a Microsoft Management Console (MMC) snap-in. MMC is a shell program that lets you run most of Windows XP's system administration applications. An MMC snap-in typically has two panes. You select an item in the left (scope) pane to see information about it displayed in the right (detail) pane.

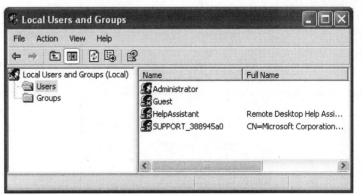

In this console, you have complete control over the local accounts (and groups, as described in a moment) on your computer. This is the real, raw, unshielded command center, intended for power users who aren't easily frightened.

The truth is, you probably won't use these controls much on a domain computer. After all, most people's accounts live on the domain computer, not the local machine. You might occasionally have to log in using the local Administrator account to perform system maintenance and upgrade tasks, but you'll rarely have to create *new* accounts.

Workgroup computers are another story. Remember that you'll have to create a new account for each person who might want to use this computer—or even to access its files from across the network. If you use the Local Users and Groups console to create and edit these accounts, you have much more control over the new account holder's freedom than you do with the User Accounts control panel.

Creating a New User Account

To create a new account in the Local Users and Groups console, start by clicking the Users folder in the left side of the console (technically called the *scope pane*). On the right side of the console (the *detail pane*), you see a list of the accounts already on the machine. It probably includes not only the accounts you created during the Windows XP installation (and thereafter), but also the Administrator and Guest accounts described earlier in this chapter.

To create a new account, choose Action→New User from the Action menu. In the New User dialog box (Figure 17-9), type a name for the account (the name this

Figure 17-9:
When you first create a new user, the "User must change password at next logon" checkbox is turned on. It's telling you that no matter what password you make up when creating the account, your colleague will be asked to make up a new one the first time he logs in. This way, you can assign a simple password (or no password at all) to all new accounts, but your underlings will still feel free to devise passwords of their own choosing, and the accounts won't go unprotected

person will type or choose when logging in), the person's full name, and if you like, a description. (Microsoft no doubt has in mind "Shipping manager" rather than "Short and balding," but the description can be anything you like.)

In the Password and Confirm Password text boxes, specify the password that your new colleague will need to access the account. Its complexity and length are up to you and your innate sense of security paranoia.

Tip: If you can't create a new account, it's probably because you don't have the proper privileges yourself. You must have an Administrator account (page 501) or belong to the Power Users or Administrators *group* (page 517).

If you turn off the "User must change password at next logon" checkbox, you can turn on options like these:

- **User cannot change password.** This person won't be allowed to change the password that you've just made up. (Some system administrators like to maintain sole control over the account passwords on their computers.)

- **Password never expires.** Using software rules called *local security policies*, an administrator can make account passwords expire after a specific time, periodically forcing employees to make up new ones. It's a security measure designed to foil intruders who somehow get a hold of the existing passwords. But if you turn on this option, the person whose account you're now creating will be able to use the same password indefinitely, no matter what the local security policy says.

- **Account is disabled.** When you turn on this box, this account holder won't be able to log on. You might use this option when, for example, somebody goes on sabbatical—it's not as drastic step as deleting the account, because you can always reactivate the account by turning the checkbox off. You can also use this option to set up certain accounts in advance, which you then activate when the time comes by turning this checkbox off again.

Note: When an account is disabled, a red circled X appears on its icon in the Local Users and Groups console. (You may have noticed that the Guest account appears this way when you first install Windows XP.)

When you click the Create button, you add the new account to the console, and you make the dialog box blank again, ready for you to create another new account, if necessary. When you're finished creating accounts, click Close to return to the main console window.

Groups

As you may have guessed from its name, you can also use the Local Users and Groups window to create *groups*—named collections of account holders.

Suppose you work for a small company that uses a workgroup network. You want to be able to share various files on your computer with certain other people on the network. You'd like to be able to permit them to access some folders, but not others. Smooth network operator that you are, you solve this problem by assigning *permissions* to the appropriate files and folders (page 528).

In Windows XP Pro, you can specify different access permissions to *each file for each person*. If you had to set up these access privileges manually for every file on your hard drive, for every account holder on the network, you'd go out of your mind—and never get any real work done.

That's where groups come in. You can create one group—called Trusted Comrades, for example—and fill it with the names of every account holder who should be allowed to access your files. Thereafter, it's a piece of cake to give everybody in that group access to a certain folder, in one swift step. You end up having to create only one permission assignment for each file, instead of one for each *person* for each file.

Furthermore, if a new employee joins the company, you can simply add her to the group. Instantly, she has exactly the right access to the right files and folders, without your having to do any additional work.

Creating a group

To create a new group, click the Groups folder in the left side of the Local Users and Groups console (page 513). Choose Action→New Group. The New Group dialog box appears, as shown in Figure 17-10. Into the appropriate boxes, type a name for the group, and a description if you like. Then click Add.

Figure 17-10:
The New Group dialog box lets you specify the members of the group you are creating. A group can have any number of users as members, and a user can be a member of any number of groups.

A Select Users or Groups dialog box appears (the same box shown in Figure 17-20). Here, you can specify who should be members of your new group. (You can always add more members to the group, or remove them later.)

Finally, click OK to close the dialog box, and then click Create to add the group to the list in the console. The box appears empty again, ready for you to create another group.

Built-in groups

You may have noticed that even the first time you opened the Users and Groups window, a few group names appeared there already. That's because Windows XP comes with a canned list of ready-made groups that Microsoft hopes will save you some time.

For example, when you use the User Accounts control panel program to set up a new account, Windows automatically places that person into the Limited or Computer Administrator group, depending on whether or not you made him an administrator (page 501). In fact, that's how Windows knows what powers and freedom this person is supposed to have.

Here are some of the built-in groups on a Windows XP Professional computer:

- **Administrators.** Members of the Administrators group have complete control over every aspect of the computer. They can modify any setting, create or delete accounts and groups, install or remove any software, and modify or delete any file.

  But as Spiderman's uncle might say, with great power comes great responsibility. Administrator powers make it possible to screw up your operating system in thousands of major and minor ways, either on purpose or by accident. That's why it's a good idea to keep the number of Administrator accounts to a minimum—and even to avoid using one for everyday purposes yourself, as described in the Tip on page 502.

- **Power Users.** Members of this group have fewer powers than Administrators, but still more than mere mortals in the Users group. If you're in this group, you can set the computer's clock, change its monitor settings, create new user accounts and shared folders, and install most kinds of software. You can even modify some of the critical system folders, including the Windows folder and Windows→ System32 folder—but only for the purpose of installing applications that deposit files into those folders.

  Clueless Power Users members can still cause trouble, so you should reserve the status for people who know what they're doing. On the other hand, Power Users aren't allowed to delete, move, or change core operating system files, so the damage they can inflict is relatively limited. This is a good kind of account for you, the wise administrator, to use for everyday work.

- **Users.** Limited account holders (page 509) are members of this group. They can access their own Start menu and desktop settings, their own My Documents folders, the Shared Documents folder, and whatever folders they create themselves—but they can't change any computer-wide settings, Windows system files, or program files.

  If you're a member of this group, you can install new programs—but you'll be the only one who can use them. That's by design; any problems introduced by that program (viruses, for example) are limited to your files and not spread to the whole system.

  If you're the administrator, it's a good idea to put most new account holders into this group.

- **Guests.** If you're in this group, you have pretty much the same privileges as members of the Users group. You lose only a few nonessential perks, like the ability to read the computer's *system event log* (a record of behind-the-scenes technical happenings).

In addition to these basic groups, there are also two special-purpose groups:

- **Backup Operators.** People in this group can back up and restore any of the files on the computer, even if those files are technically off-limits to these account holders. Members of this group can also log onto the system and shut it down, although they can't modify any security settings.

Figure 17-11:
In the Properties dialog box for a user account, you can change the full name or description, modify the password options, and add this person to, or remove this person from, a group. The Properties dialog box for a group is simpler still, containing only a list of the group's members.

- **Replicator.** If you're in this group, you can replicate files across a domain, a technical bit of bookkeeping of absolutely no interest to anyone outside the thrilling world of network administration.

Remember: You can add an individual account to as many groups as you like. That person will have the accumulated rights and privileges of all of those groups.

Modifying Users and Groups

To edit an account or group, just double-click its name in the Local Users and Groups window. A Properties dialog box appears, as shown in Figure 17-11.

You can also change an account password by right-clicking the name and choosing Set Password from the shortcut menu. But see page 504 earlier in this chapter for some cautions about this process.

Setting Up the Logon Process

On a Windows XP computer in a workgroup, the dialog box that greets you when you turn on the PC (or when you relinquish your turn at the PC by choosing Start→Log Off) looks something like Figure 17-14. But a few extra controls let you, an administrator, set up the logon screen for either more or less security—or, put another way, less or more convenience.

Open the User Accounts program in the Control Panel, and then click "Change the way users log on or off." As shown in Figure 17-12, Windows XP now offers you two extremely important logon options.

Figure 17-12:
The first option here governs the appearance of the user-friendly Welcome screen shown in Figure 17-14. The second lets one person duck into his own account without forcing you to log off completely, as described on page 520. Note that these options are related—you can't turn off the first without first turning off the second.

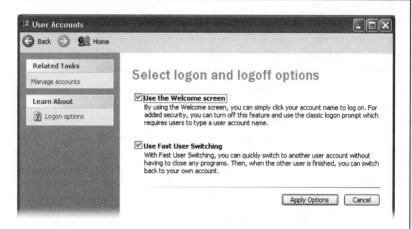

Use the Welcome Screen

Under normal circumstances, the logon screen presents a list of account holders when the PC is first turned on, as shown in Figure 17-14.

If you're worried about security, however, you might not even want that list to appear. If you turn off "Use the Welcome screen," each person who signs in must type both his name *and* password into blank boxes—a very inconvenient, but secure, arrangement (Figure 17-13). (You can't turn off "Use the Welcome screen" if Fast User Switching is turned on, as described in the next section.)

Tip: Even when you're looking at the standard, friendly Welcome screen (Figure 17-14), you can switch to the older, Classic logon screen: just press Ctrl+Alt+Delete. (If you're having trouble making it work, try pressing down the Alt key *before* the other ones.)

You may be used to using the Ctrl+Alt+Delete keystroke for summoning the Task Manager, as described on page 158, but at the Welcome to Windows box, it means something else entirely.

Figure 17-13:
If you turn off the new Welcome screen, you sign into Windows XP just as Windows 2000 fans have for years. You're expected to type in your name and password and then click OK. (By the way, you also see this display if you joined a domain when installing Windows XP Pro.)

Use Fast User Switching

If you've used any version of Windows before, the business about separate user accounts for everybody who uses a certain PC is old hat. One aspect of this feature, however, is dramatically new in Windows XP—and extremely welcome: *Fast User Switching.*

How Fast User Switching works

Suppose you're signed in, and you've got things just the way you like them: You have eleven programs open in carefully arranged windows, your Web browser is downloading some gigantic file, and you're composing an important speech in Microsoft Word. Now Chris, a co-worker/family member/fellow student, wants to duck in to do a quick email check.

In the old days, you might have rewarded Chris with eye-rolling and heavy sighs, or worse. If you chose to accommodate the request, you would have had to shut down your whole ecosystem, interrupting the download, closing your windows, saving your work and exiting your programs. You would have had to log off completely.

If Fast User Switching is turned on, however, none of that is necessary. All you have to do is press the magic keystroke, Windows logo key+L. (Or, if you've misplaced your keyboard, you can choose Start→Log Off, and then click Switch User in the Log Off dialog box.)

Now the Welcome screen appears, ready for the next person to sign in. Looking at the screen now, you may *think* you've just logged off in the usual way.

But look at it closely (Figure 17-14): You haven't actually logged off at all. Instead, Windows has *memorized* the state of affairs in your account—complete with all open windows, documents, and programs—and shoved it into the background. Chris (or whoever) can now sign in normally, do a little work, or look something up. When Chris logs out again, the Welcome screen comes back once again, at which point *you* can log on again. Without having to wait more than a couple of seconds, you find yourself exactly where you began, with all programs and documents still open and running.

This feature requires a good deal of memory, of course (don't even think about it on a machine with less than 96 MB of RAM). Otherwise, however, it's an enormous timesaver.

NOSTALGIA CORNER

The Double-Thick Security Trick

If you use Windows XP Pro in a corporation, you may see the startup box shown here when you first turn on the machine. You don't proceed to the Classic logon box (Figure 17-13) until you first press Ctrl+Alt+Delete.

This somewhat inconvenient setup is intended as a security feature. By forcing you to press Ctrl+Alt+Delete to bypass the initial Welcome box, Windows rules out the possibility that some sneaky program (such as a Trojan-horse program), designed to *look* like the Classic logon box, is posing *as* the Classic logon box—in order to "capture" the name and password you type there.

This two-layer logon system is what you get when you add

your PC to a network domain during the Windows XP Pro installation. If you want to use it on a workgroup machine, you can, but you have to do a little digging to find it. Choose Start→Run; type *control Userpasswords2*, and then press Enter. You see the program shown on page 512—the old-style User Accounts box. Click the Advanced tab.

At the bottom of the Advanced tab, turn on "Require users to press Ctrl+Alt+Delete," and then click OK. From now on, turning on the PC greets you not with a logon screen, but with the un-fakeable Welcome box shown here. (Of course, this presumes you've also turned off "Use the Welcome screen," as shown in Figure 17-12.)

Tip: If Fast User Switching is turned *off,* its special keystroke—Windows logo key+L—is still special. Now it *locks* your PC, hiding all of your open programs and windows. The only thing on the screen is an Unlock Computer dialog box (which looks almost exactly like the one shown in Figure 17-14). At this point, nobody can even get into the machine except you or somebody with an Administrator account.

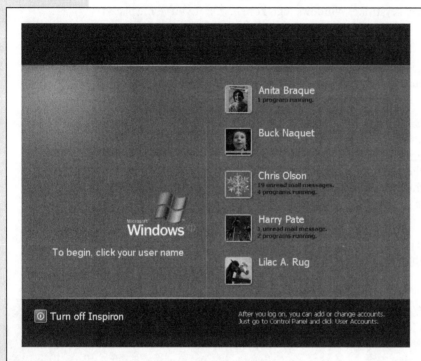

To begin, click your user name

Anita Braque
1 program running.

Buck Naquet

Chris Olson
19 unread mail messages.
4 programs running.

Harry Pate
1 unread mail message.
2 programs running.

Lilac A. Rug

Turn off Inspiron

After you log on, you can add or change accounts. Just go to Control Panel and click User Accounts.

Figure 17-14:
When Fast User Switching is turned on, you can call up the Welcome screen shown here without even quitting your programs and closing your windows. If Outlook Express or Windows Messenger is running, the Welcome screen even shows you how many unread email messages are waiting for you. (Point without clicking to produce a tooltip that breaks down which email accounts they came in on.)

How to turn on Fast User Switching

To turn on this optional feature, open the User Accounts program in the Control Panel. Click "Change the way users log on or off"; the dialog box shown in Figure 17-12 appears. Make sure "Use the Welcome screen" is turned on (it's a requirement for Fast User Switching), and then turn on "Use Fast User Switching." Finally, click the Apply Options button.

Note: You can't turn Fast User Switching off if anybody else's account is still open in the background. Before you can turn off the feature, you must first switch to each account in turn (press Windows key+L) and then sign off from each account.

From now on, you have two options each time you decide that you're finished working for the moment. You can log off normally, closing all of your programs and windows—or you can *fast switch,* logging off temporarily, leaving your work open on the screen behind the scenes. Figure 17-15 shows you the difference.

Tip: Here's the power user's version of fast user switching (Administrator account required). Press Ctrl+Alt+Delete to open the Task Manager dialog box, whose Users tab reveals the list of logged-on accounts. Right-click the account you want, choose Connect from the shortcut menu, and *boom!*—you're switched. You don't even have to listen to the two-note musical switching theme.

Figure 17-15:
Top: If you choose Start→Log Off when Fast User Switching is turned off, you get this limited dialog box.

Bottom: When you choose Start→Log Off while Fast User Switching is turned on, you get this choice: you can either log off for real (click Log Off), or use Fast User Switching to cede control of the computer to another account holder and put your work into background memory (click Switch User).

Logging On

Once your account is set up, here's what it's like getting into, and out of, a Windows XP Professional machine.

Identifying Yourself

When it comes to the screens you encounter when you log onto a Windows XP computer, your mileage may vary. What you see depends on how your PC has been set up. For example:

You zoom straight to the desktop

If you are the sole account holder, and you've set up no password at all for yourself, you cruise all the way to the desktop without any stops.

This password-free scenario, of course, is not very secure; any evildoer who walks by your machine when you're in the bathroom has complete access to all of your files (and all of your password-protected Web sites). But if you work in a home office, for example, where the threat of privacy invasion isn't very great, it's by far the most convenient arrangement.

You get the "Log On to Windows" dialog box

If you've turned off "Use the Welcome screen" (page 520), you don't get the usual Welcome screen shown in Figure 17-14 at startup. Instead, you must *type in* your name, as shown in Figure 17-13, rather than simply clicking it in a user-friendly list. (If you were the last person to use the machine, you might not have to type in the name, because Windows automatically fills the box with the name of the most recent user.)

You get the "Press Ctrl-Alt-Delete to Begin" dialog box

Either you added your PC to a domain while installing Windows XP Professional, or you have turned off the "Use the Welcome screen" feature and activated the "Require Users to Press Ctrl-Alt-Delete" option mentioned earlier. This is the most secure configuration, and also the least convenient.

You get the Windows XP Welcome screen

This is what people on stand-alone or workgroup computers see most of the time (Figure 17-14).

At this moment, you have several alternatives. If you click the "Turn off [computer name]" button (in the lower-left corner of the screen)—maybe in a sudden panic over the amount of work you have to do—you'll be offered the "Turn off computer" dialog box. It contains Stand By, Turn Off, Restart, and Cancel buttons. (If you press the Shift key, the Stand By button becomes a Hibernate button.)

Otherwise, to sign in, click your account name in the list. If no password is required for your account, you proceed to your personal Windows world with no further interruption.

If there *is* a password associated with your account, you'll see a place for it (Figure 17-16). Type your password and then press Enter (or click the green arrow button).

There's no limit to the number of times you can try to type in a password; with each incorrect guess, a tooltip balloon appears, tactfully inquiring, "Did you forget your password?" It reminds you that capitalization counts.

Figure 17-16:
If you can't remember the password, click the ? icon. It produces a balloon that reveals your password hint. And if you still can't remember, it's time to take out the Password Reset Disk (page 506).

Tip: If your Caps Lock key is pressed, another balloon lets you know. Otherwise, because you can't see anything on the screen as you type except dots, you might be trying to type a lowercase password with all capital letters.

Profiles

As you've read earlier in this chapter, every document, icon, and preference setting related to your account resides in a single folder: by default, it's the one bearing your name in the Local Disk (C:)→Documents and Settings folder. This folder is technically known as your *user profile*.

The All Users Profile

Each account holder has a separate user profile. But your PC also has a couple of profiles that aren't linked to human beings' accounts.

Have you ever noticed, for example, that not everything you actually see in your Start menu and on your desktop is, in fact, in *your* user profile folder?

The solution to this mystery is the All Users profile, which also lurks in the Documents and Settings folder (Figure 17-17). As you can probably tell by its name, this

Figure 17-17:
Behind the scenes, Windows XP maintains another profile folder, whose subfolders closely parallel those in your own. What you see—the contents of the Start menu, Desktop, Shared Documents folder, Favorites list, Templates folder, and so on—is a combination of what's in your own user profile folder and what's in the All Users folder.

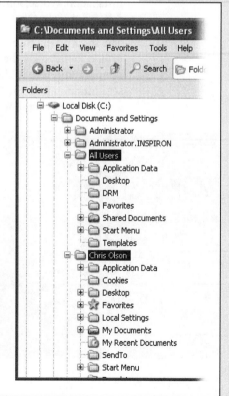

folder stores the same kinds of settings your profile folder does—except that anything in All Users appears on *everybody's* Start menu, desktop, and so on.

All of this is a long-winded way of suggesting another way of making some icon available to everybody with an account on your machine. Drag it into the corresponding folder (such as Desktop or Start Menu) in the All Users profile folder.

Whose software is it, anyway?

The All Users folder also offers a handy solution to the "Whose software is it, anyway?" conundrum: the burning question of whose Start menu and desktop reflects new software that you've installed using your own account.

As noted in Chapter 6, some software installers ask if you would you like the new program to show up only in your Start menu, or in *everybody's* Start menu. But not every installer is this thoughtful. Some installers automatically deposit their new software into the All Users folder, thereby making its Start menu listing available to everybody when they log on.

On the other hand, some installers may deposit a new software program only into *your* account (or that of whoever is logged in at the moment). In that case, other account holders won't be able to use the program at all, even if they know that it's been installed, because their own Start Menu and Desktop folders won't reflect the installation. Worse, some people, not seeing the program's name on their Start menus, might not realize that you've already installed it—and may well install it *again*.

The solution, of course, is to open the Start Menu→Programs folder in your user profile folder, copy the newly installed icon, and paste it into the All Users→Start Menu→Programs folder. (Repeat with the Desktop folder, if you'd like everyone to see a desktop icon for the new program.) You've just made that software available and visible to everybody who logs onto the computer.

TROUBLESHOOTING MOMENT

The Missing Security Tab

If you don't see a Security tab in the Properties dialog box for a file or folder, several things may have gone wrong.

You could be looking at a file or folder on a hard drive that uses the *FAT 32* formatting scheme instead of the NTFS file system. As the name implies, the NTFS permissions system is available only on drives formatted with NTFS. (See page 620 for definitions and instructions.)

You yourself might not have the appropriate permissions to view or change the permissions for a certain file or folder.

The easiest way around this obstacle is to log on using the local Administrator account (page 512), or an account with equivalent privileges that you've created yourself.

Finally, you might have Windows XP's Simple File Sharing feature turned on (page 574), which hides the entire NTFS permissions system from you. To turn off Simple File Sharing, choose Tools→Folder Options in any desktop window, click the View tab, scroll down, and then turn off the "Use simple file sharing" checkbox. Then click OK.

The Default User Profile

When you first create a new account, who decides what the desktop picture will be—and its Start menu configuration, assortment of desktop icons, and so on?

Well, Microsoft does, of course—but you can change all that. What a newly created account holder sees is only a reflection of the Default User profile. It's yet another folder—this one usually hidden—in your Documents and Settings folder, and it's the common starting point for all profiles.

If you'd like to make some changes to that starting point, start by tweaking a regular account—your own, for example. Make its desktop picture, Start menu, Web favorites, and other decorations look just the way you'd like the new default to be.

Then you need to fire up a little program called Profile Manager, whose job is to copy, move, and delete items among user profiles. Figure 17-18 has full instructions.

Figure 17-18:
Top: To open Profile Manager, open the System program in the Control Panel. Click the Advanced tab, and then click the Settings button in the User Profiles section, as shown here.

Bottom: To copy the settings from a person's profile into the Default User profile, highlight the name of the account whose settings you want to copy. Then click Copy To; in the next dialog box, click Browse, and then navigate to and select, the My Computer→Local Disk (C:)→ Documents and Settings→Default User folder. Click OK—and the deed is done.

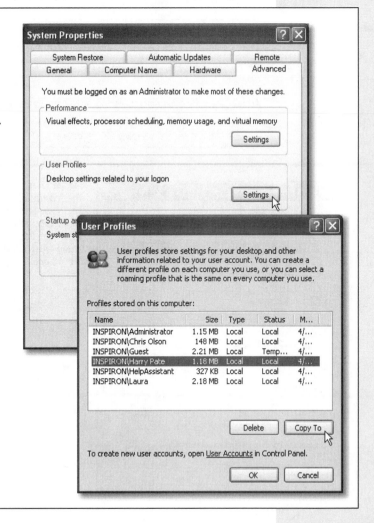

NTFS Permissions: Protecting Your Stuff

There's one final aspect of user accounts that's worth mentioning: *NTFS permissions*, a technology that's the heart of Windows XP Pro's security system. Using this feature, you can specify exactly which co-workers are allowed to open which files and folders on your machine. In fact, you can also specify *how much* access each person has. You can dictate, for example, that Gomez and Morticia aren't allowed to open your Fourth-Quarter Projections spreadsheet at all, that Fred and Ginger can open it but not make changes, and George and Gracie can both open it and make changes.

Your colleagues will encounter the permissions you've set up like this in two different situations: when tapping into your machine from across the network, or when sitting down at it and logging in using their own names and passwords. In either case, the NTFS permissions you set up protect your files and folders equally well.

Tip: In Chapter 20, you can read about a very similar form of access privileges called *share permissions*. There's a big difference between share permissions and the NTFS permissions described here, though: share permissions keep people out of your stuff only when they try to access your PC from *over the network*.

Actually, there are other differences, too. NTFS permissions offer more gradations of access, for example. And using NTFS permissions, you can declare individual *files* accessible or inaccessible to specific co-workers—not just folders. See page 581 for details.

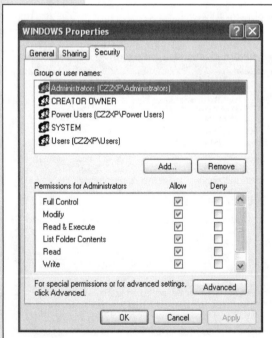

Figure 17-19:
The Security tab of an NTFS folder's Properties dialog box. If you have any aspirations to be a Windows XP power user, get used to this dialog box. You're going to see it a lot, because almost every icon on a Windows XP system—files, folders, disks, printers—has a Security tab like this one.

Using NTFS permissions is most decidedly a power-user technique because of the added complexity it introduces. Entire books have been written on the topic of NTFS permissions alone.

You've been warned.

Setting Up NTFS Permissions

To change the permissions for an NTFS file or folder, you open its Properties dialog box by right-clicking its icon, and then choosing Properties from the shortcut menu. The Properties dialog box appears; click the Security tab (Figure 17-19).

Step 1: Specify the Person

The top of the Security tab lists the people and groups that have been granted or denied permissions to the selected file or folder. When you click a name in the list, the Permissions box at the bottom of the dialog box shows you how much access that person or group has.

The first step in assigning permissions, then, is to click the person or group whose permissions you want to change.

If the person or group isn't listed, click the Add button to display the Select Users or Groups dialog box, where you can type them in (Figure 17-20).

Tip: Instead of typing in names one at a time, as shown in Figure 17-20, you can also choose them from a list, which lets you avoid spelling mistakes and having to guess at the variations. To do so, click the Advanced button to display an expanded version of the dialog box, and then click Find Now to search for all of the accounts and groups on the computer. Finally, in the resulting list, click the names of the people and groups you want to add (Ctrl-click to select more than one at once). Click OK to add them to the previous dialog box, and click OK again to add the selected users and groups to the Security tab.

If you've used Windows 2000, in the meantime, you might wonder why this process is so much more convoluted in XP Pro that was in Windows 2000. The answer is: good question!

Figure 17-20:
Type the names of the people or groups in the "Enter the object names to select" box at the bottom, trying not to feel depersonalized by Microsoft's reference to you as an "object." If you're adding more than one name, separate them with semicolons. Because remembering exact spellings can be iffy, click Check Names to confirm that these are indeed legitimate account holders. Finally, click OK to insert them into the list on the Security tab.

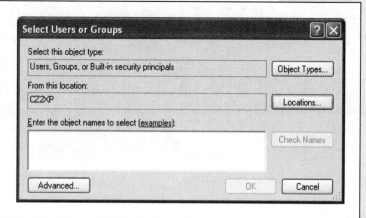

Step 2: Specify the Permissions

Once you've added the users and groups you need to the list on the Security tab, you can highlight each one and set permissions for it. You do that by turning on the Allow or Deny checkboxes at the bottom half of the dialog box.

The different degrees of freedom break down as follows (they're listed here from least to most control, even though that's not how they're listed in the dialog box):

- **List Folder Contents,** available only for folders, means that the selected individuals can see (but not necessarily open) the files and folders inside. That may sound obvious—but believe it or not, if you *don't* turn on this option, the affected people won't even be able to see what's in this folder. The folder will just appear empty.

- **Read** lets people examine the contents of the file or folder, but not make changes. (They can also examine the permissions settings of these files and folders—the ones that you're setting up right now.)

- **Read & Execute** is a lot like Read, except that it also lets people run any programs they find inside the affected folder. When applied to a folder, furthermore, this permission adds the ability to *traverse* folders. (Traversing means directly opening inner folders even when you're not allowed to open the outer folder. You might get to an inner folder by double-clicking a shortcut icon, for example, or by typing the folder's path into the Address bar of a window.)

- **Write** is like Read, but adds the freedom to make and save changes to the file. When applied to a folder, this permission means that people can create new files and folders inside it.

- **Modify** includes all of the abilities of the Write and Read & Execute level, plus the ability to *delete* the file or folder.

FREQUENTLY ASKED QUESTION

Allow vs. Deny

Why do I see both Allow and Deny checkboxes in the Permissions dialog box? Isn't not allowing permission the same as denying it?

In this case, no. "Deny" permissions always take precedence over "Allow" permissions.

For example, if somebody has been granted access to a file or folder because he's a member of a group, you can explicitly revoke his permission by using the Deny

checkboxes for his account. You've just overridden the group permission, just for him, leaving the rest of the group's permissions intact.

You can also use the Deny checkboxes to override permissions granted by *inheritance* from a parent folder. For example, you can grant somebody access to the C: drive by sharing it and assigning her Allow permissions to it, but then prevent her from accessing the C:\Program Files folder by sharing that and *denying* her permission.

- **Full Control** confers complete power over the file or folder. The selected person or group can do anything they like with it, including trashing it or its contents, changing its permissions, taking ownership of it (and away from you, if they like), and so on.

Of course, turning on Allow grants that level of freedom to the specified user or group, and turning it off takes away that freedom. (For details on the Deny checkbox, see the box on the facing page.)

Note: If you're not careful, it's entirely possible to "orphan" a file or folder (or even your entire drive) by revoking everyone's permission to it, even your own, making it *completely* inaccessible by anyone. That's why, before you get too deeply into working with NTFS permissions, you might consider creating an extra user account on your system and granting it Full Control for all of your drives, just in case something goes wrong.

Groups and Permissions

Once you understand the concept of permissions, and you've enjoyed a thorough shudder contemplating the complexity of a network administrator's job (6 levels of permissions $\times$ thousands of files $\times$ thousands of employees = way too many permutations), one other mystery of Windows XP Pro will fully snap into focus: the purpose of groups, introduced on page 515.

On those pages, you can read about groups as canned categories, complete with predefined powers over the PC, into which you can put different individuals to save yourself the time of adjusting their permissions and privileges individually. As it turns out, each of the ready-made Windows XP Pro groups also comes with predefined *permissions* over the files and folders on your hard drive.

Here, for example, is how the system grants permissions to your Windows folder for the Users, Power Users, and Administrators groups:

POWER USERS' CLINIC

Special Identities

When you open the Select Users or Groups dialog box, you may notice a number of groups listed there that you didn't create. What's going on?

These elements, which include Everyone, Authenticated Users, Creator Owner, and Terminal Service User, aren't exactly traditional groups. Microsoft calls them *built-in security principals*, or alternatively, *special identities*, but neither term is especially helpful. Whatever you want to call them, the idea is the same: these security principals are *roles*, not specific individuals. They're designed to give you more flexibility in applying permissions en masse.

For example, the Authenticated Users security principal affects anybody who logs on by supplying a user name and password (which is just about everybody except Guest people); everybody in this category automatically inherits any permissions you've set up for the Authenticated Users group. Similarly, the Everyone group—the most commonly used of the built-in security principals—means everybody.

	Users	Power Users	Administrators
Full Control			X
Modify		X	X
Read & Execute	X	X	X
List Folder Contents	X	X	X
Read	X	X	X
Write		X	X

If you belong to the Users group, you have the List Folder Contents permission, which means that you can see what's in the Windows folder; the Read permission, which means that you can open up anything you find inside; and the Read & Execute permission, which means that you can run programs in that folder (which is essential for Windows XP itself to run). But people in the Users group aren't allowed to change or delete anything in the Windows folder, or to put anything else inside. Windows XP is protecting itself against the mischievous and clueless.

Members of the Power Users group have all of those abilities and more—they also have Modify and Write permissions, which let them add new files and folders to the Windows folder (so that, for example, they can install a new software program on the machine).

When Permissions Collide

If you successfully absorbed all this information about permissions, one thing should be clear: people in the Power Users group ought to be able to change or delete any file in your Windows folder. After all, they have the Modify permission, which ought to give them that power.

In fact, they can move or delete anything in any folder *in* the Windows folder, because the first cardinal rule of NTFS permissions is this:

NTFS permissions travel downstream, from outer folders to inner ones

In other words, if you save the Modify and Write permissions to a folder, then you ought to have the same permissions for every file and folder inside it.

But if you are indeed in the Power Users group, you'll find that you can't, in fact, delete any of files or folders in the Windows folder. That's because each of them comes with Modify and Write permissions turned *off* for Power Users, even though the folder that encloses them has them turned on.

Why would Microsoft go to this trouble? Because it wants to prevent people in this group from inadvertently changing or deleting important Windows files—and yet it wants these people to be able to put *new* files into the Windows folder, so that they can install new programs.

This is a perfect example of the second cardinal rule of NTFS permissions:

NTFS permissions that have been explicitly applied to a file or folder always override inherited permissions

Here's another example: Suppose your sister, the technical whiz of the household, has given you Read, Write, Modify, Read & Execute, and List Folder Contents permissions to her own My Documents folder. Now you can read, change, or delete every file there. But she can still protect an individual document or folder *inside* her My Documents folder—the BirthdayPartyPlans.doc file, for example—by denying you all permissions to it. You'll be able to open anything else in there, but not that file.

Believe it or not, NTFS permissions get even more complicated, thanks to the third cardinal rule:

Permissions accumulate as you burrow downward through folders inside folders

Now suppose your sister has given you the Read and List Folder Contents permissions to her My Documents folder—a "look, but don't touch" policy. Thanks to the first cardinal rule, you automatically get the same permissions to every file and folder *inside* My Documents.

Suppose one of these inner folders is called Grocery Lists. If she grants you the Modify and Write permissions to the Grocery Lists folder, so that you can add items to the shopping list, you end up having Read, Modify, *and* Write permissions for every file

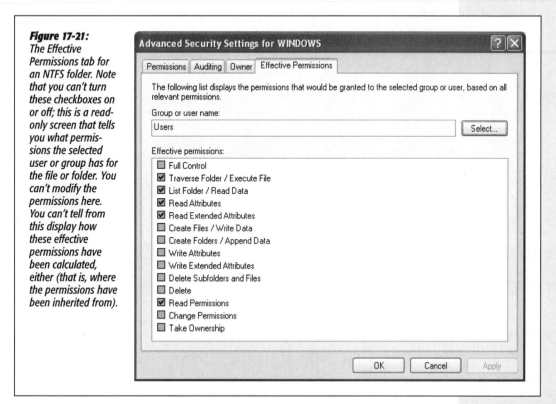

Figure 17-21:
The Effective Permissions tab for an NTFS folder. Note that you can't turn these checkboxes on or off; this is a read-only screen that tells you what permissions the selected user or group has for the file or folder. You can't modify the permissions here. You can't tell from this display how these effective permissions have been calculated, either (that is, where the permissions have been inherited from).

in that folder. Those files have *accumulated* permissions—they got the Read permission from My Documents, and the Modify and Write permissions from the Grocery Lists folder.

Because these layers of inherited permissions can get dizzyingly complex, Microsoft has prepared for you a little cheat sheet, a dialog box that tells you the bottom line, the net result—the *effective* permissions. To see it, follow these steps:

1. **Click the Advanced button on the Security tab.**

   The Advanced Security Settings dialog box appears.

2. **Click the Effective Permissions tab; finally, click Select.**

   Now you see the same Select User or Group dialog box you saw earlier when you were creating permissions.

3. **Click the user or group whose effective permissions you want to see, and then click OK.**

   You now see checkmarks next to the permissions that are in effect, taking into account folder-permission inheritance and all other factors, for the user or group for that particular file or folder, as shown in Figure 17-21.

Setting Up a Workgroup Network

I t's a rare Windows XP Pro machine indeed that isn't connected, sooner or later, to some kind of office network (technically known as a *local area network,* or *LAN*). And no wonder: the payoff is considerable: Once you've created a network, you can copy files from one machine to another just as you'd drag files between folders on your own PC. Everyone on the network can consult the same database, phone book, or calendar. When the workday's done, you can play games over the network. You can even store your MP3 music files on one computer and listen to them on any other. Most importantly, you can share a single laser printer, cable modem or DSL Internet connection , fax modem, or phone line among all the PCs in the house.

If you work at a biggish company, you probably work on a *domain network,* which is described in the next chapter. You, lucky thing, won't have to fool around with building or designing a network; your job, and your PC, presumably came with a fully functioning network (and a fully functioning geek responsible for running it).

If you work at home, or if you're responsible for setting up a network in a smaller office, this chapter is for you. It guides you through the construction of a less formal *workgroup network,* which ordinary mortals can put together.

You'll soon discover that, when it comes to simplicity, setting up a network has a long way to go before it approaches, say, setting up a desk lamp. It involves buying equipment, installing adapters, and configuring software. Fortunately, Windows XP's Network Setup Wizard makes the software part as painless as possible.

Kinds of Networks

You can connect your PCs using any of several different kinds of gear. Most of the world's offices are wired with *Ethernet cable,* but all kinds of possibilities await, including networking systems that rely on the phone or power lines already in your walls, and even wireless systems that don't need cables at all. Here's an overview of the most popular networking systems.

Note: Be sure that whatever networking gear you buy is compatible with Windows XP by checking the compatibility list at *www.microsoft.com/hcl.* Networking is complicated enough without having to trouble-shoot some gadget that's not designed for XP.

Ethernet

Ethernet is the world's most popular networking protocol. It gives you fast, reliable, trouble-free communication that costs very little and imposes few limitations on where you can place the PCs in a home or small office.

In addition to the computers themselves, an Ethernet network requires three components:

- **Network adapters.** You need an adapter for each computer. (You may also hear a network adapter called a *network interface card* or NIC ["nick"].)

  The network adapter provides the jack, shown in Figure 18-1, where you plug in the network cable. If you have a desktop PC that doesn't already have an Ethernet jack, you can buy a network adapter either in the form of a PCI card (which you must open up your computer to install) or a USB box (which connects to the back of the computer and dangles off of it).

  If you have a laptop, you can use one of these USB adapters or a PC Card that slips into your computer's PC Card slot.

Tip: You can generally order a new PC with an Ethernet card preinstalled, often for less than what it would cost to buy one at your local computer store.

- **A hub.** An Ethernet network also requires an Ethernet *hub* (also shown in Figure 18-1), the nexus into which you plug the network cable from each PC. Hubs come in different sizes; five- and eight-port hubs are popular for home networking.

Tip: Buy a hub with a few more ports than you need. You may eventually add another computer to the network, not to mention shared network equipment like laser printers or a *router* (which lets you share a cable modem among all of the PCs on the network).

Of course, you can always expand your network by adding on *another* hub when the time comes, thanks to a special connector called an *uplink port* that lets you hook one hub into another.

If you have a cable modem or DSL connection to the Internet, you may want consider buying a combination *router/hub* instead of a standard hub. (The dialog boxes in Windows XP call these boxes *residential gateways,* although almost no one else does.) In addition to serving as a hub, a special connector on this gizmo also accommodates your cable modem or DSL box, so that all of the PCs on your network can share the high-speed magic of just one Internet connection. (You can also purchase a router and hub separately.)

- **Ethernet cables.** The cables used for most Ethernet networks look something like telephone cables, but they're not the same thing—and they're definitely not interchangeable. Both the cable itself (called *10BaseT, 100BaseT cable,* or *Cat 5* cable) and the little clips at each end (called an *RJ-45* connector) are slightly fatter than those on a phone cable (Figure 18-1). You can buy ready-made Ethernet cables (that is, with the connectors already attached) in a variety of lengths and in many different colors. Each computer must be connected to the hub with a cable that's no longer than 100 yards or so long.

Figure 18-1:
Top: The Ethernet cable is connected to a computer at one end, and the hub (shown here) at the other end. The computers communicate through the hub; there's no direct connection between any two computers. The front of the hub has little lights for each connector port, which light up only on the ports that are in use. You can watch the lights flash as the computers communicate with one another.

Bottom: Here's what a typical "I've got three PCs in the house, and I'd like them to share my cable modem" setup might look like.

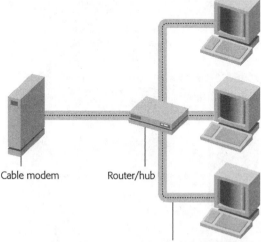

Cable modem   Router/hub

Wiring (Ethernet, Powerline, HomePNA) or radio waves
(if you're using a wireless network)

Tip: Ethernet gear can be shockingly inexpensive; a search at *www.buy.com,* for example, reveals Ethernet cards for $10 and five-port Ethernet hubs for $30 from no-name companies. If you're willing to pay slightly more–$20 for the card, $50 for the hub, for example–you can get brand-name gear (like Microsoft, Netgear, 3Com, or LinkSys) whose support with installation, phone help, and driver updates through the years may reward you many times over. Setting up an Ethernet network generally goes very smoothly–but in the few cases where trouble arises, cheapo equipment is often the problem.

Network Hookups

On paper, the hardware part of setting up the network is simple: Just install a network adapter in each computer, and then connect each one to the hub using an Ethernet cable. It's that "using an Ethernet cable" part that sometimes gets sticky. Depending on where your PCs are and how concerned you are about the network's appearance, this wiring process may involve drilling holes in floors or walls, stapling cables to baseboard trim, or calling in an electrician to do the job.

When all of your computers are in the same room, you can run the cables along the walls and behind the furniture. Buying cables that are the same color as your walls or floors can help to hide the installation. If you have to run cables between rooms,

---

UP TO SPEED

Network Devices Have Speed Limits

Ethernet cards and hubs are available in different speeds. The most common are *10BaseT* (10 megabits/second, or Mbps) and *100BaseT* (100 megabits/second, sometimes cleverly called *Fast Ethernet*).

For most home or small business networks, which you choose won't have much bearing on speed, unless you frequently transmit huge files between the computers on your network. For example, you can play MP3 music files stored on another computer over a 10BaseT connection with no problems at all. However, if you plan to install video cameras all around your palatial estate and want to watch all of the video feeds simultaneously, opt for Fast Ethernet– or even Gigabit Ethernet, the current Ethernet speed champ (1,000 megabits/second).

Note, however, that the speed of the network has no effect on your computers' *Internet* speed–Web surfing, email downloading, and so on. The reason: Even the slowest network operates far faster than your Internet connection. Remember, dial-up modems run no faster than 56 kilobits/second, and even a cable modem or DSL connection

maxes out at 512 to 1,024 kilobits/second–still 10 to 20 times slower than a 10BaseT network. Even a T-1 line (a permanent leased telephone line commonly used for corporate Internet connections, costing thousands of dollars a month) only runs at 1,544 megabits/second.

Much of the Ethernet equipment on the market today is designed to run either at Fast Ethernet speed, or at *both* 10 and 100 Mbps. If you buy a *dual-speed* hub (often labeled "10/100"), each networking card connected to it will run at its own maximum speed. If one computer has a 10BaseT network card and one has 100BaseT, they'll still be able to communicate. But if your hub operates *only* at 100BaseT speed, then 10BaseT cards won't work at all.

That's the story on the hubs. As for the cards, virtually all of them these days are all dual-speed 10/100 devices.

The bottom line: As you shop for gear, buy Fast Ethernet (or 10/100) hubs, which aren't much more expensive than the slower, 10 Mbps hubs. You may as well go for the higher speed, so you'll be ready for any high-bandwidth application that comes down the pike.

---

you can secure the cables to the floor or baseboards using staples (use the round kind that won't crush the cables) or plastic raceways with an adhesive backing.

Of course, you might not be thrilled about having *any* exposed cables in your home or office. In that case, the installation process can be much more complicated. You should probably hire a professional cable installer to do the job—or don't use cables at all. Read on.

Phone line networks

Instead of going to the trouble of wiring your home with Ethernet cables, you might consider using the wiring that's already *in* your house—telephone wiring. That's the idea behind a kind of networking gear called HomePNA. With this system, you can use the network even when using the modem or talking on the phone, although you can't make a modem and voice call simultaneously.

Unfortunately, the average American household has only two or three phone jacks in the *entire house,* meaning that you don't have much flexibility in positioning your PCs. If you're trying to avoid the plaster-dust experience of installing additional wiring, consider one of the networking types described next.

Power outlet networks

Here's another way to connect your computers without rewiring the building: use the electrical wiring that's already in your walls. Unlike phone jacks, electrical outlets are usually available in every room in the house.

If you buy *Powerline adapters* (also called HomePlug adapters), you get very fast speeds (14 megabits/second), very good range (1,000 feet, although that includes the twists and turns your wiring takes within the walls), and the ultimate in installation simplicity: You just plug the Powerline adapter from your PC's Ethernet or USB jack into any wall power outlet. Presto—all of the PCs are connected.

This isn't the cheapest avenue; at this writing, Powerline adapters cost about $100 apiece. But they afford a great deal of convenience, and a five-year-old could perform the installation.

Wireless networks (WiFi or 802.11b)

All of the networking methods described so far involve various schemes for wiring your computers together. Thousands of people, however, have embraced the flexibility of a networking system that involves no wires at all—a cordless networking technology that's based on a standard called *WiFi* or *802.11b* ("eight-oh-two dot eleven B"). (Your Macintosh friends probably call the same thing *AirPort,* because that's what Apple calls it.)

To create a WiFi network, you equip each PC with a special network adapter (about $60) whose little antenna pokes out of the computer. If all of your equipment is wireless, that's it: your PCs can now communicate with one another.

If you want to be able to get onto the Internet with them via a shared cable modem or DSL connection, though, you also need an *access point* (about $100)—a box that connects to your Ethernet hub and lets your wireless computers communicate with the cabled network. The usual gang—Microsoft, LinkSys, Netgear, 3Com, and others—sell these access points (also called base stations).

802.11 equipment has a range of about 150 feet, even through walls. In concept, this setup works much like a cordless phone, where the base station is plugged into the wall phone jack and a wireless handset can talk to it from anywhere in the house.

Wireless networking is not without its downsides, however. You may get intermittent service interruptions from 2.4-gigahertz cordless phones and other machinery, or even the weather. Furthermore, big metal things, or walls *containing* big metal things (like pipes) can sometimes interfere with communication among the PCs, much to the disappointment of people who work in subways and meat lockers.

Wireless networking isn't as secure as a cabled network, either. If you drive around a typical middle-class American neighborhood these days with your wireless-equipped laptop turned on, you'll be surprised at how many home wireless networks you can get onto, piggybacking onto other people's cable modems because they failed to turn on the optional password feature of their wireless systems.

Still, nothing beats the freedom of wireless networking, particularly if you're a laptop lover; you can set up shop almost anywhere in the house or in the yard, slumped into any kind of rubbery posture. No matter where you go within your home, you're online at full speed, without hooking up a single wire.

FREQUENTLY ASKED QUESTION

802.11b vs. 802.11a

I've been reading about a new wireless standard called 802.11a, which is supposed to be much faster than 802.11b. Which should I get?

The idea is exactly the same: wireless cards for the laptops or PCs, and wireless base stations for your hub or cable modem/DSL.

But 802.11a gear is newer, more expensive, and much faster: It can transfer up to 54 megabits per second (Mbps) instead of 11 Mbps, like 802.11b. It also operates on a frequency that doesn't clash with 2.4-gigahertz cordless phones—a distinct advantage in some homes and small offices.

It has its downsides, however. First of all, although it permits faster data transfer *between your PCs,* it doesn't make

Internet transactions any quicker (Web browsing, for example). Your cable modem or DSL is drastically slower than even 11 Mbps, so you won't feel any difference with 802.11a.

Second, and maybe more important, 802.11a's range isn't as good as 802.11b—about 60 feet instead of 150.

Finally, remember that the "a" and "b" technologies are not compatible. Your standard WiFi laptop won't be able to talk to an 802.11a laptop or base station.

Opt for 802.11a, in other words, only if your entire office uses it; you don't need the greater range of "b"; and your work entails frequent transfer of massive files or live video between machines.

FireWire Networks

Not many PCs have FireWire jacks (which are technically called, unpoetically, *IEEE-1394* connectors). If yours has a FireWire card, you probably bought it because you wanted to edit video you've captured on a DV camcorder (page 235).

But if you have a handful of computers with FireWire cards installed, Windows XP offers one of the world's simplest and fastest methods of connecting them in a network: just hook them together with six-pin-to-six-pin FireWire cables. That's it—no hubs or boxes to buy. (Because a typical FireWire card has *two* jacks, you can link several computers together this way, like a chain.)

Of course, this arrangement connects your computers only. It won't help if you want two computers in your house to be able to share a single cable modem or laser printer. Furthermore, FireWire cables can't be longer than 15 feet, which may cramp your networking style.

GEM IN THE ROUGH

Two-Computer Ethernet—and Direct Cable Connections

If your network has modest ambitions—that is, if you have only two computers you want to connect—you can ignore all this business about hubs, routers, and wiring. Instead, you just need an Ethernet *crossover cable,* costing about $10 from a computer store or online mail-order supplier. Run it directly between the Ethernet jacks of the two computers. Everything else in this chapter works exactly as though you had purchased a hub and were using a "real" Ethernet network.

Of course, even that solution requires a networking card in each PC. If that expenditure is a stretch for you, there's yet another way to connect two machines: a direct connection. You can create this kind of miniature homemade network only if (a) the computers are close to each other, (b) they both have parallel or USB ports, and (c) you've bought a high-speed DirectParallel or USB Net-LinQ cable from *www.lpt.com.*

To begin, open the Network Connections icon in your Control Panel. Click the "Create a new connection" link to start the New Connection Wizard.

Click Next. On the second screen, click "Set up an advanced connection," and then click Next. Click "Connect directly to another computer," and hit Next again.

Now Windows wants to know if the computer you're using will be the *host* (the machine whose files will be shared) or the *guest* (the one that will be accessing shared resources on the other machine). Choose Host (an option only if you're using an Administrator account), and then click Next.

On the next wizard screen, specify the port you're using to connect the machines (from the list of unused USB, serial, parallel, or infrared ports). Select USB or Parallel, as appropriate. Plug in the cable, if you haven't already.

Click Next again to view the list of user accounts; turn on the checkboxes of the people who should be allowed to tap into your machine via this direct-connect cable. Click Next, then Finish. The host computer starts "listening" for the guest to visit it.

Repeat all of this on the other machine, this time designating it the Guest (you don't need an Administrator account this time).

Once the two machines are connected by cable, you can open the My Network Places window on the guest machine. You'll see the shared folders, disks, and printers, just as though they were connected by a "real" network, as described in Chapter 20.

Installing Drivers

Regardless of which kind of network adapters you install in your computers, your next obligation is to install their software drivers. Fortunately, Windows XP comes with built-in drivers for almost all recent networking cards. When you turn the PC on after installing the card, you'll generally see XP install its driver almost automatically. If you're not so lucky—say you're using an old or nonstandard (read: cheap) network adapter—see Chapter 14 for advice on what to do when Plug and Play fails.

Sharing an Internet Connection

If you have cable modem or DSL service, you're a very lucky individual. Not only do you get spectacular speed when surfing the Web or doing email, but you also have a full-time connection. You never have to wait for some modem to dial (screeching all the way), and wait again for it to disconnect. It's just too bad that only one PC in your household or office can enjoy these luxuries.

Fortunately, it doesn't have to be that way. You can spread the joy of high-speed Internet to every PC on your network in either of two ways:

- **Buy a router.** A *router* (a *residential gateway* in Microsoft lingo) is a little box, costing about $80, that connects directly to the cable modem or DSL box. In some cases, it doubles as a hub, providing multiple Ethernet jacks into which you can plug your PCs. Others offer only a single jack into which you plug your existing hub. As a bonus, the router provides excellent security, serving as a firewall that isolates your network computers from the Internet and keeps out hackers.

  You're supposed to change a router's settings (in the rare event that they need changing) using your Web browser. You "sign onto" it using the account name and password you use to log onto the cable or DSL network. The router then logs onto your Internet service and stands ready to transmit Internet data to and from all of the computers on your network.

- **Use Internet Connection Sharing (ICS).** ICS is a built-in feature of Windows XP Professional that serves as a software router. Like a hardware router, ICS distributes a single Internet connection to every computer on the network—but unlike a router, it's free. You just fire it up on the *one* PC that's connected directly to your cable modem or DSL box—or, as networking geeks would say, the *gateway* or *host* PC.

  But there's a downside: If the gateway PC is turned off, nobody else in the house can go online. Furthermore, you have to install *two* Ethernet cards into the gateway PC: one that goes to the cable modem or DSL box, and the other that connects it to the hub.

  Most people think of ICS in terms of high-speed Internet accounts like cable modems and DSL. But it offers advantages even for PCs with standard dial-up modems. For example, more than one PC can be online at the same time, which can be a sanity saver in certain households. ICS also lets you park PCs in rooms that don't actually have phone jacks.

Even if you don't intend to share an Internet connection in this way, it's important to have some understanding of these concepts before running the Network Setup Wizard. Many of the questions it will ask pertain to the notion of connection sharing.

Tip: If you do intend to use Internet Connection Sharing, make sure the gateway PC can already get onto the Internet, on its own, before you attempt to run the Network Setup Wizard. The gateway PC should also be running Windows XP, although the other computers can be running earlier versions of Windows.

The Network Setup Wizard

Once you've set up the networking equipment, you have to inform Windows XP Pro about what you've been up to. You also have to configure your computers to share their files, folders, printers, modems, Internet connections, and so on. Fortunately, the Network Setup Wizard handles this duty for you. (You must have an Administrator account to run this wizard.)

To launch the wizard, choose Start→Control Panel, and then open Network Connections. In the task pane at the left side of the window (Figure 18-2), click the link that says, "Set up a home or small office network."

Tip: If you've chosen to hide your task pane, you can choose Start→All Programs→Accessories→ Communications→Network Setup Wizard instead.

A welcome message appears; click Next. The remaining screens of the wizard are as follows.

"Before you continue"

The screen contains a link called "checklist for creating a network." If you click it, you see a help page that guides you through the steps of setting up a network. It incorporates much of the information you've read so far in this chapter.

It also reminds you that if you plan to use Internet Connection Sharing, described earlier, you should ensure that your gateway Windows XP machine can get online *before* proceeding with the wizard. When you're finished reading the checklist, close its window and then click Next.

"Select a connection method"

The next wizard window starts the process of setting up Internet Connection Sharing (see Figure 18-2, right).

Your next step depends on your plans for your network and Internet use:

• **Each PC will go online independently.** If sharing a single Internet connection isn't the point of your networking efforts, click the Other button (Figure 18-2); on the next screen, click "This computer connects to the Internet directly or through a network hub." In other words, your various networked PCs will each connect directly to the Internet. No connection sharing is involved.

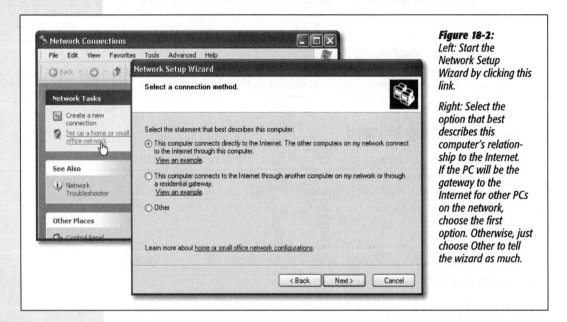

Figure 18-2:
Left: Start the Network Setup Wizard by clicking this link.

Right: Select the option that best describes this computer's relationship to the Internet. If the PC will be the gateway to the Internet for other PCs on the network, choose the first option. Otherwise, just choose Other to tell the wizard as much.

• **This is the computer with the connection.** If the computer you're at now is the one connected to the Internet—that is, if it's the gateway computer—click the first option: "This computer connects directly to the Internet. The other computers on my network connect to the Internet through this computer" (Figure 18-2).

Tip: *If your DSL service is for* multiple fixed IP addresses, *then your computers can share the connection without having to choose one single computer as the host.*

• **This isn't the computer with the connection.** If you like the idea of sharing a PC's Internet connection, but the machine you're using now isn't the gateway machine, choose the second option: "This computer connects to the Internet through another computer on my network or through a residential gateway."

• **You have a router.** If you've bought a router (residential gateway), you won't be needing the built-in Windows Internet Connection Sharing feature. Once again, you should click the second option ("This computer connects to the Internet through another computer on my network or through a residential gateway").

• **You don't plan to use the Internet at all.** If you just want to set up connections among your computers—but none of them ever goes online—click Other, then click Next, and then turn on "This computer belongs to a network that does not have an Internet connection."

"Select your Internet connection"

If you indicated that the computer you're setting up will indeed be connecting to the Internet, the wizard now shows you a list of the ways you've set up for your PC to get online (Figure 18-3). Each represents a different method of getting onto the Internet—network (Local Area Connection), America Online dial-up, your DSL account, or whatever. Turn on the one you want to use, and then click Next.

"Give this computer a description and name"

On this wizard screen (Figure 18-3), you see a place to give your PC its unique name. For example, if you have a laptop and a desktop PC, you might give them names like *Portegé* and *Millennia* (or *Kirk* and *Spock,* for all Windows cares). Of course, you already gave your computer a name when you installed Windows XP; that should be the name you see here.

Figure 18-3:
Top: Every computer on a Windows network (even a big network in a business environment) must have a unique name. Computer names and workgroup names are limited to 15 characters, without spaces. Hyphens and apostrophes are OK, but most other punctuation is forbidden.

Bottom: Tell the wizard how this machine connects to the Internet. See Chapter 10 to find out how these account names got here.

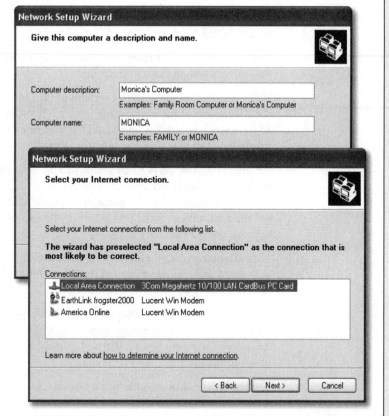

"Name your network"

On the screen, you're supposed to make up a name for your *workgroup* (mini-network). Every PC on your network should have the same workgroup name (it doesn't have to be *MSHome,* as much as Microsoft might like it).

"Ready to apply network settings"

Click Next. On the next wizard screen, you see a summary of your settings. If it all looks good, click Next, and wait a few minutes while the wizard scurries around, applying various internal settings.

"You're almost done"

Your first PC may now be correctly configured to be part of an office network, but it faces the problem of the first telephone owner: Who ya gonna call?

Your next step, therefore, should be to run the Network Setup Wizard again on each of your other PCs. As indicated by the wizard screen before you now, getting the wizard onto those other machines depends on what version of Windows they're using:

- **If the next PC has Windows XP.** Click the bottom option here, "Just finish the wizard." Click Next, and then click Finish.

  Now move to the next computer; start the Network Setup Wizard on *it,* exactly the way you did on the first machine.

- **If the next PC has some earlier version of Windows.** You'll probably want to run the XP version of the networking wizard. (If you're comfortable plugging in IP addresses, subnet mask numbers, and default gateway settings, you can enter them manually—but the wizard automates all of this.)

  XP offers you two ways to go about it: First, you can insert your Windows XP Professional CD-ROM into each of the other PCs. When the Windows Setup program opens up, click the link at the left side called "Perform additional tasks." On the next screen, click "Set up home or small office networking." The wizard appears, and you're ready to go.

  Second, you can create a *networking setup disk* for your older computers. That is, the wizard will transfer a copy of itself to a floppy disk that you can carry to the non-XP machines on your network.

  If you select this option and then click Next, you're instructed to put a blank formatted disk into the floppy drive. Click Next again to create the disk, which takes only a moment or two. Then eject the disk; for best results, label it for easy identification.

  Now insert the disk into the floppy drive on the older PC. Open the My Computer icon on your desktop, double-click the floppy drive icon, and double-click the Setup.exe icon. The by-now-familiar Network Setup Wizard appears.

No matter how you get the wizard onto the other machines, the experience of using it is precisely as described on the preceding pages—with two exceptions:

- If you've decided to set up the first computer as the gateway for Internet Connection Sharing, you don't see the complex array of choices illustrated in Figure 18-2. Instead, you see only the simplified options of Figure 18-4.

- There's no need to create a network setup floppy disk on the final wizard screen.

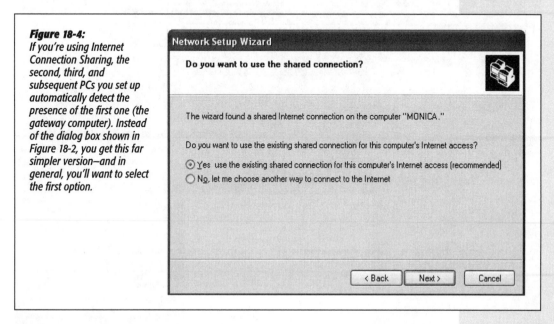

Figure 18-4:
If you're using Internet Connection Sharing, the second, third, and subsequent PCs you set up automatically detect the presence of the first one (the gateway computer). Instead of the dialog box shown in Figure 18-2, you get this far simpler version—and in general, you'll want to select the first option.

When it's all over, Windows lets you know that you should restart the computer. At that point, each PC you've visited is ready for network action.

Testing the Network

After all of this setup, here's how you can find out whether or not the gods are smiling on your new network. Seated at your Windows XP Pro machine, choose Start→My Network Places.

The network window opens, revealing the folders and disks that your machine can "see" (detect) on other computers of the network. The first time you try this experiment, there may not be much to see here.

Tip: All recent generations of Windows can "see" each other and work joyously side-by-side on the same network. On the older machines, you would open the equivalent window by double-clicking the My Network Places or Network Neighborhood icon on the desktop instead of using the Start menu.

However, if you click "View workgroup computers" in the task pane at the left side of the window, you should see the names and icons of the other computers you've set up, as shown in Figure 18-5. In Chapter 20, you'll find out how to burrow into these icons, using the files and folders of other networked PCs exactly as though they were on your own computer.

If you don't see the icons for your other computers, something has gone wrong. Check to see that:

TROUBLESHOOTING MOMENT

Troubleshooting Internet Connection Sharing

The Internet Connection Sharing (ICS) feature of Windows XP is worth its weight in gold—or, to be more precise, it's worth $80. That's about how much you would spend on a piece of equipment called a router, which you would otherwise need to share one Internet connection among all the PCs on your network.

If you have a high-speed connection like a cable modem or DSL, keeping your shared Internet system working is fairly simple. Just remember that the gateway PC must be turned on— and turned on *before* the other computers on the network—in order for the other PCs to get online. Remember, also, that the Personal Firewall feature should be on for all PCs *except* the gateway computer. (See page 312.)

If you use a dial-up modem, however, you may wind up having to do a little more fine-tuning. For example, if you open your Web browser on a *client* computer (that is, not the one with the Internet connection), the host computer dials. Unfortunately, dialing and connecting take time; before the host computer has finished making the connection, your Web browser may already have reported that the Web page can't be opened. Similarly, your email program may report that "the server isn't available," simply because it took an especially long time for the host computer to make the connection.

In either case, simply wait a moment and then try again: in your Web browser, click the Refresh button; in the email

program, click the Send/Receive button again. This time, your PC should find the connection and succeed in getting online.

Another typical problem: The host computer insists on connecting to your Internet service provider 24 hours a day, tying up the household phone line all day long, redialing every time it loses the connection.

Fortunately, it's easy enough to give Internet connection sharing some behavior-modification therapy. On the gateway PC, open the Network Connections icon in your Control Panel. Right-click the connection icon for your Internet service provider; from the shortcut menu, choose Properties, and click the Options tab. Make sure "Redial If line is dropped" is turned off, and set "Idle time before hanging up" to a reasonable number—say, ten minutes.

While you're here, you may as well turn off "Prompt for name and password" and "Prompt for phone number" to streamline the connection process, so that Windows XP won't bother you for this information every time you try to connect.

Also while you're here, you may as well visit the Advanced tab. On the gateway PC—the one connected directly to the Internet—all of these checkboxes should be turned on. On the other machines, these checkboxes should be turned off.

• Your cables are properly seated in the network adapter card and hub jacks.

• Your Ethernet hub (if any) is plugged into an electrical outlet.

• Your networking card is working. To do so, open the System program in the Control Panel. Click the Hardware tab; click the Device Manager button. Look for an error icon next to your networking card's name (see Chapter 13 for more on the Device Manager).

If you don't find a problem, rerun the Network Setup Wizard. If that doesn't work, you'll have to call Microsoft or your PC company for help.

Figure 18-5:
We have network! Your My Network Places window should reveal the presence of other PCs in your network, complete with the names you gave them when plowing through the Network Setup Wizard. This illustration shows Tiles view for clarity, but Windows starts out in Details view.)

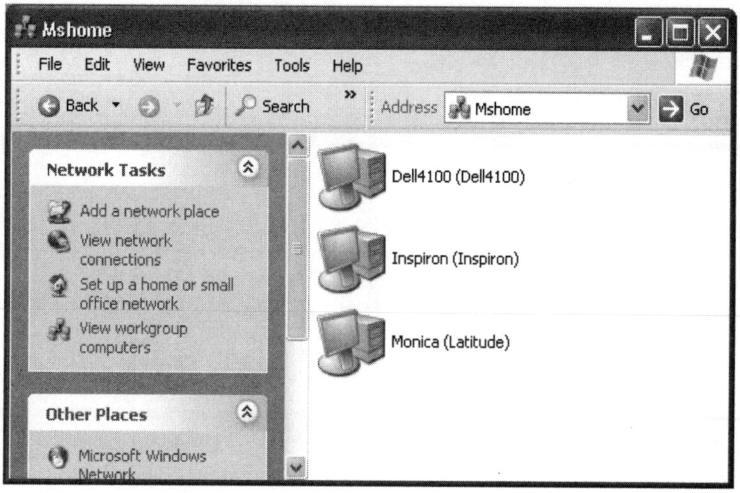

Introducing
Network Domains

As you may remember from page 23, Windows XP Pro was designed to thrive on two very different kinds of network worlds: the *workgroup* (an informal, home or small-office network) and the *domain* (a hard-core, security-conscious corporate network of dozens or thousands of PCs). Depending on which kind of network your PC belongs to, the procedures and even dialog boxes you experience are quite a bit different.

Chapter 18 guides you through the process of setting up a workgroup network, but no single chapter could describe setting up a corporate domain. That's a job for Super Geek, otherwise known as the network administrator—somebody who has studied the complexities of corporate networking for years.

This chapter is designed to help you learn to *use* a corporate domain. If your PC is connected to a workgroup network or no network at all, on the other hand, feel free to use these pages as scratch paper.

Note: In the context of this chapter, the term *domain* refers to a group of Windows computers on the same network. It's not the same as an *Internet* domain, which you may occasionally see mentioned. An Internet domain is still a group of computers, but they don't have to be connected to the same network, and they don't have to be running Windows. In addition, the domain name (like *amazon.com*) must be registered to ensure that there's no duplication on the Internet. Because Windows domains are private, they can be named any way the administrator chooses.

The Domain

As you may remember from Chapter 18, nobody else on a workgroup network can access the files on your PC unless you've created an account for them on your machine. Whenever somebody new joins the department, you have to create another new account; when people leave, you have to delete or disable their accounts. If something goes wrong with your hard drive, you have to re-create all of the accounts.

What's Wrong with Workgroups

You must have an account on each shared PC, too. If you're lucky, you have the same name and password on each machine—but that isn't always the case. You might have to remember that you're *pjenkins* on the front-desk computer, but *JenkinsP* on the administrative machine.

Similarly, suppose there's a network printer on one of the computers in your workgroup. If you want to use it, you have to find out whose computer the printer is connected to, call him to ask if he'll create an account for you, and hope that he knows how to do it. You either have to tell him your user name and password, or find out what user name and password he's assigned to you. In that case, every time you want to use that printer, you might have to log on by typing that user name and password.

If you multiply all of this hassle by the number of PCs on your small network, it's easy to see how you might suddenly find yourself spending more time managing accounts and permissions than doing the work the PC was supposed to help you with.

The Domain Concept

The solution to all of these problems is the network domain. In a domain, you only have a single name and password, which gets you into every shared PC and printer on the network. Everyone's account information resides on a central computer called a *domain controller*—a computer so important, it's usually locked away in a closet or a data-center room.

A domain controller keeps track of who is allowed to log on, who *is* logged on, and what each person is allowed to do on the network. When you log onto the domain, your PC communicates with a domain controller, which verifies your credentials and permits (or denies) you access.

Most domain networks have at least two domain controllers with identical information, so that if one computer dies, the other one can take over. (Some networks have many more than two.) This redundancy is a critical safety net; without a happy, healthy domain controller, the entire network is dead.

Without budging from their chairs, network administrators can use a domain controller to create new accounts, manage existing ones, and assign permissions. The domain takes the equipment-management and security concerns of the network out of the hands of individuals and puts them into the hands of trained professionals. You may sometimes hear this kind of networking called *client/server networking*. Each *workstation*—that is, each mere mortal PC like yours—relies on a central server machine for its network access.

If you use Windows XP Professional in a medium- to large-sized company, you probably use a domain every day. You may not even have been aware of it.

In fact, knowing what's been going on right under your nose isn't especially important to your ability to get work done. After all, it's not your job—it's the network administrator's. But understanding the domain system can help you take better advantage of a domain's features.

Active Directory

You may be aware that Microsoft sells two versions of Windows XP: Home Edition and Professional. One key difference is that Windows XP Home Edition computers can't join a domain.

There are other versions of Windows, however: the specialized ones that run on the above-mentioned domain controller computers. To create a domain, at least one computer must be running either Windows .NET Server 2003 or Windows 2000 Server. These are far more expensive operating systems (the price depends on the number of machines that they connect) and they run only on high-octane PCs. They also require high-octane expertise to install and maintain.

One key offering of these specialized Windows versions is an elaborate application called *Active Directory*. It's a single, centralized database that stores every scrap of information about the hardware, software, and people on the network. (The older operating system called Windows NT Server can create domains, but it doesn't include Active Directory.)

After creating a domain by installing Active Directory on a server computer, network administrators can set about filling the directory (database) with information about the network's resources. Every computer, printer, and person is represented by an *object* in the database and *attributes* (properties) that describe it. For example, a *user object's* attributes specify that person's name, location, telephone number, email address, and other more technical elements.

Active Directory lets network administrators maintain an enormous hierarchy of computers. A multinational corporation with tens of thousands of employees in offices all over the world can all be part of one Active Directory domain, with servers distributed in hundreds of locations, all connected by wide-area networking links. (A group of domains is known as a *tree*. Huge networks might even have more than one tree and are called, of course, a *forest*.)

The objects in an Active Directory domain are arranged in a hierarchy, something like the hierarchy of folders within folders on your hard drive. Some companies base their directory-tree designs on the organization of the company, using departments and divisions as the building blocks. Others use geographic locations as the basis for the design, or use a combination of both.

Unless you've decided to take up the rewarding career of network administration, you'll never have to install an Active Directory domain controller, design a directory tree, or create domain objects. You very well may encounter the Active Directory at your company, however; you can use it to search for the mailing address of somebody else on the network, for example, or locate a printer that can print on both sides of the page at once. Having some idea of the directory's structure can help in these cases.

Domain Security

Security is one of the primary reasons for Active Directory's existence. First of all, all of the account names and passwords reside on a single machine (the domain controller), which can easily be locked away, protected, and backed up. The multiple domain controllers automatically *replicate* the changes to one another, so that every one of them has up-to-date information.

Active Directory is also a vital part of the network's other security mechanisms. When your computer is a member of a domain, the first thing you do is log on, just as in a workgroup. But when you log into a domain, Windows XP Professional transmits your name and password (in encrypted form) to the domain controller, which checks your credentials and grants or denies you access.

Joining a Domain

If you work in a corporation, the computer supplied to you generally has Windows XP already installed and joined to the domain, ready to go.

But if you ever have occasion to add a PC to a domain yourself, here's how you go about it. (You can make your PC join a domain either during the installation of Windows XP Pro, or any time afterward.)

1. **Log on using the local Administrator account.**

   See page 512 for details.

2. **Choose Start→Control Panel→System. In the resulting dialog box, click the Computer Name tab (see Figure 19-1).**

   You should now be able to see the names of your computer and any workgroup or domain it belongs to.

3. **Click the Network ID button.**

   The Network Identification Wizard appears.

4. **Click Next to bypass the Welcome screen.**

   The Connecting To The Network screen appears.

5. **Click "This computer is part of a business network," and then click Next.**

   Now the wizard wants to know: "What kind of network do you use?"

6. Click "My company uses a network with a domain" and click Next.

A Network Information screen appears. It lets you know that, before you can join a domain, you need both a domain user account and a computer account. Your network administrator should create and give these to you in advance.

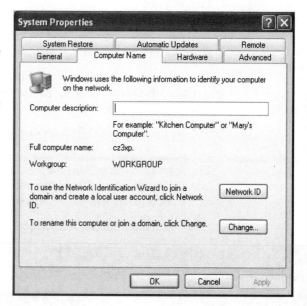

Figure 19-1:
The Computer Name tab of the System control panel displays the name of your computer and the workgroup or domain of which it is currently a member. From here, you can change the computer or workgroup name or join a new domain. The Network ID button launches a Network Identification Wizard, while the Change button displays a dialog box in which a more experienced person can perform the same tasks.

7. Click Next. On the User Account and Domain Information page, enter the user account name and password supplied by your administrator, plus the name of the domain in which your account has been created.

Remember this domain name; you'll need it again later to log on.

8. Click Next again.

A Computer Domain screen may appear next, requiring you to specify the name of your computer and the domain the *computer object* is in. If you see this page, it means that your computer isn't listed in the Active Directory domain you specified on the previous wizard screen. Flag down your network administrator and point out the problem. Then click Next to proceed.

In any case, you should now arrive at the User Account page, where you can create a *local* account for your computer. Of course, if you're going to be logging onto a domain, you don't really need a local account on your PC.

9. Click "Do not add a user at this time." Click Next, and finally click Finish to complete the wizard.

Restart the computer for your changes to take effect.

Five Ways Life Is Different on a Domain

As described in Chapter 18, the domain and workgroup personalities of Windows XP Professional are quite a bit different. Here are some of most important differences.

Logging On

What you see when you log onto your PC is very different when you're part of a domain. Instead of the standard Welcome screen (which shows a list of people with accounts on your PC), you generally encounter a two-step sign-in process:

- First, you see a Welcome to Windows dialog box. It instructs you to press Ctrl+Alt+Delete to begin. (As noted on page 521, this step is a security precaution.)

- Now the Log On to Windows dialog box appears (see Figure 19-2).

Tip: You can turn off the requirement to press Ctrl+Alt+Delete at each log on, if you like. Log on using the local Administrator account (or another administrator account), and then choose Start→Control Panel→User Accounts. Then click the Advanced tab and turn off the "Require users to press Ctrl-Alt-Delete" checkbox.

UP TO SPEED

Knowing What You're Logging Onto

You may remember from Chapter 18 that there are two kinds of accounts: *domain* accounts, maintained by a highly paid professional in your company, and *local* accounts—accounts that exist only on the PC itself. It's actually possible to find domain accounts and local accounts that have the same name—a perennial source of confusion for beginners (and occasionally experts).

For example, you know that every Windows XP Pro computer has an Administrator account, which the Windows XP installer creates automatically. The trouble is, so does the domain controller.

In other words, typing *Administrator* into the User Name text box might log you onto either the local machine or the

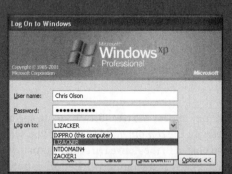

domain, depending on what password you supply. (With luck, the two accounts won't have the same password, but you never know.)

To avoid this kind of confusion, click the Options button on the Log On to Windows screen. As shown here, you're now privy to the "Log on to" drop-down menu. It lists the name of the domain you just joined, any other domains on the network, and your computer's name (which is marked "this computer"). It's important to select the correct item before you click OK.

For this reason, it's a good idea to keep the Log On to Windows dialog box in its expanded state all the time, so that you can easily see whether you are logging onto the domain or the local machine.

As you see in Figure 19-2, the Log On to Windows dialog box provides a place for you to type your user name and password. To save you time, Windows fills in the User Name box with whatever name was used the last time somebody logged in.

Figure 19-2:
Joining a domain disables Fast User Switching and the Windows XP Welcome screen, presenting a simple Log On to Windows dialog box instead. If you know Windows 2000, you should feel right at home, because this is the standard Welcome screen for that operating system, too.

Browsing the Domain

When your PC is part of the domain, all of its resources—printers, shared files, and so on—magically appear in your desktop windows, the My Network Places window, and so on (see Figure 19-3).

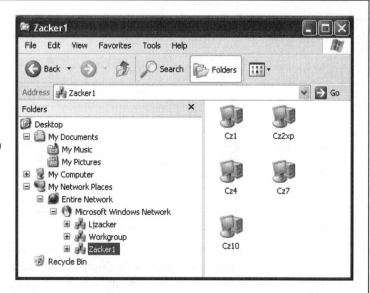

Figure 19-3:
When you open a Windows Explorer window and expand the My Network Places and Microsoft Windows Network icons, you see an icon for each workgroup on the network (see Figure 19-4). You can browse through the computers in a domain and access their shared folders (if you have the appropriate permissions) just as you would those of a workgroup. On a large network, you'll just see a lot more computers.

Searching the Domain

You can read all about the Windows XP Search command in Chapter 2. But when you're on a domain, this tool becomes far more powerful—and more interesting.

For example, when you choose Start→Search, the Computers or People search option changes to say Printers, Computers, or People. (Microsoft figures that you wouldn't need a search command for printers on a small network workgroup. After all, if you've only got two printers in your small office, you probably don't forget where they are very often. It's a different story if you work in a huge building with hundreds of computers and printers.)

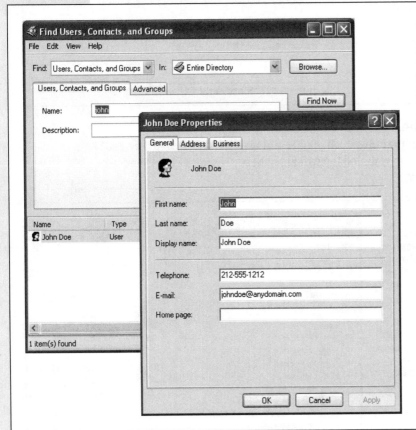

Figure 19-4:
Top left: Searching for people in your network's Active Directory is like using a phone book. You supply the information you know about the person.

Lower right: When you find that person (technically, her user object), you can view the information stored in its attributes. Of course, the usefulness of this feature depends on how much information your network administrators enter when creating the user objects.

When you choose Start→My Computer and click the My Network Places link on the left side of the window, the screen changes to show the list of your network places (if any). On the left side of this window, you can click the Search Active Directory link to open the dialog box shown at top left in Figure 19-4.

The name of this dialog box changes depending on what you're looking for. Your choices are:

- **Users, Contacts, and Groups.** Use this option to search the network for a particular person or network group (Figure 19-4). If your search is successful, you can find out someone's telephone number, email address, or mailing address, for example, or see what users belong to a particular group.

- **Computers.** This option helps you find a certain PC in the domain. It's of interest primarily to network administrators, because it lets them open a Computer Management window for the computers they find and manage many of its functions by remote control.

- **Printers.** In a large office, it's entirely possible that you might not know where you can find a printer with certain features—tabloid-size paper, for example, or double-sided printing. That's where this option comes in handy (see Figure 19-5).

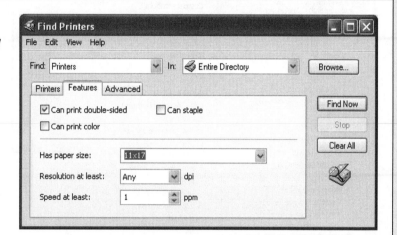

Figure 19-5:
Searching for a printer in Active Directory lets you find the printing features you need. Network administrators may also record the physical locations of the network printers. This way, when your search uncovers a printer that can handle 11 x 17-inch paper and print double-sided too, you can simply look at its attributes to find out that it's located on the fourth floor on the west side of the building.

- **Shared Folders.** In theory, this option lets you search for shared folders on the domain's computers—but you'll quickly discover that searches for a certain shared folder generally come up empty-handed.

  That's because just sharing a folder on your computer doesn't "publish" it to Active Directory, which would make it available to this kind of search. Only network administrators can publish a shared folder in Active Directory.

- **Organizational Units.** You may not have heard of organizational units, but your network administrator lives and breathes them. (They're the building blocks of an Active Directory hierarchy.) You, the mere mortal, can safely ignore this search option.

Custom Searches

In addition to these predefined searches, you can also create a custom search of your own by looking for information in specific fields (that is, attributes) of Active Directory, as shown in Figure 19-6.

When used creatively, these custom searches can be powerful indeed, in ways you might not expect. For example, suppose your car won't start, and you need a ride home from the office. You can open this dialog box, click the Field button, and choose User→Home Phone. Change the Condition drop-down menu to Starts With; type your own area code and telephone exchange into the Value text box. When you click the Find Now button, you'll get a list of co-workers who live in your neighborhood (as indicated by the first three digits of their phone numbers).

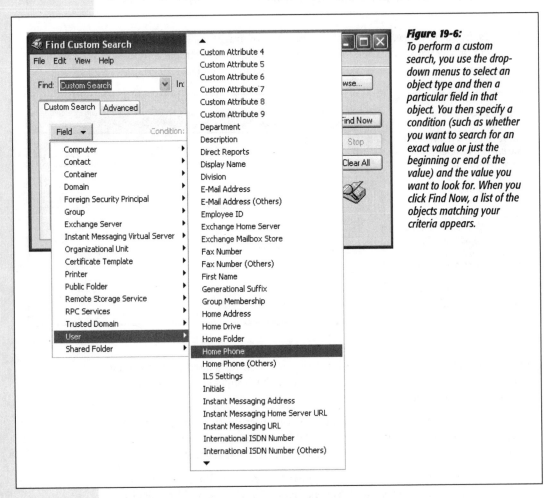

Figure 19-6:
To perform a custom search, you use the drop-down menus to select an object type and then a particular field in that object. You then specify a condition (such as whether you want to search for an exact value or just the beginning or end of the value) and the value you want to look for. When you click Find Now, a list of the objects matching your criteria appears.

Assigning Permissions to Domain Members

Chapter 17 describes the process of assigning permissions to certain files and folders, so that only designated people and groups can open them from across the network. When you're a member of a domain, the process is the same, except that you can select people and groups from the domain as well.

When you open the Properties dialog box for a file or folder, click the Security tab, and then click Add, you don't get the same dialog box that you'd see on a workgroup network. On a domain, it's called the Select Users, Computers, or Groups dialog box (Figure 19-7).

Figure 19-7:
When you click the Object Types button, you can specify whether you want to search for Built-in Security Principals (special-purpose groups like Everyone and Authenticated Users), Computers, Groups, or Users. Also, the standard location for the objects is your current domain. You can still click the Location button and select your computer's name (to specify local user and group accounts), or even choose another domain on the network, if others are available.

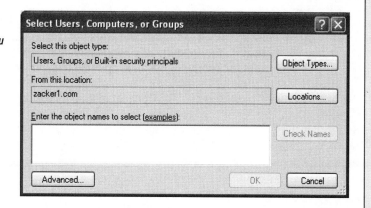

Logging Off and Shutting Down

When you're on a domain PC, you sacrifice one useful feature of Windows XP Pro: the Fast User Switching feature described on page 520. (On the other hand, you're less likely to need it, since you're less likely to share your PC with other employees

Figure 19-8:
Top: Logging off on a Windows XP Professional domain computer is simpler than on a workgroup, because you can't switch users.

Bottom: Selecting Shut Down on a Windows XP Pro computer that's a member of a domain lets you log off the domain or perform one of the usual shutdown options.

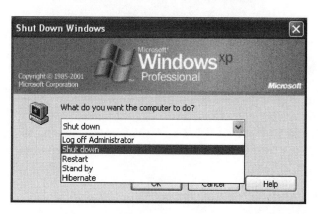

during the course of the workday.) Instead, you must completely log off before other people can access their accounts.

When you choose Start→Log Off, you don't get the Switch User and Log Off buttons you'd see in a workgroup. Instead, you see a simple Log Off Windows dialog box, as shown at top in Figure 19-8.

When you Start→Shut Down, on the other hand, you see the dialog box shown at bottom in Figure 19-8. This dialog box, too, is slightly different from the one you see on a workgroup—but the idea is the same. You specify whether you want to log off, shut the computer down completely, restart it, or put it into hibernation.

Sharing Network Files

Whether you built the network yourself (Chapter 18) or work in an office where somebody has done that work for you (Chapter 19), all kinds of fun can come from having a network. You're now ready to share the following components among the various PCs on the network:

- **Your Internet connection.** Having a network means that all the PCs in your home or office can share a single connection. This is a *huge* feature, one that can save you hundreds of dollars a year if you have a cable modem or DSL. On a small network, it's called Internet Connection Sharing, and it's described in Chapter 18.

- **Printers.** Another excellent justification for creating a network is that you don't need a printer for every PC; all of the PCs can share a much smaller number of printers. If several printers are on your network—say, a high-speed laser printer for one computer, a color printer for another—everyone on the network can use whichever printer is appropriate to a particular document. You'll find step-by-step instructions starting on page 401.

- **Files, folders, and disks.** No matter what PC you're using on the network, you can open the files and folders on any *other* networked PC (and its mounted disks), as long as the other PCs' owners have made these files available for public inspection. That's where *file sharing* comes in, and that's what this chapter is all about. (File sharing also lets you access your files and folders using a laptop on the road.)

The uses for file sharing are almost endless. At its simplest, you can use file sharing to finish writing a letter in the bedroom that you started downstairs at the kitchen table—without having to carry a floppy disk around. But you can also store your library of MP3 music files on one computer and play them from any other computer on the network. You can even run a program like Microsoft Bookshelf from any computer on the network without removing the CD-ROM from the drive.

Note: Your network may include only one Windows XP computer, along with a Windows 95, 98, or Me machine or two. That's perfectly OK; all of these PCs can participate as equals in this party. This chapter points out whatever differences you may find in the procedures.

Accessing Other Computers

Later in this chapter, you can read the steps for making one of your own disks or folders public, so that other people on the network can rifle through it and enjoy its contents.

More often, though, you'll probably be on the receiving end of that transaction—that is, you'll connect to other PCs whose disks and folders have been shared.

Fortunately, doing so is extremely easy.

Method 1: My Network Places

Most people view their network contents using a special window:

- **In Windows XP or Windows Me:** Choose Start→My Network Places.

- **In earlier versions:** Double-click the desktop icon called Network Neighborhood or My Network Places.

The very first time you open the network window, you see icons that correspond to the shared folders and files on the computers of your network (including those on your own machine), as shown in Figure 20-1. Just double-click one to open it.

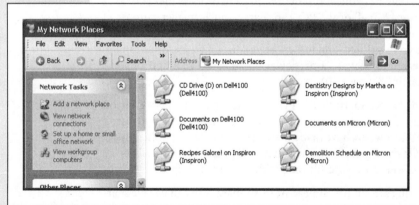

Figure 20-1:
In Windows XP, all of the shared disks and folders show up automatically in the My Network Places window—including shared disks and folders on your own PC, which can be a bit confusing.

"View workgroup computers"

If you find the My Network Places window overwhelmingly crowded as your network grows, you might find clarity in the "View workgroup computers" link at the left side of the window. It shows you the icons of the *computers* on your network—not every last shared folder on all of them. Double-click one of these computer icons to see a list of the shared folders and printers on it (Figure 20-2).

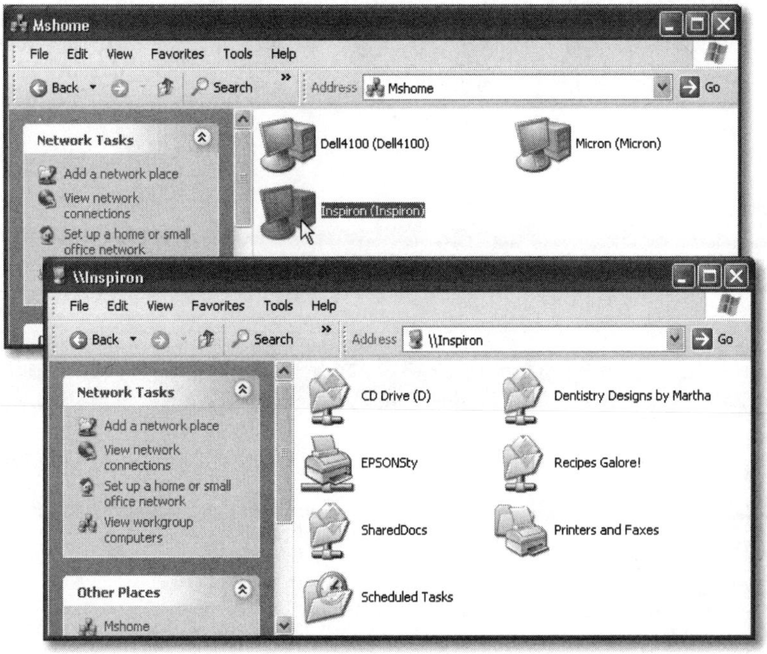

Figure 20-2:
Top: If you know that the folder or file you're looking for resides on a particular PC, it's often more convenient to start your quest at this window.

Bottom: Double-click one of these computers to see a list of its shared resources (folders, disks, and printers), as shown here.

Older PCs: Network Neighborhood

If you're using a networked PC that's still running Windows 95 or Windows 98, you won't find a My Network Places icon on the desktop. Instead, you get its ancestor: Network Neighborhood.

When you open Network Neighborhood, Windows displays an icon in the window for each computer it finds on the workgroup (see Figure 20-3), along with an Entire Network icon. (If you're on a domain network, you may see a list of domains here. Click the one you want.) Just double-click a computer's icon to see the shared disks, folders, and printers attached to it. (Once again, you may have to type in the correct password to gain access.)

Method 2: Windows Explorer

Instead of using the My Network Places or Network Neighborhood icon on the desktop, some people prefer to survey the network landscape using Windows Explorer. (See page 116 for details on opening Windows Explorer.)

The left pane of the window lists an icon for My Network Places or Network Neighborhood. As shown in Figure 20-4, you can click the + button to see a list of the computers and shared resources on them.

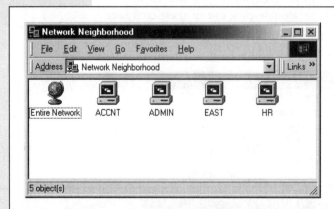

Figure 20-3:
This workgroup has four computers. The Entire Network icon lets you drill down from the workgroup to the computers—but because you see the networked workgroup PCs immediately, there's little reason to do so.

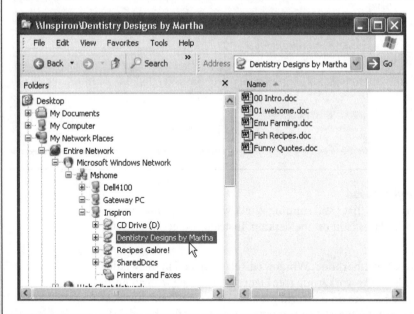

Figure 20-4:
The advantage of using Windows Explorer to look over your network is that you can simultaneously access folders and files on your own computer from this window, making it easier to copy files between the computers. You get a good overview of the network all at once.

Method 3: Universal Naming Convention (UNC)

For hard-core nerds, that business of burrowing into the My Network Places folder is for sissies. When they want to call up a shared folder from the network, or even a particular document *in* a shared folder, they just type a special address into the

Address bar of any folder window, or even Internet Explorer—and then press the Enter key. You can also type such addresses into the Run dialog box, accessible from the Start menu.

It might look like this: *\\laptop\shared documents\salaries 2002.doc.*

Tip: Actually, you don't have to type nearly that much. The AutoComplete feature proposes that full expression as soon as you type just a few letters of it.

This path format (including the double-backslash before the PC name and a single backslash before a folder name) is called the *Universal Naming Convention (UNC)*. It was devised to create a method of notating the exact location of a particular file or folder on a network. It also lets network geeks open various folders and files on networked machines without having to use the My Network Places window.

You can use this system in all kinds of interesting ways:

• Open a particular folder like this: *\\computer name\folder name.*

• You can also substitute the IP address for the computer instead of using its name, like this: *\\192.1681.44\my documents.*

• You can even substitute the name of a shared *printer* for the folder name.

• As described later in this chapter, Windows XP can even access shared folders that sit elsewhere on the Internet (offline backup services, for example). You can call these items onto your screen (once you're online) just by adding *http:* before the UNC code and using regular forward slashes instead of backwards slashes, like this: *http://Computer Name/Folder Name.*

Tip: A great place to type UNC addresses is in the address bar that you can bring to the top of any desktop window.

Working with Network Files

Now that you know how to open shared drives and folders from across the network, you can start using the files you find there. Fortunately, there's nothing much to it. Here are some of the possibilities.

At the Desktop

When you're working at the desktop, you can double-click icons to open them, drag them to the Recycle Bin, make copies of them, and otherwise manipulate them exactly as though they were icons on your own hard drive. Chapter 4 contains much more detail on manipulating files. (Of course, if you weren't given permission to change the contents of the shared folder, you have less freedom.)

Tip: There's one significant difference between working with "local" icons and working with those that sit elsewhere on the network: When you delete a file from another computer on the network (if you're allowed to do so), either by pressing the Delete key or by dragging it to the Recycle Bin, it disappears instantly and permanently, without ever appearing in the Recycle Bin.

Using Start→Search

As noted in Chapter 2, the Windows XP Search program stands ready to help you find files not just on your own machine, but also elsewhere on the network. When the Search window opens up (choose Start→Search), open the "Look in" drop-down list and choose Browse. You're offered a list of disks and folders to search—and one of them is My Network Places. Click it and then click OK. You've just confined your search to the shared disks and folders on your network. In the Search Results list, you'll be able to see, along with each found file, the name of the PC that contains it.

Inside Applications

When you're working in a program, opening files that sit elsewhere on the network requires only a couple of extra steps. Just summon the Open dialog box as usual (choose File→Open) and then, when it appears, click the My Network Places icon in the left-side panel (or choose My Network Places from the "Look in" drop-down menu).

Now just double-click your way to the folder containing the file you want to use. Once you've opened the file, you can work on it just as though it were sitting on your own computer.

At this point, using the File→Save command saves your changes to the original file, wherever it was on the network—unless you weren't given permission to make changes, of course. In that case, you can choose File→Save As and then save a copy of the file onto your own PC.

Shared Folders Online

One of Windows XP's slickest features is its ability to treat hard drives out on the Internet as though they were directly connected to your system. You can create short-cuts that bring servers like these directly onto your screen, where they appear in standard folder windows:

- FTP sites (private, password-protected sets of folders on the Internet).

- Web sites that have been specially prepared to serve as online "folders." Certain data-backup Web sites work this way: they provide you with, say, a 50 MB hard drive in the sky—actually on the Internet—that you can use to store whatever files you like.

- Folders on corporate intranets.

The trick to bringing these servers online is the "Add a network place" link, which you'll find in the task pane at the left side of the My Network Places window.

Tip: There's actually a quicker, simpler way to immortalize a server as a shortcut on your desktop: just drag its icon out of the Address bar of Internet Explorer or an open folder, as shown in Figure 20-5.

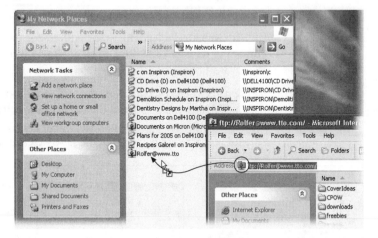

Figure 20-5:
If you've already connected to some network server—whether on your network or on the Internet—here's a very quick way to create a shortcut of it on your desktop for faster access next time. Just drag the tiny folder icon out of the Address bar. (You can put it on your desktop or, if it feels more consistent to do so, into your My Network Places folder.)

Bringing an FTP or Web Server Online

To view the contents of an FTP server or an offline backup service, start by clicking the "Add a network place" link. When the wizard appears (see Figure 20-6), click Next. Wait, if necessary, while your PC goes online. Then, on the second screen, click "Choose another network location." Click Next.

Tip: You can also use this wizard to sign up for one of the above mentioned Web-based "offline disk" services. The second wizard screen lists, for example, the MSN Communities service ("Share your files with others, or store them for your personal use"). In theory, Microsoft may add other, similar services to this screen.

Finally you arrive at the critical screen, where you can type in the address of the Web site, FTP site, or other network location that you want your new shortcut to open.

Into the first text box, you can type any of these network addresses:

- **The UNC code.** As described earlier in this chapter, a UNC code pinpoints a particular shared folder on the network. For example, if you want to open the shared folder named FamilyBiz on the computer named Dad, enter *dad\familybiz*. Capitalization doesn't matter. Or, to open a specific file, you could enter something like *dad\finances\budget.xls*.

Tip: Remember that you're specifying the *share name,* which isn't necessarily the same as the actual folder name. If you get an error message when you try to add a folder or file to your My Network Places window, this distinction may be at the heart of the problem.

- **http://website/folder.** To see what's in a folder called Customers on a company Web site called BigBiz.com, enter *http://bigbiz.com/customers.* (You can't just type in any old Web address. It has to be a Web site that's been specifically designed to serve as a "folder" containing files.)

- **ftp://ftp.website/folder.** This is the address format for FTP sites. For example, if you want to use a file in a folder named Bids on a company site named WeBuyStuff.com, enter *ftp://ftp.webuystuff.com/bids.*

What happens when you click Next depends on the kind of address you specified. If it was an FTP site, you're offered the chance to specify your user name. (Access to every FTP site requires a user name and password. You won't be asked for the password until you actually try to open the newly created folder shortcut.)

Figure 20-6:
Left: The Add Network Place Wizard (top) walks you through setting up a desktop icon for your Web, FTP, or intranet site, including (middle) entering the location of the folder or file for which you want to create a shortcut in your My Network Places window—in this case, an FTP server (bottom).

Right: When you double-click the newly created FTP icon (top), you'll be asked for your password (middle). Thereafter, depending on the speed of your connection, the files in the FTP folder might show up on your screen as though they were sitting on a very, very slow floppy disk (bottom).

Click Finish to complete the creation of your network shortcut, which now appears in the My Network Places window. To save you a step, the wizard also offers to connect to and open the corresponding folder.

The beauty of all this is that these remote folders appear in everyday, ordinary folder windows (or in Internet Explorer), as shown at bottom right in Figure 20-6. You can work with them exactly as though they were sitting on your own hard drive. The only difference is that because you're actually communicating with a hard drive via the Internet, the slower speed may make it feel as if your PC has been drugged.

Mapping Shares to Drive Letters

If you access network shares on a regular basis, you may want to consider another access technique called *mapping shares*. Using this trick, you can assign a *letter* to a particular shared disk or folder on the network. Just as your hard drive is called C: and your floppy drive is A:, you can give your Family Stuff folder the letter F: and the Jaz drive in the kitchen the letter J:.

Doing so confers several benefits. First, these disks and folders now appear directly in the My Computer window. Getting to them can be faster this way than navigating to the My Network Places window. Second, when you choose File→Open from within one of your applications, you'll be able to jump directly to a particular shared folder instead of having to double-click, ever deeper, through the icons in the Open File dialog box. You can also use the mapped drive letter in pathnames anywhere you would use a path on a local drive, such as the Run dialog box, a File→Save As dialog box, or the command line.

To map a drive letter to a disk or folder, open any folder or disk window. Then:

1. **Choose Tools→Map Network Drive.**

   The Map Network Drive dialog box appears, as shown in Figure 20-7.

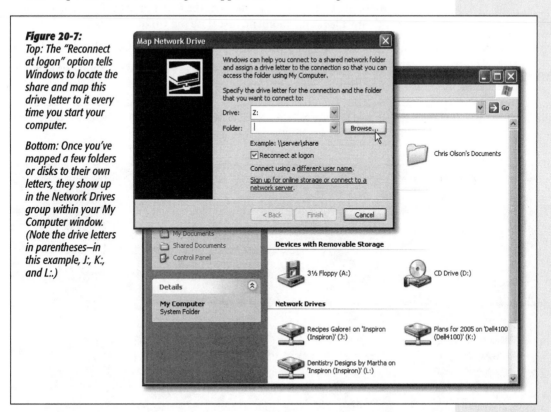

Figure 20-7:
Top: The "Reconnect at logon" option tells Windows to locate the share and map this drive letter to it every time you start your computer.

Bottom: Once you've mapped a few folders or disks to their own letters, they show up in the Network Drives group within your My Computer window. (Note the drive letters in parentheses—in this example, J:, K:, and L:.)

2. **Using the drop-down list, choose a drive letter.**

   You can select any unused letter you like (except B, which is still reserved for the second floppy disk drive that PCs don't have anymore).

3. **Indicate which folder or disk you want this letter to represent.**

   You can type its UNC code into the Folder box, choose from the drop-down list of recently accessed folders, or click Browse.

Tip: Most people use the mapping function for disks and drives elsewhere on the network, but there's nothing to stop you from mapping a folder that's sitting right there on your own PC.

---

4. **To make this letter assignment stick, turn on "Reconnect at logon."**

   If you don't use this option, Windows will forget this assignment the next time you turn on the computer. (Use the "Connect using a different user name" option if your account name on the shared folder's machine isn't the same as it is on this one.)

5. **Click Finish.**

   A window opens to display the contents of the folder or disk. If you don't want to work with any files at the moment, just close the window.

From now on (depending on your setting in step 4), that shared disk or folder will show up in your My Computer list alongside the disks that are actually in your PC, as shown at bottom in Figure 20-7.

Tip: If you see a red X on one of these mapped icons, it means that the PC on which one of the shared folders or disks resides is either off the network or turned off completely.

WORKAROUND WORKSHOP

Automatic Reconnections Can Be Tricky

If you select "Reconnect at logon" when mapping a shared disk or folder to a letter, the order in which you start your computers becomes important. The PC containing the shared disk or folder should start up before the computer that refers to it as, say, drive K:. That way, when the second computer searches for "drive K:" on the network, its quest will be successful.

On the other hand, this guideline presents a seemingly insurmountable problem if you have two computers on the network, and each of them maps drive letters to folders or disks on the other.

In that situation, you get an error message to the effect that the permanent connection is not available. It asks if you want to reconnect the next time you start the computer. Click Yes.

Then, after all the computers have started up, open My Computer or Windows Explorer. You can see the mapped drive, but there's a red X under the icon. Ignore the X. Just double-click the icon. The shared folder or disk opens normally (because the other machine is now available), and the red X goes away.

Two Roads to File Sharing

But enough about accessing the shared folders on *other* computers. Half the fun is sharing your *own* folders, making them available to other people on the network. This can be a much more complex proposition, which is why the rest of this chapter covers only this part of the equation.

First, however, a word of warning: As with so many other features, Windows XP Pro has two different personalities, depending on where you're using it (see Figure 20-8). In this case, Microsoft has created two different file-sharing systems:

- **Simple file sharing.** If you're working on a home network, and you have nothing to hide from the other people in the house, you may appreciate Windows XP's new *Simple file sharing* feature. It lets you share certain folders with a minimum of red tape and complexity. If you need a peek at the spreadsheet that Harold was working on yesterday, no big deal—you just open up his My Documents folder from across the network.

  If it's just you and your spouse, or you and a co-worker, this scenario is almost ideal: maximum convenience and minimum barriers. On the other hand, when you share a folder this way, anybody on the network can not only read your files, but also change or delete them. In other words, Simple file sharing isn't especially secure. Kids horsing around on the computer, young geniuses experimenting with your data, or a disgruntled co-worker could, in theory, send important data to Never-Never Land.

Note: Simple file sharing is the *only* form of file sharing in Windows XP Home Edition.

- **Standard file sharing.** If you want to specify exactly who has access to your files, and how much access they have, then you may prefer Windows XP Pro's *Standard* file sharing option, which it inherited from Windows 2000. This method is more complicated than Simple file sharing, but it gives you much more flexibility and protection.

WORD TO THE WISE

Job Number One?

In workgroup (or nonnetworked) PCs, the factory setting is the Simple file sharing system. Among Windows critics, that's yet another example that Microsoft doesn't take security seriously.

Some experts, therefore, strongly recommend that the first thing you should do on a new Windows XP machine is to turn off Simple file sharing.

That advice may be a bit on the extreme side. In an office

environment, sure, you may want to consider turning off Simple file sharing. In its place, either learn how to use the Standard file sharing method or store your shared files on a server, where a network administrator controls the shared files and their security.

If you use your PC at home, or in a small office with a few trusted employees, Simple file sharing is a viable option that can save you a lot of bother.

Of course, you may not have a choice of these two methods at all. If your PC is part of a corporate domain, Standard is the only method available. (You can actually turn on the Simple file sharing checkbox, but doing so has no effect.)

In any case, the following pages tackle the two file sharing systems one at a time.

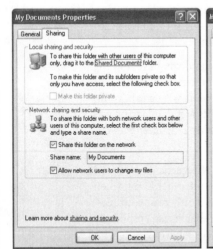 

Figure 20-8:
Left: When Simple file sharing is on, you share designated folders and files with everyone in your workgroup whether you like it or not.

Right: In Standard file sharing, this Sharing tab appears. You can click the Permissions button to specify who is allowed to access it on a person-by-person (or group) basis.

Turning Simple File Sharing On and Off

On any Windows XP Pro machine that isn't part of a corporate domain network, Simple file sharing is turned on automatically.

File Sharing Without a Network

Most people think of file sharing in the context of an office network. But in fact, you can use file sharing to your advantage even if your PC isn't connected to anything but the desk. You can also use file sharing to make certain folders available to other account holders on the *same* PC (see Chapter 17).

As described in Chapter 17, the mere act of assigning a password to your user account triggers Windows XP—with your approval—to make all of your files and folders private, so that no other account holders can access them.

If you try to open anybody else's files or folders, you see a dialog box so nice, it tells you twice: "[This folder] is not accessible. Access is denied."

That's all well and good if you'd just as soon your fellow PC users keep their noses out of your stuff. But it doesn't bode well for the kinds of exciting collaboration that computers are supposed to make possible. If your worlds are completely separate, how can you collaborate on a document? What are you supposed to do, email the thing to another account on the exact same computer?

Fortunately, you don't have to do that. You can share your files with the other users on the computer using any of the techniques described in this chapter.

To turn it off or on again, choose Tools→Folder Options from the menu bar of any desktop window (or open the Folder Options icon in the Control Panel). Click the View tab, scroll all the way down to the bottom of the Advanced Settings list, and click "Use Simple File Sharing (Recommended)" to turn Simple file sharing on or off.

Strangely enough, this checkbox still appears when your PC is connected to a domain; you can even click it on or off. But it's a trick—don't fall for it. No matter what this checkbox says, you'll be using all Standard file sharing, all the time.

Simple File Sharing

This section is for you, workgroup (or nonnetworked) PC fans.

Sharing Your Own Folders

It's easy enough to "publish" any of your folders or disks for inspection by other people on your network. (Actually, sharing a folder, as you're about to do, also makes it available to other people who log into this PC under their own accounts, sitting at it in person.)

The trick is to use the Properties dialog box, like this:

1. **Locate the icon of the folder or disk that you want to share.**

   Your disk icons, of course, appear when you choose Start→My Computer. You can share any kind of disk; hard drive, floppy, CD-ROM, removable drive, and so on.

   Sharing an entire disk means that every folder on it, and therefore every file, is available to everyone on the network. If security isn't a big deal at your place (because it's just you and a couple of family members, for example), this feature can be a timesaving convenience that spares you the trouble of sharing every new folder you create.

   On the other hand, people with privacy concerns generally prefer to share individual *folders*. By sharing only a folder or two, you can keep *most* of the stuff on your hard drive private, out of view of curious network comrades. For that matter, sharing only a folder or two does *them* a favor, too, by making it easier for them to find files you've made available. This way, they don't have to root through your entire drive looking for the appropriate folder.

Note: If you're logged in using a normal account, of course, you may share only the disks and folders to which you've been given access. If you've logged in using the local Administrator account, on the other hand, you can share *any* disk or folder, but you should still avoid sharing critical system folders like the Windows folder and the Program Files folder. There's no reason other people on the network would need to get to these folders anyway—and if they did, they could do serious damage to your PC.

---

2. **Right-click the disk or folder icon. From the shortcut menu, choose Sharing and Security.**

   The Sharing tab of the Properties dialog box opens (Figure 20-9). (The shortcut menu includes the Sharing command only if you've set up the computer for networking, as described in Chapter 18. And if you don't see a Sharing and Security command, just choose Properties from the shortcut menu—and then, in the resulting dialog box, click the Sharing tab.)

   If you're trying to share an entire disk, you now see a warning to the effect that, "sharing the root of a drive is not recommended." Click the link beneath it that says, "If you understand the risk but still want to share the root of the drive, click here" and then proceed with the next step.

3. **Turn on "Share this folder on the network" (see Figure 20-9).**

   The other options in the dialog box spring to life.

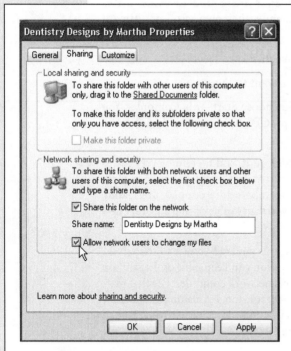

Figure 20-9:
The Sharing tab for a disk or folder on a Windows XP workgroup computer. (The dialog box refers to a "folder" even if it's actually a disk.) You can turn on "Share this folder on the network" only if "Make this folder private" is turned off. (If a folder is private, you certainly don't want other network citizens rooting around in it.)

4. **Type a name for the shared disk or folder.**

   This is the name other people will see when they open their My Network Places windows.

   Make this name as helpful as possible. For example, you may want to name the kitchen computer's hard drive *Kitchen Documents Drive.*

Tip: If any of the other PCs on your network aren't running Windows XP, the shared folder's name can't be longer than twelve characters, and most punctuation is forbidden. You can type it here, all right, but–as a warning message will tell you–the other machines won't be able to see the shared disk or folder over the network.

5. Turn off "Allow network users to change my files," if you like.

If the "Allow network users to change my files" checkbox is turned *off,* you create a "look, don't touch" policy. Other people on the network can open and read what's inside this disk or folder, but won't be able to save changes, rename anything, delete anything, or deposit any new files. (In technical lingo, you've established a "read-only" shared folder.)

Otherwise, your co-workers can theoretically run wild, trashing your files, renaming things at random, and painting a mustache onto your face in the JPEG family photo.

Remember, however, that making the shared folder read-only means that *you* won't be able to modify its files from another computer on the network, either. You've just run up against one of the fundamental shortcomings of Simple file sharing: You must give full access to your files to either *everybody on the network*—or nobody.

Note: Turning off the "Allow network users to change my files" checkbox isn't much of a security safeguard. True, other people on the network won't be able to change what's *in* your folder–but there's nothing to stop them from copying stuff *out* of it. Once they've saved copies of your files on their own hard drives, they can do with them whatever they like. They just can't copy the changed files back *into* your shared folder or disk. In other words, if you don't want other people to see or distribute what's in your folders (using Simple file sharing), don't share them.

6. Click OK.

As shown in Figure 20-10, the icon changes for the disk or folder you just shared. It's also gained a new nickname: you may hear shared folders geekily referred to as *shares.*

Figure 20-10:
When you share a folder or a disk, a tiny hand cradles its icon from beneath–a dead giveaway that you've made it available to other people on the network.

Shared Documents   Local Disk (C:)   CD Drive (D:)

Notes on Simple File Sharing

The preceding steps show you how to make a certain folder or disk available to other people on the network. The following footnotes, however, are worth skimming, especially for Windows 2000 veterans:

- You can't share individual files—only entire folders or disks.

- The "Share this folder on the network" checkbox is dimmed for *all* folders if your PC is not, in fact, on the network—or, more specifically, if you haven't experienced the thrill of the Network Setup Wizard described in Chapter 18.

- Unless you specify otherwise, sharing a folder also shares all of the folders inside it, including new ones you create later. Your "Allow network users to change my files" setting gives permission to change or delete files in all of those folders, too.

  If you right-click one of these inner folders and inspect the Sharing tab of its Properties dialog box, you'll find the Sharing checkbox turned off, which can be a bit confusing. But you'd better believe it: those inner folders are actually shared, no matter what the checkbox says.

- On the other hand, it's OK to right-click one of these inner folders and *change* its sharing settings. For example, if you've shared a folder called America, you can make the Minnesota folder inside it off-limits by making it private. Similarly, if you've turned *off* "Allow network users to change my files" for the America folder, you can turn it back *on* for the Minnesota folder inside it.

- Be careful with nested folders. Suppose, for example, that you share your My Documents folder, and you permit other people to change the files inside it. Now suppose that you share a folder that's *inside* My Documents—called Spreadsheets, for example—but you turn *off* the ability for other people to change its files.

  You wind up with a strange situation: Both folders, My Documents and Spreadsheets, show up in other people's Network Places windows, as described earlier in this chapter. If they double-click the Spreadsheets folder, they won't be able to change anything inside it. But if they double-click the My Documents folder and open the Spreadsheets folder inside *it*, they *can* modify the files.

- You're not allowed to share important system folders like Windows, Program Files, and Documents and Settings. If you've set up your PC with multiple user accounts (Chapter 17), you can't share folders that belong to other people, ei-

---

POWER USERS' CLINIC

Un-Hiding Hidden Folders

As sneaky and delightful as the hidden-folder trick is, it has a distinct drawback: *You* can't see your hidden folder from across the network, either. Suppose you want to use another computer on the network—the one in the upstairs office, for example—to open something in your hidden My Novel folder (which is downstairs in the kitchen). Fortunately, you can do so—if you know the secret.

On the office computer, choose Start→Run. In the Run dialog box, type the path of the hidden folder, using the format *Computer Name**Folder Name*.

For example, enter *kitchen**my novel$* to get to the hidden folder called My Novel$ on the PC called Kitchen. (Capitalization doesn't matter, and don't forget the $ sign.) Then click OK to open a window showing the contents of your hidden folder. (See page 566 for more on the Universal Naming Convention system.)

---

ther—only your own stuff. The exception: You can share them when you've logged in using an Administrator account (page 501).

Hiding Folders

If a certain folder on your hard drive is really private, you can hide the folder so that other people on the network can't even *see* it. The secret is to type a $ symbol at the end of the share name (see step 4 on page 576).

For example, if you name a certain folder My Novel, anyone else on the network will be able to see it. But if you name the share My Novel$, it won't show up in anybody's My Network Places window. They won't even know that it exists. (It still shows up on *your* machine, of course. And it will also be visible to other network computers if you shared the *disk* on which the folder sits.)

Standard File Sharing

If you need more security and flexibility than Simple file sharing affords—or if your computer is part of a corporate domain—then the time has come to tackle Standard file sharing.

The process of sharing a folder is much the same as it is in Simple file sharing, except that there's an additional step: specifying who else on the network can access the share, and what they're allowed to do with it.

Note: Before you can create Standard file shares, you must disable Windows XP's Simple file sharing feature, as described on page 575.

Step 1: Turn on Sharing

After you've located the icon of the drive, folder, or printer you want to share, proceed like this:

1. **Right-click the disk or folder icon. From the shortcut menu, choose Sharing and Security.**

   The Sharing tab of the Properties dialog box opens (see Figure 20-11). If you've ever seen this dialog box when using Simple file sharing, you'll notice that it looks quite a bit different now.

2. **Turn on "Share this folder."**

   The other options in the dialog box become active.

3. **Type a name for the shared disk or folder.**

   This is the name other people will see when they open their My Network Places windows. Windows XP proposes the name of the folder as the share name, which is fine, but you can change it to anything you like.

If you want to limit the number of network users that can access the shared file or folder simultaneously—to avoid slowing down your PC, for example—click "Allow this number of users" radio button, and specify the maximum number of people who can access the share at one time (3 or 5, for example).

If you were to click OK at this point, you would make this item available to everyone on the network. But before leaving the dialog box, take a moment to survey the security options. This, after all, is one of the big advantages of Standard file sharing.

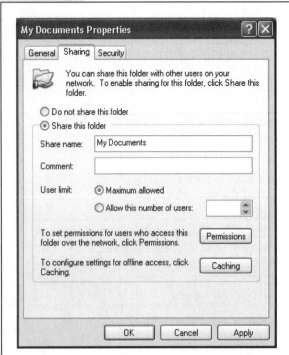

Figure 20-11:
The Sharing tab for a disk or folder on a Windows XP domain system. From here, you can share this folder, specify the maximum number of people who can access it at once, and specify who can access the share and to what degree.

Step 2: Limit Network Access

When you make a folder or drive available to the network, you don't necessarily want to give your co-workers permission to run wild, running roughshod over the files inside it. In many cases, you may prefer to share a folder or drive *selectively*. If you're in Accounting, for example, you might want to make the company salary spreadsheet accessible by the other accountants in your workgroup, but off-limits to everyone else in the company.

Fortunately, you can limit people's access on an individual (or group-by-group) basis, thanks to the Permissions button shown in Figure 20-11.

When you click it, you get the dialog box shown at left in Figure 20-12. Setting up permissions involves two steps: identifying the person (or group) to whom you're granting permission, and then specifying how much access you want to grant them.

NTFS permissions vs. share permissions

If you read the discussion of NTFS permissions in Chapter 17, you should at this point be getting a distinct feeling of déja vu. Both the Permissions dialog box and the entire concept of protecting your folders should be familiar.

To put it bluntly, Windows XP Pro offers two separate and overlapping systems for protecting folders. First, there are the *NTFS permissions* described in Chapter 17; second, there are the *share permissions* described below. Each system lets you choose which network citizens (or groups of them) may view, make changes to, or have full control over certain folders.

Understanding the ramifications of two separate and overlapping permissions systems involves some serious technical slogging. Here are the most important differences:

- NTFS permissions guard a folder no matter how someone tries to get at it: from across the network or seated in person at the PC. Share permissions, on the other hand, govern access only from over the network.

  So suppose you've got a folder full of confidential files. Hoping to protect them from inspection by your co-workers, you might turn off *all* forms of access (Figure 20-12)—but all you've done is keep people *elsewhere on the network* out of it. People who sit down at your machine can still rifle through your private file stash.

- Nobody can access shared files from across the network unless they have *both* share permissions *and* NTFS permissions to those files. Even if somebody has given you Full Access using one permissions system, if the other is set to No Access, you're out of luck.

- NTFS permissions are more flexible than share permissions. For example, there are five or six degrees of NTFS standard permissions, compared with only three levels of share permissions. NTFS permissions can also protect individual *files,* whereas share permissions affect only entire *folders.*

If you think maintaining a duplicate set of overlapping permissions is complex and confusing, imagine being a network administrator whose job it is to keep them all straight—not only for each folder on each computer, but for each person on the network. It's just an overwhelming number of permutations.

As a result, most network administrators simply grant everyone Full Access to network shares, effectively eliminating share permissions as the complicating factor. The administrators then use NTFS permissions to control access to specific files and folders, confident that these settings will correctly protect shared folders and disks *both* from across the network and in person.

Specify whose freedom you're about to limit

If you've read the preceding paragraphs of warning, but you've decided to protect certain folders with share permissions anyway, read on. This discussion assumes that you're poised with the Sharing tab (Figure 20-11) open before you.

1. Click the Permissions button.

A Permissions dialog box appears (Figure 20-12), a close cousin to the Security tab you use to set NTFS permissions (page 528). The top half lists the people or groups that have been allowed or denied permission to the share; the bottom half tells you how much access the selected person or group has been given.

When you first share a folder or disk, you'll see only Everyone in this list. If you're on a workgroup network, you'll see that Everyone starts out with Full Control permission, on the assumption that security isn't such a big deal in your household or small business. If you're using a *domain* computer, on the other hand, Everyone starts out with only Read permission, which affords more security. More about these permissions settings in a moment.

Tip: When a permission checkbox is selected but also shaded gray, it means that its permissions settings have been inherited from the folder that it's in.

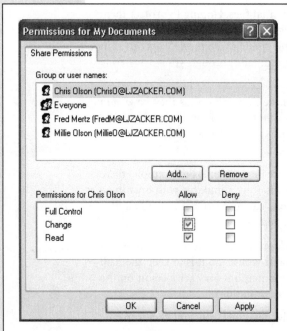

Figure 20-12:
Top: The Permissions dialog box lets you control how much access each person has to the folder you're sharing. Using the top list, specify which people (or groups of people) can access your shared folder over the network.

Bottom: When you click Add in the box above, this box appears. Click Find Now to locate a person's name; click the name and then click OK.

Now you can start assigning permissions on a person-by-person (or group-by-group) basis. (If the person's name doesn't appear here, click Add. The dialog box shown back in Figure 17-20 appears, providing you the delightful opportunity of adding a name to the list by typing it, letter-perfect, into the "Enter the object names to select" box and then clicking OK. The users and groups you selected appear in the "Group or user names" list.)

Note: See page 515 for details on groups—and remember that an individual account's permissions take precedence over group permissions.

2. **Click the name of a person or group in the list. Set the appropriate permissions by turning on the relevant checkboxes.**

   You have three options. If you turn on **Read,** this person (or group of people) will encounter a "look, don't touch" policy when they try to open this folder from across the network. They'll be allowed to open and read what's inside (and run any programs they find there), but won't be able to save changes, rename anything, delete anything, or deposit any new files.

Note: Other people on the network can *copy* folders and files from a Read folder or disk onto their own computers. From there, they can do whatever they like. But they can't copy the changed files back to your shared folder or disk.

   If you choose **Change** instead, the people you've identified can not only open the shared files, but also edit and even delete them. They can also put new files and folders into the shared folder or disk.

POWER USERS' CLINIC

Administrative Shares

When you try to share a disk when your PC is a member of a domain, you may be surprised to see that the "Share this Folder" option is already selected, and it already has a share name (the drive letter followed by a $ symbol). As it turns out, Windows XP Professional automatically shares the outer level (the *root* level) of all hard drives on a domain computer.

To be specific, it creates what's known as an *administrative* share: a shared disk that's invisible to ordinary peons on the network, but available to administrators who know its secret, hidden name. (See page 579 for more on hidden shares, which also have the $ symbol at the end of their names.)

You're not allowed to change the permission settings for the administrative shares. You can stop sharing them, but Windows XP will re-share them automatically the next time you start up the computer.

But what if you want to share a drive yourself, so that other people on the network can access it?

Open its Properties dialog box, click the New Share button, and—in the New Share dialog box—specify a share name, a maximum number of users (if you like), and then click the Permissions button to set access permissions for the new share. (The administrative share permissions remain unaffected.) When you click OK, the new share name appears on the Sharing tab in the Share Name text box instead of the administrative share's name.

Notice, however, that the Share Name text box has now become a drop-down list. You can use it to choose either of the shares at the root of the drive, so that you can change the properties of each independently. You can also click the Remove Share button to delete the currently displayed share name, or click New Share to create as many shares at the root of the disk as you want. (Why you would want to so is another question.)

Finally, if you choose **Full Control,** the selected person or group can run wild, fooling around not only with the contents of the disk or folder, but also with its permissions. They can change whatever permissions settings you make here, and even claim *ownership* of the folder or disk—they could even lock you out of your own stuff.

Note: When you first turn on sharing for a folder, it inherits the permission settings from the disk or folder it's in (that is, its *parent* folder). But if you *change* the settings for one of these inner folders, your new settings override any permissions that are inherited from parent folders.

---

3. **Click OK to close the Properties dialog box.**

   You'll see that the icon for the resource you just shared has changed. A hand now cradles the icon to help you remember what you've made available to your network colleagues.

Clever Share Tricks

Sharing files and folders using Standard file sharing may be a lot more trouble than Simple file sharing, but it has its rewards. Only in Standard file sharing, for example, can you interesting scenarios like these:

- You can access your files from different computers on the network, but still protect them from interference by other people. To do that, share the file or folder, give yourself the Full Control permission, and deny all permissions to the Everyone group.

  Yes, you are also part of the Everyone group—but an individual's permissions always override any group permissions that may affect that person. As a result, you end up with Full Control over your files, and no one else can even read them. On a home network, you can start working on a document in the bedroom upstairs—and then, when you go downstairs to cook dinner, you can continue working on the kitchen computer while the pasta is boiling. Meanwhile, the kids can be using their own computer, but won't be able to see what's in your file or folder.

- You can also create a drop box: a folder into which people can deposit documents for your inspection, but which is otherwise off-limits to them.

  For example, you might create a drop box so that your fellow employees can leave insurance claim forms they've filled out with a word processor. After sharing the folder, you could grant yourself (and other people in your department) Full Control—but you would give everyone else in the company only the Change permission. Now people in other departments can copy their claim forms into the drop-box folder, because they have permission to create new files in it. But because they lack the Read permission, they can't open the folder to see what's inside.

Offline Files

The Windows XP Professional feature called *offline files* is designed primarily for laptop lovers. It lets you carry away files that generally live on your office network, so that you can get some work done while you're away.

Then, when you return and connect your laptop to the office network, Windows automatically copies your edited, updated documents back to their original locations on the network, intelligently keeping straight which copies are the most recent. (And vice versa: If people changed the network copies while you were away, Windows copies them onto your laptop.) It's a great feature, and, by the way, one that isn't available in Windows XP Home Edition.

Note: Although Microsoft developed Offline Files primarily for laptops that sometimes leave the network, it can also be a useful feature for desktop computers that belong to a network that isn't always up and running. Even so, this chapter refers to your computer as *the laptop,* to avoid having to repeat "the laptop or desktop computer that isn't always on the network" 50 million times.

Phase 1: Turn on Offline Files

To turn on this feature, open any window at the desktop, such as My Documents. Choose Tools→Folder Options, click the Offline Files tab, and then make sure that Enable Offline Files is turned on (see Figure 20-13).

Figure 20-13:
You must turn on Enable Offline Files to activate this feature. This is also your opportunity to specify when the synchronizing takes place, so that the process is automated and the files are kept up-to-date on both your hard drive and the network.

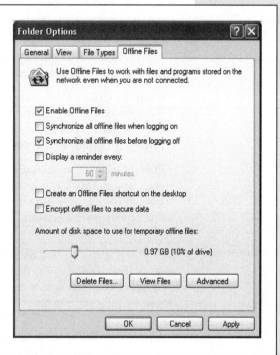

Note: If you can't seem to turn this feature on, it's probably because Fast User Switching is turned on. Unfortunately, you're not allowed to use both features at the same time. Turn Fast User Switching off as described on page 520.

Here are some of the options you should inspect before closing this dialog box:

- **Synchronize all offline files when logging on.** This setting is meant for laptop luggers who are often away from the network (or for people with shaky connections to the network even at the best of times). It means that has soon as you're back on the network, whatever files you edited while you were away get transferred back to the appropriate places on the network.

Note: If you don't select this setting, you'll get a Quick synchronization (page 592) each time you log onto the network. As you'll find out in a moment, that means that your documents may not be the most current versions.

- **Synchronize all offline files before logging off.** You'll almost certainly want this option turned on. It ensures that whenever you leave the office with your laptop, it will contain copies of the most recent version of your files.

Note: This setting isn't available when you connect to the network by dialing in as described in Chapter 21.

- **Display a reminder every _____ minutes.** A reminder balloon will appear on your taskbar at regular intervals to let you know that you're off the network. If you suffer from intermittent network dropouts, it can be nice to know when you just been cut off; otherwise, these reminders can be annoying.

- **Create an Offline Files shortcut on the desktop.** When you select this box, Windows places a handy Shortcut to Offline Files icon on your desktop. When you double-click it, you open a window that lists all of the files and folders that you've marked for offline use, as described later in this chapter.

- **Encrypt offline files to secure data.** This option encodes the copies of the files on your laptop, which can be useful if you carry confidential files with you away from the office. (It doesn't do anything to the corresponding copies of these files that remain on the network.)

Note: Some programs, including Microsoft Word, create temporary copies of open documents (for example, in a folder called Temp). A dedicated spy who stole your laptop could, in theory, view some of your confidential information by opening these folders. That's a good argument for learning which folders these are and encrypting them too.

- **Amount of disk space to use for temporary offline files.** You can set an upper limit for the amount of hard drive space Windows XP uses for files you've copied from the network. (If XP Pro reaches whatever limit you've set, it begins to delete older offline files to make room for the new ones.)

- **Delete Files button.** Use this button when you're desperate to reclaim some disk space on your laptop; it deletes your laptop copies of the offline files. (This option doesn't affect the master copies of these documents that reside on the network.)

- **View Files button.** This button opens a list of all of the files you've marked for offline use.

- **Advanced button.** The Advanced dialog box lets you tell Windows how to handle specific computers when they become unavailable: to stop working with the offline files, or to notify you and start working with offline files (see Figure 20-14).

Figure 20-14:
"Never allow my computer to go offline" doesn't actually prevent your computer from disconnecting from the network; it means that you'd rather stop working with offline files when the network connection is lost.

Phase 2: Choose the Files You Want

To tell Windows XP Pro which files and folders you want to take away with you on the laptop, navigate to them on the network. Right-click each of them, choosing Make Available Offline from the shortcut menu. (Alternatively, highlight some file or folder icons and then choose File→Make Available Offline.)

Note: When you select a folder that contains other folders, Windows asks how you want to handle its subfolders. You have two choices: "Yes, make the folder and all its subfolders available offline," or "No, make only this folder available offline."

Now your machine takes a quick moment to copy the files onto your own hard drive (that is, on the client machine—your laptop).

Phase 3: Log Off

As long as your laptop's still connected to the network, double-clicking a file or folder icon opens the original network copy. But when you log off the network, Windows checks to make sure that your computer has the most recent copies of the files. (All of this works only if you choose Log Off or Turn Off Computer from the Start menu. If you just yank out the network cable, you catch Windows by surprise, and you don't get the benefit of its intelligent Offline Files copying.)

If you don't, in fact, have the latest copy of all the files you've selected, Windows performs the necessary copying (assuming you've turned on "Synchronize all offline files before logging off" as described earlier).

When your computer disconnects from the network, two new icons and a "network is unplugged" reminder appear in your notification area (see Figure 20-15).

POWER USERS' CLINIC

Making Files and Folders Available for Other People

On a corporate network, the network administrator generally decides which files and folders are available for offline use. But if *you* are the network administrator—for example, if you work on a workgroup network—*you* will have to specify which folders are available for offline use.

To do so, navigate to the file or folder you want to share, right-click its icon, and choose Properties from the shortcut menu. Click the Sharing tab, turn on Sharing, and then click Caching. The Caching Settings dialog box appears, as shown here. Turn on "Allow caching of files in this shared folder," and then select the desired caching setting from the Setting drop-down list. You have three choices:

Manual caching of documents makes your files available for offline use, but they won't be automatically synchronized when other computers connect or disconnect.

Your co-workers are responsible for triggering the synchronization themselves.

Automatic caching of documents means that whenever one of your co-workers opens one of one of the files that you've made available for offline use, it will automatically be copied to their machines, ready for offline editing.

Automatic caching of programs and documents. Select this option only for shared folders that contain files and applications that people aren't allowed to change (software programs, for example).

The first time you mark a network folder or file for offline use, the Offline Files Wizard guides you through the process. When you click Finish, a Synchronizing dialog box displays a progress bar until synchronization is complete. The item(s) you've selected are now available for your offline use.

Phase 4: Working Offline

Once you're untethered from the network, you can find the synchronized files in any of several ways:

- Open the Offline Files icon on your desktop (if you chose to put one there). The Offline Files window appears (Figure 20-16).

Figure 20-15:
Top: Each offline file and folder icon is marked with this double arrow badge for easy recognition. Middle: When your computer disconnects from the network (or when it disconnects from you you), the Offline Files and Local Area Connection icons (the first two pictured here) appear, along with a balloon, to make sure you know about it.

Bottom: When your computer reconnects, the Local Area Connect icon disappears, and the little "i" logo appears on the Offline Files icon. You can manually synchronize your offline files by double-clicking the Offline Files icon, selecting the files you want (in the resulting window), and then clicking OK.

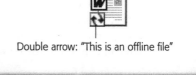

Double arrow: "This is an offline file"

Red X: "You're off the network, pal"

Little i: "You're back online and ready to sync"

- In any desktop window, choose Tools→Folder Options. Click the Offline Files tab; click View Files.

- Browse your network just as you normally would, using My Network Places as described earlier this chapter. You will, however, notice something strange: the

Figure 20-16:
When you're using the Details view, special information columns show you some useful details about each file: the type of file, whether or not it's been synchronized, where it is, and whether or not the server (or whatever computer stores the "real" copies of the files) is online.

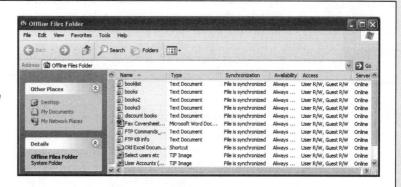

shared drives and folders on the network appear to be completely empty *except* for the files and folders that you marked for offline use.

It's easy enough to tell when you're working on a document that's been swiped from the network: a tiny, telltale double arrow appears on its icon (Figure 20-15, top), at least when your viewing the window in an icon view. (Alternatively, highlight its icon, open the File menu, and look for a checkmark next to the Make Available Offline option.)

Now you're free to work with these offline files and folders exactly as you would if you were still connected to the network. You can revise, edit, and duplicate files, and even create new documents inside offline folders. The permissions remain the same as when you connect to the network.

Phase 5: Reconnecting to the Network

Now suppose you return from your jaunt away from the office. You plop your laptop down on your desk and reconnect the network cable.

Once Windows discovers that it's home again, it whirls into action, automatically comparing your set of offline files and folders with the master set on the network, attempting to handle discrepancies between the two as best it can. For example:

• If your copy and a network copy of a file don't match, Windows wipes out the older version with the newer version, so that both locations have exactly the same edition.

• If you deleted your copy of a file, or somebody on the network deleted the original, Windows deletes the corresponding file so that it no longer exists on either machine. (That's assuming that nobody edited the file in the meantime.)

• If somebody added a file to the network copy of a folder, you get a copy of it in your laptop's copy of the folder.

• If you've edited an offline file that somebody on the network has deleted in the meantime, Windows offers you the choice to save your version on the network or delete it from your computer.

• If you delete a file from your hard drive that somebody else on the network has edited in the meantime, Windows deletes the offline file from your hard drive but doesn't delete the network copy from the network.

• If both your copy and the network copy of a file were edited while you were away, Windows asks you which one should "win" (and also gives you the option of keeping both of the copies under different names).

Synchronization Options

You could spend a lifetime fiddling with the settings for Offline Files. If you want proof, open any desktop window, open any folder window, choose Tools→ Synchronize, and then, in the Items to Synchronize dialog box, click the Setup button. The Synchronize Settings dialog box opens, shown in Figure 20-17.

The Logon/Logoff tab lets you specify which network connection you want to use, which files and folders you want to synchronize automatically, and when you want synchronization to take place (at log on, log off, or both). Here, too, is your chance to make Windows ask permission before performing any of its synchronizations: just turn on "Ask me before synchronizing the items." (That's a handy option when you're working toward a tight deadline and you don't want this process to slow down your computer.)

The other two tabs in this dialog box (On Idle and Scheduled) offer specialized synchronization features, discussed later in this section.

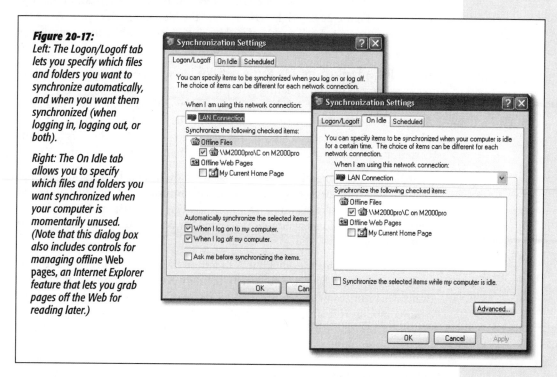

Figure 20-17:
Left: The Logon/Logoff tab lets you specify which files and folders you want to synchronize automatically, and when you want them synchronized (when logging in, logging out, or both).

Right: The On Idle tab allows you to specify which files and folders you want synchronized when your computer is momentarily unused. (Note that this dialog box also includes controls for managing offline Web pages, an Internet Explorer feature that lets you grab pages off the Web for reading later.)

When synchronization happens

In general, automatic synchronization is the most convenient. But you can gain more control over exactly when the two-way updating takes place, using any of these scenarios:

- **Manual synchronization.** Windows doesn't always synchronize your files automatically. For example, it can't synchronize a file that's open on your laptop at the moment you log on or log off, and it doesn't try to do automatic synchronization when you're connected to the network via a slow connection (like a dial-up modem).

  In these cases, you have to trigger the synchronization yourself, like this: Open any folder window. Choose Tools→Synchronize. In the Items to Synchronize dialog box, select the folders you want to synchronize, and then click the Synchronize button. Windows does the rest.

- **On Idle synchronization.** Some people have no problem with the delay caused by automatic synchronization when they disconnect from, or reconnect to, the network. They just sit back with a cup of coffee, waiting while Windows updates the files. There is, however, an alternative: telling Windows to do this copying quietly in the background throughout the workday, finding little pauses in your work when the computer isn't being used.

  To turn on this option, open the On Idle tab of the Synchronization Settings dialog box (Figure 20-17, right). Now select the files and folders you want synchronized; turn on the "Synchronize the selected items while my computer is idle" option.

  If you click Advanced, the Idle Settings dialog box appears, where you can set up regular intervals for the updating (every 60 minutes, for example). The idea here is that if your laptop's quietly keeping things in sync all day long, you'll be able to disconnect quickly, content that you probably have the latest versions of your files. If your computer is a laptop, this dialog box also offers the "Prevent synchronization when my computer is running on battery power" option.

- **Scheduled synchronization.** The Scheduled tab of the Synchronization Settings dialog box (Figure 20-8) lets you establish synchronization at specified times and frequencies. (If you're planning to leave the office for a trip at 4 p.m., for example, you could conceivably set up a sync for 3:45 so that you can grab the laptop and go.)

  To set up such a schedule, click the Add button. In the Scheduled Synchronization Wizard, you'll be asked to specify the network connection, what files you want synchronized, whether or not you want Windows to automatically connect your computer if it isn't already on the network at the designated moment (by dialing in, for example), and how often you want the automatic synchronizing to occur.

A Full and Quick synchronization

The Offline Files synchronization process in general doesn't always leave identical copies on your laptop and on the network; sometimes, Windows copies files only in one direction. To use the technical terminology, Windows sometimes performs a *Quick* synchronization, and sometimes a *Full* one.

In a Full synchronization, Windows copies all offline files both to and from your computer, thus ensuring that the latest and greatest versions of the files are in both locations—the best possible arrangement. But you get Full synchronization only when you trigger synchronization in these ways:

- On a schedule

- Manually, by choosing Tools→Synchronize

- When you've turned on "Synchronize all offline files before logging off" (see page 586)

Quick synchronization, on the other hand, is a much faster, one-way process. It merely checks to ensure that there is *some* copy of every designated offline network file on your hard drive.

If, for example, somebody else on the network has deposited a new file into a folder that you've marked for offline use, Quick synchronization will make sure you have a copy of it. Note, however, that Quick synchronization doesn't compare the network and laptop copies, to make sure that you have the *latest* copy—it just makes sure that you have *a* copy.

Quick synchronization is what you get when:

- You log onto the network with automatic synchronization turned on.

- You've turned on "On Idle" synchronization, as described earlier.

- You've turned off "Synchronize all offline files before logging off" (page 586).

Three Ways to Dial In from the Road

W indows XP Professional provides a long list of avenues for dialing into one PC from another. If you're a road warrior armed with a laptop, you may be delighted by these features. If you're a corporate employee who used to think that you could escape the office by going home, you may not.

In any case, each of these *remote access* features requires a good deal of setup and some scavenging through the technical underbrush, and each offers slightly different benefits and drawbacks. But when you're in Tulsa and a spreadsheet you need is on your PC in Tallahassee, you may be grateful to have at least one of these systems in place.

Remote Access Basics

The two most common scenarios for using these remote access features are (a) dialing your home PC using a laptop and (b) dialing into your office network from your PC at home. To help you keep the roles of these various computers straight, the computer industry has done you the favor of introducing specialized terminology—and learning these terms now will help keep your brain from tying itself in knots:

- The *host computer* is the home-base computer—the one that's sitting there, waiting for you to connect to it. It could be your office computer (you'll dial into it from home), or your home computer (you'll dial into it from your laptop on the road).

- The *remote computer* is the one that will do the dialing: your laptop on the road, for example, or your home machine when you tap into the office network.

The remaining pages of this chapter cover all three systems, but here's a quick summary:

- **Dialing direct.** The remote computer can dial the host PC directly, modem to modem, becoming part of the network at the host location. At that point, you can access shared folders exactly as described in the previous chapter.

  The downside: The host PC must have its own phone line that only it answers. Otherwise, its modem will answer every incoming phone call, occasionally blasting the ears of hapless human callers.

- **Virtual private networking.** Using this system, you don't have to make a direct phone call from the remote PC to the host. Instead, you use the Internet as an intermediary. This way, you avoid long distance charges, and the host PC doesn't have to have its own phone line. Once again, the remote computer behaves exactly as though it has joined the network of the system you're dialing into.

- **Remote Desktop.** This feature, new in Windows XP, doesn't just make the remote PC join the network of the host; it actually turns the remote computer *into* the host PC, filling your screen with its screen image. When you touch the trackpad on your laptop, you're actually moving the cursor on the home-base PC's screen, and so forth.

UP TO SPEED

Remote Networking vs. Remote Control

As noted above, when you connect to a PC using direct-dial or virtual private networking (VPN), you're simply joining the host's network from far away. If you've dialed into your home PC using your laptop, and you try to open a Word document that's actually sitting on the home PC, your *laptop's* copy of Word opens and loads the file. Your laptop is doing the actual word processing; the host just sends and receives files as needed.

Windows XP's new Remote Desktop feature is a completely different animal. In this case, you're using your laptop to *control* the host computer. If you double-click that Word file on the home-base PC, you open the copy of Word *on the host computer.* All of the word processing takes place on the distant machine, the one you've connected to; all that passes over the connection between the two computers is a series of keystrokes, mouse movements, and screen displays. The host is doing all the work. Your laptop is just peeking at the results.

Once you understand the differences between these technologies, you can make a more informed decision about which to use when. For example, suppose your PC at the office stores a gigantic 100-megabyte video file, and you want to edit it from your PC at home. Using a remote networking connection means that you'll have to wait for the file to be transmitted to your home machine before you can begin working. If you've connected to the office machine using a standard dial-up modem, you'll be waiting, literally, for several *days.* If you use a Remote Desktop connection, on the other hand, the video file remains right where it is: on the host computer, which does all the processing. You see on your screen exactly what you would see if you were sitting at the office.

On the other hand, if the computer doing the dialing is a brand-new Pentium 7, zillion-megahertz screamer, and the host system is a five-year old rustbucket on its last legs, you might actually prefer a remote network connection, so that the faster machine can do most of the heavy work.

To make this work, you have to dial *into* a computer running Windows XP Pro. But the machine doing the dialing can be running any relatively recent version of Windows, including Windows XP Home Edition.

Tip: The world is filled with more powerful, more flexible products that let you accomplish the same things as these Windows XP features, from software programs like LapLink, Carbon Copy, and PC Anywhere to Web sites like *www.gotomypc.com*.

On the other hand, Remote Desktop is free.

Note, by the way, that these are all methods of connecting to an *unattended* machine. If somebody is sitting at the PC back home, you might find it far more convenient to dial in using Windows Messenger, described in Chapter 11. It's easier to set up and doesn't require XP Professional on one end, yet offers the same kind of "screen sharing" as Remote Desktop.

Dialing Direct

To set up the host to make it ready for access from afar, you first must prepare it to answer calls. Then you need to set up the remote computer to dial in.

Setting Up the Host PC

If your host PC has its own private phone line—the lucky thing—here's how to prepare it for remote access:

1. **Choose Start→Control Panel. In the Control Panel window, double-click Network Connections.**

   You see the icons for the various network connections you've created.

2. **In the task pane at the left side of the window, click "Create a new connection."**

   As you might have predicted, something called the New Connection Wizard appears (Figure 21-1, top).

3. **Click Next. On the next screen, click "Set up an advanced connection," and then click Next.**

   Now the Advanced Connections Options screen appears.

4. **Ensure that the "Accept incoming connections" option is selected (Figure 21-1, middle). Then click Next.**

   Now you're shown a list of the communication equipment your PC has—including its modem.

5. **Turn on the checkbox for your modem.**

   At this point, you could also click the Properties button and, in the resulting dialog box, turn on "Disconnect a call if idle for more than __ minutes." Doing so

---

makes sure that your home PC won't tie up the line after your laptop in the hotel room is finished going about its business. Click OK.

6. **Click Next. Leave "Do not allow virtual private connections" selected, and then click Next.**

As shown in Figure 21-1 at bottom, you're now looking at a list of every account holder on your PC (Chapter 17).

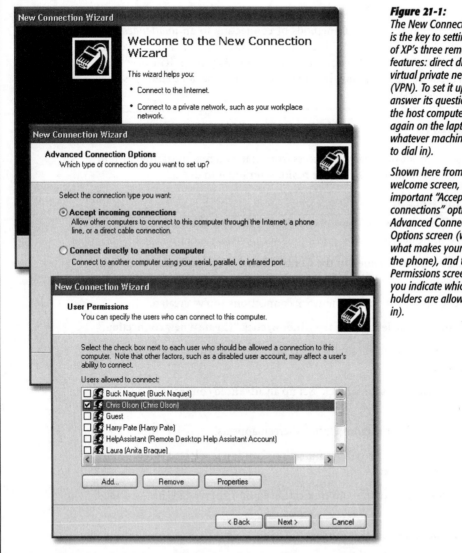

Figure 21-1:
The New Connection Wizard is the key to setting up two of XP's three remote access features: direct dialing and virtual private networking (VPN). To set it up, you answer its questions once on the host computer, and again on the laptop (or whatever machine you'll use to dial in).

Shown here from top: the welcome screen, the all-important "Accept incoming connections" option on the Advanced Connection Options screen (which is what makes your PC answer the phone), and the User Permissions screen (where you indicate which account holders are allowed to dial in).

7. **Turn on the checkboxes corresponding to the people who should be allowed to dial into this host PC.**

Don't turn on Guest, which amounts to a welcome mat for hackers.

If you highlight a name and then click Properties, you can turn on the *callback* feature—a security feature that, after you've dialed in, makes your host PC hang up and call you back at a specific number. You can either (a) specify a callback number at the host machine in advance, so that outsiders won't be able to connect, or (b) let the remote user specify the callback number, which puts most of the telephone charges on the host computer's bill (so that you can bypass obscene hotel long distance surcharges). Click OK to close the dialog box.

8. **Click Next.**

You're shown a list of networking protocols that Windows XP will make available to you when you call in. In general, you should simply confirm that all the checkboxes are turned on. (Highlighting "Internet Protocol (TCP/IP)" and clicking the Properties button may be useful to the paranoid, however. It lets you limit a remote caller to just this particular PC, instead of having full access to the network.)

9. **Click Next again, and then click Finish.**

A new icon in your Network Connections window, called Incoming Connections, is born. Your home-base PC is ready for connections. When the phone rings, the modem will answer it. (Of course, you shouldn't use this feature with the same phone line as your answering machine or your fax.)

Setting Up the Remote PC

Next, go to the remote computer and get it ready to phone home. Here's what to do:

1. **Choose Start→My Network Places. At the left side of the My Network Places window, click "Create a new connection."**

The New Connection Wizard appears.

2. **Click Next. Select "Connect to the network at my workplace," and then click Next.**

Now Windows wants to know if you'll be connecting via modem ("Dial-up connection" or via Internet ("Virtual Private Network connection").

3. **Click "Dial-up connection," and then click Next. Type a name for your connection (like "Phone home"), and then click Next. Type a phone number for the line your home PC is connected to, and then click Next again.**

You'll have an opportunity to specify area codes and dialing codes later.

4. **On the final screen, turn on "Add a shortcut to this connection to my desktop," and then click Finish.**

You're now ready to establish a connection between the two computers.

Making the Call

Once you've configured both computers, fire up the remote system and follow these steps to connect:

1. **Double-click the shortcut icon you created in step 4 above.**

   If it isn't on your desktop, you should find it in your Network Connections window (which you can open from the Control Panel). The dialog box shown in Figure 21-2 appears.

Note: If you're using a laptop while traveling, you might have to tell Windows XP where you are before you attempt to connect. If you're in a different area code, open the Phone and Modem Options icon in the Control Panel. Make sure that you've specified your current location, complete with whatever fancy dialing numbers are required by it (see page 320 for instructions on establishing these locations). Click the current location and then click OK. Now Windows knows what area code and prefixes to use.

Figure 21-2:
You're ready to phone home. If you click the Properties button, you can invoke one of the dialing rules you prepared while reading page 320, which can save you a bit of fiddling around with area codes and access numbers.

2. **Type in your name and password, and double check the phone number.**

   This is the same name and password you'd use to log in at the Welcome screen if you were sitting in front of the host PC (Chapter 17). If you've set up dialing rules (page 320), you can choose the appropriate set of phone number segments by clicking the Properties button.

3. Click Dial.

That's all there is to it. Windows dials into your home PC, makes the connection, and—if the phone number, name, and password are all correct—shows you a balloon on your taskbar (Figure 21-3).

You're free to open up any shared folders, even use shared printers, on your network back home. And although it may make your brain hurt to contemplate it, you can even surf the Internet if your home PC has, say, a cable modem.

Note: Don't try to run any *programs* that reside on your host PC, however; you'll be old and gray by the time they even finish opening. If you try, the host computer must transmit all of the files that make up the program to your remote machine as it loads (see the box on page 596).

When you're finished with your email check, address lookup, document transfer, or whatever, right-click the little network icon in your notification area and choose Disconnect from the shortcut menu (Figure 21-3, top).

Tip: If you're having trouble connecting, confirm that the name and password you're using are correct—that's the number-one source of problems. If the remote system still doesn't recognize you, click the Properties button in the dialog box shown in Figure 21-2. On the General tab, make sure that your laptop's dialing the right number; on the Networking tab, confirm that all the checkboxes are turned on.

Figure 21-3:
Top: Congratulations—you're in. (When two 56 K modems connect, alas, they're limited to the top uploading speed of either—and that's about 33 K.)

Bottom: Disconnect by right-clicking the notification area icon. (The X'ed-out network icon, by the way, represents the office Ethernet cable that's currently disconnected from this laptop, which is in a hotel room somewhere.)

Virtual Private Networking

If you're a frequent traveler who regularly connects to a distant home or office by dialing direct, you must be the toast of your long-distance phone company.

Fortunately, there's a more economical solution. Virtual private networking (VPN) is a fancy way of saying, "Your remote computer can become part of your host network, using the Internet as a connection instead of a long distance phone connection." Yes, this does sound exactly like the direct-dialing feature described above—

WORKAROUND WORKSHOP

Getting a Fixed IP Address

Several of the remote-connection methods described in this chapter require that your home-base PC have a *fixed* IP address. An IP address is a unique number that identifies a particular computer on the Internet. (It's made up of four numbers separated by periods.) A *fixed* IP address is one that's been permanently assigned to your computer.

Furthermore, these remote-connection technologies require that you have a registered IP address (one that, behind the scenes, has been filed with a group called the Internet Assigned Numbers Authority).

A few PCs with high-speed Internet connections (cable modem, DSL) have this kind of permanent, unchanging address. But in most cases, your ISP assigns your computer a new address each time you connect, thus giving you a *dynamic* IP address. That's always what you have, for example, when you connect using a dial-up modem.

Even if your cable modem or DSL connection has a fixed IP address (because you're connected continuously), you don't necessarily have a *registered* IP address. (Want to find out? Connect to the Internet, and then choose Start→All Programs→Accessories→Command Prompt. In the Command Prompt window, you'll see all kinds of network configuration information about your computer, including its IP address [or addresses, if you're connected to a network]. Your IP address is not registered if it falls within any of these ranges: 10.0.0.0 through 10.255.255.255, 172.16.0.0 through 172.31.255.255, or 192.168.0.0. through 192.168.255.255. Or just ask your Internet service provider or network administrator.)

If it turns out that you don't have a fixed, registered IP

address, you might assume that you can't use the remote-connection technologies described in this chapter. After all, your Internet address *changes* every time you connect, making it impossible to provide a single, permanent address. Fortunately, there are workarounds.

One solution is to contact your ISP and ask if it offers a fixed, registered IP address service. Some ISPs can be persuaded to assign you the same registered address every time you connect (for an additional fee, of course).

Another solution is to sign up for a *dynamic DNS service* that gives your PC a name, not a number. Whenever you're online, these free services automatically update the IP address associated with the name you've chosen (such as *pcnut.dyndns.org*), so that you (and your colleagues) can memorize a single address for your machine.

To sign up for one of these services, just go to its Web site—*www.dyndns.org, www.dhs.org, www.dtdns.com, www.hn.org,* or *www.no-ip.com,* among others.

If you bought a router for your home or small-office network—a small box that shares your cable modem or DSL connection with several computers on the network—there may be a third solution. Some routers let you map the unregistered address of a computer on your local network to a registered address inside the router, making that computer visible to the Internet. To find out if your router can pull off this stunt, you'll have to dig out the manual for the router, or contact its manufacturer.

In any case, once you obtain a fixed, registered IP address for your host system, don't forget to bring it with you. You'll need it when setting up the remote computer.

---

except this time, you don't pay any long-distance bills, your host PC doesn't necessarily have to have its own phone line, and (if the computers on both ends have fast connections) you're not limited to the sluglike speeds of dial-up modems.

With a VPN connection, both the host and the remote computers connect to the Internet by making *local* calls to your Internet service provider (ISP). If you travel with a laptop, that's a good argument for signing up with a national or international ISP that has local access numbers wherever you plan to be. On the other hand, if you don't move your computers around much, you can just use your regular ISP as you always do, whether you connect using a dial-up, a cable modem, DSL, or whatever.

If you're connecting to your corporate network, no problem: your company probably has its own Internet service. If you are the sole proprietor of both machines, however, all of this may mean that you'll actually have to have *two* different ISP accounts, so that both machines can be online at once.

Not only can VPN save the frequent traveler quite a bit of money, but it's also extremely secure. When you connect using VPN, the information traveling between the two connected computers is encoded (encrypted) using a technology called *tunneling*. Your connection is like a reinforced steel pipe wending its way through the Internet to connect the two computers.

To create a VPN connection, your host computer must have two important components:

- It must be on the Internet at the moment you try to connect. Usually, that means it needs a full-time Internet connection, like cable modem or DSL. But in a pinch—if it has only a dial-up modem, for example—you could phone a family member or co-worker just before you need to connect, with the direction to go online with your home PC.

- It needs its own, fixed *IP address*. (See the box on the previous page for a workaround.)

The remote computer, on the other hand, doesn't have any such requirements.

Setting Up the Host Machine

To set up the host PC for the VPN connection, do exactly as you would for direct-dial connections (page 597)—but in step 6, choose "Allow virtual private connections." When the wizard finishes its work, the host machine is ready for action. Instead of setting up the modem to answer incoming calls, Windows XP now listens for incoming VPN connection requests from the Internet.

Making the Connection

Now move to the laptop, or whatever machine you'll be using when you're away from the main office. These steps, too, should seem familiar—they start out just like those that began on page 599, except that in step 3, you should choose "Virtual Private Network connection." Then proceed like this:

1. On the Public Network screen before you, leave "Automatically dial this initial connection" selected. Use the drop-down list to select the connection you use to access the Internet.

   Now Windows XP can automatically dial up your ISP when you launch the VPN connection.

2. Click Next. On the VPN Server Selection screen, type the host name or registered IP address of the VPN host—that is, the computer you'll be dialing into.

   If you've signed up for one of the dynamic DNS services described in the box on page 602, you know what the host computer's name is. Otherwise, specify its registered IP address.

3. Click Next, turn on "Add a shortcut to this connection to my desktop," and then click Finish.

   The result is a new icon on your desktop (and in the Network Connections window). When you double-click it, you see a dial-up box like the one shown in Figure 21-2. As with direct-dial connections, you can use dialing rules (page 320) to simplify your life as you move from area code to area code in the course of your life.

At this point, you've once again joined your home network. Exactly as with the direct-dial connections described earlier, you should feel free to transfer files, make printouts, and so on. Avoid actually running programs on the distant PC, at least if one computer or the other is connected to the Internet using a dial-up modem; the situation improves if both are using high-speed connections.

When you want to hang up, right-click the connection icon in your notification area and choose Disconnect.

Note: All of this sounds simple enough—and it is, if you have only one PC at home, or several that rely on Internet Connection Sharing (Chapter 18).

Unfortunately, setting up virtual private networking (and, for that matter, Remote Desktop, described next) on larger networks, or on networks that don't use Internet Connection Sharing, can be extremely complex. If you've installed a *router* to share an Internet connection with your network (page 542), for example, some hairy technical bushwhacking is involved in setting it up to accommodate remote-access requests from the road. A consultant, or call to the router company, may be in your future.

Remote Desktop

If you opt to set up your host computer to use Remote Desktop instead of a standard direct-dial or VPN connection, dialing into it from your remote offers some spectacular advantages. When you use Remote Desktop, you're not just tapping into your home computer's network—you're actually bringing its screen onto your screen. You can run its programs, print on its printers, "type" on its keyboard, move its cursor, manage its files, and so on, all by remote control.

Remote Desktop isn't useful only when you're trying to dial into the office or reach your home computer from the road; it even works over an office network. You can actually take control of another computer in the office—to troubleshoot a novice's PC without having to run up or down a flight of stairs, perhaps, or just to run a program that isn't on your own machine.

If you do decide to use Remote Desktop over the Internet, the requirements are the same as they are for a VPN connection. That is, the host computer must be connected to the Internet when you try to access it, and it must have a fixed, registered IP address.

Tip: Windows XP Pro contains the software that lets you create both ends of the Remote Desktop connection: the host (server) piece and remote (client) piece.

As noted earlier, the remote PC can be running any version of Windows all the way back to 95. To install the Remote Desktop Connection client on one of these other operating systems, insert the Windows XP Professional CD-ROM into the drive. When the Welcome to Microsoft Windows XP window appears, click Perform Additional Tasks→Setup Remote Desktop Connection. The InstallShield Wizard for Remote Desktop Connection appears, and leads you through the process of installing the software.

Setting Up the Host Machine

To make your Windows XP Pro machine ready for invasion—that is, to turn it into a host—proceed like this:

1. **Choose Start→Control Panel. Double-click the System icon.**

   The System control panel program opens.

2. **Click the Remote tab.**

   The dialog box shown in Figure 21-4 appears.

3. **Turn on "Allow users to connect remotely to this computer."**

   You've just turned on the master switch that lets outsiders dial into your machine and take it over.

4. **Click the Select Remote Users button.**

   The Remote Desktop Users dialog box appears. You certainly don't want casual teenage hackers to visit your precious PC from across the Internet, playing games and reading your personal info. Fortunately, the Remote Desktop feature requires you to specify precisely who is allowed to connect. Anybody not on your list will be shut out.

5. **Click Add. In the resulting dialog box, type the names of the people who are allowed to access your PC using Remote Desktop.**

   This dialog box might seem familiar—it's exactly the same idea as the Select Users, Computers, or Groups dialog box shown on page 529.

Choose your lucky comrades carefully; remember that they'll be able to do anything to your system, by remote control, that you could do while sitting in front of it. (To further ensure security, Windows XP Pro insists that the accounts you're selecting here have passwords. Password-free accounts can't connect.)

Note: The Administrator account (page 510) always has Remote Desktop access.

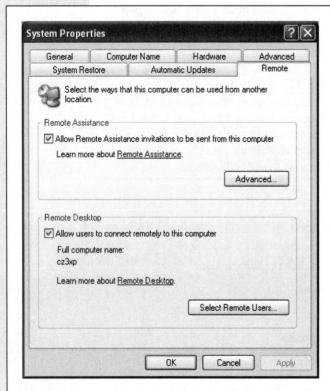

Figure 21-4:
Turning on the "Allow users to connect remotely to this computer" checkbox makes Windows XP listen to the network for Remote Desktop connections. Now you can specify who, exactly, is allowed to dial in.

6. **Click OK three times to close the dialog boxes you opened.**

The host computer is now ready for invasion. It's listening to the network for incoming connections from Remote Desktop clients.

Making the Connection

When you're ready to try Remote Desktop, fire up your laptop, home machine, or whatever computer will be doing the remote connecting. Then:

1. **Connect to the Internet just as you always do.**

   If the host computer is elsewhere on your local network—in the same building, that is—you can skip this step.

2. **Choose Start→All Programs→Accessories→Communications→Remote Desktop Connection.**

   The Remote Desktop Connection dialog box appears.

3. **Click the Options button to expand the dialog box (if necessary). Fill it out as shown in Figure 21-5.**

   The idea is to specify the IP address (or DNS name) of the computer you're trying to reach.

Figure 21-5:
Type in the IP address or registered DNS name of your host computer. Then fill in your name and password (and domain, if necessary), exactly the way you would if you were logging onto it in person.

4. **Click the Connect button.**

Now a freaky thing happens: after a moment of pitch-blackness, the host computer's screen fills your own (Figure 21-6). Don't be confused by the fact that all of the open windows on the computer you're using have now *disappeared*. You can now operate the distant PC as though you were there in the flesh, using your own keyboard (or trackpad) and mouse. You can answer your email, make long-distance printouts, and so on. All the action—running programs, changing settings, and so on—is actually taking place on the faraway host computer.

Tip: You can even shut down or restart the faraway machine by remote control. Choose Start→Windows Security (a command that appears only when you're connected). In the resulting dialog box, use the Shut Down menu to choose the command you want—Restart, Turn Off, Disconnect, or whatever.

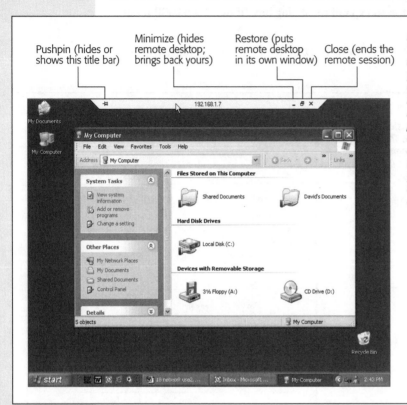

Pushpin (hides or shows this title bar)

Minimize (hides remote desktop; brings back yours)

Restore (puts remote desktop in its own window)

Close (ends the remote session)

Figure 21-6:
The strange little title bar at the top of your screen lets you minimize the distant computer's screen or turn it into a floating window. To hide this title bar, click the pushpin icon so that it turns completely horizontal. After a minute, it slides into the top of the screen, out of your way until you move the cursor to the top edge of the screen.

Keep in mind a few other points:

- You don't need to feel completely blocked out of your own machine. The little title bar at the top of the screen offers you the chance to put the remote computer's screen into a floating window of its own, permitting you to see both your own screen and the home-base computer's screen simultaneously (Figure 21-7).

- You can copy and paste highlighted text or graphics between the two machines (using regular Copy and Paste), and even transfer entire documents back and forth (using Copy and Paste on the desktop icons). Of course, if you've made both desktops visible simultaneously (Figure 21-7), you can also copy icons just by dragging them.

- Even Windows XP Pro can't keep its mind focused on two people at once. If somebody is trying to use the host machine in person, you'll see a message to the effect that you're about to bump that person off the PC. In fact, unless Fast User

Switching is turned on (page 520) *and* the person back home clicks Yes in the "Do you want to allow this connection?" dialog box that appears, your colleague at home will lose all unsaved work.

Figure 21-7:
By putting the other computer's screen into a window of its own, you save yourself a little bit of confusion—and open up some unique possibilities. For example, you can now transfer documents back and forth just by dragging them between the two windows. You can even minimize the remote computer's screen entirely, reducing it to a tab on your taskbar until you need it again.

Your office PC's desktop back home

Your current PC's desktop

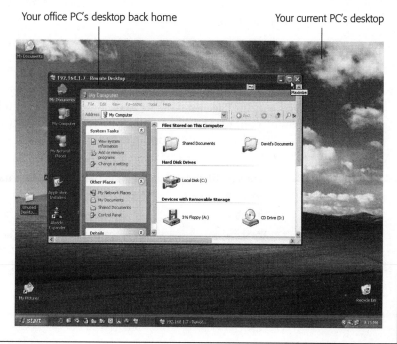

- Similarly, if somebody tries to log on at the host computer while you're connected from the remote, *you* get unceremoniously dumped off. (You just get a message that tells you, not exactly accurately, that your session has been terminated "by means of an administration tool.") Fortunately, you don't lose work this way—your account remains logged on behind the scenes, just as in Fast User Switching. When you connect again later (after the interloper has signed off), you'll find all your programs and documents open exactly as you left them.

- Back at the host computer, nobody can see what you're doing. The standard Welcome screen appears on the remote PC, masking your activities.

Keyboard Shortcuts for the Hopelessly Confused

When the Remote Desktop Connection window is maximized (that is, it fills your entire screen), all of the standard Windows keyboard shortcuts operate on the *host* computer, not the one you're actually using. When you press Ctrl+Esc, for example, you see the host computer's Start menu. When you press Ctrl+Alt+Delete, you see the host computer's Task Manager dialog box.

But when you turn the Remote Desktop Connection into a floating window that doesn't fill your entire screen, it's a different story. Now your current computer (the remote machine) "hears" your keystrokes. Now, pressing Ctrl+Esc opens the *remote* computer's Start menu, and Ctrl+Alt+Delete displays the *remote* computer's Task Manager. In this situation, how are you supposed to operate the host computer by remote control?

Microsoft has thought of everything. It's even given you alternatives for the key combinations you're accustomed to using. For example, suppose you've connected to your office PC using your laptop. When the Remote Desktop window isn't full-screen, pressing Alt+Tab switches to the next open program on the laptop—but pressing Alt+Page Up switches to the next program on the host computer. Here's a summary of the special keys that operate the distant host computer—a table that can be useful if you are either an extreme power user or somebody who likes to win bar bets:

Standard Windows Key Combination	Remote Desktop Key Combination	Function
Alt+Tab	Alt+Page Up	Switches to the next open program
Alt+Shift+Tab	Alt+Page Down	Switches to the previous open program
Alt+Esc	Alt+Insert	Cycles through programs in the order in which you open them
Ctrl+Esc	Alt+Home	Opens the Start menu
Ctrl+Alt+Delete	Ctrl+Alt+End	Displays the Task Manager or the Windows Security dialog box. (Actually, you should use the alternative key combination whether the Remote Desktop window is maximized or not, because Ctrl+Alt+Delete is always interpreted by the remote computer—the one you're currently using.)

Disconnecting

To get out of Remote Desktop mode, click the close box in the strange little title bar at the top of your screen, as shown in Figure 21-6 (or choose Start→Turn Off Computer).

Note, however, that this method leaves all your programs running and your documents open on the distant machine, exactly as though you had used Fast User Switching. If you log on again, either from the road or in person, you'll find all of those programs and documents still on the screen, just as you left them.

If you'd rather log off in a more permanent way, closing all your distant documents and programs, choose Start→Log Off (the home-base computer's Start menu, not yours).

Fine-tuning Remote Desktop Connections

Windows XP Pro offers all kinds of settings for tailoring the way this bizarre, schizophrenic connection method works. The trick is, however, that you have to change them *before* you connect, using the tabs on the dialog box shown in Figure 21-8.

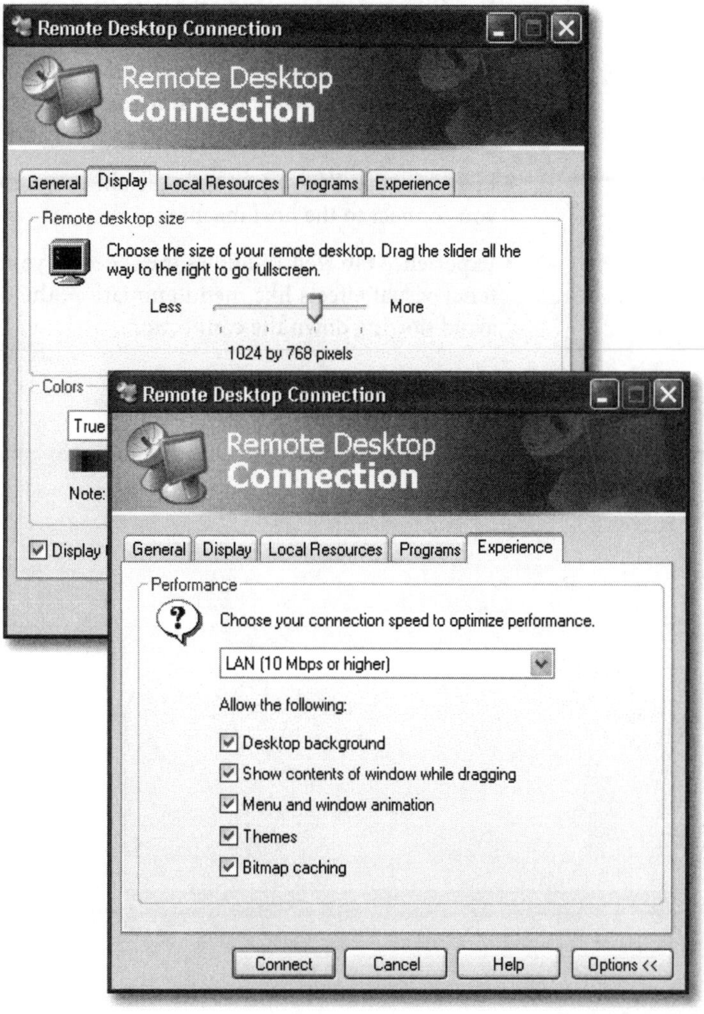

Figure 21-8:
Click the Options button if you don't see these tabs. Once you've made them appear, though, a few useful (and a lot of rarely useful) settings become available. On the Display tab (left), for example, you can effectively reduce the size of the other computer's screen so that it fits within your laptop's. On the Experience tab (right), you can turn off special-effect animations to speed up the connection.

Here's what you'll find:

- **General tab.** Here's where you can tell Windows to memorize your password, or to save all of the current settings as a shortcut icon, which makes it faster to reconnect later. (If you connect to a number of different distant computers, saving a setup for each one in this way can be a huge timesaver.)

- **Display tab.** Use these options to specify the *size* (resolution) of the host computer's display—an especially useful option if it's different from your remote computer's screen size.

- **Local Resources tab.** Using these controls, you can set up local peripherals and add-ons so that they behave as though they were connected to the remote computer. This is also where you tell Windows which PC should "hear" keystrokes like Alt+Tab, and whether or not you want to hear sound effects played by the distant machine.

- **Programs tab.** You can set up a certain program to run automatically as soon as you connect to the host machine.

- **Experience tab.** Tell Windows the speed of your connection, so that it can limit fancy visual effects like menu animation, the desktop wallpaper, and so on, to avoid slowing down the connection.

Part Six:
Appendixes

6

Installing Windows XP Pro

I f your computer came with Windows XP Professional already installed on it, you can skip this appendix—for now. But if you're running an earlier version of Windows and want to savor the XP experience, this appendix describes how to install the new operating system on your computer.

Before You Begin

Believe it or not, most of the work involved in installing Windows XP takes place well before the installation CD so much as approaches your computer. You have a lot of research and planning to do, especially if you want to avoid spending a five-day weekend in Upgrade Hell.

To start with, before you even think about installing Windows XP, you must ensure that your PC is beefy enough to handle it. You also have to decide which of two types of installation you want to perform: an *upgrade* or a *clean install*. (More on this in a moment.)

If you opt for the clean install (a process that begins with *erasing your hard drive completely*), you must back up your data. Finally, you have to choose a *file system* for your hard drive and gather all of the software bits and pieces you'll need in order to perform the installation.

Checking Hardware Requirements

Before you even buy a copy of Windows XP, your first order of business should be to check your computer against the list of hardware requirements for Windows XP, as published by Microsoft:

- A computer with 300 megahertz (MHz) or higher processor clock speed recommended (233 MHz minimum required); Intel Pentium/Celeron family, AMD K6/Athlon/Duron family, or compatible processor recommended

- 128 megabytes (MB) of RAM or higher recommended (64 MB minimum)

- 1.5 gigabytes (GB) of free hard disk space

- Super VGA (800 x 600) or higher resolution video adapter and monitor

- CD-ROM or DVD drive

- Keyboard and Microsoft mouse or compatible pointing device

At this point, of course, anyone who really knows Windows is writhing on the carpet, convulsed in laughter. Run Windows XP on a 233 MHz Pentium with 64 MB of RAM? It would take three weeks just to get past the Windows logo at startup time. You'd get your work done faster by using an abacus.

Microsoft does make a distinction between what is "recommended" and what is "required," but even the "recommended" statistics are wishful thinking. Glaciers exhibit more speed than an underpowered computer running Windows XP.

In short, if you care about your sanity, treat the first two recommendations (processor and memory) as bare minimums—especially the memory. (256 MB makes Windows XP much happier than 128.) And keep in mind that even on a 1 GHz Pentium machine with 256 MB of memory, it still takes a second or two for the Start→All Programs menu to appear on the screen.

If your computer doesn't meet these requirements, then consider a hardware upgrade—especially a memory upgrade—before you even attempt to install Windows XP. With memory prices what they are today (read: dirt cheap), you'll thank yourself later for adding as much RAM as you can afford.

Adding more hard disk space is also a reasonably easy and inexpensive upgrade. The one place where you may be stuck, though, is on the processor issue. The state of the art in processor speeds seems to advance almost weekly, but it's safe to say that a PC running at 300 MHz or less is certifiably geriatric. It may be time to think about passing the old girl on to the kids or donating it to a worthy cause and getting yourself a newer, faster computer. As a bonus, it will come with Windows XP preinstalled.

Hardware Compatibility

Once you've had a conversation with yourself about your equipment, it's time to investigate the suitability of your existing add-on gear for use with Windows XP.

Microsoft maintains a list of the hardware components that have been tested with Windows XP (and other Microsoft operating systems): the hardware compatibility list (HCL), which is at *www.microsoft.com/hcl*. On this Web page, you can search for a particular component to make sure that it has been tested and works with XP.

If some of the hardware components in your computer don't appear on the HCL, you don't necessarily need to assume that they won't work with Windows XP—only that they haven't been tested by Microsoft. In general, products released since November 2001 are Windows XP–compatible, but you should still proceed with caution before using them with Windows XP. You should by all means check the Web sites of these components' manufacturers in hopes of finding updated driver software.

Checking Software Compatibility

Most programs and drivers that worked with Windows 2000 work fine in Windows XP, but not all of them—and programs designed for Windows 95, 98, and Me may well cause you problems.

If you have a lot of older programs for which XP–compatible updates aren't available, you'd be wise to run the Windows XP Professional Upgrade Advisor program. To do so, insert the Windows XP CD-ROM, and on its welcome screen (Figure A-2), click "Check system compatibility," and then click "Check my system automatically."

Tip: The same compatibility checker runs automatically during the installation process itself.

The Upgrade Advisor first offers to download updated setup files from Microsoft's Web site. If you can get online, it's an excellent idea to take it up on this offer. You'll get all the patches, updates, and bug fixes Microsoft has released since the debut of Windows XP.

Tip: You can download the Windows XP Professional Upgrade Advisor from Microsoft's Web site at *http://www.microsoft.com/windowsxp/pro/howtobuy/upgrading/advisor.asp* so that you can check your computer's hardware and software compatibility before you purchase Windows XP Professional.

Next, the advisor shows you a report that identifies potential problems. Almost everybody finds some incompatibilities reported here, because Microsoft is particularly conservative with its judgment about which programs will work with Windows XP. But if the report lists a serious incompatibility, it's not worth proceeding with the XP installation until you've updated or deleted the offending program.

Note: Utilities like hard-drive formatting software, virus checkers, firewall programs, and so on are especially troublesome. Don't use them in Windows XP unless they're specifically advertised for Windows XP compatibility.

Upgrade vs. Clean Install

If your PC currently runs an older version of Windows, the next big question is whether or not you should upgrade it to Windows XP.

About the Upgrade Installation

You can upgrade to Windows XP Professional from Windows 98, Windows 98 SE, Windows Millennium Edition (Me), Windows NT Workstation 4.0, Windows 2000 Professional, or Windows XP Home Edition. If your PC currently runs Windows 3.1, Windows 95, or Windows NT Workstation 3.51, you can't upgrade to Windows XP Professional at all—you have to perform a *clean install*, as described in the following pages.

Upgrading the operating system retains all of your existing configuration settings and data files. Your desktop colors, font choices, and wallpaper all remain the same, as do some more important elements, including your Favorites list and the files in your My Documents folder.

Upgrading might seem like a convenient option because you don't have to go back and redo all your preferred settings. Unfortunately, upgrading can bring along some unwelcome baggage, too. Outdated drivers, fragmented disk drives, and a clutter of unneeded registry settings are just some of the things that Windows preserves when you upgrade. If all this artery-clogging gunk has already begun to slow down your computer, upgrading to Windows XP will only make things worse.

Furthermore, following an upgrade installation of Windows XP, you may find that some of your software doesn't run as well as it used to, and various other system glitches may pop up from time to time. That's not to say that your software won't run well on Windows XP—only that it would prefer to be installed fresh on the new operating system. In short, upgrading can save you some time and aggravation now, but you might end up paying for it later.

Buying Windows XP

If you do decide to upgrade your existing version of Windows, you can save some money. As with other versions of Windows, XP is available in both an Upgrade version and a Full version.

The Upgrade Edition can only install Windows XP Professional on a computer that already has Windows 98, Windows 98 SE, Windows Me, Windows NT Workstation 4.0, Windows 2000 Professional, or Windows XP Home Edition on it. If your computer is currently running any other version of Windows, and you want Windows XP Professional, you have to buy the Full version and perform a clean install.

Here, too, there's a caveat: If you upgrade your computer to Windows XP Pro using the Upgrade Edition, and some time later, a computer catastrophe wipes out your hard drive, you'll have to reinstall Windows XP the second time the same way you did it the first time: by first installing the older version of Windows, and then running the XP upgrade installer on top of it. Here again, you can pay now, or risk having to pay later.

About the Clean Install

The alternative to an upgrade is the *clean install* of Windows XP. During a clean install, you repartition and reformat your hard disk, wiping out everything on it.

The overwhelming advantage of a clean install is that you wind up with a fresh system, 100 percent free of all of those creepy little glitches and inconsistencies that have been building up over the years. Ask any Windows veteran: the best way to boost the speed of a system that has grown sluggish is to perform a clean install of the operating system and start afresh.

Backing up

The drawback of a clean install, however, is the work it will take you to back up all of your files and settings before you begin. If your computer has a tape backup drive, that's not much of a problem. Just perform a full backup, test it to make sure that everything you need has been copied to tape and is restorable, and you're ready to install Windows XP.

If you have a CD-R or CD-RW drive, backing up is almost equally easy. If you have a second computer, you can also consider backing up your stuff on to it, via a network (Chapter 18). And, of course, you can always buy a Zip drive or external hard drive. In any of these cases, you'll probably want to use the new Files and Settings Transfer Wizard for this purpose, which is included with Windows XP Professional. It's described later in this appendix.

Even having a full backup plan, however, doesn't mean that a clean install will be a walk in the park. After the installation, you'll still have to reinstall all of your programs, reconfigure all your personalized settings, re-create your dial-up networking connections, and so on.

Tip: It's a good idea to spend a few days writing down the information you need as you're working on your computer. For example, copy down the phone number, user name, and password that you use to connect to your Internet service provider (ISP), and the user names and passwords you need for various Web sites you frequent.

Performing a clean install also means buying the Full Edition of Windows XP. It's more expensive than the Upgrade Edition, but at least you can install it on a blank hard disk without having to install an old Windows version first.

Overall, performing a clean install is preferable to an upgrade. But if you don't have the time or the heart to back up your hard drive, wipe it clean and re-establish all of your settings, the upgrade option is always there for you.

Dual Booting

Here's yet another decision you have to make before you install Windows XP: whether or not you'll want to be able to *dual boot*.

In this advanced scenario, you install Windows XP onto the same PC that contains an older version of Windows, maintaining both of them side by side. Then, each time you turn on the PC, it *asks you* which operating system you want to run for this computing session (see Figure A-1).

Dual booting comes in handy when you have some program or hardware gadget that works with one operating system but not the other. For example, if you have a scanner with software that runs on Windows 98 but not Windows XP, you can start up the PC in Windows 98 only when you want to use the scanner.

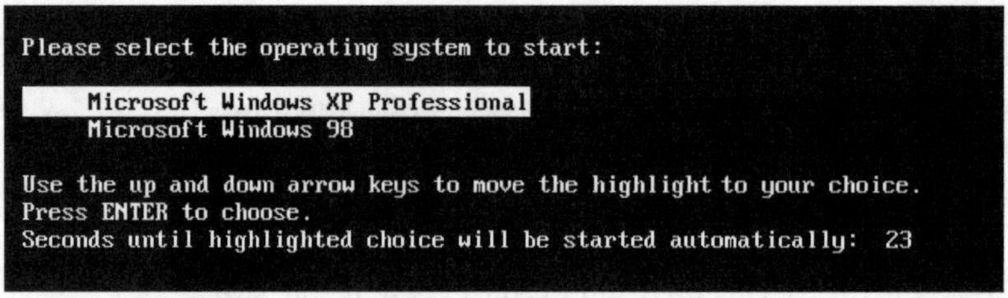

```
Please select the operating system to start:

    Microsoft Windows XP Professional
    Microsoft Windows 98

Use the up and down arrow keys to move the highlight to your choice.
Press ENTER to choose.
Seconds until highlighted choice will be started automatically:   23
```

Figure A-1:
When you dual boot, this menu appears each time you turn on your PC, offering you a choice of OS. (If you don't choose in 30 seconds, the PC chooses for you.)

If you intend to dual boot, here's some important advice: *Don't install both operating systems onto the same hard drive partition.* Your programs will become horribly confused.

Instead, keep your two Windows versions separate using one of these avenues:

• Buy a second hard drive. Use it for one of the two operating systems.

• Back up your hard drive, erase it completely, and then *partition* it, which means dividing it so that each chunk shows up in the My Computer window with its own icon, name, and drive letter. Then install each operating system on a separate disk partition.

One way to partition your drive is free, but not especially user-friendly: use the built-in DOS program called FDISK (see the box on the facing page).

• If you're less technically inclined, you might prefer to buy a program like PartitionMagic (*www.partitionmagic.com*). Not only does it let you create a new partition on your hard drive without erasing it first, but it's more flexible and easier to use than FDISK.

There's just one wrinkle with dual-booting. If you install Windows XP onto a separate partition (or a different drive), as you must, you won't find any of your existing programs listed in the Start menu, and your desktop won't be configured the way it is in your original operating system. You'll generally wind up having to reinstall every program into your new Windows XP world, and re-establish all of your settings, exactly as though the Windows XP "side" were a brand-new PC.

Choosing a File System

There's one final decision you have to make: which *file system* you want to use for formatting your hard drive.

A file system is a scheme of formatting your hard drive, a system of dividing up its surface into little parking spaces for data. It's a very technical issue, and, mercifully, one that's largely invisible to you except for the day you install the operating system.

POWER USERS' CLINIC

Using FDISK to Partition a Drive

If you're an old-time Windows user, the idea of using an old DOS program like FDISK might be no big deal. But scan the following instructions and confirm that they're worth slogging through just to save yourself the price of a simpler formatting program like PartitionMagic. Remember that FDISK *erases your entire hard drive;* don't use it until you're confident you have a good backup.

Here, then, is how you'd create a two-partition setup so that you can have Windows 95, 98, Me, NT 4.0, or 2000 installed simultaneously with Windows XP on different partitions. (Note: After you make each selection in the following instructions, press the Enter key to proceed.)

Start up the PC from the Windows 95/98/Me/NT/2000 CD-ROM. On the first two screens, choose "Boot from CD-ROM" and then "Start computer with CD-ROM support." After a moment, you wind up at the A:/> prompt; type *fdisk*.

When asked if you "wish to enable large disk support," accept the Y (yes) option by pressing Enter. The FDISK Options screen appears.

If your drive has already been in use: Choose 3 ("Delete partition or Logical DOS Drive"), then 1 ("Delete Primary DOS Partition"), and then 1 (which corresponds to your C: drive's main partition). Type Y to confirm that you want to wipe it out, then Esc to continue. Continue with the steps in the next paragraph, because your drive is now completely empty.

If your drive is completely empty: On the FDISK Options screen, type 1 ("Create DOS partition or Logical DOS Drive"). On the next screen, choose 1 again ("Create Primary DOS Partition"). After FDISK checks your drive, it asks if you "wish to use the maximum available size." Type N (no, you don't—you want to partition it, dividing its space in half).

After a moment, you're asked for the size you want for the first partition, which will contain the older Windows version. In general, you'll need at least 1500 MB; leave room for your programs, too. So type, for example, *2500,* press Enter, and then press Esc to return to FDISK Options. This time, press 2 ("Set active partition") and then, on the next screen, press 1 (for the main partition) to establish your first partition as the active one. Press Esc to return to the FDISK Options screen.

Back at FDISK Options, create the second partition by choosing 1 ("Create DOS partition…") and then, on the next screen, 2 ("Create extended DOS partition"). If two partitions are all you need, then you don't have to specify the size of this second one—FDISK automatically proposes using all the space that's left. Just press Enter, then Esc.

FDISK now wants you to format the second partition, which will house Windows XP. Here again, you'll generally want to use the full amount of space available—so just press Enter, then Esc. You're at the FDISK Options screen one last time. Press Esc twice more to say goodbye. Finally, press Ctrl+Alt+Delete to restart the PC.

At last you're ready to install Windows 95, 98, Me, NT, or 2000. Start up from its installation CD, choosing "Start Windows Setup from CD-ROM," "Format Drive C:," and "Format this drive (Recommended)" when you get the chance. After a quick disk check by ScanDisk (press X for Exit when it's done), the usual Windows Setup program appears. When you're offered a choice of partitions, allow it to install Windows onto the C:\WINDOWS folder as usual.

When that's all over, just install Windows XP as though you're performing a clean install. Follow the instructions that begin on page 625, paying special attention to the notes pertaining to dual-booting.

Windows XP offers a choice of two file systems, geekily named *FAT* 32 and *NTFS*. FAT 32 (file allocation table) is the descendant of the original DOS formatting scheme. NTFS (NT file system) is far more advanced and modern; it was introduced with Windows NT in 1993.

NTFS offers a long list of attractive features:

- It can handle bigger hard drives than FAT—in fact, it can handle drives with capacities up to two terabytes (that's 2,048 gigabytes). No, drives that big aren't available today, but it's only a matter of time. The FAT scheme can handle any of today's hard drives, but Microsoft recommends that you use NTFS for all drives larger than 32 gigabytes.

- It offers automatic file compression, conserving disk space (page 449).

- It makes your hard drive much more immune to corruption (of the sort that used to require the old ScanDisk program to scurry around, cleaning up glitches).

- It lets you take advantage of a long list of advanced hard drive and file features, including *mounted drives* (Chapter 15) and *private folders* that nobody else on the network can see (Chapter 17).

There's only one significant drawback of formatting your drive with NTFS: older versions of Windows don't recognize it. If you format your drive with NTFS when you install Windows XP, and then at some future time start up the computer using a DOS floppy disk, you won't be able to "see" the NTFS drive.

Although Windows NT and 2000 do recognize NTFS disks, Windows 95, 98, and Me don't. That's a problem if you plan to dual boot between Windows XP and one of these older versions. The bottom line: If you intend to dual boot between Windows XP and Windows 95, 98, or Me, your startup drive *must* use the FAT file system.

If the lack of complete operating system support isn't a problem, then you should opt for NTFS when installing Windows XP. Otherwise, use FAT.

Tip: If you are unsure about which file system to use, start out choosing FAT. You can never convert an NTFS drive to the older FAT system, but you can convert a FAT drive to NTFS at any time.

Here's how. Choose Start→All Programs→Accessories→Command Prompt. Type *convert C: /FS:NTFS* and then press Enter. (Of course, replace *C:* with whatever drive letter you're trying to reformat.) If the drive you're converting is the one with Windows XP on it, the conversion will occur the next time you restart the computer.

Installing Windows XP

Once you've decided to take the plunge and install Windows XP, you can begin your final preparations.

Preparing for the Installation

If you've made all the plans and done all the thinking described so far in this chapter, you have only a short checklist left to follow:

- Update your virus program and scan for viruses. Then, if you're updating an existing copy of Windows, *turn off* your virus checker, along with other auto-loading programs like non-Microsoft firewall software and Web ad blockers.

- Decompress the data on any Windows drives that are compressed with DriveSpace.

- Confirm that your computer's BIOS—its basic startup circuitry—is compatible with Windows XP. To find out, contact the manufacturer of the computer or the BIOS. *Don't skip this step.* You may well need to upgrade your BIOS if the computer was made before mid-2001.

- Gather updated, Windows XP–compatible drivers for all of your computer's components. Graphics and audio adapters are particularly likely to need updates, so be sure to check the manufacturers' Web sites—and driver-information sites like *www.windrivers.com* and *www.driverguide.com*—and download any new drivers you find there.

- Disconnect any gear that's older than Windows XP itself to prevent it from making the PC freeze during the installation. You'll have better luck if you reconnect them *after* Windows XP is in place.

If you've gone to all this trouble and preparation, the Windows XP installation process can be surprisingly smooth. You'll spend most of your time waiting around and reading the commercials on the screen as the installer does its thing.

Performing an Update Installation

Here's how you upgrade your existing version of Windows to full Windows XP status. (If you prefer to perform a clean install, skip these instructions.)

1. **Start your computer. Insert the Windows XP Professional CD-ROM into the drive.**

   The Setup program generally opens automatically (Figure A-2). If it doesn't, open My Computer, double-click the CD-ROM icon, and run the Setup.exe program in the CD's root folder.

2. **Click Install Windows XP.**

   The Windows Setup Wizard appears.

3. **From the Installation Type drop-down list, choose Upgrade (Figure A-2, bottom). Click Next.**

   A screen full of legalese appears.

4. **Review the work of Microsoft's lawyers, and then click "I Accept This Agreement." Click Next.**

Now you're asked to find the 25-character serial number that came with your Windows CD.

5. **Enter the 25-character product key.**

Note that you don't have to press Tab or click to move from box to box. As you fill up each text box, your insertion point moves automatically to the next one.

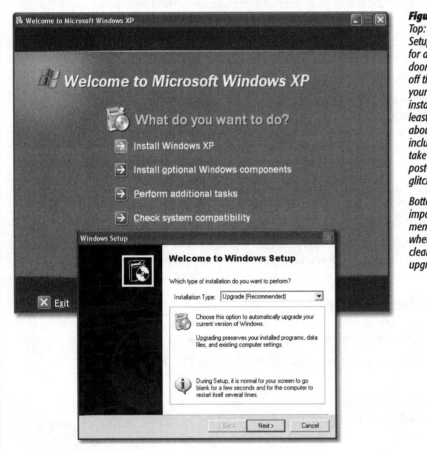

Figure A-2:
Top: The Windows XP Setup program is ready for action. Close the doors, take the phone off the hook, and cancel your appointments. The installer will take at least an hour to go about its business—not including the time it will take you to iron out any post-installation glitches.

Bottom: Use this important drop-down menu to indicate whether you want a clean installation or an upgrade installation.

6. **Click Next.**

Now Microsoft offers you the opportunity to check for updates and patches for the installer program itself. If you're online, and you have the time, letting it perform this check is a very good idea.

7. **Click Yes to download updated installation files from the Internet, or No to by-pass this option. Click Next.**

Now the installer checks to see if any of your PC's components are incompatible with Windows XP. If so, the Report System Compatibility screen appears, shown in Figure A-3. There's not much you can do about it at this point, of course, other than to make a note of it and vow to investigate XP-compatible updates later. Click Next.

Figure A-3:
This screen lists any programs and drivers that Microsoft considers incompatible with Windows XP Pro. You can save any information that shows up in this list to a file by clicking the Save As button.

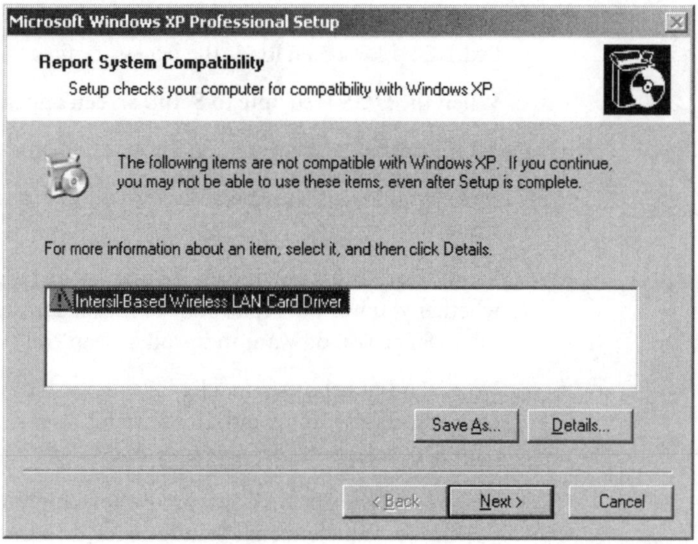

Microsoft Windows XP Professional Setup

Report System Compatibility
Setup checks your computer for compatibility with Windows XP.

The following items are not compatible with Windows XP. If you continue, you may not be able to use these items, even after Setup is complete.

For more information about an item, select it, and then click Details.

Intersil-Based Wireless LAN Card Driver

Save As...   Details...

< Back   Next >   Cancel

Either way, the installation program begins copying files and restarting the computer several times. Finally, the familiar Welcome to Microsoft Windows screen appears, so that you can log back on. This step completes the upgrade process.

Performing a Clean Install (or Dual-Boot Install)

To perform a clean installation of Windows XP Professional, or to install Windows XP onto an empty partition for the purpose of dual booting, the steps are slightly different:

1. **Start up your PC from your Windows XP Professional CD-ROM.**

   Almost every Windows XP–compatible computer can start up from a CD instead of from its hard drive. Sometimes, if you start up the computer with a CD in the drive, instructions for booting from it appear right on the screen (you may be directed to hold down a certain key, or any key at all). If you don't see such an instruction, you might have to check with the computer's maker for instructions on this point.

Tip: If your computer can't start up from a CD-ROM, download the English version of the Windows XP startup disk utility from *www.microsoft.com/downloads/release.asp?ReleaseID=33291.* (The utility is also available in other languages: *http://support.microsoft.com/default.aspx?scid=kb;en-us;Q310994.*)

This download contains a program that builds a set of six boot floppies needed to start Windows XP Professional. You can substitute the first of these floppies for the CD in this instruction.

At the beginning of the setup process, you'll wait for quite a while as an ugly, all-text DOS-like screen loads the necessary files.

2. **When the DOS Welcome to Setup screen appears, press Enter to continue.**

After a moment, the usual legal notice appears.

3. **Review the licensing agreement, if you like, and then press the F8 key to continue.**

Setup searches for previous Windows XP installations. If it finds one, Setup asks whether you want to repair it or to install a fresh (or clean) copy without repairing it. Since you do want to install a clean copy of XP, press the Esc key.

Now Windows shows you a list of the *partitions* on your hard drive (page 470). Unless you've set up your hard drive for *dual booting* as described in the box on page 620, you probably have only one.

4. **By pressing the up and down arrow keys, highlight the name of the partition on which you want to install Windows XP, and then press Enter.**

If you selected a partition that already contains another operating system, you have to confirm your decision by pressing the C key.

5. **Specify whether you want to format the partition you selected, and whether you want to use NTFS or FAT, with or without the Quick option, and press Enter.**

See page 620 for a discussion of these formatting options.

If you elect to format the partition, and there are files on it, the installation program forces you to confirm—by pressing the letter F key—that you really want to wipe out all of the partition's data.

Dual-booters note: If you choose NTFS, remember that you won't be able to "see" that partition when you're running your Windows 95/98/Me. Stick with FAT if you want to be able to share documents between your two worlds.

After the formatting process is complete, the Setup program begins copying files to the partition you selected, and eventually restarts the computer.

When the PC begins detecting the hardware components of your computer, the Setup program steps in to ask you some questions. At this point, you'll notice that the Setup program has finally started to look more like Windows than DOS.

6. **Click Next to bypass the Regional and Language Options screen.**

   Bypass it, that is, unless you don't speak English or don't live in the United States.

7. **On the Personalize Your Software screen, type your name and the name of your organization. Click Next. On the Your Product Key screen, enter the 25-character product key.**

   "Product key" refers to the serial number that came with your Windows XP Professional CD-ROM. As noted earlier, you don't have to click or press Tab to move from box to box—the insertion point jumps automatically as you type.

8. **Click Next. On the Computer Name and Administrator Password screen, specify a name for your computer and a password for the Administrator account.**

   The computer name should be short and punctuation-free. (You can always change it later; see page 296.) If you're installing Windows XP on your home computer, you probably don't need an especially secure password. If you're in a business environment, consider using a password that's not easy to guess.

9. **Click Next.**

   If your computer has a modem, the Modem Dialing Information screen appears at this point. (If not, skip to step 11.)

10. **Select your country, phone system type (tone or pulse dialing), your area code, and the number you dial to get an outside line (if any). Click Next.**

    The Date and Time Settings screen appears now.

11. **Set the date, time, and time zone, and then click Next.**

    Next stop: The Network Settings screen.

Note: If you don't have a network card installed, you won't see the Network Settings screen or the Workgroup or Computer Domain screen. Skip to step 14.

---

12. **Click Typical Settings, and then click Next to continue.**

    Now, on the Workgroup or Computer Domain screen, you face an important question: whether your PC will be part of a *workgroup network* or a *domain network*. (You can find many glorious paragraphs of prose describing these concepts beginning on page 23.)

    If your PC will be part of a domain, select "Yes, make this computer a member of the following domain," and then enter the name of the domain. (Of course, if you really are joining a domain, then a network administrator, or just a really smart computer whiz, is probably on hand to help you with this step.)

    If your PC won't be part of a network, or will be part of a home or small-office network instead, select "No, this computer is not on a network, or is on a network without a domain." Then type in a name for your workgroup network (or accept Microsoft's suggestion: "WORKGROUP").

13. **Click Next.**

   If you've indicated that you want your PC to be part of a domain network, but the administrator hasn't yet added your computer to the domain, you now see the Join Computer to <name of the domain> Domain dialog box.

   Unless you know the Administrator-account password, an error message asks you if you want to proceed for now and join a domain later. Click Yes; your network administrator will have to sort this problem out later.

14. **Click Next.**

When it's all over, the Setup Wizard appears, as described next.

Setup Wizard

Most of the installation procedures described here wind up at the Setup Wizard, which debuts with a Welcome to Microsoft Windows screen. When you click Next, this wizard guides you through the process of:

- Identifying how you plan to connect to the Internet (dial-up modem, cable modem/DSL, or network).

WORKAROUND WORKSHOP

Using an Image Disk

It's becoming increasingly common for computer manufacturers to sell you a new PC without including an operating system CD-ROM. (Every 11 cents counts, right?) The machine has Windows installed on it—but if there's no Windows installation CD, what are you supposed to do in case of emergency?

Instead of a physical Windows CD, the manufacturer provides something called an *image disk*—a CD-ROM containing a complete copy of the operating system *and* other software that was installed on the computer at the factory. If the contents of the computer's hard disk are ever lost or damaged, you can, in theory, restore the computer to its factory configuration by running a program on the image disk.

Of course, this image is a bit-by-bit facsimile of the computer's hard disk drive, and therefore, restoring it to your computer *completely erases* whatever files are already

on the drive. You can't restore your computer from an image disk without losing all of the data you saved since you got the computer from the manufacturer. (Talk about a good argument for keeping regular backups!)

But completely reinstalling Windows isn't the only time that you need a Windows CD. As you can read in various chapters of this book, you'll also be prompted to insert the original Windows CD whenever you want to install a new Windows component that wasn't part of the original installation.

In these situations, if your PC came with only an image disk, you're still covered. This image CD generally contains a copy of the operating system installation files, so that whenever you install a new Windows feature, your PC can grab it from the disk. (Furthermore, some manufacturers install a copy of these installation files right on the hard drive, so that you won't even have to hunt for your CD.)

- Entering the settings for your network connection (your IP and DNS numbers).

- *Activating* your copy of Windows (Figure A-4).

- Registering it (an optional process—if you'd rather not get junk mail, click "No, not at this time").

- Configuring your Internet connection, if you don't already have one.

- Setting up names for the first five user accounts (Chapter 17), if they aren't already set up.

Tip: The Setup Wizard asks only for names, not passwords. When the installation is complete, you might consider making a beeline for the User Accounts program in the Control Panel, in order to set up passwords for your newly hatched accounts (and to set up more than five accounts, if necessary).

This is an important step, too, if you've just upgraded from a previous version of Windows, one that had user accounts already set up. Windows XP imports the old accounts—but strips away their passwords. You might want to take a moment to reinstate them.

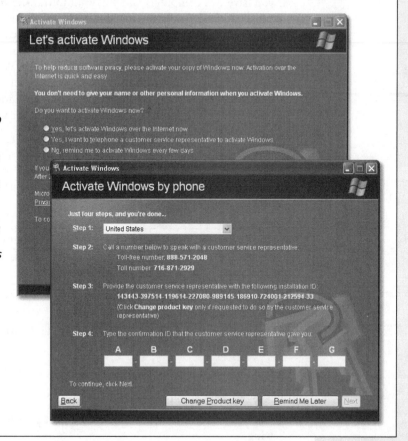

Figure A-4:
Top: Let's activate Windows! During activation, your PC sends Microsoft a list of 10 internal components of your PC. This, ladies and gentleman, is copy protection. If you ever try to install Windows XP onto a second machine, it will notice that the components aren't identical, and you'll be locked out after 30 days (see page 18).

Bottom: If you don't have an Internet connection, you can do this process by telephone, although it's less convenient and takes a lot longer.

Network Identification Wizard

If you weren't able to add your computer to a corporate domain network earlier in the installation process, the Network Identification Wizard appears at this point to give you another shot at it. It's not an especially self-explanatory process; in fact, most of the questions this wizard poses are best answered by your network administrator. After all, adding PCs to network domains wasn't in *your* job description.

(Besides, you can always join the domain later, following the instructions in Chapter 19.)

Files and Settings Transfer Wizard

The Files and Settings Transfer Wizard is a new tool included with Windows XP Professional. It's designed to round up the files and preference settings from one computer—and copy them into the proper places on a new one. For millions of upgrading Windows fans, this little piece of software is worth its weight in gold.

You can use the Files and Settings Transfer Wizard in several ways:

• If you have two computers and you want to transfer files and settings from the old one to the new one, you can run the wizard on the old computer, package its files and settings, and then transfer them to the new computer. You can make the transfer over a network connection, a direct cable connection, or via floppy disks, Zip disks, CD-Rs, or some other kind of disk. The Windows XP CD-ROM includes a version of the wizard that you can run directly from the CD on another Windows computer, even one that's not running Windows XP. You can also create a wizard disk on your Windows XP computer for use on another system.

• If you have only one computer, you can run the wizard from the Windows XP CD-ROM before you install Windows XP, saving the files and settings to a disk or a second hard drive. Then, after performing a clean install of Windows XP, you can run the wizard again, neatly importing and reinstating your saved files and settings.

Tip: If you'd like more power, versatility, or automation in transferring settings between machines or between installations, you can use a commercial program like LapLink PC Sync *(www.laplink.com)* or PC Upgrade Commander *(www.v-com.com)* instead of Microsoft's own wizard.

Phase 1: Backing up the Files

To save the files and settings on your old computer (or your old operating system), proceed like this:

1. **Insert the Windows XP Professional CD-ROM into the drive.**

   The Setup program opens automatically.

2. **Select Perform Additional Tasks; on the next screen, select Transfer Files and Settings.**

The Files and Settings Transfer Wizard opens up (Figure A-5).

3. **Click Next.**

If you're running the wizard on a Windows XP computer, the "On which computer is this?" screen appears. Tell it that this computer is the old one.

(The old computer can be running Windows 95 or later. The new computer must be a Windows XP machine.)

4. **Click Next. On the Select A Transfer Method screen, specify where you want to store the files and settings you intend to transfer (Figure A-5, middle).**

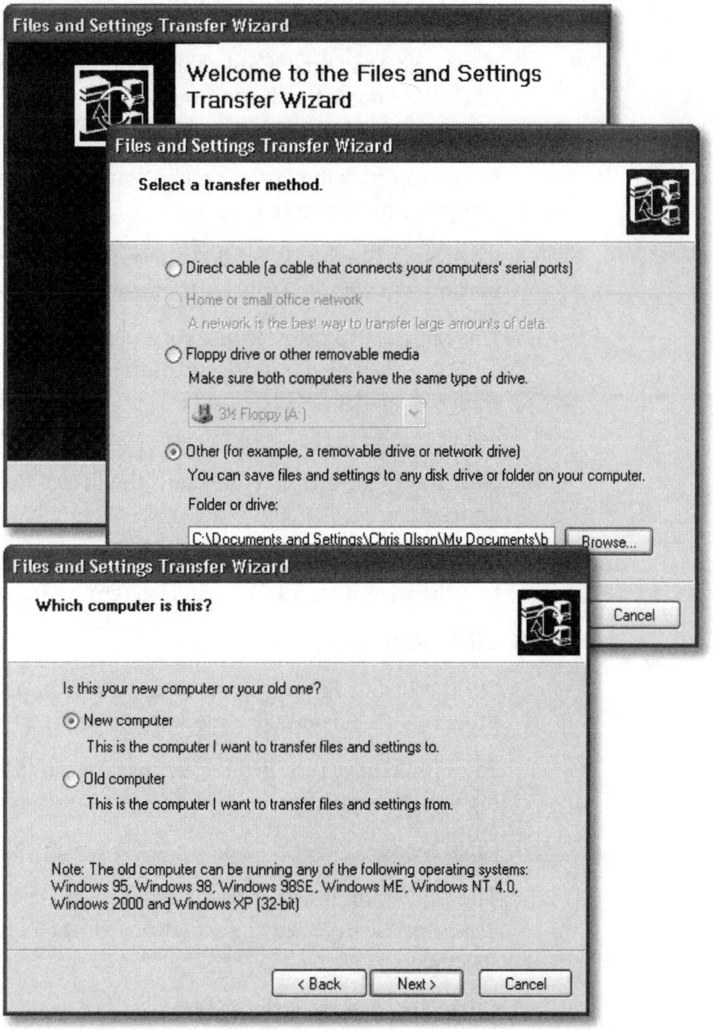

Figure A-5:
Top: The Files and Settings Transfer Wizard, new to Windows XP, can be a sanity-saving convenience. Middle: It lets you save all of the files and settings into a folder, which can be on your hard drive, for example, across a network cable, or onto a disk.

Bottom: After you've installed Windows XP or bought a new Windows XP computer, you can reinstate all of your old files and settings using the same wizard. Just locate the folder that it saved originally.

This location can be a link to another computer using a direct cable or network connection, or to a folder on a hard drive, or to a floppy or other removable disk.

When storing the information on a floppy, you'll need one or two floppies if you want to transfer only your settings, and five to ten floppies to store both settings and files. Don't forget to number the floppies as they are created. When you transfer the information, the wizard will prompt you to insert the floppies in the order that they were copied.

Tip: If you click Other, you can save the files and settings onto the built-in hard drive, where they become a single, special backup file. You can then copy this file to any medium you wish, like a backup tape or CD-R.

---

5. **Click Next.**

   If you selected Direct Cable, the "Set up your serial connection" screen appears. Click the Autodetect button on both wizards after you've connected your two computers with the cable.

   Before you click the Autodetect button, make sure that you've advanced the other computer to this screen.

6. **Click Next. On the "What do you want to transfer?" screen, specify which information you want to transfer to the other computer.**

   You can elect to transfer just your personalized settings, just your data files, or both. You can also build a customized list of the *specific* files and settings you want to transfer.

7. **Click Next. If you click "Let me select a custom list of files and settings when I click Next (for advanced users)," the Select Custom Files and Settings screen appears.**

   This screen lets you add settings, folders, files, and file types to your list of items that the wizard stores. You can also remove items from the list.

8. **Click Next.**

   On the Install Programs on Your New Computer screen, the wizard lists the programs associated with the settings you're saving.

   You should have installed these programs on the new computer before proceeding with the transfer.

9. **Click Next.**

   The Collection in Progress screen appears. The wizard proceeds to search your drives for the necessary information, compress it, and send it to the location you specified.

10. **Click Finish to close the wizard.**

Phase 2: Restoring the Files

To transfer the settings and files you've saved to your new Windows XP computer, use the following procedure.

1. **Choose Start→All Programs→Accessories→System Tools→Files and Settings Transfer Wizard.**

   The Files and Settings Transfer Wizard appears.

2. **Click Next. On the "Which computer is this?" screen, select "New computer" (Figure A-5, bottom) and then click Next.**

   The "Do you have a Windows XP CD?" screen appears.

3. **Click "I don't need the wizard disk."**

   If you don't have the Windows XP CD-ROM handy, you can use this screen to create a wizard disk that runs on other Windows operating systems.

4. **Click Next. On the next screen, specify the location of the files and settings you saved on the other computer.**

   The location you specify could be a path to a hard drive folder, a floppy or CD-ROM drive, or a direct cable/network connection to another computer running the wizard.

5. **Click Next.**

   If you selected Direct Cable, the "Set up your serial connection" screen appears. Click the Autodetect button on both wizards after you've connected your two computers with the cable.

   Before you click the Autodetect button, make sure that you've advanced the wizard on the other computer to this screen.

6. **Click Next.**

   The wizard proceeds to copy the files and apply the saved settings on the new computer.

POWER USERS' CLINIC

User State Migration Tool

The Files and Settings Transfer Wizard is meant for use on a small scale, like home networks. If you're an administrator who needs to transfer files and settings on a larger scale, as in a corporate environment, you should consider using the User State Migration Tool (USMT), a command-line utility. It requires Windows XP Pro on the destination machine, a client machine that's connected to a Windows Server domain controller, and an administrator who knows what's what.

The USMT tools are in the Valueadd→MSFT→USMT folder on the Windows XP installation CD. For details, visit this Web page: *www.microsoft.com/windowsxp/pro/techinfo/deployment/userstate/UserStateMigrationinWindowsXP.doc.*

---

7. **Click Finish to close the wizard.**

If Windows couldn't restore some of your settings, you'll see them listed on the final screen; you'll have to re-create these settings manually. Depending on the settings you saved, you may have to log off and log on again before the transferred settings take effect.

Backing Out of Windows XP

Hard though it may be to imagine, even after going to all of the trouble to switch to Windows XP, you may pine for the old days. Some people find Windows XP too intrusive and too much of a nag. Other people find too many incompatibilities with

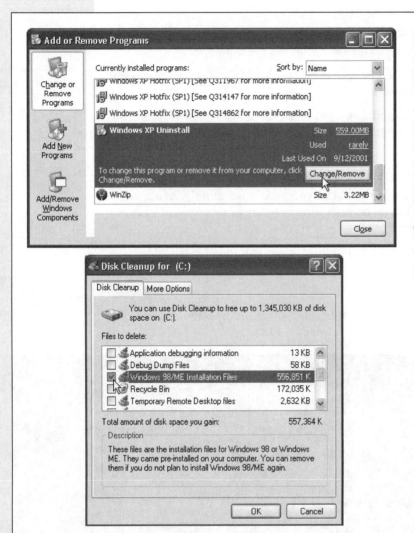

Figure A-6:
Whenever you perform an upgrade installation from Windows 98, Windows 98 SE, or Windows Me, you actually retain both the old and the new versions of Windows. If, as the months go by, you decide that you'd like to reclaim the disk space being used by the dormant operating system, you can delete it. You can delete Windows XP (top), restoring your older version, or you can delete the older version (bottom), committing to Windows XP forever.

their old gear. Fortunately, Microsoft has made it very easy for you to back out, reinstating your older operating system.

Note: This option is available only if you upgraded your PC from Windows 98, Windows 98 SE, or Windows Me. If you erased the hard drive and performed a clean install, or if you upgraded from Windows NT 4.0 or Windows 2000, this option isn't available. Furthermore, you lose this option if you repartitioned your drive, or converted it to NTFS, since you upgraded.

Ditching Windows XP

To get rid of Windows XP and reinstate the good old days, open the Add or Remove Programs program in your Control Panel. As shown in Figure A-6 at top, Windows XP is listed among the other programs currently installed in your machine.

Click Windows XP Uninstall, then the Change/Remove button, then Uninstall Windows XP. When you're asked if you really want to uninstall Windows XP and restore your old operating system, click Yes. When the process is complete, your computer will shut itself down, restart, and then start up with your old copy of Windows 98, Windows 98 SE, or Windows Me.

Ditching the Older Windows

Conversely, if you just love Windows XP and never want to go back, you may prefer to reclaim the hundreds of megabytes of disk space that your old copy of Windows 98, 98 SE, or Me is taking up.

Here, too, there's not much to it. Choose Start→All Programs→Accessories→System Tools→Disk Cleanup. As shown in Figure A-6 at bottom, the Disk Cleanup program lists a lot of stuff that you can permanently delete—and in the list, you'll see the name of your original Windows version ("Windows 98/Me Installation Files," for example).

Just turn on the checkbox and then click OK. The 600 megabytes you save could be your own.

Windows XP, Menu by Menu

A menu bar tops every Windows desktop window and almost every application window. Along this menu bar, of course, are the names of the menus that, when clicked, produce lists of the commands available to you.

Most menu bars have a menu named File on the extreme left side, and Help is always the last menu on the right. What comes between depends on the program you're using. This appendix covers the menu commands in the Windows XP desktop windows.

Tip: You can choose almost any Windows XP menu command entirely from the keyboard; the necessary keystrokes are described in this appendix. (If you open a submenu that doesn't bear the telltale keystroke-hint underlines, press the arrow keys to highlight the command you want, and then Enter to trigger it.)

If you open a menu and then change your mind, press the Esc key to close the menu.

File Menu

Most of these commands operate on a *selection*—that is, you're supposed to highlight an icon, or several icons, before using the menu. It's worth noting, too, that the File menu *changes* depending on what you've highlighted. For example, you see one set of commands when you've highlighted an icon, and a longer set when nothing is selected.

Note: Certain software installations may add other commands to your File menu.

Open, Open With..., Preview

Opens a highlighted document, program, folder, or disk into a window, exactly as though you had double-clicked its icon. (If Windows doesn't know what program it's supposed to use for opening a highlighted document, the command says Open With..., so that you can choose the program you want. And if you've highlighted a graphics file, the command says Preview instead of Open.) *Keyboard equivalent:* Enter.

Print

Available for documents only. Sends the highlighted document to your printer after first opening the necessary application (such as your word processor) and offering you the Print dialog box, where you can specify, for example, how many copies you want. *Keyboard equivalent:* Alt+F, P.

Explore

Opens Windows Explorer, which shows you what's in the highlighted disk or folder in the Explorer two-pane format (see page 116). This command is available only if the selected icon is a drive or folder. *Keyboard equivalent:* Alt+F, X.

Search

Opens a Search window that's ready to look in the selected drive or folder (the Search command isn't available if you select a file). See page 41 for more on the Search command. *Keyboard equivalent:* F3.

Sharing and Security

Available only for folders and disks. Opens the Sharing tab of the icon's Properties dialog box. As described in Chapter 20, this dialog box is exclusively for people with networks; it lets you make a folder or disk available to other people on the network. *Keyboard equivalent:* Alt+F, H.

Run As...

Available for programs only, this handy command lets you run a program as though you have an Administrator account (or somebody else's account), provided you know the account's password. It's described on page 509. *Keyboard equivalent:* Highlight the program name, then press Alt+F, A.

Pin to Start menu

Here's another option for programs (and shortcuts of programs) only. It forces the highlighted icon to be listed in the top left section of your Start menu for easy access. *Keyboard equivalent:* Alt+F, I.

Send To

Offers submenu commands that move or copy the highlighted icon(s) to the desktop, to a floppy disk, to the My Documents folder, and so on. (For files and folders only.) *Keyboard equivalent:* Alt+F, N.

New

This command's submenu lets you create a new folder, shortcut, text file, or other new item, depending on the programs you've installed. For example, if you have Microsoft Office installed, you'll find a New→Microsoft Word Document command here. *Keyboard equivalent:* Alt+F, W.

Create Shortcut

Creates a shortcut to the selected icon. (See page 134 for more on shortcuts.) If you've highlighted a folder or document icon, the shortcut appears in the same window as the original icon; at this point, you haven't accomplished much. To make it useful, drag the shortcut to, for example, the desktop or the Quick Launch toolbar.

If the selected icon is a drive, Windows XP displays a message that says: "Windows cannot create a shortcut here. Do you want the shortcut to be placed on the desktop instead?" Click Yes. *Keyboard equivalent:* Alt+F, S.

Delete

Moves the highlighted folder or file to the Recycle bin, after first requesting confirmation. *Keyboard equivalent:* Delete or Ctrl+F, D.

Rename

Opens an editing box for the name of the highlighted icon. *Keyboard equivalent:* F2.

Properties

Opens the Properties dialog box for the highlighted icon. Folder and file properties display creation-date and modification-date information. Disks display information about free and used space, along with a Tools tab that lets you open the disk-maintenance tools described in Chapter 16. If you've set up a network (Chapter 18), disk and folder Properties dialog boxes also offer a Sharing tab. *Keyboard equivalent:* Alt+Enter.

Close

Closes the window, just as if you'd clicked the X in the upper-right corner of the window (or double-clicked the icon in the upper-left corner). *Keyboard equivalent:* Alt+F4.

Edit Menu

When you work in, say, your word processor, you use the Edit menu quite a bit—its Cut, Copy, and Paste commands are very useful for moving bits of text. At the desktop, these commands operate on icons, providing an easy way for you to move files and folders from one window or disk to another.

Undo

Reverses the last action you performed. The name of the command changes to reflect what you've just done: Undo Delete, Undo Rename, and so on. (Alas, there's no Undo Print feature.) *Keyboard equivalent:* Ctrl+Z.

Cut, Copy, Paste, Paste Shortcut

Let you move or copy files or folders from one window to another, as described on page 129. (The Paste Shortcut command offers yet another method of creating a shortcut icon.) *Keyboard equivalents:* Ctrl+C (for Copy), Ctrl+X (for Cut), Ctrl+V (for Paste), Alt+E, S (for Paste Shortcut).

Copy To Folder, Move To Folder

If the Cut/Paste and Copy/Paste routines for moving or copying a file or folder to a different window aren't your cup of tea, you can use these commands instead. When you choose either command, a dialog box opens so you can select a destination folder (see Figure B-1). *Keyboard equivalents:* Alt+E, F (for Copy to Folder), Alt+E, V (for Move to Folder).

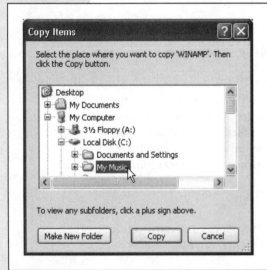

Figure B-1:
Click the + button to "expand" your drive's contents, so that you can choose a destination folder for the icon you're moving or copying. You can create a new folder inside the selected folder by clicking the Make New Folder button.

Select All

Highlights all of the icons in the open window—or, if no window is open, on the desktop. Windows applies any subsequent command (Copy, Delete, Print, Rename, or whatever) to all of them at once.

If you're editing an icon's name, and your cursor is blinking in the renaming rect-angle, this command highlights the entire filename instead. *Keyboard equivalent:* Ctrl+A.

Invert Selection

If there are 50 icons in a folder, and you want to highlight 49 of them, don't bother trying to click and Shift-click all 49. Instead, use this trick: Click the one icon (or Shift-click the handful of icons) you *don't* want. Then choose Edit→Invert Selection. Windows highlights the icons that weren't selected, and vice versa. *Keyboard equivalent:* Alt+E, I.

View Menu

The commands in the View menu apply only to the *active* desktop window: the one that's open and in front of all the others.

Toolbars

Offers a submenu of toolbars you can add to the top of the window. For details on these toolbars and their functions, see page 91. *Keyboard equivalent:* Alt+V, T.

Status Bar

Makes the status bar appear or disappear at the bottom of the window. The status bar displays information about the contents of the current window, or the selection you've made inside it. (It may say, for example, "3 object(s) selected" or "Type: Microsoft Word Document.") *Keyboard equivalent:* Alt+V, B.

Explorer Bar

Splits the window, creating a new left-side pane. In this special panel, you can summon your choice of extra information; make your choice using the View→Explorer Bar submenu. The choices are described on page 77. *Keyboard equivalent:* Alt+V, E.

Thumbnails, Filmstrip, Tiles, Icons, List, Details

Let you view the files in a window as icons (which you move by dragging freely), as a list (a neat list view that's automatically sorted), as a filmstrip (a slide show of graphics files), and so on. Page 82 begins a complete description of these views and their relative advantages.

Arrange Icons By

Tidies a window filled with randomly spaced icons, placing them into an orderly grid according to the criteria you select from the submenu here. These commands appear only in windows you've displayed in icon (not list) views. Page 83 has complete details. *Keyboard equivalent:* Alt+V, I.

Choose Details

If you've put a window into Details view, you can use this command to specify which columns of information you want the window to show (date, size, type, author, and so on). *Keyboard equivalent:* Alt+V, C.

Customize This Folder

This command launches a wizard that walks you through the process of changing the folder window's background (such as the identifying text and graphics that appear on the left side of the window). See page 83 for details. *Keyboard equivalent:* Alt+V, F.

Go To

This command's submenu lets you move forward or backward through desktop windows you've recently opened, much like the Back and Forward buttons in your Web browser. (View→Go To→Home Page launches your Web browser, connects to the Internet, and takes you to the page you've designated as your home page.)

Keyboard equivalents: Backspace or Alt+left arrow (for Go To→Back), Alt+right arrow (for Go To→Forward), Alt+V, O, U (for Up One Level), Alt+Home (for Home Page), Windows logo key+D (for Desktop).

Refresh

Updates the contents of the window. Use this command if you've just cut, pasted, or deleted icons and the window doesn't yet reflect the changes. *Keyboard equivalent:* F5.

Favorites Menu

The Favorites menu shows the list of Web pages you've "bookmarked" when using Internet Explorer *and* desktop windows you've designated as Favorites to which you'd like quick access.

Add to Favorites

Adds the currently open Web page or desktop window to the Favorites list. *Keyboard equivalent:* Alt+A, A.

Organize Favorites

Opens the window shown in Figure B-2. Here, you can edit your Favorites list items in several ways:

- **Rearrange them** by dragging your Favorites items up or down in the right-side list.

Tip: Windows can sort your Favorites alphabetically, but not in the Organize Favorites dialog box. Instead, right-click any item *in the Favorites menu itself* and choose Sort by Name from the shortcut menu.

- **Delete or rename one** by clicking its name and then clicking Delete or Rename, respectively.
- **Organize them into folders.** For example, you may want a folder for all the favorite folders on your PC, another folder for all the Internet sites related to cooking, and another folder for all the Internet sites you visit to get help on computing.

Click the Create Folder button to add a new, empty folder to the right-side list; type a name for it and then press Enter. Then file a Favorites listing away by dragging it onto the folder icon (see Figure B-2). *Keyboard equivalent:* Alt+A, O.

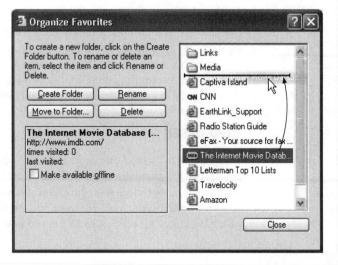

Figure B-2:
Click a folder to see what's in it. Drag a Favorites item up or down the list to reposition it; drag it onto a folder icon to file it away into a subcategory. Click its name once to read, in the lower-left panel, about its origin and when you last looked at it.

Favorites List

Choose a name from this list to open the desktop window, or visit the Web site, in question. If you choose a folder name, a submenu appears that lists all of the windows or Web pages you filed in that "folder," as described in the previous paragraphs.

Tools Menu

This menu offers a handful of leftover commands that didn't quite belong in any of the other menus.

Map Network Drive

This command, exclusively for people on a network, lets you assign a drive letter to a folder to which you've connected over the network. For details, see page 643. *Keyboard equivalent:* Alt+T, N.

Disconnect Network Drive

This command, also just for networked people, summons a dialog box that lets you *delete* a drive mapping you've established. *Keyboard equivalent:* Alt+T, D.

Synchronize

Synchronize, in Microsoft-ese, means, "copy files so both computers contain the identical contents." Using the Briefcase, for example, you can ensure that your laptop and desktop computers contain the same updated files (see page 585 for details). Synchronizing also means updating the Web pages you've told Internet Explorer that you want to read when you're not online, a trick described on page 335. *Keyboard equivalent:* Alt+T, S.

Folder Options

The dialog box summoned by this command lets you change several global desktop-window options. For example, you can specify that you want a new window to appear every time you double-click a folder (instead of the single-window approach); that you want one click, not two, to open a folder; and so on. You can read about these settings in detail starting on page 87. *Keyboard equivalent:* Alt+T, O.

Help Menu

This menu has three commands: Help and Support Center, which opens the Windows XP help system discussed in Chapter 5; "Is this copy of Windows legal?" which takes you to a Web page that shows you the various clues that you have a genuine, non-counterfeit version of Windows; and About Windows, which tells you precisely which Windows XP version you have and how much memory your PC has.

Index

Colophon

This book was created in Microsoft Word XP, whose revision-tracking feature made life far easier as drafts were circulated from authors to technical and copy editors. SnagIt (*www.techsmith.com*) was used to capture illustrations; Adobe Photoshop and Macromedia Freehand were called in as required for touching them up.

The book was designed and laid out in Adobe PageMaker 6.5 on a Macintosh PowerBook G3, PowerBook G4, and Power Mac G4. The fonts used include Formata (as the sans-serif family) and Minion (as the serif body face).

The book was generated as an Adobe Acrobat PDF file for proofreading and indexing, and finally transmitted to the printing plant in the form of PostScript files.